14

Ultrapurification of Semiconductor Materials

ULTRAPURIFICATION OF SEMICONDUCTOR MATERIALS

Proceedings of the Conference on Ultrapurification
of Semiconductor Materials

BOSTON, MASSACHUSETTS

APRIL 11–13, 1961

EDITED BY

M. S. Brooks and J. K. Kennedy

sponsored by the

ELECTRONICS RESEARCH DIRECTORATE
Air Force Cambridge Research Laboratories
Bedford, Massachusetts

The Macmillan Company

A Division of The Crowell-Collier Publishing Company

Printed in the United States of America

First Printing

THE MACMILLAN COMPANY, NEW YORK
BRETT-MACMILLAN LTD., GALT, ONTARIO

Library of Congress catalog card number: 62-13030

PREFACE

This volume contains 49 papers and discussion presented at an International Conference on the Ultrapurification of Semiconductor Materials held in Boston, Mass. from the 11th to the 13th of April, 1961. The Conference was sponsored by the Electronics Research Directorate of the Air Force Cambridge Research Laboratories.

The subject matter of the Conference was divided into three topic areas: chemical preparation and purification; physical preparation and purification; analysis. The papers were presented at four sessions. A full session was given to each of the topic areas and an evening session was devoted to ten minute papers. For convenience these three topic divisions have been retained in assembling the papers in these proceedings. The table of contents differs from the conference program only in two respects. The ten minute papers of the evening session have been arranged according to subject content and placed in one of the three divisions. The opening remarks of General B. Holzman, Commander, Air Force Cambridge Research Laboratory and Dr. L. M. Hollingsworth, Director, Electronics Research Directorate, are not included in the proceedings. However, their help and encouragement as well as that of R. M. Barrett, Deputy Director of the Electronics Research Directorate is gratefully acknowledged.

The Chairman of the sessions were F. Rosi (R.C.A. Laboratories), C. Rosenblum (Merck, Sharpe and Dohme), A. J. Rosenberg (Tyco, Inc.) and W. Tiller (Westinghouse Research Laboratories). The discussion portion of each of the three aforementioned divisions of the book were summarized and edited by B. Rubin, P. Cali and J. O'Connor, respectively.

The editors would like to take this opportunity to thank the authors, chairmen, and summary editors for their fine cooperation and efforts. The successful organization and smooth functioning of the conference was aided by the wholehearted support of many members of the staff of our laboratory. Miss Helen Turin, as conference secretary, undertook all of the manifold difficult duties associated with this task. We are also grateful to L. Woods, C. D. Turner, and B. Rubin for their efforts. In addition J. O'Connor of Lincoln Laboratory was most helpful in many stages of the planning. The conference also benefited greatly from the efforts of R. J. Young and his associates of Wentworth Institute. This institute coordinated many aspects of the conference and was especially helpful in extending aid to overseas participants. This work was performed under Air Force Contract AF 19(604)-8364.

For speed, proofreading was done by the editors. Thus, for any misjudgements that may have been made in necessary condensation and for any uncorrected mistakes in the printing, the editors with to apologize both to the authors and readers.

TABLE OF CONTENTS

Page

I. CHEMICAL PREPARATION AND PURIFICATION OF SEMICONDUCTOR MATERIALS

Introduction

The Role of Impurities in Semiconductor Research 3
Calvin S. Fuller, Bell Telephone Laboratories,
Murray Hill, New Jersey

A. Elements

The Development of a Method for the Removal of Boron
from Silicon Tetraiodide by Zone Refining 25
J. T. Buford and R. J. Starks, The Eagle-Picher
Research Laboratories, Miami, Oklahoma
The Preparation of Semiconductor Grade Silicon by the
Iodide Process 34
H. Baba and H. Araki, Nippon Telegraph and Tele-
phone Public Corp., Tokyo, Japan
The Preparation of High Purity Silicon from Silane 55
C. H. Lewis, M. B. Giusto and S. Johnson, Metal
Hydrides, Inc., Beverly, Mass.
High Purity Boron for Semiconductor Research........ 67
L. Sosnowski, T. Niemyski, and Z. Olempska, Polish
Academy of Sciences, Warsaw, Poland
The Preparation of High Purity Bismuth by the Reduc-
tion of Bismuth Trichloride with Lithium Aluminum
Hydride 80
W. Brenner, C. G. Kumar, H. Hellman and C. J.
Marsel, New York University, New York, N. Y.
The Purification of Tellurium by Distillation 84
B. Wedlock and F. M. Norton, Massachusetts Insti-
tute of Technology, Cambridge, Mass.
The Preparation of High Purity Gallium by Hydride
Reductions 94
Y. Okamoto, W. Brenner, E. Bierig and C. J.
Marsel, New York University, New York, N. Y.

Organometallic Compounds in the Preparation of High-
Purity Metals   106
    W. A. G. Graham, Arthur D. Little, Inc., Cambridge,
    Mass.
Purification of Rare Earth Metals.   145
    B. Love and E. V. Kleber, Nuclear Corporation of
    America, Burbank, California
Preparation of Chromium   164
    N. W. Silcox, A. F. Armington and G. F. Dillon, Air
    Force Cambridge Research Laboratories, L. G.
    Hanscom Field, Bedford, Mass.
Ultrapurification of Indium, Antimony, Bismuth, Arsenic
and Tellurium   173
    Raymond Beau, Les Produits Semi-Conducteurs,
    Antony (Seine) France

B.   Compounds

Preparation of Luminescent Aluminum Nitride   186
    I. Adams and T. R. AuCoin, U. S. Army Signal Re-
    search and Development Laboratories, Fort Mon-
    mouth, N. J. G. A. Wolff, Harshaw Chemical Co.,
    Cleveland, Ohio
The Preparation and Purification of Transition Metal
Silicides.   192
    R. M. Ware, The Plessey Co., Ltd., Towcester,
    Northants, England
Purification Effects in Silicon Carbide Under Thermal
Gradients   205
    R. S. Braman, E. H. Tompkins, S. Susman and
    V. Raziunas, Armour Research Foundation, Chicago,
    Illinois
Purification of Some II-VI Compounds Using Ion Ex-
change Resins   219
    M. J. Presland, Associated Electrical Industries
    (Woolwich) Ltd., Harlow, Essex, England
Arene-Metal π-Complexes and their Purification.   224
    M. Tsutsui, New York University, New York, N. Y.

C.   Chromatographic Techniques

The Potential of Gas Chromatography for Purifying
Semiconductor Materials.   239
    J. H. Bochinski and K. W. Gardiner, Bell & Howell
    Research Center, Pasadena, California. R. Juvet,
    University of Illinois, Champaign, Illinois

Synthesis and Gas Chromatographic Purification of
Organometallic Compounds for Semiconductor
Applications   253
    J. I. Peterson, L. M. Kindley and H. E. Podall,
    Melpar, Inc., Falls Church, Virginia

II. THE DETECTION OF TRACE IMPURITIES
IN SEMICONDUCTOR MATERIALS

A. Introduction

Determination of Ultratrace Impurities in Semiconductor
Materials   267
    G. H. Morrison, General Telephone and Electronics
    Laboratories, Inc., Bayside, N. Y.

B. Emission and Mass Spectroscopy

Analysis of Trace Impurities by Spark Source Mass
Spectrometry   279
    R. Brown, R. D. Craig, J. A. James and C. M.
    Wilson, Associated Electrical Industries (Rugby)
    Ltd., Rugby, Warwickshire, England
The Application of Solid-Source Mass Spectrometry to
Determine the Purity of Materials for Semiconductor
Purposes   294
    J. F. Duke, National Physical Laboratory, Tedding-
    ton, Middlesex, England
Electrical and Mass Spectrographic Analysis of III-V
Compounds   316
    R. K. Willardson, Bell & Howell Research Center,
    Pasadena, California
Mass Spectrographic Evidence for Deviations from
Stoichiometry in Gallium Antimonide   340
    E. B. Owens and A. J. Strauss, Lincoln Laboratory,
    Massachusetts Institute of Technology, Lexington,
    Mass.
Specific Detectabilities by Several Spectrographic
Procedures   349
    W. C. Myers, Battelle Memorial Institute, Columbus,
    Ohio
A Spectrochemical Method for the Determination of
Trace Impurities in Indium   356
    J. F. Duke, National Physical Laboratory, Tedding-
    ton, Middlesex, England

Electron Gun Type Excitation Source for Spectrographic
Determination of O_2, N_2, H_2, P, S and Halogens in Gallium Arsenide   373
    D. Andrychuk and C. E. Jones, Texas Instruments,
    Inc., Dallas, Texas
Analysis of Impurities in Semiconductors by Means of
Spectroscopy and Paramagnetic Resonance   382
    M. Balkanski, Universite de Paris, Ecole Normale
    Superieure Paris, France

C.   Electrical Measurements

The Hall Effect as an Analytical Tool in Ultrapure Silicon
and Germanium   397
    C. A. Klein, Raytheon Company, Waltham, Mass.
Space-Charge Current Measurements as a Technique for
the Detection of Trace Impurities in Ultrapure
Materials   416
    R. W. Smith, RCA Laboratories, Princeton, N. J.

D.   Other Techniques

Determination of Small Stoichiometric Deviations in
Oxide Monocrystals   423
    H. B. Sachse, Keystone Carbon Co., St. Marys, Pa.
Trace Analysis in Semiconductor Crystals by X-Ray
Diffraction Microscopy   434
    G. H. Schwuttke, General Telephone and Electronics
    Laboratories, Inc., Bayside, N. Y.
Polarographic and Colorimetric Determination of
Selenium in Gallium Arsenide   454
    E. H. Cornish and E. L. Bush, Standard Telecom-
    munications Laboratories, Ltd., Harlow, Essex,
    England
New Determination Method of Traces of Carbon in Some
Elements—Application to Silicon   461
    L. Ducret and C. Cornet, Centre National d'Etudes
    des Telecommunications, Issy-les-Moulineaux,
    Seine, France

III. PHYSICAL PREPARATION, PURIFICATION, AND MEASUREMENTS OF SEMICONDUCTOR MATERIALS

A. Zone Purification Processes

The Horizontal Zone Leveling of Silicon in Non-Reactive
Crucibles   469
    D. Lamb, Sylvania Electric Products, Inc., Towanda,
    Pa. J. L. Porter, Sylvania Electric Products, Inc.,
    Woburn, Mass.
Free Convection in Zone Melting   481
    W. R. Wilcox, Pacific Semiconductors, Inc., Culver
    City, California. C. R. Wilke, University of Cali-
    fornia
An Experimental Study of Zone Refining   502
    A. F. Armington and G. H. Moates, Air Force Cam-
    bridge Research Laboratories, L. G. Hanscom Field,
    Bedford, Mass.
Floating Zone Refining of Gallium Arsenide   513
    F. A. Cunnell, Services Electronics Research
    Laboratory, Baldock, Hertfordshire, England

B. Crystal Growing Processes

Dislocations of Silicon Single Crystals Grown by the
Floating Zone Method   521
    K. Akiyama, Matsushita Electric Industrial Co.,
    Ltd., Kadoma, Osaka, Japan. J. Yamaguchi, Osaka
    University, Higashinoda, Osaka, Japan
Experiments on Floating Zone Silicon   534
    A. J. Goss, Marconi's Wireless Telegraph Co., Ltd.,
    Chelmsford, Essex, England
Crystal Growth of III-V Compounds   550
    W. P. Allred, Bell & Howell Research Center,
    Pasadena, California
The Role of Contamination in Gallium Arsenide Crystal
Growth   568
    L. Ekstrom and L. R. Weisberg, RCA Laboratories,
    Princeton, N. J.
Preparation of Crystals of the Alloy System
Bi-Sb-Se-Te   585
    D. A. Poutinen, Massachusetts Institute of Tech-
    nology, Cambridge, Mass.

Condensation of Evaporated Zinc and Cadmium on Silicon Surfaces   595
   G. Helwig, Standard Elektrik Lorenz Ag., Nurnberg,
   West Germany

C.   Measurements of Semiconductor Materials

Purification Methods in the Study of Semiconductor
Surfaces   604
   J. A. Dillon, Jr., Brown University, Providence,
   Rhode Island
Grain Boundaries as Imperfections of Planar Extent,
Their Model and Electronic Properties   614
   H. F. Matare, TE KA DE, Nuremberg, Germany
Application of the Siemens Method for the Measurement
of Lifetime and Resistivity of Small Slices of Silicon . . .   636
   J. Nishizawa, Tohoku University, Sendai, Japan
Thermodynamic Properties of Cubic BP and of Rhombohedral B_6P   645
   B. D. Stone, F. V. Williams, R. A. Ruehrwein and
   G. B. Skinner, Monsanto Chemical Co., Dayton,
   Ohio
Thermodynamic Properties of II-IV and V-VI Compounds   652
   B. W. Howlett and M. B. Bever, Massachusetts
   Institute of Technology, Cambridge, Mass.

Ultrapurification of Semiconductor Materials

I

CHEMICAL PREPARATION
AND PURIFICATION OF
SEMICONDUCTOR MATERIALS

ROLE OF IMPURITIES IN
SOLID STATE RESEARCH

C. S. Fuller
Bell Telephone Laboratories, Incorporated
Murray Hill, New Jersey

I.   INTRODUCTION

It is perhaps a sad commentary on social progress that only under the urgency of World War II were Si and Ge of sufficient purity obtained to demonstrate clearly the vital importance of trace impurities in semiconductors. It was the fact that apparently insignificant amounts of certain impurities produced unexpectedly large electrical effects that provided the impetus for ultrapurification. For example, one part in 10^{10} of Ni in Ge, or of Au in Si, is easily detected by its effect in reducing carrier lifetimes. About a thousandth of a monolayer of Cu is detectable on the surface of Ge simply by the change caused in the room temperature resistivity upon heating the crystal. Because such effects exist, germanium and silicon are the purest elements known today.

In support of this, Figure 1 shows some results of ultrapurification by vacuum zone refining of silicon, obtained at Siemens Co. [1]. True intrinsic behavior, almost down to the room temperature range, indeed has been achieved - a total active impurity concentration of about one part in 10^{12}.

Indium antimonide and other III-V compounds are not far behind Si and Ge in their purity. However, considering the large number of potential semiconductors these accomplishments are only a beginning and much work remains to be done before the binary and multicomponent semiconductors are equal to Ge and Si in controlled purity.

I should like in what follows to review briefly some special aspects of the effects of impurities in semiconductors. Burton [2] has given a summary of solubilities, distribution coefficients, diffusion coefficients and ionization energies of donor and acceptor impurities in Ge and Si up to the year 1954. It is not intended here to attempt to bring the information on these topics up-to-date, many other articles have done this [3], but rather to

3

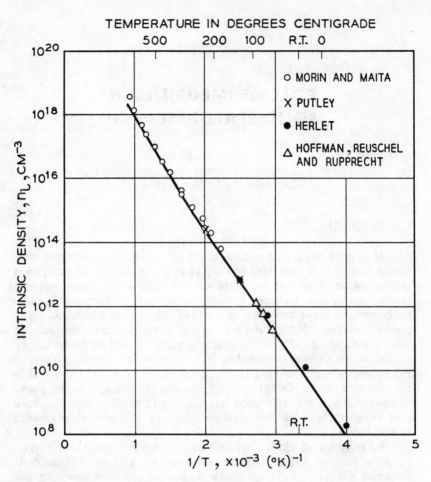

Figure 1. Plot of intrinsic carrier concentration versus 1/T for silicon after 76 zone passes. Results taken from Morin and Maita, Phys. Rev. 96, 28 (1954); Putley and Mitchell, Proc. Phys. Soc. 72, 193 (1958); and Herlet, Z.Angew. Phys. 9, 155 (1957) are shown. (After Hoffmann, Reuschel, and Rupprecht, J. Phys. Chem. Solids 11, 284 (1959).)

indicate by means of examples some recent applications of impurity effects to solid-state problems, and vice versa, to indicate how some of the solid-state problems react on attempts to control the effects of impurities. Let us first review some of the effects of impurities in the elementary semiconductors, Si and Ge.

II. IMPURITY BEHAVIOR IN Ge AND Si

One of the early triumphs of semiconductor chemistry was the proof, by means of radio-tracer techniques, that group V donors in Ge produced one electron per ionized donor atom [4]. The substitutional nature of the group III and group V impurities was thus confirmed. However, it was not long before hypothetical elements like "thermium" and "deathnium" [5] were required in order to explain anomalies which occurred during the processing of Ge into devices. Once again the radio-tracer method proved invaluable [6, 7], and Cu and Ni were identified as major causes of the phenomena. Another important fact was learned. Attempts to account for the diffusion properties of Cu and Ni showed that these elements belonged to a general class of impurities, the so-called "rapid diffusers." Thus, was introduced the interstitial nature of many impurities in semiconductors. Not only was it found that elements, like Cu and Ni, diffused as interstitials at relatively low temperatures, but it was found that they were able likewise to substitute in the lattice to produce unusual electrical effects. A new way of doping, namely by diffusion, became possible. This had the big advantage that elements could be introduced into doped crystals without disturbing the dopants already present.

Interest next focussed on other elements than the group III acceptors and the group V donors. Multiple ionization levels were discovered and, to unravel these, it became necessary to control the concentrations of the group III and group V elements within very narrow limits. Two remarkable examples of this are the determination in Ge of the 4 electronic states of gold [8], and the determination of the three electronic states of copper by means of Hall effect measurements. Figure 2, taken from the work of Woodbury and Tyler [9], shows how controlled doping of Ge with As, enabled the Fermi level to be adjusted so that the individual ionization levels of Cu could be determined. Many investigations of this kind could be mentioned, but the important point to be stressed here is that, had it not been for the existence of pure Ge and Si, such experiments could not have been carried out.

When group I impurities came to be investigated it was found that H and Li behaved as pure interstitials. However, only Li was found to be electrically active. Tracer analyses could not be made on Li, but fortunately emission spectroscopy and flame analysis were applicable here. By these means accurate curves for the solubilities were able to be determined [10, 11].

Because Li is essentially a pure interstitial donor which is singly ionized in Ge and Si, it has been an invaluable tool in the investigation of interactions between it and other impurities.

5

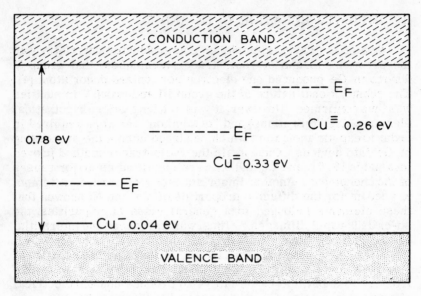

Figure 2. Energy level scheme for Cu in Ge showing Fermi level positions for filling of the Cu levels to occur. (After Woodbury and Tyler, Phys. Rev. 105, 84 (1957).)

The coulombic interactions between Li^+ ion with singly- and doubly-charged acceptor ions resulting in ion pairs are of particular interest. The properties of such "ion pairs" are now fairly well understood [12]. They show reversible association and dissociation with temperature and, since the binding energies for multiply-charged ions can be appreciable, pairs stable at relatively high temperatures are possible. Figure 3, taken from Reiss and Morin [13] shows by the nearly parallel slopes of the mobility curves versus temperature, for example, that $(Li^+ Zn^=)$ pairs are stable up to at least 400°C. Likewise, the effects of pairing on the rate of diffusion of interstitial atoms can be very large. For example, the diffusion coefficient of Li in Ge is reduced by a factor of about 10^6 at 300°K in the case of the Li-Zn pairs mentioned above.

As an example of the importance of having available a variety of analytical tools, the case history of oxygen deserves some discussion. Because oxygen hardly affects the properties of Si or Ge when it is present as dispersed atoms, its presence in Si was missed for several years. But effects from it showed up, like a dormant malady, when the Si was incubated at 400-500°C. Even then its presence was obscure until chemical tests were made, and in particular, until the observation of the 9μ and 11.5μ absorption bands in the infrared spectra of Si and Ge were

6

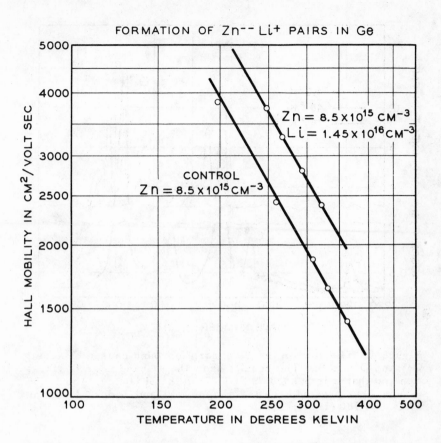

Figure 3. Hall mobility versus T on log scales for Ge containing Zn⁻⁻Li⁺ pairs and for Ge containing Zn alone (control). The higher mobility for the Ge containing both Li and Zn and the slow approach of this line to the line for the control with increasing T, show a high degree of stability of the pairs. (After Morin and Reiss, Phys. Rev. 105, 384 (1957).)

discovered [14]. The final proof was furnished [15] by the isotopic shift in the infrared produced by doping Si with O^{18} (Figure 4). At present, the infrared method, standardized against gas analytical techniques [16], offers the most convenient method of quantitative analysis for oxygen in these crystals. Strangely enough it required an air leak in a zone refining machine to show that Ge, unlike Si, had been essentially free of oxygen all along [17]. It is, however, easy to dope Ge with oxygen by growing under different partial pressures.

A very large number of investigations have been devoted to the behavior of oxygen in Si and Ge [18]. These have shown that atomic oxygen can react with itself to form a tetraoxide-type of

7

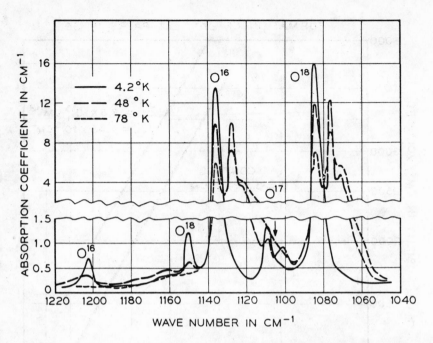

Figure 4. The shift in the 9μ absorption band caused by adding O^{18} and O^{16} to Si. The results show the 9μ band is an O vibration and that O is bonded as Si-O-Si in the Si lattice. About 1.5% O^{17} is also present. (After Hrostowski and Alder, J. Chem. Phys. 33, 980 (1960).)

"molecule" which remains in solid solution and acts as a donor; dioxide and trioxide molecules also form. These likewise appear to be donors. Oxygen reacts strongly with Li in solid solution to produce the donor LiO^+. Pell [19] has shown that this reaction can be studied by its effect on the kinetics of Li precipitation (Figure 5) and can be used to determine O analytically. Oxygen also has been shown to react with Al, B, and Ga in Si [20], a donor molecule being formed with Al (Figure 6). Finally oxygen is found to react with Cu, both in Si and in Ge. In the latter case a neutral or compensated structure is formed [21].

These reactions of oxygen are excellent examples of diffusion-controlled processes. In fact, the activation energies for the diffusion of oxygen agree well with direct measurements of oxygen diffusion.

The foregoing discussion of impurity effects in Ge and Si is obviously incomplete. It is not intended to leave the impression that the work is in any sense done. Even the qualitative behavior of many impurities is still far from clear and the characteristics

8

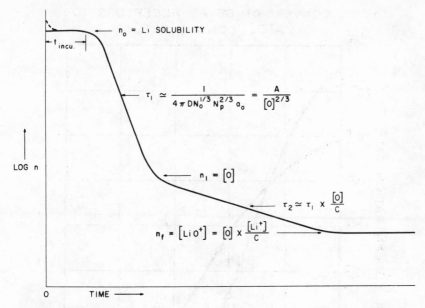

Figure 5. Log of electron concentration as a function of time of Li precipitation in Si. The change at n_i corresponds to the oxygen concentration whereas the final level of n corresponds to the LiO concentration. (After E. M. Pell, Proc. Conf. on Semiconductors, Brussels (1958).)

of many, remain to be quantitatively understood. This, in fact, promises to be a fertile field for the chemist for many years to come. Nevertheless, the main technological problems in the elementary semiconductors have been sufficiently well answered so that the urgent need for analytical and purification skills lies elsewhere, namely with the preparation and investigation of the binary and other multicomponent semiconductors.

III. GROUPS III-V SEMICONDUCTORS

In attacking multicomponent systems physicists and chemists are not starting anew. Faraday[22] discovered semiconductivity in AgS in 1833. Wagner [23] found non-stoichiometric behavior in Cu_2O when the oxygen pressure was varied. As was well realized by some at the time, however, the problem of purity, to say nothing of single crystal production, was a major stumbling block to precise work and understanding. Today with the experience of the elementary semiconductors behind us, we are in a much stronger position. At the same time, there are new facets to the old problems. Let us briefly review some of the knowledge about the III-V semiconductors.

9

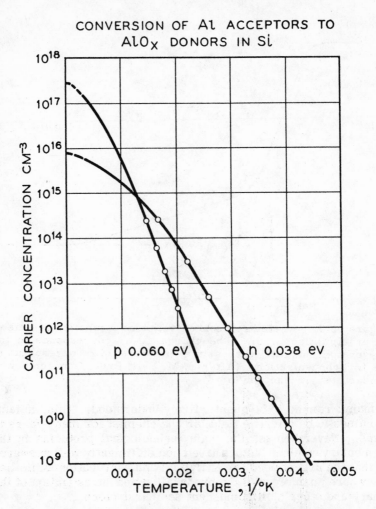

CONVERSION OF Al ACCEPTORS TO
ALO$_x$ DONORS IN Si

Figure 6. Hall measurements on Al-doped Si containing dissolved O, before and after annealing at
800°C showing formation of donor from Al and O.
(After Fuller, Doleiden and Wolfstirn, J. Phys. Chem.
Sol. 13, 187 (1960).)

Of the III-V semiconductors only InSb and GaAs have been
obtained in purity approaching that of Ge and Si. This is true in
spite of the fact that most of these compounds can be zone
refined. Even with careful purification of the starting elements,
the final purity of the single crystal leaves much to be desired.
There are good reasons why III-V semiconductors present more
difficult problems: In the first place more impurities are electrically active in the III-V compounds than in the elementary

10

semiconductors because impurities can substitute for both elements. Secondly, the III-V compounds themselves are more reactive chemically. For example, AlSb attacks both quartz and carbon vessels and its surface instability is only too well known. AlP, AlAs, InP also are highly reactive materials. Finally, unlike Ge and Si, in which the effects of vacancies and dislocations can now largely be eliminated and in which non-stoichiometry plays no part, the effects of structural factors in the III-V compounds are still largely unevaluated. So far, no electrical effects attributable to non-stoichiometry have been reported, but only by constant effort toward the attainment of completely pure crystals can the magnitudes of these effects be determined.

One of the most interesting phenomena in the III-V compounds is shown in the behavior of the group IV impurities. By their position in the periodic table, it might be anticipated that atoms of these elements can occupy both group III and group V element sites and that the proportion on each site might vary depending upon concentration and other external factors. Such has indeed been found to be the case. Si, for example, when added to GaAs, shares the two lattice sites about equally at high concentrations [24]. But as the concentration is decreased, more Si atoms go onto the Ga sub-lattice than go on the As sub-lattice, thus providing over-all donor activity. By means of Hall effect measurements combined with radiochemical analyses, the results shown in Figure 7 have been obtained [25]. A theory to account

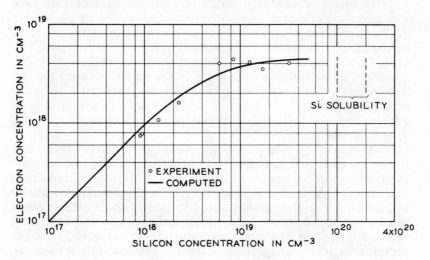

Figure 7. Log plot showing concentration of electrons as determined from Hall measurements as a function of added concentration of Si[31] to GaAs. (After Whelan, Struthers, and Ditzenberger, Conference on Semiconductors, Prague (1960).)

for this behavior has also been worked out. Work of this kind needs to be extended to other III-V compounds.

Although a considerable amount of work has been done on the solubilities and electrical properties of group II acceptors and group VI donors in the III-V semiconductors, this has been impeded by the lack of sufficiently pure crystals and much remains to be done. Where radiotracer elements are applicable, distribution coefficients are able to be determined, but in materials like GaP which are always extrinsic at the melting point, k will depend greatly on purity.

Work relating to the behavior of fast-diffusing elements such as Cu, Ag, Ni, Au, Li, etc., in the III-V compounds has been limited. Considerable attention has been given to the effects of copper in GaAs which it enters interstitially and in which it becomes a substitutional acceptor, much as in Ge. Results obtained with Cu^{64} show, however, that its solubility can approach $10^{19} cm^{-3}$ in GaAs at high temperatures and that one Cu atom produces one hole when completely ionized in n-type material [26]. This result suggests that Cu only substitutes on the Ga sub-lattice and that it does so by raising an electron from the d-shell to the valence shell. Ni and Ag behave similarly to Cu in GaAs. Li has been found to diffuse rapidly into III-V compounds and to produce compensation in some, such as AlSb [27]. Although oxygen has been found in GaAs crystals and various effects have been attributed to it, its role still remains obscure.

The diffusion characteristics of a number of elements have also been investigated, particularly in GaAs. Zn in particular has been the subject of much attention because of the peculiar shapes of the penetration curves obtained [28]. Self-diffusion [29], using Ga and As and Sb in GaAs and GaSb, as well as chemical diffusion [30] indicates a difference in energy for vacancy formation on the "cation" and "anion" sub-lattices, the latter being the larger. Diffusion studies offer a useful way in which to gain information about the III-V crystals, but much remains to be done here also.

Summarizing, this very brief review of the III-V compounds it can be said that definite facts about impurities are meager. Work seems to be concentrating on InSb, InAs, GaSb, GaAs, and GaP, and it is to be hoped that crystals of all of sufficient purity will soon exist so that effects of impurities in controlled amounts can be evaluated more fully. InSb and GaAs have practically reached this stage and much profitable chemical work, aimed at studying impurity properties in them, can now be carried out.

IV. OXIDE AND SULFIDE SEMICONDUCTORS

This class of materials includes a very large number which we shall discuss together.

As mentioned previously, the oxides and sulfides were among the earliest semiconductors investigated and the first to find practical application. Only in recent years, however, have methods progressed far enough to provide relatively pure single crystals some like Cu_2O, of large size [31].

It was perhaps unfortunate that the pioneers, who chose to work on the oxides and sulfides were denied the luxury of pure elemental crystals, for they were presented immediately with all of the complications of the subtle semiconductor art. Not the least of these was the occurrence of non-stoichiometry which, as we have seen is so weak in the III-V semiconductors as to go so far undetected. The electrical properties in most of the other compounds are, however, greatly dependent upon the environment in which the materials are prepared because of the effects of non-stoichiometry.

Although these effects were correctly interpreted on early polycrystalline specimens particularly on PbS, studies of single crystals of PbS, PbSe, and PbTe emphasized the importance of partial pressures of oxygen and sulfur during the preparation [32]. The remarkable effects of S on PbS and its high rate of diffusion as shown by Brebrick and Scanlon [33] left no doubt about the control of stoichiometry by the S pressure over the crystal (Figure 8). A complete study of PbS was recently carried out by Bloem, Kroger and Vink who showed the effects of added Bi, Ag, and Cu [34]. It is no wonder therefore the intrinsic properties of PbS crystals were originally obscure. The generation of anion vacancies during the heating incident to measurement, could hardly have been anticipated and it is to the credit of early workers that the true explanation of this complicated behavior was found.

The behavior of Cu and Ni in PbS has been investigated by Bloem and Kroger [35]. The interstitial-substitutional properties of these impurities is once more evident here as in previous materials. A significant impurity effect found by these workers was that doping PbS with Ag (also an acceptor like Cu and Ni) favored the occupation of interstitial (donor sites) by these latter elements. Effects such as these illustrate the importance of small energy differences in determining the course of reactions in crystals.

Inasmuch as the behavior of CdS, CdSe, and CdTe is similar to that of the corresponding Pb compounds, they will not be discussed here. Because the Cd compounds have large energy gaps (2.4 ev for CdS), deep levels due to impurities can and do occur, particularly for acceptors. As a consequence optical methods have been used extensively to investigate these materials. A higher state of purity however, is desirable if their electrical properties are to be understood.

13

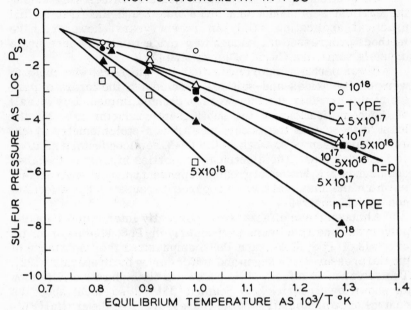

Figure 8. Effect of S pressure in converting n-type PbS to p-type PbS at various temperatures. (After Brebrick and Scanlon, Phys. Rev. 96, 598 (1954) and Bloem, Philips Res. Repts. 11, 273 (1956).)

ZnO is another example in which non-stoichiometry (this time of the interstitial kind) plays an essential role. Interstitial Zn always appears to be present in excess in this crystal, giving rise to donor behavior [36]. As for other semiconductors having large energy gaps, (ZnO gap is ~ 3.5 ev), the electrical conductivity of "pure" ZnO crystals is too low to measure. It thus becomes necessary to carry out controlled doping experiments if the effects of impurities are to be determined. Diffusion doping is the most practicable, and experiments using Cu, Zn, H, Li, O and In have been carried out [37]. Oxygen under various pressures produces no effect,* but the results with H_2 are revealing. It is found that the conductivity varies as the one-fourth power of the H_2 pressure, showing that one H atom provides one conduction electron. From the change in conductivity, the activation energy for H diffusion can be determined. The

_____

*It has been calculated that an extremely high pressure of oxygen would be required to make ZnO p-type, see J. J. Lander, J. Phys. Chem. Sol. 15, 324 (1960).

large value of 0.91 ev, suggests that H reacts with O in ZnO to give OH$^=$ groups. The diffusion consists of H, hopping from one O$^=$ to another [38].

In addition to the II-VI semiconductors there exist a host of other sulfides and oxides (as well as silicides, nitrides, etc.) possessing semiconductor properties; binary, ternary and quaternary compounds having semiconducting properties are known [39]. In view of what has been said already, it is evident that the problem of specifying the role of impurities in these materials is a still more difficult task. It will not be attempted here to cite specific problems connected with their preparation and investigation. It is obvious that the problems of chemical analysis and purification become more severe as the number of atoms increases, to say nothing of the interpretation of the electrical properties. Because, in multicomponent systems the highest melting points frequently do not occur at the stoichiometric composition (incongruent melting), zone refining is not always applicable to the final compounds so that methods of growing stoichiometric crystals must be devised in these instances.

The lesson to be learned from the work on the II-VI and other compounds (which has been very inadequately reviewed above) is that if we are to correlate the electrical behavior of semiconductor crystals (conductivity, temperature dependence of conductivity, mobility, lifetime, etc.) with added chemical impurities, we must be prepared to carry out many different kinds of investigations. Preferably we should first evaluate the "pure" crystal in order properly to assess the importance of such factors as non-stoichiometry and site-interchange effects as discussed above. The final objective should be to achieve a complete understanding of the mechanisms and free energies of the reactions, as well as the free energy changes in the phase diagrams.

V. NEW METHODS

It is evident from the above discussion that chemists, metallurgists and physical chemists need to be continually aware of new physical methods applicable to solid state chemistry problems. That this awareness in the past has been acute is attested by the long list of tools the chemist has adapted to his use: chromatography, colorimetry, flame, emission, x-ray, and mass spectrography, neutron activation analysis, x-ray fluorometry, infrared absorption analysis, to mention only a few.

Perhaps still in the realm of chemical physics are such procedures as Hall effect measurements, infrared absorption (solids), nuclear magnetic resonance (NMR) absorption, electron

15

paramagnetic resonance (EPR) absorption, magnetic suscepti-
bility and photoconduction - the order is not of significance.

In what follows, a few examples of the applications of some
of these methods will be indicated.

The use of electrical conductivity to measure the concentrations of chemical species is well known. However, this method
can only be applied when the degree of ionization of the species
is known and the carrier mobilities are available. Conductivity
is non-specific; it does not tell what the impurity species is. By
measuring in a magnetic field (Hall effect), the carrier mobility
can be independently determined. But Hall measurements, too
are non-specific, although conductivity and mobility can provide
useful information, for example, in studying chemical kinetics in
crystals. Also, as with most physical methods, conductivity and
Hall effect measurements can be made specific if they are combined with another parameter. Thus, variations with temperature
in these instances lead to the evaluation (under the proper conditions) of "ionization energies" which are specific to each solute
atom. Of the greatest importance today, however, are the new
additions to the list of spectroscopic methods: photoconductivity,
infrared absorption applied to solids, electron or paramagnetic
resonance absorption and nuclear resonance absorption. The
relations among these various procedures are illustrated by
Figure 9.

Photoconductivity and infrared methods supplement one
another. The former is most useful as a qualitative or semi-
quantitative method, since it is relatively easy to apply and can
be extremely sensitive to small amounts of impurities. Figure
10, taken from Newman and Tyler [40], illustrates this for Ge
containing ~ 10^{14}cm^{-3} of Fe. The ionization energy of the Fe
atoms is given approximately by the center of the 3 decade
response at the left. The response at the right corresponds to
exciting electrons across the forbidden gap. Photoconductivity
measurements, except for very deep-lying levels, must be carried out at very low temperatures or in compensated specimens,
when the interpretation becomes difficult. This subject has
recently been thoroughly treated by Bube [41].

Although infrared methods have been employed in analysis
for many years, their application to semiconductors has been
largely in research where they have yielded and continue to yield
invaluable information on band structures and impurity behavior.
By far the most precise ionization information relating to
impurities has been obtained from infrared absorption. Figure
11, taken from a paper by H. J. Hrostowski and R. H. Kaiser [42]
illustrates the details in the spectrum of Al (present to
6×10^{15}cm^{-3}) in Si.

16

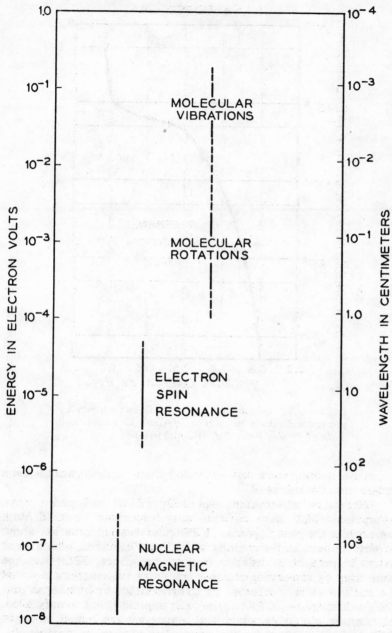

Figure 9. Energies of electromagnetic waves in relation to various spectrographic methods.

17

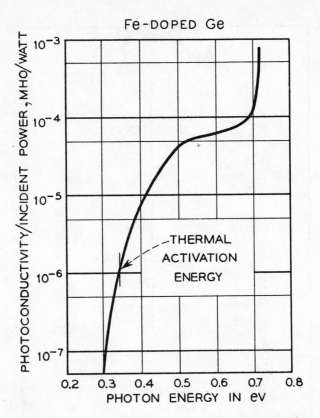

Figure 10. Ionization of Fe in Ge as shown by photoconductive response. (After Newman and Tyler, Phys. Rev. 96, 882 (1954).)

More recent work has extended these investigations even farther into the infrared.

Microwave absorption especially (EPR) and radio wave absorption (NMR) have become very important in solid state research in the past 5 years. EPR provides information about the environment in the vicinity of the "odd" electron, which must always be present in order to observe the effect. NMR does the same thing by observing changes involving the magnetic moment of a nucleus as it is affected by internal fields or by interactions with electron spins. EPR is generally applied to extremely dilute solutions of atoms to which odd electrons are bound, whereas NMR is best applied to the pure elements or to compounds. Although it can provide useful data on semiconductors, NMR is not as effective in studying impurity effects and therefore will not be discussed here.

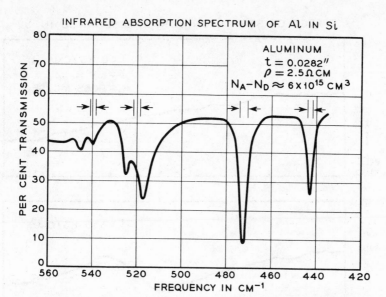

Figure 11. Excited states of the Al acceptor in Si is revealed by infrared absorption. (After Hrostowski and Kaiser, J. Phys. Chem. Sol. 4, 148 (1958).)

In EPR, the atom investigated must have, as mentioned, unpaired electrons. The resonance energy of interest is given by $g\beta H$ where $g = 2$ for the free electron (slightly different for an electron in a crystal), β is the Bohr magneton and H is the external magnetic field. The single line, due to this transition is, however, split into $(2I + 1)$ lines by the nuclear spin moment, I, of the atom itself. Such resonances were first observed for donors in Si [43] and have only recently been found for acceptors in Si (Figures 12, 13) [44]. The separations of the lines provide information about the electron wave functions at the nuclei of the atoms and the number of lines gives data on the nuclei themselves. By means of a different technique (electron nuclear double resonance), it is possible also to determine the nature of the environment about a particular donor or acceptor being investigated [45].

Finally, EPR has become extremely valuable in the study of the interactions between vacancies and impurities in semiconductors [46]. In this manner pairing reactions between charged vacancies and impurities have been examined and the pairing energies and equilibria determined [46] (Figure 14). The ionization energies associated with the early bombardment defects in Si have in fact been found to be associated with oxygen - vacancy pairs rather than with vacancies as was first believed [48]. Very interesting reactions between vacancies and impurities have been

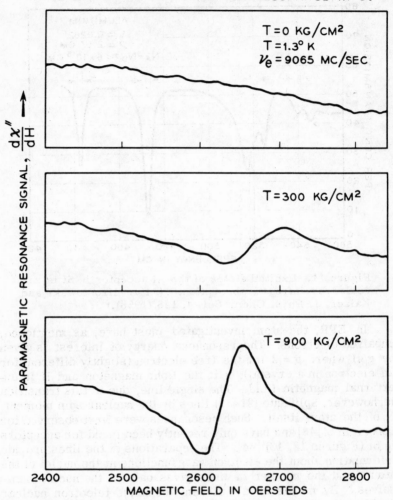

Figure 12. EPR spectra of "holes" bound to acceptors in Si under uniaxial stress. (After Feher, Hensel and Gere, Phys. Rev. Letters 5, 309 (1960).)

investigated in NaCl by Watkins [49]. In addition, vacancies have been found to react with interstitial Mn^{++} in Si [50]. Finally, EPR measurements have shown that pair formation occurs between ions such as Cr^{++}, Mn^{++} and Fe^{++} in the presence of acceptors like Al, B, Ge and In in Si solutions [51]. The EPR technique, therefore, seems destined to add greatly, not only to our knowledge of the state of ions in very dilute semiconductor

20

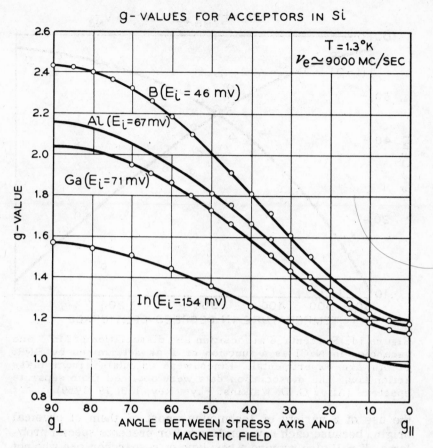

Figure 13. G-values for "holes" showing order of differences for various acceptors in Si presence at ~ 10^{17} cm^{-3}. A stress of 700-900 kg/cm^2 was applied along [100] direction. (After Feher, Hensel and Gere, Phys. Rev. Letters 5, 309 (1960).)

solutions, but also to the chemistry of the reactions among impurities, including the reactions with vacancies.

VI. CONCLUSION

The conclusion to be drawn from the above brief summary is simply that a great deal more solid-state chemical research needs to be done. Much work on the solubilities and diffusion coefficients of impurities remains. In particular, we must understand a great deal more about interactions which occur in semiconductors, often under relatively mild conditions if we are to employ them successfully in devices. This work will require

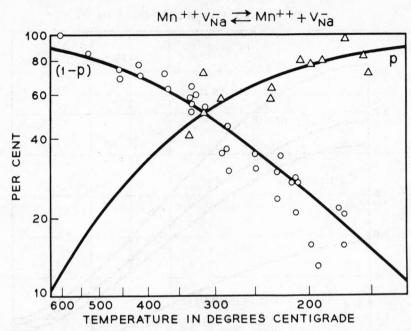

Figure 14. Percentage association and dissociation of Mn^{++} and vacancies in NaCl as a function of T as determined by EPR. Points are experimental. Lines were calculated from mass action law. The dissociation data were obtained from separate spectra. (After G. D. Watkins, Phys. Rev. 113, 79 (1959).)

the use of a variety of techniques, most of them of physical origin, because each new semiconductor presents special problems. It will also require a new type of researcher, one who not only understands the electronic processes in crystals but who understands as well, the kinetics and thermodynamics applicable to reactions in solids. Perhaps, then, a much needed systematic knowledge of the chemistry of solids can be acquired.

REFERENCES

1. A. Hoffmann, K. Reuschel and H. Rupprecht, J. Phys. Chem. Sol. 11, 286 (1959).
2. J. A. Burton, Physica 20, 845 (1954).
3. F. A. Trumbore, Bell System Tech. J. 39, 205 (1960).
4. G. L. Pearson, J. D. Struthers, and H. C. Theuerer, Phys. Rev. 77, 809 (1950).
5. These terms were first used by W. Shockley.
6. C. S. Fuller and J. D. Struthers, Phys. Rev. 87, 526 (1952).
7. W. P. Slichter and E. D. Kolb, Phys. Rev. 87, 527 (1952).
8. W. C. Dunlap, Jr., Phys. Rev. 100, 1629 (1955).

9. H. H. Woodbury and W. W. Tyler, Phys. Rev. 102, 647 (1956), ibid., 105, 84 (1957).
10. E. M. Pell, J. Phys. Chem. Sol. 3, 74, 77 (1957); R. N. Hall, ibid., 3, 63 (1957).
11. C. S. Fuller and H. Reiss, J. Chem. Phys. 27, 318 (1957).
12. H. Reiss, C. S. Fuller, and F. J. Morin, Bell System Tech. J. 35, 535 (1956).
13. F. J. Morin and H. Reiss, Phys. Rev. 105, 384 (1957).
14. W. Kaiser, P. H. Keck, and C. F. Lange, Phys. Rev. 101, 1264 (1956).
15. H. J. Hrostowski and R. H. Kaiser, Phys. Rev. 107, 966 (1957); H. J. Hrostowski and B. Alder, J. Chem. Phys. 33, 980 (1960).
16. W. G. Guldner and A. L. Beach, A.S.T.M. Special Tech. Pub. #222 (1958).
17. G. Elliot, Nature (London) 180, 1350 (1959).
18. C. D. Thurmond and W. Kaiser, J. Appl. Phys. 32, 115 (1961).
19. E. M. Pell, Solid State Phys. in Elect. Telecom. Vol. I, Pt. I, p. 261, M. Desirant and J. L. Michiels, Eds., Academic Press (1960).
20. C. S. Fuller, F. H. Doleiden and Katherine Wolfstirn, J. Phys. Chem. Sol. 13, 187 (1960).
21. C. S. Fuller, J. Phys. Chem. Sol. 19, 18 (1961).
22. M. Faraday, Experimental Researches Series IV (1833) 433-9.
23. Carl Wagner and Walter Schottky, Z. Phys. Chem. 11B, 163 (1930); ibid., 22, 195 (1933).
24. C. Kolm, S. A. Kulin, and B. L. Auerbach, Phys. Rev. 108, 965 (1957).
25. J. M. Whelan, J. D. Struthers, and J. A. Ditzenberger, Conference on Semiconductors, Prague (1960).
26. J. M. Whelan and C. S. Fuller, J. Phys. Chem. Sol. 6, 173 (1958).
27. H. J. Hrostowski and C. S. Fuller, J. Phys. Chem. Sol. 4, 155 (1958).
28. F. A. Cunnell and C. H. Gooch, J. Phys. Chem. Sol. 15, 127 (1960); ibid., J. W. Allen, 15, 134 (1960).
29. F. H. Eisen and C. E. Birchenall, Acta Met. 5, 265 (1957).
30. B. Goldstein, Phys. Rev. 118, 1024 (1960); ibid., 121, 1305 (1961); A. Schillman, Naturforsch. 11a, 472 (1956).
31. R. S. Toth, R. Kilkson, and D. Trivich, J. Appl. Phys. 31, 1117 (1960).
32. E. H. Putley, Proc. Phys. Soc. 65B, 388, 736, 992 (1951).
33. R. E. Brebrick and W. W. Scanlon, Phys. Rev. 96, 598 (1954); W. W. Scanlon, Solid State Physics 9, 83 (1959).
34. J. Bloem, F. A. Kroger, and J. H. Vink, London Physical Society Conference on Defects in Crystalline Solids (Bristol) London Phys. Soc. 1955, p. 73.
35. J. Bloem and F. A. Kroger, Philips Res. Rept. 12, 281 (1957).
36. D. G. Thomas, J. Phys. Chem. Sol. 3, 229 (1957).
37. E. Mollwo, Z. Physik 138, 478 (1954); G. Bogner and E. Mollwo, J. Phys. Chem. Sol. 6, 136 (1958); J. J. Lander, ibid., 15, 324 (1960).

38. D. G. Thomas and J. J. Lander, J. Chem. Phys. 25, 1136 (1956).
39. E. Mooser and W. B. Pearson, J. Electronics 1, 629 (1956).
40. R. Newman and W. W. Tyler, Phys. Rev. 96, 882 (1954).
41. R. H. Bube, Photoconductivity of Solids, John Wiley & Sons (1960).
42. H. J. Hrostowski and R. H. Kaiser, J. Phys. Chem. Sol. 4, 148 (1958).
43. R. C. Fletcher, W. A. Yager, G. L. Pearson and F. R. Merritt, Phys. Rev. 95, 844 (1954).
44. G. Feher, J. C. Hensel, and E. A. Gere, Phys. Rev. Letters, 5, 309 (1960).
45. G. Feher, Phys. Rev. 114, 1219 (1959).
46. Schneider and Caffyn, Conference on Defects in Crystalline Solids (Bristol) London Phys. Soc. 1955, p. 74.
47. G. D. Watkins, Phys. Rev. 113, 79 (1959).
48. G. D. Watkins, J. W. Corbett and Walker, J. Appl. Phys. 30, 1198 (1959).
49. G. D. Watkins, Phys. Rev. 117, 102 (1960); G. Bemski, J J. Appl. Phys. 30, 1195 (1959).
50. H. H. Woodbury and G. W. Ludwig, Phys. Rev. Letters 5, 96 (1960).
51. H. H. Woodbury and G. W. Ludwig, J. Phys. Chem. Sol. 8, 81, 490 (1959).

THE DEVELOPMENT OF A METHOD FOR THE REMOVAL OF BORON FROM SILICON TETRAIODIDE BY ZONE MELTING

J. T. Buford and R. J. Starks
The Eagle-Picher Research Laboratories
Miami, Oklahoma

ABSTRACT

The preparation, primary purification by distillation, zone melting and thermal dissociation processes for silicon tetraiodide developed in this study are discussed. Emphasis is given to the development of a continuous zone melting process which utilizes the void-zoning technique for material transport. The boron concentration in the silicon produced from silicon tetraiodide through various stages of the process is presented. A comparative evaluation of the purification factor obtained to the theoretical purification is made. Possible reasons for the significant deviation from the theoretical are discussed.

INTRODUCTION

The general purpose of this study was the development of a continuous system for the preparation of transistor grade silicon via the iodide process. This system included the processes of synthesis, primary purification by distillation, zone melting and thermal dissociation of silicon tetraiodide.

The specific area of interest was in the investigation of the continuous zone melting technique applied to the iodide process by Rubin, Moates and Weiner [2]. This continuous zone melting process utilized the principles of void-zoning, as expressed by Pfann [1], for material transport.

The interest of applying a zone melting purification step to the iodide process developed after an investigation of the segregation coefficients of various impurities found in silicon tetraiodide. These segregation coefficients in the SiI_4 matrix were found to be less than unity in all cases investigated.

Table I gives the effective segregation coefficients of various impurities in a SiI_4 matrix [2].

Table 1

Effective Segregation Coefficients
of Various Impurity Species
in a SiI_4 Matrix.

Impurity Species	K_{eff}
B*	0.16 ± 0.07‡
Al	0.70 ± 0.35
Na	0.10 (single run)
Mg*	0.16 ± 0.01
Cu	0.64 ± 0.17
Fe*	0.15 ± 0.08
Ti	0.91 ± 0.08
Mn*	0.09 ± 0.04
Boron Triiodide†	0.42 ± 0.22

* = Values obtained by extrapolation.
† = Doped samples.
‡ = Maximum variability of results.

The segregation coefficients found for the boron and boron triiodide species led to the application of the continuous zone melting theory to the silicon tetraiodide process used in the preparation of transistor grade silicon.

EXPERIMENTAL

A continuous system was developed using the processes of synthesis, primary purification, zone melting and thermal dissociation of silicon tetraiodide. The purpose for this continuous system was to provide a process as free from theoretical sources of contamination as possible. Figure 1 is a schematic of the continuous system developed.

SYNTHESIS

The synthesis of silicon tetraiodide was carried out in a fused silica apparatus employing a fluid-bed reactor. The reaction tube was 3-1/4 inches I.D. and 20 inches in length. An iodine dispersion tube was positioned in the center of the reaction tube and extended 9 inches into the silicon bed. This enabled the introduction of elemental iodine through approximately

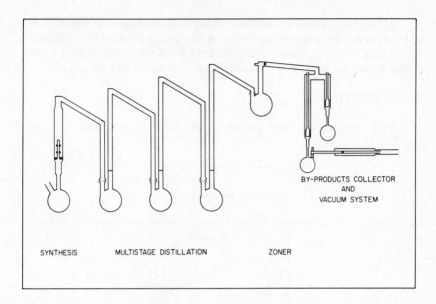

SYNTHESIS   MULTISTAGE DISTILLATION   ZONER

BY-PRODUCTS COLLECTOR
AND
VACUUM SYSTEM

Figure 1. Schematic of the Continuous System for the Synthesis, Distillation, Zone Melting and Thermal Dissociation of Silicon Tetraiodide.

one-half the length of the silicon bed and produced a greater rate of synthesis. The silicon used was screened to minus 14 plus 35 mesh. The iodine boiler was a three-liter transparent silica flask that was fused to the reaction chamber eliminating the necessity of any joints.

The reaction temperature of the synthesis was 800°C. The average rate of synthesis was 4-kilograms per hour with a maximum production capacity of 20 kilograms per silicon charge.

DISTILLATION

The multi-stage distillation unit was constructed of transparent fused silica. The height of the columns through the three stages were - 36 inches, 42 inches and 48 inches, respectively. The silicon tetraiodide boilers were three-liter transparent fused silica flasks. These boilers also served as the SiI_4 collector from the previous stage. The boilers were fused to the fractionating columns to provide as nearly a contaminant-free system as possible. The first cut of the distillate was removed before the system was connected to the next stage. An inert gas was used to sweep the following stage before and during the coupling of the two stages to prevent atmospheric contamination.

27

An external heating element around the condensing chambers at the top of the column provided a means of controlling the reflux ratio. Vacuum insulating jackets enclosing the reflux area of the columns provided adiabatic conditions in the columns.

ZONE MELTING

The continuous void zoner is shown schematically in Figure 2.

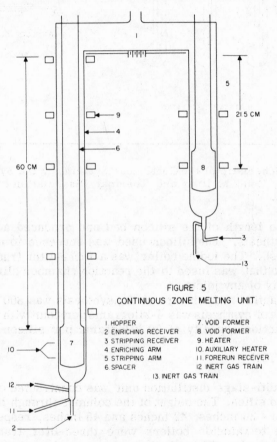

FIGURE 5
CONTINUOUS ZONE MELTING UNIT

1. HOPPER	7. VOID FORMER
2. ENRICHING RECEIVER	8. VOID FORMER
3. STRIPPING RECEIVER	9. HEATER
4. ENRICHING ARM	10. AUXILIARY HEATER
5. STRIPPING ARM	11. FORERUN RECEIVER
6. SPACER	12. INERT GAS TRAIN
	13. INERT GAS TRAIN

Figure 2. Schematic of the Continuous
Zone Melting Unit.

The apparatus was constructed of transparent fused silica. The hopper (1) was 50 mm I.D. and 12 inches in length. The enriching receiver (2) and stripping receiver (3) were two-liter flasks. (Enriching applies to the zoned silicon tetraiodide, and

28

stripping designates the waste product.) The enriching arm (4) was 50 mm I.D. and 60 cm in length. The stripping arm (5) was also 50 mm I.D. but only 21.5 cm long. Tubes 38 mm O.D. and sealed on the lower end were inserted in both the enriching and stripping arms to serve as spacers (6). These spacers were introduced in scaling up the experimental zoner to provide an increase in the material flow without sacrificing the more desirable planar condition of the solid-liquid interface.

The calculations to determine the theoretical separation ratio α for boron triiodide in this zoner are as follows:

Given
$\qquad K_{eff} = .4$ (Boron triiodide) [2]
$\qquad$ Height of molten zone $= l = 1.18$ inches
$\qquad$ Heater height $= h = 1.417$ inches
$\qquad$ Length of enriching arm $= L_e = 22.8$ inches

Applying Pfann's equations for the enriching arm we have

$$B_e = .935 \text{ from } e^{B(1.417)} = 1 + B\frac{(1.18)}{(.4)} \qquad (1)$$

This is a transcendental equation and has no exact algebraic solution but if it can be placed in the form $f(x) = 0$ then $f_1(x) = f_2(x)$ where one side is only algebraic terms. A solution for this equation can be found by setting each side equal to y and plotting on the same set of axes. Where the curves intersect (other than $B = 0$) the value for B will satisfy the original equation. From Pfann's "Limit of α Table," we know that all B values will be positive for $K < l/h$, therefore it is only necessary to plot positive values of B for any K from 0.16 to 0.7. Using this value of B in the subsequent equations in the series, $\alpha = 1.22 \times 10^{-24}$ for the enriching arm for a segregation coefficient of 0.4. Pfann defines the separation ratio α as C_p/C_f where C_p is the solute concentration in the product and C_f is the concentration in the feed material.

For the stripping side the separation ratio β was calculated to be 4.32×10^5. Pfann defines β as C_w/C_f where C_w is the solute concentration in the waste and C_f is the concentration in the feed material.

The void-formers (7) and (8) were 46 mm O.D. and 3 inches in length. The molten zones were created by external heaters (9) positioned 10 cm apart. These heaters were regulated to create zones 3 cm long. These zones are carried to the top of the enriching arm where the solute is mixed with the feed material. Separation in the opposite direction is effected in the stripping arm by the downward passage of the zones.

The flow of material is produced by voids that travel up the enriching and stripping arms. The collection of the enriched material and the waste material provides for the creation of the voids.

The distillation unit was connected to the iodide reservoir of the zoner to provide continuity of the system. The reservoir was sealed from the zoner by a breakseal positioned in the cross-arm. This permitted thorough cleaning and outgassing of the zoning system prior to operation. The system was vacuum dried and outgassed with helium. With a positive helium pressure the breakseal was fractured and the unit was charged with silicon tetraiodide. Figure 3 shows the zoner in operation.

Figure 3. Continuous Zone Melting Unit in Operation.

Silicon tetraiodide was melted from the void former to a point just opposite the bottom heater by an auxiliary heater. The lower heater was then turned on. When the SiI_4 became molten the drive mechanism was activated. The molten SiI_4 solidifies at a point just above the auxiliary heater forming a plug. The distance was determined by the volume required to create a void 6 mm high in the enriching arm.

The heaters travel 10 cm at a rate of 5 cm per hour and then reciprocate rapidly to their original position. The heaters were activated at a rate of one per cycle until all heaters were on and the zoning could continue indefinitely. Figure 4 is a close-up of a molten zone and void on the enriching arm.

Figure 4. Molten Zone and Void on the Enriching Arm.

Voids travel continuously with the zones on the enriching side but intermittently with the zones on the stripping side.

To obtain a state of equilibrium in the zoner it was necessary to remove a forerun resulting from one hundred passes. The number of passes required was based on the number of passes calculated to obtain the ultimate distribution in the experimental zoner - 60 passes plus 40 passes arbitrarily selected as an insurance factor.

Upon completion of the forerun the solid silicon tetraiodide plug sealing the enriching receiver was removed by sublimation to prevent contamination of the zoned material receiver.

The visual evidence of the segregation of elemental iodine from the bottom zone of the enriching arm through the stripping arm supports the theory of the geometry of this continuous zoner. Color gradation, as created by elemental iodine, showed a purification in the feed material in the hopper supporting the purification factor indicated by the calculation of the separation ratio. Figure 5 is a photograph of the enriched material.

THERMAL DISSOCIATION

The thermal dissociation unit was sealed from the enriched material receiver by a series of breakseals. The thermal dissociation unit was thoroughly cleaned, dried and vacuum checked before fracturing the breakseal. The breakseal on the dissociation

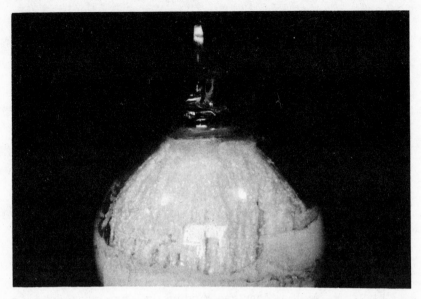

Figure 5. Zoned Silicon Tetraiodide.

unit was fractured and a vacuum check made on the weld coupling
the unit to the receiver. A positive helium atmosphere was restored to the system and the breakseal of the enriched receiver
was fractured. The small orifice, through which to insert the
transparent fused silica rod used to fracture the breakseal, was
sealed.

The temperature of the thermal dissociation was $1,100°C \pm$
$10°C$. The pressure of the system as determined by a McLeod
gauge downstream from the by-products collector was 1×10^{-3}
mm Hg.

The substrate for the silicon deposition was a transparent
fused silica tube. The silicon recovered was 155 grams representing a yield of 83 percent.

The purification factor obtained from the zone melting
process, as determined by the base boron level of the silicon
recovered was 5x. The base boron level of the final product
was 2 ppb, as compared to 10 ppb for the starting material to
the zoner.

CONCLUSIONS

Possible reasons for some deviation from the theoretical
may be attributed to a non-planar condition in the solid-liquid
interface, variation in length of the molten zones and height of
the voids. It is considered that any of these conditions would

effect the ultimate distribution, but not to a degree sufficient for the significant deviation from the theoretical reported in this paper.

The purification factor obtained, as well as the magnitude of the base boron concentration was disappointing; but these results are considered inconclusive with the limited date available.

The application and successful operation of a continuous zone melting technique is considered the significant accomplishment of this study.

ACKNOWLEDGMENTS

The authors wish to acknowledge The Electronic Research Directorate, Air Force Cambridge Research Laboratories, for the sponsorship of this study.

REFERENCES

1. Pfann, W. G., "Zone Melting," John Wiley & Sons, Inc., New York, N. Y., 1958, pp. 115-130.
2. Rubin, B., Moates, G. H., and Weiner, J. R., J. Electrochem. Soc., 104, 656 (1957).

DISCUSSION

W. R. WILCOX (Pacific Semiconductors): What zone velocity did you use and how did you determine your effective distribution coefficient?

J. T. BUFORD (Eagle-Picher): The zones traveled at a rate of two inches per hour. The segregation coefficients were not determined by us. The information is in the literature by Rubin, Moates and Weiner.

W. R. WILCOX (Pacific Semiconductors): Was this at the same zone velocity?

J. T. BUFORD (Eagle-Picher): Yes, that is correct.

M. J. URBAN (General Electric): Will this technique be applied to your commercially available silicon tetraiodide?

J. T. BUFORD (Eagle-Picher): I am not in a position right now to state whether it will or not. This is just a pre-pilot scale apparatus.

A. J. ROSENBERG CHAIRMAN (Tyco): Did you state what the highest purity that you obtained was?

J. T. BUFORD (Eagle-Picher): In the base boron level it was two parts per billion.

THE PREPARATION OF SEMICONDUCTOR GRADE SILICON BY THE IODIDE PROCESS

H. Baba* and H. Araki
Electrical Communication Laboratory, N. T. T.
Tokyo, Japan

INTRODUCTION

The crude silicon of 97% purity is produced for alloy use by reducing the natural silex in an arc furnace. Usually the purification of silicon for semiconductor use starts from this material, and the principal impurities and their approximate concentrations are 10^{-3} of Fe, Al, Ca, 10^{-4} of C, Ti, Mg and 10^{-5} of P and B respectively.

The purification of this material had been tried since 1927, and the purity of 99.8% was attained by treating the finely powdered elemental silicon with mixed acid, but its purity was far from semiconductor grade. Silicon can also be purified by segregating it from solvent metal such as zinc or aluminum. Since the silicon itself forms solid solutions with these metals in some extent, the purity attainable by this process is limited [1]. At any rate, it is difficult to attain semiconductor grade purity without employing a chemical purification process. That is, the crude silicon must be converted to some intermediate which can easily be refined, and it should be capable of being reduced to its elemental state without contamination. Elemental germanium can be obtained by reducing germanium dioxide with hydrogen, but in the case of silicon, a silicon halide must be thermally decomposed or reduced with hydrogen to obtain the element directly.

In the quest for a practical solution, several purifying methods have been tried besides the well known duPont method, [2] which was the first process used successful on an industrial scale. To date, the following have been proposed; namely, 1) silane process, [3], 2) trichlorosilane process, 3) reduction of silicon tetrachloride by hydrogen, [4,5] and 4) thermal decomposition [6] or hydrogen reduction [7] of silicon tetraiodide. Among these, the second one has been succeeded industrially in several countries.

---

*Present Address:
IBM Research Center, Yorktown Heights, New York.

34

We expected that the silicon iodide method could be promising if further improvement was made on the purification processes, and we have devoted considerable effort to this process to make it applicable to industry.

PROCESSES AND STUDIES ON THE INDIVIDUAL REFINING STEPS

Figure 1 shows a systematic diagram of the author's process. The purification process consists of seven successive steps. They are: the iodination reaction, three repetitions of recrystallization from toluene, a second distillation under reduced pressure, a fractional distallation, zone refining of the iodide, and thermal decomposition of the iodide to its elements.

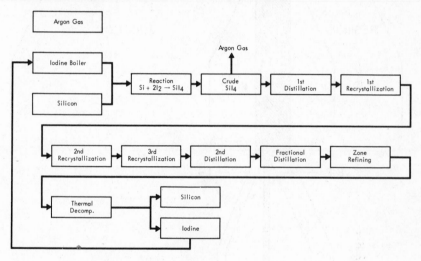

Figure 1. Systematic Diagram for Purifying Silicon by the Iodide Process.

Individual purification steps were studied as the preliminary experiments. Silicon tetraiodide can be prepared by passing iodine vapor over the starting silicon at 850°C. The reaction proceeds almost quantitatively and there remain few problems as reported elsewhere [8,9]. In order to clarify the behavior of impurities during the recrystallization process, radio isotope ^{32}P was used as a tracer.

Silicon tetraiodide containing radioactive phosphorus was prepared by dissolving the iodide in hot toluene, in which activated red phosphorus had been reacted with iodine to form phosphorus iodide, and after filtration the iodide was crystallized by cooling the solution. The silicon iodide thus obtained was

35

dissolved in toluene at 120°C and argon gas saturated with water vapor at room temperature was introduced into the solution to form suspending hydrolyzed products, which were filtered off through a glass filter while the solution was hot. The filtrate was then cooled to crystallize out the silicon iodide. The behavior of impurity phosphorus during the recrystallization was followed by measuring the activity in various samples at each step.

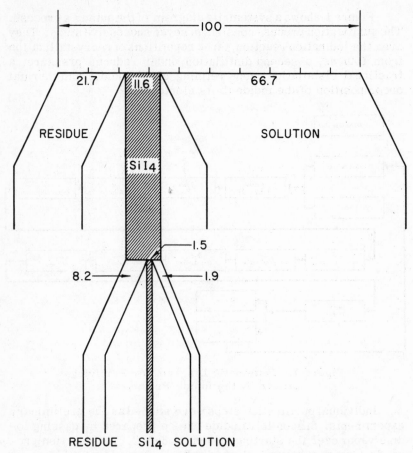

Figure 2. Distribution of ^{32}P in Fractions of the Recrystallizational Purification Process

Figure 2 shows the distribution of phosphorus in the hydrolyzed product, the silicon tetraiodide, and the filtrate solution of each step of recrystallization, as the relative concentration of phosphorus in per cent to that in the starting iodide. It indicates that impurity phosphorus in silicon tetraiodide can be removed effectively by the recrystallization process, and the hydrolyzed

36

products suspending in the iodide solution play the predominant role because of their high adsorptivity. The results of the emission spectroscopic analysis indicated that other impurities could also be removed by this process.

Phosphorus, arsenic, and boron are difficult to remove by zone melting elemental silicon, because their effective segregation coefficients are close to unity. The behavior of these elements in silicon tetraiodide should be different from in elemental silicon.

Rubin, et al studied the zone melting of silicon tetraiodide and they determined the segregation coefficients of several elements by spectrographic analysis [10]. We studied the behavior of trace quantities of boron and phosphorus in silicon tetraiodide during normal freezing and zone melting of the material [11]. Tracer techniques were applied for phosphorus, while boron was determined by a colorimetric technique using curcumin. The results are shown in Fig. 3. After passing three molten zones, the ratio of the concentration of radioactive phosphorus from the head to the tail of the matrix was in the order of 10^{-3}. A complete profile of the distribution of boron could not be obtained because of the relatively poor determination limit of the analysis used comparing to the radiochemical method. Spectral analysis also showed that impurity elements such as Mn and Ti were concentrated in the tail portion of the zone refined iodide matrix. It is believed that the hydrolyzed colloidal products play an important role in the segregation because of their high adsorptivity with respect to these impurity elements.

Silicon iodide is thermally decomposed at above 1000°C in a high vacuum according to the following equation: $SiI_4 \rightarrow Si + 2I_2$. The possibility of industrialization of this process is mainly determined by the decomposition rate, yield, and the amount of contamination by foreign impurities during the decomposition process.

Deposition of silicon on a heated tantalum ribbon [6] has been tried by several investigators, but the contamination from tantalum and other accompanying impurities with it could not be avoided. Decomposition on the inner surface of a high purity quartz tube heated at a high temperature is one of the best methods to obtain highly pure silicon. The yield depends on the diameter of the decomposition tube, flow rate of silicon iodide, and decomposition temperatures. The correlations between these factors were obtained by using small scale apparatus. Correlations between the flow rate of the iodide and the yield of the reaction are shown in Fig. 4.

The decomposition temperature was kept constant at 1100°C and the diameter of the quartz tube was 10mm. The decomposition temperature also influenced the yield of the reaction, however the decomposition rate was determined mainly by the flow

Table 1. Spectrographic Data

Element	Wavelength	Iodine Product SiI_4	1st Distillation		Recrystallization			2nd Distilled SiI_4	Fractional Distillation			Blank
			Distilled SiI_4	Residue	1st Recryst Residue	3rd Recryst Residue	3rd Recryst-ed SiI_4		First Fraction	Middle Fraction	Last Fraction	
Al	3082.1	+5	+2	str	str	+2	(+2)	±	(+)	(+)	±	tr
	3092.7	+5	+3	str	str	+3	+2	(+)	+	(+)	(+)	tr
Ag	3280.6	tr	-	(+2)	(+)	tr	-	-	-	-	-	-
	3382.8	-	-	+	±	-	-	-	-	-	-	-
B	2496.7	tr	tr	+2	+4	+2	tr	-	-	-	-	-
	2497.7	±	tr	(+3)	+5	(+3)	tr	-	-	-	-	-
Ca	3158.8	±	-	+	±	-	-	-	-	-	-	-
	3179.3	±	-	(+2)	±	-	-	-	-	-	-	-
Cu	3247.5	+5	+	+5	+4	(+4)	+2	tr	(+)	tr	tr	-
	3273.9	(+5)	(+)	+5	(+4)	+3	(+2)	tr	+	tr	tr	-
Fe	2599.3	+	±	(+3)	(+3)	+2	tr	-	tr	-	-	-
	2719.0	+	±	(+3)	(+3)	+2	±	±	(+)	+	tr	-
	3020.6	(+2)	(+)	+3	+3	(+3)	(+)	+	+	+	tr	-
Ge	3039.0	-	-	±	-	-	-	tr	+	-	tr	-
Mn	2794.8	+4	-	+5	+4	+	-	-	±	-	-	-
	2798.2	+4	-	+5	+4	tr	-	-	+	-	-	-
Mg	2795.5	+4	(+3)	+4	+4	(+4)	(+2)	+2	(+4)	+2	+2	+
	2852.1	+5	+3	+5	+5	+4	(+3)	(+3)	+4	(+3)	(+3)	(+2)
Ni	3002.4	tr	-	+	±	tr	-	-	-	-	-	-
	3050.8	tr	-	(+2)	(+)	±	-	-	-	-	-	-
Na	3302.3	tr	±	±	(+)	(+)	-	(+)	+	tr	tr	-
	3302.9	tr	tr	tr	+	+	tr	±	(+)	tr	tr	-
Pb	2802.0	-	-	±	(+)	-	±	-	-	-	-	-
	2833.0	-	-	(+)	+	tr	tr	-	-	-	-	-
Ti	3234.5	+	(+2)	(+4)	+5	+	-	-	-	-	-	-
	3236.5	+	(+2)	(+4)	+5	+	-	-	-	-	-	-

str > +5 > (+5) > ...... + > (+) > ± > tr > -

38

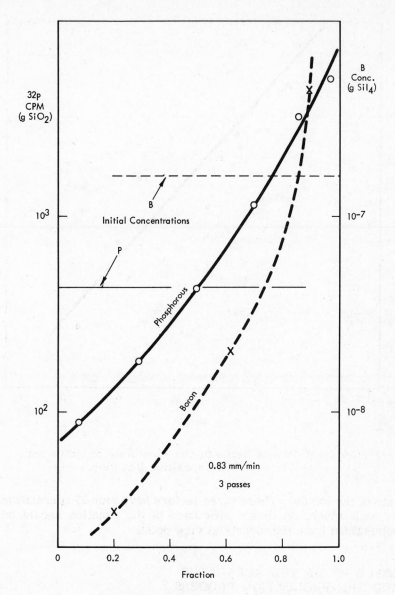

Figure 3. Redistribution of B and P after Three
Passes of Molten Zone.

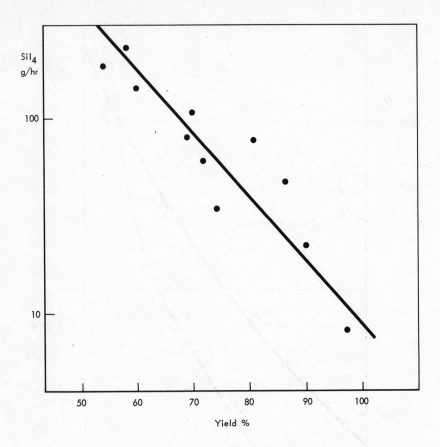

Figure 4. Relations Between the Flow Rate of Iodide and
the Yield of Decomposition Reaction.

rate of the iodide. These three factors have mutual correlation
to each other, maximum efficiency of the reaction should be
determined from the industrial view point.

SCALE UP OF THE APPARATUS
AND THE PRODUCTION PROCESS

Construction: The determination of the purity of the material
requires knowledge of the electrical and physical properties of
the single crystal. For this purpose, a substantial amount of the
material is required; and, also, in order to determine its adapta-
bility to industrialization, some magnification of the apparatus
is required.

Figure 5. The First Apparatus.

The iodination system consisted of five sections; namely, purification of argon gas which was used as a carrier of the iodine vapor, device for the concentration measurements of the iodine in the gas stream by the absorption of a soft γ-ray, iodine saturation, iodination reaction tube, and iodide reservoir.

The iodine reservoir had a capacity of 5 kg of iodine, and it could be heated electrically to the boiling temperature. Argon gas which was used as the carrier of iodine vapor was passed through the iodine boiler at a flow rate of 1ℓ/min. The iodine vapor carried by argon was introduced into the reaction tube (made of quartz with 80 mm diameter and 660 mm length) in which about 1 kg of crushed raw silicon could be charged.

The recrystallization system consisted of three double walled flasks equipped with valves and filters. Each of the flasks could be heated or cooled by circulating the thermomedia oil in the

41

jacket so that three repetitions of recrystallization could be carried out continuously without exposing the contents to atmosphere. The silicon iodide dissolved in toluene was transferred from one flask to another through filters by changing the pressure of the system. During the dissolving process, water vapor accompanied by air was introduced into the solutions to form the suspension of hydrolyzed products in the solution.

This step was followed by the sublimation of the iodide under a reduced pressure. Free iodine and any residual solvent in the iodide were removed by this process. The silicon tetraiodide purified by sublimation was then transferred to the fractional distillation system. This system was a plate type distillation tower equipped with fifteen plates made of quartz.

The main fraction of the distilled iodide was then zone refined. As the zone refining of the iodide was the final step of the purification, all vessels and tubes were made by quartz in order to avoid the contamination from the vessels. The tube (40 mm diameter and 1000 mm length) was placed horizontally and the iodide was charged to about 80% of the tube leaving small spaces on the surface to avoid breakage of the tube by expansion and shrinkage of the material. The molten zone was about 50 mm width and the space between the two molten zones was maintained at about 150 mm; the traveling speed of the zone was 1.5 mm/min.

The decomposition apparatus was composed of the quartz reaction tube in which a thin wall quartz tube with 30 mm diameter and 600 mm length was mounted, the iodide flask, the free iodine trapping flask, and a vacuum system. The reaction tube was set vertically and the iodide flask was attached at the bottom so that the iodide gas was vaporized up and was decomposed to its elements on the inner surface of the decomposition tube at 1100°C in the vacuum of 10^{-4} mm Hg.

Operating data: The operating data are listed in Table 2. The results showed that the iodination reaction proceeds almost quantitatively at 850°C when the iodine input was around 500 g/hr. After three repetitions of the recrystallization, using about 1200 ml of toluene as a solvent, 4.3 kg of fine light yellow crystalline iodide were obtained. The material was then distilled under the pressure of about 45 mm Hg to remove the toluene. Starting with 4.0 kg of iodide, about 3.0 kg of middle fraction of the distillate were used for succeeding steps.

About 2.3 kg of zone refined iodide was decomposed. The yields of this process were about 50-70%. The fluctuations of yield arise from the irregular evaporation of the iodide.

RESULTS

Any improvement of the purification process requires a thorough understanding of the behavior of impurity elements. It

42

Table 2. Operating Data of the First Apparatus

PROCESSES	RUN NO. 5		RUN NO. 6		RUN NO. 7	
A) Iodination Reaction						
Si charged	860	g	934	g	1093	g
I_2 charged	5.0	kg	5.0	kg	8.0	kg
Reaction temp.	850°C		850°C		850°C	
Iodine boiler temp.	180 ~248°C		180 ~256°C		170°C	
Argon Gas flow rate	1	1/m	1	1/m	1	1/m
Reaction time	9	hrs	7	hrs	10	hrs
Iodine consumed	5.0	kg	5.0	kg	7.2	kg
Silicon consumed	280	g	256	g	----	
B) Recrystallization					Iodide	
1) Iodide	----		----		6,065	g
Toluene	1500	ml	1100	ml	1st distill.	
Iodide (contg. toluene)	5.2	kg	4.8	kg	5,785	g
2) Toluene	1200	ml	1300	ml		
Iodide (contg. toluene)	4.8	kg	4.7	kg		
3) Toluene	1200	ml	1300	ml		
Iodide (contg. toluene)	4.3	kg	4.3	kg	4.7	kg
C) Distillation under reduced						
pressure (atmosphere)	(Vacuum)		(Argon)		(Argon)	
Temp.	111°C		140 ~179°C		165°C	
Pressure	Vac.		45 mm Hg		45 mm Hg	
Iodide charged	4.3	kg	4.3	kg	4.6	kg
Distilled	4.0	kg	4.0	kg	3.9	kg
Time	4	hrs	2	hrs	4.5	hrs
D) Fractional Distillation						
Iodide charged	4.0	kg	4.0	kg	3.8	kg
1st Fraction	0.6	kg	0.3	kg	0.25	kg
Middle Fraction	3.0	kg	3.5	kg	3.2	kg
Time	4.5	hrs	7.0	hrs	19.0	hrs
E) Zone Refining						
Zone passed	16		22		13	
Zone refined SiI_4	2.3	kg	2.8	kg	2.4	kg
F) Thermal Decomposition	1100°C		1100°C		1100°C	
Si metal obtained	36.4	g	65.5	g	45.7	g
Yield	----		71.5%		----	

is advantageous, of cource, to have quantitative data on the distribution of impurity elements for each step in the purifying processes. The authors determined the arsenic content in the iodide samples taken from each purification step of the process. The samples were hydrolyzed by adding a sufficient amount of water to form silicon dioxide and were dried up in a quartz

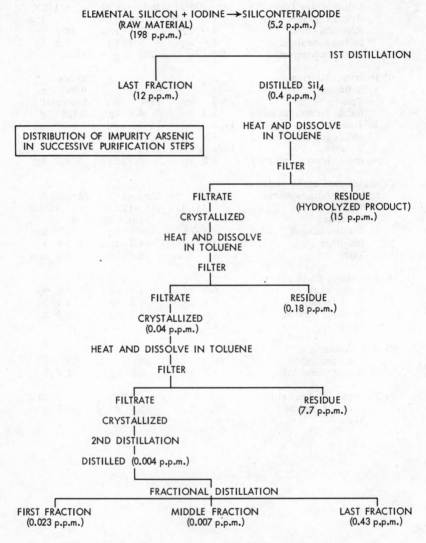

Figure 6. Distribution of Impurity Arsenic in Successive Purification Steps.

44

vessel on a hot plate. By this treatment, the arsenic, which would be present as iodide, was hydrolyzed to oxide. The oxide samples were irradiated under a neutron flux of about 4×10^{11} n/cm^2 sec. for five hours.

The activated samples were fused with potassium hydroxide containing arsenious acid as a carrier. The fused cake was treated with concentrated hydrochloric acid, and the arsenic was distilled out and converted to arsenic sulfide for β-ray counting. The results show that the arsenic in silicon tetraiodide is also concentrated in hydrolyzed products and its concentration in iodide may be reduced to the order of 10^{-8} after the fractional distillation.

As the elemental silicon is deposited in the atmosphere of iodine, it is unavoidably contaminated by traces of iodine. The results of activation analysis of iodine as deposited in silicon showed a concentration of several p.p.m. of iodine, but this was reduced to 0.3 p.p.m. by fusing in an argon gas atmosphere for one hour. The silicon sample which was irradiated under a thermal neutron flux of about 6×10^{11} n/cm^2 sec for one hour was carefully fused by alkaline. The fused cake was treated with sulfuric acid and molecular iodine was liberated by adding sodium nitrite, distilled and purified by solvent extraction, and then converted into silver iodide for counting and weighing. The distribution of iodine throughout a silicon single crystal is shown in

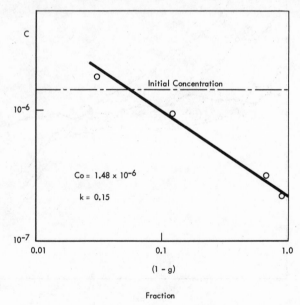

Figure 7. Distribution of Iodine Concentration in a Single Crystal of Silicon Prepared by the Iodide Process.

Fig. 7. This indicates that the iodine is segregated during the crystal growing and the distribution constant is estimated to be 0.15 from this data.

Results of the spectrographic analysis are shown in Table 1. As shown in the Table, many kinds of impurities which were detected in starting iodide became lower in concentration as the purification proceeded. After the fractional distillation, trace amounts of Al, Cu, Fe, Mg and Na were detected.

The distribution of resistivity throughout the zone refined silicon rod gives helpful information about the purity of the material and the type of impurity present in the material. Fig. 8 shows the redistribution of resistivity by the repetition of zone melting. This indicates that the impurity is of one type, and it is assumed to be Al and B. After 67 passes, the top of the bar reached to 1.8 kΩcm.

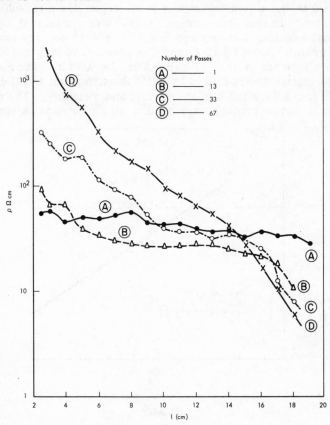

Figure 8. Resistivity Profile of Floating Zone Refined Silicon.

46

IMPROVED PROCESS AND APPARATUS

Several difficulties were found in the previous apparatus especially in the recrystallization system. The system was too complicated to handle, and the heating and cooling systems were also causes of troubles.

The improved method of recrystallization was a combination of the principles of recrystallization and zone refining.

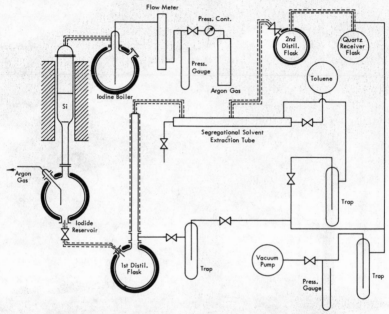

Figure 9. Flow Sheet of the Improved Apparatus.

The schematic flow sheet is shown in Fig. 9. Argon gas was introduced into the iodine boiler after passing a flow meter. The iodine boiler consisting of a round flask 30 cm in diameter was heated by a mantle heater. The reaction tube was the same as used in the previous apparatus. The iodination products were melted from the iodide reservoir into the first distillation flask. The first distillation flask was pumped out through the trap without passing the tower to separate the free iodine from the main fraction of the distillate. The main fraction was distilled into the segregational recrystallization tube. The tube was then filled with toluene from the toluene flask. After three repetitions of this process, the remaining solvent was pumped out. The molten iodide in the tube was transferred into the second distillation flask. The packed column distillation tower made of quartz was used in the new apparatus. The tower was 28 mm in

47

diameter and 2100 mm high, and was packed with 5 mm x 10 mm quartz tips. The tower was covered by a 50 mm diameter glass tube and was heated from outside by nichrome windings.

Segregational Extraction: The principle of solvent extraction is based on a solubility difference at different temperature, but the process presents some difficulties for industrial applications because a large amount of solvent is consumed and the

Figure 10. The Improved Apparatus.

process must be continuous and executed without exposing the material to moisture in this case. The authors designed the previous apparatus with these facts in mind but found many technical difficulties in operation such as heating and cooling systems, and transferring of the material to the next step of purification. The authors tried to combine the principles of the solvent extraction and segregation effects.

Suppose that a solvent phase is present in addition to the iodide layer so that the saturated impurities in the liquid phase

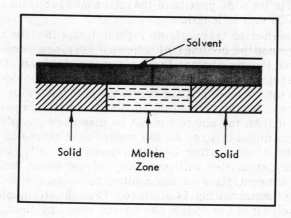

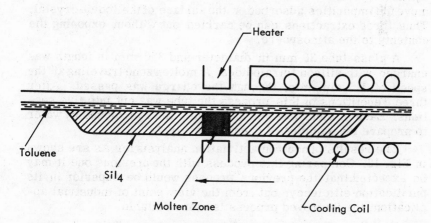

Figure 11. Schematic Diagram of the
Segregational Solvent Extraction.

49

of the iodide may move to the solvent phase by the principle of solvent extraction. Thus segregation as well as solvent extraction effects can be expected simultaneously. One problem concerning this process is the diffusion of impurities in the solvent phase because the purified solid iodide is always in contact with the solvent, and it causes the recontamination of the purified material. This fault may be eliminated by washing the iodide crystal after the solvent is drained out from the tube. A schematic diagram of this process is shown in Fig. 11. Both ends of the tube are narrowed as shown in the figure so that the iodide can be charged in the wide portion of the tube which is 60 mm in diameter and 1000 mm in length.

The zone heater travels from right to left of the tube as shown in the figure and the cooling coil follows it keeping a constant distance. First, the zone heater is placed at the right end of the tube to melt the top portion of the matrix. A part of the iodide is dissolved into the toluene until the solvent is saturated with it at that temperature. As the amount of solvent is small compared with that of the iodide, the solute can not be dissolved completely but exists in two liquid layers. As the molten zone moves to the left, the impurity concentration in it increases gradually, but some parts of the impurities will go to the solvent phase before the maximum concentration in the molten zone, as defined by the principles of zone melting, is attained. Thus the attainable purity by zone melting of the iodide can be improved by the existence of a solvent phase in addition to the iodide.

After passing the molten zone, the solvent is drained out of the tube while the cooling coil covers the whole length of the tube, and the crystal is washed by fresh toluene several times to remove the impurities adsorbed on the surface of the iodide crystal. Thus three extractions can be carried out without exposing the contents to the atmosphere.

A glass tube 20 mm in diameter and 350 mm in length was charged with silicon tetraiodides. A molten zone traveling at the speed of 1.5 mm/min. through the charge was passed. After three repetitions of this process the tube was cut into five sections. Each of them was weighed rapidly and hydrolyzed by water to prepare the samples of chemical analysis.

The results of neutron activation analysis for As are shown in Fig. 12. Comparing this process with the previous one it may be expected that the previous process would be superior in its purification efficiency, but from the view point of industrial application, the improved process is more suitable.

Results: The operating data are shown in Table 3. Each run started with a charge of 5.0 kg iodine and was operated under similar conditions.

50

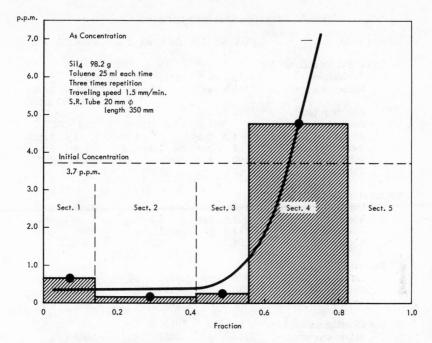

Figure 12. Redistribution of As after Three Repetitions of the Segregational Solvent Extraction Process. (Activation analysis).

The resistivity profile of a single crystal prepared by this process is shown in Fig. 13. Examining these two processes, the purity of the products was assumed to be comparable but judging from the industrial aspects, the improved process is more promising because of its simplicity and ease of operation.

ACKNOWLEDGEMENTS

The writers with to thank Drs. Z. Kiyasu, T. Niimi and K. Mizuma for much helpful discussions and many suggestions.

51

Table 3. Operating Data of the Improved Apparatus

PROCESSES	RUN NO. 2-1		RUN NO. 2-2		RUN NO. 2-3	
A) Iodination Reaction						
Si charged	1071	g	1281	g	1160	g
Iodine charge	5.0	kg	5.0	kg	5.0	kg
					(industrial grade)	
Reaction temp.		850°C		850°C		850°C
Iodine boiler temp.		300°C	300 ~350°C		250 ~300°C	
Argon Gas flow rate	1.5	1/m	1.5	1/m	1.0	1/m
Reaction time	4	hrs	3.3	hrs	4	hrs
Iodide	5190	g	4975	g	4558	g
Yield	98%		94.5%		----	
B) 1st Distillation						
Iodide	5190	g	4975	g	4558	g
Time	2.5	hrs	4.0	hrs	3.0	hrs
Distilled Iodide	4890	g	4744	g	3830	g
Yield	94.5%		95.2%		84.1%	
C) Solvent Extraction						
1st time, Toluene	645	ml	300	ml	300	ml
2nd time, Toluene	500	ml	200	ml	200	ml
3rd time, Toluene	300	ml	200	ml	200	ml
D) 2nd Distillation						
Iodide charged	3184	g	3638	g	2665	g
Iodide distilled	2945	g	----		2420	g
Time	3	hrs	----		3	hrs
E) Fractional Distillation						
Charge	2945	g	3560	g	2420	g
First Fraction	1055	g	1315	g	578	g
Middle Fraction	1483	g	1470	g	1335	g
F) Thermal Decomposition						
Temp.		1100°C		1100°C		1100°C
SiI_4 consumed	1483	g	1433	g	1335	g
Si metal obtained	70	g*	68	g*	66	g*
(after etching)	(47.6)		(62.0)		(52.0)	
Yield	66%		91%		74%	
Reaction time	6	hrs	26	hrs	22	hrs

*Including small amounts of quartz

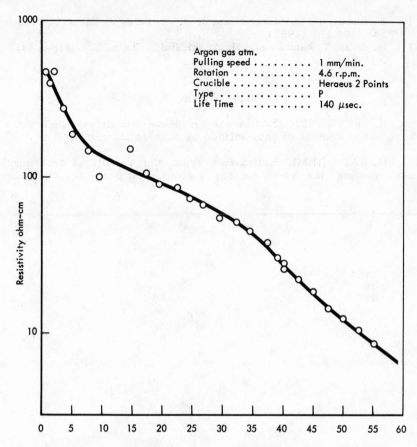

Figure 13. Resistivity Distribution in Silicon Single Crystal.

REFERENCES

1. H. V. Wartenberg, Z. f. Anorg. u. Allgem. Chem. 265 186 (1951).
2. D. W. Lyon, C. M. Olson and E. D. Lewis, J. Electrochem. Soc. 96 359 (1949).
3. S. I. Kleshchevnikova, et al, Soviet Physics. Technical Physics 2 152 (1957).
4. R. Holbling: Z. f. Angew. Chem. 40 655 (1927).
5. H. C. Theuerer, Bell Lab. Record 33 327 (1955).
6. F. B. Litton and H. C. Anderson, J. Electrochem. Soc. 101 287 (1954).
7. G. Szekely, J. Electrochem. Soc. 104 663 (1957).
8. A. C. Loonam, J. Electrochem. Soc. 106 238 (1959).
9. U. V. McCarty, J. Electrochem. Soc. 106 1036 (1959).

10. B. Rubin, G. H. Moates and J. R. Weiner, J. Electrochem. Soc. 104 656 (1957).
11. H. Baba, T. Nozaki and H. Araki, Bull. Chem. Soc. Japan 32, 5 (1959).

DISCUSSION

H. G. VERNER (Mallinckrodt): Have you determined the base boron content of your silicon by zone refining it?

H. BABA (IBM): Estimating from the results of troating zone melting, the boron content is about eight parts per billion.

THE PREPARATION OF HIGH-PURITY
SILICON FROM SILANE

Charles H. Lewis, Mario B. Giusto,
Henry C. Kelly and Sidney Johnson
The Research and Development Laboratories,
Metal Hydrides Inc., Beverly, Massachusetts

In the past five years, the electronics industry has developed a requirement for ultra-pure silicon for semiconductor applications. To fulfill this need, a number of alternative processes for the preparation of high-purity silicon have been investigated by various laboratories throughout the world. Starting in 1956, a research program was conducted to evaluate silane as an intermediate material for the preparation of ultra-pure silicon [1, 2]. The silane was generated by interaction of silicon tetrachloride with lithium aluminum hydride, and then thermally decomposed in accordance with the following equations

$$SiCl_4 + LiAlH_4 \xrightarrow{\text{tetraglyme}} SiH_4 + LiCl + AlCl_3$$

$$SiH_4 \xrightarrow{\Delta} Si + 2 H_2$$

Since silane, SiH_4, is a highly volatile gas which forms spontaneously explosive mixtures with air and presents severe handling problems not common to other intermediates, the advantages to be gained by its use are summarized:

1. Silane is the least stable intermediate with respect to decomposition to the elements. Thermodynamically there is less energy to overcome to achieve decomposition - a factor which can only be beneficial for the preparation of silicon. The favorable comparison is readily seen from the standard heat of formation values in Table I below.

2. Silane contains a greater percentage of silicon than other intermediates. The quantity of various silicon compounds required to contain unit weight of silicon is given in Table II.

3. The silicon tetrachloride-lithium aluminum hydride silane generator operates by mixing two solutions and is a homogeneous reaction. Silane is essentially instantaneously evolved. It is easy to start, stop, control, and regulate.

Table I

Standard Heats of Formation at 25°C

Compound		ΔH_f	Reference
SiH$_4$	(g)	+7.8	a
SiI$_4$	(s)	-31.6	b
SiBr$_4$	(l)	-95.1	b
SiCl$_4$	(l)	-153.0	b
SiF$_4$	(g)	-370	b

(a) E. O. Brimm and H. M. Humphreys, J. Chem. Phys., 61, 829 (1957).

(b) "Selected Values of Chemical Thermodynamic Properties," F. D. Rossini, D. D. Wagman, W. H. Evans, S. Levine, and I. Jaffe, Natl. Bur. Standards Circ. 500, U. S. Government Printing Office, Washington, 1950.

Table II

Si Compound	Mol. Wt.	$\dfrac{\text{Wt. Si Compound}}{\text{Wt. Si}}$
Si	28.06	1.00
SiH$_4$	32.092	1.14
SiF$_4$	104.060	3.71
SiHCl$_3$	135.439	4.83
SiCl$_4$	169.888	6.05
SiBr$_4$	347.724	12.39
SiI$_4$	535.740	19.09

4. Use of the dimethyl ether of tetraethyleneglycol (b.p. 275°C) virtually eliminates solvent entrainment as a consideration.

5. The generation step is an exceedingly powerful purification procedure. It completely and quantitatively eliminates all elements which do not form volatile hydrides, or whose volatile hydrides are protonic in nature.

6. The silane gas stream is particularly susceptible to complete quantitative removal of trace impurities by gas scrubbing techniques. Quality control of the product is relatively independent of starting materials.

7. Only hydrogen is evolved as a decomposition by-product. Hydrogen chloride and chlorine evolved in other processes present corrosion problems—significant only to semiconductor applications.

8. No boron is evolved when excess lithium aluminum hydride is present. The relatively high acidity of the borane group, BH_3, compared to silane greatly enhances the separation of this element.

Where ultra-pure silicon is the prime objective, these considerations indicate the advantages of silane as an intermediate and they far outweigh its disadvantages.

GENERATION OF SILANE

The investigation started with a consideration of various methods of generating silane. A hydride reduction of a silicon halide in an ether solvent was most suitable. Lithium aluminum hydride and either silicon tetrachloride or trichlorosilane gave quantitative yields of silane. Any number of ethers are suitable, but its low volatility made the dimethyl ether of tetraethylene glycol the solvent of choice (variously referred to as "tetraglyme," "E-181," or "M4M").

The reaction was carried out at room temperature by adding the glycol ether solution of the chloride dropwise into a magnetically stirred glycol ether solution or slurry containing an excess of lithium aluminum hydride. This afforded a ready and convenient means of controlling the reaction by adjusting the rate of addition. The reaction vessel was under evacuation and the evolved silane passed through a Dry Ice condenser, a purification train, and into the decomposition chamber. Here the purified silane is decomposed to yield a polycrystalline deposit of ultra-pure silicon metal, and the by-product hydrogen is expelled through vacuum pumps.

The reaction proceeds by the stepwise replacement of silicon-chlorine bonds with hydrogen. A donor solvent is necessary for the reaction [3]. This serves to displace a hydride ion from the AlH_4^- ion, which in turn displaces a chloride ion from the silicon atom. In subsequent steps, chloride rather than ether displaces the hydride ion. The overall reaction may be represented by the equation

$$R_2O + LiAlH_4 + SiCl_4 \longrightarrow R_2OAlCl_3 + SiH_4 + LiCl$$

PURIFICATION OF SILANE

The generation step is itself a powerful purification, quantitatively separating many impurities. Contaminants in the effluent gas stream are limited to, (a) solvent vapor, (b) unreduced or partially reduced chlorosilanes, as $SiCl_4$ and SiH_xCl_{4-x}, and (c) those elements, originally present as impurities in the silicon tetrachloride, which form volatile hydrides and are liberated from the reaction mixture with silane.

57

Solvent vapor is removed from the gas stream by the use of Dry Ice (-78.5°) and isopentane (-160°) slush baths. The latter bath also is effective in controlling the flow rate of silane and the quantity of undecomposed silane present in the system. At that temperature, liquid silane exerts a vapor pressure of 9 mm. Any silane gas surge from the generator which increases the pressure above this value causes condensation of liquid silane in the trap, and is not transmitted to the decomposition chamber. Additionally, one can observe any accumulation of liquid silane in this bath. By keeping this accumulation small, one can readily assure that the hazard from accidental admixture of silane and air does not exceed the safety limits of the facilities being used.

No evidence for incomplete reduction of silicon tetrachloride was found. An excess of lithium aluminum hydride was always used. The silicon tetrachloride solution was introduced from the dropping funnel through capillary tubing which terminated in a hook at the very bottom of the reaction flask. This caused the evolved gas to pass up through the lithium aluminum hydride solution. The excess lithium aluminum hydride not only assured complete reduction of the silicon tetrachloride, but also reacted with any boron trichloride present to yield nonvolatile lithium borohydride, rather than gaseous diborane, which is evolved in the presence of excess chloride [4, 5]. In some runs, a lithium aluminum hydride-glycol ether solution gas scrubber was placed in the purification train to insure complete reduction, but this precautionary measure is not necessary.

Chemical absorption was considered to offer a most effective means of purifying silane. Differences in acid or base character were considered in selecting absorbents. Thus, on a relative basis, the silane molecule might be considered neutral; a Group III hydride (B_2H_6), acidic; and a Group V hydride (PH_3), basic. The silicon atom has more than four bonding orbitals, and certain of its tetravalent compounds are therefore susceptible to nucleophilic attack by a strong base. A given base, then, in order to function as an effective purifying agent (e.g., absorption of diborane) must be selective, i.e. inert to silane.

Amines are known to coordinate with boron compounds. An amine may be added directly to the silicon tetrachloride - glycol ether solution. Any boron trichloride present will coordinate with the amine, and the B-N bond will persist through the reaction, even though the substituents may undergo reaction. The evolution of any volatile boron compounds is thereby prevented. Alternatively, a liquid amine or amine solution gas scrubber can be inserted in the purification train, or a solid amine in a packed column. The latter methods preclude the possibility of the amines reacting with lithium aluminum hydride, although avoiding this is not essential since only small quantities of amine are required, and a substantial excess of lithium aluminum hydride is always used. Tertiary alkyl amines are unreactive in any event.

Activated carbon proved to be an excellent adsorbent. Tests indicated a strong affinity for both diborane and arsine. Arsine is not eluted at room temperature under vacuum. Diborane adsorbed at 0° is desorbed to the extent of 23-24% at room temperature [6]. For maximum effectiveness, therefore, the activated carbon should be kept at 0° or below. It is undoubtedly also an excellent adsorbent for other polar molecules, as solvent vapor, chlorosilanes, amines, phosphine, etc.

A final property which may be utilized to purify silane is its relative thermal stability compared with possible contaminating hydrides. Although "decomposition temperature" is a rather imprecise term for these compounds, the approximate temperature necessary to achieve rapid decomposition of various hydrides to their elements is shown in Table III below.

Table III

Thermal Stability of Hydrides
Temperature (°C) necessary for rapid decomposition to elements

$(BH_3)_2$ (g)		
300°		
$(AlH_3)_x$ (s)	SiH_4 (g)	
110-160°	>600°	
$(GaH_3)_2$ (l)	GeH_4 (g)	AsH_3 (g)
130°	340-360°	300°
$(InH_3)_x$ (s)	SnH_4 (g)	SbH_3 (g)
	150°	200°
	PbH_4 (g)	BiH_3 (g)
	25°	25°

We found that passing silane through a quartz tube having a twelve-inch zone heated to 600-636° resulted in only 2 to 6% decomposition under normal operating conditions. This is a temperature far in excess of that required to completely decompose the other hydrides listed in Table III. To purify silane, the gas stream was passed through a quartz-packed quartz tube heated to 350° before being introduced to the decomposition chamber.

Other volatile hydrides, as ammonia, water, other Group VI hydrides, and the hydrogen halides are not present in the silane gas stream because their protonic hydrogens react with the hydridic hydrogens of lithium aluminum hydride to give hydrogen and nonvolatile aluminum compounds. In fact, lithium aluminum hydride ether solutions are perhaps the best protonic scavengers known, so that a more effective reagent for removal of these materials is unlikely.

DECOMPOSITION OF SILANE

Initially, the purified silane was decomposed by passing through a heated tube of fused transparent quartz. The decomposition efficiency was poor at 600-636° but quantitative at 777° and above. Due to the difference in thermal contraction of quartz and silicon, the tubes cracked on cooling. This led to the use of a quartz vacuum jacket over the decomposition tube. The silicon proved very difficult to remove from the quartz, and required prolonged leaching with hydrofluoric acid. Generally, the heavier the deposit of silicon, the better the purity. Thus, it became apparent that the impurities were coming primarily from the quartz and the leaching operation, and efforts were directed to depositing the silicon on inductively heated high-purity silicon with the apparatus illustrated in Figures 1 and 2. Utilizing a 4 MC output frequency, induction heating of a silicon rod was accomplished by first coupling to a quartz-enclosed graphite rod adjacent to the silicon substrate. After the silicon had been heated by radiation, coupling to silicon was achieved. Silane, in vacuo, was directed at the base of the silicon substrate by means of a water-cooled jet. The quartz apparatus containing the substrate was cooled by running water down the outside jacket to prevent the deposition of metallic silicon on the inner wall of the cracking chamber. The substrate was raised and lowered by a magnetic device outside of the chamber.

Silicon deposits obtained in this manner are shown in Figures 3 and 4. They are easily fractured along definite angular boundaries, which may be indicative of a preferred orientation in the crystal growth.

The temperature of the substrate, as measured by an optical pyrometer, ranged between 930-1375°. The temperature was controlled to ± 25°. Operating at temperatures from 1250-1375°, it was noted that elongation of the substrate deposit was enhanced if the R.F. coil was 5 to 8 mm. below the bottom of the substrate. At lower temperatures, the position of the coil did not influence elongation, provided it was positioned at the widest section of the substrate or below. The substrate was attached at the top by a quartz holder. Better decomposition efficiencies were obtained

60

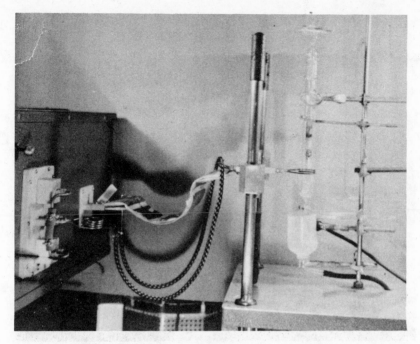

Figure 1. Picture showing a portion of the induction unit on the left and the quartz cracking chamber on the right. Although the silicon substrate is shown fixed, the apparatus was later modified so that it could be raised or lowered by a magnetic assembly. The center of the picture shows the R.F. coil which may be hydraulically adjusted to any desired level.

by adjustment of the distance between the base of the silicon substrate and the orifice of the silane jet. During the early stages of a run, the distance should be less than 20 mm. As the deposit grows, the distance between the substrate and orifice was increased to as much as 150 mm.

Progress was followed by spectrographic analyses in the early phases of the project. When the impurities were below the limits of spectrographic detection, a limited number of neutron activation analyses were made. Values obtained are shown in Table IV. Eight of the tabulated values are from a single sample, the other four are from another sample where either the limit of detection was lower, or more effective purification for the particular element was utilized.

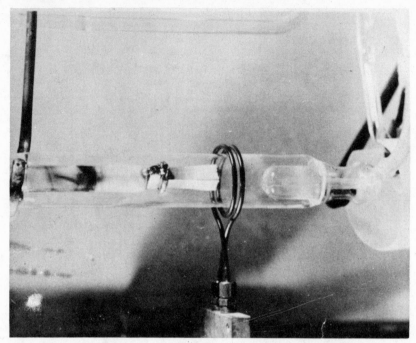

Figure 2. A close-up view of the silane cracking chamber. At the bottom of the quartz chamber extending almost to the coil is the water-cooled orifice where the silane gas is jetted into the chamber. The R.F. coil is on the outside of the chamber to reduce contamination. The silicon substrate is machined, leached, hung on a quartz holder and leached again before inserting into the chamber. Directly above the silicon substrate is the carbon preheater enclosed in quartz under vacuum. This radiantly heats the silicon to a temperature where the R.F. unit will couple to it. At the top of the picture is the water cooling tube which washes over the entire outer surface of the chamber.

Table IV

Impurities in Silicon Metal from Thermal Decomposition of Silane
Neutron activation analyses (parts per billion)

Fe	17.0*	As	1.0	Zn	0.41*	Ga	0.0062*
Cu	11.0	P	1.0*	Ni	0.27*	Sb	0.0037*
Bi	1.6*	Tl	0.91*	In	0.032*	Mn	0.00062*

*Not detected. Value shown is limit of detection in ppb.

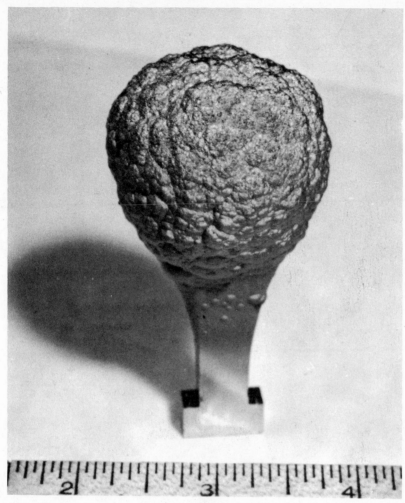

Figure 3. Silicon deposit from thermal decomposition of silane on silicon substrate.

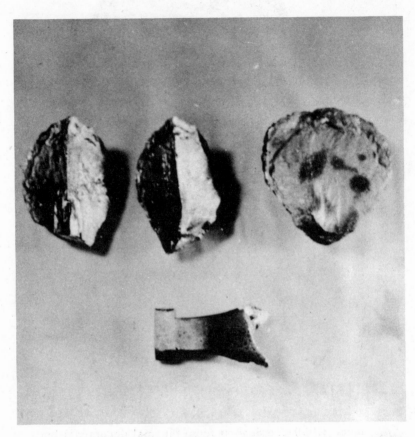

Figure 4. Fragments of silicon deposit showing cleavage angles.

ACKNOWLEDGEMENT

The authors thank Mr. J. Paul Cali of the Air Force Cambridge Research Laboratories who performed the neutron activation analysis shown in Table IV.

REFERENCES

1. H. C. Kelly, T. J. Flynn, C. W. Davis and S. Johnson. AFCRC-TR-57-198; AD 133701. "The Preparation of Transistor Grade Silicon from Silane or Analogous Compounds," Final Report under Contract AF19(604)-1928, 31 August 1957.
2. C. H. Lewis, M. B. Giusto and S. Johnson. AFCRC-TR-59-354; AD 228538. "The Preparation of Transistor Grade Silicon from Silane or Analogous Compounds," Final Report under Contract AF19(604)-3464, 30 October 1959.
3. N. L. Paddock, Nature, 167, 1070 (1951).
4. J. M. Wilson, Research, 10, 166 (1957).
5. J. M. Wilson, U. S. Patent 2,888,328, May 26, 1959.
6. V. I. Mikheeva and T. N. Dymova, Zhur. Neorg. Khim., 2, 2539 (1957).

DISCUSSION

H. M. MANASEVIT (Autonetics, North American Aviation): Did the silane that was decomposed at $700°$ yield a single crystal or a polycrystalline deposit?

S. JOHNSON (Metal Hydrides): The deposit was polycrystalline. The substrate was, in some cases, a single crystal substrate, but the deposit was polycrystalline.

R. FOEHRING (Sperry Semiconductor): Have you any quantitative measures of the lithium and aluminum content of the silicon?

S. JOHNSON (Metal Hydrides): None, other than that they are below the limit of spectroscopic detectability.

O. J. MARSH (Hughes Aircraft): Would you comment about the boron content which, in the past, has been the largest contributer to impurities in silicon?

S. JOHNSON (Metal Hydrides): Boron unfortunately cannot be determined by neutron activation analysis but I can say that it is below the limit of spectroscopic detectability.

O. J. MARSH (Hughes Aircraft): Have you done anything to prepare single crystals for resistivity measurements?

S. JOHNSON (Metal Hydrides): We had two single crystal samples evaluated by resistivity measurements and they were not outstanding.

F. D. ROSI, CHAIRMAN (RCA Lab.): Is the relative acidity of borane to trichlorosilane comparable to the relative acidity between the borane and the silane?

S. JOHNSON (Metal Hydrides): Yes, I think so. I am not saying that this method is unique to hydrides. The amine dust could be put in with the trichlorosilane, and boron trichloride is certainly far more acidic than trichlorosilane.

F. D. ROSI, CHAIRMAN (RCA Lab.): What is the highest resistivity you measured of the silicon you prepared by the silane decomposition?

S. JOHNSON (Metal Hydrides): I think it was about 75 ohm-centimeters.

M. RUBENSTEIN (Westinghouse): What is the impurity content of the lithium aluminum hydride and what company makes the pure material?

S. JOHNSON (Metal Hydrides): The commercial grade of lithium aluminum hydride is sold by Metal Hydrides Inc. It is specified to be 95 per cent pure by hydrogen evolution analysis. Metal Hydrides also sells laboratory quantities of crystalline grade lithium aluminum hydride which is 99-plus per cent pure.

I think the consideration here is the presence of any impurities which would lead to a volatile hydride which would come out of the generator and, as far as I know, there are not contaminants in lithium aluminum hydride giving rise to such impurities. For example, iron and aluminum, I am sure, are impurities in lithium aluminum hydride. I don't believe that the impurity content of these materials would really effect the product. I think that one advantage of the process is that, by putting a purification train in the gas stream, one can make the product relatively independent of the starting materials. You should be able to get a purification train that will take out any of the impurities that I indicated--solvent vapor, unreduced chlorosilane, or volatile hydrides which come out of the reaction mixture.

W. BRENNER (New York Univ.): We ran some emission spectroscopic analyses on the lithium aluminum hydride from Metal Hydrides, and the following impurities were found: calcium, sodium, potassium, magnesium, aluminum, copper, iron, lead, barium and silicon. The percentages of impurities vary from .5 per cent to .006 per cent, the various impurities giving different percentages. They don't seem to effect the quality of the product.

S. JOHNSON (Metal Hydrides): Thank you. I think that answers your question. I do not believe that the presence of these impurities would effect the gas evolved, because the impurities would not give rise to volatile species.

G. CHIZINSKY (Solid State Products): I have worked with this type of reaction in the past and have obtained resistivities of well over 1,000 ohm-centimeters and boron contents of below 1 part per billion regularly.

HIGH PURITY BORON FOR
SEMICONDUCTOR RESEARCH

T. Niemyski, Z. Olempska and F. Sosnowski

Boron has been known to be a semiconductor for many years. Compared to other semiconductors, however, little is known about its properties. This is undoubtedly due to the technological difficulties such as its very high melting point (about 2300°C) and its extreme reactivity at high temperatures. The latter is particularily true when boron is in the liquid state.

For some time our laboratory has been engaged in investigating methods for obtaining boron having impurity levels low enough for semiconductor research. In a manner analogous to investigations in Si and Ge, a compound of boron was sought which would be suitable for purification and subsequent decomposition to free boron.

Of the several possible compounds boron trichloride was chosen. After purification by fractional distillation the chloride was reduced at a high temperature in a stream of hydrogen.

PREPARATION OF BORON TRICHLORIDE

The choice of boron trichloride as an intermediate was a compromise based on several considerations.

Table I

Boiling Points of Boron Halides

Compound	BF_3	BCl_3	BBr_3	BJ_3
Boiling point °C	-101	12.6	91.3	210

The boiling points of the halogens of boron are shown in Table I. The halogen to boron bond energies decrease from fluoride to iodide while the ease of decomposition decreases from iodide to fluoride. Despite this fact the chloride was chosen because of the ease with which it can be purified, its greater content of boron by weight and its less toxic nature when compared with the bromide or iodide. Also, the danger of contamination due to the leaching of contaminents from glass equipment is reduced because of its low boiling point.

The bromide and iodide are obtained by direct synthesis from the elements at high temperatures. An additional advantage of the chloride is that it can be produced from more easily available starting materials. A method for obtaining the chloride based on a reaction of gaseous chlorine with a mixture of boron oxide and carbon was worked out and proceeds according to the following equation:

$$B_2O_3 + 3C + 3\,Cl_2 \rightleftharpoons 2\,BCl_3 + 3\,CO$$

An outline of the equipment is shown in Figure 1.

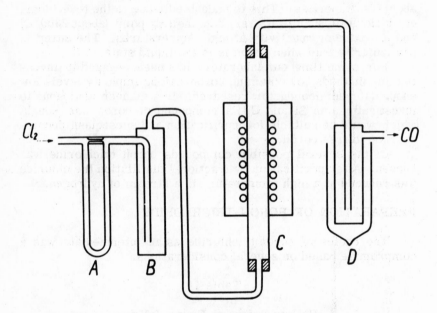

Figure 1. Schematic Drawing of Equipment for Obtaining Boron Trichloride.

It consisted of:

(1) A ceramic tube, C, heated to a temperature of 700°C, in which the reaction took place.

(2) A flowmeter, A, used for measuring the flow of chlorine.

(3) A cleaning trap, B, containing concentrated sulfuric acid.

(4) A condenser, D, cooled with solid CO_2.

The mixture of boron oxide and carbon was prepared by sintering commercial grade boron oxide and powdered carbon.

68

The porosity of the sintered mixture was found to facilitate the reaction.

Spectral analysis showed that the concensed boron trichloride was contaminated with chlorine, silicon tetrachloride and small amounts of Mg, Al, Fe, Ti, Cu and Ca.

PURIFICATION OF BORON TRICHLORIDE

The boron trichloride was separated from the aforementioned impurities by fractional distillation. The chemical and physical properties of the chloride made this distillation a little unusual. At room temperature BCl_3 can be distilled only at elevated pressures. To avoid this difficulty the distillation was carried out at normal pressure in a chamber where the temperature was maintained at $-5°C$.

Thirty plate columns with vacuum mantle and head were used for the distillation. The equipment was cooled with solid CO_2. The head construction is shown in Figure 2.

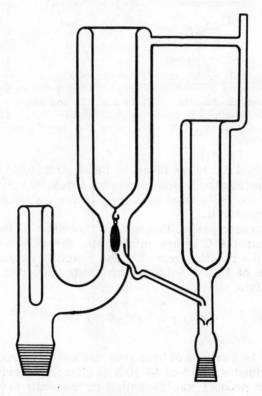

Figure 2. Head of Distilling Column
for Boron Trichloride.

The collection of distillate was regulated by an electro-magnetic device. The apparatus was protected from moisture to eliminate hydrolysis of the BCl_3.

Spectral analysis of the triple distilled BCl_3 showed only traces of Si.

REDUCTION OF BORON TRICHLORIDE

Elemental boron was obtained by reducing the triple distilled BCl_3 in a stream of excess pure hydrogen at high temperature.

The apparatus is shown in Figure 3.

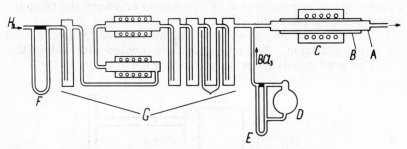

Figure 3. Schematic Drawing of Equipment for
Obtaining Free Boron from Boron Trichloride.
A-quartz tube; B-mantle; C-furnace; D-container with boron chloride; E-flowmeter for regulating the BCl_3 flow speed; G-purifier of hydrogen; F-flowmeter for regulating the hydrogen flow speed.

The reduction takes place in the quartz tube A which is placed in the mantle B and heated by a resistance furnace C. The flow of the BCl_3 from container D was regulated by reference to flowmeter E.

The hydrogen passes through the flowmeter F and the purification apparatus G before mixing with the BCl_3 immediately in front of the reaction tube A. The reaction carried out at a temperature of $1100°C$ - $1200°C$ proceeds according to the following equation.

$$BCl_3 + \frac{3}{2}H_2 \rightleftharpoons B + 3\ HCl$$

A forty fold excess of hydrogen was used. Under the conditions described a yield of 40-50% of elemental boron was obtained. The product was deposited on the walls of the tube in two forms, polycrystalline blades and, nearer the center of the tube, an amorphous form.

70

Figure 4 a, b. Powdered Boron, Obtained by Thermal
Decomposition in Hydrogen Atmosphere.

71

The purity of both forms was determined by spectral analysis. The crystalline form contained: $10^{-2}\%$ Si and $10^{-5}\%$ Mg. The amorphous form contained $10^{-4}\%$ Si.

MELTING AND CRYSTALLIZATION

The great reactivity and high melting point of boron is the cause of the main difficulties encountered during its melting and recrystallization. At these temperatures chemical reaction or diffusion takes place between almost all elements.

Figure 5. Induction Furnace for Melting Boron.

Investigations using several melting techniques were carried out. The boron was melted in resistance, induction and electron bombardment furnaces. In the first two cases vacuum or a protecting atmosphere of argon or hydrogen was used. The electron beam meltings were carried out in vacuum only. Simultaneous with the investigations of melting methods, a search for suitable crucible materials and investigations of melting without a crucible were undertaken.

As a result of these investigations it has been concluded that melting by resistance furnaces is unsatisfactory. This technique leads to the danger of melt contamination by the heater material and also the possibility of reaction between the heater

72

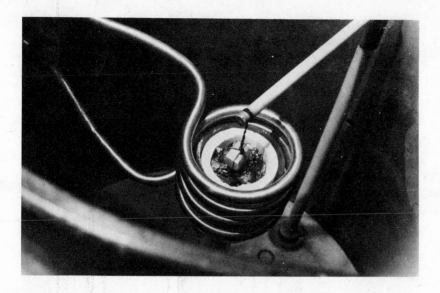

Figure 6. Electron Bombardment Furnace for Melting Boron.

and crucible materials. These difficulties are lessened in the case of induction and electron bombardment heating.

The investigations of crucible material show that the most suitable material for melting boron is boron nitride. All other refractories tried reacted with boron at temperatures above 2000°C. Among these were Zr, Be, Hf, Ca and Zn oxides. The boron nitride proved satisfactory over the entire temperature range up to the boiling point of boron.

The boron nitride used in the preparation of all crucibles and containers was obtained by the gaseous reaction between BCl_3 and ammonia. The product of the reaction was then heated, pressed into the proper form and sintered to a kind of ceramic. It may be mentioned, that the presence of boron oxide causes the destruction of the crucibles during the melting of boron.

SOME PROPERTIES OF BORON SAMPLES

The pure boron obtained thus far has been in the form of polycrystalline ingots containing some crystals a few millimeters in size.

The mechanical and electrical properties varied appreciably depending upon whether the melting process was carried out in vacuum or in a protective atmosphere of hydrogen or argon. "The vacuum" samples possessed great mechanical strength and relatively low electrical resistance whereas "the gaseous" samples tended to be porous and to crack easily. On

73

Figure 7 a, b. Boron Nitride Crucible for Melting Boron.

Figure 8. The Ingot of Melted Boron.

microscopic examination of the fractures, small red ruby-like crystals could be seen. The electrical resistance at room temperature was in the megohm range.

Although some measurements on conductivity, Hall coefficients, thermoelectric power and infrared absorption have been made, the results were inconclusive and it is felt that further work on crystallization and structure is needed before any significance can be attached to them. Further study is now being carried out.

Typical results of electrical measurements on "gaseous" samples are shown in Figures 9a, 9b, and 10. As can be seen, the room temperature conductivity is of the order $G \cong 10^{-6}$ ohm^{-1} cm^{-1}, while the corresponding concentration of current carriers (holes) is: $P = 10^{15}$ cm^{-3}. Forbidden energy gap measurements, $\Delta E = 1.1$ ev, agree well with the absorption edge in the infrared (approximately one micron).

For "vacuum" samples the following measurements were typical $G \cong 10^{-2}$ ohm^{-1} cm^{-1}, $P \cong 10^{14} - 10^{15}$ cm^{-3}. The energy gap inferred from infrared absorption measurements was $\Delta E \cong 0.6 - 0.7$ ev.

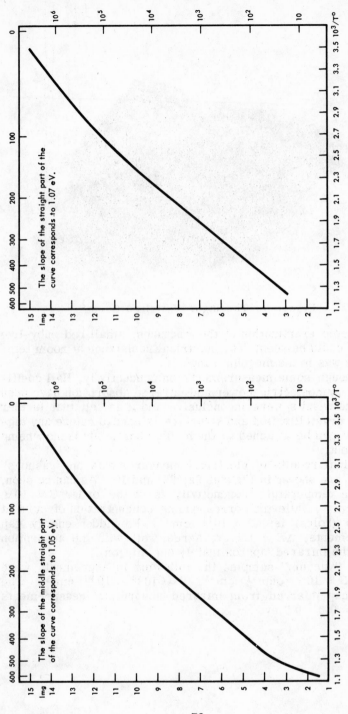

Figure 9 a, b. The Plots of Resistance vs. Temperature.

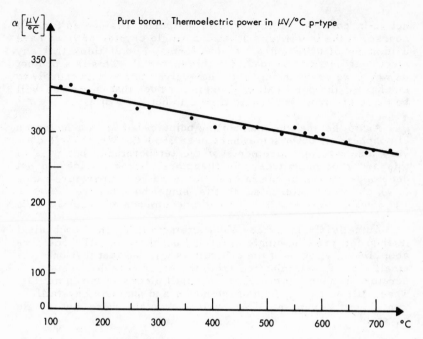

Figure 10. The Plot of Thermoelectric Power vs. Temperature.

REFERENCES

1. E. Weintraub, J. Ind. Eng. Chem., 106-115, 1913.
2. J. Lagrenaudie, J. Chim. Phys., 50, 629-33, 1953.
3. E. S. Greiner, and J. A. Gutowski, J. Appl. Phys. 28, 1364-5, 1957.
4. F. H. Horn, J. Appl. Phys. 30, 1611-12, 1959.
5. F. H. Horn, J. Appl. Phys. 30, 1612-13, 1959.

DISCUSSION

P. H. R. SCHOLEFIELD (Ministry of Aviation): I wonder if Dr. Sosnowski would first discuss the prospective use for boron in the semiconductor field--and secondly, it was stated that boron nitride was stable up to the boiling point of the boron. Should this be the melting point?

I would like to confirm the use of electron beam melting on this substance. It is very convenient, indeed. I have done quite a lot of work on this technique.

L. SOSNOWSKI (Polish Academy of Sciences): The prospective use of boron depends on the properties of large single crystals, which we still have not attained. Anyone can easily obtain, for instance, the diode characteristics in a single crystal but not so in polycrystalline boron of the purity attained so far. Of course, if the mobility is low for a single crystal or if we have a mixture of different allotropic forms, I don't think that any electronic use will be made for this material. This is a project on which we are working, and I have given this report merely to emphasize the purification process. I hope that some use will be made of boron, but at this time I do not know of any.

As to the melting and boiling point of boron in a hydrogen atmosphere, it boils somewhere near 2550°C. We haven't done very accurate measurements of the temperature, but it is of this order of magnitude. Furthermore, boron nitride did not decompose at this temperature. In the whole temperature range in which we are interested, that is, somewhere between 2000°C and 2500°C, it is stable. It should decompose at about 3000°C.

Actually, we have made some attempts to use the Czochralski method for growing single crystals, but there is still considerable difficulty. One of the difficulties was the fact that one gets small bits of contamination from the boron nitride. This temperature causes the break-off of small pieces of boron nitride. These fall on the surface of the boron and nucleate crystallization. Thus, even our Czochralski crystals were not single crystals.

Actually we started the work on the crystallization recently so that we don't know much about it.

L. R. WEISBERG (RCA Lab.): Ordinarily, to make boron nitride crucibles, a binder is necessary to hold the boron nitride particles together. Did you find it necessary to use a binder in making crucibles of boron nitride?

L. SOSNOWSKI (Polish Academy of Sciences): Yes. I mentioned that we need a binder, but we cannot use it because it causes contamination. We tried to make a crucible from boron nitride without a binder and were successful. However it had very undesirable mechanical properties. It cracked very easily. With sufficient care, with just the right pressure and temperature, it was successful. It is not an easy kind of operation.

L. R. WEISBERG (RCA Lab.): In mass spectrographic analysis, Dr. Honig of our laboratories has seen boron nitride decompose in a vacuum at temperatures as low as 1100 and 1200°C. Did you have any excess nitrogen in your system? That may explain the lack of decomposition in your experiments on boron nitride. Or do you think that it just does not decompose, even at temperatures over 2000°C?

L. SOSNOWSKI (Polish Academy of Sciences): We haven't noticed decomposition on any large scale. I have observed traces of decomposition, but what is the consequence? We melt boron in boron nitride, which gives off nitrogen and there is no harm. However, when we melt in the atmosphere, as we usually do, the material completely changes appearance, and thus is not a pure boron. It is believed that vacuum purification yields a material that is closer to pure boron. We are now carrying on x-ray investigations. The structure seems to be a complicated one.

C. P. TALLEY (Texaco Experiment, Inc.): I believe the currently acceptable value for the heat of formation of boron nitride is around 60 kilocalories per mole. If this be the case, we have a dissociation pressure of around 1 atmosphere in the vicinity of 2500 degrees Kelvin. It may be that the boiling that you observed was nitrogen bubbling through the boron and coming to the surface. At any rate, you would have to have very high nitrogen pressures to suppress the dissociation of boron nitride.

I might add that I was very much interested in forming other allotropic forms of boron from the melt. Generally, it is conceded that the beta rhombohedral phase is the one that is formed from the melt, if you cool at a reasonably slow rate. If you have observed other modifications, this would be extremely interesting.

I would also like to confirm the application of electron bombardment heating as a very useful method. We have prepared single crystals of the beta rhombohedral phase of boron and are measuring its properties at the present time.

R. FOEHRING (Sperry Semiconductor): What pressure was used in fabricating the boron nitride crucibles?

L. SOSNOWSKI (Polish Academy of Sciences): Several hundred kilograms per square centimeter.

THE PREPARATION OF HIGH PURITY BISMUTH BY THE REDUCTION OF BISMUTH TRICHLORIDE WITH LITHIUM ALUMINUM HYDRIDE

W. Brenner, C. G. Kumar, H. Hellman and C. J. Marsel
New York University, New York, N. Y.

ABSTRACT

The reduction of bismuth trichloride by lithium aluminum hydride has been experimentally investigated for the preparation of high purity bismuth metal. The impurity level of the metal thus produced is described using emission spectrographic analyses.

In view of the considerable amount of success obtained on the purification of metals by means of hydride reductions [1,3], it was desired to investigate this technique for the preparation of high purity bismuth metal. Commercial production of bismuth metal has been described in the literature [1,2,7]. While both pyrometallurgical and electrochemical processes have been developed the former are apparently in wide use and capable of yielding quite pure metal on an industrial scale [4,6]. More recently the zone refining of bismuth metal has also been investigated [5]. Hydride reductions are of definite interest because they offer the possibility of obtaining high purity metal by a simple low temperature reaction instead of the rather complex multi-step pyrometallurgical processes now employed.

Commercial reagent grade bismuth trichloride was reduced by lithium aluminum hydride in order to ascertain the feasibility of preparing high purity bismuth metal via hydride reductions. The reaction was studied by adding diethyl ether solutions of bismuth trichloride dropwise to an excess of lithium aluminum hydride, also in diethyl ether solution. While this reduction of the bismuth trichloride was carried out in a rather wide range of temperatures, a majority of the runs were performed under ambient conditions. Under these conditions, rapid reduction of the trichloride took place with the formation of a very finely divided black powder. The reactions were carried out in a nitrogen atmosphere. However, this precaution may not be necessary as some reductions have yielded equivalent results without this precaution.

It is believed that the reduction of bismuth trichloride to the metal with lithium aluminum hydride may occur via an unstable intermediate hydride, bismuthine, as follows:

$$4 \ BiCl_3 \ + \ 3 \ Li \ AlH_4 \rightarrow \ 4 \ BiH_3 \ + \ 3 \ LiCl \ + \ 3 \ AlCl_3$$

$$4 \ Bi \ + \ 6H_2$$

Low reaction temperatures would appear to be conducive for the isolation of bismuthine. However, under the reaction conditions investigated, no evidence for the existence of bismuthine was obtained even below -80°C.

After completion of the addition of the bismuth trichloride the reaction mixture was then hydrolyzed carefully in an acid medium. Thus unreacted lithium aluminum hydride was decomposed under acid conditions to soluble reaction products. The resulting bismuth metal powder was then washed successively with 6N hydrochloric acid, water, and absolute alcohol. The final processing steps consisted of heating this powder in a quartz tube under a helium atmosphere and casting to produce ingots. Portions of the ingots were subjected to emission spectrographic analysis. Yields of bismuth metal were in the order of 60-70% based upon the bismuth trichloride used.

Typical semiquantitative emission spectrographic analyses are shown in Table 1.

Table 1

Spectrographic Analysis of Bismuth Samples

Im-purities	Bismuth Chloride Starting Material	Bismuth Metal Powder Form	Bismuth Metal Ingot Form
Bi	major	major	major
Fe	0.0X (low)	NF	NF
Si	0.00X	0.000X (low)	NF
Cu	0.000X	0.000X (low)	NF
Ag	0.000X	0.000X (low)	0.000X
Mg	0.000X	NF	NF
Cr	0.000X	NF	NF
Al	NF	NF	NF

Elements checked but not found: Mn, Pb, Sn, Ni, Cr, Co, Mo, Va, W, Sb, As, Zn, Cd, In, Th, Ga, Ge

0.000X = 0.0001~0.0009% estimated
0.000X (low) = 0.0001~0.0005% estimated

81

The data show that the simple reduction of bismuth trichloride to the metal eliminated iron, magnesium and chromium as contaminants and either reduced or removed other interfering metal elements, i.e., silicon, copper, silver. No additional impurities were introduced during the reduction.

Experiments were also carried out during which the amount of excess of lithium aluminum hydride used was varied. No substantial improvements in product quality were obtained beyond a 3/1 molar ratio of $LiAlH_4/BiCl_3$.

Pyrex glass equipment was employed throughout these experimental studies. Care was taken to avoid the use of silicone grease in the apparatus as it was found that such grease could result in silicon contamination of the product. It was also essential to carry out the hydrolysis of the reduction mixture promptly under acid conditions in order to avoid possible reaction of lithium hydroxide upon the Pyrex glass reaction vessels.

The reduction of bismuth trichloride with lithium aluminum hydride offers a promising low temperature route for the preparation of high purity bismuth.

REFERENCES

1. W. Brenner, E. Bierig, D. Lum, F. Pollara and C. Marsel, "The Preparation of Pure Tin via the Thermal Decomposition of Stannane," XII International Congress of Pure and Applied Chemistry, Munich Germany, September 1959.
2. C. L. Mantell, "Industrial Electrochemistry," 3rd Edition, McGraw Hill Publishing, New York, N. Y. (1950).
3. "Research On the Preparation of Pure Metals," Scientific Reports No. 2-4 (1958-1960), Contract AF19(604)-4124, New York University, New York, N. Y.
4. Kirk Othmer Encyclopedia Vol. II, Interscience Publishers, New York, N. Y.
5. W. G. Pfann, Zone Melting, John Wiley and Sons, Inc., New York, N. Y. (1955).
6. W. C. Smith, Metals and Alloys 22, 397-402 (1945).
7. W. C. Smith, "Bismuth" in "Lidell Handbook of Non-Ferrous Metallurgy" Vol. II, 3rd Edition, McGraw-Hill Publishing Company, New York, N. Y. (1951).

DISCUSSION

R. A. KRAMER (Alcoa): In the last slide (Table I), you listed the spectrographic analysis of the metal and I noticed a few particular absences. There was no aluminum or magnesium found. Also, calcium was not listed. In many of these materials which are done by spectrographic analysis, it seems you always find these impurities. Are these listed as "Not Found" because they are a blank problem or were there actually no spectral lines visible?

W. BRENNER (New York Univ.): There were no spectral lines visible. There were others which were checked, but I thought some of the ones I used for the slide were of most interest.

R. A. KRAMER (Alcoa): Do you use a DC arc or an AC spark?

W. BREMMER (New York Univ.): This is with an AC spark.

R. A. KRAMER (Alcoa): Then you have rather limited sensitivity, I take it?

W. BRENNER (New York Univ.): It is a new model.

PURIFICATION OF TELLURIUM
BY DISTILLATION*

Bruce D. Wedlock and Frank M. Norton
Massachusetts Institute of Technology
Cambridge, Mass.

ABSTRACT

A rapid method is described by which tellurium and materials of similar vapor pressures may be separated from less
volatile impurities such as copper, antimony, and various oxides.
The technique consists of multiple distillation under a continuously pumped vacuum. A mechanical arrangement has been
devised which employs a reusable crucible, thereby increasing
the speed of the operation. Evaluation indicates that one operation will produce tellurium with an electrically active impurity
concentration of 4×10^{14}/cc from material with considerable
surface oxides.

I. INTRODUCTION

The increasing interest in thermoelectric energy converters
during the past few years has resulted in a large research effort
in the area of intermetallic semiconducting tellurides, notably
bismuth telluride and lead telluride. In addition, mercury telluride, cadmium telluride, and molybdenum telluride are also
receiving increased attention. As research in each of these
materials progresses, it is necessary to produce crystals of
the highest possible perfection, both chemically and crystallo-
graphically speaking, if detailed experiments on their transport
properties and band structure are to yield meaningful results.
In an effort to produce such high-quality single crystals by both

*The research reported in this paper has been sponsored by the
Electronics Research Directorate of the Air Force Cambridge
Research Center, Air Research and Development Command,
under contract AF19(604)-4153. This paper, although based on
work sponsored by the U. S. Air Force, has not been approved
or disapproved by that Agency.

the Bridgeman and Czochralski techniques, it was experimentally determined that the "high purity" tellurium as commercially supplied* required further purification. Accordingly, the scheme of multiple distillation under a continuously pumped vacuum was employed with considerable success.

A system was designed to employ a reusable sample tube. This feature reduced the time required to purify a given sample, inasmuch as glass blowing operations associated with individual sample tube preparation have been eliminated. At present, using a 25 mm tube the system has an output capability of approximately 35 grams of purified tellurium per hour.

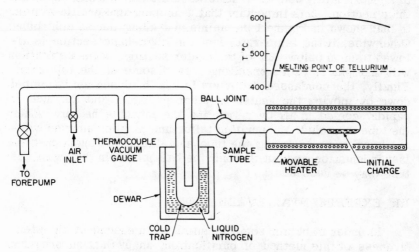

Figure 1. Tellurium Distillation Apparatus.

II. SYSTEM DESCRIPTION

A schematic diagram of the tellurium distillation apparatus is shown in Figure 1. It consists of a sample tube surrounded by a movable heater and connected to a vacuum system by means of a ground-glass ball joint. The sample tube, made entirely of Vycor, consists of three sections formed by semi-circular indentations of the tube wall. The tube is sealed at one end, and provided with a Vycor ground ball joint at the other. This ball joint mates with a Pyrex ball joint on the vacuum system, thereby eliminating the need for a graded seal. The heater power is controlled by a Variac, and the temperature is

---

*American Smelting and Refining Co., South Plainfield, N. J.; semiconductor grade, 99.999% pure tellurium.

monitored by a thermocouple mounted on the inside wall of the heater.

The tellurium to be distilled is placed at the closed end of a clean, dry sample tube. The tube is then connected to the vacuum system and pumped down to a pressure of approximately 1 micron. The movable heater is placed so that only the end section of the sample tube will be above the melting point of tellurium. The heater temperature is then brought up to approximately 500°C, whereby the molten tellurium condenses in the center section of the tube. The heater is then moved so that the center section is now included and the temperature raised to approximately 600°C. The tellurium then recondenses in the third section. It is important that a temperature profile similar to that shown in Figure 1 be maintained along the sample tube. Otherwise, if the temperature of the right-hand section is allowed to drop below that of the center section, back-distillation will take place, with a resulting loss of some of the tellurium. Finally, the condensed tellurium in the third section is melted down by moving the heater to form an ingot, and the tube is rapidly cooled in air by retracting the movable heater. After the tube is cooled, the purified tellurium may be removed without breakage by rotating the tube and sliding the ingot past the last indentation and out through the ball joint. In this way, the tube may be reused.

III. EXPERIMENTAL EVALUATION

In order to obtain some quantitative measure of the effectiveness of this method of purification, an evaluation program was proposed and executed. Considerable information is available [3,4] on the effects of impurities on electrical conductivity in tellurium. Since this data establishes that most acceptors are nearly fully ionized down to liquid nitrogen temperature and for impurity concentrations less than 10^{20}/cc the mobility may be assumed constant at a given temperature, it was decided to employ electrical conductivity measurements as a measure of the purity of tellurium. By eliminating Hall effect measurements the experimental work was considerably reduced. In addition to measurements of improvement upon commercially supplied "high purity" tellurium, the effect on impurities of copper and antimony were also investigated.

Sample Preparation

In order to reduce the effect of anisotropy ($\sigma_{||}/\sigma_{\perp} = 2$) [4] in the conductivity measurements, samples were taken from large grain material and the current axis was chosen along the parallel direction. Samples measured approximately 0.2 x 0.2 x 1 centimeters. Current contacts were soldered with indium solder and voltage probes were attached by welding fine gold wires or by soldering to nickel plated spots in the case of copper doping. Samples were etched in dilute aqua regia momentarily prior to measurements.

Estimation of Carrier Concentration

The dashed line in Figure 2 represents an experimentally determined curve of hole concentration as a function of electrical

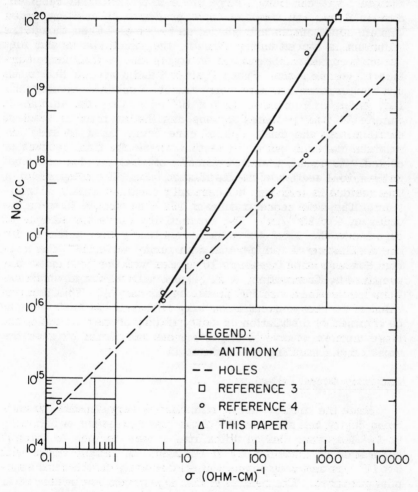

Figure 2. Impurity and Carrier Concentrations in Tellurium as a Function of Conductivity at 167°K.

conductivity at $167°K$ ($10^3/T = 6.0$). This relationship will be used to estimate the carrier concentrations quoted in the following sections. We believe that these estimations will be accurate within perhaps a factor of two and hence sufficient for this evaluation program.

Commercial High Purity Tellurium

It has been found that by distillation commercial high purity tellurium can be further purified. This material as supplied consists of large lumps as well as small pieces and fine powder. Sample 8 was cut from a large piece of tellurium as received. Sample 3 was cut from an ingot produced by melting under vacuum small pieces and powder as received. Even though the tellurium is stored under vacuum, the small pieces and dust absorb a considerable amount of oxygen due to their large surface to volume ratio. From Figures 2 and 3 we find that in the low temperature extrinsic range sample 3 exhibits greater than 10^{18} holes/cc compared to 8×10^{14} holes/cc for sample 8. Sample 10 was produced by one distillation from a batch of small pieces and dust, special care being taken to keep the oxidized material out of the section where the final product is cooled. As usual, a sizable quantity of white residue remained in the initial section of the distillation tube. The composition of this residue is unknown, but certainly contains oxides of tellurium. The hole concentration at $167°K$ in sample 10 is on the order of 4×10^{14}/cc. The conductivity curve for sample 10 represents the limit which has consistently been achieved for one distillation of commercial high purity material. The carrier concentration in sample 10 agrees with the best materials prepared by Kronmuller, et al. [4] and with tellurium which has been zone refined with 300 passes by Aigrain [1]. This limiting value of carrier concentration may represent the best that can be obtained by distillation or zone refining or may be due to the large number of crystal imperfections introduced by even the most careful handling of the material.

Antimony Doped Tellurium

Since the conductivity of tellurium is very sensitive to antimony doping and since at $600°C$ the vapor pressure of antimony is 10^3 less than that of tellurium, it was decided to attempt separation of antimony by distillation. A sample doped with 5×10^{19}/cc antimony atoms was successively distilled and samples prepared. The results of this experiment are presented in Figure 4. Using Figure 2 we see that one distillation reduced the antimony concentration to 6×10^{17}/cc and two distillations

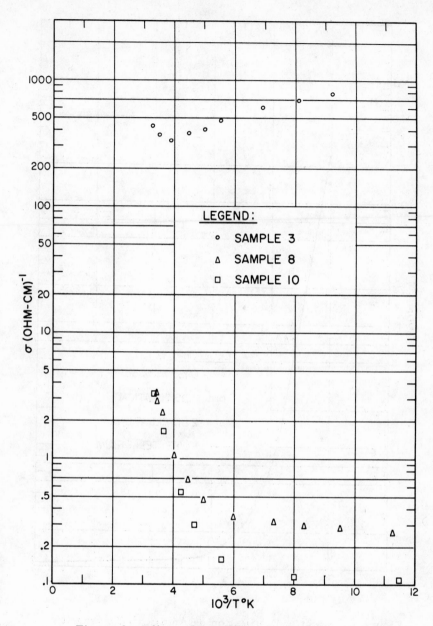

Figure 3. Effect of Distillation on Commerical
High Purity Tellurium.

89

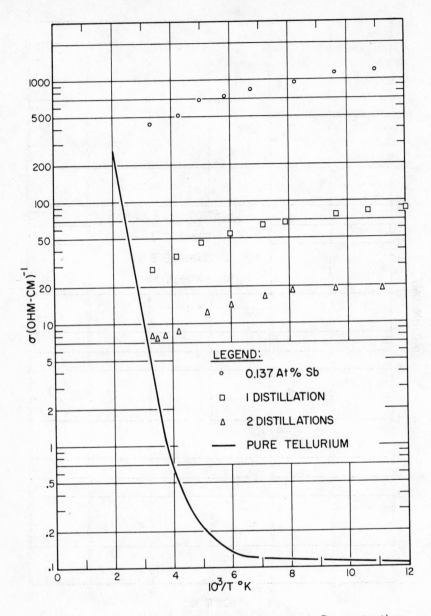

Figure 4. Effect of Distillation on Antimony Concentration in Tellurium.

reduced it to 7×10^{16}/cc. A third distillation yielded essentially the same result as two distillations, indicating that we have reached an equilibrium situation with two operations.

Copper Doped Tellurium

Distillation proved even more effective in reducing the carrier concentration resulting from copper impurities than from antimony. A single distillation was all that was required to reduce the low temperature hole concentration to less than 10^{15}/cc from a sample doped with 4 At % copper (1.44×10^{21}/cc). However, as copper is relatively inactive as an electrical impurity, we can only estimate the residual copper after one distillation to be less than 10^{18}/cc.

IV. CONCLUSIONS

It has been shown that the quality of commerical high purity tellurium can be substantially improved by a simple vacuum distillation technique. The success of this method has been measured directly by carrier concentration improvement as summarized in Table 1, and indirectly by success in growing high-quality single crystal material by both the Bridgeman and Czochralski techniques. In the case of antimony, a limiting impurity level of 7×10^{16} was obtained after two distillations.

Table 1

Summary of Purification of Tellurium by Distillation

Impurity	Initial Hole Concentration No./cc T = 167°K	Number of Distillations	Final Hole Concentration No./cc T = 167°K
Oxides (Large Lumps)	8×10^{14}	1	4×10^{14}
Oxides (Small Pieces and Powder)	10^{18}	1	4×10^{14}
Antimony	5×10^{19} *	3	7×10^{16} *
Copper	--	1	10^{15}

*Antimony Concentration

91

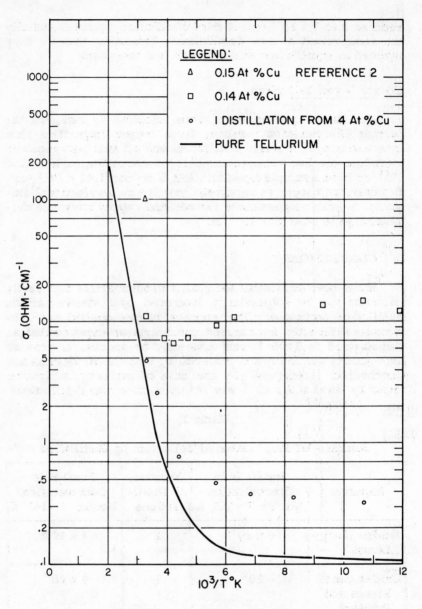

Figure 5. Effect of Distillation on Copper Concentration
in Tellurium.

With heavy cooper concentrations a usable product was obtained after one operation.

V. ACKNOWLEDGMENTS

The authors would like to acknowledge many helpful discussions with Messrs. D. A. Puotinen, R. J. Schwartz, and R. E. Nelson. Credit is also due Mr. L. R. Johnson and Mrs. M. A. Wedlock for assistance with the experimental measurements.

VI. REFERENCES

1. P. Aigrain, private communication.
2. C. H. Cartwright and M. Haberfield-Schwarz, Proc. Roy. Soc. 148 A, 648 (1935).
3. T. Fukuroi, S. Tanuma and S. Tobisawa, Sci. Rep. Res. Insts. Tohoku Univ. A 4, 283 (1952).
4. Von H. Kronmuller, J. Jaumann and K. Seiler, Z. Naturforschg. 11 a, 243 (1956).

DISCUSSION

F. D. ROSI CHAIRMAN (RCA Lab.): Has this material ever helped you in your thermoelectric work?

B. WEDLOCK (MIT): To the extent that we are able to get high quality material in order to perform transport measurements. For example, in mercury telluride, where you have a very small energy gap, we like to get single crystal material in order to perform the transport measurements. I don't think we have seen any order of magnitude improvement in the figures of the thermoelectric material by using distilled tellurium instead of commercially supplied material.

F. D. ROSI CHAIRMAN (RCA Lab.): That is why I asked. You have to dope these down so much anyway.

A. TANG (Tang Industries): I have a question on the last graph that you had. You have a curve of conductivity versus temperature and you have different levels of copper doping. I wonder if, in between the two curves that you have, you would expect a perfect temperature compensation characteristic?

B. WEDLOCK (MIT): Yes, that is certainly quite possible. There is possible compensation in the copper.

THE PREPARATION OF HIGH PURITY GALLIUM
BY HYDRIDE REDUCTIONS

Y. Okamoto, E. Bierig, W. Brenner and C. J. Marsel
New York University
New York 53, N. Y.

ABSTRACT

The preparation of high purity gallium has been experimentally studied via the synthesis and subsequent decomposition of lithium gallium hydride. This intermediate was obtained from the reaction of gallium trichloride with lithium hydride. Data are presented to illustrate the mechanism of purification and characterize product quality in terms of emission spectrographic analyses. High purity gallium metal can thusly be prepared by a sequence of rather simple low temperature reactions.

Some experiments have also been carried out on the reduction of gallium trichloride with lithium aluminum hydride. As the products include aluminum and lithium as well as gallium this reaction does not offer promise for the preparation of high purity gallium metal.

That class of inorganic substances known as intermetallic compounds is being increasingly researched for their possible utility as semiconductor materials. In the recent past particular emphasis has been given to the study of gallium arsenide. Because the greater band gap and potentially greater mobility of this intermetallic compound it could offer very distinct advantages for both high frequency and high temperature performance over such established semiconductor materials as silicon and germanium. It is generally recognized that our knowledge of the characteristics of gallium arsenide—as well as other intermetallic semiconductor materials—lags far behind that of germanium and silicon. It has been stated correctly that "this is due in part to the great difficulties involved in both the purification and growth of large single crystals [11]." The importance of adequate raw materials purification techniques on pertinent device properties has been amply demonstrated with the elemental semiconductors silicon and germanium and is especially critical with the newer intermetallic compounds requiring multiple element purifications.

The subsequent paper is concerned with the preparation of high purity gallium for possible semiconductor applications. Previously reported experimental studies on the synthesis of pure gallium have been limited in both number and scope. Purification methods have been described by Hoffman and Scribner [5], Detricler and Fox [3], and Richards [10]. Electrolytic techniques which were first studied at the National Bureau of Standards in 1935 [5] have also been investigated at Lincoln Laboratories [7]. Gallium purification methods have been studied at RCA [9], Bell Telephone Laboratories [12], etc. One important consideration is that conventional zone refining is known to be inefficient in removing impurities which have segregation coefficients >1 [11]. The reported segregation coefficients of many of the most significant impurities are greater than 1 necessitating therefore the use of other purification techniques for the optimization of gallium purity [2].

In view of the considerable measure of success attained in the preparation of various high purity metals by hydride reductions [1, 8], it was decided to evaluate this approach experimentally for the synthesis of pure gallium metal. The careful study of pertinent literature references revealed that the compound lithium gallium hydride was reported to decompose rather readily to gallium metal and could therefore be a useful intermediate for the preparation of the pure metal [4, 13]. Accordingly an experimental investigation was carried out on the synthesis of pure gallium metal via the formation and subsequent decomposition of lithium gallium hydride.

Lithium gallium hydride was first prepared by A. E. Finholt et al. who reduced gallium chloride with lithium hydride as shown [4]:

$$GaCl_3 + 4\ LiH \xrightarrow{\text{ether}} LiGaH_4 + 3\ LiCl \qquad (1)$$

This compound was also synthesized by Wiberg and Schmidt who found that lithium gallium hydride decomposes, even at ambient temperatures, slowly into lithium hydride, gallium and hydrogen [13]:

$$LiGaH_4 \xrightarrow{20^\circ C} LiH + Ga + 1.5\ H_2 \qquad (2)$$

It has been speculated that the decomposition of lithium gallium hydride is autocatalytically hastened by the presence of any finely divided gallium.

The apparently limited thermal stability of lithium gallium hydride was considered to offer a definite advantage for the preparation of gallium metal. A successful low temperature synthesis would of course minimize container contamination problems which become increasingly serious when reactions have to be carried out at elevated temperatures. It also renders more convenient certain chemical processing operations associated with decomposition reactions.

The gallium purification methods developed in this laboratory are based on the formation and subsequent thermal decomposition of the intermediate lithium gallium hydride. The synthesis of this compound was accomplished by suitable modifications of the reaction between gallium trichloride and lithium hydride in diethyl ether which was first described by Finholt et al [4]. Appropriate methods for the decomposition of lithium gallium hydride and the recovery of purified gallium metal were then developed after extensive laboratory studies of various pertinent processing conditions. Spectroscopic analyses were employed throughout these studies to help ascertain impurity levels.

The starting materials for these purification studies were either gallium chloride or gallium metal. Gallium chloride was obtained both from a commercial supply house and by the chlorination of gallium metal, also procured from a commercial source. A spectrographic analysis of a typical batch of gallium chloride is shown in Table I. The total impurity content was in the order of 7000 ppm with iron and silicon most prominent.

Table I

Spectrographic Analysis of
Gallium Trichloride in ppm

Gallium	major
Iron	2500
Silicon	2500
Sodium	700
Aluminum	730
Calcium	680
Cadmium	70
Magnesium	90
Manganese	9
Lead	10
Tin	8
Silver	2
Zinc	80

With a commercial grade (purity >95%) gallium metal as the starting material, conversion to the trichloride was first carried out. This was accomplished essentially as reported in the literature [6]. Commercial grade chlorine gas was passed through a concentrated sulfuric acid scrubber and then through calcium chloride. Gallium metal contained in a porcelain boat was heated gently with a Bunsen burner while dried chlorine gas was passed over it. Gallium trichloride was formed and collected in the colder region of the tube. A sketch of the equipment (Pyrex glass) set up is shown in Fig. 1. This gallium chloride was also subjected to emission spectroscopic analysis before use.

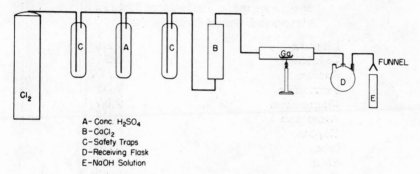

A- Conc. H_2SO_4
B- $CaCl_2$
C- Safety Traps
D- Receiving Flask
E- NaOH Solution

Figure 1. Diagram for Gallium Trichloride Synthesis.

The reduction of gallium trichloride with lithium hydride was carried out at -80°C. Finely divided lithium hydride was reacted in a diethyl ether solution of gallium chloride. A two-fold molar excess of lithium hydride was used in many of the more successful experiments. The reaction mixture was then allowed to warm up to ambient temperatures.

Two grades of lithium hydride were experimentally investigated as a reducing agent for gallium chloride. Preliminary experiments were carried out with a 95% (nominal purity) grade of lithium hydride supplied by Maywood Chemical Co., Maywood, N. J. A spectroscopic analysis of this reagent is shown in Table II.

Table II

Spectroscopic Analysis of 95%
Maywood Lithium Hydride (in %)

Lithium	major
Sodium	0.6
Calcium	0.07
Potassium	0.05
Strontium	0.006
Barium	0.004
Copper	0.002
Iron	0.003
Silicon	0.001
Aluminum	0.003

97

Later work was carried out with a "purified" grade of lithium hydride. This material, designated as "99% lithium hydride", was also procured from Maywood. A spectrographic analysis is given in Table III.

Table III

Spectrographic Analysis of 99%
Maywood Lithium Hydride (in %)

Lithium	major
Calcium	0.2
Sodium	0.006
Potassium	0.04
Magnesium	0.04
Aluminum	0.03
Copper	0.03
Iron	0.005
Lead	0.005
Barium	0.004
Silicon	0.001

The spectrographic analysis did not in fact show a lower impurity level for the 99% material than for the so called 95% grade. The main difference was found to be the amount of active material, as determined by hydrogen evolution. On this basis the 99% lithium hydride was found to contain substantially more active material—close to 99.24% as against 88.62% for the initially used 95% grade.

The reaction mixture resulting from the gallium chloride-lithium hydride interaction was filtered in an inert atmosphere, and ether was evaporated under vacuum at room temperature. As the evaporation of the ether proceeded a white powder precipitated from the solution. A greyish colored solid precipitate remained after removal of ether had been completed.

A quantitative analysis of this precipitate agreed with the formula composition for lithium gallium hydride, $LiGaH_4$. This is shown in Table IV. Repeated runs gave average yields above 95% for the lithium gallium hydride obtained (weight basis!).

Table IV

Quantitative analysis of the $LiGaH_4$ precipitate

Element	Molar Ratios	
	Experimental	Theoretical
Lithium	1.02	1
Gallium	0.98	1
Hydrogen	2.04	2

This lithium gallium hydride was then decomposed thermally. A wide range of temperatures was experimentally investigated in order to ascertain optimal decomposition conditions. Temperatures in the order of 100-200°C were found to be quite satisfactory. The thermal decomposition products were then carefully treated with water, followed immediately with 3N hydrochloric acid. The resulting gallium metal was then thoroughly washed with water, acetone, etc. and transferred into Teflon containers.

Spectroscopic analyses were performed on representative samples of thusly purified gallium metal products. The results of three typical runs are summarized and also compared with a sample of commercially procured electronic grade gallium in Table V. The starting material used was the batch of gallium chloride whose spectroscopic analysis was shown in Table I.

Table V

Typical spectroscopic Analyses of Gallium Metal
Obtained by Hydride Reduction in ppm

	Run #E 115B*	Run #E 36C	Run #E 36	Alcoa
Ni	5	< 1	1	< 1
Fe	7	1-2	< 1	< 1
Cr	1	2-3	1	1-2
Cu	3	.5	2-3	0.5-1
Mg	.2	1	1	1
Ag	< 0.1	< 0.5	< 0.5	< 0.5
Ca	NF	< 2	< 2	< 2
Pb	NF	< 2	< 2	< 2
Zn	NF	< 2	< 2	< 2
Al	4	< 1	< 1	< 1
Si	< 1	NF	NF	NF

Elements checked but not found: As, Co, In, Mo, Sb, Th, Va, W, Zr, Zn

---

*Air Force Cambridge Research Laboratories Analysis

Appropriate materials balances showed that based on the starting material gallium chlorides, the yields of purified gallium metal were in the 50-60% range. Since—as noted previously—the intermediate lithium gallium hydride could be prepared in almost quantitative amounts, losses of gallium metal must occur in the processing steps following thermal decomposition, i.e., hydrolysis, etc. This was confirmed when quantitative analyses indicated that the missing 40-50% of the gallium was indeed present in the aqueous hydrolysis solution.

Some experiments were carried out in order to study the feasibility of the recovery of the gallium contained in these hydrolysis solutions. It was found possible to convert this metal rather readily to sodium gallate and then recover it via electrolysis on the cathode.

It has been speculated that during the thermal decomposition of lithium gallium hydride some polymeric gallium hydride $(GaH)_x$ may be formed which in turn is hydrolized by the dilute aqueous hydrochloric acid solution to water soluble gallium compounds. Experimental studies are in progress to gain a better understanding of the hydrolysis reaction in order to minimize, if possible, the loss of gallium due to this reaction step.

As the above described procedures consistently resulted in a substantial reduction of the impurity level of gallium metal it was considered of interest to investigate more closely the nature of the purification processes involved in this process. Accordingly gallium metal was chlorinated, the trichloride reduced with lithium hydride to lithium gallium hydride and the lithium gallium hydride decomposed back to the metal with spectroscopic analyses carried out at every step of the way. Electronic grade gallium metal procured from Alcoa was the starting material. A porcelain boat was used to contain the gallium during chlorination.

The analytical sequence shown in Table VI indicates rather clearly that the major purification step occurs in the preparation and subsequent sublimation of the gallium trichloride. The subsequent low temperature reduction of the gallium trichloride by the hydride reductant results in the introduction of only small quantities of additional impurities because container contamination etc., are minimized at these reaction conditions.

Also these data show that during chlorination all impurities present in the gallium starting material were either eliminated (lead, tin) or reduced (copper) but that an additional impurity, namely aluminum, was introduced--almost certainly from the boat material used. In the reduction of the halide the reducing agent effectively removes this aluminum impurity but reintroduces rather small amounts of copper and lead. The impurities are seen to concentrate in the gallium metal residue in the boat after completion of the chlorination reaction. In view of these results the suitability of other boat materials for the chlorination, particularly high purity graphite, deserves experimental evaluation.

Some experimentation was also carried out to ascertain the effects, if any, of a secondary purification, i.e., secondary chlorination and subsequent reduction of the chloride starting with a gallium metal obtained by the same process sequence. Analyses of the product of one such series of runs (E 38) follows in Table VII.

100

Table VI

Qualitative Spectroscopic Analyses of Gallium
Purification Process
(Run E 36)

	Gallium metal supplied (ALCOA)	Gallium chloride produced from ALCOA gallium	Gallium metal left in the chlorination boat	Gallium metal product
Boron	NF	NF	NF	NF
Gallium	major	major	major	major
Copper	0.00X	0.000X	0.0X	0.000X
Lead	0.00X	NF	0.0X	0.000X
Tin	0.00X	NF	0.0X	NF
Iron	NF	NF	0.00X (low)	NF
Aluminum	NF	0.00X (low)	NF	NF

Elements checked but not found: Ag, As, Bi, Cd, Co, Cr, Ge, In, Mg, Mn, Mo, Ni, Sb, Si, Ti, Th, V, W, Zn, Zr.
0.000X = 0.0001 ~ 0.0009% estimated
0.000X (low) = 0.0001 ~ 0.0005% estimated

Table VII

Effect of Secondary Purification of Gallium Metal
on Impurity Concentrations

	Gallium metal supplied (ALCOA)	Gallium metal obtained from first reduction	Gallium metal obtained after second reduction
Boron	NF	NF	NF
Gallium	major	major	major
Copper	0.00X	0.000X	0.000X
Lead	0.00X	NF	0.000X
Tin	0.00X	NF	NF
Iron	NF	NF	NF
Aluminum	NF	0.000X (low)	0.000X
Silver	NF	NF	0.000X (low)
Magnesium	NF	NF	0.000X (low)

Elements checked but not found: As, Bi, Cd, Co, Cr, Ge, In, Mn, Mo, Ni, Sb, Si, Ti, Th, V, W, Zr, Zn.

It is apparent that at least in this series of experiments the secondary reduction not only did not improve product purity but resulted in the introduction of additional trace impurities. Further experiments are planned to obtain the additional data which are considered necessary before any conclusions can be drawn. The additional trace impurities found after the second reduction may, for example, have been introduced in the necessarily more extensive handling of the samples.

GALLIUM CHLORIDE—
LITHIUM ALUMINUM HYDRIDE REACTION

Experiments were also carried out to study the possible use of lithium aluminum hydride as a reductant for gallium chloride. The reaction of gallium trichloride with this complex metal hydride has been reported previously by Wiberg et al to result in the preparation of a thermally unstable gallium aluminum hydride which at $0°C$ decomposes to gallium hydride etherate. The gallium hydride etherate was reported to break down to the metal above $35°C$ [14]:

$$GaCl_3 + 3 \; LiAlH_4 \xrightarrow[\text{Et}_2\text{0}]{\text{low temp.}} Ga(AlH_4)_3 + 3 \; LiCl$$

$$Ga(AlH_4)_3 \xrightarrow[\text{Et}_2\text{0}]{0°C} GaH_3 + 3 \; AlH_3$$

$$GaH_3 \xrightarrow[\text{Et}_2\text{0}]{35°C} Ga + 1.5 \; H_2$$

Accordingly gallium trichloride in diethyl ether solutions were reacted with lithium aluminum hydride, also in diethyl ether, at $-80°C$. The resulting solutions were filtered and ether removed under reduced pressure. The product melted at $20 \sim 25°C$ and decomposed between $125-130°C$, even below 1 mm Hg pressure. Analysis of the gray colored decomposition products showed substantial amounts of aluminum and lithium as well as gallium. A rather extended further study of the gallium trichloride - lithium aluminum hydride reaction fully confirmed these results. No further work is therefore planned along these lines.

REFERENCES

1. W. Brenner, Abstracts of papers, XII International Congress of Pure and Applied Chemistry, Munich, Germany, September 1959.
2. F. A. Cunnel, J. T. Edmond, and W. R. Harding, Solids State Electronics 1, 97 (1960).

3. D. P. Detricler, and W. M. Fox, J. Metals 7, 205 (1935).
4. A. E. Finholt, A. C. Bond, Jr., H. I. Schlesinger, J. Am. Chem. Soc., 69, 1199 (1947).
5. J. I. Hoffman, and B. J. Scribner, J. Research National Bur. Standards, 15, 205 (1935).
6. W. C. Johnson, and C. A. Haskew, "Inorganic Synthesis", Vol. 1, p. 26, McGraw Hill Book Co., New York, (1939).
7. Lincoln Laboratory, M.I.T., Lexington, Mass. Personal Communication.
8. New York University, "Research on the Preparation of Pure Metals", Scientific Reports No. 2 and 3, Contract AF19(604)-4124.
9. RCA Somerville Research Laboratory, Somerville, N. J. Personal Communications.
10. J. L. Richards, Nature, 117, 182 (1956).
11. L. R. Weisberg, F. O. Rosi, and P. G. Herkart, "Materials Research on GaAs and InP" Properties of elemental and compound semiconductors, Metallurgical Society Conferences Vol. V (1960). Interscience Publishers, New York/London.
12. J. M. Whelan, and J. H. Wheatley, J. Phys. Chem. Solids 6, 169, (1958).
13. E. Wiberg, and M. Schmidt, Z. Naturforsch. 6b, 171 (1951).
14. E. Wiberg, and M. Schmidt, Z. Naturforsch, 6b, 172 (1951).

DISCUSSION

A. J. LEFFLER (Arthur D. Little): I have not worked with lithium gallium hydride, but I have worked with lithium hydride, and I know that it is necessary to heat the material to about 70 degrees Centigrade in vacuum to remove the last traces of ether. Have you found this to be true, also, with lithium gallium hydride and, if so, was there any decomposition during the removal of the ether?

DR. Y. OKAMOTO (New York Univ.): We removed the ether from the product and we found a gray product which we analyzed. The data of analysis showed that there was decomposition of lithium gallium hydride, and I imagine small amounts of lithium gallium hydride could be decomposed during the removal of the ether.

F. D. ROSI CHAIRMAN (RCA LAB.): The way your gallium is prepared may be, as you state, a simple method, but I observed, that it showed several parts per million of spectrographic impurities, whereas the gallium currently required and used, for example, in the preparation of compounds like gallium arsenide show no spectrographically detectable impurities and we have to resort to mass spectrography for analysis. Can you comment on this?

DR. Y. OKAMOTO (New York Univ.): The Gallium is about 99.999 per cent pure, and we are trying for further purification.

W. BRENNER (New York Univ.): The gallium metal which is required for this type of application is supposed to be free of spectrographic impurities. Without going into details, we have obtained at least two samples of gallium metal which were supposed to be spectrographically pure but it has been analyzed and spectrographic impurities have been found.

F. D. ROSI CHAIRMAN (RAC Lab.): I was referring to the availability of gallium from the Aluminum Company of America and also from a Swiss Company. Although the sources have various lot numbers, generally speaking, one can obtain gallium in a form where it is below at least a part per million total impurities, and this is what I was referring to specifically. Would you care to comment on that?

W. BRENNER (New York Univ.): I would like to make two points. The first point is that, we do not claim that we made ultimate-purity gallium. We claim that we had a procedure which, with a minimum of investment, gave a rather interesting grade product.

Now, as regard lot numbers which you mentioned, I think it is known that each grade of gallium which one obtains is different. And there are certain lot numbers which have been analyzed by one analyst who claims them to be free from impurities while another analyst will take the same sample, run an emission spectroscopic analysis and find impurities in it in the part per million range. We have given conservative values throughout. We have also run an analysis on gallium which was made by Alcoa and by the Swiss people and, in the complete paper, we have a comparison of various specific lot numbers. In none of the samples at which we have looked so far have we found spectrographically pure material?

F. D. ROSI CHAIRMAN (RCA Lab.): To what level did you find impurities?

W. BRENNER (New York Univ.): One to three parts per million.

F. D. ROSI CHAIRMAN (RCA Lab.): What was the total concentration?

W. BRENNER (New York Univ.): I am talking about individual impurities.

F. D. ROSI CHAIRMAN (RCA Lab.): I will also say--and Dr. Weisberg, who is sitting there, can probably say more about this than I--that in working with gallium, you run into serious sources of contamination just in handling the material and waiting to analyze it after it is received by the people.

L. R. WEISBERG (RCA Lab.): In discussions of the purity of a metal such as gallium, I think it is worth while for people to become aware of the use of the residual resistivity ratio at liquid helium to room temperature in characterizing the material. We have found this particularly useful. We have seen samples that have shown no spectrographically detectable impurities and yet have seen differences in the residual resistivity ratio. I would like to encourage people engaged in purification work to use a characterization that may have more meaning than spectrographic analysis.

C. J. MARSEL (New York Univ.): I would like to point out that this is part of a continuing program and is sponsored by the Air Force Cambridge Research Laboratories to illustrate methods and general procedures for preparing high purity metals by this interesting hydride technique. Our purpose was not really to work out a completely detailed procedure, but to illustrate the principles.

L. CORRSIN (Xerox): I believe you mentioned electrolytic reduction of gallium salts to gallium. Does this method produce good purity, too?

DR. Y. OKAMOTO (New York Univ.): No, about 95 per cent purity. But the gallium we obtained by electrolysis could be chlorinated and purified by sublimation.

ORGANOMETALLIC COMPOUNDS IN THE PREPARATION OF HIGH PURITY METALS

W. A. G. Graham and A. R. Gatti
Arthur D. Little, Inc.
Cambridge, Mass.

INTRODUCTION

As a result of advances in solid-state physics and electronics, materials with impurity levels of one part per billion or lower are required. Not enough is known of the general methods that may be useful in the production of such materials. This chapter surveys the literature related to the use of organometallic compounds for that purpose, and describes some previously unreported attempts to use them to purify mercury, magnesium, gallium, and rhenium.

The preparation of ultra-pure metals via organometallic compounds involves two more or less separate steps: first, preparation of the compound and its isolation from all other compounds which would contaminate the final product; second, recovery of the metal from the compound in suitable physical form, and without contamination from container materials or other constituents of the compound itself.

The first step is the less difficult one. Organometallic compounds fall into several distinct classes, and the chemical reaction used to prepare the compound will result in effective separation from other classes. To achieve separation from more similar compounds of the same class, conventional purification techniques such as distillation can be used in favorable cases.

To achieve the second step requires that a molecule such as tetraethyllead, $(C_2H_5)_4Pb$, be decomposed in such a way that no more than one part per billion of the carbon and hydrogen content remains with the lead. It implies a conversion of at least 99.9999999% in the decomposition reaction.

Accordingly, emphasis is placed in this chapter on methods of recovering the metal from its compounds. Four are considered: pyrolysis, photolysis, electrolysis, and hydrogenolysis. Although other methods can certainly be used to excite and

decompose molecules, they have not been used with organometallic compounds to our knowledge.

General Properties of Organometallic Compounds

Since some readers of this report may not be familiar with
organometallic chemistry, it is appropriate to review here some
of the general background. Excellent detailed accounts are
available elsewhere [25, 107].

Organometallic compounds are those which have metal-
carbon bonds. Their properties vary widely with the particular
metal, but the following categories provide a useful guide. Figure 1 indicates this classification from the standpoint of the
periodic table.

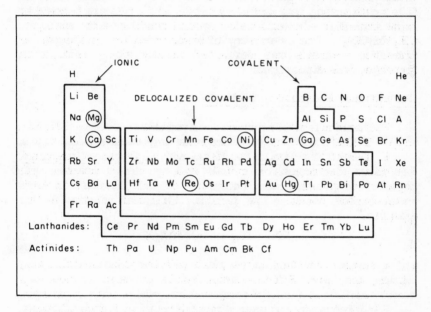

Figure 1. Periodic Classification of Organometallic Compounds.

Ionic organometallic compounds are formed by the most
electropositive metals. They are salt-like in nature, with the
organic radical carrying a negative charge—for example,
ethylsodium, $Na^+C_2H_5^-$, which gives rise to extremely high
reactivity with air and water. The compounds are nonvolatile
and insoluble in organic solvents. Lithium and beryllium organometallics approach the covalent type in many of their properties,
and to a lesser extent this is true of magnesium. Scandium,
yttrium, lanthanium, and the rare earth metals are included in

107

this category, since their only stable organometallic derivatives (formed with the $C_5H_5^-$ group) are ionic in nature.

Covalent organometallic compounds are formed by the main group elements other than the sodium and calcium groups. The alkyls of this group, apart from those of copper, silver and gold, are distillable liquids, varying in their sensitivity to water and air. Thus, for example, triethylboron (bp. 95°C) is stable to water but reactive to air; triethylaluminum (bp. 185.6°C) reacts with air and violently so with water; tetraethyltin (bp. 175°C) is stable to both air and water.

Delocalized Covalent compounds are formed by the transition elements with certain organic groups. Examples are ferrocene, $(C_5H_5)_2Fe$, and dibenzene chromium, $(C_6H_6)_2Cr$, both of which possess a "sandwich" structure. In general these are sublimable solids, soluble in organic solvents, and some are easily oxidized. It is worth noting that ordinary alkyls and aryls are formed by some transition elements under special conditions, for example, $CH_3Mn(CO)_5$. The chemistry of organometallic compounds of transition elements has developed rapidly since 1951, when ferrocene was discovered.

Conventional Preparative Methods

Full accounts of this subject are available elsewhere [107, 65], and we indicate here only the two most important general types.

1. Direct Reaction of the Metal with an Organic Compound: The more electropositive metals undergo direct reaction with organic compounds, most commonly organic halides, to form metal-carbon bonds. The familiar Grignard reaction is one example,

$$RX + Mg \longrightarrow RMgX$$

and a similar reaction takes place with the alkali metals, aluminum, and zinc. Silicon-carbon bonds are also formed in a direct reaction at elevated temperatures with a copper catalyst.

A limited number of metals react directly with hydrocarbons. The addition of alkali metals to double bonds is well known. Reaction of iron and magnesium with cyclopentadiene has been observed more recently.

2. Formation from Other Organometallic Compounds: In general, organometallic compounds of the more electropositive metals react with metal halides of less electropositive metals in reactions such as the following:

$$3\ RMgBr + BBr_3 \longrightarrow R_3B + 3\ MgBr_2$$

$$4\ RNa + SnCl_4 \longrightarrow R_4Sn + 4\ NaCl$$

Another general reaction is that of electropositive metals with organometallic compounds of less electropositive metals, in particular of mercury:

$$R_2Hg + Mg \longrightarrow R_2Mg + Hg$$

RECOVERY OF METALS FROM ORGANOMETALLIC COMPOUNDS

Thermal Decomposition

For almost 30 years the thermal decomposition of organometallic compounds has been recognized as a convenient source of free radicals. Short-lived and very reactive free radicals are formed from organometallic compounds at relatively low temperatures, which simplifies the interpretation of their behavior. The detailed mechanisms which account for the observed products, and the energetics of the elementary processes derived from rate measurements are not of primary importance for the purposes of this survey. Our interest centers on the fraction of a material which is decomposed in a given time under particular conditions, on the purity of the metallic product, and on whether nonvolatile by-products are formed which may contaminate the metal; some published papers on the subject pay little attention to these very practical considerations.

Experiments on thermal decomposition may involve simple or fairly complex apparatus. Most commonly, the decomposition is studied in the gas phase. There are two experimental methods, one using a static system, the other a flow system. In the former, materials are placed in a reaction vessel, which is heated at a given temperature for a given time; the vessel is then cooled and the products are analyzed. In a flow system, materials being studied are swept continuously through a furnace; the products are trapped as they leave the furnace and later analyzed. The time variable is expressed as a contact time, equal to the volume of the decomposition vessel divided by the volume rate of flow of the gas.

Mercury: The pyrolysis of organomercury compounds is a classical method for the study of free radicals. More is known about the thermal decomposition of organic compounds of mercury than about those of any other metal, and it seems likely that the behavior of other organometallic compounds will, upon closer investigation, parallel to some extent that of organomercury compounds.

Among organomercury compounds, dimethylmercury has been the subject of many investigations. The pyrolysis of dimethylmercury in a static system has been studied by a number of workers [69, 145, 112, 32]. The work of Cunningham and Taylor [32] offers a complete description of the experiment. The pyrolysis vessel was filled with gaseous dimethylmercury at pressures ranging from 20 to 50 mm. No measurable decomposition was observed after long heating at 255°C; at 290°C, decomposition amounted to 2% in 5 hours; and at 348°C, decomposition was relatively rapid. About 60% of the carbon resulting from the decomposition was in the form of methane and ethane. The balance remained as a dark brown deposit on the walls of the reaction vessel, presumably a $(-CH_2-)_n$ polymer. This residue would complicate the recovery of pure mercury. It was found, however, that in the presence of hydrogen (initial pressures of 40 mm for dimethylmercury and 200 mm for hydrogen) there was no dark coating of the reaction vessel, and almost all the carbon from decomposed dimethylmercury was accounted for in the form of methane. In addition, the reaction was accelerated by hydrogen; complete decomposition resulted after heating for one hour at 348°C with hydrogen, while complete decomposition of dimethylmercury alone required 11 hours at this temperature.

Quite recently, it has been found that the presence of cyclopentane also eliminates the formation of a nonvolatile carbonaceous residue [112]. Thus, in an experiment at 375°C using a 20-fold excess of cyclopentane, in which decomposition of dimethylmercury was carried to completion, 98% of the carbon was accounted for in the volatile products. The postulated CH_2 intermediate was presumed to react with the cyclopentane instead of polymerizing.

The formation of a residue in these experiments was attributed to a wall reaction [120]. This would account for its absence when the decomposition is carried out in a flow system, as is evidently the case in reported studies using this technique. Typical conditions in such experiments are 530°C, about 5 mm Hg partial pressure of dimethylmercury and the use of a carrier gas [52].

Experiments in flow systems are frequently carried out in the presence of toluene, which acts as a "radical trap," thus simplifying a kinetic interpretation of the results. This was done for dimethylmercury [94], but the presence or absence of toluene makes little difference [52] in this case.

Studies of the thermal decomposition of other organomercury compounds are as follows: diethylmercury [20], di-n-propylmercury [21, 22], diisopropylmercury [23], di-n-butylmercury [41], di-n-heptylmercury [105], and diphenylmercury [20].

Lithium: Methyllithium, CH_3Li, decomposes between 200-240°C forming methane and Li_2CH_2, a yellow-brown, air-sensitive powder. Strong heating of the residue forms Li_2C_2, LiH, and perhaps lithium metal [150]. Methyllithium showed no signs of decomposition on long heating in phenetole at 150°C [8].

Ziegler and Gellert [148] have studied the thermal decomposition of ethyllithium and butyllithium. Ethyllithium reacts mainly as follows:

$$CH_3CH_2Li \longrightarrow LiH + C_2H_4$$

Butylene and butane are found in smaller amounts among the gaseous products, since ethylene can react with undecomposed ethyllithium to form butyllithium. Butyllithium forms lithium hydride and butene-1 in a similar way, beginning at 100°C and rapidly at 150°C. Contact of butene-1 with unchanged butyllithium forms butadiene, which contaminates the products with resin. This can be overcome to a considerable extent by operating at 80-100°C in high vacuum.

Sodium: Thermal decomposition of ethylsodium begins slowly at room temperature and is rapid at 100°C. At 90-100°C, ethylene is the chief product, implying that the main reaction is

$$CH_3CH_2Na \longrightarrow NaH + C_2H_4$$

Ethane is formed in smaller amounts, and a materials balance suggests that it is formed in the over-all reaction:

$$4\,NaC_2H_5 \longrightarrow 3\,C_2H_6 + H_2 + 2\,Na + NaCCNa$$

These reactions take place below 142°C. When heated above this temperature with a free flame, nearly pure hydrogen was evolved, from decomposition of sodium hydride. The residue was pyrophoric [19].

It has been reported that preparations of amylsodium decompose to form the metal

$$NaC_5H_{12} \longrightarrow Na + C_5H_{11}$$

and that the reaction is catalyzed by alkoxides [77]. This finding has been questioned, since free amyl radicals could not be detected [16].

Beryllium: Decomposition of diethylberyllium begins at 65°C and is rapid at 190-200°C; the product is a viscous oil (formula corresponding to $HBeCH_2CH_2BeH$) and crystals (formula $[HBe_2(CH_2)_3]_x$ or $[Be_2(CH_2)_3]_x$) [51]. Paneth was able to deposit a bright mirror of beryllium on gold foil by pyrolysis at unstated conditions [89].

111

Di-t-butylberyllium etherate gives beryllium hydride on pyrolysis [26]; under the best conditions, the hydride contained 20% of ether impurity [56]. When pure di-t-butylberyllium was pyrolized, the product again contained 80% of beryllium hydride with a residue of t-butyl groups. It seems probable that vapor-phase pyrolysis of di-t-butylberyllium above 210°C would yield beryllium metal directly [56].

Pyrolysis of isopropylberyllium hydride at 220-250°C gives beryllium metal with an orange residue [27].

Magnesium: Dimethylmagnesium decomposes in the range 220-240°C according to the equation:

$$(CH_3)_2Mg \longrightarrow MgCH_2 + CH_4.$$

The reaction is complete by 260°C, and can be carried out in a high-boiling solvent [150].

Pyrolysis of diethylmagnesium in high vacuum to a final temperature of 200°C evolves a mixture of ethylene (80%) and ethane (20%). Higher temperatures favor ethylene formation. The residue is reported to be pure magnesium hydride, formed according to

$$Mg(C_2H_5)_2 \longrightarrow MgH_2 + C_2H_4.$$

Ethane is formed in a side reaction

$$Mg(C_2H_5)_2 \longrightarrow MgC_2H_4 + C_2H_6$$

but the MgC_2H_4 is volatile, and passes from the pyrolysis apparatus. The MgC_2H_4 is initially crystalline, but changes to a nonvolatile oil, presumably $(MgC_2H_4)_n$, which on further heating at 200°C in high vacuum is partly volatilized and partly converted to magnesium hydride [40, 136].

Dibutylmagnesium begins to evolve gas (80% butene) at 170-180°, forming the hydride as the chief product. A secondary reaction also takes place, as above, leading to MgC_4H_8. Yet another side reaction is observed, however:

$$(C_4H_9)_2Mg \longrightarrow Mg + (C_4H_9)_2.$$

Diphenylmagnesium, heated in high vacuum to 210°C, decomposes chiefly according to the reaction

$$Mg(C_6H_5)_2 \longrightarrow Mg + (C_6H_5)_2.$$

In this case also, a side reaction forms MgC_6H_4, which contaminates the magnesium residue. The extent of the side reaction is unknown [136].

112

Magnesium hydride decomposes to the metal in vacuum at 280-300°C [136, 137].

Boron: Decomposition of alkylboranes at moderate temperatures forms alkylboron hydrides [110, 140]. Thus at 100-130°C, tri-n-butylborane decomposes as follows:

$$2 (n-C_4H_9)_3B \longrightarrow [(n-C_4H_9)_2BH]_2 + C_4H_8$$

Complete conversion to boron hydrides seems probable on continued heating, but rather high temperatures are required for conversion of the hydride to pure boron [117, 123].

Aluminum: A kinetic study of the thermal decomposition of trimethylaluminum has been carried out [144]. When a static system and temperatures of 300°C and higher were used, the reaction vessel was in some cases coated with a thin film having a blue metallic sheen. At higher temperatures, a complex mixture of metallic and brownish polymeric material was formed. At an initial pressure of 85 mm, a heavy yellowish deposit formed, probably aluminum carbide. Formation of aluminum carbide was also reported when trimethylaluminum was heated in a sealed Carius tube at 230°C [72]. Ziegler has confirmed that the over-all reaction for thermal decomposition of trimethyl-aluminum is [151]:

$$4 (CH_3)_3Al \longrightarrow Al_4C_3 + 9 CH_4$$

Ziegler and Gellert [149] pointed out that triisobutylaluminum, formed by the direct reaction of aluminum, hydrogen, and isobutylene, was converted to diisobutylaluminum hydride at 150°C:

$$[(CH_3)_2CH-CH_2]_3Al = [(CH_3)_2AlCH-CH_2]_2AlH + (CH_3)_2C = CH_2$$

and that the hydride decomposed smoothly at 250°C:

$$[(CH_3)_2CH-CH_2]_2AlH = Al + 1 1/2 H_2 + 2 (CH_3)_2C = CH_2$$

They suggested that these equations formed the basis for an aluminum purification process.

Ziegler recently reported a more detailed study of the pyrolysis of a number of organoaluminum compounds [151]. In the decomposition of diisobutylaluminum hydride at 200-250°C, some of the evolved isobutylene adds to the hydride in a side reaction:

$$[(CH_3)_2CH-CH_2]_2AlH + (CH_3)_2C = CH_2 = [(CH_3)_2CH-CH_2]_3Al$$

113

Decomposition of triisobutylaluminum at these temperatures is complex, and gives rise to aluminum carbide. Using gaseous diisobutylaluminum hydride in a vacuum system, conditions designed to minimize the side reaction, the carbide content was reduced to 0.04%.

A recent patent [11] cites the decomposition of triisobutyl-aluminum at 275-350°C to give high-quality deposits of aluminum. This patent also claims that triethylaluminum and diethyl-aluminum hydride are satisfactory for aluminum plating.

Silicon: Decomposition of tetramethylsilane in a static system between 660 and 720°C has been studied [59]. At 678.7°C, with an initial pressure of 33 mm, decomposition was 40% complete in 9 minutes and 80% complete in 24 minutes. A sooty deposit of silicon and carbon was formed.

Decomposition of tetraethylsilane was complete in 25 minutes at 580°C in a static system [129]. Up to within 5 minutes of completion, the only deposit on the walls of a new flask was a white coating of silicon. At completion, however, the walls show a blackish-gray deposit which eventually assumes the shiny-black appearance of carbon particles. Decomposition of tetra-propylsilane has also been studied, but nothing is said about the nature of the solid products [129]. A patented process claims the use of silicon alkyls, in particular tetraamylsilane, to prepare pure silicon by thermal decomposition [47]. A novel feature of the patent is the use of nitric oxide to inhibit the formation of carbon deposits, presumably by breaking free-radical chain processes.

The importance of pyrolysis conditions is indicated by the isolation of new types of high-boiling or crystalline compounds with Si-C-Si bonds from the thermal decomposition of tetramethyl- and tetraethylsilane [42]. Formation of silicon carbide from methyltrichlorosilane at 1500°C has also been observed [75].

Germanium: In a study of the kinetics of thermal decomposition of tetraethylgermane in a static system at 420-450°C, it was reported that a semimirror of metallic germanium was deposited on the walls of the reaction vessel [43].

Thermal decomposition of germanium tetraalkyls, tetra-amylgermane in particular, is one of the claims in a patent on the preparation of pure germanium [47].

Tin: The thermal decomposition of tetramethyltin in a static system has been investigated [114, 130]. In the short runs of up to five minutes at 440-493°C, a whitish-gray coating, presumed to be tin, formed on the flask. In longer experiments, the coating became blackish-gray because of the deposition of carbon.

A study of the pyrolysis of dimethyltin dichloride made no mention of the solid products, but the kinetic scheme suggested that stannous chloride was formed [96].

114

Lead: In static experiments on tetramethyllead, Simons, McNamee, and Hurd found that high temperatures resulted in less carbon deposition. At 265°C, there was considerable tarring and carbonization; this decreased until between 550 and 620°C, the deposit resembled a sputtered film of lead and contained little or no carbon [119]. Meinert reported that tetraethyllead decomposed at its boiling point, leaving a residue of finely divided lead in which no carbon could be detected [74]. Smooth decomposition took place when tetraethyllead vapor was passed through a tube in the range 300-500°C, leaving the lead loosely deposited on the sides in the form of a fine dust. The pyrolysis of tetraethyllead in a static system with hydrogen and ethylene has also been studied [125].

Cornish [29] has reported deposition of lead mirrors on a substrate heated to 375-525°C, when nitrogen at 10-63 mm was bubbled through tetraethyllead at 20°C and directed through the apparatus at 3 liters per hour.

Arsenic: Decomposition of trimethylarsine in a flow system between 400 and 460°C forms polymeric material and a coherent layer of free carbon in the reaction vessel. Arsenic sublimed from the furnace at these temperatures [2]. The same workers carried out a parallel study of tristrifluoromethylarsine in the range 350-410°C. In a silica reaction vessel, silicon tetrafluoride and carbon dioxide were formed, and a little arsenic trifluoride; in a platinum reactor, appreciable amounts of arsenic trifluoride were formed, as well as small amounts of a white polymer resembling polytetrafluoroethylene. It was suggested that platinum acted to hold the arsenic in the reaction vessel, perhaps as an arsenide, so that the following reaction could take place:

$$3 CF_3 \cdot + As \longrightarrow AsF_3 + 3 \cdot CF_2 \cdot$$

Antimony: In the pyrolysis of trimethylstibine in the range 475-664°C with toluene carrier, all the methyl groups could not be accounted for in the gaseous products, and it was supposed that a polymer $(SbCH_3)_x$ was produced [96].

A recent report indicates that very pure antimony has been produced from triisobutylstibine, but details of the work have not been reported [91].

A preliminary report of the thermal decomposition of tristrifluoromethylstibine, $(CF_3)_3Sb$, has been given [2]. Formation of antimony trifluoride and polytetrafluoroethylene is considerable in the range 180-220°C. At these temperatures, antimony does not sublime from the furnace, and hence is available for reaction with $CF_3 \cdot$ radicals, as indicated above for arsenic.

115

Bismuth: In the decomposition of trimethylbismuth with toluene carrier in the range 346-584°C, all the methyl groups could be accounted for as methane and ethane [96]. Thus carbon deposition is probably slight.

Tellurium: Diphenylditelluride is reported to yield crystalline tellurium quantitatively, but the temperature was not stated [37]. Likewise, crystals of tellurium formed on the heating of an amyltellurium compound [141].

Zinc: Diethylzinc does not decompose appreciably at temperatures up to 250°C [76]. In dimethylzinc pyrolysis [95], 98% of the methyl groups could be accounted for as methane and ethane, but there is no statement concerning the zinc residue. Various zinc alkyls are thermally decomposed to the metal in examples cited in a patent [33a].

Cadmium: In a static system, metallic cadmium is formed by pyrolysis of dimethylcadmium at 212-337°C. A yellowish solid product, presumed to be a hydrocarbon polymer, deposited on the walls of the vessel [58]. In a flow system, using a toluene carrier, decomposition of dimethylcadmium was complete with 5.6 seconds contact time at 595°C, and 98.7% of the carbon was accounted for in the volatile products [94].

Transition Metals: Since the simple alkyls of transition metals are—with one or two exceptions—unstable, and because stable organometallic derivatives of any kind have been few in number until recently, it is not surprising that systematic studies of thermal decomposition have not been made. A close reading of papers dealing with the organometallic chemistry of the individual elements sometimes reveals important incidental observations. Thus, a few lines in the experimental section of a paper on dibenzene chromium indicate that the compound decomposes at 250-300°C to form a bright metallic mirror [147]. A paper on dicyclopentadienylnickel mentions that the compound decomposes above its melting point (173-174°C) with formation of a metallic mirror [38].* These brief observations, however, may be of greater value than a lengthy study of the kinetics of the decomposition which makes no reference to the nature of the metallic product. Thermal decomposition of metal derivatives of cyclopentadiene, in particular those of manganese, titanium, magnesium and vanadium, at relatively high temperatures (500-700°C) has been claimed as a method of depositing metal coatings [18]; the same process apparently yields metal carbide as well [18].

---

*In unpublished experiments (Final Report, Contract No. AF 19(604)-4975), a black, shiny material containing 50% carbon was obtained when dicyclopentadienylnickel in an evacuated sealed tube was heated at 210°C for 90 minutes.

The case of metal deposition from metal carbonyls presents a special problem, since carbon monoxide resulting from the decomposition can enter the equilibrium:

$$2\ CO = C(graphite) + CO_2$$

At 500°C, 95% CO_2 is found, but the amount drops to 0.06% at 1200°C [68b]. At low temperatures, formation of carbon from carbon monoxide is extremely slow, but is catalyzed by numerous metals. These facts account for the carbon content of metals prepared by decomposition of metal carbonyls. Clearly, carbon contamination will be minimized by using low deposition rates in a high vacuum system, so that carbon monoxide liberated in the reaction has minimum contact with the metal surface. In addition, high temperature decomposition favors low carbon content, but at the same time increases contamination by diffusion from the substrate.

The reaction of metals with carbon monoxide has been studied extensively from the viewpoint of the Fischer-Tropsch synthesis [63]. Nickel deposited from the carbonyl in a static system contains up to 12% carbon [111], but under suitable conditions hydrogen gas apparently converts the carbon in Ni_3C quantitatively to methane [4]. The general problem has been considered for chromium, molybdenum and tungsten, with consideration of the effect of hydrogen and/or water vapor in reducing the carbon content of the metal [68, 108, 109].

Photolysis

Contamination of pure materials can result from contact with container materials or other surfaces. This is a diffusion process and increases exponentially with temperature. An attractive aspect of the use of organometallic compounds in purification is that decomposition takes place thermally at lower temperatures than with metal halides, for example. Since some organometallic compounds are sensitive to ultraviolet light, it appeared that decompositions might be carried out at room temperature in this way. It is also possible that in cases where metals formed by thermal decomposition were contaminated by carbon and hydrogen, photolysis—here taken to mean decomposition by ultraviolet light—might result in a purer product.

The action of ultraviolet light on organometallic compounds has not been studied extensively. Available data indicate that the metal is formed in a number of cases, and the subject deserves more thorough investigation.

Mercury: Steacie has surveyed the many studies of the kinetics of the photochemical decomposition of mercury alkyls [121].

117

The majority are unimportant from the viewpoint of this survey and are not included. Dimethylmercury absorbs continuously at wavelengths shorter than 2800 Å, but the decomposition is most efficient in the range 2000-2100 Å [126, 97]. The quantum yield was unity at room temperature [127], rising to 2.21 at 189°C [128]. Photolysis of dimethylmercury vapor in a static system formed no carbonaceous deposit, as was found on thermal decomposition [32]. Aerosols of mercury have been prepared by dimethylmercury photolysis [55].

Aluminum: A thin film with a bluish metallic sheen was deposited on the photolysis of trimethylaluminum, which apparently did not differ from the deposit formed by thermal decomposition [144].

Gallium: A remarkable patent by Plust describes the production of gallium of semiconductor purity by photolysis of organogallium compounds [92]. Triethylgallium, triisopropylgallium, and triisobutylgallium were found to be suitable. Decomposition of the compounds, which could be carried out either with or without a solvent, was accelerated by heating to a temperature just below that at which thermal decomposition sets in. Gallium separated as large drops, and could be drawn off continuously from the reactor. Only gray-black powders were formed on thermal decomposition.

Lead: Tetramethyl- and tetraethyllead are decomposed in the vapor or liquid state or in solution to yield metallic lead. Ultramicroscopic particles of lead were observed a few seconds after the solutions were irradiated [70]. A lead film was produced in flash photolysis of tetramethyllead [24].

Zinc: The action of a quartz mercury arc brings about rapid decomposition of liquid diethylzinc to ethane and zinc metal [12]. Photolysis of diethylzinc vapor in a static system deposited a film of zinc on the walls of the vessel; higher temperatures favored the formation of higher hydrocarbons, including, perhaps, polyethylene [76].

Cadmium: A cadmium mirror was formed in photolysis of dimethylcadmium in a static system at 50°C. The deposit was not mirror-like in the range 150-275°C, but consisted of bright particles of metal covering a part of the irradiated area. In the presence of hydrogen, the deposit formed at elevated temperatures contained black specks, presumably carbon [1].

Hydrogenolysis

The reactions of several organometallic compounds with hydrogen at elevated temperatures and pressures have been observed. In the presence of a nickel catalyst, tetraphenyllead and dibutylzinc formed the respective metals, diphenylmagnesium was converted to magnesium hydride, and triphenylantimony was unchanged by hydrogen [146].

In another study, tetraphenyllead was converted without catalyst to metal in 97% yield, by use of hydrogen at 200°C and 60 atmospheres. Tetraphenyltin was converted in a similar way to tin in 76% yield, and in the majority of cases, metallic tin occurred as a button of high purity [44].

It was recently reported that diethylmagnesium is converted in 98% yield to magnesium hydride under rather mild conditions (ether solvent, 75°C, 800 psig, no catalyst). The authors review the available data and conclude that the ease of hydrogenolysis of the metal-carbon bond is greater the more electropositive the metal and the more ionic the bond [93]. This conclusion is gratifying, since satisfactory recovery of metal from the more ionic compounds by photolysis or pyrolysis is likely to be difficult.

Electrolysis

The conductivity and electrolysis of organometallic compounds of a limited number of metals have been studied. Brenner [15] attributes an important role to the solvent in determining the conductivity of solutions of organometallic and related compounds; he considers that a loose ionic complex between solvent and solute must be formed.

Electrolysis of Grignard reagents has been studied extensively, most generally from the standpoint of the organic products at the anode. References to early work are given by Overcash and Mathers [83], who first examined the process as a method for electrodeposition of magnesium. Ethylmagnesium iodide gave magnesium as loose, crystalline trees which could not be removed from the bath without loss; addition of dimethylaniline gave brighter and more adherent deposits, but the purity was not determined [83]. Brenner reported white, metallic deposits from electrolysis of ethylmagnesium bromide, but the metal content was only 71%, the rest presumably organic material [28].

Ether solutions of diethylmagnesium are reported to conduct, but electrolysis has not been studied [33, 35].

Electrodeposition of aluminum from baths containing organo-aluminum compounds has yielded good deposits of aluminum metal, but aluminum halides and an aromatic solvent have been involved. It is likely that the conductivity is due to a Friedel-Crafts complex, with the presence of organoaluminum compounds only incidental [13, 14, 115, 116].

Deposits of beryllium from electrolysis of dimethylberyllium in diethyl ether were brittle, black, and treed, and contained only 63-77% of the metal. Black, coherent deposits were obtained in tetrahydrofuran. A gray, metallic deposit with 95% beryllium resulted from addition of beryllium chloride. A solution of diphenylberyllium apparently does not conduct [142].

Alkyl derivatives of the alkali metals form conducting solutions in diethylzinc, dipropylzinc, trimethylaluminum, and triethylaluminum [57]. Electrolysis of diethylzinc solutions plates zinc at the cathode.

FREE-RADICAL REACTIONS

In the Gas Phase

The existence of free gaseous methyl radicals was first demonstrated by Paneth in 1929 [85]. The radicals were formed by the pyrolysis of tetramethyllead in a flow system at low pressure, and detected by their reaction with zinc, antimony, and lead mirrors, which they caused to disappear. The mirrors were converted to volatile metal alkyls, which could be trapped out and identified. This mirror technique was extensively used during the following 10 years to capture or fix free radicals, and so demonstrate their transient existence in gas reactions. During that period, mirrors of a number of metals were found to be converted to organometallic compounds by free radicals, and it was even suggested that this reaction might prove to be a useful synthetic method [84]. This work was fully reviewed in 1935 by Rice and Rice in their book, The Aliphatic Free Radicals [106], and more recently by Steacie [122].

In experiments of the Paneth type, by proper adjustment of conditions, a mirror can be removed from one position in a tube and made to reappear downstream. This transport of metal raised the possibility that metal purification processes utilizing this technique might be designed. We have reviewed the literature on reactions of organic free radicals with metals from this viewpoint.

Organic Radicals Used: In the great majority of experiments methyl, $CH_3\cdot$, ethyl, $C_2H_5\cdot$, and methylene, $\cdot CH_2\cdot$, constituted the free radical species. The lifetime of more complex alkyl radicals is too short for them to react with the mirror. Thus, when Paneth used tetrapropyllead or tetraisobutyllead as a source of free radicals, antimony or zinc mirrors disappeared, but only methyl derivatives of antimony and zinc were formed [88]. The propyl and butyl radicals expected as primary products evidently decompose very rapidly:

$$(C_3H_7)_4Pb \longrightarrow Pb + 4\,C_3H_7\cdot$$

$$C_3H_7\cdot \longrightarrow CH_3\cdot + C_2H_4$$

120

The resonance-stabilized benzyl free radical, $C_6H_5CH_2\cdot$, is an exception. Benzyl radicals, formed by thermal decomposition of tetrabenzyltin, survived long enough to react with mirrors of selenium and mercury; dibenzylselenide and dibenzylmercury were isolated [88].

Products of the Reaction: Metals whose reaction with free radicals has been described in the literature are listed in Table I. In addition to the elements listed there, Rice and Rice [106a] refer to unpublished work which shows that free radicals react with lithium, potassium, calcium, tin, cadmium, lanthanum, and thallium. Similarly, unpublished work indicates that magnesium, copper, silver, gold, and cerium give negative results in Paneth-type experiments.

At least two factors appear to determine whether a metallic mirror will be transported by a free-radical stream. First, it would appear that the organometallic compound formed must be stable and volatile; an interesting exception, however, is the case of lanthanum, since no organolanthanum compounds could be prepared by conventional methods [45]. The second factor is a property of the metal itself, or perhaps of the metal surface.

The condition of the metal surface plays an important role. The activity of tellurium, arsenic, and especially lead and antimony mirrors is diminished or completely inhibited by traces of oxygen admitted during or after their preparation; the activity of a mirror diminishes on standing, an effect which may be due to traces of oxygen from the walls of the apparatus, or to crystallization of the mirror [48]. Preliminary heating of the mirror in a hydrogen stream causes it to react more readily [104]. Paneth was unable to obtain a positive reaction with beryllium when it was deposited on quartz, but a reactive beryllium mirror was formed when it was deposited on gold foil by pyrolysis of diethylberyllium [89]. In the case of mercury, a particularly satisfactory technique was worked out by Rice, Johnston, and Evering [104], who directed a radical stream at a water-cooled finger on which mercury was continuously condensing.

The temperature of the mirror can influence the rate of mirror removal and the kind of organometallic products. It was found that the rate of combination of free radicals with lead diminished with rising temperature, and fell to zero above 350°C. Antimony, in contrast, reacted at a rate which was essentially independent of temperature [106b]. Paneth observed that heating arsenic, antimony, and bismuth mirrors favored the formation of less volatile, less highly alkylated products. In the reaction of arsenic with methyl radicals, for example, it would appear that the sequence was:

$$(CH_3As)_5 \longrightarrow (CH_3)_2AsAs(CH_3)_2 \longrightarrow (CH_3)_3As$$

Table I

Organometallic Compounds from Gaseous Free Radicals and Metallic Mirrors

Metal	Products	Remarks	References
Na	CH_3Na, C_2H_5Na	Less than one millimole of product formed. Forms coating on mirror.	118
Be	$(CH_3)_2Be$, $(C_2H_5)_2Be$	Mirror deposited on gold foil by diethyl-beryllium decomposition.	89
Pb	$(CH_3)_4Pb$, $(C_2H_5)_4Pb$		85, 87
As	$(CH_3)_2As$, $(CH_3)_2AsAs(CH_3)_2$ $(C_2H_5)_3As$, $(C_2H_5)_2AsAs(C_2H_5)_2$ $(CH_3As)_5$, $(C_2H_5As)_5$(?)	Diarsines are main products at room temperature. Pentamers formed by use of heated mirrors.	89
Sb	$(CH_3)_3Sb$, $(CH_3)_2SbSb(CH_3)_2$ $(C_2H_5)_3Sb$, $(C_2H_5)_2SbSb(C_2H_5)_2$	$(C_2H_5)SbSb(C_2H_5)_2$ formed only with hot mirrors.	89
Bi	$(CH_3)_3Bi$, $(C_2H_5)_3Bi$ $(CH_3)_2BiBi(CH_3)_2$(?)	Cold mirrors formed only trialkyls.	89
Se	$(C_6H_5CH_2)_2Se$, $(CH_2Se)_x$ $(C_6H_5CH_2Se)_2$		89, 90

Table I—Continued

Metal	Products	Remarks	References
Te	$CH_3TeTeCH_3$, $(CH_2Te)_x$ $(C_6H_5CH_2)_2Te$ (?)	Telluroformaldehyde formed from methylene radicals.	89, 102 90, 103
Zn	$(CH_3)_2Zn$, $(C_2H_5)_2Zn$		85, 87
Hg	$(CH_3)_2Hg$, $(C_2H_5)_2Hg$ $(C_6H_5CH_2)_2Hg$ CH_3Hg (?)	The methyl mercurous compound is extremely unstable.	89, 104 101, 10
I	CH_2I_2	Iodine mirror is cooled to $-65°$.	9

123

When the mirror was heated, the yield of the first was greatly increased, since it volatilized before it could be methylated further [89].

Specificity—The Problem of Methylene: The behavior of methylene free radicals, formed, for example, in the decomposition of diazomethane, is of particular interest. Those radicals exhibit a selectivity in their reactions with metals. Rice and Glasebrook demonstrated convincingly that methylene removes tellurium, antimony, selenium, and arsenic mirrors, but does not attack zinc, cadmium, bismuth, thallium, or lead, all of which are removed by alkyl radicals [102]. More recent work has not confirmed this specificity [82], and the discrepancy is probably related to the extreme sensitivity of the reactions to impurities, as well as to the complex behavior of methylene itself.

A related area of controversy is the nature of the supposed telluroformaldehyde obtained from methylene and tellurium. Rice and Glasebrook isolated it as a nonvolatile red solid of composition $(CH_2Te)_x$ [102], whereas the telluroformaldehyde obtained by Belchetz and Rideal was more volatile and was obtained only by use of a hot mirror [9]. Later work seems to have resolved the problem [90].

Leighton and Mortensen, in tracer experiments with invisibly thin mirrors, found that a lead isotope was transported, while its daughter, a bismuth isotope, remained in the position of the original mirror [70]. The discrepancy here could be due to the minute amounts involved, however.

Discussion: On the basis of the literature on the subject, there are two principal reasons for questioning the value of the mirror technique in the purification of metals. The first is the small scale on which the reactions have been carried out, and the second is whether the reactions are indeed very specific.

The scale on which these experiments can be carried out is limited by the necessity of maintaining low pressures (1-2 mm Hg) and high flow rates (10-15 m/sec). If these conditions are not met, free radicals do not survive until they reach the mirror. In a typical Paneth experiment, less than 10 milligrams of lead constitutes the mirror [86]. The only paper dealing primarily with the use of these reactions in synthesis makes no reference to the yield, absolute or fractional [89]; the impression is gained, however, that the amounts are no more than enough for characterization by micro techniques. In most reported work on this method, positive identification of the organometallic compound has been a serious problem because of the small amounts formed.

Rice and his coworkers simplified the apparatus greatly by using a condensable carrier gas, and in the case of mercury, which was condensed continuously on a cooled surface as

124

previously mentioned, obtained a gram of product in a three-hour period. They suggested that with larger apparatus, 10-gram lots could be made in a day's run [104]. Their products, however, were contaminated by other reaction products, carrier gas, and excess mercury, and a series of fractional sublimations was required to obtain pure products.

Of the elements which form covalent alkyls (see Figure 1), only copper, silver, and gold have been reported not to undergo reaction with free alkyl radicals. The literature on the subject thus provides no evidence that the reaction is any more specific than are many of the standard preparative methods. The specificity of methylene in comparison with methyl, and the effect of mirror temperature represent variables which could have great importance in a purification process; their generality has been little investigated, however.

In Solution

It has been recognized for a considerable time that free radicals can react directly with certain metals in solution. Such reactions were used to prove the transitory existence of free radicals in solution. The parallel with investigations of gaseous free radicals, outlined in the preceding section, is noteworthy. As synthetic methods, the reactions discussed here have not been attractive in comparison with the standard methods. In passing, we may note that free radicals may be involved to some extent in even the standard methods [17]. Nevertheless, the reaction of free radicals in solution with metals appeared to merit consideration from the special viewpoint of ultra-pure materials.

Radicals from Diazo Compounds: The only systematic study of the reaction of metals with free radicals in solution was carried out by Waters and reported in a series of papers between 1937 and 1939 [71, 132-135]. As a source of free radicals, Waters used benzene diazonium chloride, which decomposed on heating in acetone or ethyl acetate with elimination of nitrogen:

$$PhN_2Cl \longrightarrow Ph\cdot + N_2 + Cl\cdot \qquad (Ph = C_6H_5)$$

Calcium carbonate, suspended in the reaction medium, eliminated the possibility that the metal was attacked by hydrochloric acid; the latter could be formed from reaction of chlorine atoms with solvent. Incidentally, the chlorine radicals attacked many metals, including gold and silver, forming the chlorides.

Using the system PhN_2Cl-acetone-$CaCO_3$, Waters tested 38 elements in all, of which seven formed organometallic compounds: mercury, tin, arsenic, antimony, sulfur, selenium, and tellurium [135].* The results of Waters and others are summarized in Table II. Only phenyl derivatives are considered in the table, but in many of the references cited, a series of substituted phenyl groups has been used, the yield depending markedly on the particular aromatic group.

Reaction of diazonium double salts with copper or other metals also produces organometallic compounds, in some cases: Ph_3Bi in 22% yield from $PhN_2Cl \cdot BiCl_3$ [46]; Ph_2Hg in 65% yield from $PhN_2Cl \cdot HgCl_2$ [78]; Ph_2SnCl_2 from $(PhN_2Cl)_2SnCl_4$ [67]; and Ph_2PbCl_2 from $PhN_2Cl \cdot PbCl_2$ [66]. It is of interest that elemental bismuth was not attacked by the PhN_2Cl-acetone-$CaCO_3$ system [135].

<u>Radicals from Organic Peroxides</u>: It has been reported that organomercury compounds are formed by reaction of the metal with acyl peroxides in refluxing benzene [99]. From benzoyl peroxide, phenylmercuric benzoate was formed in 31.5% yield, while acetyl peroxide gave a 64.7% yield of methylmercuric acetate. According to the author, this is the first report of the reaction of an alkyl radical with a metal in solution. Tin and antimony formed acetates and benzoates, not organometallic compounds, under similar conditions [100].

<u>Radicals of Long Life</u>: Triphenylmethyl, $(C_6H_5)_3C\cdot$, is the best known member of a class of "stable" free radicals [131]. Its reaction with alkali metals forms conducting solutions containing the triphenylmethyl anion:

$$Ph_3C\cdot + Na \rightleftharpoons (Ph_3C:)^- + Na^+$$

The reaction is reversible, since when the ether solution is shaken with mercury, some sodium amalgam is formed. Analogous lithium and potassium derivatives are known.

The behavior of magnesium with triphenylmethyl is of considerable interest. Gomberg and Bachmann observed [49] that formation of triphenylmethyl Grignard took place in two successive stages:

$$2\,Ph_3CBr + Mg \longrightarrow 2\,Ph_3C\cdot + MgBr_2 \qquad (i)$$

$$2\,Ph_3C\cdot + MgBr_2 + Mg \longrightarrow 2\,Ph_3CMgBr \qquad (ii)$$

---

*Waters could not detect organometallic compound formation with the following elements: Cu, Ag, Au, Mg, Zn, Cd, B, Al, In, Tl, C, Si, Ge, Pb, P, Bi, Ti, Zr, V, Ta, Cr, W, Mo, Mn, Fe, Co, Ni, Pd, Pt, Ce, Th. It has since been shown that alloys of Pb or Tl with sodium undergo the reaction (see Table II).

Table II

Reaction of Metals with Phenyl Radicals in Solution

Element	Radical Source and Conditions	Products and Yield	References
Hg	PhN_2Cl, acetone, $CaCO_3$	PhHgCl	133
	PhN_2BF_4, acetone–water	PhHgCl (60%)	34
	PhN_2Cl, water	PhHgCl (45%)	73
	$(PhCOO)_2$, benzene	PhHgOOCPh (31.5%)	99
	$Ph_2I^+I^-$, n-PrOH	PhHgCl	113
Tl	PhN_2Cl, acetone, $CaCO_3$	none	135
	PhN_2BF_4, acetone, NaTl-alloy	Ph_2TlCl (10–20%)	79
Sn	PhN_2Cl, acetone, $CaCO_3$	Ph_2SnCl_2	135
Pb	PhN_2Cl, acetone, $CaCO_3$	none	135
	PhN_2BF_4, acetone, NaPb alloy	Ph_4Pb (30%)	80
As	PhN_2Cl, acetone, $CaCO_3$	Ph_3AsCl_2	135
Sb	PhN_2Cl, acetone, $CaCO_3$	Ph_3Sb, Ph_3SbCl_2, Ph_2SbCl	71
	$PhN_2Cl \cdot ZnCl_2$, acetone	Ph_3Sb, Ph_2SbCl, Ph_3SbCl_2	71
	$Ph_2I^+Cl^-$, water, Na_2S	Ph_3SbS	113
S	PhN_2Cl, acetone, $CaCO_3$ (reflux)	Ph_2S	134

Table II—Continued

Element	Radical Source and Conditions	Products and Yield	References
Se	PhN$_2$Cl, acetone, CaCO$_3$ (reflux)	Ph$_2$Se	134
Te	PhN$_2$Cl, acetone, CaCO$_3$ (cold) PhN$_2$Cl·ZnCl$_2$, acetone Ph$_2$I$^+$Cl$^-$, n-PrOH	Ph$_2$TeCl$_2$ Ph$_2$TeCl$_2$ Ph$_2$Te	134 134 113

Bachmann later showed that triphenylmethyl reacted with magnesium metal in the presence of a small amount of magnesium bromide [3]. Waters suggests that this combination behaves as "magnesious bromide":

$$Mg + MgBr_2 = 2 \cdot MgBr \qquad\qquad (iii)$$

$$Ph_3C \cdot + \cdot MgBr \longrightarrow Ph_3CMgBr \qquad\qquad (iv)$$

followed by reaction (i).

Although this is generally assumed to be a free-radical reaction, hexaphenylethane can undergo ionic dissociation, and the observations could be accounted for in this way.

Apart from Mg and the alkali metals, there have been no reports of the reaction of triphenylmethyl or other stable radicals with other metals. This area is perhaps worthy of investigation.

Discussion: The scale of operation and simplicity of apparatus involved suggest that metal-radical reactions in solution should be compared with conventional preparative methods, rather than with the Paneth technique. As with Paneth-type experiments, however, there is the question of the condition of the surface.

It would appear that the seven elements which are converted to organometallic compounds in this way could be freed from all other members of the covalent group (Figure 1), with the possible exception of gallium, which was not investigated. This is equivalent to a separation from all other metals of the periodic table. The surface question makes such a conclusion doubtful, for there is reason to suspect that zinc, cadmium, lead, bismuth, and possibly others would react under proper conditions.

As suggested by Waters [135], the metallic character of an element probably determines its behavior toward free radicals. Thus tin reacts, but the inertness of silicon and germanium can be ascribed to their diamond-type structure, in which electrons are paired. This sharp distinction may be contrasted with the reaction which the halides of these elements undergo, for example, with Grignard reagents. This kind of specificity might of course be expected in other reactions where a metal, as opposed to a metallic halide, is involved.

SOME SPECIFIC EXAMPLES

The foregoing constitutes a literature-based appraisal of the value of organometallic compounds as intermediates in metal purification. In addition, we have utilized these intermediates in a laboratory program with the object of obtaining high-purity samples of a number of metals of interest to Air Force Cambridge Research Laboratories. In four cases, mercury, magnesium,

129

gallium, and rhenium, the results are of sufficient interest to warrant inclusion here. Calcium and nickel were also investigated, but the results for the most part are negative or in need of additional study.

Mercury

As Coates [25] points out, there are three major groups of organomercury compounds: the type RHgX, where X is an electronegative radical; the type R_2Hg; and the more complicated types derived from olefins. We have confined our work to compounds of the R_2Hg type, primarily because they can be purified by the convenient and powerful technique of distillation. Mercury dialkyls are volatile liquids, e.g., diethylmercury $(C_2H_5)_2Hg$, b.p. 159°C. They are stable to air and water, differing in this respect from the alkyls of metals of periodic groups II and III. In this property, and in their lack of acidic or basic properties, they resemble alkyls of group IV metals; the latter are the most probable contaminants.

Diethylmercury was selected as the intermediate compound on account of the ease with which it could be prepared in quantity using commercially available triethylboron as the alkylating agent [64]. The product was purified by distillation at reduced pressure using a 60-cm, vacuum-jacketed, helix-packed column, fitted with a total reflux, partial take-off distilling head. After several distillations, the product was homogeneous by gas chromatography (Barber Colman instrument with ionization detector, Dow-Corning High Vacuum Grease on 30-mesh glass beads) except for a single very weak impurity peak.

The pure product was transferred from the distillation receiver to a round-bottom quartz flask with a single quartz standard taper joint. A Pyrex water condenser was attached and the flask was centered about 20 cm in front of a 325-watt Hanovia Analytic Model ultraviolet lamp. After irradiation of 73 g. diethylmercury for four days, most of the pool of mercury at the bottom of the flask was transferred to a storage vessel, washed six times with anhydrous ether, and dried in a nitrogen stream. The weight of mercury recovered was 26 g. (46% yield). Emission spectroscopic analysis by Metal Hydrides, Inc. (Beverly, Massachusetts) detected no impurities in the sample at levels greater than were present in the blanks. Estimated sensitivities in parts per million for the elements sought are as follows:

Zn						2-3
Au,	B,	Ca,	Cr,	Mn,	Mo	< 0.2
Ag,	Al,	Co,	Fe,	Sn		< 0.03
Cu,	Mg,	Si				< 0.003

130

It is probable that an additional purification results during the photolysis stage, since potential impurities such as tetra-ethylsilane (b.p. 153°C) are not readily decomposed by ultraviolet light. Irradiation could probably have been continued to achieve higher yields, and recovery and redistillation of the undecomposed diethylmercury would also increase the yield substantially. Mercury proved to be almost ideally suited for purification by means of organometallic compounds. The intermediate compound was readily prepared and purified; ultraviolet light efficiently decomposed the intermediate organomercury compound at room temperature, reducing contamination by diffusion from the container material to low values; finally, collection and handling of the purified metal was simplified by its unique physical properties. Thus it is not surprising that we were ultimately successful in preparing spectroscopically pure mercury by photolysis of diethylmercury. A review of mercury purification by conventional methods is of interest; the appearance of the surface is altered by extremely small amounts of certain impurities [50].

Magnesium

The properties of organomagnesium compounds raise certain difficulties insofar as their use in the preparation of pure magnesium is concerned. Our work is, in fact, less concerned with high purity than with the gross aspects of possible processes, hopefully to define objectives worth pursuing.

Diethylmagnesium: The pyrolysis or hydrogenolysis of diethylmagnesium to yield magnesium hydride was noted above. Diethylmagnesium is also reduced to the hydride by lithium aluminum hydride, although the reaction is not clean and the product contains aluminum [5]. Magnesium hydride decomposes to the metal above 280–300°C.

We followed Wiberg's procedure [136] for the preparation of magnesium hydride by pyrolysis of diethylmagnesium. It was clear that this method was not well suited to large scale preparation; the pyrophoric residue, after heating to decompose magnesium hydride, contained 9% carbon. This probably arises from the side reaction mentioned above, due to trapping of the $(MgC_2H_4)_n$ in the large amount of solid present. This finding emphasizes that pyrolysis of a solid organometallic compound is likely to give a metal product heavily contaminated with carbon. It would appear that hydrogenolysis of a solution of diethylmagnesium is a more attractive method of obtaining magnesium hydride, but this possibility was not explored.

Electrolysis was an attractive alternative to thermal decomposition. We chose not to work with Grignard reagents due to the probability of halogen contamination, and investigated

131

diethylmagnesium instead. For a 1.0 molar diethylmagnesium solution prepared by the dioxane method, we found a specific conductance of 4.3×10^{-5} ohm^{-1} cm^{-1}, in good agreement with the literature [75]. This was sufficient to permit rapid deposition of magnesium at 100 volts, although the deposit consisted of loose dendrites. Examination showed that the metal was contaminated by bromine, which could only mean that the "halogen-free" diethylmagnesium [143] prepared by the dioxane method contained appreciable amounts of bromide ion. This fact was recognized by earlier workers [81], but more recently had been overlooked.

To eliminate halogen completely, we returned to the original method for preparing diethylmagnesium, the reaction of magnesium with diethylmercury. The reaction was conveniently carried out in dibutyl ether, which acted as a solvent for the product, and provided at its normal boiling point a convenient reaction rate. The final diethylmagnesium solution was red in color, owing presumably to free radical attack of the solvent. Surprisingly, the solution was non-conducting to the limit of sensitivity of our apparatus. We were able to conclude that the specific conductance was less than 3.2×10^{-7} ohm^{-1} cm^{-1} for an approximately 0.25 molar solution. Thus, truly halogen-free diethylmagnesium is not suitable for electrodeposition of magnesium in diethyl ether. This finding is nonetheless of considerable interest in connection with studies of the structure of the Grignard reagent [33].

Ethylmagnesium hydride: It occurred to our colleague, Dr. Amos J. Leffler, that halogen contamination might be eliminated by converting the Grignard reagent to an alkylmagnesium hydride. A species of this type had not been reported, but we were able to prepare it by the reaction of ethylmagnesium bromide with sodium hydride:

$$C_2H_5MgBr + NaH \xrightarrow{\text{tetrahydrofuran}} C_2H_5MgH + NaBr$$

The new compound was not isolated, but its presence in solution was shown by evolution of hydrogen and ethane on hydrolysis, and a negative halide test with aqueous silver nitrate.

A tetrahydrofuran solution of ethylmagnesium hydride conducted well, forming a dendritic deposit at the cathode (Figure 2) and evolving a gas (presumed to be hydrogen) at the anode. The cell shown in Figure 3 was designed to avoid shorting of the electrodes by the streamer-like magnesium deposit. The magnetic stirrer dislodged the dendrites and permitted operation for several days at a steady current of 50 milliamps at 300 volts.

The most serious defect of the ethylmagnesium hydride process is the lack of a suitable physical method of purification, a feature common to most known organomagnesium compounds.

132

Figure 2. Cathode During Electrolysis of
Ethylmagnesium Hydride.

Magnesium cyclopentadienide: This unique compound possesses a "sandwich" structure, similar geometrically to that of ferrocene. It was first prepared by pyrolysis of cyclopentadienyl-magnesium bromide [138, 139] but is most conveniently obtained by passing cyclopentadiene over heated magnesium metal [6, 7]. The compound forms white, air-and-moisture-sensitive crystals, and alone among organomagnesium compounds, it can readily be purified by a physical method, i.e., sublimation. The properties of the compound suggest appreciable ionic character, which is explicable in terms of the theory of bonding in sandwich compounds [31]. Its solution in liquid ammonia is conducting [139].

Hydrogenolysis of the compound in tetrahydrofuran under the conditions used for diethylmagnesium did not produce magnesium hydride. This was apparent from the absence of insoluble product and from the fact that no hydrogen was liberated on treatment of the tetrahydrofuran solution with methanol. Surprisingly, in view of the ionic character of the compound, its diethyl ether solution was non-conducting, and addition of the more basic tetrahydrofuran did not increase the conductance. We did not investigate other solvents; the conductivity in liquid ammonia, mentioned above, is sufficient for purposes of electrolysis, but the reaction of alkaline earth metals with liquid

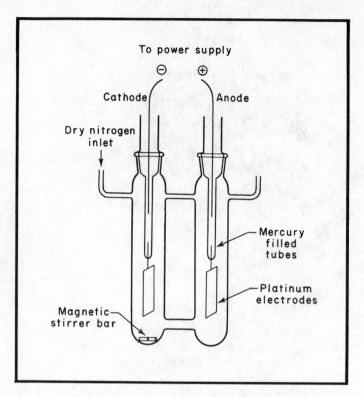

Figure 3. Apparatus for Electrolysis of
Ethylmagnesium Hydride.

ammonia would complicate the preparation of magnesium in that
solvent.

Gallium

Relatively few organic compounds of gallium have been
described [25]. Our attention was confined to trialkylgallium
compounds, air-and-water-sensitive liquids obtained by the
reaction of gallium with dialkylmercury compounds, or by the
action of Grignard reagents, zinc alkyls, or aluminum alkyls on
gallium trichloride.

Thermal decomposition of trimethylgallium was first
investigated. When the vapor from a room temperature reservoir
of trimethylgallium was admitted to a quartz tube at 400°C, the
pressure in the system increased; methane was evolved, with no
ethane or ethylene. After three hours, a thin, gallium-containing
film had formed in the tube, but an X-ray diffraction pattern
revealed no spacings characteristic of gallium metal. Using

134

argon as a carrier gas, trimethylgallium formed a dark, somewhat metallic-looking deposit on the walls of a tube heated to 520°C; microanalysis of the deposit showed 8.0% carbon, 0.0% hydrogen. Since the metal-carbon bond energy is comparable in trimethylgallium and trimethylaluminum, one may expect a similarity in their behavior on pyrolysis. Thus methane formation and a carbon residue are also found with trimethylaluminum [151].

The patent to Plust on photolytic decomposition of trialkylgallium compounds has already been mentioned [92]. In our hands, this method was less than satisfactory. We irradiated triethylgallium (20 g.) in a quartz flask placed 15 cm, in front of a 325-watt Hanovia Analytic Model Lamp; heat from the lamp kept the flask at about 50°C. After 18.5 hours, the solution was dark brown and contained a small amount of finely divided gray-black solid. Remaining triethylgallium was decanted, but addition of ether to remove residual organic material caused the solid to form a film of somewhat metallic appearance; the film could not be made to coalesce into a drop of gallium metal. Results were the same in repeated attempts. After several days' irradiation, only small amounts (estimated at less than 100 mg.) of solid formed, and this could not be recovered because it formed a thin, adherent film on the walls of the quartz container.

Triisobutylgallium was irradiated while it was heated at 145°C for 47 hours. Ultimately, 0.3 g. of a dull, gray-black solid was recovered, in which the presence of metallic gallium was demonstrated by X-ray diffraction.

Rhenium

Rhenium carbonyl, $Re_2(CO)_{10}$, was prepared in 1941 by the reaction of rhenium (VII) oxide and carbon monoxide at 200 atmospheres and 250°C; it is a white, crystalline, sublimable solid [62]. Simple alkyl or aryl compounds of rhenium cannot be prepared [30], but alkyl derivatives of rhenium carbonyl have recently been prepared [60, 61]. Various other compounds are formed by rhenium with the versatile cyclopentadienyl group [39, 53, 54, 98]. We chose to work with rhenium carbonyl since it was apparently readily prepared in quantitative yield. Actually, our yields were far from quantitative, owing perhaps to our use of a rocking autoclave instead of the rotating type used by Hieber. At the conclusion of our preparations, substantial lumps of unreacted rhenium oxide were found. Impurity levels were reduced to fairly satisfactory levels by repeated sublimation; if this had not been the case, it would have been desirable to carry out an additional, more selective chemical step, such as conversion to an alkylrhenium pentacarbonyl. Our preparation of rhenium carbonyl was carried out in an autoclave heavily plated with silver to avoid formation of iron carbonyl.

Photolysis: Metallic rhenium is not formed in the photolysis of rhenium carbonyl in a hydrocarbon solvent. Instead, a brown solid results, of empirical formula $ReC_{3.87}O_{3.96}H_{1.85}$, perhaps $[Re(CO)_4H]_n$; a determination of molecular weight fixes n as about 20. The hydrogen may well be due to small amounts of trapped solvent or to analytical errors. Irradiation of metal carbonyls in the presence of other ligands such as pyridine results in replacement of one or two moles of carbon monoxide by pyridine [124]. Presumably, carbon monoxide is ejected during irradiation of rhenium carbonyl, and we suggest as a hypothesis that the species so formed polymerizes to achieve the inert gas configuration, in the absence of other ligands.

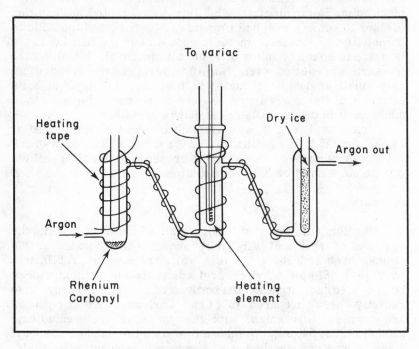

Figure 4. Apparatus for Pyrolysis of Rhenium Carbonyl in Argon Stream.

Pyrolysis: Using the apparatus shown in Figure 4, rhenium carbonyl was carried in an argon stream over a quartz finger heated to 150°C. Microanalysis of the deposit showed 0.6% carbon. Under these conditions, part of the deposit is in the form of whiskers. This phenomenon, shown in Figure 5, appears

136

Figure 5. Rhenium "Whiskers" by Carbonyl Pyrolysis.

to depend markedly on the temperature of the surface on which deposition takes place. It seemed possible that the needle-like growths were single-crystal whiskers, but an X-ray diffraction study of a single needle (1 mm in length) by Dr. James R. Aronson showed that it was polycrystalline. The needles appear under magnification to be rolled-up sheets, which suggests an interesting growth mechanism.

Best results were obtained when rhenium carbonyl was sublimed onto a heated quartz finger in high vacuum. Carbon levels below the sensitivity of our analytical method (0.1%) were obtained and yields were almost quantitative. The temperature of the surface of the quartz finger was estimated at 300°C, although measurement of the actual temperature during decomposition is a difficult problem. At this temperature, the deposit is smooth and mirror-like initially, becoming dull as deposition proceeds. The deposit was loosened by pouring ice water into the quartz finger. Analysis of a rhenium sample prepared from triply-sublimed carbonyl was as follows (by Metal Hydrides, Inc., Beverly, Massachusetts):

Si < 0.5 ppm   Mg < 0.2 ppm   Al < 0.2 ppm
Fe < 0.1   Cu   0.1

137

The limits of sensitivity based on the blank and the method are:

Cu	<0.05 ppm
Ag, Al, B, Mg, Mn, Ni, Pb, Sn	<0.1
Fe	<0.3
Ca, Cr, Si, Ti	<0.5
Ba, Hg	<1.0

We wish to acknowledge support of this work by the Electronics Research Directorate, Air Force Cambridge Research Laboratories, under Contract No. AF19(604)-4975.

REFERENCES

1. R. D. Anderson and H. A. Taylor, J. Phys. Chem., 56, 498 (1952).
2. P. B. Ayscough and H. J. Emeleus, J. Chem. Soc., 3381 (1954).
3. W. E. Bachmann, J. Am. Chem. Soc., 52, 4412 (1930).
4. H. A. Bahr and T. Bahr, Ber., 61B, 2177 (1928).
5. G. D. Barbaras, C. Dillard, A. E. Finholt, T. Wartik, K. E. Wilzbach and H. I. Schlesinger, J. Am. Chem. Soc. 73, 4585 (1951).
6. W. A. Barber, J. Inorg. Nuclear Chem. 4, 373 (1957).
7. W. A. Barber, Inorganic Syntheses 6, 11 (1960).
8. C. E. H. Bawn and F. J. Whitby, Discussions Faraday Soc. 2, 228 (1947).
9. L. Belchetz and E. K. Rideal, J. Am. Chem. Soc. 57, 1168 (1935).
10. L. Belchetz and E. K. Rideal, J. Am. Chem. Soc. 57, 2466 (1935).
11. C. Berger, U.S. 2,921,868; January 19, 1960 (to Union Carbide Corporation).
12. D. Berthelot and H. Gaudechon, Compt. rend. 156, 1243 (1913).
13. R. D. Blue and F. C. Mathers, Trans. Electrochem. Soc. 65, 339 (1934).
14. R. D. Blue and F. C. Mathers, Trans. Electrochem. Soc. 69, 519 (1936).
15. A. Brenner, J. Electrochem. Soc. 103, 652 (1956).
16. D. Bryce-Smith, J. Chem. Soc. 1712 (1955).
17. D. Bryce-Smith and G. F. Cox, J. Chem. Soc. 1050 (1958).
18. J. J. Bulloff, U.S. 2,898,235; August 4, 1959 (to The Commonwealth Engineering Company of Ohio).
19. W. H. Carothers and D. D. Coffman, J. Am. Chem. Soc. 51, 588 (1929).
20. H. V. Carter, E. I. Chappell and E. Warhurst, J. Chem. Soc. 106 (1956).
21. E. J. Caule and E. W. R. Steacie, Can. J. Chem. 29, 103 (1951).
22. H. T. J. Chilton and B. G. Gowenlock, Trans. Faraday Soc. 50, 824 (1954).

23. H. T. J. Chilton and B. G. Gowenlock, Trans. Faraday Soc. 49, 1451 (1953).

24. J. C. Clouston and C. L. Cook, Trans. Faraday Soc. 54, 1001 (1958).

25. G. E. Coates, "Organo-metallic Compounds," Second Edition, Wiley, New York, 1960.

26. G. E. Coates and F. Glockling, J. Chem. Soc. 2526 (1954).

27. G. E. Coates and F. Glockling, J. Chem. Soc. 22 (1954).

28. J. H. Connor, W. E. Reid and G. B. Wood, J. Electrochem. Soc. 104, 38 (1957).

29. E. H. Cornish, J. Appl. Chem. 11, 41 (1961).

30. F. A. Cotton, Chem. Rev. 55, 551 (1955).

31. F. A. Cotton and L. T. Reynolds, J. Am. Chem. Soc. 80, 269 (1958).

32. J. P. Cunningham and H. S. Taylor, J. Chem. Phys. 6, 359 (1938).

33. R. E. Dessy and R. M. Jones, J. Org. Chem. 24, 1685 (1959).

33a. F. E. Drummond, U.S. 2,898,227; August 4, 1959 (to The Commonwealth Engineering Company of Ohio).

34. M. F. W. Dunker, E. B. Starkey and G. L. Jenkins, J. Am. Chem. Soc. 58, 2309 (1936).

35. W. V. Evans and R. Pearson, J. Am. Chem. Soc. 64, 2865 (1942).

36. W. V. Evans, R. Pearson and D. Braithwaite, J. Am. Chem. Soc. 63, 2574 (1941).

37. W. V. Farrar, Research (London) 4, 177 (1951).

38. E. O. Fischer and R. Jira, Z. Naturforsch. 8b, 217 (1953).

39. E. O. Fischer and A. Wirzmuller, Z. Naturforsch. 12b, 737 (1957).

40. W. Freundlich and B. Claudel, Bull. soc. chim. France 967 (1956).

41. F. E. Frey and H. J. Hepp, J. Am. Chem. Soc. 55, 3357 (1933).

42. G. Fritz and B. Raabe, Z. anorg. allgem. Chem. 286, 149 (1956).

43. R. L. Geddes and E. Mack, Jr., J. Am. Chem. Soc. 52, 4372 (1930).

44. L. L. Gershbein and V. N. Ipatieff, J. Am. Chem. Soc. 74, 1540 (1952).

45. H. Gilman and R. G. Jones, J. Org. Chem. 10, 505 (1945).

46. H. Gilman and H. L. Yablunky, J. Am. Chem. Soc. 63, 949 (1941).

47. P. R. Girardot, U.S. 2,927,004; May 31, 1955 (to Bjorksten Research Laboratories, Inc.)

48. H. H. Glazebrook and T. G. Pearsons, J. Chem. Soc. 567 (1937).

49. M. Gomberg and W. E. Bachmann, J. Am. Chem. Soc. 52, 2455 (1930).

50. C. L. Gordon and E. Wichers, Ann. N.Y. Acad. Sci. 65, 369 (1957).

51. J. Goubeau and B. Rodewald, Z. anorg. allgem. Chem. 258, 162 (1949).

52. B. G. Gowenlock, J. C. Polanyi and E. Warhurst, Proc. Roy. Soc. (London) 218A, 269 (1953).

53. M. L. H. Green, L. Pratt and G. Wilkinson, J. Chem. Soc. 3916 (1958).

54. M. L. H. Green and G. Wilkinson, J. Chem. Soc. 4314 (1958).

55. J. Harms and G. Jander, Kolloid-Z. 77, 267 (1936).

56. E. L. Head, C. E. Holley, Jr. and S. W. Rabideau, J. Am. Chem. Soc. 79, 3687 (1957).

57. F. Hein, E. Petzchner, K. Wagler and F. A. Segitz, Z. anorg. allgem. Chem. 141, 161 (1924).

58. C. A. Heller, Jr. and H. A. Taylor, J. Phys. Chem. 57, 226 (1953).

59. D. F. Helm and E. Mack, J. Am. Chem. Soc. 59, 60 (1937).

60. W. Hieber and G. Braun, Z. Naturforsch. 14b, 132 (1959).

61 W. Hieber, G. Braun and W. Beck, Chem. Ber. 93, 901 (1960).

62. W. Hieber and H. Fuchs. Z. anorg. allgem. Chem. 248, 256 (1941).

63. L. J. E. Hofer, U.S. Bureau of Mines Report of Investigations 3770 (1944).

64. J. B. Honeycutt, Jr. and J. M. Riddle, J. Am. Chem. Soc. 82, 3051 (1960).

65. R. G. Jones and H. Gilman, Chem. Rev. 54, 835 (1954).

66. K. A. Kocheshkov, A. N. Nesmeyanov and N. K. Gipp, J. Gen. Chem. U.S.S.R. 6, 172 (1936); Chem. Abs. 30, 4834 (1936).

67. K. A. Kocheshkov, A. N. Nesmeyanov and V. A. Klimova, J. Gen. Chem. U.S.S.R. 6, 167 (1936); Chem. Abs. 30, 4834 (1936).

68. J. J. Lander and L. H. Germer, Am. Inst. Mining Met. Engrs., Inst. Metals Div., Metals Technol. 14, No. 6, Tech. Pub. No. 2259 (1947).

68b. W. M. Latimer and J. H. Hildebrand, "Reference Book of Inorganic Chemistry," The Macmillan Company, New York, Third Edition, 1951.

69. C. M. Laurie and L. H. Long, Trans. Faraday Soc. 51, 665 (1955).

70. P. A. Leighton and R. A. Mortensen, J. Am. Chem. Soc. 58, 448 (1936).

71. F. B. Makin and W. A. Waters, J. Chem. Soc. 843 (1938).

72. C. J. Marsel, E. O. Kalie, A. Reidlinger and L. Kramer, in "Metal Organic Compounds," Advances in Chemistry Series No. 23, American Chemical Society, Washington, 1959, p. 176.

73. R. E. McClure and A. Lowy, J. Am. Chem. Soc. 53, 319 (1931).

74. R. N. Meinert, J. Am. Chem. Soc. 55, 979 (1933).

75. K. M. Merz and R. F. Adamsky, J. Am. Chem. Soc. 81, 250 (1959).

76. W. J. Moore, Jr. and H. S. Taylor, J. Chem. Phys. 8, 396 (1940).

77. A. A. Morton and E. F. Cluff, J. Am. Chem. Soc. 74, 4056 (1952).

78. A. N. Nesmeyanov and E. I. Kahn, Ber. 62B, 1018 (1929).

79. A. N. Nesmeyanov and L. G. Makarova, Doklady Akad. Nauk U.S.S.R. 87, 417 (1952); Chem. Abs. 48, 622 (1954).

80. A. N. Nesmeyanov and L. G. Makarova, Isvest. Akad. Nauk U.S.S.R., Otdel. Khim. Nauk 380 (1954); Chem. Abs. 49, 5346 (1955).
81. C. R. Noller, J. Am. Chem. Soc. 53, 635 (1931).
82. R. G. W. Norrish and G. Porter, Discussions Faraday Soc. No. 2, 97 (1947).
83. D. M. Overcash and F. C. Mathers, Trans. Electrochem. Soc. 64, 305 (1933).
84. F. A. Paneth, Trans. Far. Soc. 179 (1933).
85. F. A. Paneth and W. Hofeditz, Ber. 62B, 1335 (1929).
86. F. A. Paneth, W. Hofeditz and A. Wunsch, J. Chem. Soc. 372 (1935).
87. F. Paneth and W. Lautsch, Ber. 64B, 2702 (1931).
88. F. A. Paneth and W. Lautsch, J. Chem. Soc. 380 (1935).
89. F. A. Paneth and H. Loleit, J. Chem. Soc. 366 (1935).
90. T. G. Pearson, R. H. Purcell and G. S. Saigh, J. Chem. Soc. 409 (1938).
91. D. A. Petrov, V. A. Butlov and N. G. Gil'yadova, Russian Journal of Inorganic Chemistry, 4, 894 (1959) (English Translation); Zhurnal Neorganicheskoi Khimii 4, 1970 (1959).
92. H. G. Plust, U.S. 2,898,278; August 4, 1959 (to Aktiengesellschaft Brown, Boveri and Cie., Baden, Switzerland).
93. H. E. Podall, H. E. Petree and J. R. Zeitz, J. Org. Chem. 24, 1222 (1959).
94. S. J. W. Price and A. F. Trotman-Dickenson, Trans. Faraday Soc. 53, 939 (1957).
95. S. J. W. Price and A. F. Trotman-Dickenson, Trans. Faraday Soc. 53, 1208 (1957).
96. S. J. W. Price and A. F. Trotman-Dickenson, Trans. Faraday Soc. 54, 1630 (1958).
97. N. Prilezhaev and A. Terenin, Trans. Faraday Soc. 31, 1483 (1935).
98. R. L. Pruett and E. L. Morehouse, Chem. and Ind. 980 (1958).
99. G. A. Razuvaev, Yu. A. Ol'dekop and L. N. Grobov, Zhur. Obshchei Khim. 23, 589 (1953); (English Translation): J. Gen. Chem. U.S.S.R. 23, 613 (1953).
100. G. A. Razuvaev, B. N. Moryganov, E. P. Dlin and Yu. A. Ol'dekop, Zhur. Obshchei Khim. 24, 262 (1954); English Translation: J. Gen. Chem. U.S.S.R. 24, 265 (1954).
101. F. O. Rice and B. L. Evering, J. Am. Chem. Soc. 56, 2105 (1934).
102. F. O. Rice and A. L. Glasebrook, J. Am. Chem. Soc. 56, 2381 (1934).
103. F. O. Rice and A. L. Glasebrook, J. Am. Chem. Soc. 56, 2472 (1934).
104. F. O. Rice, W. R. Johnston and B. L. Evering, J. Am. Chem. Soc. 54, 3529 (1932).
105. F. O. Rice and O. L. Polly, Ind. Eng. Chem. 27, 915 (1935).
106. F. O. Rice and K. K. Rice, "The Aliphatic Free Radicals," Johns Hopkins Press, Baltimore, 1935.
106a. Reference 106, p. 58.
106b. Reference 106, p. 60.

141

107. E. G. Rochow, D. T. Hurd and R. N. Lewis, "The Chemistry of Organo-metallic Compounds," John Wiley and Sons, Inc., New York, 1957.
108. A. A. Rosen, Ukrain, Khim. Zhur. 25, 735 (1959).
109. A. A. Rosen, Ukrain. Khim. Zhur. 26, 151 (1960).
110. L. Rosenblum, J. Am. Chem. Soc. 77, 5016 (1955).
111. A. L. Rotinyan and D. G. Katsman, Russ. J. Inorg. Chem. 5, 115 (1960).
112. M. E. Russell and R. B. Bernstein, J. Chem. Phys. 30, 607 (1959).
113. R. B. Sandin, F. T. McClure and F. Irwin, J. Am. Chem. Soc. 61, 2944 (1939).
114. T. V. Sathyamurthy, S. Swaminathan and L. M. Yeddanapalli, J. Indian Chem. Soc. 27, 509 (1950).
115. H. Scheibler and H. Menzel, German Patent 694,738; July 11, 1940. Chem. Abs. 35, 5038 (1941).
116. H. Scheibler and W. Menzel, German Patent 721,201; April 23, 1942. Chem. Abs. 37, 4636 (1943).
117. I. Shapiro and R. E. Williams, J. Am. Chem. Soc. 81, 4787 (1959).
118. J. H. Simons and M. F. Dull, J. Am. Chem. Soc. 55, 2696 (1933).
119. J. H. Simons, R. W. McNamee and C. D. Hurd, J. Phys. Chem. 36, 939 (1932).
120. R. Srinivasan, J. Chem. Phys. 28, 895 (1958).
121. E. W. R. Steacie, "Atomic and Free Radical Reactions," Reinhold, New York, 1954, p. 386.
122. E. W. R. Steacie, "Atomic and Free Radical Solutions," Reinhold, New York, 1954, p. 37.
123. F. G. A. Stone, Quart. Rev. (London) 9, 174 (1955).
124. W. Strohmeier, K. Gerlach and G. Matthias, Z. Naturforsch. 15b, 621 (1960).
125. H. S. Taylor and W. H. Jones, J. Am. Chem. Soc. 52, 1111 (1930).
126. A. Terenin, J. Chem. Phys. 2, 441 (1934).
127. H. W. Thompson and J. W. Linnett, Trans. Faraday Soc. 33, 501 (1937).
128. H. W. Thompson and J. W. Linnett, Trans. Faraday Soc. 33, 874 (1937).
129. C. Waring, Trans. Faraday Soc. 36, 1142 (1940).
130. C. E. Waring and W. S. Horton, J. Am. Chem. Soc. 67, 540 (1945).
131. W. A. Waters, "The Chemistry of Free Radicals," Oxford, Clarendon Press, 1946, p. 35 ff.
132. W. A. Waters, J. Chem. Soc. 113 (1937).
133. W. A. Waters, J. Chem. Soc. 2007 (1937).
134. W. A. Waters, J. Chem. Soc. 1077 (1938).
135. W. A. Waters, J. Chem. Soc. 864 (1939).
136. E. Wiberg and R. Bauer, Chem. Ber. 85, 593 (1952).
137. E. Wiberg and R. Bauer, Z. Naturforsch. 5b, 396 (1950).
138. G. Wilkinson and F. A. Cotton, Chemistry and Industry 307 (1954).
139. G. Wilkinson, F. A. Cotton and J. M. Birmingham, J. Inorg. Nuclear Chem. 2, 95 (1956).

140. P. F. Winternitz and A. A. Carotti, J. Am. Chem. Soc. 82, 2430 (1960).
141. F. Wohler and J. Dean, Ann. 97, 1 (1856).
142. G. B. Wood and A. Brenner, J. Electrochem. Soc. 104, 29 (1957).
143. J. H. Wotiz, C. A. Hollingsworth and R. E. Dessy, J. Am. Chem. Soc. 78, 1221 (1956).
144. L. M. Yeddanapalli and C. C. Schubert, J. Chem. Phys. 14, 1 (1946).
145. L. M. Yeddanapalli, R. Srinivasan and V. J. Paul, J. Sci. Ind. Research (India), 13B, 232 (1954).
146. W. H. Zartman and H. Adkins, J. Am. Chem. Soc. 54, 3398 (1932).
147. H. H. Zeiss and W. Herwig, Ann. 606, 209 (1957).
148. K. Ziegler and H. G. Gellert, Ann. 567, 179 (1950).
149. K. Ziegler and H. G. Gellert, Angew. Chem. 67, 424 (1955).
150. K. Ziegler, K. Nagel and M. Patheiger, Z. anorg, allgem. Chem. 282, 345 (1955).
151. K. Ziegler, K. Nagel and W. Pfohl, Ann. 629, 210 (1960).

DISCUSSION

L. M. FOSTER (Alcoa): You said that you were not able to duplicate Plust's work with gallium. I was wondering in what respect you were not able to. Carbon presents no problem in gallium. There is no carbide formed and no solubility of carbon in gallium. From a preparative standpoint, I wonder what the difficulty was.

W. A. G. GRAHAM (A. D. Little): It was not a question of contamination by carbon. The situation was this: when we took the compounds suggested in the patent and purified them, and exposed them for long periods to intense ultraviolet light, there was marked darkening of the solution. However, no appreciable amount of gallium formed. It was granular and when it was washed with ether, it formed a film which adhered to the walls of the flask and could not be removed.

L. R. WEISBERG (RCA Lab.): When you talk about gallium in aluminum or carbon in aluminum or gallium, is there so much carbon that you can see it visibly or are you detecting it by some analytical technique?

W. A. G. GRAHAM (A. D. Little): Carbon was not visible. At least, there was a metallic phase in our photolytic experiments, namely, a film on the walls of the flask. Some of this was scraped off and was analyzed for carbon. Initially, we used combustion and microanalysis, which is very crude. But when you have 8 per cent of carbon, it is good enough.

L. R. WEISBERG (RCA Lab.): It could have as much as 8 per cent carbon and not be visible, then?

W. A. G. GRAHAM (A. D. Little): It was not good looking gallium but it wasn't obvious that there was carbon in it.

M. TSUTSUI (New York Univ.): Would you state the wave lengths of the ultraviolet light used?

W. A. G. GRAHAM (A. D. Little): The lamp was a conventional Hanovia, model 325 watt analytic type, a commercially available lamp. I do not know the wave length.

M. TSUTSUI (New York Univ.): Did you check the ultraviolet absorption of the alkyl gallium?

W. A. G. GRAHAM (A. D. Little): No, we did not. The only indication we had of reaction was a fairly marked darkening of the solution after a few hours exposure.

C. J. MARSEL (New York Univ.): Did you prepare the alkyl derivative of the gallum and, if so, how, and did you attempt thermal decomposition of this material?

W. A. G. GRAHAM (A. D. Little): The answer to the first question is that we did prepare the gallium alkyl. Trimethyl gallium was prepared from dimethyl mercury using Coates' procedure, and that was the compound whose thermal decomposition we studied initially in a vacuum system, and then, with an argon carrier. That product was the one that had the gross contamination by carbon. We worked with triethyl gallium and tri-isobutyl gallium. These were both prepared by reaction of gallium trichloride with the appropriate aluminum alkyl.

PURIFICATION OF RARE EARTH METALS

Bernard Love and Eugene V. Kleber
Research Chemicals
Division of Nuclear Corp. of America
Burbank, California

ABSTRACT

The state of the art of purification of rare earth metals is considered from two viewpoints - separation of mixed rare earths into constituent chemical species, and reduction of the purified chemical species to high purity metals. Most of the impurities in rare earth metals are introduced during the reduction process. Various reduction methods designed to minimize contamination, and various purification methods designed to remove impurities are reviewed. Analytic methods and problems are discussed.

INTRODUCTION

Considerable interest has recently been indicated in a number of rare earth compounds as semi-conductor materials. Many of these may best be prepared from the rare earth metals. The behavior of semi-conductor materials is well-known to be markedly a function of impurity content. The preparation of rare earth metals of highest purity, and the delineation and estimation of those impurities present has, therefore, become of increasing significance in rare earth technology. The purpose of this report is to indicate the state of the art of preparation and purification of rare earth metals, and to describe the more commonly used methods of analysis and their limitations. It is obviously beyond the scope of this report to reference all work in the field and to detail complete procedures. Literature references are indicated as guides only. A more complete literature survey covering the preparation and properties of rare earth compounds and metals has been published by one of the authors [18].

The term "rare earths" is used in this report in a generic sense, and thus designates the group of elements irrespective of their chemical state. Included are the elements of atomic numbers 57 through 71 and also scandium and yttrium. The first half of the series, elements 57 through 63 (lanthanum-europium), are commonly known as the cerium group. The second half of the series, elements 64 through 71 (gadolinium-lutetium, and yttrium and scandium) are termed the yttrium group elements.

ISOLATION OF INDIVIDUAL RARE EARTHS

The preparation of high purity individual rare earth metals is more difficult than the preparation of many other semiconductor materials due to the initial requirement for the isolation of each rare earth from the other rare earths with which it occurs in nature. The chemical properties of the various rare earths, although showing some marked differences for a few individual elements, are in general quite similar. A number of methods have been developed for such separations, and the principal methods of historical importance, as well as those most commonly in use today, are discussed below.

Valance Change Methods. The most common valence state for rare earth ions in solution is the trivalent state. Several of the elements, however, may be either oxidized or reduced to quadrivalent or divalent states respectively, and as such ions have chemical properties which are significantly different from the trivalent ions.

Trivalent cerium may be oxidized in solution by permanganate, bromate, or peroxydisulfate ions, by chlorine, or electrolytically. Cerous hydroxide in alkaline suspension may be oxidized by air or oxygen. The oxidized cerium may be separated from the other rare earths by taking advantage of differences in basicity properties, by solvent extraction, or ion exchange procedures [26, 46].

Praseodymium and terbium cannot be oxidized above the trivalent state in aqueous solutions. In alkaline melts, however, chlorate will oxidize these elements to a higher oxidation state in which form they precipitate as basic compounds. The separations are fractional in nature, and although they may be repeated, the procedure does not lend itself to the rapid purification of these elements [24].

Europium, samarium, and ytterbium are reduced to the divalent state with increasing difficulty in the order indicated. Europium may be reduced by passage through a Jones reductor, and the divalent europium may be precipitated as the relatively insoluble sulfate. Europium is also reduced by electrolysis over a mercury cathode from a neutral alkaline citrate solution. The proper control of experimental procedure will effect rather good separations and several repetitions of the procedure will produce high purity europium. Samarium and ytterbium are

146

reduced by treatments with sodium amalgam. The reductions are somewhat more difficult, but good separations can be obtained if preliminary separations have isolated the samarium from europium and ytterbium, and the ytterbium from europium and samarium, respectively [20,21,23,30].

Fractional Precipitation. A number of fractional precipitation techniques have been developed for the separation of rare earths, but these are primarily useful at the present time for separation of the elements into smaller groups rather than into individual elements. The addition of sodium or ammonium sulfate to a mixed rare earth solution will precipitate the cerium group as a relatively insoluble double sulfate. The more soluble yttrium group elements may be recovered by precipitation with sodium hydroxide or oxalic acid.

Basic precipitations have been used to effect concentration or even separations, but these may be considered crude except possibly for the purification of lanthanum and yttrium. There is a considerable difference in basicity between lanthanum and the next most basic elements cerium and praseodymium. Lanthanum is also at one end of the series and therefore need be separated from elements of higher atomic number only. After removal of cerium from the most common sources of mixed rare earths, lanthanum is the most abundant element. By repeated fractional precipitations at controlled pH, all other elements may therefore be removed, and lanthanum of reasonable purity obtained.

One other element, yttrium, has been obtained in reasonable purity by a combination of basicity and double sulfate precipitations. When precipitations of rare earths are made by the addition of sodium sulfate, the elements precipitate in increasing order of atomic number with yttrium behaving as though it were approximately element No. 66 or 67. When the rare earth elements are fractionally precipitated by the addition of basic solutions, the elements precipitate in inverse order of atomic number with yttrium behaving approximately like element No. 62. The combination of the two procedures may therefore be used to separate cerium group elements in the one case, and yttrium group elements in the other, leaving yttrium of reasonable purity.

Fractional Crystallization. Many of the classical separations were based upon the fractional crystallization of various rare earth compounds. These procedures had to be repeated many times in order to achieve high purities, but it may be noted that processing on a large scale was possible, and that fractionation of double ammonium nitrates or double magnesium nitrates could be continued to produce high purity lanthanum, praseodymium, neodymium and samarium [7].

Ion Exchange. The methods of separation of rare earths by ion exchange techniques were developed as a perquisite to the

147

study of the fission products in the Manhattan project. The methods were extended to macroscopic, and commercial scale separations in the subsequent 15 year period. One comment is in order with respect to the processes which result in the rare earth separations. While most ion exchange separation procedures are dependent upon the relative absorption constants between the solution and the resin for the various elements present, rare earth fractionation is dependent upon the relative complexing constants of the various rare earths with a complexing agent present in the eluant solution. The resin acts primarily as a reservoir to hold the initial rare earth mixture and to recover the rare earths in successive separation stages. Commonly used eluants were initially citric, tartaric, or similar organic acids. More recently ethylenediaminetetraacetic acid and other polycarboxylic amino acids have been used [8,13, 22,32,39,42].

The primary advantage of the ion exchange method lies in the many stages which may be obtained per unit length of column. Good separation is attained, and there is apparently no theoretical limit to the purity attainable for a major constituent [40]. The disadvantages of the method are associated with the generally dilute solutions which must be used, and the long residence times, which indicate a relatively low rate of productivity.

Solvent Extraction. Current practice in solvent extraction is primarily based upon the separations attained with tributyl phosphate and strongly acidic solutions, although other organic phosphates or organo-phosphoric acids may be utilized. These methods were first proposed by Warf [46] and subsequently extended by Peppard and co-workers [31]. The advantages of solvent extraction methods lie in the concentrated solutions and rapid flow rates which may be used, thus giving high rare earth throughput, but there are disadvantages involved in the engineering problems of attaining a large number of stages.

Volatilization. Several systems have been proposed for the separation of rare earths by distillation or volatilization processes. The acetylacetonates have been used to separate scandium and thorium [27]. The anhydrous chlorides have been investigated, and significant differences have been found in the vapor pressures of many pairs of rare earths [45]. Spedding and Daane [38] have fractionally distilled a synthetic mixture of rare earth metals, and obtained partial separations. The elements europium, samarium, and ytterbium are particularly more volatile than the other rare earths.

Chemical Separations of the Rare Earths from Other Elements. The above discussion has been primarily concerned with the separation of individual rare earths from the rare earth group. Many of the procedures, by their nature, also result in

148

separation from most other elements. The recovery of rare earths from solution is most commonly effected by precipitation of the oxalate with oxalic acid from dilute acid solution. Most other elements do not precipitate under these conditions. The rare earths may also be recovered as a hydroxide by precipitation with either sodium hydroxide or ammonium hydroxide. The former is most suitable for separations from amphoteric elements, the latter, for separation from those forming complexes in the presence of ammonium ions or for separation from alkali elements.

The separation of many elements from rare earths may be accomplished by standard chemical procedures such as precipitation by chloride, sulfate, sulfide, etc.

REDUCTION TO THE ELEMENT

Metallothermic Reduction of the Halide. Most of the rare earth elements have been prepared in their highest purity states by the metallothermic reduction of rare earth halides with active metals according to the equation:

$$REX_3 + \frac{3}{y} M \rightarrow \frac{3}{y} MX_y + RE$$

The halide is most commonly chloride or fluoride, since these are easiest to prepare in pure form, are most economical, and contain proportionately the greatest amount of rare earth. The active metal is most commonly sodium, calcium, or magnesium, although lithium, potassium, aluminum, zirconium and other metals have been used [3,14,37,44].

Assuming that one starts with a highly purified rare earth oxide, the problems of preparing high purity metal are associated with two basic properties of the rare earths. The first is the extreme affinity for oxygen in any form, the second is the high reactivity of the metal at elevated temperatures with almost all other materials. The problem of oxygen affinity becomes apparent even in the preparation of the halide. If prepared from aqueous solution the halides are first recovered with water of hydration. Dehydration of these materials without dissociation into basic salts is extremely difficult. The halides may also be prepared by the direct reaction of rare earth oxides with ammonium chloride or ammonium fluoride, or by the high temperature hydrofluorination of the oxide, but again, complete conversion without the formation of basic salts seems to be virtually impossible. Oxygen remaining in the halide appears to be transferred almost quantitatively to the metal produced.

149

Problems associated with the reactivity of the metal at elevated temperatures are to a considerable extent a function of the temperature which must be reached to obtain the metal. The melting points of europium and ytterbium are 826 and 824°C respectively. The melting points of the other rare earths increase in a general way with atomic number, ranging from 804°C for cerium to 1652°C for lutetium. The metals at these temperatures combine rapidly with oxygen, nitrogen, or moisture vapor from the air, and to varying extent with crucible or container materials. Although stainless steel, quartz, carbon and refractory oxides have been used for the lower melting elements, these react in varying degree. The high melting elements react very rapidly with these materials, and it has been found necessary to use molybdenum, niobium, or preferably, tantalum as containers for these elements. Even for the low melting elements it may frequently be necessary to heat the system considerably above the melting point of the element in order to reach the melting point of the slag so that consolidation and separation may occur.

Efforts to produce yttrium metal (one of the higher melting elements) in large quantity at Iowa State University have resulted in the development of a eutectic system method which permitted the use of zirconium or titanium crucibles rather than the more difficultly fabricable tantalum. Yttrium fluoride is reduced with calcium, and magnesium is added to produce a lower melting yttrium-magnesium composition. Simultaneously other halides are added to form a eutectic with the calcium fluoride produced, and thus a lower melting point for the entire system [1]. Contamination with titanium or zirconium may run in the order of 0.1 to 1%. On a small scale, where tantalum crucibles could perhaps be economically used, it is almost certain that tantalum contamination would be at a much lower level. The yttrium metal is purified from magnesium by distilling away the magnesium at elevated temperatures in a vacuum, and is then consolidated by consumable arc melting, both procedures are discussed under purification techniques below.

Metallothermic Reduction of Oxides. Rare earth oxides and metals re-equilibrate at elevated temperatures in accordance with the example illustrated below for europium oxide and lanthanum metal:

$$Eu_2O_3 + 2La \rightleftharpoons La_2O_3 + 2Eu$$

If the two metals, in this case europium and lanthanum, have greatly different vapor pressures, and if the temperature is so maintained that one will distill in preference to the other, then the reaction is carried to completion in the direction of the production of the more volatile metal. Lanthanum, although it has a low melting point, has a very low vapor pressure. Europium, samarium, and ytterbium have relatively high vapor pressures at temperatures from 1000 to 1300°C, and they may be produced and distilled at these temperatures [2].

Electrolytic Reduction Methods. Electrolytic reduction of molten halides has been used for the preparation of the lower melting elements of the cerium group. A graphite or metal container is used as a cathode and the rare earth metal is collected as a molten pool [36]. Higher melting point metals have been produced by electrolysis of the chloride or of alkali chloride eutectic mixtures, utilizing a molten zinc or cadmium cathode [43]. The alloy formed is then heated in a vacuum, and the zinc or cadmium, respectively, distilled away from the rare earth metal.

Morrice and co-workers [28,29] have recently described an electrolytic process in which cerium oxide is continuously added to a cerium fluoride - alkali fluoride bath, and electrolyzed in a skull type cathode crucible utilizing a graphite anode. Electrolysis is continuous, and results in the decomposition of the fluoride to form metal which settles to the bottom of the melt, but which comes in contact only with the frozen skull of melt rather than the crucible itself.

Attempts to prepare rare earth metals by electrolysis from aqueous or alcoholic solution have in general been unsuccessful. The best results have been obtained using mercury cathodes followed by attempts to remove the mercury by distillation. Mercury, however, forms thermally stable intermetallic compounds with the rare earth elements, and it is difficult to remove the last traces by distillation. The rare earth metal which is obtained, furthermore, is finely divided and extremely reactive, and must be handled in an inert atmosphere until it can be consolidated by melting, thus reintroducing contamination problems.

In summary, the nature and sources of impurities in rare earth metals as produced by the currently used methods are as follows:

Metals produced by the reduction of halides may have impurities present in the acid or ammonium salt initially used to prepare the rare earth halide. Such impurities may be iron, copper, nickel, or other heavy metals, and there may also remain in the final elemental rare earth unreacted oxygen, chlorine, or fluorine.

From the containers in which the halides are prepared, whether glass or metal (as in high temperature hydrofluorination) impurities such as boron, silicon, iron, nickel, chromium, etc., may be introduced.

151

Those elements reduced metallothermically may have residual reductant metals such as calcium or magnesium present, and also impurities which may have been present in the starting reductant metal.

Whether produced metallothermically or electrolytically, there is a serious contamination problem from the crucible used to hold the reaction. Oxide crucibles such as those prepared from magnesia, zirconia, beryllia, etc., may introduce both oxygen and the respective cation. Metallic crucibles will introduce varying quantities of tantalum, columbium, titanium, iron, or whatever metal is utilized. Molten cathode materials such as mercury, zinc, or cadmium may be impossible to remove completely.

And additionally, impurities such as oxygen, nitrogen, or hydrogen may be introduced from residual quantities of these elements present in the vacuum or inert atmosphere or from the difficulties inherent in complete out-gassing of systems.

PURIFICATION METHODS

A number of purification methods have been evaluated in attempts to obtain metal of higher purity than can be prepared by direct reduction. Those methods which have proven useful, and those which have been evaluated on the basis of their successful application to the purification of other materials used for semi-conductor purposes are described below.

Washing and Re-melting. If a rare earth metal which is relatively unreactive to water is prepared as a sponge or in easily divisible form, soluble halides may be removed by washing with water. The metal is then quickly dried in vacuum and consolidated by re-melting. This method of course, does not remove insoluble materials, and it may introduce oxygen and hydrogen.

Slagging. Those metals prepared by the metallothermic or electrolytic reduction of anhydrous halides may be re-melted with excess rare earth halide. Some oxygen is removed as oxyhalide compound, and some impurity metals may be reduced [1]. The procedure, however, involving treatment of a molten metal for some prolonged period of time in a container, may reintroduce or further introduce container elements, especially for the high melting point rare earth metals.

Vacuum Melting. Re-melting of the metal in a vacuum will remove by volatilization calcium, magnesium, and other volatile constituents. Again, however, the crucible elements may be introduced as contaminants. Non-consumable arc-melting, generally used for consolidation purposes, may simultaneously aid in removing some of the volatile impurities.

152

Distillation. Distillation of the rare earth element metal is an extremely efficient method for the purification of europium, samarium, and ytterbium from a number of commonly present impurities. It is also effective for the higher melting yttrium group elements which have significant vapor pressures below approx. 1800°C [11,16]. It is, however, much more difficult to apply for the purification of the low melting, low vapor pressure, cerium group elements. The difficulty in purification of these materials lies in the fact that the metals must be heated to 1700°C or higher to attain significant volatilization rates. The inner surfaces of the retort must similarly be maintained above 1700°C to minimize condensation as liquid and consequent reflux. The condenser surface, however, must be kept below the melting point (804°C for cerium) to permit recovery of the metal. The sharp thermal gradient is difficult to achieve and maintain.

The method is particularly effective for reducing the oxygen content of metals and the content of the refractory elements which may be used as crucible materials. Furthermore, if a "fractional" process can be arranged, in which the first material distilled is physically separated from the bulk of rare earth element, separation from both volatile and less volatile constituents can be attained. Tables 1 and 2 indicate the analytic results for distillation of specific lots of europium and of erbium, and indicate the extent of purification attained in each case (the value for oxygen in Table 1 summarizes the results of a number of different distillations).

Table 1

Purification of Europium by Vacuum Distillation

	Feed	Distillate		Feed	Distillate
Lanthanum	0.02%	<0.007	Iron	0.02	<0.005
Cerium	0.08	<0.01	Aluminum	0.007	<0.005
Samarium	0.05	<0.01	Strontium	0.005	0.001
Gadolinium	0.01	0.008	Silicon	0.001	<0.001
Ytterbium	0.007	0.005	Magnesium	0.001	0.001
Tantalum	0.08	0.01	Copper	0.0001	<0.0001
Calcium	0.04	0.01	Oxygen*	0.1-1%	≤0.02

*Various starting materials

Table 2

Purification of Erbium Scrap by Vacuum Distillation

	Feed	Distillate		Feed	Distillate
Oxygen	0.5	0.02	Silicon	2.0	<0.01
Gadolinium	0.04	<0.01	Iron	0.3	0.07
Yttrium	0.1	0.04	Molybdenum	0.1	0.04
Holmium	0.1	0.05	Nickel	0.01	<0.01
Tantalum	0.1	<0.01	Aluminum	0.1	0.07
Magnesium	0.02	0.02	Cobalt	0.07	0.03

Zone Refining. Reported results of attempts to purify rare earth metals by zone refining have not indicated marked success. Illustrative are the results of Huffine [10] as indicated in Table 3 for the zone refining of yttrium. It is noted that only slight improvement was observed for most elements, and that improvement in oxygen content was overcome by the apparent contamination during the course of the run.

Table 3

Zone Refining of Yttrium. Analysis in PPM

Element	Original	Near Beginning	Center	Near End
Oxygen	5000	7600	6200	5300
Nitrogen	270	280	250	250
Iron	500	500	300	100
Chromium	10	10	<1	<1
Copper	10	2	0.5	5
Nickel	50	50	50	50
Titanium	100	100	100	100
Zirconium	4700	4300	3100	2750

<u>Electron Beam Melting</u>. Attempts to purify yttrium and yttrium group metals by electron beam melting have not indicated satisfactory results [10,17]. Electron beam melting requires maintenance of a high vacuum system. The vapor pressure of these elements at their melting point may be too high to permit satisfactory operation of the electron beam.

ANALYSIS

Analytic problems may be divided into two types; first, the determination of rare earth impurities, and second, the determination of all other impurities. The emphasis in the concluding portion of this report will be upon the methods commonly used for the detection of rare earth impurities in the rare earth matrix.

<u>Chemical Methods</u>. The general chemical similarity of the rare earth elements precludes the extensive use of ordinary chemical methods for the analysis of one rare earth in the presence of another. Those rare earths which may be oxidized, or reduced to other than the trivalent state, may be determined volumetrically or polarographically.

<u>Optical Absorption Methods</u>. The absorption spectra of many of the rare earth elements in solution are characterized by the presence of a number of sharp absorption peaks [33]. Although the spectrum of a mixture of all the elements is quite complex, the usual problem of the detection of one or two impurity elements in a matrix element becomes considerably simpler and interferences disappear or may be compensated for. Table 4 lists the concentration in grams per liter at which the absorption density is 0.01 for useful peaks of the various elements in chloride solution [25,34,35,41]. These values are for a one centimeter path length in the wavelength range 200-1000 millimicrons. The values become percentage values if the total rare earth concentration in the solution is 100 grams/liter (100 mg/ml). The value for cerium is that measured at 253 millimicrons in a portion of its broad absorption band. The value for terbium is determined at 219 millimicrons and the more sensitive (0.02) value for europium is at 210 millimicrons. These wave length values are at the lower limit of detectability for some spectrophotometric instruments, and may be somewhat more difficult to measure. The sensitivity may be increased through increasing the concentration or through use of longer optical paths, but it appears that it would be difficult to extend analysis below levels of approximately 100 parts per million for most elements.

The absorption peaks for praseodymium, neodymium, samarium, dysprosium, holmium, and erbium are in the visible

155

Table 4

Nominal Spectrophotometric Sensitivity of Rare Earth Ions

GMS/Liter for $\Delta I = 0.01$, 1 cm. path, chloride solution			
Cerium	0.002	Terbium	0.005
Praseodymium	0.1	Dysprosium	0.7
Neodymium	0.2	Holmium	0.4
Samarium	0.5	Erbium	0.3
Europium	0.5 (0.02)	Thulium	0.7
Gadolinium	0.5	Ytterbium	0.8

wave length regions, and can be seen and detected at about the same concentration levels through approximately a 5 to 10 centimeter path length. The method is useful for the rapid detection of impurities at the concentration levels indicated.

Although not strictly absorption measurements in the commonly accepted sense, the presence of praseodymium and terbium may be detected in the adjacent elements by visual examination of the color of the oxides. Praseodymium oxide (Pr_6O_{11}) is black, and the presence of approximately 0.003 - 0.01% is detectable in the white lanthanum oxide, and approximately 0.01-0.05% in the light blue neodymium oxide. Terbium oxide (Tb_4O_7) is brown and about 0.01% is visible as a discoloration in white gadolinium, yttrium, or dysprosium oxides.

Flame spectrophotometric procedures have been reported using oxy-hydrogen and oxy-acetylene flames. There is considerable interference between various elements, but there may be some possibility for the sensitive detection of lanthanum, europium, and ytterbium [6].

Emission Spectrographic Analysis. Spectrographic analysis detection limits are markedly dependent upon the particular technique used. The type of excitation, whether arc or spark, the speed and dispersion of the instrument, the form of the sample, whether oxide, metal, or solution, the wave length region covered, etc., are all variables of importance in establishing the sensitivity and reproducibility of analytic results. Table 5 has been compiled to illustrate the nominal spectrographic limits of detection for rare earths in rare earth matrices. These values are for arc excitation of the oxide (and probably equally well for the metal) at approximately 10-18 amperes direct current in the first order on a diffraction grating instrument giving dispersion of approximately 5 Angstroms per millimeter. It is emphasized that these are nominal limits only and that they may vary by a factor of 2 or more for a particular matrix due to the presence or absence of interfering lines. Increased sensitivity by a factor of some 3-10 times may be obtained by analysis in the second order, and further increased sensitivity may be obtained through use of special conditions such as controlled atmospheres or the cathode layer technique. Under such conditions it becomes apparent that analytic limits of from less than 1 to perhaps 10 to 20 parts per million may be attainable for virtually all rare earths, and that the spectrographic method may therefore be the most suitable for rapid and economical analysis of rare earth metals. There will, of course, be coincidental detection and analysis of the many other elements which may be determined spectrographically [5,6,15].

Table 5

Nominal Spectrographic Limits of Detection for
Rare Earths in Rare Earth Matrix

Lanthanum	0.005%	Dysprosium	0.01%
Cerium	0.05	Holmium	0.007
Praseodymium	0.03	Erbium	0.005
Neodymium	0.02	Thulium	0.007
Samarium	0.05	Ytterbium	0.0005
Europium	0.005	Lutetium	0.005
Gadolinium	0.005	Scandium	0.001
Terbium	0.01	Yttrium	0.002

X-Ray Fluorescence Methods. These methods have been investigated by a number of analysts and found quite suitable for the non-destructive analysis of complex mixtures. The limits of sensitivity, however, are not very great and it is difficult to determine elements at concentrations below approximately 0.1% [9,19].

157

Neutron Activation Methods. The high thermal neutron absorption properties of many of the rare earths indicate that these elements may be detected at very low levels by neutron activation and subsequent analysis of the radiation produced. With intensive activation, as obtained in a high flux reactor, detection of some individual rare earths to the order of parts per billion may be attained [12,47]. It is noted, however, that the high neutron cross section of many of the elements imposes an inherent limit to the use of activation analysis where these elements are the matrix elements, since they will absorb a large percentage of the incident neutron flux. The intense radio-activity coincidentally produced in some elements, such as europium, may exceed the limits of handling facilities and make analysis difficult.

Mass Spectrometry. Spark source mass spectrometry has not been reported for the analysis of rare earth matrix materials. The method is inherently sensitive to low concentration of all elements, but the analysis of rare earth materials may be complicated by the presence of the many overlapping isotopes of the adjacent rare earth elements.

Analysis for Non-Metallic Constituents. The rare earth elements may be analyzed for oxygen, nitrogen, and hydrogen by vacuum fusion methods in the customary manner; additionally, nitrogen may be determined by the Kjeldahl method. Oxygen may be determined by a number of methods based on the reactivity of oxygen with excess carbon. The metal is melted in inert gas or vacuum systems (preferably in a platinum bath), in a graphite crucible. The oxygen combines with the excess carbon to produce carbon monoxide which may be oxidized to carbon dioxide and analyzed directly, or if iodine pentoxide is used as the oxidant, the liberated iodine may be determined [15]. Fassel [4] has developed a spectrographic technique in which the spectrographic arc is used to heat the metal to liberate the carbon monoxide, and the gases are simultaneously excited to record oxygen spectra. The sensitivities of the various methods range from approximately 5-10 up to several hundred parts per million oxygen.

Analysis for carbon is customarily reported as analysis by combustion and determination of the carbon dioxide produced. The limits of detection are usually indicated as being 100 parts per million or perhaps slightly less.

Determination of Non-rare Earth Constituents. The direct determination of non-rare earth impurities may be made by spectrographic methods, or by many of the standard chemical procedures. It may be noted, however, that the rather efficient methods of removal of rare earths from solution by precipitation with oxalic acid, by precipitation with alkali, by solvent

158

extraction, and by ion exchange, may be used to effectively concentrate impurities by factors of several orders of magnitude, and may thus lead to methods for determination of non-rare earths at very low levels of concentration in the initial metal being examined.

SUMMARY

Methods are available for the separation and purification of the rare earths in aqueous solution to produce oxides or salts of very high purity. The current limit of purity attainable is apparently dictated by the methods of analysis available. The most sensitive general method currently in use is emission spectrographic analysis. The limits of detection by this method indicate that rare earth oxides approaching 99.999% purity are attainable.

Metals prepared from these oxides will be pure with respect to other rare earth contaminants, but the metal preparation methods and the reactivity of the rare earth metals result in the retention of oxygen impurities and the introduction of contaminants from the atmosphere, from reagents, and from container materials. Methods of metal purification have been developed, but these are not as efficient as the methods (such as zone refining) which have been developed for the purification of other materials used in semiconductor applications.

The reactivity of the rare earth metals indicates the need for careful and complete analysis. A limiting factor in the determination of ultimate purity of rare earth metals appears to be the limitations imposed by the analytic methods available for analysis of all other constituents, both metallic and nonmetallic.

High purity metals as currently commercially available are generally of 99% to 99.9% purity. The principal impurities are generally of three types; reductant elements such as calcium, magnesium, sodium, or lithium; container materials such as tantalum, niobium, molybdenum, titanium, or zirconium; atmospheric impurities oxygen and nitrogen; and contaminant impurities such as iron, silicon, chlorine, fluorine, etc.

REFERENCES

1. C. V. Banks, O. N. Carlson, A. H. Daane, V. A. Fassel, R. W. Fisher, E. H. Olson, J. E. Powell and F. H. Spedding, Studies on the Preparation, Properties and Analysis of High Purity Yttrium Oxide and Yttrium Metal at the Ames Laboratory IS-1, Iowa State Univ. of Science and Technology, Ames, Iowa (July 1959).
2. A. H. Daane, D. H. Dennison and F. H. Spedding, J. Am. Chem. Soc. 75, 2272 (1953).
3. A. H. Daane and F. H. Spedding, J. Electrochem. Soc. 100, 442 (1953).
4. V. A. Fassel, W. A. Gordon and R. W. Tabeling, Am. Soc. for Test. Matl's., Spec. Tech. Publ. No. 221, 3 (1958).
5. V. A. Fassel, B. Quinney, L. C. Krotz and C. F. Lentz, Anal. Chem. 27, 1010 (1955).
6. V. A. Fassel, Analytical Chemistry, 32, 19A (1960).
7. W. C. Fernelius, Inorganic Synthesis, Vol. II, McGraw-Hill Book Co. Inc., N. Y. (1946).
8. D. H. Harris and E. R. Tompkins, J. Am. Chem. Soc. 69, 2792 (1947).
9. R. H. Heidel and V. A. Fassel, Anal. Chem. 50, 176 (1958).
10. C. L. Huffine, Presented at the Joint ASM-AEC Symposium on the Rare Earths and Related Metals, Chicago, Ill. (Nov. 1959).
11. Iowa State College, Ames, Iowa, ISC-1116 (1959).
12. A. A. Jarrett and S. Berger, Nucleonics 13, 64 (1955).
13. B. H. Ketelle and G. E. Boyd, J. Am. Chem. Soc. 69, 2800 (1947).
14. W. Klemm and H. Bommer, Z. anorg. u. allgem. Chem. 231, 138 (1937).
15. B. Love, Selection and Evaluation of Rare or Unusual Metals for Application to Advanced Weapons Systems. The Metallurgy of Yttrium and the Rare Earth Metals. WADC Technical Report TR 57-666 Part II. Wright Air Development Center, Wright-Patterson Air Force Base, Ohio (March 1959).
16. B. Love, The Metallurgy of Yttrium and the Rare Earths. Part I. Phase Relationships. WADD Technical Report TR 60-74 Part I. Wright Air Development Division, Wright-Patterson Air Force Base, Ohio (May 1960).
17. B. Love, The Metallurgy of Yttrium and the Rare Earths. Part II. Mechanical Properties. WADD Technical Report TR 60-74 Part II. Wright Air Development Division, Wright-Patterson Air Force Base, Ohio (June 1960).
18. B. Love, The Technology of Scandium, Yttrium and the Rare Earth Metals. A Literature Survey. WADD Technical Report TR 60-864. Wright Air Development Division, Wright-Patterson Air Force Base, Ohio (April, 1960).
19. F. W. Lytle, J. I. Botsford and H. A. Heller, U. S. Bur. Mines, Rept. Invest. No. 5378 (Dec. 1957).
20. H. N. McCoy, J. Am. Chem. Soc. 61, 2455 (1939).
21. H. N. McCoy, J. Am. Chem. Soc. 63, 1622 (1941).

22. J. A. Marinsky, L. E. Glendenin and C. D. Coryell, J. Am. Chem. Soc. 69, 2781 (1947).
23. J. K. Marsh, J. Chem. Soc. (1943) 531.
24. J. K. Marsh, J. Chem. Soc. (1946) 20.
25. T. Moeller and J. C. Brantley, Anal. Chem. 22, 433 (1950).
26. T. Moeller and H. E. Kremers, Chem. Rev. 37, 97 (1945).
27. G. T. Morgan and H. W. Moss, J. Chem. Soc. 105, 196 (1914).
28. E. Morrice, J. Darrah, E. Brown, C. Wyche, W. Headrick, R. Williams and R. G. Knickerbocker, U. S. Bur. Mines, Rept. Invest. No. 5549 (1960).
29. E. Morrice and R. G. Knickerbocker, Presented at Joint ASM-AEC Symposium on the Rare Earths and Related Metals, Chicago, Ill. (Nov. 1959).
30. E. I. Onstott, J. Am. Chem. Soc. 81, 4451 (1959).
31. D. F. Peppard, J. P. Faris, P. R. Gray and G. W. Mason, J. Phys. Chem. 57, 294 (1953).
32. J. E. Powell and F. H. Spedding, Trans. AIME 215, 457 (1959).
33. W. Prandtl and K. Scheiner, Z. anorg. u. allgem. Chem. 220, 107 (1934).
34. C. J. Rodden, J. Research Nat. Bur. Standards 26, 557 (1941).
35. C. J. Rodden, J. Research Nat. Bur. Standards 28, 265 (1942).
36. E. E. Schumacher and F. F. Lucas, J. Am. Chem. Soc. 46, 1167 (1924).
37. F. H. Spedding and A. H. Daane, J. Am. Chem. Soc. 74, 2783 (1952).
38. F. H. Spedding and A. H. Daane, Presented at Annual Meeting of AIME, N. Y. (Feb. 1954).
39. F. H. Spedding, E. I. Fulmer, T. A. Butler, E. M. Gladrow, M. Gobush, P. E. Porter, J. E. Powell and J. M. Wright, J. Am. Chem. Soc. 69, 2812 (1947).
40. F. H. Spedding and J. E. Powell, J. Am. Chem. Soc. 76, 2545, 2550 (1954).
41. D. C. Stewart and D. Kato, Anal. Chem. 30, 164 (1958).
42. E. R. Tompkins, J. X. Khym and W. E. Cohn, J. Am. Chem. Soc. 69, 2769 (1947).
43. F. Trombe, Compt. rend. 220, 603 (1945).
44. F. Trombe and F. Mahn, Compt. rend. 217, 603 (1943).
45. R. C. Vickery, J. Soc. Chem. Ind. (London), 65, 388 (1946).
46. J. C. Warf, AECD-2524 (Aug. 1947).
47. John W. Winchester, Radioactivation Analysis in Inorganic Geochemistry. Dept. of Geology and Geophysics, Mass. Inst. of Tech. Cambridge, Mass. (1959).

DISCUSSION

M. J. VOGEL (IBM): In your europium oxides, you analyzed for various metals. Do you have an analysis for the sodium and potassium content?

B. LOVE (Research Chemicals): The only analysis we have is that they are below the limits of spectrographic detectability by the techniques which we used. In this particular case, I must say that these limits of analysis are quite poor because, for general analytical purposes, we used the first order of the diffraction grating to get as much work done with one shot as possible. The limit of analysis by this method is not very good. I feel that the concentrations of impurities probably are quite low, below 100 parts per million, based on the fact that the europium oxide for many stages back, never came into contact with sodium and that the method of reduction is with lanthanum which, again, has been pre-vacuum melted at close to 2000 degrees Centigrade to remove as many volatiles as possible that are similar to europium.

M. J. VOGEL (IBM): The other question I had was what other rare earth impurities are present with the europium oxide?

B. LOVE (Research Chemicals): The major rare earths impurity would most certainly be samarium, with probably the next major impurity, ytterbium, because both are also volatile.

J. F. MILLER (Battelle): I note that you mentioned electron beam-melting but did not elaborate on it. Would you say something about which elements you have worked on with this technique?

B. LOVE (Research Chemicals): I skipped over it quickly because I was running out of time and because it turns out to be relatively ineffective.

One of the difficulties, although there is now some equipment which overcomes this difficulty in part, is that for effective electron beam-melting you have to maintain a very high vacuum, and many of these metals have sufficiently high vapor pressures at the temperatures which are attained, so that the vacuum is broken by the metal itself.

We have tried purification of yttrium, in particular, and it was not effective, except for the removal of small amounts of calcium and magnesium which were somewhat more volatile.

J. F. MILLER (Battelle): Have you investigated removing and analyzing gaseous impurities such as oxygen and nitrogen?

162

B. LOVE (Research Chemicals): We have done both but there are limitations. We have developed methods for oxygen, nitrogen, and carbon. The limits of detection currently are at about a hundred parts per million. With respect to eliminating these elements, there are two things that can be done. The first is to be as careful as possible to avoid introducing them in the first place. This is sometimes difficult. The second and most effective means that we have found has been distillation in which the rare earth oxide remains behind as a nonvolatile constituent.

R. L. SMITH (Michigan Tech.): The zone melting results were not very effective. Was this due to poor distribution coefficients?

B. LOVE (Research Chemicals): These results were reported by Huffine of General Electric at the A.S.M. - A.E.C. Symposium on Rare Earths and Related Metals in Chicago in 1959. I don't recall all of the details but the results are indicated in Table 3. Six passes were made by the "floating zone" technique. Slight movement is noted for a few elements but no estimate of distribution coefficients was presented.

PREPARATION OF HIGH PURITY CHROMIUM

N. Silcox, G. Dillon, A. Armington
Air Force Cambridge Research Laboratories,
L. G. Hanscom Fld., Bedford, Mass.

INTRODUCTION

Metallic chromium and chromium salts are among the many materials desired in high purity by the Air Force for electronic and magnetic applications. Several methods have been used successfully for producing high purity chromium metal [2,3,6,7,8] and relatively high purity metal can be obtained commercially. However, chromium salts are not available in the high purity necessary for Air Force applications. Thus, in this study, it was decided to purify a chromium intermediate via chemical techniques so that it would be possible to convert the intermediate into either a salt (such as the sulfate) or to the metal. Two chemical purification techniques have been used in this study which are described below.

THERMAL DECOMPOSITION

The thermal decomposition method used was similar to the iodide or Van Arkel process that has been applied to several other elements. In this process, the metal is reacted with a vapor, usually iodine, to form a volatile intermediate which diffuses to a filament, usually at a higher temperature than the initial charge, where the intermediate is decomposed to the metal and starting vapor. The vapor then diffuses back to the initial charge where it again reacts. The apparatus used in the study consisted of a closed bottom quartz tube (12" long, 1" I.D.) held in a vertical position and fitted with a vacuum outlet on the top. A tungsten filament could be attached between electrical leads passing through the top of the apparatus. In operation the whole assembly, except the vacuum outlet and electrical leads, was placed in a vertical tube furnace. The furnace was held at about 800°C during a run while the filament temperature was approximately 1100°C. Normally about 20 grams of chromium and two to three grams of iodine were used as starting materials. It should be mentioned that not all of the iodine was available for the reaction since some condensed out at the cooler portion of the tube near the top. Uneven heating of the filament and slow rate of transport of the iodide to the filament contributed to the low yield which was in the order of ten percent for a forty-eight hour run.

In addition to experiments using the iodide in a closed vessel, several runs were made in an apparatus designed so that the iodide could be collected prior to decomposition in order that it could be further purified. This apparatus consisted of a 500 ml. iodine sublimer connected to a quartz reaction tube (24 inches long, 1" I.D.), enclosed in a furnace, which in turn was connected to a small collection vessel. All connections were made with 35/20 ball and socket joints. The iodine sublimer and collection flask both had an additional outlet so that carrier gases could be used in the experiments. The iodine flask was held at 60°C (iodine pressure about 4 mm.) during a run and the carrier gas flow (Argon) was 3 to 4 liters per hour. The furnace temperature during an experiment was about 900°C. Attempts to prepare the iodide by direct passage of iodine over powdered chromium in a graphite boat within the reaction tube were unsuccessful. After a forty hour run, a hard crust was formed on the metal surface and only a small amount of iodide was visible at the tube exit. An alternate method, passing iodine through the reaction tube packed with chromium chips (average dimention 1/4 inch.) proved successful. In runs varying from twenty to forty hours, 8-12 gms of iodide could be collected. However, it was found that increasing the carrier gas flow about ten-fold could produce this amount in about five hours. Analysis of the iodide showed it was about 95% CrI_2. After some runs, small nodules of chromium were formed on the larger chips of chromium, near the exit end, possibly resulting from the iodide decomposition taking place on the metal chips. These nodules were removed for analysis.

Decomposition of the iodide was accomplished by placing it in a quartz tube supported in a graphite holder which was heated inductively to 1100°C. The operation could be carried out either in a protective gas or vacuum and required only 10-12 minutes for one-two gram sample. A thin chromium film was formed which adhered very strongly to the quartz wall. It was usually necessary to break the quartz and chip out the product for analysis.

Attempts to further purify the iodide by recrystallization from toluene or ethyl alcohol were unsuccessful presumably because of the presence of water and/or oxygen. Thermal decomposition of CrI_2 after recrystallization produce insufficient metal for analysis. The residues in this case appeared to be chromium oxides.

ELECTROLYTIC DECOMPOSITION

Electrolysis of a chromium (VI) oxide - sulfuric acid solution is a standard method of preparation for chromium metal. This is also a source of commercial chromium. The availability of several references on the techniques, as well as its simplicity, seemed to justify investigation as part of this study. The reactions were performed in a jacketed vessel of approximately 100 ml. Capacity. Thermostated water was circulated through the jacket during a run to control the bath temperature. The operating conditions for this electrolysis are shown in Table I.

TABLE I ELECTROLYTIC BATH	
TEMPERATURE	62° C
ANODE	7% tin - 93% lead
CATHODE	copper
ANODE/CATHODE AREA	2:1
CURRENT DENSITY	450-600 amps/ft^2
VOLTAGE	5-6 volts
BATH COMPOSITION	CrO_3:sulfate, 100:1

The CrO_3 used in this study was Fisher Certified Reagent Grade while the Sulfuric acid was Baker and Adamson C.P. Deionized and triply distilled water was used; the major impurity in the water was silicon. The concentration of the CrO_3 in the bath was not allowed to drop below a 50:1 ratio of $CrO_3 : H_2SO_4$. No attempt was made to control the current density within narrow ranges in order to obtain a bright adherent deposit. However, such a deposit could be obtained at current densities below 400 amps/ft. [2], while above this figure the deposit occurred as trees [2]. Trees were desirable in this study because of the ease of separation of such a deposit. Prior to the deposition, the electrodes were washed with absolute ethyl alcohol or acetone, air dried, and then dipped in a 6N. hydrochloric acid solution. It was desirable to operate in a hood since during electrolysis large amounts of hydrogen and oxygen are released entraining some CrO_3, which is a nose and throat irritant. The circulating bath for the water jacket was thermostated with a Bronwill constant temperature circulator.

166

CHROMIUM SALTS

A. Chromium VI Oxide

Since CrO_3 was the starting material for both the chromium metal and chromium (III) salts prepared in this study, some effort was given to its preparation and purification. Two methods were investigated; one physical (sublimation) and one chemical (via the preparation of chromyl chloride). Chromyl chloride (CrO_2Cl_2) was prepared by reacting CrO_3 with an excess of hydrochloric acid in the presence of sulfuric acid [5]. The chromyl chloride (B.P. + 117.6°C.) was separated from the bath by distillation. The material was then redistilled two times, the center third of the distillate being taken as the purified material. It has been reported that chromyl chloride will decompose on exposure to light [5] but no such reaction was observed when the chloride was exposed for several weeks in a closed container. Chromium (VI) oxide was prepared from hydrolysis of the purified chromyl chloride. The hydrolysis was conveniently carried out by allowing chromyl chloride either to distill into the water or to be carried into the water in a stream of inert gas. After hydrolysis, the product was heated to drive off excess water and hydrochloric acid, a co-product of the hydrolysis. Complete removal of hydrochloric acid was effected by heating the solid below 200°C. A higher temperature will cause a reduction of CrO_3 to intermediate mixtures of oxides, finally producing Cr_2O_3. Addition of a silver nitrate solution to aqueous CrO_3 produced only a very faint trace of AgCl, indicating only a small amount of chloride was present after drying. The material was further purified by recrystallization using water as a solvent since CrO_3 has a tendency to react with organic solvents.

CrO_3 has an appreciable vapor pressure slightly above its melting point (190°C.) indicating that sublimation might offer a possible route to purification. Two sublimers were used for this work; 1, a vertical vacuum sublimer and 2, a horizontal entrainer sublimer. The horizontal apparatus consisted of two interconnecting glass vessels (32 x 170 mm) enclosed in a large tube (40 mm). One interconnecting vessel contained the CrO_3 while the other served as the collection vessel. Dry argon was passed over the CrO_3 driving it into the collection vessel. A slow flow rate was used in order to minimize loss of solids which condensed on the larger outside tube. It was necessary to dry the oxide, at 110°C for several hours, prior to sublimation since residual water condensed on the cooler parts of the apparatus, causing unsatisfactory deposits. The vertical sublimer consisted essentially of an evacuated quartz tube, the bottom of which was heated driving the CrO_3 to the top of the tube where it condensed on the

167

walls. In this sublimer, two deposits of different colors were observed: one red-orange and the other a deep maroon much like that of the original sample. These were collected separately for analysis.

B. Chromium III Sulfate

Chromium Sulfate is important for the production of synthetic rubies used as magnetic materials. The presence of alkali or alkaline earth ions distort the crystal structure while transition metal ions affect the magnetic properties. Thus the purity of the sulfate is important. Three methods of preparing the sulfate were attempted.

(1). At $0°C.$, sulfur dioxide was reacted with a concentrated solution of CrO_3 to produce $Cr_2 (SO_4)_3 \cdot XH_2O$ [4]. Sulfur dioxide of 99.98 percent minimum purity supplied by the Matheson Company was used without further treatment. The solid was recovered by partial evaporation and washing with absolute ethyl alcohol. The solid can also be recovered by addition of ethyl alcohol to the solid. However, in this case the color varies from blue-green (the usual color) to gray. These samples all gave an x-ray powder pattern, indicating they were crystalline, but no crystal data is available for chromium sulfate-alcohol compounds. X-ray powder patterns indicated that chromium sulfate hydrates produced in this work were amorphous.

(2). Aqueous CrO_3 and sulfuric acid were reacted at $0°C.$ in the presence of ethyl alcohol [5]. The alcohol (U S I, Reagent Grade), which acted as a catalyst, was cooled to $0°C.$ and added slowly because of the strong heat of reaction and the necessity of maintaining the temperature near $0°C.$ At higher temperatures, "oxo" and "ol" bridges are formed which result in the chromium sulfate separating as a polymeric substance which is difficult to recover.

(3). Solvent extraction. Samples of commercial (III) sulfate (Mallinckrodt Anal. Reagent) were extracted with absolute alcohol and varying amounts of water, up to 8.5 percent, using a Soxhlet extractor. The length of extraction varied from four hours to twelve hours. W and R Balston, Ltd, thimbles were used.

RESULTS

This section deals with the analytical results obtained as a result of the various purifications procedures for chromium metal and salts. All results were obtained by enission spectrograph, some performed in this Laboratory and some performed by Metal Hydrides, Inc., under contract. The limit of detection of impurities in these samples is not known, but is assumed to be less than a part per million.

(1). Chromium Metal - The Van Arkel process and its modifications produced chromium which was consistently reduced in metallic impurities. Spectrographic analyses for this portion of the work are shown on Table 2. This includes the impurities in the starting chromium, the closed Van Arkel system product, the chromium nodules discussed previously, and chromium produced by induction heating of the CrI_2 in an argon stream.

TABLE 2
CHROMIUM BY THERMAL DECOMPOSITION

METAL	INITIAL	VAN ARKEL	NODULES	INDUCTION HEATING
Ag	10	ND	1	< 1.0
Al	1.0	< 1.0	< 1.0	< 1.0
Ca	1.0	< 1.0	ND	ND
Cu	2	< 1.0	< 1.0	< 1.0
Fe	20	2	4	2
Ge	6	ND	ND	ND
In	2	ND	ND	ND
Mg	1.0	< 1.0	< 1.0	< 1.0
Si	2	3.0	< 1.0	5
Mn	ND	< 1.0	ND	ND
Ni	ND	< 1.0	9	9

ND = Not detected

The starting material was obtained from the Varlacoid Company. The major metallic impurities removed were iron and germanium. The increase of silicon in the induction heated samples was probably the result of a small amount of silica being retained when the sample was removed from the quartz wall.

The electrolytic method also produced metal of fairly good quality as shown in Table 3. It is noteworthy that neither lead nor tin, the electrode materials, appear in the spectroscopic analysis. Unlike the Van Arkel process the electrolytic chromium probably contains some gases, principally hydrogen and oxygen, in the deposit which would not be detected spectroscopically.

(2). CrO_3 - The results of the Chromium(VI) oxide purification indicate that the methods employed were not successful. Sublimation of CrO_3 (Table 4) produces a large pickup of silicon and aluminum without significant improvement of the impurity concentrations initially present. The aluminum and the silicon are probably due to contamination from the container.

Table 5 shows the analysis of CrO_3 prepared from the purified CrO_2Cl_2. These results also indicate more contamination than purification.

169

TABLE 3
CHROMIUM BY ELECTROLYSIS

	Ag	Al	Cu	Fe	Mg	Mn	Mo	Ni	Si
INITIAL	<1	8	3	2	<1.0	4	11	11	11
FINAL	<1	4	1.0	<1.0	ND	ND	ND	6	1

ND = Not detected

TABLE 4
SUBLIMATION OF CrO_3

	Ag	Al	B	Cu	Fe	In	Ni	Si	Ti
INITIAL	<1.0	<1.0	ND	1	<1.0	7	ND	<1.0	ND
HORIZONTAL SUBLIMER	<1.0	20	15	8	<1.0	8	<1.0	240	2
VERTICAL SUBLIMER	<1.0	16	ND	2	<1.0	8	ND	120	1

ND = Not detected

TABLE 5
PREPARATION OF CrO_3 FROM CrO_2Cl_2

	Ag	Al	B	Cu	Fe	In	Ni	Si	Ti	Mn
INITIAL	<1.0	<1.0	ND	1.0	<1.0	7	ND	<1.0	ND	ND
CrO_3	ND	2	<1.0	<1.0	8	ND	<1.0	4	ND	<1.0

ND = Not detected

(3). $Cr_2(SO_4)_3$ - Analysis of the chromium sulfate prepared by synthesis indicates more contamination than purification when compared to the purity of the starting CrO_3 (Table 6). The sulfur dioxide is the simplest reaction and gives a slightly better product. This product is of a considerably better purity than the commercial sulfate (Table 7, column 1).

170

TABLE 6
SYNTHETIC CHROMIUM (III) SULFATE

	Ag	Al	B	Cu	Fe	In	Ni	Si	Ti	Mg
INITIAL	<1.0	<1.0	ND	1.0	<1.0	7	ND	<1.0	ND	ND
SULFATE (ALCOHOL)	ND	ND	ND	<1.0	2	ND	ND	30	ND	13
SULFATE (SO$_2$)	ND	<1.0	ND	ND	2	ND	ND	8	ND	3

ND = Not detected

TABLE 7
EXTRACTION OF $Cr_2(SO_4)_3 \cdot XH_2O$

METAL	INITIAL	100% C_2H_5OH	7% H_2O-C_2H_5OH	8.5% H_2O-C_2H_5OH
Ag	17	4	ND	ND
Al	13	ND	2	2
B	ND	ND	ND	ND
Cu	12	<1.0	<1.0	<1.0
Ca	10	ND	ND	ND
Fe	287	7	5	6
Mg	2	4	7	2
Mn	7	<1.0	<1.0	<1.0
Ni	33	ND	ND	ND
Si	12	2	3	4

ND = Not detected

The extraction of commercial chromium sulfate reduced the metallic impurity content. This technique was as favorable as the synthetic approach, particularly in the case of silicon. The silicon content in all cases is two to four parts per million which is considerably better than any previous result. To test for metallic contamination by impurities in the Sohxlet thimbles, the extraction of empty thimbles was performed using the same liquid concentration as was used in the chromium sulfate extractions. No noticeable change was determined in the thimble impurities, indicating that leaching from the thimbles was not a serious source of contamination.

171

SUMMARY

Several methods have been evaluated for the preparation and purification of chromium metal, chromium (VI) oxide and chromium III sulfate - XH_2O. Metallic chromium of highest purity can be obtained by the Van Arkel process. Chemical preparation and sublimation of CrO_3 does not offer any improvement over the commercial product. Solvent extraction of commercial chromium III sulfate - XH_2O is the most effective purification technique for this material.

Acknowledgements - Some of the Spectroscopic analysis were made by Metal Hydrides, Inc. under Contract AF19 (604) - 3469. The authors should also acknowledge Luther N. Nolen for his assistance in the work.

REFERENCES

1. W. C. Fernelius, (ed.) "Inorganic Synthesis," Vol. II, McGraw-Hill Book Co., New York, N. Y., 1946, p. 205.
2. S. Field and A. D. Weill, "Electroplating," 6th Ed., Pitman and Sons, Ltd., London, 1951, p. 379.
3. A. K. Graham, (ed.), "Electroplating Engineering Handbook," Reinhold Publishing Co., New York., N. Y., 1955, p. 173.
4. F. Kraus, Z. anorg. Chem., 179, 143 (1929).
5. J. W. Mellor, "Comprehensive Treatise of Inorganic and Theoretical Chemistry," Vol. XI, Longmans Green Co., New York, N. Y., 1931, p. 436.
6. A. H. Sully, "Chromium," Academic Press, Inc., London, 1954, p. 158.
7. M. J. Udy, "Chromium," Vol. II, Reinhold Publishing Corp., New York, N. Y. 1956, p. 65.
8. A. E. Van Arkel, Metalwirtschaft, 13, 405 (1934).

DISCUSSION

P. R. ROBERTS (Trancoa Chemical Copr.): Is the 10% yield from the Van Arkel process standard for this method?

N. W. SILCOX (AFCRL): Yes.

P. R. ROBERTS (Trancoa Chemical Corp.): How do you propose to strip the chromium from the filament?

A. F. ARMINGTON (AFCRL): We merely straightened out the filament and the deposit fell off. There was a film on the deposit, and there was also some microcrystallinity to it which fell off. I wouldn't say that the entire deposit stripped off clean.

ULTRAPURIFICATION OF INDIUM, ANTIMONY, BISMUTH, ARSENIC AND TELLURIUM

Raymond Beau
Les Produits Semi-Conducteurs
Antony (Seine) France

Our Laboratories have set as a goal the ultrapurification of elements used as semiconductors or in compound semiconductors such as III - V compounds. The first objective was to prepare hyperpure silicon and then to extend our experience to other elements such as Ga, As, In, Sb, Bi, Te and P. Several techniques have been developed to purify these elements by chemical means. The elements and the compounds made from them are then purified by zone refining whenever possible.

The purity of the elements and compounds have been determined by analytical techniques such as colorimetry, polarographic measurements and X-ray spectrometry. Semiconducting element or compounds are analyzed by Hall effect measurements which give the carrier concentrations and the mobilities, by lifetime measurements, by infrared absorption and radiative recombination techniques and by electron paramagnetic and nuclear magnetic resonance.

INDIUM -

The purification of indium by chemical means has been worked out in detail since the purification of this material by zone refining has not proved to be very efficient.

Various authors have found that the electrolysis of indium salts with soluble anodes of indium or with insoluble anodes (graphite or platinum) was a practical and efficient means for the purification of In. Some impurities such as Tl and Cd could not be removed by this technique due to the fact that their deposition potential was very close to that of indium. We have checked this point by performing:

(a) an electrolysis in HCL- NaCl at pH 2 to 2.5 with soluble anodes of indium.

(b) an electrolysis in H_2SO_4 with platinum electrodes and in HCl with graphite electrodes.

173

ppm	Initial In.	1st Section	2nd Section	3rd Section	4th Section	9th Section
Ag	1	<1	<1	<1	<1	.... <1
Cu	3	1	1	1	<2	 6
Zn		23	<1	<1	<1	.... <1
Fe	10	2.5	1	8	1	 2
Ni		<2	<2	<2	<1	.... <1
Pb	200	3	8	9	15	 268
Cd	150	<1	<1	<1	<2	.... <2
Tℓ	80	11	11	16.5	18	 50
Bi		7.5	11	<1	<2	 2
Sn	100	3	3	3.5	5	 60
As		<1	<1	<1	<2	.... <2

Successive Deposits

ppm	Initial Indium	Elec. H_2SO_4	Elec. H_2SO_4	Extr.+Elec.*
Pb	460	15	<2	2.8
Cu	300	9	<1	<1.5
Cd	4000	2160	1820	<1
Ni	310	263	44	<1
Zn	4250	<10	<15	<1
Fe	15340	14	15	<1
Tℓ	360	925**	715**	<1
Ag	3	<1	<1	<1
As	2.5	<1	<1	<1.5
Hg	—			<2
Bi	—			<1.5

Electrolysis with Insoluble Anodes
* (Last Column-Extraction with TBP and Precipitation with Sodium Sulfite followed by Electrolysis)
** (Electrolysis not complete-enrichment of Tℓ)

Figure 1. Electrolysis with Soluble Indium Anodes
(HCl-NaCl, Ph 2-2.5)

Figure 1 shows the results. On the top table the purity becomes rich in Pb and Tl. The lower table also shows that with insoluble anodes Cd, Ni and Tl are deposited.

It is then necessary to eliminate these elements before the electrolysis and for this purpose the technique of counter current extraction was used.

The process of purification is composed of two stages:
(1) Elimination of Tl, Cd, Ni by extraction.
(2) Electrolysis at a controlled potential to eliminate the remaining impurities.

174

When the starting material is rich in Fe, the Fe is eliminated between operation 1 and 2 by precipitation of the basic sulfate of indium with sodium sulfite at 70°C. This precipitation eliminates 99% of any Fe, Zn, Cd and Ni present. (Heavy metals such as Cu, Pb, Sb, Bi and Tl are not eliminated.)

Figure 2 shows the variation of the partition coefficients of various elements against HCl concentration. All the elements which have a partition coefficient greater than 1 tend to go into the solvent phase and all the elements with a partition coefficient smaller than 1 tend to stay in aqueous solution.

Tributyl phosphate was as a solvent, the addition of benzene permits a spreading of the partition coefficient for the various elements.

In concentrated acidic solutions (8 to 11 normal) the partition coefficient of In is:

$$C = \frac{\text{Solv. conc.}}{\text{aq. conc.}} \quad \# 4$$

Whereas the partition coefficients of Tl, Cd and Ni are less than 1.

Cu, Pb, Bi, Zn are partially eliminated (a small quantity remain in the solvent phase).

Sn, Fe remain with In.

Tl should be monovalent and this naturally occurs when In is dissolved in HCl, Tl^+ being the stable valency.

For the extraction we used the Procedure designed by O'Keefe in which the solution to be purified is admitted laterally (Figure 3).

The equipment is made of:
- 5 stages for the extraction of In from the aqueous phase.
- 10 stages for the purification, that is, washing with 10 N HCl.
- 5 stages for removing In from the tributyl phosphate.

Tributyl phosphate goes through the apparatus and is recycled. The concentrated solution of Indium (200 g/l) is admitted laterally between the stages of purification and of extraction and is added to the 10N acid solution containing some In. The 10N acid carries the impurities not extracted out of the apparatus (Tl, Cd, Ni, Cu, etc. . .) while the T B P phase which has extracted In (Mn, Fe, Sn) is washed with water. The resulting solution is slightly acidic and contains 40 g/l of In.

The apparatus has 20 stages (5 + 10 + 5) fixed on the same rotation axis. Each stage performs the agitation, the decantation and the partition of the two phases which are then distributed in counter current manner to the neighboring stages.

175

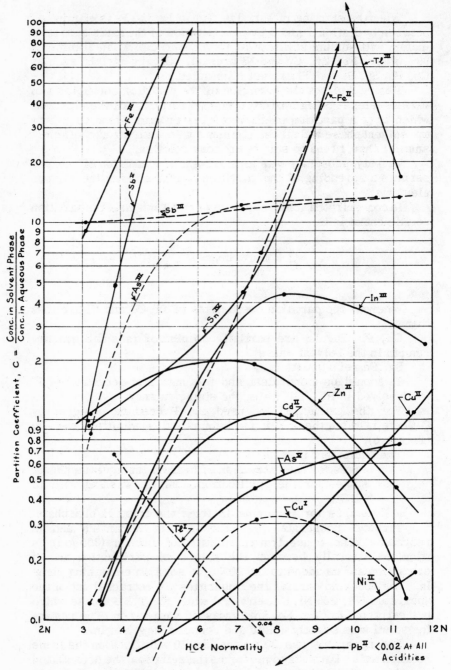

Figure 2. Partition Coefficient of Different Metals between TBP-Benzene (40-60) and HCl Phase.

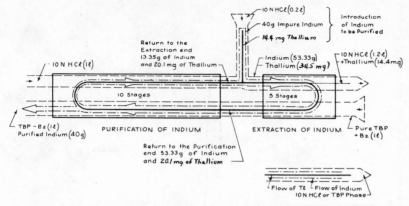

The quantities in grams or milligrams and liters are expressed per unit time.

Figure 3. Method of O'Keefe for the Extraction and
Purification of Indium.

Figures 4 and 5 show the functioning of the apparatus.
Between 1 and 2 agitation (10 times). In 3, separation. In 4, the
pouring of the light phase is over (the interface is at the neck E).
In 5, the heavy phase is poured into the higher bulb. In 6, the
phases are distributed into the next stages in a counter current
manner, the light phase goes the stage situated behind the board,
the heavy phase goes towards the stage situated in front of the
board. The cycle is then repeated.

ELECTROLYSIS -

Initially the electrolyses were carried out in sulfuric acid
since the starting material contained 1.5% Fe which was eliminated by precipitation of the In with sodium sulfite. Electrolysis
from a hydrochloric acid solution is preferred, however, in this
case it is necessary to wash twice with benzene to eliminate any
dissolved T B P. In either case the electrolysis is made in two
stages.

The current-density vs cathode potential (potential between
the cathode and a calomel electrode) curves depicted in Figure 6
show that an electrolysis at 600 MV eliminates the metals more
noble than indium, namely Pb, Cu, Sn and Bi, which extracted
with a little amount of indium. The electrolysis itself is run at
700 MV eliminating Fe, Zn, etc. The complete process is shown
in Figure 7.

The two cells are built the same way. The cathodes are made
of indium (impure for the first one and pure for the second one)
and the anodes made of nuclear grade graphite 99.999% pure are
surrounded by Pyrex Tubes with sintered glass diaphragms.

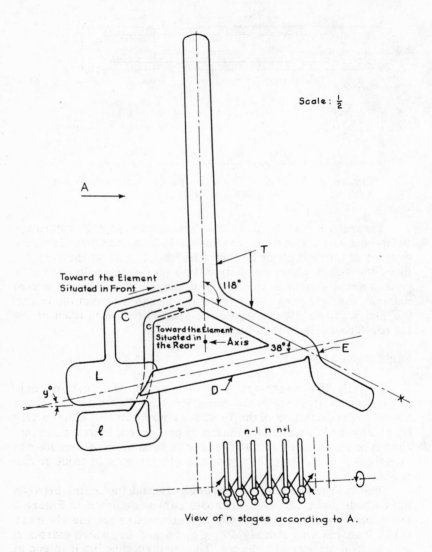

Scale: $\frac{1}{2}$

A

T

Toward the Element
Situated in Front

118°

C

c Toward the Element
Situated in
the Rear ← Axis

38°

E

L

D

9°

ℓ

n-1 n n+1

View of n stages according to A.

Figure 4.   Continuous Counter-Current Liquid-Liquid
Extraction Apparatus - One Stage.

178

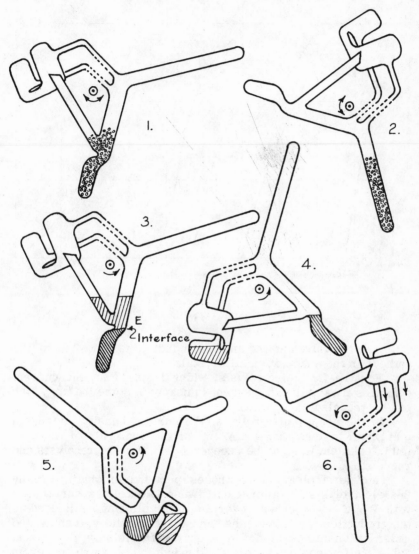

1.

2.

3.

4.

E
Interface

5.

6.

Figure 5. Apparatus for Continuous Counter Current Extraction.

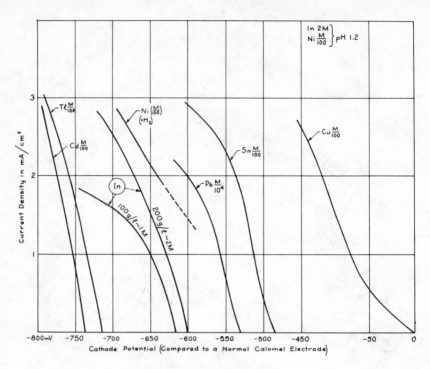

Figure 6. Curves for the Deposit of Indium and its
Impurities in H_2SO_4, pH 0.5.

Chlorine is evolved at the anode and indium is deposited at the
cathode in the shape of small crystals.

For the first electrolysis, which lasts 48 h., the current
densities are small. The current is nearly 0; some indium which
can be recycled is deposited.

In the second electrolysis, the current density goes from
5 mA/cm² to less than 1 mA/cm² at the end. 10% of the In is
left in solution, this can be recovered in a third electrolysis and
recycled.

In order to obtain new cathodes, pure indium obtained in the
2nd electrolysis is laminated between two rollers surrounded
with P V C. The excess over the initial dimensions is used as
the production and it is washed and dried carefully, then melted
under potassium cyanide in a quartz crucible with a ground
valve. After cooling to 200°C, the indium is poured under an
argon atmosphere into a teflon boat. The indium obtained in this
manner is 99.999% pure (Figure 1).

The indium is then zone refined in a quartz boat under
vacuum and then mixed with antimony which has been purified
chemically and zone refined. After 10 passes under argon

180

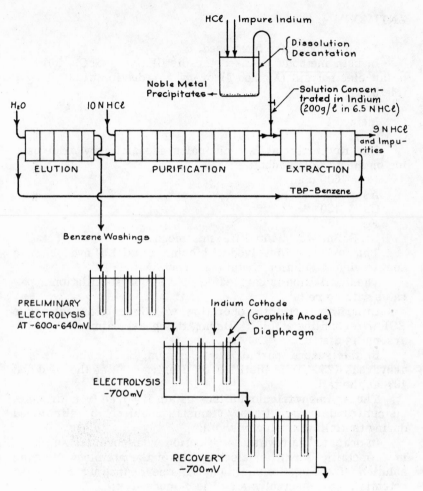

Figure 7. Production of Pure Indium by
Extraction and Electrolysis.

atmosphere we obtained the following characteristics at room
temperature:

Type N
Carrier concentration $2.4 \times 10^{16}/cm^3$
Mobility $73.000\ cm^2v^{-1}\ s^{-1}$
Resistivity $4.16 \times 10^{-3}\ \Omega$ -cm

The impurities determined in indium are:
Fe, Tl, Ag, Hg, Cu, Ni, As, by colorimetry
Pb, Cu, Cd, Ni, Zn, Fe, Tl, Bi, by polarography.

181

ANTIMONY -

Two methods have been used.

In both methods we used the distillation of $SbCl_3$ followed by an electrolysis (Method I) or by a reduction with hydrogen (Method II).

Method I

The raw material is technical grade antimony oxide used for pigments which contains:

Pb   600 ppm
As   600 "
Cu   150 "
Fe   150 "
Bi, S, Sn, etc. . . in different amounts.

This oxide is dissolved with commercial 12N hydrochloric acid to yield a solution containing about 6N free HCl.

The distillation is carried out in a simple distillation apparatus with no reflux.

In the first part of the operation, we eliminate the azeotrope HCl-water boiling at 108°. During this phase, almost all of the arsenic is distilled.

In the second part of the operation, $SbCl_3$ which is now anhydrous (200°C) is distilled off leaving 10% as the head and 10% as the tail.

The Antimony trichloride thus obtained is free from arsenic, bismuth and copper (these elements could not be eliminated during the following electrolysis).

In order to improve the purification and recover the antimony in a metallic form, an electrolysis of the antimony chloride solution (40 to 50 g/l of antimony) was performed at a controlled potential. The electrolysis cell is composed of:

- anodes of 99.999 pure graphite (bars 27 mm. in diameter) with diaphragms to prevent the formation of hypochlorous acid.
- platinum cathodes 2/10 mm thick.
- a calomel electrode
- an electric device to maintain the cathode at a constant potential.

The electrolysis is carried out at a cathode potential of -210 mV (with respect to the calomel electrode) giving a current density of about 3 to 4 mA/cm^2. 90% of the antimony is deposited from the solution.

At this potential only Sb is deposited (Cu, As and Bi being already eliminated).

Antimony is melted under pure hydrogen or under pure potassium cyanide and poured as ingots under an argon atmosphere. It is 99.999% pure, the analysis being made chemically on 11 elements.

Method II

The first operation (distillation) is the same as in Method I but the distillate is rectified again carefully in a 24 stage column, 10% is eliminated for the head and 10% for the tail. Antimony chloride is then reduced by hydrogen (purified through a palladium tube) at 800°C in a quartz tube. The reaction rate is great enough to produce 300 g. a day in a tube 35 mm. in diameter. An ingot of antimony is directly produced within the tube.

This antimony is purer than that produced by Method I.

BISMUTH -

Three different techniques have been tried.
1. Precipitation of bismuth phosphate
2. Electrolytic refining
3. Distillation of bismuth.
The various methods can be coupled.

Precipitation of Bismuth Phosphate

The method used in analysis, gives a good separation of some elements such as Ag, Cu, Hg, Cd, Al, Zn.

The raw material (Bi from Salsigne at 99.5%) is dissolved in nitric acid at 60°C. Neutralized with ammonia and then the solution is made slightly acid. After filtration, precipitation is accomplished with diammonium phosphate at 5-10%.

A preparation at the boiling point allows a good filtration. The precipite is dried at 300°C. The phosphate is hydrolyzed with concentrated sodium hydroxide in a Teflon flask. The oxide is washed and dried and then reduced by hydrogen at 550° in a silica furnace.

Electrolytic Refining

Three different bath compositions have been tried.
1. Hydrochloric acid media 100 g/l of Bi - 100 g/l free HCl
2. Tartric media. Solution of basic tartrate and bismuth chloride. (150 g. $BiCl_3$ in 100 ml HCl 37% + 150 g tartric acid + 250 g. NaOH for liter).
3. Acetic media. For one liter, 30 g. $Bi(NO_3)_3$ + 25 ml HNO_3 70% + acetic acid until complete dissolution).

Anodes are of technical bismuth at 99.5%, cathodes are of platinum.

183

Purity rises from 99.5 to 99.995%.

Distillation of Bismuth

A bidistillation is carried out in a quartz apparatus under vacuum (10^{-4} mm Hg). Bismuth is collected in a side tube in the shape of an ingot suitable for zone refining. We have not been successful in obtaining 99.999% pure bismuth by either one of these methods but by coupling two of these procedures like $BiPO_4$ - distillation, or refining-distillation. This purity can be obtained.

ARSENIC -

For the purification of As, several techniques can be used:
- Sublimation of As
- Production of $AsCl_3$ and thermal cracking for obtaining As
- Purification of $AsCl_3$ by distillation
- Purification of As_2O_3 of various salts by crystallization or precipitation followed by a reduction.

A reliable, and safe method (toxicity) was finally chosen:

1. Arsenious anhydride is purified by crystallization in hydrochloric acid.

2. The anhydride is reduced by purified H_2.

In order to purify the anhydride, it is dissolved in 6 N hydrochloric acid in a reflux apparatus. After complete dissolution, the solution is cooled to room temperature than below 0°C. The crystallized anhydride is then filtered. This treatment is repeated three times giving a very pure As_2O_3 with a total yield of 70%. The reduction is carried out in a quartz tubular furnace with three heating sections at different temperatures.

(a) A sublimation section for As_2O_3 at 300-350°C (therefore an additional purification). Mixture with pure H_2.

(b) A reduction section at 800°C.

(c) A condensation section at 350°C in which As crystallizes. Traces of anhydride not reduced are deposited before this section along with amorphous As.

The yield of crystallized arsenic is 85%. It contains some silica. The arsenic is then sublimed under hydrogen in another quartz apparatus and a 99.999% pure product is obtained. The sulfur content is less than 2×10^{-2} ppm. The main impurities are SiO_2 and C.

TELLURIUM -

We have undertaken very recently the purification of tellurium by various processes. Only the simplest one, distillation will be described. It should be noticed that by this process we cannot remove all the selenium present in tellurium and this, in spite of a rather large difference in their vapor pressure.

It is then necessary to separate selenium from tellurium prior to distillation, this is accomplished by precipitating insoluble TeO_2. Technical tellurium is attacked with chlorine to obtain $TeCl_2$ and then $TeCl_4$ (temperature is raised from 200°C to 230°C).

$TeCl_4$ is hydrolyzed at the boiling temperature by neutralization at pH 4 or 5. TeO_2 is insoluble whereas SeO_2 is soluble.

TeO_2 is reduced by H_2 at approximately 600°C, eliminating traces of Se as SeH_2.

Two sublimations under a vacuum of 5 mm to 10^{-3} mm of Hg are carried out. It was noticed that the pressure was not a determining factor for the purification.

The tellurium obtained is spectrographically pure, but for some elements, the detectable level is rather high and the purity cannot be specified.

DISCUSSION

O. J. MARSH (Hughes): Did you measure the indium antimonide at liquid nitrogen temperatures for concentration and mobility?

R. DEGEILH (Les Produits Semiconducteurs, France): No, it was at room temperature.

F. J. REID (Battelle): Do you feel, then, on the same point, that this number of 2.4 times 10 to the minus 16th is actually the extrinsic carrier concentration impurities or is this number the intrinsic carrier concentration?

R. DEGEILH (Les Produits Semiconducteurs, France): We think it is intrinsic.

PREPARATION OF
LUMINESCENT ALUMINUM NITRIDE

I. Adams, T. R. AuCoin, and G. A. Wolff *
U. S. Army Signal Research and Development Laboratory
Fort Monmouth, New Jersey

Aluminum nitride has been found to display electroluminescence, as well as phosphorescence and cathodoluminescence [1, 2]. The material had been made by several investigators in the past [3], but they had considered it too unstable to be useful. Recent work, however, [2, 4, 5, 6, 7, 8] produced a relatively inert product by a number of methods involving high temperature reactions of aluminum and aluminum compounds with nitrogen or ammonia. While the product produced by these methods is inert and satisfactory for refractory use, a relatively purer product is needed for research on its luminescent properties.

Pure, crystalline AlN is prepared by the reaction of high purity (99.999%) aluminum powder with prepurified nitrogen (99.996%), at high temperature and pressure (Fig. 1). The Al powder, contained in a refractory crucible is placed inside of a tungsten resistance coil. The reactor is evacuated, and N_2 gas is admitted in excess of the amount necessary for the completion of the reaction. When the aluminum has reached about 1000°C, the reaction takes place as is indicated by a sudden drop in pressure and a rapid increase in temperature. The reaction takes only a few seconds for completion. The product is removed as a porous, sintered agglomerate, pulverized, and treated with Cl_2 gas at about 600°C, to remove unreacted aluminum and other impurities as volatile chlorides (Fig. 2). The purified powder is found by spectrochemical analysis to contain less than 0.01% total detectable impurities (Fig. 3). X-ray analysis reveals no trace of any other phase.

Care in selection of a refractory crucible to contain the aluminum powder is very important since the reaction of aluminum and nitrogen is exothermic and drives the temperature high enough to cause melting and a chemical attack on the crucible by the aluminum. Aluminum nitride emerges as the only material that has complete chemical inertness to aluminum under these

---

*Present address: Harshaw Chemical Company, Cleveland, Ohio

AUTOCLAVE PRESSURE REACTOR

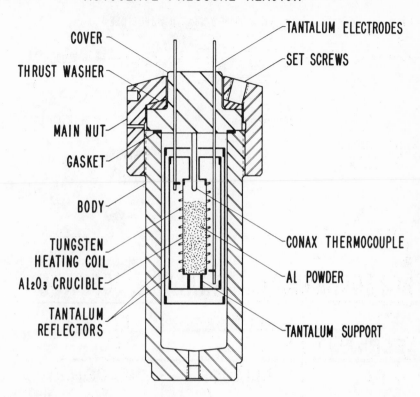

Figure 1. Autoclave Pressure Reactor.

conditions [7]. High density, impervious, AlN crucibles have been made by hot pressing techniques [8]. The AlN used for fabrication of crucibles can be obtained in a pure state by using high purity 99.7% Al_2O_3 crucibles. The simultaneous reaction of aluminun and nitrogen with Al_2O_3 results in a spinel structure of the composition $Al_{(2+x/3)}$ $O_{(3-x)}$ N_x. This spinel is stable at high temperatures. The composition of this phase cannot exceed the value x = 0.75 [Al_3 (O_3N)]. Above this value a wurtzite phase appears. When analyzed for nitrogen and aluminum, this phase consistently showed an aluminum excess which could accurately be accounted for by oxygen. The wurtzite structure was found to exist for $2 \leq x \leq 3$. The spinel phase can be partially separated from AlN by gently crushing the sintered mass extracted from the Al_2O_3 crucible and sieving to 270 mesh or finer.

Yields can be increased by reducing the rate of heating near the reaction temperature. This apparently permits the aluminum

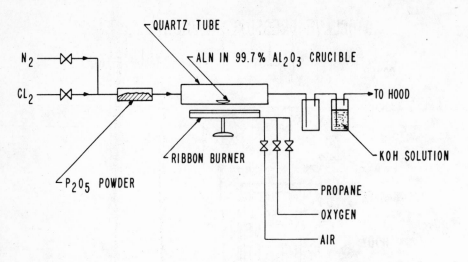

Figure 2. Apparatus for Aluminum Nitride Purification.

SPECTROCHEMICAL ANALYSIS OF ALN

ELEMENT	BEFORE Cl_2	AFTER Cl_2
AL	MAJOR	MAJOR
Si	0.005	0.001
Fe	0.005	0.003
Mg	0.003	0.0005
Mn	0.001	nd
Ca	0.01	0.001
Cu	0.0005	0.0007
Cr	0.005	nd
Ni	0.001	nd
TOTAL	0.0305	0.0062

Figure 3. Spectrochemical Analysis of AlN.

188

to absorb more nitrogen and gives more even and complete reaction. The product is seldom homogeneous, but usually consists of three distinct regions or zones: a hard crust in contact with the walls of the crucible, an intermediate gray-white zone, and an unsintered pale yellow interior zone. This pale yellow region is usually of the highest purity, and is easily crushed. Variations in N_2 pressure from 50 psi to several thousand psi did not seem to affect the reaction.

The AlN, before purification with Cl_2, emits a blue phosphorescence peaking at about 4300Å when excited by 2537Å Hg radiation. When AlN has been doped with Cl and a suitable activator, it exhibits AC and DC electroluminescence, the wavelength varying with the activator used. Blue, green and red electroluminescence has been observed. αAl_2O_3, prepared by the decomposition of AlN in oxygen at 1300°C, emits a similar phosphorescence and when suitably doped, emits a red electroluminescence. Since attempts to produce electroluminescence in αAl_2O_3 not produced in this manner were unsuccesful it was concluded that minor amounts of nitrogen may act as an activator.

ACKNOWLEDGMENTS

The authors are indebted to Mr. Joseph LoCicero and Mr. Edward Nolan for valuable assistance in the design of the pressure reactor used to prepare the aluminum nitride.

REFERENCES

1. G. A. Wolff, I. Adams, and J. W. Mellichamp, Phys Rev, 114, No. 5, 1262-1264, June 1, 1959.
2. I. Adams, J. W. Mellichamp, and G. A. Wolff, Electrochemical Soc, Electronics Div Abstracts, 9, No. 1.
3. J. W. Mellor: Comprehensive Treatise on Inorganic and Theoretical Chemistry, Vol VIII, Nitrogen and Phosphorus, Longmans, Green and Co., New York, 1928, 1110 pp.
4. J. A. Kohn, Perry G. Cotter, and R. A. Potter, Am. Mineral 41, 355 (1956).
5. M. Rey, Silicates Industries, 22, 453 (1958).
6. Von Th. Renner, Zanorg u Allgem Chem 298 [1-2] 22 (Jan 1959).
7. G. Long and L. M. Foster, J. Am. Ceram Soc., 42, No. 2, 53 (1959).
8. K. M. Taylor and C. Lenie, J. Elec. Soc., 107, No. 4, Apr 1960.
9. Zh. L. Vert, M. V. Kamentsev, V. I. Kudryavtsev, and M. I. Sokhor, Doklady Akad Nauk SSSR, 116, 834-7 (1957).
10. N. E. Filonenko, I. V. Lavrov, O. V. Andreeva, and R. L. Pevzner, Doklady Akad Nauk SSSR, 115, No. 3, 583-585 (1957).

DISCUSSION

L. R. WEISBERG (RCA Lab.): What size were the largest crystallites?

I. ADAMS (U. S. Army Signal R & D Lab.): The material is very crystalline. It is hexagonal. We have made single crystals of aluminum nitride by firing in the same apparatus with a carbon heater. These crystals were about 1 centimeter long by about 1 millimeter or a half a millimeter in diameter.

J. I. PETERSON (Melpar): I am interested in how you assayed the aluminum nitride.

I. ADAMS (U. S. Army Signal R & D Lab.): The chemical analysis of the AlN leaves much to be desired. We analyzed the aluminum as aluminum oxide. In these analyses, we would always get a slight excess of nitrogen and a slight deficiency of aluminum, which leads me to suspect that either the aluminum oxide reaction is not quantitative or there is a certain amount of the spinel phase being formed by the action of aluminum nitride and oxygen. The presence of the spinel phase was detected by x-ray powder diffraction patterns and the analysis of the impurities was by spectrochemical analysis.

L. M. FOSTER (Alcoa): I would like to say that there is actually another crystalline phase in the phase diagram. The cubic alumina is a reasonably stable alumina phase, and the nitrogen simply stabilizes it more. You pass over to a delta alumina at even lower nitrogen content. There are crystalline phases in the system.

These materials are analyzed quite easily if you encapsulate and seal them in about 50 per cent hydrochloric acid in a glass capsule, and heat to about 200 degrees. The nitride or oxynitride or oxide dissolves completely and a nitrogen determination on the solution gives a very excellent analysis.

F. D. ROSI CHAIRMAN (RCA Lab.): Would you draw a phase diagram if there is any?

I. ADAMS (U. S. Army Signal R & D Lab.): We don't know what the phase diagram looks like and I hesitate to draw one.

F. D. ROSI CHAIRMAN (RCA Lab.): I just wanted to put it on the record that there was no phase diagram.

I. ADAMS (U. S. Army Signal R & D Lab.): No. All that I am trying to indicate here is that aluminum nitride apparently is soluble in aluminum oxide and that variations in nitrogen content of the aluminum nitride give rise to a spinel-like phase which looks like γ-aluminum oxide but actually contains nitrogen as an impurity.

G. A. WOLFF (Harshaw Chemical): Dr. Foster mentioned the high temperature stability of the spinel type "γ - Al_2O_3" grown in the presence of nitrogen. Aluminum oxide of spinel structure grown in the presence of nitrogen has also been found by us to be stable up to 1600°C and higher. In its pure form, γ - Al_2O_3 normally converts to the α - form at temperatures as low as 900°C. We suggest the following explanation. An ideal simple oxide of spinel structure corresponds to the composition Al_3B_4. The γ - Al_2O_3 can therefore be formulated in a different way: as $Al_{8/3}\,\square_{1/3}O_4$ where $\square$ represents octahedral or tetrahedral cationic vacancies. When nitrogen is taken up by the oxide, then for each three nitrogen atoms replacing three oxygen atoms in the structure, one additional Al atom will have to occupy one of the available vacancies in the structure. The formula in this way changes to

$$Al_{(2+x/3)}\square_{3-4x/12}O_{3-x}N_x$$

where x represents the number of nitrogen atoms taken up. From this it can be seen that all the spinel vacancies are occupied when x = 3/4 and the composition of the compound corresponds to Al_3O_3N. In α - Al_2O_3 it is apparently possible only to replace Al atoms, but not to introduce more Al or other atoms in excess of those present in the pure compound. Probably for this reason a γ - to α - transformation does not occur in a solid solution of Al_2O_3 - AlN, in which the spinel vacancy sites are all or partly occupied by Al atoms. How much of the AlN actually is taken up by the "γ - Al_2O_3" and whether or not the compound Al_3O_3N of maximum AlN content of spinel structure can actually be obtained, cannot be stated. However, on the AlN side of the Al_2O_3 - AlN phase diagram, it appears that as much as 20 mole % of $(Al_2O_3)_{1/2}$ is taken up by AlN without changing its (wurtzite) structure. This has been concluded by an indirect determination from sample analyses for Al and N and calculation of the oxygen content from the measured Al excess of this material. The errors observed were in the order of 1.5 wt %. In this Al_2O_3 - AlN solid solution of wurtzite structure it is assumed that tetrahedral cationic wurtzite vacancies are present. Again we are not able to say how much Al_2O_3 can be taken up, but it is suspected that toward the center of the Al_2O_3 - AlN phase diagram a miscibility gap exists.

F. D. ROSI CHAIRMAN (RCA Lab.): Are you saying that your phase diagram shows limited solubility on both terminal components, but in between you have these other lower complex structures?

G. A. WOLFF (Harshaw Chemical Company): Yes. You can not say more at the moment. The important thing is that if you have nitrogen present, you fill up the remaining vacancies, stabilize the Al_2O_3 spinel this way, to much above 900 degrees where normally the γ - Al_2O_3 spinel would convert. You can heat it up to 1600° or higher without any difficulties. Essentially the phase diagram γ - Al_2O_3 - AlN may best be described as representing isodimorphism, with an unidentified phase observed in the center region.

THE PREPARATION AND PURIFICATION
OF TRANSITION METAL SILICIDES*

R. M. Ware
The Plessey Co. Ltd., Caswell Research Laboratories
Towcester, Northants, England

ABSTRACT

Two main purification processes were employed. The first consisted of the purification of cobalt by a chemical method, the second of the purification of the silicides by zone refining on a water cooled copper hearth.

To obtain pure cobalt a solution of laboratory grade cobalt chloride was oxidized in the presence of excess ammonia to yield the insoluble cobalt hexammine chloride. Nickel, which constituted the main impurity, does not form a hexammine and its pentammine is soluble in water. Filtration of the cobalt hexammine chloride and its reprecipitation from acid solution yielded a material with no spectrographically detectable impurities. Metallic cobalt was obtained by electrolysis of an aqueous solution of the hexammine onto a tantalum cathode. Impurities in the final product did not exceed 5 ppm. The cobalt silicides were prepared by melting the purified cobalt plate together with pure silicon by induction heating on a water cooled copper hearth.

Isolation of the stoichiometric compounds and further purification was achieved by zone refining in the copper cold hearth. This method reduces the risk of crucible contamination and is considerably simpler to operate than floating zone refining.

The method has been applied to several other transition metal silicides including Cr, Mn, Fe, Ni, Rh, Ir, and appears to be generally applicable to the purification of reactive materials.

1. INTRODUCTION

In the course of a programme of work on thermoelectric materials a systematic study of the properties of transition metal silicides has been carried out. For the purposes of this study it was necessary to prepare the stoichiometric compounds, purify

---

*This work was supported by The Ministry of Aviation.

them and also to prepare a range of their alloys. It was decided that a total impurity content not greater than ten parts per million should suffice for this work. The available methods for the preparation of silicides are as follows:-

(1) Direct combination of the elements.
    (a) By fusion.
    (b) By sintering of mixed powders.
(2) Reduction of metal oxides with silicon.
(3) Reaction of metal oxides with silica in the presence of carbon.
(4) Reduction of mixed oxides with aluminum or magnesium.
(5) Reaction of the Metals with silicon in a copper menstruum.
(6) Reaction of metal with silicon halide or of metal halide with silicon.
(7) Fused salt electrolysis.

Direct reaction of the elements was selected as most likely to yield a pure product. Of the two possible methods of direct reaction, sintering of powders was first attempted but soon abandoned in favour of fusion since it was difficult to avoid significant oxygen contamination from the considerable quantity of oxygen usually present on the surface of silicon powder. The chief difficulty of the fusion method was the reactivity of the molten silicides which, together with their high heats of formation, caused attack upon crucible materials. However, the development of the water cooled copper hearth provided a convenient means of both synthesising and zone refining the silicides, and it has been applied to a wide range of these materials with complete success. The first silicides prepared were those of cobalt. At the time of their preparation it was not known what degree of purification of the compounds could be achieved and so a chemical method of purifying cobalt was developed. This is described in the next section.

2. PURIFICATION OF COBALT

The major impurity in commercially available cobalt is nickel. From the nickel-cobalt phase diagram it seems unlikely that an efficient separation of nickel from cobalt could be achieved by zone refining. This was confirmed in practice. Starting with electroplated cobalt and using the cold hearth zone refiner, ten passes were made along a bar of cobalt 13 inches long. As can be seen from Table 1 there was no evidence of any movement of nickel.

Since zone refining of cobalt did not seem an effective way of removing nickel a chemical process was developed. This method is based upon the preparation of cobalt hexammine chloride

Table 1

Zone Refining of Cobalt

Specimen	Distance from front of ingot	Nickel Content Wt. %
Original Material	-	0.25
Zone refined	1"	0.26
	4"	0.29
Ingot	8"	0.26
(ten passes)	12"	0.29

described by Bjerrum and Reynolds [1]. The separation of cobalt from nickel depends upon the fact that whilst cobalt pentammine nitrate can be oxidised to an insoluble hexammine complex the nickel remains as soluble pentammine. The two may therefore be separated by filtration.

The preparation of the cobaltic hexammine chloride from cobalt chloride may be represented overall by the equation.

$$4CoCl_2 + 4NH_4Cl + 20NH_3 + O_2 \rightarrow 4[Co(NH_3)_6] Cl + 2H_2O$$

In practice cobaltous pentammine chloride is first formed and an equilibrium is established between pentammine and hexammine. Activated charcoal is employed as a catalyst and serves to establish the equilibrium at room temperature and atmospheric pressure. The presence of a large excess of ammonia displaces the equilibrium in the direction of the formation of hexammine. The process as described by Bjerrum is as follows:-

240 g (1 mol) of cobalt (II) chloride hexahydrate and 160 g (3 mols) of ammonium chloride are added to 200 ml of water. The mixture is shaken until most of the salts are dissolved. Then 4 g of activated decolourizing charcoal and 500 ml of concentrated ammonia are added. Air is bubbled vigorously through the mixture until the red solution becomes yellowish-brown (usually about 4 hr). The air inlet tube is of fairly large bore (10 mm) to prevent clogging with the precipitated hexammine cobalt (III) salt.

The crystals and carbon are filtered on a Buchner funnel and then added to a solution of 15-30 ml of concentrated hydrochloric acid in 1500 ml of water; sufficient acid should be used

194

to give the entire mixture an acid reaction. The mixture is heated on a hot plate to effect complete solution and is filtered hot. The hexammine cobalt (III) chloride is precipitated by adding 400 ml of concentrated hydrochloric acid and slowly cooling to 0°C. The precipitate is filtered, washed first with 60 percent and then with 95 percent alcohol and dried at 80°C. Following this process, yields of hexammine varying from 10-44% of the theoretical were obtained.

Improved yields were obtained by the following modifications to the process.

1. Oxygen was used instead of air.
2. Bubbling was continued for fifteen hours.
3. To maintain the necessary excess of ammonia the proportion of ammonia in the reaction mixture was increased.

Using the original technique the average yield obtained over a series of ten preparations was 19.5% of the theoretical. The modified procedure gave an average yield over 20 preparations of 66.7% with some runs yielding more than 80% of the theoretical quantity.

In order to obtain cobalt as metal, electrolysis of an aqueous solution of the cobalt hexammine chloride was carried out. The electrolyte consisted of a saturated solution of the hexammine in distilled water. A further quantity of solid hexammine rested on the bottom of the plating bath and dissolved during the course of the run to replace that plated out from solution. The anode was platinum gauze, the cathode tantalum sheet. During the course of plating there was a continuous evolution of ammonia from the plating bath. The electrodeposited cobalt was easily stripped from the tantalum cathode and no tantalum was ever detected in the cobalt. The results of several preparations of cobalt by this method are shown in Table 2. The impurities present were detected spectrographically and none was found to be present in quantities greater than a "slight trace," i.e., a few parts per million. The total impurities in the final product were estimated at less than 10 ppm in all cases.

3. SYNTHESIS AND ZONE REFINING OF THE SILICIDES

After the preliminary work with powdered materials mentioned in the Introduction, attention was turned to preparation by fusion of the elements. First attempts involved the use of refractory crucibles but invariably some reaction between melt and crucible occurred. As can be seen from the results of these experiments, shown in Table 3, silicon nitride appeared to be the most promising material of those tried, but even in this case some reaction occurred. The search for suitable crucible materials was not carried further due to the success of the cold hearth method.

195

Table 2

Impurities in "Hexammine Cobalt"

| Run No. | Hexammine | | Cobalt Plating |
	Yield %	Impurities† present	Impurities Present*
1	65.6	None detected	Cu, Ag, Ca, Mg
2	84.6	None detected	Ca, Mg, Al
3	66.9	Cu, Ca, Si	Cu, Ca, Mg
4	72.7	Fe+, Cu, Zn, Al, Si, Mn	Cu, Ca, Mg, Al
5	75.5	None detected	Cu, Ca, Mg

†Trace
*Slight traces

Table 3

Reaction of Molten $CoSi_2$ With Refractory Crucibles

Crucible Material	Observed Effect
Quartz	Severe sticking, crucible invariably shattered.
Alumina	Some sticking, bright blue colouration, crucible cracked.
Zirconia	Severe sticking, crucible cracked.
Silicon Nitride	No sticking, slight reaction.

Cold hearth melting is a well established technique (e.g., in arc melting) and the use of induction heating for cold hearth melting of refractory metals is described by W. H. Shepherd [5] and by G. H. Schippereit et al. [4] The method was applied successfully both to the synthesis of the transition metal silicides and their purification by zone refining.

196

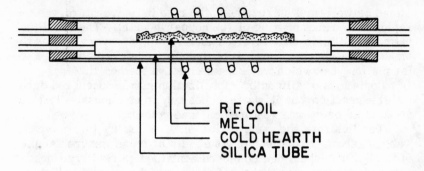

R.F. COIL
MELT
COLD HEARTH
SILICA TUBE

Figure 1. The Cold Hearth Zone Refiner.

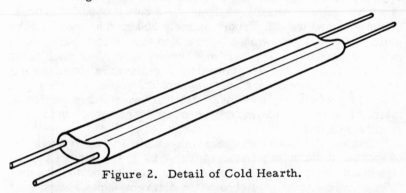

Figure 2. Detail of Cold Hearth.

The apparatus used is illustrated diagrammatically in Fig. 1 and the shape of the cold hearth itself can be seen from Fig. 2. For zone refining a single depression extends along the length of the hearth; for reactions several small depressions are used, each 3-4 inches long, so that a homogeneous melt can be obtained.

The material to be reacted or refined rests in the depression on the upper surface of the cold hearth. The cold hearth is constructed of copper and the surface of the depression is highly polished. An inert atmosphere is maintained in the quartz outer tube. The induction coil is mounted on a small trolley and connected to the high frequency generator by flexible leads. By means of a motor and pulley system the trolley can be moved along the length of the silica tube. The generator employed had an output of 7-1/2 kilowatts at 260,000 cycles.

The method was first applied to the silicides of cobalt. To carry out a reaction several lumps of silicon plus a portion of the cobalt required were first melted together in an atmosphere of 97% argon 3% hydrogen. Further quantities of cobalt were added until the required compound was formed. (This stepwise method was necessary due to the highly exothermic nature of the reaction. On occasions when stoichiometric quantities of the

197

elements were melted together, the rise in temperature was so rapid as to cause melting of the copper hearth.) The resulting button of silicide was inverted and remelted several times to ensure homogeneity. Several of these buttons were combined to form a long bar which was zone refined on the hearth.

Some loss of silicon by volatilization usually occurred during the reaction but it was unnecessary to compensate for this as stoichiometry was restored on zone refining.

To illustrate the purification of silicides by this method, Table 4 shows the effect of zone refining on an impure sample of $CoSi_2$. The specimen employed contained fairly large quantities of impurities so that purification could be readily followed by analysis.

The refining was carried out on a bar of cobalt disilicide 30 cm long and weighing approximately 200 g. The length of the molten zone was approximately 2 cm and the speed of zone movement 25 cm/hour. The bar was turned over after each pass. Iron and nickel were determined by chemical analysis, the remainder of the impurities spectrographically.

Using cobalt prepared by the method described in Section 2, material with a total impurity content less than 10 ppm. was readily obtained.

The method has been successfully applied to a large number of silicides which are listed in Table 5. In the case of CrSi it was found to be impossible to purify this compound by zone refining. Although the published phase diagram shows a maximum melting point for CrSi, the compound seems to decompose on melting and zone refining produces a bar with $Cr_5 Si_3$ at one end and $CrSi_2$ at the other.

Neither was it possible to zone refine IrSi and RhSi with the available equipment since their melting points were too high for a stable molten zone to be formed. The problem of zone refining high melting point materials does not appear to be solely a question of available power. The apparatus was tried with several high frequency generators with the following outputs and frequencies.

1. 7-1/2 kw, 260,000 cycles/sec.
2. 14 kw, 350,000 cycles/sec.
3. 25 kw, 450,000 cycles/sec.

Of these the 7-1/2 kw generator was by far the most effective, and it may be that lower frequencies are more favourable. It is interesting to note that only part of the power is induced in the specimen directly from the work coil. The copper hearth itself acts as a single turn coil and the side of the specimen resting on the cold hearth can be seen to heat more rapidly than its upper surface.

Table 4

Purification of CoSi$_2$ by Zone Refining

Specimen	Phase present‡	Impurities									
		Ni	Fe	Mn	Al	Ag	Ca	Cu	Ga	Mg	Na
Before refining	CoSi + 2% CoSi$_2$	0.25%*	0.12%*	s.t.	tr.	s.t.	s.t.	s.t.	s.t.	s.t.	s.t.
Starting end after 8 passes	CoSi	0.19%*	0.05%*	n.d.	s.t.	n.d.	n.d.	n.d.	n.d.	n.d.	n.d.
Finishing end after 8 passes	CoSi + 10% CoSi$_2$	0.69%*	0.25%	tr.	tr.	n.d.	n.d.	tr.	n.d.	n.d.	n.d.
Starting end after 14 passes	CoSi	tr.	s.t.	n.d.	n.d.	n.d.	n.d.	s.t.	n.d.	n.d.	n.d.
Finishing end after 14 passes	CoSi + 10% CoSi$_2$	Small + quantity		tr.	tr.	n.d.	s.t.	tr.	tr.	n.d.	n.d.

*Chemical analysis of Ni and Fe content
n.d. = not detected
tr. = trace 10-50 parts per million

s.t. = slight trace 1-10 parts per million
+ = chemical analysis not carried out
‡ = determined by X-ray powder photography

Table 5

Silicides Synthesized and Refined on Cold Hearth

Silicide	Melting Point °C	Crystal Structure	Final Impurity (1) Content
Co_2Si	1330		Sn*, Cu, Fe
CoSi	1460	Cubic, B20	Al, Ca, Fe
$CoSi_2$	1326	CaF_2 type	Ca, Mg
FeSi	1410	Cubic, B20	Cu, Mg
$FeSi_2$ (H)	1220		Not analysed
(L)	Dec. 995°C.		Mn*, Cu, Mg
CrSi	1600	Cubic, B20	Cu, Mg, Fe
$CrSi_2$	1550	Hexagonal	
MnSi	1275	Cubic, B20	Ca, Cu, Sn
$MnSi_2$		Tetragonal	
VSi_2	1750	Hexagonal	
IrSi		MnP type, B31	Fe*, Cu
RhSi		B31	Fe*, Cu, Al

(1) All slight traces, (i.e., 1-10 ppm.) except where marked * which contain trace quantities (10-50 ppm.) of the elements so marked.

(2) $FeSi_2$ (L) and CrSi were synthesized on the cold hearth but could not be zone refined owing to decomposition

$$CrSi \rightarrow Cr_5Si_3 + CrSi_2$$
$$FeSi_2 \rightarrow FeSi + FeSi_2 \text{ (H)}$$

IrSi, RhSi were only prepared in small quantities and not zone refined.

It has been found that a considerable improvement is obtained by winding the rf coil with a reverse turn at each end. The use of a reverse turn has been described by C. J. Frosch and L. Derick [2] for the zone refining of gallium phosphide where a flatter meniscus to the melt was obtained. However it was found that using the coil with a reverse turn at each end actually seemed to increase the power into the melt. Vanadium disilicide which could not be melted on the hearth with the ordinary coil was readily zone refined with the modified coil.

One point of considerable interest is the extent to which pickup of copper from the hearth occurs. It is evident from the spectrographic analysis that such pickup, if it occurs at all, is very slight. The reasons for the lack of copper contamination are thought to be:

(1) The high thermal conductivity of the copper ensures that the temperature of the upper surface of the hearth is comparatively low. Measurements of heat flow through a copper hearth indicate that the surface temperature of the copper is 50-60°C. [6]

(2) A thin layer of the silicide in contact with the hearth remains solid. This is proved by the fact that a bar with a molten zone in the middle can be pushed along the hearth. Under these conditions the diffusion of copper into the specimen should be small.

The successful application of cold hearth zone refining to a considerable number of silicides indicates that it should have general application to the purification of reactive materials. In this respect it may be considered as an alternative to floating zone refining. It has the advantage that it is much simpler to carry out in practice. However there are several disadvantages:

1. It does not appear possible to grow single crystals due to nucleation at the copper surface. However, it should be possible to pull single crystals from the water cooled crucible described by Schippereit [4].

2. Considerable stresses are introduced into the specimens due to the very large thermal gradients involved.

3. It is restricted to materials which do not wet copper. However cold hearths have also been successfully operated made of aluminium and silver. For example, an attempt to prepare $MoGe_2$ on a copper hearth was unsuccessful due to wetting and subsequent reaction with the copper. No reaction occurred on an aluminium hearth.

ACKNOWLEDGEMENTS

Thanks are due to Mr. John Knight for suggesting the method of cobalt purification, to Mr. Gordon Spence for very valuable work on the development of the cold hearth and to the Plessey Company Limited for permission to publish this paper.

REFERENCES

1. J. Bjerrum and J. P. Reynolds, Inorganic Syntheses Vol. II, McGraw-Hill (1946).
2. C. J. Frosch and L. Derick, J. Electrochem. Soc., 108, 251 (1961).

3. P. Schwarzkopf and R. Kieffer, Refractory Hard Metals, Macmillan (1953).
4. G. H. Schippereit, A. F. Leatherman and D. Evers, J. Metals 13, 140 (1961).
5. W. H. Shepherd, J. Sci. Inst. 37, 177 (1960).
6. W. H. Shepherd, private communication.

DISCUSSION

S. H. SKALKA (Transitron): Will you comment on the physical properties of the disilicides prepared by this method?

R. M. WARE (Plessey, U.K.): Vanadium Disilicide is quite solid and quite sound. There was no difficulty with this material. With chromium disilicide, some difficulties occurred due to shattering of the material. However, by very slow zoning and by annealing the compound afterwards, it was possible to obtain sound ingots.

S. H. SKALKA (Transitron): What about iron disilicide?

R. M. WARE (Plessey, U.K.): Iron disilicide, as I pointed out, has two forms; one, which is of interest and which is a semiconductor, can't be made on the cold hearth since it decomposes well below the melting point. The other disilicide forms a good mechanically sound bar. If one wants to make the low temperature disilicide by melting the required quantities of iron and silicon and then by annealing below the transformation point, it is found that, due to considerable volume changes involved in the phase transformation, the bar disintegrates on annealing. However, this can be overcome if one carries out the reaction on the cold hearth. The product, when thus formed, is no longer quite as reactive and it can be melted in quartz. If it is melted in quartz, the temperature then dropped to just below the transformation point, and then annealed for long periods--three or four weeks are necessary very often at this temperature--then one can obtain sound bars of the low temperature form of iron disilicide at the low temperature of iron disilicide.

J. F. MILLER (Battelle): In respect to the hearths, could you say something about the thickness of copper that is used?

R. M. WARE (Plessey, U.K.): An ordinary piece of 1 inch copper tubing is deformed into the shape of the hearth. I am not sure of the exact thickness, but it would be about 1/16 of an inch.

J. F. MILLER (Battelle): Have you attempted to use a cold hearth for crystal pulling?

R. M. WARE (Plessey, U.K.): I noted a publication recently by Battelle on the cold hearth crucible and it occurred to me that one could probably use this to maintain a melt and pull a crystal from it in this way, but we haven't tried it yet.

R. H. L. LESCARTS (Societé Générale Métallurgique de Hoboken, Belgium): What is the melting temperature of cobalt silicide?

R. M. WARE (Plessey, U.K.): Cobalt monosilicide melts at 1450 Centigrade, and the disilicide is somewhat lower, about 1320 or 1330.

R. H. L. LESCARTS (Societé Générale Métallurgique de Hoboken, Belgium): I do not understand what the difficulties are that you encounter to obtain single crystals in your copper crucible.

R. M. WARE (Plessey, U.K.): The material is always in contact with the cold surface and nucleation appears to take place readily from the surface, so that a large number of crystals probably 3 or 4 millimeters wide by a centimeter or 2 centimeters long are obtained in the course of zone refining on this hearth.

I. M. RITCHIE (Transitron): How successful were you in your purification as measured by the resistivity profile down the bar after zone refining?

R. M. WARE (Plessey, U.K.): I showed in the cobalt disilicide the impurities building up in the lower end of the bar, and this is generally found in practice in other materials as well.

I. M. RITCHIE (Transitron): I appreciate that in zone refining you get a build-up of impurities at one end. In the bulk of the bar, how did the resistivity vary?

R. M. WARE (Plessey, U.K.): This depends very much on the individual material. In the case of the more metallic silicides, there is not a very great variation in resistivity. In the case of the disilicides, there is considerable variation. I do not have the figures available here. The results of measurements of the electrical properties of these materials are all in the course of publication elsewhere and I will gladly provide you with a reprint.

H. B. SACHSE (Keystone Carbon): You mentioned the sticking density on certain substrates. Is there a definite reaction which can be found in this case?

R. M. WARE (Plessey, U.K.): I think in the case of the oxide crucibles that there was a reaction with oxygen and silicon to form a silicate. In the case of alumina, one gets some aluminum silicate and this caused sticking.

F. D. ROSI CHAIRMAN (RCA Lab.): Have you measured the thermoelectric power versus temperature, above room temperature, and, if so, what was the highest temperature that you achieved before intrinsic conduction set in as evidenced by a sharp decrease in the thermoelectric power?

203

R. M. WARE (Plessey, U.K.): This depends upon the individual materials. In the case of the cobalt monosilicide, for instance, there is a steady drop. At room temperature, it is about 100, falling to about 60 to 70 at about 600 degrees Centigrade. In the case of iron silicide, work has not reached a very high state of development in that this is a much more difficult material to work with. However, at 600 degrees Centigrade, it appears to be still rising. The other materials vary between these two extremes.

A. SNOWMAN (High Purity Metals): In 1959, the Russians did considerable investigation into the thermoelectric properties of the silicides. Do you have any indication of whether your methods yielded any improvement in the general thermoelectric properties of the silicides?

R. M. WARE (Plessey, U.K.): Yes. In general, silicides prepared by these methods tend to have a higher thermoelectric power and, in many cases, lower resistivity; in other words, the thermoelectric properties are generally better than the figures quoted by the Russians. Again, these will be reported in full elsewhere. I think the reason is that most of the Russian work appears to be done purely by melting together the elements without any attempt to isolate the stoichiometric compound afterwards. Invariably, there is some silicon loss, so that in my opinion, a good deal of the Russian work was done on two-phase material.

PURIFICATION EFFECTS IN SILICON CARBIDE
UNDER THERMAL GRADIENTS

R. S. Braman, E. H. Tompkins, S. Susman and V. Raziunas
Armour Research Foundation
Chicago, Illinois

Much progress has been made in recent years in the development of semiconducting materials which exhibit a high efficiency as thermoelectric materials. (Many of these cannot be used at temperatures above 400°C and, so, are limited in efficiency.) Emphasis has therefore been placed on the development of high temperature materials to take advantage of improved Carnot efficiency. At elevated temperatures, however, undesirable effects can occur such as the diffusion of doping materials and electrode materials and decomposition or reaction of the thermoelectric matrix material.

Because of the importance of these effects, this program was undertaken with the objective of developing methods for studying the behavior of impurity elements in refractory materials under thermal gradients. Part of the objective of the program was also to ascertain if the impurity transport effects could be used in the purification of high temperature semiconducting materials.

Impurity transport was first considered from a theoretical point of view. A model for diffusion in a homogenous medium was assumed and a mathematical treatment of this model was developed. Of the possible forces acting to cause impurity diffusion, the main ones considered were concentration gradient, electric field and thermal gradient. At the high temperatures used electric fields were relatively small. Experiments were designed to determine, (1) the magnitude of the thermal transpiration effect, and (2) the relative rate of diffusion or diffusibility of different elements under similar combinations of forces. The combination of forces included uncertainties due to interactions between different diffusing components, but the general ordering of the elements according to ease of diffusion indicated which elements were most useful as doping agents in thermoelectric devices.

Silicon carbide was chosen as the main study material because of its ready availability in the form of single crystals and polycrystalline rods. Impurity elements were of sufficient variety and concentration to permit the use of spectrographic analytical methods.

Two types of experimental arrangements were employed to study impurity transport in silicon carbide. The intense thermal gradient method, involved establishing a temperature gradient by means of a high frequency induction heater at one end of a silicon carbide rod, sectioning the rod after the heat treatment, and then analyzing the rod slices for impurity element concentration. The second type of experiment was a spectrometric diffusibility method in which a crystal of silicon carbide (or rod) was mounted in an inert gas chamber and arced with a d.c. arc. Moving plate studies were performed to obtain a time versus impurity concentration plot. All work was done in an inert atmosphere to avoid rapid oxidation reactions.

PROCEDURE FOR THE SPECTROMETRIC
DIFFUSIBILITY STUDIES

The inert gas chamber used for spectrometric diffusibility studies is shown in Figure 1. Following alignment of the sample (rod or crystal) and counter electrodes with the optical axis of the spectrograph, a d.c. arc was struck between the auxiliary and sample electrodes until the silicon carbide crystal (or rod) specimen became heated to glowing. The auxiliary arc was then extinguished, followed immediately by ignition of the discharge across the analytical gap. This preheating technique decreased crystal shattering from thermal shock upon initiation of the discharge. All electrodes used were ultra pure spectroscopic grade graphite to prevent possible contamination of the crystal surface.

After considerable experimentation, the following conditions were established as optimum for the spectrometric diffusibility studies.

d.c. arc current	- 7.5 amps
Inert gas flow	- 3.8 cu ft He per hour
Slit width	- 30 microns
Photographic Plates	- Eastman Kodak 103-0
Sectoring	- 4 step rotating sector with 2.51 step height ratio
Ignition (pretreatment)	- 57 sec preheat time - 3 sec initiation of the arc (not on the plate)
Exposure Interval	- 7 sec with 3 sec dead time

206

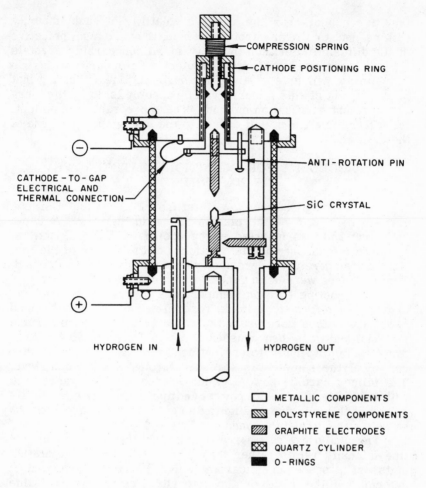

Figure 1. Inert Gas Chamber for Spectrometric
Diffusibility Experiments

    Consecutive exposures of the arc were taken without inter-
rupting it by moving the photographic plate detector of the
spectrograph at timed intervals of ten seconds with seven seconds exposure time per plate. Photometric analysis of the
consecutive spectrograms obtained yielded integrated intensity
ratios over each exposure interval. The data were obtained by
measuring the intensity ratio between a given impurity line and
a silicon line in each exposure. The intensity ratio method was
used to compensate for variations in the amount of sample
vaporized during each exposure interval. The curves are
strictly only plots of intensity ratio versus exposure time, but

207

they are indicative of the relative volatility of each impurity with respect to silicon carbide. Hence, they are also indicative of the diffusibility of each impurity in silicon carbide crystals under the action of a thermal gradient. An impurity with zero diffusibility will give a straight horizontal line indicating that no movement of this impurity can be accomplished by the thermal gradient purification method. The more rapid the boilout, the faster the element will diffuse to the low temperature end of the crystal.

PROCEDURE FOR INDUCTION HEATING TYPE OF EXPERIMENTS

The working chamber for direct induction heating of silicon carbide rods at 5 megacycles is shown in Figure 2. A 2 to 3 inch long rod was inserted in the cooled base piece, and the single turn focusing coil was positioned at the top end of the rod. Various temperatures were used with a two hour heating period. Temperatures were determined with an optical pyrometer.

After cooling to room temperature pieces of rod approximately 2-3 millimeters thick were sliced off with a diamond saw. The slices were washed in nitric acid to remove surface material and were then crushed in a steel mortar with molybdenum shielding plates to prevent contamination. Each crushed portion of the sample was screened through a 150-mesh sieve. The silicon carbide powder which passed through was mixed with two parts of graphite powder and approximately eight milligrams of this mixture was ignited in a 10-amp d.c. arc until the sample was completely consumed.

The analytical data were obtained in the form of spectral line intensity ratios rather than in conventional concentration units. The spectrochemical analytical technique consisted of determining the ratio of the impurity element spectral line intensity to the matrix element spectral line intensity. This ratio is designated the spectral line intensity ratio and is related to concentration of impurity element in samples by:

$$I_{impurity}/I_{matrix} = k(C_{impurity}/C_{matrix})p$$

Normally, the relation between the intensity ratio and concentration ratio can be established using standard samples of known composition, but such standard samples were not available for the type of silicon carbide used. Consequently, the intensity ratios were utilized as a direct measure of concentration. This procedure was considered to be satisfactory for the purposes of this study since the significant information desired was the relative variation in concentration produced by the thermal gradient technique rather than the precise determination of the

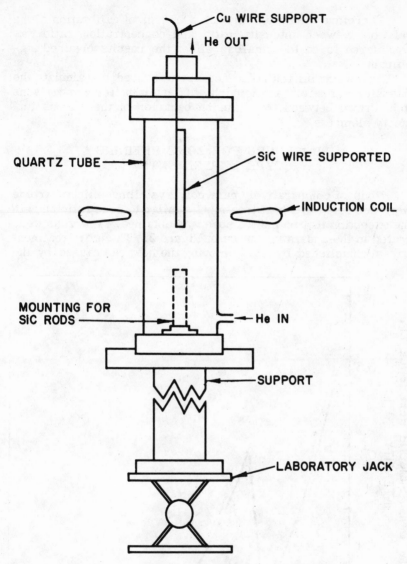

Figure 2. Inert Gas Chamber for Induction
Heating Experiments.

true impurity element concentrations. It was recognized that an
error in concentrations variations exists if the exponent p in the
aforementioned relation is not unity. Tests made with National
Bureau of Standards silicon carbide powder indicated that the
analytical lines used were homogenous with the 2970 and 2631 Å
silicon lines.

Therefore the error introduced by lack of calibration of the relation between intensity ratio and concentration ratio was considered to be too small to effect the results obtained significantly.

The same silicon reference line was used to calculate the intensity ratios for each impurity to permit better comparisons to be drawn between the diffusion behavior of the various impurity elements.

PROCEDURE FOR ZONE REFINING
TYPE EXPERIMENTS

Rods of comparatively pure polycrystalline silicon carbide were subjected to a heat treatment similar to zone refining with the exception that no melted zone was obtained. The rods were heated in the apparatus shown in Figure 2. The heat treatment was accomplished by slowly moving the hot zone caused by the

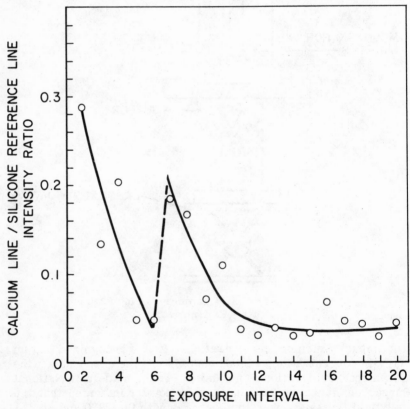

Figure 3. Diffusibility of Calcium in SiC Crystal.

210

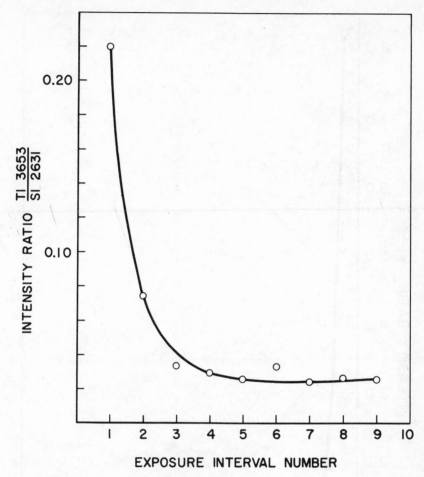

Figure 4. Diffusibility of Titanium in SiC Crystal.

focusing coil down the rod; one inch of rod was treated per hour; two passes were used on each heat treated rod. An alternative procedure was to lower a rod through a carbon susceptor ring in one-eighth inch increments at a rate of one inch per hour with two passes per rod.

RESULTS AND DISCUSSION-SPECTROMETRIC
DIFFUSIBILITY EXPERIMENTS

Selected results of spectrometric diffusibility experiments are shown in Figures 3, 4, 5 and 6. In all cases the predicted change in impurity element concentration was observed. Figure 3 illustrates the effect observed when a crystal cracks during the arcing process. Cracking the crystal exposes a new

211

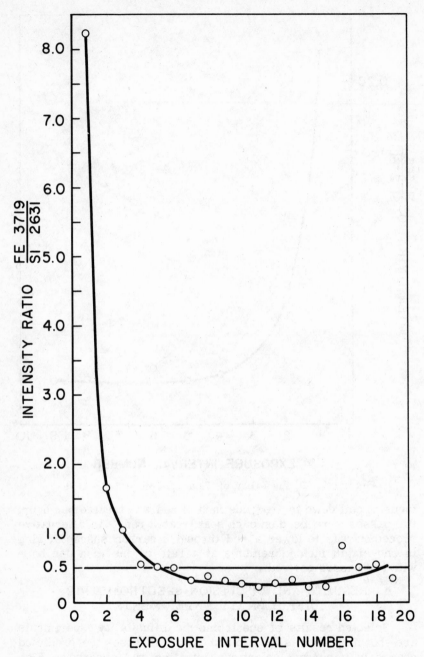

Figure 5. Diffusibility of Iron in SiC Crystal.

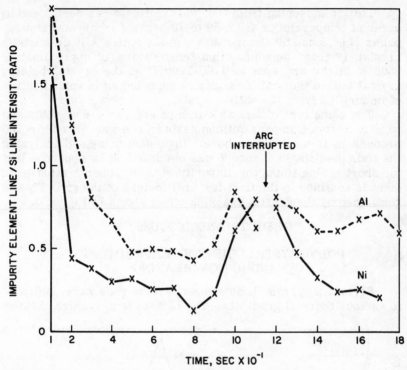

Figure 6. Impurity Element Concentration as a Function
of Time in an Arced SiC Crystal.

crystal surface not yet subjected to an intense thermal gradient
and the sharp decrease in the impurity element concentration
relative to the matrix concentration is again observed. Nickel,
iron vanadium and aluminum (not illustrated here) all showed
the same effect. Figures 4, 5, and 6 all show the impurity diffusion effect when no cracking of the single crystal is encountered. In the experiment from which the data for Figure 6 was
obtained, the spectrographic arc was interrupted after 110 seconds of burning time. A black powdery layer was observed on
the partially burned crystal surface. This was removed by
polishing with silicon carbide powder and a piece of cloth. No
sharp decrease in impurity concentration was observed upon
re-ignition of the spectrographic arc indicating that the impurity
diffusion takes place in the silicon carbide crystal and not just
over a surface layer. No great increase in impurity element
concentration was observed throughout the burning of the crystal. This may be due to the loss of impurity elements by volatilization from the side of the crystal away from the arc or by
transfer of impurity elements to the graphite holder.

213

Lattice loosening from thermal treatment has been found to occur at temperatures from 50 to 70 percent of crystal melting points [1]. Since the temperature in the entire silicon carbide crystal is from decomposition temperature of approximately 2500°K at the arc spot to 1700-1800°C at the crystal holder, crystal lattice thermal loosening is expected as is volatilization of impurities from the entire crystal.

The same type of data as shown in Figures 4-6 was obtained when a Norton Company silicon carbide rod was arced for 200 seconds in an inert atmosphere. Upon sectioning and analyzing the rod, the data in Figure 7 was obtained. It is apparent that for short arcing times the impurity element concentration gradient is confined to the first few millimeters of the rod. This is confirmed by the crystal cracking effect shown in Figure 3.

RESULTS AND DISCUSSION

POLYCRYSTALLINE ROD EXPERIMENTS - INDUCTION HEATING

Several polycrystalline silicon carbide rods were subjected to various thermal gradients. The highest temperature of these

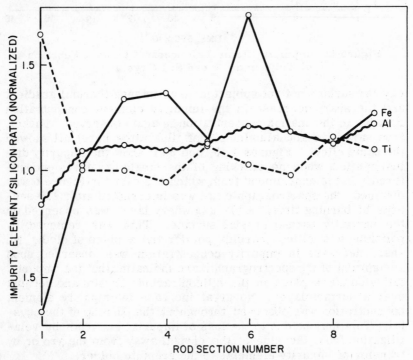

Figure 7. Normalized Impurity Distribution in an Arced SiC Rod.

214

gradients ranged from 975°C to 1650°C. One rod was arced in a d.c. spectrographic arc to give a gradient with approximately 2500°C highest temperature. The rod was sectioned and analyzed spectrographically using the intensity ratio method described previously. Data were plotted by normalizing the impurity element ratios and plotting this value versus the rod section number or length along the heat treated rod. Data was rather scattered but definite impurity diffusion was observed at the highest gradient temperature above approximately 1000°C; impurity element diffusion was towards the cold part of the gradient and was found to be dependent upon the diffusing element (see Figure 8). This is probably due to the molecular form of the element. For example, the mobility of aluminum metal atoms in a polycrystalline silicon carbide rod must be much different from the mobility of aluminum oxide molecules. The spectrographic technique measures total element concentration and gives an indication of total regardless of chemical combination, however, and the total diffusion effect observed would illustrate a combined effect. This undoubtedly can cause erratic results, depending upon the relative amount of impurity element in combined or uncombined state and the relative mobility of the atoms and molecules of the element in question.

Zone refining experiments were performed on the rods in an attempt to utilize the diffusion effect in a purification process. Impurity bands were observed to move down the rod but there still appeared to be a residual impurity concentration present. In no case was a marked change in nitrogen concentration observed.

CONCLUSION

Two methods have been developed for studying the effect of thermal gradients on impurity elements in refractory materials. From these methods information can be obtained on the expected behavior of thermoelectric materials at high temperatures and on the feasibility of employing a high thermal gradient as a purification technique. Silicon carbide has been studied and found to exhibit impurity element diffusion above 1000°C in the presence of a thermal gradient. The polycrystalline silicon carbide rods studied can be purified by approximately a factor of 10 by the application of a thermal gradient, however this is dependent upon the diffusing element. Nitrogen did not appear to diffuse under the experimental conditions employed.

A suggested study for future work would be to determine the effect of molecular form of the impurity elements on diffusion. Techniques other than emission spectrography would be required.

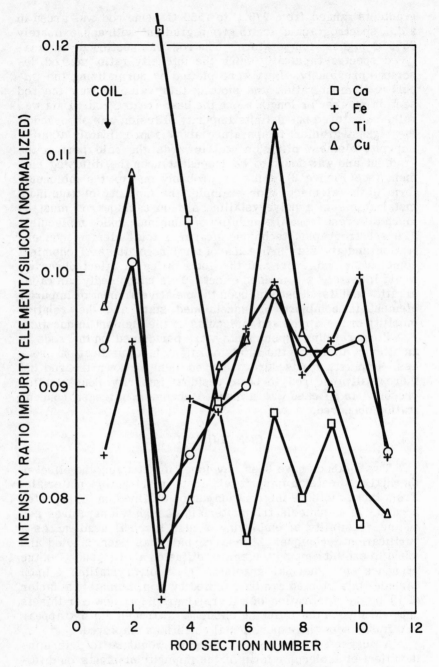

Figure 8. Normalized Impurity Distribution in an
Induction Heated SiC Rod.

ACKNOWLEDGEMENT

The work described in·this study was supported by the Air Research and Development Division, USAF.

REFERENCE

1. J. R. O'Connor and J. Smiltens, Silicon Carbide, A High Temperature Semiconductor, Permagon Press, New York, 1960, p. 232.

DISCUSSION

B. LOVE (Research Chemicals): In the spectrographic treatment, did you check back to a lower portion of the rod to see whether there was actually diffusion of the elements? Did you check to make sure that there was just not fractional sublimation and removal of these elements at different rates?

R. S. BRAMAN (Armour): As pointed out in the experimental part we performed analyses of a sectioned, arced silicon carbide rod. The period of heating was comparatively short in this experiment and marked changes in impurity element concentration were confined to the heated end of the rod.

B. LOVE (Research Chemicals): The thing I was wondering about was whether in ordinary spectrographic analysis, even where you burn the sample completely, you frequently find that there is a different rate of volatilization of the various elements.

R. S. BRAMAN (Armour): Yes, this is precisely what we were trying to point out. This is dependent upon the diffusibility of the elements.

B. LOVE (Research Chemicals): Is it the diffusibility or the selected rate of volatilization?

R. S. BRAMAN (Armour): The relative rate of volatilization is undoubtedly at least partially dependent upon diffusion of impurities to the surface of arced samples.

L. R. WEISBERG (RCA Lab.): How large were the crystals that you were working with?

R. S. BRAMAN (Armour): Most of them were about four or five millimeters high by a couple of millimeters across. We also worked with some very thin single crystals which were about a half a centimeter in width and about a centimeter high, and a couple of multimeters thick.

L. R. WEISBERG (RCA Lab.): Did you ever measure the thermal gradients across these samples from end to end?

R. S. BRAMAN (Armour): The decomposition temperature of silicon carbide is approximately 2500 degrees which is above the range of an optical pyrometer. With the rod we were able to measure the thermal gradient with an optical pyrometer. It was comparatively linear with length, when heated with an induction heater. In the case of the rods we went from 950 at the bottom of the rod down to about 2000 degrees. The impurity transport effect seemed to stop at about 1000 degrees, and we found that there was no diffusibility in eight hours in the rod experiment performed with the maximum temperature of 1000 degrees.

L. R. WEISBERG (RCA Lab.): Do you mean diffusibility outward or do you mean diffusibility down the rod?

R. S. BRAMAN (Armour): Down the rod.

A. J. ROSENBERG CHAIRMAN (Tyco): The question the previous speaker asked was whether there was diffusion from the surface or was it down the rod, in which case the thermal gradient would have nothing to do with it. Do you know whether it diffused down the rod specifically?

R. S. BRAMAN (Armour): We realized that an impurity element gradient effect may occur in a single section of silicon carbide rod. Sections were treated with nitric acid to remove sublimed loosely bound surface material before analysis of each section and we assume, therefore, that the major effect observed in diffusion of impurity elements down the rod.

L. R. WEISBERG (RCA Lab.): I am surprised that solubility plays no role here. For example, if an element has a retrograde solubility, that is, a higher solubility at higher temperatures, it would be somewhat surprising if it diffused from that section to a lower temperature section where the solubility is lower.

218

PURIFICATION OF SOME II-VI COMPOUNDS USING ION-EXCHANGE RESINS

M. J. Presland
Associated Electrical Industries
(Woolwich) Ltd.
Harlow, Essex, England

For some applications in the fields of luminescence and photo-conductivity there is a need for very pure zinc and cadmium sulphides. Neither of these materials are easily purified once they have been prepared, and because of this difficulty it is usual to purify the reagents used in their preparation, or to synthesise the sulphides from the pure elements.

It is with the former methods of preparation that this paper is concerned, whereby zinc sulphide is precipitated from an ammoniacal solution of a soluble zinc salt by hydrogen sulphide, and cadmium sulphide is similarly precipitated from an acid solution of a soluble cadmium salt.

To obtain materials of adequate purity the solutions are passed through ion-exchange resin columns [1]. This method has been adopted because, firstly, there is no theoretical limit to the amount of purification possible; secondly the process takes place in a closed system thus reducing the risk of contamination without the necessity of providing special clean rooms, and thirdly the process is fairly cheap since the resins are easily regenerated.

Because of these features the ion-exchange method is particularly suited to small scale production of high purity material in a research laboratory, although large-scale production is also possible.

In order to secure a high degree of purity efficiently it is necessary to work with a concentrated solution and to utilise a system in which there is a large distribution coefficient.

Special emphasis has been laid upon the separation of copper, manganese, iron and nickel from zinc and cadmium since these metals have insoluble sulphides and their presence affects the electrical and optical properties of zinc and cadmium sulphides.

In order to obtain the high degree of separation required it is necessary to employ complexing agents.

219

Published data on the separation of zinc and cadmium for analytical purposes suggest the use of the halide complexes in conjunction with anion exchange resins [3,4]. Kraus and Nelson [2] have carried out an extensive investigation of the adsorption of elements from hydrochloric acid onto anion exchange resins in connection with the analysis of fission products. Our work differs slightly in requirements from the analyst in that we require a separation greater by several orders of magnitude, but do not require a quantitative yield. Often both analytical and purification requirements are met by the same system, as in the case of the chloride complexes.

A series of equilibration experiments between 0.1M solutions of the various metal chlorides in hydrochloric acid of varying concentration, and air dried Amberlite IRA-401 in the chloride form were conducted. The high degree of adsorption of zinc and cadmium in 2N hydrochloric acid compared with the negligible adsorption of copper and the complete absence of adsorption of manganese, iron and nickel is ideal for purification purposes. This inference is borne out in practice. A column of Amberlite IRA-401 was loaded with zinc to which had been added small amounts of cadmium, copper, manganese, iron and nickel. The latter four elements are removed quickly on elution with 2N hydrochloric acid and their concentration rapidly drops below the limits of trace analysis using organic reagents. Continued elution failed to remove zinc or cadmium but changing the eluant to water allowed rapid removal of both zinc and cadmium. The zinc leads the cadmium owing to the fact that cadmium is rather more strongly adsorbed in neutral solution. This difference is insufficient for the removal of traces of zinc from cadmium or of traces of cadmium from zinc. If such a separation is required the iodide complexes offer a possible solution but the separation is not nearly as great as that of copper manganese iron and nickel from zinc and cadmium.

According to Baggot and Wilcocks [3] the absence of sulphate allows some adsorption of the zinc at lower concentrations, therefore the zinc and cadmium were added as sulphates. The graphs show that the optimum concentration of potassium iodide is about 10 gm/ℓ. A 50-50 mixture of zinc and cadmium, as sulphates, was introduced onto a column of Deacidite-FF and elution was carried out with a solution of 10 gm/ℓ potassium iodide and 17 gm/ℓ (0.1M) potassium sulphate. Recent experiments showed that the zinc is removed early as expected, but it tails badly. In addition traces of cadmium are removed from the column and appear with the zinc in the effluent. These traces are too small to be shown on the graph but amount to a contamination of about 0.3%. The column was then washed with water. Only traces of cadmium were detected. Subsequent elution with 5N ammonium hydroxide removed the cadmium but the final traces of zinc were also removed so that the contamination was again about 0.3%. The eluting solutions were analysed and were shown not to be the source of these contaminations.

Further investigations of the zinc - cadmium separation are at present in progress. Disproportionate quantities of zinc and and cadmium have not yet been used in this experiment.

The sulphides may be required free of halogen. Conversion of zinc or cadmium chlorides or iodides to sulphates, nitrates, etc., is conveniently achieved by means of anion exchange resins. Thus conversion of zinc chloride to zinc sulphate occurs when the chloride solution is passed down a column in the sulphate form.

The purification of the other reagents by similar means has not yet been completed. It may prove advantageous to use ammonium sulphide rather than hydrogen sulphide as a precipitating agent.

Although very few elements have so far been considered in this work it is possible to predict from the published data that many other metals should also be removed, for instance the alkali and alkaline earth metals show no tendency to be adsorbed from hydrochloric acid solutions [2].

The work has so far been carried out on a small scale and by such methods as have been described the amount of sulphide required per batch determines the size of the column required. A yield of 100 gm of zinc sulphide would require about two kilograms of resin.

The ideal process would be the removal of all impurities from the zinc or cadmium solutions in one stage by complete adsorption of the impurities onto the resin, when the process would resemble the de-ionisation of water, and a small resin column could then purify large quantities of zinc or cadmium.

REFERENCES

1. R. Kunin "Ion Exchange Resins" John Wiley & Sons, Inc., New York, N. Y., 1958 (general).
2. K. A. Kraus and F. Nelson "Proceedings of the International Conference on the Peaceful Uses of Atomic Energy" Vol. 7, United Nations, New York, N. Y., 1956. Anion Exchange Studies of Fission Products, pp. 113-125.
3. E. R. Baggott and R. G. W. Wilcocks, The Analyst 83, 53, (1955).
4. J. A. Hunter and C. C. Miller, The Analyst 79, 483, (1954).

DISCUSSION

D. H. WILKINS (General Electric): I would like to make a few comments. I believe you mentioned iron and nickel were comparable on your ion exchange resins. This is not correct. I believe you will find that iron shows stronger absorption than nickel. Also, on the zinc-cadmium separation, I think you will find this works very well if you go to dilute hydrochloric instead of using water. If you go down to about a hundredth normal hydrochloric, you will take the zinc out ahead of the cadmium. Also on the cadmium ion exchange, you can take zinc and cadmium through the resins very easily and leave the other elements behind, which is advantageous for the separation you are using. I would also recommend that you stay away from a hydroxide formula or you are going to have trouble.

M. J. PRESLAND (Assoc. Electrical Ind.): I would like to comment on the use of very dilute hydrochloric acid. In order to get the enormous separations required you really want a system which takes out one ion very strongly and which rejects the other completely. Otherwise you have to fractionate the solution by continued dilution. The zinc and cadmium are both taken up by the solutions, even the neutral solutions, and I feel that in order to try to keep the process suitable it is necessary to use the very high separation regions. I know this has been done, using very dilute solutions of hydrochloric acid.

D. H. WILKINS (General Electric): This is true, and actually the separation using the dilute hydrochloric is not particularly good for large quantities. You have a problem in that, if you try to load the resin too heavily, you will find that the cadmium will get through. This is using a hundredth normal hydrochloric. It is not the kind of a separation you want. You prefer the kind where the minor constituent hangs on and the other shows no absorption. I am afraid you are not going to find this to be the case with zinc and cadmium. With a cation resin you will find that both cadmium and zinc can be taken through quite readily by virtue of forming the chloride complexes, whereas the other metals, such as iron, nickel, magnesium, and copper, are not taken through the resin. You will find mercury is going to remain with the cadmium and zinc. Tin is another one and there are a few others that will come through.

M. J. PRESLAND (Assoc. Elect. Inc.): I know there are a few others, but we haven't been troubled by these elements in the past in making the preparations of zinc sulfide.

W. C. BENZING (Merck): Does the speaker have any data comparing the sulfides made by this technique with the more conventional solution purifications.

M. J. PRESLAND (Assoc. Elect. Ind.): We haven't arrived at the stage of being able to run the complete process in order to make this sort of comparison yet.

W. C. BENZING (Merck): Have you performed chemical analyses? What was the highest separation you were able to achieve between cadmium and zinc by using this process?

M. J. PRESLAND (Assoc. Elect. Ind.): The elution curves were done using fractions, and starting from a 50/50 mixture, the results yielded about 0.3 per cent of contamination by weight.

ARENE-METAL π-COMPLEXES AND THEIR PURIFICATION

Minoru Tsutsui
New York University
College of Engineering
Research Division
New York, New York

I. INTRODUCTION

Since the discoveries of ferrocene (1952) by Kealy and Pauson[4] and bis-diphenyl-chromium (1954) by Tsutsui, Onsager and Zeiss [7, 8], representatives of transition metals or "sandwich" compounds, π-complex chemistry has progressed remarkably.

In addition to metal derivatives of the cyclopentadienyl anion and arenes (Figures 1 and 2), a great number of related compounds have been synthesized.

Mixed arene-metal π-complexes, five and six-membered [2] and five and eight-membered ring [5] metal complexes have been reported. (Figure 3).

The use of metal carbonyls stimulated the progress of synthesis of arene-metal π-complexes, particularly half-sandwich-π-complexes, cyclopentadiene-, benzene-, cycloheptanium-, cyclooctatetraene-, cyclobutadiene-, and other π-complexes [1, 6, 14, 16]*.

This paper reports several new arene π-complexes which have been synthesized in our laboratory, and also discusses the preparation, the stability and the purification of arene π-complexes.

II. METHODS FOR PREPARATION

The preparation methods for charged and uncharged arene-metal-π-complexes are listed as follows:

---

*Review articles on cyclopentadienyl and arene π-complex chemistry.

224

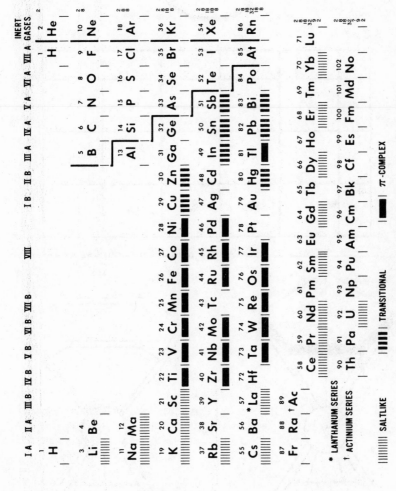

Figure 1. Cyclopentadienyl Metal Compounds.

225

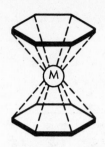

	V	VI	VII	VIII	
4	V	Cr	Mn	Fe	Co
5		Mo		Ru	Rh
6		W	Re	Os	Ir

Figure 2. Bis-Arene Metal Compounds.

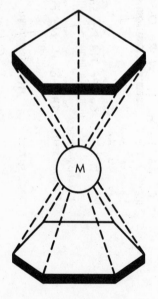

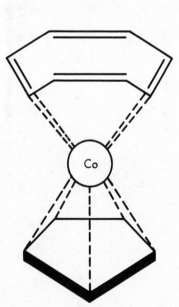

Figure 3.

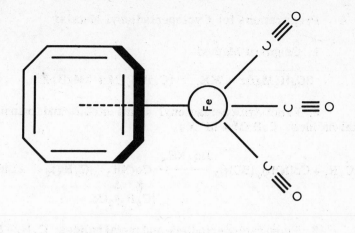

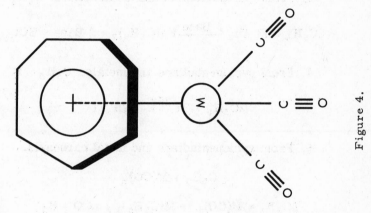

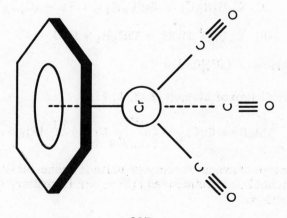

Figure 4.

A. Preparations for Cyclopentadienyl Metals:

1. Grignard Method

$$2C_5H_5MgBr + MX_n \rightarrow (C_5H_5)_2 M + 2MgBr\overset{.}{X}$$

2. From cyclopentadienyl alkali metals and transition metal halides: $C_5H_5M + M'X_n$

$$2LiC_5H_5 + Co(NH_3)_4(SCN)_2 \xrightarrow{\text{liq. NH}_3} Co(NH_3)_6(C_5H_5)_2 + 2LiSCN$$
$$\downarrow \Delta$$
$$(C_5H_5)_2Co$$

3. From cyclopentadiene and metal halides: $C_5H_6 + MX_n$

$$2C_5H_6 + Fe Cl_2 \xrightarrow{\text{2 Base}} Fe(C_5H_5)_2 + 2 \text{ Base} \cdot HCl$$

4. From cyclopentadiene and metals: $C_5H_6 + M$

$$2C_5H_6 + Tl \xrightarrow{358°} C_5H_5Tl$$

5. From cyclopentadiene and metal carbonyls:

$$C_5H_6 + M(CO)_n$$

$$2C_5H_6 + M(CO)_n \rightarrow M(C_5H_5)_2 + nCO + H_2$$

6. Other methods

(a) C_5H_5HgCl or $Hg(C_5H_5)_2 + Fe \rightarrow (C_5H_5)_2Fe$

(b) $C_5H_6 + TlOH \rightarrow TlC_5H_5 + H_2O$

B. Arene-π-Complexes

1. Grignard Method [2, 3, 4, 11]

$$3\langle\hexagon\rangle MgBr + CrCl_3 \rightarrow (\langle\hexagon\rangle CrBr)_5 \xrightarrow{KI} \text{(Figure 5)}$$

A new type of arene-π-complex, salts of arene-bis-dipyridyl-chromium, has been synthesized [13] in our laboratory by applying this method.

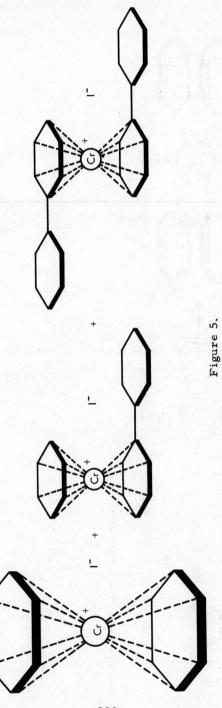

Figure 5.

229

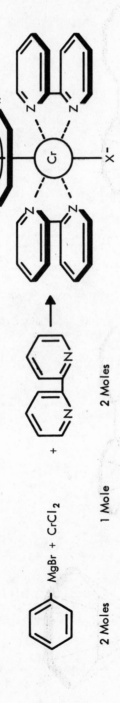

+ 2 Moles

MgBr + CrCl₂

2 Moles   1 Mole

$$2 \text{ Moles} \quad 1 \text{ Mole} \quad 2 \text{ Moles}$$

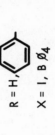

R = H,

X = I, BØ₄

Figure 6.

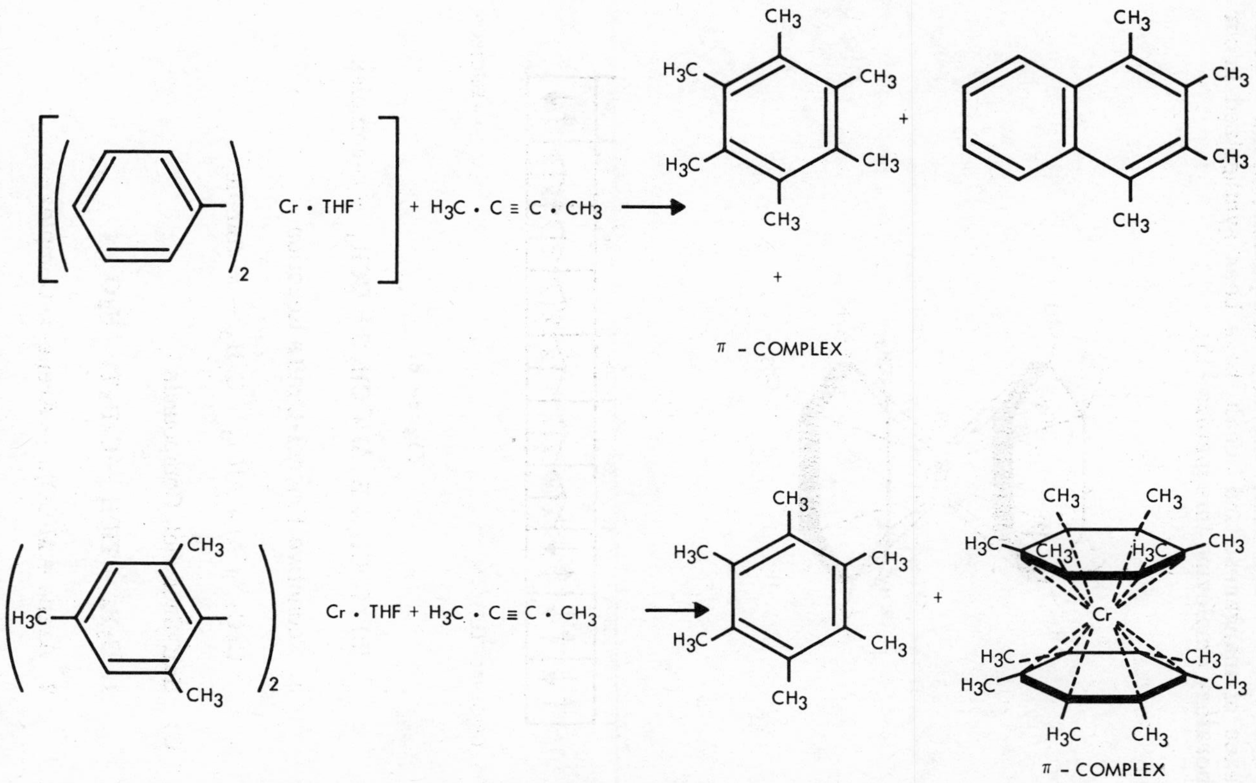

Figure 7 [14].

2. (a) Cyclization of Acetylenes

The following new compounds, arene-π-complexes of manganese and cobalt, have been synthesized in our laboratory employing this method [15].

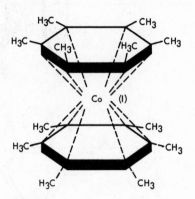

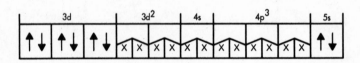

↑ = ORIGINAL ELECTRON   X = π - ELECTRON

Figure 8.

(b) $CrCl_3 + R_3Al + CH_3C \equiv CCH_3 \rightarrow \pi$-complex

3. Reductive Friedel-Crafts Reaction

$$CrCl_3 + Al + AlCl_3 + C_6H_6 \rightarrow \pi\text{-complex}$$

C. Half-Sandwich Compounds

1. $C_5H_6 + TlOH \rightarrow C_5H_5Tl + H_2O$

2. Arene + $M(CO)_n \rightarrow$ Arene-π-Complex

The use of metal carbonyls has promoted the preparation of π-complexes remarkably.

232

D.   Mixed Sandwich π-Complexes

1. Bis-Arene-π-Complex + (Aryl)' MgBr $\rightarrow$

2. Arene Metal Carbonyl + (Arene)' $\rightarrow$

III.   PURIFICATION METHODS

Almost all of the known purification methods shown as follows can be used for the purification of arene-metal-π-complexes. This suggests that arene-π-complexes may be obtained in ultra high purity and that such ultrapure arene-metal-π-complexes may be useful compounds for obtaining ultrapure metals, from their decomposition.

A.   Recrystallization
B.   Sublimation
C.   Column Chromatography and Gas Chromatography
D.   Zone Purification

IV.   THERMOSTABILITY [1, 6, 10, 14, 16]

Decomposition points of some arene-metal-π-complexes are shown in the following tables. Melting points of typical arene-metal-π-complexes are also shown.

Table 1

Bis-Cyclopentadienyl Metal Complexes.

	M.P. (°C)	Dec. (°C)
IV		
Ti		130
TiBr$_2$		319
TiMe$_2$		100
TiØ$_2$	146-48	
ZrBr$_2$		260
V		
V	167-68	
VCl$_2$		-250
VI		
Cr	172-73	
VII		
ReH	161-62	
ReH$_2$Cl		-140

233

Table 1—Continued

	M.P. (°C)	Dec. (°C)
VIII		
Fe	173	
FeI_6		125-30
Rn	195-96	
Os	218	
Co	173	
Ni		173
Pd		40
UCl		260

Table 2

Bis-Arene Metal Complexes.

	M.P. (°C)	Dec. (°C)
bZ_2Cr	282-84	
(diphenyl)$_2$Cr	112	
bZ(diphenyl)Cr	120-21	
bZ_2V	277-78	
bZ_2Mo		115
$bZ_2R_e^+$		
Reineckate		120-40

Table 3

Mono-Arene Metal Complexes.

	M.P. (°C)	Dec. (°C)
Benzene Cr(CO)$_3$	165-66	
Aniline Cr(CO)$_3$	173-75	
Benzene Mo(CO)$_3$		120-25
Benzene W(CO)$_3$		140-45 .

234

Table 4

Mono-Cyclopentadienyl Complexes.

	M.P. (°C)	Dec. (°C)
π-CpV(CO)$_4$		138
$[\pi$-CpCr(CO)$_3]_2$		163-68
$[\pi$-CpCr(CO)$_3][\pi$-Cp$_2$Cr]		190-93
π-CpMo(CO)$_3$C$_2$H$_5$		77.5-78.5
$[\pi$-(MeCp)Mo(CO)$_3]_2$		146-47
$[\pi$-CpW(CO)$_3]_2$		240-42
π-CpMn(CO)$_3$	76.8	
π-CpFe(CO)$_2$CN		120
$[\pi$-Ind Fe(CO)$_2]_2$		198
π-CpCo(C$_5$H$_6$)	98-99	
π-CpRh(C$_5$H$_6$)	121-22	
π-CpNi(CO)$_2$		139

V. SUMMARY

Although organometallic compounds have been known for over a century, the chemistry of complexes formed by metals and hydrocarbons constituted only a small part of either organic chemistry or the chemistry of inorganic complex compounds until the discoveries of dicyclopentadienyl iron, ferrocene, in 1951 and bis-biphenyl chromium in 1954. The field of metal complexes containing aromatic rings has since this time expanded very rapidly. In addition to metal derivatives of the cyclopentadienyl anion and arenes, a great number of related compounds have been synthesized in which cyclobutadiene, tropylium cation, cyclooctatetraene, thiophene, etc., are coordinated via π-electron systems with the metal. In addition, the synthesis of many mixed arene-metal complexes and arene-metal carbonyls and nitrosyls has been reported. Arene and olefin π-complex chemistry now covers almost all the elements from group I to group VIII. Purification of π-complexes is accessible by recrystallization, sublimation, chromatography and other techniques which have been utilized in organic and inorganic chemistry. Pyrolysis of some π-complexes yields pyrophoric metals or produces metallic mirrors which are probably ultrapure.

REFERENCES

1. E. O. Fischer and H. P. Fritz, "Advances in Inorganic and Radiochemistry," Vol. 1, p. 55, New York, Academic Press, 1959.
2. E. O. Fischer and H. P. Kögle, Z. Angew. Chem., 68, 462, (1956).
3. Fr. Hein, Ber. 52, 195 (1919).
4. T. J. Kealy and P. L. Pauson, Nature, 168, 1039 (1951).
5. A. Nakamura and N. Hagihara, Bull. Chem. Soc. Japan, 23, 425 (1960).
6. P. L. Pauson, Quat. Rev. 40, No. 4 (1955).
7. M. Tsutsui, Ph.D. Dissertation, Yale University, 1954.
8. M. Tsutsui, H. Zeiss and L. Onsager, Abstr., 126th Meeting, Amer. Chem. Soc., New York, N. Y. 1954, p. 29 - 0.
9. M. Tsutsui and H. Zeiss, J. Am. Chem. Soc., 81, 4117 (1957).
10. M. Tsutsui and H. Zeiss, Naturwiss., 45, 420 (1957).
11. M. Tsutsui and H. Zeiss, J. Am. Chem. Soc., 82, 6255 (1960).
12. M. Tsutsui and H. Zeiss, J. Am. Chem. Soc., 83, 825 (1961).
13. M. Tsutsui, 139th Meeting, Amer. Chem. Soc., St. Louis, Mo., 1961.
14. M. Tsutsui, Chem. & Ind., Japan, in press.
15. M. Tsutsui, Ann. N. Y. Academy of Sciences, in press.
16. G. Wilkinson and F. A. Cotton, in "Progress in Inorganic Chemistry," Vol. 1, Ed. by F. A. Cotton, p. 1, New York, Interscience Publishers, 1959.

DISCUSSION

J. K. KENNEDY (AFCRL): Can you suggest which method of purification is the most fruitful?

M. TSUTSUI (New York Univ.): We usually use the re-crystallization method for purification. However, sublimation under high vacuum is also recommended. For example the benzene-chromium complexes and the ferrocene complexes are very stable under high vacuum at about 100 degrees. We haven't noticed any decomposition at that temperature.

J. K. KENNEDY (AFCRL): You mentioned chromatographic techniques for purification. Would you comment on the useful-ness of this technique?

M. TSUTSUI (New York Univ.): Yes. Some of this has been done. For instance, the resolution of some isomers of ferro-cences has been done at the University of Illinois. I think that chromatography is a good method, of course.

J. K. KENNEDY (AFCRL): We were thinking of employing gas chromatography for the preparative purification of these compounds. In your opinion are these compounds sufficiently stable to be purified in this manner?

M. TSUTSUI (New York Univ.): Yes, at about 30 millimeters pressure.

W. A. G. GRAHAM (A. D. Little): Are you aware of any cases where the metal produced in the decomposition of these complexes has been deliberately analyzed from the point of view of metal purity?

M. TSUTSUI (New York Univ.): Pyrolysis of sandwich type complexes gives a metallic mirror. However, I do not have any data about their purity.

W. A. G. GRAHAM (A. D. Little): I have one comment, namely that the observations in the literature on this subject have to be treated with some skepticism. For instance, in our work on nickel, we were led by an observation made by E. O. Fischer to investigate the pyrolysis of dicyclopentadienyl nickel. He reported that at its melting point it decomposed to form a mirror. Actually, he did this in a melting point capillary. When we did it on a larger scale, we found that there was, indeed, a mirror formed, but that it contained, on analysis, a gross amount of carbon, on the order of 40 to 50 percent.

M. TSUTSUI (New York Univ.): I think I mentioned the pyrolysis of metallic compounds which contain carbon. Thermal decomposition of organometallics leaves, of course, the metal, but this metal contains carbon. However if you decompose dicyclopentadienyl nickel under high vacuum, you can eliminate or you can diminish the amount of carbon in the product. Have you ever done this work?

W. A. G. GRAHAM (A. D. Little): We attempted this in several ways. We attempted it at high vacuum, but found that it sublimed out at the hot regions before it decomposed. We likewise attempted to pass it over a hot finger in vacuum at temperatures of five to six hundred degrees Centigrade, and there was no deposit formed on the film. What we finally did was sublime it in a sealed tube, on the one hand, and in a slow stream of inert gas, on the other. Both led to large amounts of carbon.

M. TSUTSUI (New York Univ.): I would like to comment that the dicyclopentadienyl nickel is an ionic sandwich compound. Another compound of this type is the benzene chromium pi-complex, a neutral pi-complex. However, this benzene-chromium sandwich neutral pi-complex yields a product on decomposition which is relatively free of carbon. Have you done any decomposition of this arene-type complex?

W. A. G. GRAHAM (A. D. Little): No, but I would agree with you that the complexes of zero valent metals are probably the most promising.

J. A. ROBERTS (Transitron): Could you give me some idea of the metal-metal spacings in these kinds of structures?

M. TSUTSUI (New York Univ.): No.

C. J. MARSEL (New York Univ.): There certainly is a paucity of data on the decomposition of these materials to give metals. I think we are just beginning to scratch the surface of this very interesting area, and I think we will also have to use some new techniques. For example, it may well be that the decomposition of these materials under a hydrogen atmosphere, for example, might very well promote a cleaner breakage of the bonds and the elimination of the carbonaceous products and the subsequent preparation of the metal in a pure form. There are new techniques, I think, that will have to be studied to use this procedure.

THE POTENTIAL OF GAS CHROMATOGRAPHY
FOR PURIFYING SEMICONDUCTOR MATERIALS

J. H. Bochinski and K. W. Gardiner
Bell & Howell Research Center
Pasadena, California
R. S. Juvet, Jr.
Department of Chemistry and Chemical Engineering
University of Illinois
Urbana, Illinois

INTRODUCTION

Gas chromatography is a separation process based on the selective distribution of volatile compounds between a moving gas phase and a stationary liquid or solid phase. As most commonly practiced, gas chromatography is a batch process that is operated to separate a complex mixture into its components and, in general, to yield these components in a high state of purity. This technique has been primarily oriented toward analysis of small quantities of organic compounds but has also been used for the isolation of highly purified organic compounds in liter/day quantities using an automatic cycling instrument [1]. Although a truly continuous flow unit appears practical, very little work along these lines has been reported. The potential application of gas chromatography for purifying volatile inorganic materials with batch and continuous operation will be discussed in this paper.

HOW GAS CHROMATOGRAPHY WORKS

In gas chromatography an inert carrier gas, such as nitrogen or helium, forms a mobile phase which is allowed to flow past a finely divided inert solid, such as diatomaceous earth, coated with a stationary non-volatile partitioning solvent. The essential elements of a conventional batch scale chromatograph designed for analysis consist of a sample injection point, a thermostated chromatographic column, and some type of detector for measuring the concentration of a component in the gas phase. A schematic diagram of an apparatus is shown in Figure 1. When a

239

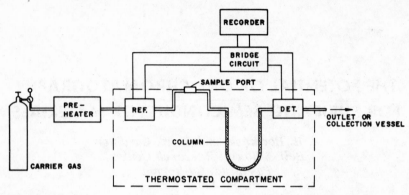

Figure 1. Schematic Diagram of Conventional Chromatograph.

sample containing volatile components A and B is injected into the pre-heated carrier gas, the sample is immediately vaporized and the components pass through the column at a rate dependent upon their relative solubilities in the stationary liquid phase. If component A is more readily absorbed by the partitioning solvent than B, it will be delayed in its transit through the column and a chromatogram similar to that shown in Figure 2 will result. In general, the shape of the concentration curves of the eluted components approximate gaussian distribution. A 4-foot packed column is easily prepared which possesses an efficiency of 2,000 theoretical plates, or equilibrium contacts between gas and partitioning solvent. By optimizing the flow rate, the particle diameter, and other variables as many as 30,000 theoretical plates may be obtained on packed columns. Recently, capillary columns coated on the inside with a non-volatile liquid phase have been prepared with an apparent efficiency of one million theoretical plates. Thus, gas chromatography is ideally suited for the separation of volatile components.

PREPARATIVE SCALE GAS CHROMATOGRAPHY

Most preparative scale gas chromatographs are based on batch operation. The columns used in analytical work are limited to the separation of milligram quantities of sample because of the relatively small diameter of the column, frequently of the order of 1/4 inch. The capacity of the column may be increased for preparative work by at least three methods: (A) the column diameter may be increased to approximately 5/8 inch without serious loss in resolution; (B) a group of columns may be arranged in parallel with a common feed and exit system; (C) an apparatus may be used which will automatically feed the sample

240

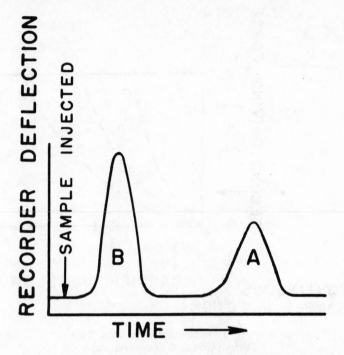

Figure 2. A Chromatogram of Two Components;
B More Volatile than A.

repetitively into the column and collect only the fractions desired. Sample introduction rates of the order of 20 g per cycle,
and cycle times of 10 minutes to one hour have been reported [2].
    The techniques described above operate in one dimension
and are limited to batchwise operation. From the point of view
of preparative work it would be desirable to operate a gas
chromatograph with continuous injection of sample. Such a gas
chromatograph would need to operate in two dimensions to permit continuous withdrawal of several purified fractions. Two
dimensional operation may be achieved by imposing a driving
force with a vector perpendicular to the carrier gas flow as
shown in Figure 3. The resulting driving force would need to
affect each component to a different degree in order to achieve
successful two dimensional operation. Movement of the packing
or solvent at right angles to the carrier gas flow has been suggested [3-5] as providing another "driving force" for two dimensional gas chromatography. However, some mechanical
design and diffusion problems need to be resolved before such a
system gives a good separation of components. In another two
dimensional gas chromatograph concept [6], a thermal gradient

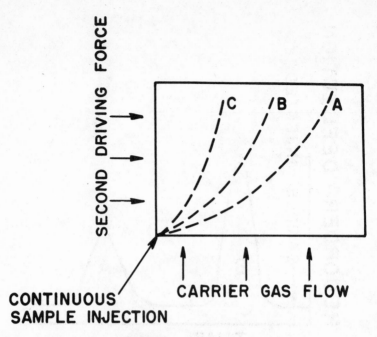

Figure 3. Flow Pattern in a Two-
Dimensional Chromatograph

induced preferential diffusion of components in the lateral direction in a packed bed might be utilized to recover one component from a multi-component mixture.

Techniques for preparation of purified organic compounds by gas chromatography can also be applied to purification of semiconductor materials. However, the specifications for allowable impurities in semiconductors are several orders of magnitude lower than the specifications normally acceptable for purified organic chemicals, and two inorganic components would therefore need to be separated more completely on the column than is often necessary in the case of organic purifications.

SEMICONDUCTOR MATERIALS PURIFICATION

In order for gas chromatography to be used as a tool for the purification of semiconductor materials, the materials being separated must be volatile at the column operating temperature. Also, in order to avoid contamination of purified fractions, the partitioning solvent, the solid support and the materials of construction must not have appreciable vapor pressures or react chemically with the semiconductor materials. Inspection of the boiling points of a number of the pure elements (Table I) used

TABLE I

BOILING POINTS OF SELECTED ELEMENTS

	3 a	4 a	5 a	6 a
	5 B	6 C	7 N	8 O
	2550	4200	-196	-183
2 b	13 Al	14 Si	15 P	16 S
	1800	2600	280	445
30 Zn	31 Ga	32 Ge	33 As	34 Se
907	1700	2700	615(s)	688
48 Cd	49 In	50 Sn	51 Sb	52 Te
767	1450	2260	1380	1390
80 Hg	81 Tl	82 Pb	83 Bi	84 Po
357	1650	1620	1450	—

in preparing semiconductors shows that temperatures in excess of 1000°C would be required in a great majority of cases. At these high operating temperatures the available materials of construction having low vapor pressure and chemical stability become quite limited in number, and the gas chromatographic separation of elements as pure elements rather than as volatile compounds looks attractive only for sulfur, selenium, phosphorous, arsenic, zinc and cadmium. Chromatographic separation of the high boiling elements may only be practical if these elements are processed as low boiling compounds.

Juvet and Wachi [7] have shown that the separation of inorganic compounds is possible if the elements are purified as the more volatile metal halides. Tables II-IV list the boiling points of several metal chlorides, bromides and fluorides. Heavy lines are placed around those elements with boiling points less than 800°C, a temperature easily accessible in inorganic gas chromatography. It has been found [7] that inorganic fused salt eutectic mixtures are ideally suited for use as partitioning solvents for inorganic separations at high temperatures. Eutectic mixtures with a useful temperature range of several hundred degrees are available. Moreover, the vapor pressure of the more volatile component of the eutectic mixture is generally decreased by the presence of the other component of the mixture.

243

TABLE II

BOILING POINTS OF METAL CHLORIDES
(DEGREES, CENTIGRADE)

TRANSITION ELEMENTS

1a	2a	3b	4b	5b	6b	7b	8b	8b	8b	1b	2b	3a	4a	5a	6a	7a	0
1 H I=-85																	2 He
3 Li I=1380	4 Be II=488(a)											5 B III=13	6 C IV=77	7 N III=71	8 O	9 F O=-34	10 Ne
11 Na I=1465	12 Mg II=1412											13 Al III=178(s)	14 Si IV=58	15 P III=180 V=76 Y=159	16 S II=138	17 Cl	18 A
19 K I=1407	20 Ca II=2027	21 Sc III=967	22 Ti II=1477 IV=136	23 V II=1377 III=d IV=152	24 Cr II=1302	25 Mn II=1190	26 Fe II=1026 III=315	27 Co II=1050	28 Ni II=987(a)	29 Cu I=1490 II=d	30 Zn II=756	31 Ga II=535 III=215	32 Ge II=83	33 As III=130	34 Se I=130(d) IV=226(d)	35 Br I=5	36 Kr
37 Rb I=1381	38 Sr II=2027	39 Y	40 Zr IV=331	41 Nb V=241	42 Mo V=268	43 Tc	44 Ru	45 Rh III=800(a)	46 Pd	47 Ag I=1557	48 Cd II=960	49 In III=500(a)	50 Sn II=623 IV=114	51 Sb III=225 V=172	52 Te II=324 IV=390	53 I I=97	54 Xe
55 Cs I=1300	56 Ba II=1560	57-71 La Series	72 Hf IV=317	73 Ta V=234	74 W V=276 VI=337	75 Re III=>550 IV=500 VI=<40	76 Os	77 Ir	78 Pt	79 Au III=265(u)	80 Hg I=384 II=304	81 Tl I=807	82 Pb II=954	83 Bi IV=d	84 Po	85 At	86 Rn
87 Fr	88 Ra II=1727	89-103 Ac Series															

LANTHANIDE SERIES	57 La III=1607	58 Ce III=1610	59 Pr III=1597	60 Nd III=1577	61 Pm	62 Sm	63 Eu II=2027 III=1547	64 Gd III=1527	65 Tb III=1517	66 Dy III=1507	67 Ho III=1502	68 Er III=1497	69 Tm III=1487	70 Yb	71 Lu III=1457?
ACTINIDE SERIES	89 Ac	90 Th IV=922	91 Pa	92 U IV=618	93 Np	94 Pu	95 Am	96 Cm	97 Bk	98 Cf	99 Es	100 Fm	101 Md	102 No	

244

TABLE III

BOILING POINTS OF METAL BROMIDES
(DEGREES, CENTIGRADE)

TRANSITION ELEMENTS

	1a	2a	3b	4b	5b	6b	7b	8b			1b	2b	3a	4a	5a	6a	7a	0
	1 H I = -67																1 H I = -67	2 He
	3 Li I = 1310	4 Be II = 474											5 B III = 91	6 C II = 187	7 N	8 O	9 F	10 Ne
	11 Na I = 1390	12 Mg II = 1227											13 Al III = 265	14 Si IV = 153	15 P III = 173 V = 841(i)	16 S	17 Cl 0 = 59	18 A
	19 K I = 1380	20 Ca II = 1827	21 Sc III = 929	22 Ti II = 230	23 V	24 Cr	25 Mn II = 1027	26 Fe II = 927	27 Co	28 Ni II = ..	29 Cu I = 1355	30 Zn II = 697	31 Ga III = 278	32 Ge IV = 187	33 As III = 221	34 Se I = 227(d)	35 Br	36 Kr
	37 Rb I = 1352	38 Sr II = 1877	39 Y	40 Zr	41 Nb	42 Mo	43 Tc	44 Ru	45 Rh	46 Pd	47 Ag I = 1533	48 Cd II = 1136	49 In III = .	50 Sn II = 638 IV = 205	51 Sb III = 280	52 Te II = 339	53 I I = 116	54 Xe
	55 Cs I = 1300	56 Ba	57-71 La Series	72 Hf	73 Ta V = 345	74 W V = 333	75 Re	76 Os	77 Ir	78 Pt	79 Au	80 Hg I = 345(s) II = 319	81 Tl I = 815	82 Pb II = 914	83 Bi III = 461	84 Po	85 At	86 Rn
	87 Fr	88 Ra II = 1677	89-103 Ac Series															

LANTHANIDE SERIES	57 La III = 1577	58 Ce III = 1557	59 Pr III = 1547	60 Nd III = 1537	61 Pm	62 Sm	63 Eu III = 1497	64 Gd III = 1487	65 Tb III = 1487	66 Dy III = 1477	67 Ho III = 1467	68 Er III = 1457	69 Tm III = 1457	70 Yb	71 Lu III = 120?
ACTINIDE SERIES	89 Ac	90 Th IV = 857	91 Pa	92 U III = vol. IV = vol.	93 Np	94 Pu	95 Am	96 Cm	97 Bk	98 Cf	99 Es	100 Fm	101 Md	102 No	

245

TABLE IV

BOILING POINTS OF METAL FLUORIDES
(DEGREES, CENTIGRADE)

1a	2a	3b	4b	5b	6b	7b	8b			1b	2b	3a	4a	5a	6a	7a	0
1 H I=20																1 H I=20	2 He
3 Li I=1681	4 Be II=1327											5 B III=-101	6 C IV=-182	7 N III=-129	8 O	9 F O=-188	10 Ne
11 Na I=1704	12 Mg II=2227											13 Al III=1272(s)	14 Si IV=-96(s)	15 P III=-101 V=-85	16 S IV=-64 VI=-40	17 Cl I=-101 III=12	18 A
19 K I=1500	20 Ca II=2467	21 Sc III=1527	22 Ti	23 V V=111	24 Cr III=1427	25 Mn II=2027	26 Fe III=1827 II=1327	27 Co	28 Ni	29 Cu I=1100(a)	30 Zn II=1502	31 Ga	32 Ge IV=-37	33 As III=-53 V=-64	34 Se IV=93 VI=-35	35 Br III=135 I=-20 V=41	36 Kr
37 Rb I=1410	38 Sr II=2427	39 Y	40 Zr	41 Nb V=225	42 Mo VI=35	43 Tc	44 Ru	45 Rh III>600(a)	46 Pd	47 Ag	48 Cd II=1747	49 In III=1170	50 Sn IV=705(s)	51 Sb III=150	52 Te VI=36(s)	53 I V=97 VII=51(a)	54 Xe
55 Cs I=1251	56 Ba II=2277	57-71 La Series	72 Hf	73 Ta V=230	74 W VI=17	75 Re VII=48 VI=797	76 Os VIII=47 VI=205	77 Ir VI=53	78 Pt	79 Au	80 Hg II=650	81 Tl I=655	82 Pb I=1290	83 Bi	84 Po	85 At	86 Rn
87 Fr	88 Ra	89-103 Ac Series															

TRANSITION ELEMENTS

LANTHANIDE SERIES	57 La III=2327	58 Ce III=2327	59 Pr III=2377	60 Nd III=2327	61 Pm	62 Sm III=2327	63 Eu III=2377	64 Gd III=2377	65 Tb III=2377	66 Dy III=2327	67 Ho III=2327	68 Er III=2227	69 Tm III=2227	70 Yb III=2377	71 Lu
ACTINIDE SERIES	89 Ac	90 Th	91 Pa	92 U VI=56(a)	93 Np	94 Pu III=2327	95 Am	96 Cm	97 Bk	98 Cf	99 Es	100 Fm	101 Md	102 No	

246

It is desirable for the fused salt partitioning solvent to have a common ion with the semiconductor compounds being purified in order to reduce the possibility of reaction on the column. Following chromatographic purification, many of the metal halides may be decomposed to the elements and the metal recovered by pyrolysis or reduction with hydrogen.

Separation of the volatile elements or volatile compounds of the elements might also be carried out on solid adsorbents. This may be the only practical approach at temperatures near 1000°C where most of the halide salts of possible partitioning solvents have appreciable vapor pressures.

The following discussions on the purification of tellurium and arsenic as the chlorides and arsenic as the pure element emphasize the important considerations that must be taken into account in designing equipment and selecting conditions for preparative gas chromatography.

Considerations for Purification of Tellurium Chloride

Tellurium (II) chloride boils at 324°C and could be separated from impurities by gas chromatography using a potassium chloride-lithium chloride eutectic mixture (41 mole % KCl) supported on 60-80 mesh Johns-Manville C-22 firebrick. The melting point of this eutectic is 352°C. The eutectic mixture should constitute about 70% by weight of the column packing material, and a 12-foot column should be adequate. Suppose the column temperature were maintained at 360°C. The large difference between the boiling points of the chlorides of the various elements (see Table II) indicates that tellurium (II) chloride may be readily separated from the other metal halides. In the preparative scale gas chromatographic separation of organic compounds a purity of 99.96% has been obtained with two components whose boiling points differ by only 0.6° and are known to form azeotropes in ordinary distillation [8]. Separation of azeotropes or compounds with identical boiling points is possible in gas chromatography only if there is a difference in the distribution ratios of the components, where the distribution ratio for a compound can be defined as partial pressure at equilibrium divided by concentration in the stationary phase. Compounds with identical boiling points can be separated by careful choice of the stationary liquid phase.

Vaporization of residual volatile components in the column packing materials itself would be a major concern, and the column would have to be "conditioned" for several hours at the operating temperature to remove trace impurities. Of the two components used in the proposed eutectic mixture lithium chloride is the more volatile (b.p., 1380°C). At 360°C the vapor

247

pressure of lithium chloride, extrapolated from the data of Horbe and Knacke [9], is of the order of 5×10^{-9} atms. If 140 mg of purified tellurium chloride are collected over a one minute interval using a carrier gas flow rate of 25 ml/minute, it may be shown that the maximum amount of lithium in the tellurium is only 7×10^{-7} atom percent. The actual lithium impurity would probably be much less than this due to complex formation with the potassium chloride present in the eutectic. Thus, perhaps compounds of elements which do not interfere with the semi-conductor properties may be chosen as the components of the liquid phase and the concentration of these impurities may be maintained very small. For larger scale work the column capacity would be increased, but this increase in capacity would not materially increase the lithium impurity present.

Consideration for Purifying Arsenious Trichloride

Arsenious trichloride is a liquid with its boiling point (120°C) well removed from the boiling points of most of the chlorides listed in Table II with the exception of those for tin and sulfur. Many other compounds, other than the halides, are found as impurities in commercial grade arsenious trichloride and some of these compounds may have boiling points within a few degrees of the boiling point of arsenious trichloride. A well controlled distillation step could remove many of the impurities, barring presence of unknown azeotropes, prior to the chromatographic purification.

The partitioning solvents or solid adsorbents selected would need to be chemically inert with respect to the arsenic and have vapor pressures below 10^{-7} atmospheres at the temperature of the column to avoid contamination of the purified fractions. This required condition of low vapor pressure would rule out most of the organic partitioning solvents currently used in gas chromatography for applications where carbon interferes and cannot be removed by further treatment. An inorganic eutectic salt mixture such as $KCl-ZnCl_2$ which has a very low vapor pressure may be satisfactory even though its melting point, 230°C, may be above the most desirable operating temperatures. About 7×10^{-6} atom percent of zinc would probably be present in the purified arsenious trichloride. Because of the large difference between the boiling points of zinc and arsenic chlorides it should be possible to remove most of the zinc chloride in a second column packed with a solid adsorbent.

The materials of construction and the possible corrosion products must also be chemically inert to arsenic and have low vapor pressures and low solubility in the liquid $AsCl_3$ product. Vapor pressure data in Figure 4 indicate that the more common materials such as nickel, copper, and iron might be suitable materials of construction because they have low vapor pressures. However, the iron might form chloride oxidation products that have appreciable vapor pressures. From the point of view of chemical inertness Vycor glass would be the wisest choice even though it is fragile and more difficult to fabricate.

Considerations for Purifying Elemental Arsenic

It may be very desirable to purify arsenic as the element rather than as the chloride because the chloride reduction step would be avoided and danger of further contamination of the ultrapure element would be reduced. Fractional distillation could not be used as a purification process for elemental arsenic because this material is a solid that sublimes at ordinary pressures. Repeated sublimations or gas chromatography may be the best techniques available. Gas chromatography would have a great advantage over repeated sublimations if a large number of sublimation steps would be required as would be the case if the undesirable impurities have vapor pressures not far removed from the vapor pressure of arsenic.

The compilation of information on the properties of the many possible impurities associated with elemental arsenic has not been completed in this report; however, some of the problems that might be encountered in purification of elemental arsenic can be anticipated from the vapor pressure data in Figure 4. The large differences in vapor pressure data indicate that it might not be too difficult to remove the oxides of arsenic and antimony from elemental arsenic. Sulfur may be a difficult impurity to remove since sulfur compounds of arsenic (As_2S_2, As_2S_3) have vapor pressures both slightly higher and slightly lower than the vapor pressure of arsenic. Selective adsorbent materials would need to be used in chromatographic columns to separate the impurities having vapor pressures very close to the vapor pressure of arsenic.

Systems for Detection of Impurities

For proper operation and control of a preparative gas chromatograph a detection system capable of sensing at least the concentration of the major components in the gaseous effluent is required. The availability of a detection system with sensitivity equivalent to a mass spectrometer capable of detecting parts per billion impurities in solids would be highly useful during the development of a separation procedure but would not be absolutely necessary for routine production of materials by gas chromatography. Below an operating temperature

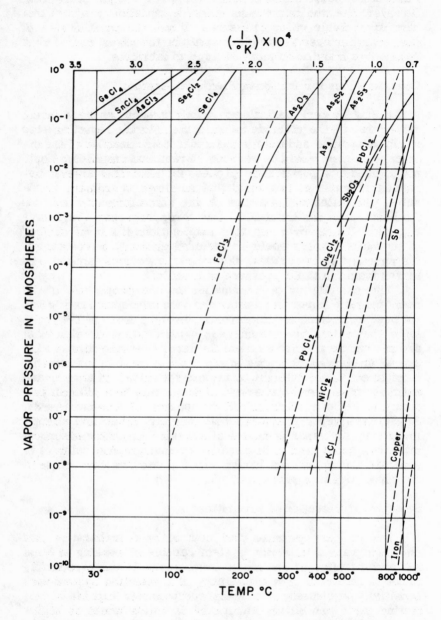

Figure 4. Vapor Pressures of Selected Compounds.

250

of 500°C a detector based on changes in thermal conductivity might prove adequate for process control. For higher operating temperature detectors based on flame ionization or chemical reaction could be used.

A simple chemical reaction detector based on the reaction of oxygen with the transition elements would have rapid response when used in conjunction with a detector based on changes in thermal conductivity. A small portion of the product stream would be consumed in the oxidation reaction step when mixed with the oxygen stream. The detector would continually measure the remaining oxygen content in the reacted gas mixture and any change in the oxygen concentration would be a quantitative indication of the product concentration in the gas chromatograph effluent. Such a detection system would be relatively insensitive to fluctuation in gas flow and temperature changes.

SUMMARY

On the basis of the work done with preparative scale organic chromatography, it should be possible to design gas chromatographs that will prepare many semiconductor halide compounds and some of the semiconductor elements in quantities greater than one kilogram per day. Further work along these lines is underway at both the University of Illinois and the Bell & Howell Research Center, and the results of this work will be reported at a later date.

ACKNOWLEDGMENT

Work at the University of Illinois was supported by NSF Research Grant G-15706.

REFERENCES

1. H. E. Felton, paper presented Chemical Institute of Canada, Toronto, Ontario, February 1, 1960.
2. Chemical & Engineering News, 38, 58 (February 15, 1960).
3. K. A. Fischer and G. Grandes, German Patent 1,033,638 (1956).
4. R. P. W. Scott, in "Gas Chromatography 1958," D. H. Desty, ed., Butterworths, London, 1958, p. 287.
5. L. G. Hall and L. G. Cole, U. S. Patent, 2,891,630 (1959).
6. K. W. Gardiner, U. S. Patent applied for (1960).
7. R. S. Juvet and F. M. Wachi, Analytical Chemistry, 32, 290 (1960).
8. G. Catalette, J. P. Beaufils, B. Gras and J. E. Germain, paper presented, Lille Section, Societe Chimique de France, November 19, 1959; summary, Bulletin Societe Chimique de France 6 (1960).
9. R. Horbe and O. Knacke, Z. Erzbergbau u. Metallhuttenw., 8, 556 (1955).

DISCUSSION

W. L. TOWLE (Mallinckrodt): Up to what temperatures is it feasible to operate this equipment?

J. BOCHINSKI (Bell & Howell): Based on the vapor pressure data of various materials of construction with nickel-chromium alloys probably six to eight hundred degrees is the limit if we are sure that we don't generate corrosion products. If we do generate corrosion products, it will be necessary to use vycor or quartz. In this case we can probably go up to a thousand or higher.

H. C. GIVENS (Union Carbide): Have you found any particular substrate or class of substrates more effective in separating the metallic chlorides in gas chromatography?

J. BOCHINSKI (Bell & Howell): We haven't actually separated any yet, and thus we have no answer to give you. You could use eutectics. There is quite a large combination of eutectics that could be used, and these are listed in three volumes titled "Phase Diagrams for Ceramicists."

R. S. BRAMAN (Armour Research): Have you looked into the possibility of using the technique of chromothermography rather than the conventional gas chromatography?

J. BOCHINSKI (Bell & Howell): We have an apparatus that we have built for testing the concept of chromothermography. We will know probably in about a month how it works. Thermochromatography has been used in some organic chemical purification. One way of doing it is to have a tube packed with the partitioning solvent on a granular material. This is described in the literature. You could have a furnace which would impose a temperature profile across it. This can be considered as a plow that plows up certain components preferentially. It is a crude explanation, but I think it will illustrate the point. The more volatile compounds will tend to be vaporized and pushed in one direction. I don't think the resolutions obtained by this technique on organic chemicals would be as good.

R. S. BRAMAN (Armour Research): I think there is still a controversey about this. The point is that this eliminates much of the diffusion that you see with long retention times in conventional chromatography.

J. BOCHINSKI (Bell & Howell): Well, I might make one comment that the apparatus that we have has a very large sized tube furnace in which we install the whole chromatograph and detector, and the furnace is so long that it gives a fairly uniform temperature profile along the length of the tube. This is very useful when you are working with something like vycor or quartz.

252

"SYNTHESIS AND GAS CHROMATOGRAPHIC PURIFICATION OF ORGANOMETALLIC COMPOUNDS FOR SEMICONDUCTOR APPLICATIONS"

J. I. Peterson, L. M. Kindley and H. E. Podall
Melpar, Inc.
Falls Church, Va.

ABSTRACT

For the past year, Melpar has been engaged in an experimental program to develop methods of formation of semiconductor films by deposition of pure elements and element combinations from atmospheres of organic compounds of the elements. The program includes compounds of boron, gallium, silicon, germanium, tin, phosphorus, arsenic and bismuth. Unusual problems in the synthesis of these compounds will be discussed. The gas chromatographic approach to achieving high purity of tetraethylgermanium for vapor deposition has been developed and applied. This technique has been shown to have tremendous potential because of the high efficiencies of separation of impurities which result. Details, techniques, and applications of this method of purification and analysis will be presented.

I.   INTRODUCTION

Melpar is engaged in a program to develop film deposition techniques in connection with their molecular electronics program. Experimentation on metal film deposition is being pursued with the techniques of metal evaporation onto a cold surface and pyrolytic decomposition of metal organic compounds upon a heated surface. In both cases, it is evident that chemical purity, and even to some extent the physical purity, of the deposited film depends upon the degree of purity of the metal or metallic compound being used in the deposition process. In the case of metal organic compounds for pyrolytic decomposition, with which this paper is concerned, purification must be achieved solely by using purification techniques commonly used in chemistry. The problem is particularly critical because the synthetic methods used to prepare the original compounds lead to a

253

product which is relatively impure in terms of both entirely organic impurities and metallic impurities. The extent to which entirely organic impurities will lead to contamination of the final metal film is not known, but the possibility of inclusion of carbon or partially pyrolyzed organic products in the metal film is high and may play an important part in determining both the chemical composition of the film and the formation and growth of its crystal structure during deposition. Since the growth of relatively large crystals during deposition is desired, and in fact the formation of larger crystals than in the metal evaporation technique is one of the advantages of vapor deposition, it is important that adsorption of miscellaneous organic compounds upon the surface of a growing crystal lattice does not occur to prevent further regular growth.

Because of these considerations, it was evident to us about a year ago that an efficient purification process should be applied to the tetraethylgermanium which was being experimentally used in the study of germanium films formed by vapor deposition. To our knowledge, gas chromatography had not been applied previously to this purpose, but since its separation efficiency for the purification of volatile compounds far exceeds that of any other known method, we developed a procedure for the purification of tetraethylgermanium using a gas chromatographic technique.

This technique has been applied on a routine basis for about six months. It is difficult to evaluate the extent to which this purification step plays a part in the success of the program because many other factors also enter into the quality of the final films; however, it is evident that a significant degree of chemical purity is achieved in the deposited films. Hall mobility measurements on these films show them to be superior to germanium films produced in this laboratory by the vacuum evaporation technique.

In the succeeding portion of the paper, further information will be given on the synthetic problems to be encountered with other metal organic compounds and details will be given of the technique and performance of the gas chromatographic purification method.

II. SYNTHESIS OF ORGANOMETALLIC COMPOUNDS

1. Criteria in Selection of Compound

In selecting an organometallic compound for use in the vapor deposition of a metal film, the following basic criteria should be met; (1) the compound must volatilize without decomposition to such an extent that its vapors can be transported by a carrier gas; (2) the vapors of the organometallic compound must be capable of decomposition at a temperature between that required for volatilization and the melting point of the metal, and (3) the organometallic vapors must decompose to give only the metal and volatile compounds. For the vapor deposition of two or more element combinations, an additional criteria is that the compound containing the elements of interest should fragment in the appropriate manner for the deposition of the element combination in the required ratio.

In general, four groups of metals are of interest to us; Groups III-A (B, Ga, In), Group IV-A (Si, Ge, Sn), Group V-A (P, As, Sb, Bi), and the transition elements. To meet the above criteria, the hydride and alkyl derivatives are of greater interest than the aryl or mixed organometallic halides primarily because of the greater volatility of the former compounds. Another reason for preferring the hydrides and alkyl derivatives of the metals is that they are generally easier to decompose thermally than the arylmetallics. This situation applies to the Group III-A, IV-A, and V-A elements. For the transition metals, the metal carbonyls are of the greatest value because of their exceptional volatility. In cases where the carbonyls are unknown, the π-cyclopentadienyl or preferably the π-arene derivatives may be employed as volatile sources of the metal.

2. Synthesis Methods

There are two basic methods for the preparation of the organometallics of the Group IIIA-VA elements, viz.,

$$(a) \quad 2M + 3R_2Hg \rightarrow 2R_3M + 3Hg \tag{1}$$

$$(b) \quad MX_3 + M'R_n \rightarrow R_3M + M'X_n \tag{2}$$

where M' = Na, Li, or XMg-

In general, for the Group III-A elements (Ga, In, Tl) method (a) is best, while for the Group IV-A and V-A elements method (b) is best. Thus, triphenylgallium was prepared by method (a) involving reaction of 99.99% pure gallium metal with diphenylmercury under argon in a sealed tube at 130° for 75 hours. The triphenylgallium was recovered and purified by repeated crystallization from benzene under dry nitrogen to afford a product which was 99.9% pure triphenylgallium prior to ultrapurification.

Tetraethylgermanium, on the other hand, was prepared by method (b) involving reaction of $GeCl_4$ with ethylmagnesium bromide in an ether-benzene solution. After hydrolyzing the reaction mixture with dilute acetic acid and extracting with

255

benzene to recover the tetraethylgermanium, the latter was fractionally distilled under reduced pressure employing diphenylether as a chaser. The resulting tetraethylgermanium was 99% pure or better prior to gas chromatographic purification, with a germanium yield of 50%. High purity $GeCl_4$ from Sylvania Electric Products was used, and the other materials were reagent grade.

For the Group III-A elements, method (b) is confined to the use of organosodium and organolithium reagents. In addition, there is a tendency here to stop at the dialkyl stage, requiring further treatment with sodium in order to obtain complete alkylation, e.g.,

$$3R_2GaX + 3Na \rightarrow 2R_3Ga + Ga + 3NaX \qquad (3)$$

The principal difficulty with method (a) is in the contamination of the product with traces of unreacted organomercury compound. In the case of method (b) which generally requires the use of an ether type solvent for conducting the reaction, the product may be contaminated with some of the etherate, e.g., $R_3Ga \times Et_2O$. In addition, some of the alkylmetallic halide may be present in the product.

In the case of the Group III-A elements in particular, the hydrides and organic derivatives are very sensitive to oxygen and moisture. In the case of the less volatile organoaluminum and gallium compounds, the various handling operations were conducted in a dry nitrogen box. In the case of the more volatile organoboron compounds, a vacuum line manifold is generally employed. Tie-in of the gas chromatographic equipment with the vacuum line manifold has given other workers a very powerful method for the preparation of ultrapure materials.

In the case of the organotransition metal compounds, three general synthetic methods have been employed, viz.,

(a) $M + x CO \rightarrow M (CO)$

(b) $MX_2 + 2Na Cy \rightarrow Cy_2 M$

$Cy_2 M + xL \rightarrow Cy M Lx$

Where Cy = cyclopentadienyl group

L = CO or PR_3 generally

(c) $M (CO)_x + arene \rightarrow \pi$-arene $M (CO)_x$

In the case of the mixed metal or element combinations, the methods are very much dependent upon the specific combination of elements required and, of course, upon the compound desired. A specific method of value for the preparation of organometallic compounds containing Group III-A and V-A elements is as follows, e.g.,

$$R_2GaX + R_2'As\ Na \rightarrow R_2GaAsR_2 + NaX$$

III. GAS CHROMATOGRAPHIC PURIFICATION OF TETRAETHYLGERMANIUM

1. Preparative Scale Chromatographic Purification Equipment and Procedure.

Preliminary experimentation led to the selection of silicone rubber as the most suitable column liquid among the commonly available materials. It has the advantage of low volatility at elevated temperature. The equipment used was the F&M Model 500B Linear Programmed Temperature Gas Chromatograph with a 244 cm long by 1.65 cm ID preparative scale column. We found the equipment entirely satisfactory for the purpose, and the feature of temperature programming presented a distinct advantage in operation because of the wide range of volatility of impurities to be removed from a sample. About 1 ml samples of tetraethylgermanium were used. The samples were collected in a Hamilton Fraction Collector using either a dry ice-acetone mixture or liquid nitrogen as a coolant. The preparative column was packed with Johns-Manville chromosorb W, regular grade, 60/80 mesh, with a 20% of the total weight coating of Union Carbide W95 silicone rubber gum stock. The injection and detector block were operated at a temperature of 200°C and during a run the column was programmed to rise from 50°C to 200°C at 7.9° per minute. A flow rate of 1400 ml a minute of helium was used, measured at atmospheric pressure at the detector. The column inlet pressure was 31 psi, giving a compressibility factor (j) of .45. The retention time of the air peak was .58 minute.

The bulk of the germanium comes through in a broad peak with a retention time range of 6 to 10 minutes over the column temperature range of 105 to 140°C. An impurity peak occurs on both the immediate front and tail of the tetraethylgermanium peak so that it is necessary to "cut off" or not collect a portion of the front and tail of the peak. Figure 1 shows the appearance of the chromatogram.

A collection efficiency or yield of 80% of the original sample is obtained. Part of the reason for this is a low efficiency of condensation in the fraction collector. An improved design of fraction collector should be used to increase collection

257

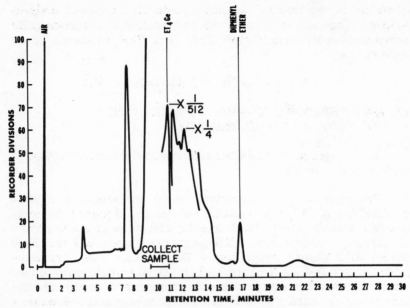

Figure 1. Preparative Scale Chromatogram of Synthesized
and Distilled Tetraethylgermanium.

efficiency, since dry ice-acetone does not give complete condensation, and liquid nitrogen causes plugging.

2. Gas Chromatographic Analysis of Tetraethylgermanium and Identification of Impurities

For analytical purposes, the same gas chromatograph was
equipped with a 300 cm long by 5 mm ID column, filled with the
same silicone rubber coated packing as the preparative column.
The conditions were the same except that a flow rate of 140 ml
per minute was used, and the column inlet pressure was 23 psi,
giving a compressibility factor (j) of .54. The air retention was
.60 minute.

Figure 2 shows the appearance of a chromatogram of a
50 μl sample of the distilled tetraethylgermanium. The tetraethylgermanium peak occurs at a retention time of 14.4 minutes.
A number of impurities can be seen in this chromatogram. A
relative area measurement to give an approximation of the
amount of impurity present indicates an assay of the synthesized
and distilled product of 99 1/4%. An idea of the amount of each
of the observed impurities can be gotten from the estimate that
the first peak appearing is about .015%, the next sharp peak is
about .1%, and the last peak observed is about .04%. The
minimum detectable peak size is about .0015%.

258

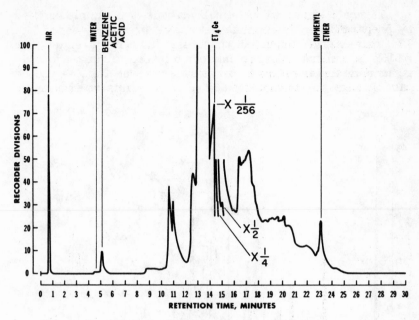

Figure 2. Analytical Chromatogram of Synthesized and Distilled Tetraethylgermanium.

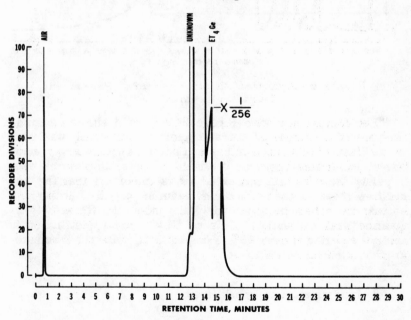

Figure 3. Analytical Chromatogram of Chromatographically Purified Tetraethylgermanium.

259

Figure 3 shows an identical analysis of a sample purified by preparative scale chromatography as previously described. The only visible impurity remaining (that is, greater than .0015% in amount) appears immediately before the tetraethylgermanium and is estimated to represent about .05%. A second pass through the chromatograph to remove this was not tried.

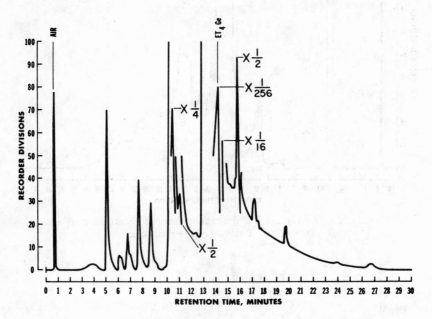

Figure 4. Analytical Chromatogram of Purchased Tetraethylgermanium.

For comparison with Figure 2, Figure 4 shows a similar analysis of a sample of tetraethylgermanium which was purchased instead of being synthesized here. A much larger number of impurities appear. It should be noted that since each impurity tends to tail somewhat, it is important that the impurities close to the tetraethylgermanium be small in amount, so that the extent to which they tail under the tetraethylgermanium peak is small. This is why a prior distillation to achieve a purity of over 99% is desirable to make the chromatographic purification efficient.

3. Identification of Impurities

An attempt was made to identify the impurities which appear on the chromatogram of the distilled product in order to evaluate their possible effect upon the deposited metal film. The techniques of identification by retention time and by collection of the impurity for infrared analysis were used.

To collect a sample for infrared analysis, a 1 ml sample was passed through the preparative scale column and when the impurity peak was observed, the sample was collected in the Hamilton Fraction Collector using liquid nitrogen as the coolant. In one method about 50 μl of carbon tetrachloride were added to the collection tube after it had warmed, and the resulting solution was put in an infrared cell. In the other method, a plug of glass wool was inserted about half way down the side of the collection tube and about 1/2 gram of spectroscopic grade potassium bromide was put on top. Following adsorption of the impurity on the potassium bromide, it was mixed with about an equal amount of additional potassium bromide and a pellet made for infrared analysis. In the case of relatively low volatility materials such as diphenyl ether, about .5 mg of sample is sufficient to get an infrared spectrogram by either method, but as the volatility of the material increases, the amount which must be in the sample also increases considerably because of the inefficiency of collection. Thus, the .04% of diphenyl ether in the sample, giving about .4 mg in a 1 ml sample, and the peaks just before the tetraethylgermanium which could not be identified, could both be collected satisfactorily for infrared analysis, but smaller peaks or more volatile materials could not be collected satisfactorily for identification.

Only the first and last peaks could be identified as reagents used in the synthesis. The last peak was identified by both retention time and infrared analysis as diphenyl ether. A measurement of retention times showed that the very small peak appearing just ahead of the first sharp peak is due to water, and that the first sharp peak appearing is due to either benzene, acetic acid, or both, since the retention times of these fall very close together at this spot. All of the other impurity peaks which show between these two peaks are due to something other than the initial reagents, and are due to either synthesis by-products or distillation decomposition compounds. A retention time check of the reagents showed no impurities present in them which would account for those observed in the distilled product. An infrared spectrogram of the combined impurities appearing with a retention time between 10 and 11 minutes was obtained but no identification could be made beyond the observation that the material contained alkane and ether groups. It was not possible to identify any of the other impurities, either because of insufficient resolution when run through the preparative scale column or inefficiency of collection.

IV. GAS CHROMATOGRAPHIC PURIFICATION OF SOLID ORGANOMETALLICS

Many of the organometallic compounds of interest are solids or high boiling liquids. In spite of this fact, it is possible to employ gas chromatography conveniently and effectively for the purification of such materials. Thus, π-cyclopentadienyl-manganese tricarbonyl, m.p. 77°, and chromium hexacarbonyl, m.p. 155°, have been so purified in previous work by one of the authors.

V. CONCLUSIONS

The preparative scale gas chromatographic purification of tetraethylgermanium has been developed and applied on a routine basis. It has been shown that the purification produces 99.95% tetraethylgermanium with only one impurity showing. The analysis of volatile impurities in tetraethylgermanium can be conducted using the gas chromatographic technique with a limit of detection of approximately 15 parts per million impurity concentration. It has been shown that most of the impurities, representing the bulk of the impurity content which appears in the synthesized and distilled tetraethylgermanium, do not originate in the reagents used for the synthesis. The deposited germanium films resulting from this purification technique have produced Hall mobilities in the range between 69 and 184 cm^2/volt-sec, indicating a good physical and chemical purity. The potential for application of gas chromatographic purification to other metal organic compounds is shown. The primary limitation of this technique is its restriction to small-scale operation. The synthesis of metal-organic compounds for film deposition has been discussed.

DISCUSSION

W. A. G. GRAHAM (A. D. Little): How do you decompose the tetraethylgermanium and what is the decomposition temperature?

J. I. PETERSON (Melpar): I might point out, that the gas chromatographic separation was operated at a maximum temperature of 200 degrees Centigrade. We used programmed temperature chromatography because this is a great convenience and, I might point out, partially negates any advantage of thermal chromatography. The vapor deposition takes place at a temperature in the range of 500 to 600 degrees Centigrade. I believe that tetraethylgermanium does not decompose appreciably below 500 degrees Centigrade. The vapor deposition technique is a fairly simple affair. It is simply a system for bubbling an inert carrier gas through the tetraethylgermanium at some temperature to lead to a particular degree of saturation. The inert gas stream carrying the vapor then goes into a chamber in which are mounted quartz slides. The whole chamber is heated and, actually, this is a very wasteful system as practiced at present. The deposition takes place not only on the slides, but it takes place all over.

R. E. JOHNSON (Texas Instruments): You used the same method for analysis as you used to prepare the material, do you have any other independent means of telling us the purity of your product?

J. I. PETERSON (Melpar): No, we haven't. We of course could and should apply emission spectrographic analysis. We have not applied this yet, partly because of the difficulty of getting a sensitive analysis of a volatile material.

O. J. MARSH (Hughes): Was the material deposited single or polycrystalline?

J. I. PETERSON (Melpar): It deposits a polycrystalline material. The crystal size is larger than is achieved by vapor deposition.

J. K. KENNEDY (AFCRL): You had one unknown in your tetraethylgermanium purification by gas chromatography. Did you make any attempt to change your substrate or change the conditions to eliminate this?

J. I. PETERSON (Melpar): No, we didn't. This of course is a very desirable thing to do.

II

THE DETECTION OF
TRACE IMPURITIES IN
SEMICONDUCTOR MATERIALS

DETERMINATION OF ULTRATRACE IMPURITIES IN SEMICONDUCTOR MATERIALS

George H. Morrison
General Telephone & Electronics Laboratories
Bayside, New York

ABSTRACT

Characterization of semiconductor materials by electrical measurements (resistivity, Hall coefficient) alone is insufficient since the chemical identity and concentration gradients of the intended and inherently present impurities remain unknown. Also, compensation effects of donors and acceptors in the same sample interfere with the understanding and, eventually, the engineering of the semiconductor for solid state devices.

Therefore, highest interest has been aroused in the powerful field of direct detection and determination of trace elements in electronic materials. This is particularly true in view of the recent favorable situation where new and refined direct analytical methods have been shown to be capable of providing sensitivities comparable to those obtained by electrical measurements.

This paper reveals the pace of the program for the determination of ultratrace impurities by presenting recent results obtained with such generally applicable techniques as activation analysis, emission spectroscopy and mass spectrometry. The role of trace analysis in the evaluation of semiconductor raw materials, purified material, single crystals, and device material will be discussed, as well as the microanalysis of very small samples. The sensitivities of the methods will be in the order of a part per million or better.

The basic role of impurities in semiconductor technology and the requirements for high purity are strongly emphasized by this Conference whose theme is the ultrapurification of semiconductor materials. In order to achieve the required degree of purification it is necessary to employ methods of analysis capable of evaluating the various impurities at the various stages of the technology.

From the viewpoint of the analyst, the evaluation of impurities in the raw materials, where the concentrations under consideration are in the range above a part per million, presents no particular problem. Many techniques including emission spectroscopy, colorimetry and other wet chemical methods have been more than adequate in the past in the evaluation of impurities in germanium, silicon, silicon carbide, and various constituents used in the synthesis of compound semiconductors.

It is in the evaluation of single crystal material of high purity that considerable demands are made on analysis, where concentrations in the parts per billion range and even lower are of significance. Although electrical measurements have been of inestimable value as a guide in the characterization of semiconductor materials, alone they are insufficient since the chemical identity and concentration gradients of the intended and inherently present impurities remain unknown. Also, compensation effects of donors and acceptors in the same sample interfere with the understanding and, eventually, the engineering of the semiconductor for solid state devices.

An all too common situation encountered in the purification of semiconductor materials is the reaching of a limit where, regardless of the purification technique employed, further refinements do not yield a significant improvement in the material as determined by electrical measurements. This limit may be one of two types—a free carrier concentration barrier or a mobility barrier. For example, in the purification of gallium antimonide a limit of 1 to 2×10^{17} acceptors per cm^3 has been reached regardless of the purification steps currently employed, indicative of the former type of limitation. The purification of gallium arsenide, on the other hand, has yielded free carrier concentrations in the vicinity of 10^{14} electrons per cm^3. The measured mobilities, however, are lower than would be expected from theoretical calculations, indicating the presence of an impurity or impurities which presents a barrier to the attainment of higher purity in terms of mobility. It is in such situations that identification of specific impurities becomes essential to prescribing the appropriate purification schemes to be employed in attaining higher purity material.

Therefore, highest interest has been aroused in the powerful field of direct detection and determination of ultratrace elements in electronic materials. This is particularly true in view of the recent favorable situation where new and refined direct analytical methods have been shown to be capable of providing sensitivities comparable to those obtained by electrical measurements. The three ultratrace techniques that presently appear to show the most promise in their general applicability to semiconductor impurity analysis are activation analysis, emission spectroscopy, and spark source mass spectrometry. This is further substantiated by the nature of the papers being presented at this session of the Conference dealing with analysis. Although there are a number of other trace analytical techniques such as spectro-photometry, flame photometry, atomic absorption spectroscopy, polarography, etc., which can be used in conjunction with pre-concentration techniques to achieve the sensitivities required, the need for large samples and the danger of contamination and loss when performing chemical separations at the parts per billion level makes their use of doubtful value.

The relative freedom from contamination using activation analysis, emission spectroscopy and mass spectrometry has prompted scientists to investigate methods for increasing the sensitivities of these techniques to the range of interest. In addition, the ability of the latter two techniques to permit direct and simultaneous analysis for many impurity elements has served as a strong stimulus. Therefore, this paper will review the recent trends in the development of these three trace techniques and their application to high-purity semiconductor materials.

ACTIVATION ANALYSIS

Since the application of neutron activation analysis to the determination of traces of arsenic in germanium by Smales and Pate in 1952 [18], many methods have been developed for the determination of a variety of impurity elements in germanium, silicon, silicon carbide, gallium arsenide, and other semiconductor materials [10]. In addition to the high sensitivity available, the unique advantage of freedom from contamination during the course of the analysis, because the species of interest are radioactive, makes the technique particularly attractive in semiconductor analysis.

The principles of the technique are well known [10], and in the past decade most emphasis has been placed on the development of appropriate radiochemical procedures in conjunction with neutron activation in order to apply the technique to the various materials of interest. Various approaches have been taken ranging from individual isolation of the radioelements of interest prior to measurement of activity all the way to the application of gamma scintillation spectrometry directly to the irradiated sample as in the case of silicon [13]. In most cases, however, it has been found that a combination of radiochemical separations and physical methods of resolution of the radiations yields the most practical procedures. Although multielement activation analysis procedures have been developed for silicon [9], [19] and silicon carbide [11], the major role of activation analysis in the determination of ultratrace impurities in semiconductor materials is for the more precise determination of a few specific elements rather than as a survey tool for the general impurity content of the material. Thus the technique is

269

ideally suited to the evaluation of the removal of specific impurity elements, to the study of diffusion processes in conjunction with device fabrication, and in fact any situation where it is necessary to determine precisely the concentration of very minute amounts of elements in samples of limited size. A precision of about 10 percent can be expected at low levels of concentration, although by careful work at somewhat higher levels, this can be extended to 1 percent.

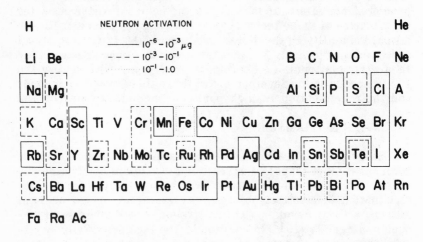

Figure 1. Neutron Activation Sensitivities [12]. Calculated sensitivities based on irradiation until saturation or for 30 days, whichever is shorter, using a flux of 1 x 10¹³ n per cm² per sec. Radioisotopes with half-lives shorter than 10 min. have been omitted.

With regard to the sensitivities currently attainable in neutron activation analysis, typical values using a thermal neutron flux of 1×10^{13} n/cm²/sec are summarized in Figure 1 [12]. The use of higher fluxes results in proportionately greater sensitivity. The values in the figure are based on measurement of the activity with a thin end-window Geiger counter, assuming complete isolation of the nuclide of interest. Although it is possible to activate aluminum, fluorine, neon, niobium, rhodium, titanium and vanadium with neutrons, the resulting short-lived isotopes would decay too rapidly during moderately prolonged chemical separation.

270

Only recently have nuclear reactions other than the (n, γ) been seriously applied during the irradiation process, primarily because of the more general availability of sources of sufficient intensity to provide the necessary sensitivity required for semiconductor problems [10]. One of the more important consequences of this development is the ability now to determine submicrogram amounts of boron in silicon using the B^{11} (p,n)C^{11} reaction.

Within the past two years laboratory neutron generators have been commercially produced which are capable of providing a convenient source of fast neutrons based on the (d,n) reaction. The multiplicity of reactions occurring in fast neutron irradiation widens the scope of the method, particularly for the lighter elements. Using a flux of 10^{10} n/cm^2/sec, sensitivities of 1 μg or better can be achieved for many elements [2]. Although the method is not applicable in the ultratrace range, with anticipated increase in neutron outputs of these laboratory accelerators some time in the future, improvements in sensitivity will be possible.

EMISSION SPECTROSCOPY

Until recently, the only method of sufficient sensitivity for the analysis of high purity semiconductor materials has been neutron activation analysis; however, because of the requirement of close proximity to a nuclear reactor of high thermal neutron flux, the large number of time-consuming radiochemical separations involved, and the inability to determine certain impurity elements of importance in semiconductor technology, more convenient and rapid methods of trace analysis of broader scope have been sought.

Emission spectroscopy has long been used as a trace analytical tool in the parts per million concentration range, and the technique is still universally employed for the survey of semiconductor raw materials. The ready availability of standard spectrographic equipment in the modern laboratory, and the ease and rapidity with which direct determinations can be made, fulfill many requirements mentioned above except that of sensitivity. Although preconcentration techniques have been applied to provide sensitivity in the parts per billion range, they are time-consuming and subject to serious errors because of the difficulty in achieving reproducible blanks and yields.

Within the past two years, however, research efforts have led to refinements in the technique of dc arc excitation so that spectrographic sensitivity has been increased by two to three orders of magnitude [17]. Among the trace determinations of semiconductor interest that have already benefited are the

271

determination of impurities in silicon carbide in the parts per billion concentration range [14], the determination of boron in silicon down to 4 parts per billion [17] and the determination of impurities in gallium arsenide in the parts per billion range [8].

In the author's laboratory, a research program sponsored by the Air Force Cambridge Research Laboratories has revealed that refinements in each of the three major components of emission spectroscopy, namely the light source, the optical system, and the detector, have yielded increased sensitivity, with the most marked results being achieved through a better understanding of the volatilization-excitation processes taking place in the light source [17]. This important increase has been achieved by better control of the impurity volatilization from a solid matrix using a dc arc in an argon atmosphere, resulting in a rate of impurity volatilization more favorable to excitation. Better temperature control results from the combined use of high currents (15 to 23 amps), an undercut carbon anode, and a flowing argon atmosphere. By proper alignment and focusing it is possible to improve the efficiency of both the external optical system and the spectrograph, thereby providing an increase in spectrographic sensitivity of at least an order of magnitude. Finally, the use of faster photographic emulsions has been of some value.

In view of the great convenience and speed of the spectrographic technique, there should be many new applications to semiconductor materials now that sensitivities for many elements in the parts per billion range are possible with direct methods. The technique is ideally suited to purification evaluation studies and control where large numbers of samples are involved. The precision of dc arc methods is about 25 percent.

It should be pointed out, however, that the emission spectrographic technique is highly matrix dependent, so that each material presents a new situation which must be investigated in order to develop appropriate quantitative methods. Also, at the present time the sensitivities for a number of the non-metallic elements are quite poor; however, research is in progress to improve the situation [1,7].

MASS SPECTROMETRY

One of the most dramatic advances in the field of ultra-trace analysis is the development of the technique of spark source mass spectrometry for the determination of impurities in solids. Although its potential value was first demonstrated by Dempster [4] in 1946, it is only since the recent availability of double focusing mass resolving instruments that the technique has attained its important status as a trace analytical tool. The

272

application of the technique to the determination of impurities in semiconductor materials by Hannay [15], [16] may be considered responsible for its rapid development in the past few years.

In essence, the samples are clamped into the electrodes of the vacuum spark ion source at right angles. The high voltage rf spark then jumps between the two samples sending ionized sample molecules into the mass resolving system where they are separated and recorded either on a photographic plate or electrically. The technique has been described in detail by Craig et al. [3] and Robinson [16]. Among the features of the method which make it particularly attractive for impurity analysis are the ability to record the spectrum of the whole range of elements from lithium (mass 6-7) to uranium (mass 234-238) in a single exposure of the photographic plate. The simple mass spectra, which are directly related to the known isotopic constituents of the elements, facilitate qualitative analysis. Of special importance is the fact that the sensitivities of the elements are approximately equal, thereby permitting semiquantitative analysis without instrument calibration, and sensitivities of the order of a part per billion (atomic) for most elements have recently been attained [15]. Among the current limitations are the high cost of the instrument and the slow rate of sample handling because of the use of a vacuum system.

At the present time there are two commercially available instruments, the Consolidated Electrodynamics Corp. Type 21-110 and the Associated Electrical Industries Model MS7. Although they have become available only recently, there have been a number of important applications to the field of semiconductor analysis. Thus, complete determinations of impurities in silicon [3] and gallium arsenide [15] have been reported, and several papers on today's program describe others. It is important to note that in the case of gallium arsenide the investigators have compared the carrier concentration that would be expected on the basis of the mass spectrographic analysis with that obtained from the Hall coefficient and found them to agree within a factor of two. The technique can be used for a variety of semiconductor problems including the analysis of raw materials, evaluation of zone refining, examination of crucible material, identification of surface contamination, and in checking the doping of semiconductors.

While enormous gains have been made in ultratrace analysis, anyone who has been involved in this work realizes that no one of these techniques can be used efficiently for all problems. Thus, mass spectrometry, which at the present time must be considered a research tool, can best serve as a survey method for new materials, so that other more convenient techniques can be prescribed for specific elements. Activation analysis still provides the greatest sensitivity and precision for certain elements, whereas emission spectroscopy fulfills the need for rapid and convenient multielement analyses for large numbers of samples. The need for sensitivity will, of course, vary with the specific purification problem at hand. In addition to the ability to analyze purified raw materials and high purity semiconductor crystals, these highly sensitive techniques are useful in the examination of micro samples such as the final device, where the concentration and distribution of minute amounts of specific elements can be ascertained.

While the role of ultratrace analysis for the identification of specific impurities has been emphasized here, there are many other difficult problems involving impurities for which new and highly specialized methods are required; a number of these will be described in this session.

REFERENCES

1. D. Andrychuk and C. E. Jones, Jr., "Electron Gun-Type Excitation Source for Spectrographic Determination of O_2, N_2, H_2, P, S and Halogens in GaAs," paper presented at the Pittsburgh Conference on Analytical Chemistry and Applied Spectroscopy, March 3, 1961.
2. R. F. Coleman, Analyst, 86, 39 (1961).
3. R. D. Craig, G. A. Errock, and J. D. Waldron, in "Advances in Mass Spectrometry," J. D. Waldron, ed., Pergamon Press, N. Y., 1959.
4. A. J. Dempster, "The Mass Spectrograph in Chemical Analysis," U. S. Atomic Energy Commission Report MDDC 370, Decl. 1946.
5. N. B. Hannay, Rev. Sci. Instr. 25, 644 (1954).
6. N. B. Hannay and A. J. Ahearn, Anal. Chem. 26, 1056 (1954).
7. C. E. Harvey, "Research Investigation of Semiconductor Impurities," Second Quarterly Report to U. S. Army Signal Engineering Labs., Fort Monmouth, N. J., Dec. 1960.
8. C. E. Jones, Jr., D. Andrychuk and J. Massengale, "The Determination of Low Trace Impurities in Semiconductor Gallium Arsenide," paper presented at the Pittsburgh Conference on Analytical Chemistry and Applied Spectroscopy, March 3, 1961.
9. A. Kant, J. P. Cali and H. D. Thompson, Anal. Chem. 28, 1867 (1956).
10. R. C. Koch, "Activation Analysis Handbook," Academic Pres, N. Y., 1960.
11. L. F. Lowe, H. D. Thompson and J. F. Cali, Anal. Chem. 31, 1951 (1959).
12. G. H. Morrison, "Metals Analysis by Radioactivation," American Society for Testing Materials Special Technical Publication No. 261, 1959.
13. G. H. Morrison and J.-F. Cosgrove, Anal. Chem. 27, 810 (1955).

14. G. H. Morrison, R. L. Rupp and G. L. Klecak, Anal. Chem. 32, 933 (1960).
15. G. D. Perkins, C. F. Robinson and R. K. Willardson, "Analysis of Impurities in Compound Semiconductors," Special Report by Consolidated Electrodynamics Corp., Pasadena, Calif., Jan. 6, 1961.
16. C. F. Robinson in "Physical Methods in Chemical Analysis," W. G. Berl, ed., Vol. 1, 2nd revised ed., Academic Press, N.Y., 1960.
17. R. L. Rupp and G. H. Morrison, "Analysis of Trace Impurities in Silicon Carbide," Scientific Report No. 2, TR 60-703.8, to Air Force Cambridge Research Laboratories, July 7, 1960.
18. A. A. Smales and B. D. Pate, Anal. Chem. 24, 717 (1952).
19. B. A. Thompson, B. M. Strause and M. B. Leboeuf, Anal. Chem. 30, 1023 (1958).

DISCUSSION

J. I. PETERSON (Melpar): Dr. Morrison, has your laboratory a solids mass spectrograph?

G. H. MORRISON (General Telephone and Electronics Laboratory): Our laboratory just acquired one at the beginning of this year (1961); however, it is still in the process of installation and adjustment.

J. I. PETERSON (Melpar): This, in my opinion, is potentially the most powerful tool available, but I understand from conversations with the group at Wright Air Development Center, that a memory problem exists, which has not yet been solved.

G. H. MORRISON (General Telephone and Electronics Laboratory): We have here quite a group of experts in this field, and I presume they will cover this problem in the course of their papers.

J. I. PETERSON (Melpar): Very well. I would like now to raise what seems to be one of the biggest shortcomings in this entire field of trace analysis: namely, the need for standards. We have the instrumental indication, but no one knows for sure what it means.

G. H. MORRISON (General Telephone and Electronics Laboratory): This is unfortunately true for the whole field of trace analysis, and, in particular, the field of emission spectroscopy. It seems no one has time to do anything except to analyze samples. What is needed are many research programs dedicated to basic understanding in this field.

C. ROSENBLUM (Chairman) (Merck): Would you say that a comparable problem exists in activation analysis?

275

G. H. MORRISON (General Telephone and Electronics Laboratory): No. I think the problems have been pretty well worked out here, and furthermore, there are many research centers dedicated to developing a basic understanding and of the techniques involved.

J. P. CALI (AFCRL): I would like to comment first on this question of standards. A good many people here today belong to the Semiconductor Analytical Group (SAG), who recognize that in the field of emission spectroscopy and now in the rapidly developing field of solids mass spectrography, this problem of standards is pressing and must be faced by the entire semiconductor industry. Indeed, it has wide applicability to any field where trace analysis is important.

Air Force Cambridge Research Laboratories is presently discussing with the National Bureau of Standards the possibility of the preparation of such standards. They are eminently qualified, if any one is, to handle such a problem. However, the Bureau of Standards will not undertake this difficult task unless it is convinced that there is a wide-spread need for such standards. If such a need is, in effect, extant, then we are going to attempt to make a set of three standards using silicon as the matrix. The three ranges to be aimed at are, one set at one part per million, one set at a tenth of a part per million and the last set at ten parts per billion. It is planned to have from ten to thirty trace elements present per set.

I should like to comment very briefly on the state of activation analysis. There are several areas of basic research being pursued, which will, I believe, tend to increase the applicability of the activation method. It is hoped this research will permit the analysis of some elements in trace concentrations, where analyses are now difficult or impossible to accomplish.

Air Force Cambridge Research Laboratories is sponsoring research at the M.I.T. Reactor aimed toward the determination of traces by the use of short-lived activated products. Magnesium, for example, with a half life of about five minutes, could be done using special techniques at reactor sites.

The whole field of prompt gamma emission is a field which, up to now, has had practically no application in trace analysis. We are actively pursuing possibilities in this area.

The last area to be mentioned is the field of charged particle activation, which has been quite neglected. Of course, in the past there was the problem of deutron or proton production. However, particle accelerators are now available which should certainly stimulate interest in this field. This field should be especially important for the trace determination of the light mass elements.

C. ROSENBLUM (Chairman) (Merck): I feel it is appropriate to devote some time to activation analysis because, later in the session, we shall concentrate primarily on spectroscopic methods.

E. A. LEARY (Martin): Dr. Morrison, I noticed in your comments on fast neutron activation, that you said zirconium, but not niobium, was detectable.

Now, as my memory serves me, the thermal cross-section for zirconium is about a sixth barn and the thermal cross-section for niobium is about one barn.

G. H. MORRISON (General Telephone and Electronics Laboratory): With regards to niobium, the problem here is its short half life.

Of course, as Mr. Cali pointed out, if one can work at a reactor site, then some of these fast half-life nuclides can be detected. Generally speaking, five to ten minutes half-life nuclides could be done using fast separations, of if possible, by direct gamma spectrometry.

With regards to the fast neutron activation work, the data quoted is from Coleman in his article in "The Analyst."

E. A. LEARY (Martin): I noticed in one of your slides that by gamma ray spectroscopy multi-element analysis can be accomplished. How about the rare earths?

G. H. MORRISON (General Telephone and Electronics Laboratory): Sorry. That is the wrong situation. This method works well with a silicon matrix. One must realize, of course, that a price is paid for this convenience, and that is sensitivity.

Gamma spectroscopy applied to trace analysis is particularly useful where the matrix is a pure beta-emitter having a short half-life, and is not strongly activated. This method has been used in silicon, aluminum and in biochemical and organic applications.

C. ROSENBLUM (Chairman) (Merck): I would like to illustrate Mr. Cali's contention that there is much to be gained from the use of the prompt nuclear reactions in the very case that we are not going to be able to discuss this morning, namely, the boron work. There is a prompt gamma emitted by the metastable state of the lithium, which is produced by the (n, γ) reaction on boron, which could certainly serve for quite sensitive measurements. No one, to my knowledge, has ever attempted that sort of an analysis, that is, by measuring the prompt gamma emitted by the metastable state of the lithium produced.

M. R. LORENZ (General Electric Research Laboratory): I would like to mention another area which merits some

277

investigation; that is, the area near the band edge where there are multiple emission peaks. At low temperatures these peaks come up quite strongly, and I wonder if this may not be a good method which should be thoroughly investigated. One advantage, of course, is that the method is non-destructive. Are you aware of any work going on in this area from an analytical viewpoint?

G. H. MORRISON (General Telephone and Electronics Laboratory): If there is work going on in this area I am not presently aware of it. What I have tried to cover this morning are the most general techniques of trace element analysis. Later in the session more specialized methods will be discussed.

ANALYSIS OF TRACE IMPURITIES BY SPARK SOURCE MASS SPECTROMETRY

R. Brown, R. D. Craig, J. A. James and C. M. Wilson
Associated Electrical Industries Ltd.
Manchester, England

INTRODUCTION

Mass spectrometric analysis of inorganic solids requires a different approach from that used for gases and organic compounds as the materials are generally refractory so that it is impractical to introduce them into the mass spectrometer in the vapour phase. Of the methods available for producing ions from solids, only three have been at all widely used:
1. The spark source technique [1-3].
2. Thermal evaporation followed by ionization in an electron beam [4].
3. Surface ionization [5].

For elemental analysis the main requirement is that the ion beam should be representative of the composition of the solid, and the spark source technique is the only one for which this requirement is satisfactorily met. A great advantage of the method is that the whole range of elements is covered in a single analysis, and it is found that all elements have essentially the same sensitivity to within about a factor of three, for metallic and non-metallic elements alike and independent of the matrix, whether it be a low melting solid or a refractory metal or compound.

The choice of a spark source for excitation gives rise to a large energy spread in the resulting ion beam and requires the use of a double focusing mass spectrometer.

The MS7 instrument made by Associated Electrical Industries Ltd. uses the Mattauch arrangement, as shown in Figure 1, in which focusing of the ions of all masses in one plane makes it possible to use a photographic plate as the ion detector.

DESCRIPTION OF THE INSTRUMENT

Positive ions, representative of the sample electrodes, are produced in the spark gap and accelerated through a system of

279

MS7 MASS SPECTROMETER

FOR THE ANALYSIS OF SOLIDS

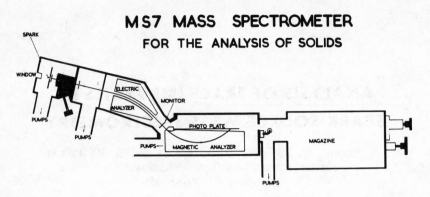

Figure 1. MS7 Mass Spectrometer.

slits by a potential difference of 20kV, finally passing into the analysers through a slit at earth potential. The ion beam is then deflected in the field of the electrostatic analyser and a fraction of the beam is intercepted by the monitor slit. The remainder passes on into the magnetic field, where the ions follow different radial paths depending on their mass to charge ratio, and are recorded on a photographic plate.

Because the conditions of sparking in the source vary with time, the exposure is measured by the charge falling on the monitor slit, and is ended when a given charge has been collected. The spark is controlled by an oscillator which allows the pulse length, and repetition rate to be altered, and permits the exposure to be varied over a range of 10^7 to 1. The photographic plate can be moved so that a series of 15 graded exposures can be made on the same plate, which is 10 inches long and 2 inches wide and coated with Ilford Q2 emulsion.

The normal mass range covered is 7-250, but the lower mass region can be recorded on an expanded scale by adjusting the magnetic field, for example to cover the mass range 1-35 on the plate.

The pressure in the analyser section is maintained at less than 10^{-8} mm Hg. and vacuum locks are provided for changing samples and photographic plates. Thus the sample can be changed, a new photographic plate inserted and the equipment pumped down ready to start the exposures again, all within 10 minutes.

METHOD OF ANALYSIS

Identification

The first step in identifying lines on the photographic plate is the calibration of the mass scale; since distance along the

280

plate is proportional to $\sqrt{m/e}$, it is possible to calculate the complete mass scale once two lines are identified. However, it is usual to work at a series of fixed values of magnetic field, so comparison between plates is simplified and a mass scale can be constructed for each setting.

Figure 2 shows a typical mass spectrum, of a silicon sample, covering the mass range 7-250, and showing a series of graded exposures. The strongest lines are a group of three which correspond in intensities to the abundance of the silicon isotopes and these are at mass 28, 29 and 30. This isotopic pattern is reproduced in a group of lines at mass 14, 14-1/2, 15 which are due to doubly ionized silicon, and this is repeated for Si^{3+} and so on.

Other obvious features of the plate are the groups of lines starting at mass 56, 84 and higher multiples of 28, which are due to molecular ions of the form Si_n^+.

The lines at 121 and 123 are identified as antimony by their position and isotope ratio and the absence of any lines due to silicon compounds in this region.

The series of graded exposures is useful in showing up any surface contamination or inhomogeneity of the samples; in the absence of these there should be a regular increase in intensity for all lines with increasing exposure.

The time taken for an analysis depends on the level of impurity it is required to detect, and Table 1 shows average times for detection to the 10^{-8} and 10^{-9} levels. Actual times however are variable as some materials give larger ion currents than others, and the electrode shape can have a large effect on the efficiency of extracting the ions produced in the spark.

Sensitivity

The sensitivity of the MS7 mass spectrometer is such that an isotope corresponding to 1 in 10^9, or .001 ppm (atomic) of the major constituent is detectable, provided the line is not masked by one due to the major constituent. This sensitivity has been confirmed by comparison with analyses of doped samples by other methods, including electrical measurements and radio-activation.

To estimate the concentration of an impurity we normally use the internal standard method, in which a comparison is made between the exposures required to produce two lines of equal optical density, one line being due to the impurity and the other to a weak line of the matrix element.

For example, in the analysis of a silicon sample for boron content the boron line at mass 11 was detectable on an exposure of 3×10^{-8} coulomb, and the silicon line at mass 30 occurred at

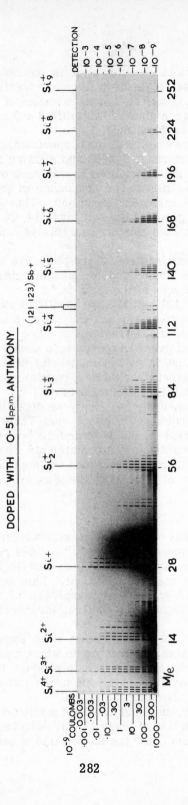

Figure 2. Mass Spectrum of a Silicon Sample.

Table 1

Times for Analysis to 10^{-8} and 10^{-9} Level

INSTRUMENT TIME

To insert sample and change photoplate	:	5 minutes
To pump down	:	5
To take thirteen exposures for detection to 10^{-8} level	:	10

Total time   :   20 minutes

To take two additional exposures for detection to 10^{-9} level	:	40

Total time   :   60 minutes

INTERPRETATION TIME

Photographic processing of the plate	:	10 minutes
To estimate one element in a known matrix	:	1/2 minute
To make a complete analysis with an unknown matrix	:	4 hours

the same density on an exposure of 10^{-13} coulomb. The boron concentration was therefore calculated as follows:

$$(\text{Boron}) \quad = \frac{E_s}{E_b} \cdot \frac{I_s}{I_b}$$

$$= \frac{10^{-13}}{3 \times 10^{-8}} \cdot \frac{0.03}{0.8} = 0.125 \text{ ppm (atomic)}$$

where

E_b and E_s are the exposures at which the boron and silicon lines are visible at the same density and

I_b and I_s are the corresponding isotope abundances.

This result, expressed in terms of atoms/cc is compared below with the value deduced from electrical measurements on the crystal.

MS7 (assuming equal sensitivity for B and Si)	:	$6.3.10^{15}$ atoms/cc
Hall Measurement	:	$7.6.10^{15}$

The minimum detectable amount of boron in silicon is largely governed by vacuum conditions for at m/e 11 there is a slight continuous background due to charge exchange processes between the silicon ions and the residual gas molecules in the analysers [3]. On the present instrument this background is normally of comparable density to a 3.10^{-9} boron line.

The sensitivity and basic detection level of 1 in 10^9 has also been checked by radio activation analysis. For example the antimony lines in the spectrum of Figure 2 were found by activation analysis to correspond to 0.51 ppm as compared with 1.2 ppm estimated from the spectrum on the assumption of equal sensitivity for Sb and Si.

The assumption of equal sensitivity for different elements has also been shown to be valid, to within a factor of about 3, for a wide range of trace elements in steel and copper spectrographic standards [3, 6].

DETECTION LIMITS

Figure 3 shows the usual practical detection limits for impurities in graphite and silicon. Most elements are readily detectable to .01 ppm, or better, but there are exceptions.

For example, the element shown with a detection level of 0.1 ppm in graphite is magnesium and the reason for the poor detection level is the masking of the magnesium line at 24 by C_2^+

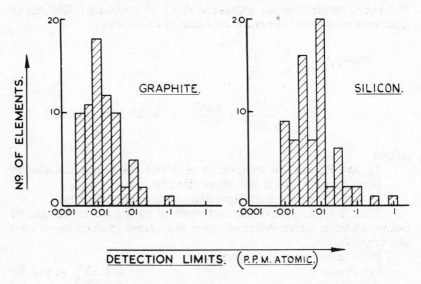

Figure 3. Detection Limits in Graphite and Silicon.

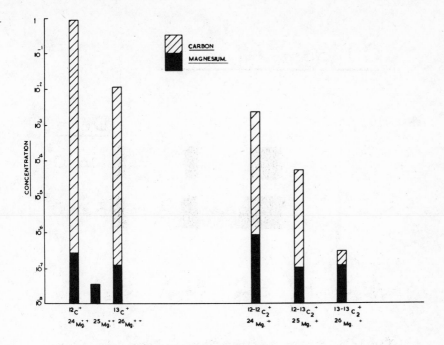

Figure 4. Overlap of Carbon and Magnesium Spectra
(1 ppm Mg in C).

as shown in Figure 4. The less abundant isotopes of magnesium at 25 and 26 are also obscured by combination of ^{12}C, ^{13}C, but the line at 12-1/2 due to $^{25}Mg^{++}$ can be used because the probability of C_2^{++} formation is very small.

However, because of the continuous background from C^+ the minimum detection level at 12-1/2 is raised to 3 in 10^9; a factor of 3 has then to be allowed for use of a doubly rather than singly charged ion and a factor of 10 for the isotopic abundance of ^{25}Mg, thus leading to the detection limit figure of 0.1 ppm.

In some cases the usual figure quoted for the detection limit can be improved on, for example by taking exposures on an expanded mass scale to reduce the effect of continuous background, or by using mass measurement to distinguish a background or matrix line from a possible impurity at the same mass number. These points are illustrated in Figure 5 which shows a part spectrum of a 0.17 ppm aluminum in silicon sample. The aluminum line at 27 is seen to be well separated from the intense Si^+ background and to be clearly resolved from an instrumental background line of $C_2H_3^+$, also at m/e 27.

285

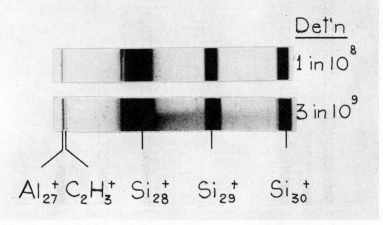

Figure 5. Silicon Spectrum Showing Resolution of the
Aluminum and Hydrocarbon Lines at Mass 27.

As an example of the sort of detection levels readily obtainable on a binary semiconductor the detection limits for impurities
in gallium phosphide are listed in Table 2.

SAMPLE HANDLING

The instrument is not limited in application to one class of
sample, but can be used in the metal, semiconductor or ceramic
fields. The sample handling technique used for a particular
sample will depend on the type of material and to some extent
on its size and crystalline state.

Ideally, a pair of electrodes 1/2 inch long and .060 inches
square are cut to size, cleaned, and inserted in the source and
sparked for various times to produce a series of graded exposures. If the sample is a single crystal of a noble metal the
etching and washing procedure is quite simple, for example
silver would be etched in aqua regia and washed in deionized
water and the process repeated twice. If the sample is a more
active metal, impurities in the etchant may plate out on the
sample and even repeated etching and washing may not remove
the last traces so that in such cases the purest reagents available should be used in minimum quantities.

286

Table 2

Detection Limits of Impurities in Gallium Phosphide
(ppm atomic)

Element	Detection Limit	Element	Detection Limit
Uranium	0.001	Silver	0.002
Thorium	0.001	Palladium	0.004
Bismuth	0.001	Rhodium	0.001
Lead	0.002	Ruthenium	0.005
Thallium	0.005	Molybdenum	0.004
Mercury	0.003	Niobium	0.3
Gold	0.001	Zirconium	0.006
Platinum	0.003	Yttrium	0.001
Iridium	0.002	Strontium	0.001
Osmium	0.002	Rubidium	0.05
Rhenium	0.002	Bromine	0.02
Tungsten	0.003	Selenium	0.02
Tantalum	0.001	Arsenic	0.01
Hafnium	0.003	Germanium	0.03
Lutecium	0.001	Zinc	0.006
Ytterbium	0.003	Copper	0.005
Thulium	0.001	Nickel	0.005
Erbium	0.003	Cobalt	0.003
Holmium	0.001	Iron	0.003
Dysprosium	0.004	Manganese	0.003
Terbium	0.001	Chromium	0.01
Gadolinium	0.004	Vanadium	0.01
Europium	0.002	Titanium	0.01
Samarium	0.004	Scandium	0.01
Neodymium	0.008	Calcium	0.01
Praseodymium	0.001	Potassium	0.01
Cerium	0.01	Chlorine	0.01
Lanthanum	0.003	Sulphur	0.03
Barium	0.2	Silicon	0.03
Cesium	0.01	Aluminium	0.003
Iodine	0.01	Magnesium	0.003
Tellurium	0.03	Sodium	3
Antimony	0.002	Fluorine	0.003
Tin	0.003	Boron	0.001
Indium	0.001	Beryllium	0.001
Cadmium	0.003	Lithium	0.003

If the sample is cracked or porous, reagents are likely to be left in the pores and it may be better not to use an etchant at all. Cleaning methods which do not involve etchants include physical techniques such as ion bombardment or turning with a diamond-tipped tool, and with brittle material it is sometimes possible to cleave crystals to produce fresh uncontaminated surfaces. When crystals are grown from the vapour phase it is often possible to select a crystal of suitable dimensions which can be examined without any other treatment.

The size of sample consumed in the analysis is quite small, about 10 mg, so that if polycrystalline material is being examined which may show segregation of impurities along the boundaries the analysis will only be representative of the whole sample if the grain size is small in relation to the sample consumed.

Sometimes the size of the sample available is insufficient to obtain an electrode 1/2" long. In this case a small fragment may be inserted into a split graphite electrode and sparked as before, but one must watch for carbon appearing in the spectrum or formation of carbides with the sample. Using this technique we have successfully analysed a single radar diode which weighed only 2 mg., showing the doping element and its approximate concentration. Individual crystals of cadmium sulphide for photocells have also been examined.

The graphite used must of course be free from impurities. We have used National Carbon Co. spectrographic electrodes, in which chlorine is the only element present at a level likely to interfere with the analysis.

Graphite has also been used to support low melting point materials such as gallium, which cannot be used as self supporting electrodes. In this case a small hole is drilled in the end of the graphite rod, and a globule of gallium weighing 20-30 mg. inserted. When a pair of such electrodes is sparked together the gallium spreads over the surface but is held by the surface tension forces. Useful spectra can be obtained this way as is shown in Figure 6 by the relatively low intensity of the C_2^+ lines at m/e 24-26 compared with the Ga^{++} lines at m/e 34-1/2 and 35-1/2. The lines at m/e 32-34 are due to a sulphur impurity in the gallium. However, when the sample is liquid there is some evidence of selective distillation of impurities and only semi-quantitative data can be given, although comparison between samples is possible.

The low melting point metals sodium (M.P..97°C) and indium (M.P.155°C) have been successfully run as self-supporting electrodes. The metalloids tellurium, arsenic and phosphorus have also been run, phosphorus being first converted to the more stable red form. With these volatile elements the amount of

288

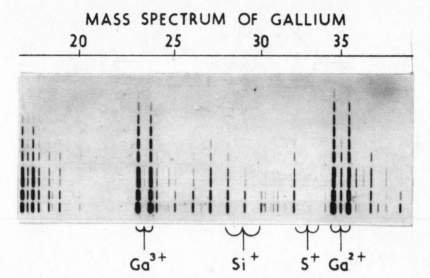

Figure 6. Gallium Spectrum Showing
Silicon and Sulphur Impurities.

sample consumed is comparatively high, and the source must be thoroughly cleaned and baked out to avoid memory effects.

The resistivity of the material is not critical provided it is less than a few thousand ohm.cm. and most semiconductors can be handled without any special technique. However, insulators do require a starting electrode as shown in Figure 7, where the samples to be analysed are clamped with graphite auxiliary electrodes. Here, one must use a different system for monitoring the exposure since the ions reaching the normal monitor will be a variable mixture of sample ions and carbon ions. However, by fitting a special collector electrode in the magnetic analyser it is possible to monitor a line from one of the major constituents. Using this system we have analysed natural and synthetic silica used for crucibles [7]. Alumina crucibles, single crystals and glasses have also been examined using this technique.

APPLICATIONS TO SEMICONDUCTORS

This analytical technique has proved useful in analysis of silicon for aluminium and boron, but recently the chief application has been to compound semiconductors where the state of the art is not so far advanced. In the past 12 months we have run about 200 "semiconductor" samples covering surveys of existing sources of supply of component elements such as aluminium, gallium, indium, phosphorus, arsenic and antimony, testing the efficiency of zone refining for a number of elements at one time,

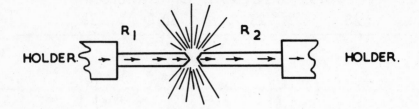

(a). CONDUCTORS

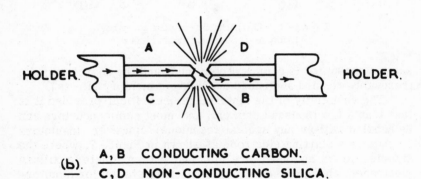

(b). A, B CONDUCTING CARBON.
     C, D NON-CONDUCTING SILICA.

Figure 7. Electrode Arangement for Insulators.

checking the purity of crucible materials and final analysis of the compounds prepared.

A particular example is shown in Figure 8, which shows how the aluminium and silicon impurities in a gallium phosphide sample are segregated to opposite ends of the ingot by zone refining.

Another series of analyses was related to the preparation of gallium arsenide by a variety of techniques and using different starting materials. As shown below the results indicate a close correlation between the silicon content and electrical properties.

ZONE REFINED GALLIUM PHOSPHIDE

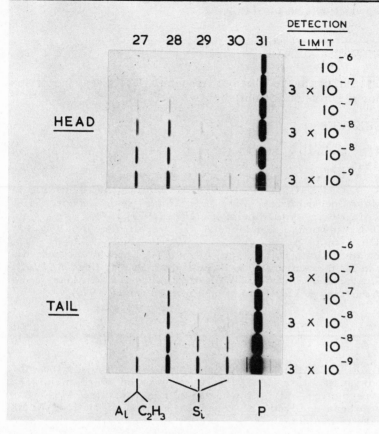

Figure 8. Gallium Phosphide Spectra Showing the Opposite Direction of Segregation of Aluminium and Silicon in a Zone Refined Sample.

Ingot	Silicon Content (MS7)	Net Donors (Hall Measurement)
58/3	3.2 ppm	2.5 ppm
58/4	9.3	10
58/5	7.4	5
58/5R	5.4	2
60/2	14	10
60/3	3.6	2

CONCLUSIONS

The technique of spark source mass spectrometry for the analysis of solids provides a general method for trace analysis with sensitivity down to 1 in 10^9 which can be used with metals, semiconductors and insulators.

ACKNOWLEDGMENTS

The authors are indebted to Associated Electrical Industries Ltd. for permission to publish this paper.

REFERENCES

1. A. J. Dempster, MDDG 370, U.S. Department of Commerce (1946).
2. N. B. Hannay, Rev. Sci. Inst. 25, 644 (1954).
3. R. D. Craig, G. A. Errock and J. D. Waldron, Advances in Mass Spectrometry, p. 136 (Pergamon Press, London, 1959).
4. R. E. Honig, Anal. Chem. 25, 1530 (1953).
5. D. C. Newton, J. Sanders, A. C. Tyrrell, The Analyst, 85, 870, 1960.
6. R. M. Elliott, R. D. Craig and G. A. Errock, Instruments and Measurements, Vol. 1 (Academic Press, London, 1961).
7. J. A. James and J. L. Williams, Advances in Mass Spectrometry, p. 157 (Pergamon Press, London, 1959).

DISCUSSION

L. R. WEISBERG (RCA Laboratories): Although you discussed sensitivities, Dr. Duke, there was not much mentioned about resolution. It is my understanding that the MS-7 has recently been involved with research on mass resolution. Would you care to comment?

J. F. DUKE (National Physical Laboratory): Yes. The first instrument was rather disappointing resolution-wise. It is not really known why this was so and, by a bit of juggling of the electrical parameters on the instrument, we have now been able to improve this to perhaps better than 1 in 1500. We haven't really done enough work to get to the final precise figure.

In my own particular instrument, I am pretty certain that it is better than 1 in 1500, as I will show in the next paper. In fact, the people at Associated Electrical Industries are getting much increased resolution and are resolving hydrocarbon from elemental lines.

L. R. WEISBERG (RCA Laboratories): I understand that 1 in 3000 has been approached. Do you know if that is true?

J. F. DUKE (National Physical Laboratory): Well, I wouldn't like to bank on this.

W. M. HICKAM (Westinghouse Research Laboratories): In the polyatomic ions associated with carbon in the spark instrument, there has been some discussion that there are intensity variations of the polyatomic ions which may be related to factors in the sample itself. Have you noticed any variation in the intensities of the polyatomic ions for silicon that might be pertinent to the sample?

J. F. DUKE (National Physical Laboratory): No. I don't think this has been even looked for at the moment.

THE APPLICATION OF SOLID-SOURCE MASS SPECTROMETRY TO DETERMINE THE PURITY OF MATERIALS FOR SEMICONDUCTOR PURPOSES

J. F. Duke
National Physical Laboratory
Metallurgy Division
Teddington, Middlesex, England

SUMMARY

An Associated Electrical Industries MS.7 solid-source mass spectrometer is being employed to analyse pure metals destined for use in the semiconductor field. The sensitivity of the instrument is such that impurity concentrations as low as 1 part in 10^9 (atomic) can be detected in a number of cases. Almost the whole of the periodic table can be covered in each single analysis. The absence of any reagent blank is a further attraction.

Some selected applications are described and details of the initial operating experiences are given.

INTRODUCTION

The MS.7 mass spectrometer [1] has been specifically designed to determine traces of impurities in solids. A more complete description of the instrument appears in another paper given at this conference [2], but essentially it consists of a Dempster radio-frequency spark source allied with a Mattauch-Herzog double focussing mass analyser. The mass spectrum is focussed on to a photographic plate, which has the advantage of acting as a simple integrating detector as well as being a permanent record.

The place of solid-source mass spectrometry as an analytical tool in pure metals research is fairly well defined. It has much greater sensitivity than X-ray fluorescence or X-ray emission analysis, and its inherently simple spectra with their relative freedom from interference effects are easier to interpret than optical emission spectra. It further yields simultaneous information for a large number of elements (including the light elements lithium and beryllium, and non-metals such as boron,

294

sulphur and the halogens) in contrast to nuclear activation or polarographic techniques. More important perhaps are its freedom from reagent blanks and the modest amounts of sample required for a complete analysis. At present the MS.7 is most useful in detecting elements in the range of concentration between 1 part in 10^5 and 1 part in 10^9.

EXPERIMENTAL TECHNIQUE

The lower limit of detection and the quality of the spectra produced are governed to a large extent by the degree of vacuum obtainable in the analyser section of the instrument, and it is desirable to maintain this below 2×10^{-8} torr. This necessitates continuous pumping and continuous use of liquid nitrogen in the cold traps serving the four diffusion pumps. Automatic refilling is essential and as much as 30 to 50 litres of liquid nitrogen may be consumed per day depending on laboratory conditions.

To assist outgassing the system there is provision for baking the analyser region to a temperature of 250°C. In practice it is found convenient to bake out every weekend, with the cold traps empty, and to refill the traps on Monday morning before allowing the metalwork to cool. The gaskets have withstood these repeated heating cycles without trouble for a year of operation.

A vacuum lock enables the source region to be opened to atmosphere so that samples may be changed. The samples are mounted in insulated clamps via the front window as shown in Figure 1. Alternative windows are provided: one with a rubber gasket, allows for rapid sample changing, but limits the pressure attainable in the source region to approximately 5×10^{-7} torr. When the lowest limits of detection are required an alternative window is attached by a metal gasket, and the source region baked overnight to reduce the source pressure to that of the analyser region.

Considerable sputtering and evaporation of samples occur during the exposure periods, and to minimise memory effects a disposable sleeve is used around the circumference of the source chamber. Since all demountable parts of the source unit and ion gun are dismantled and thoroughly etched between samples, a second complete set of source parts is of great advantage.

It is not easy to generalize over sample preparation and handling techniques since individual metals have their own problems. The source design calls for two rod-like specimens of matchstick dimensions. In the case of a soft metal such as indium it is possible to cut the sample approximately to size with a stainless steel scalpel, whereas aluminium is best cut with a fine saw blade. Hard or brittle materials demand abrasive

Figure 1. Front View of Source Chamber Showing
Sample Electrodes in Position.

or diamond-bonded slitting wheels. Separate wheels and blades
are required for each matrix material to avoid cross-contami-
nation.

After the shaping operations it is essential to etch away the
surface of the material in a drastic fashion, for trace elements
transferred from saw blades and wheel bonding agents will
show up at disproportionately high levels, since the spark only
penetrates the outer layers of the sample.

Care must be taken in choosing suitable etching media
because recontamination of the sample surface is easily possible.
Acid media are almost universally used for etching metals.
However, it has been found that chloride ions are readily absorbed
from hydrochloric acid solution and use of this reagent has been
abandoned in favour of hydrofluoric acid, frequently in the
presence of nitric acid, which is less troublesome in this respect.
Nitric acid used alone has a tendency to produce oxide films on
the surface of metals, which subsequently cause molecular oxide
ions to appear in the mass spectrum.

296

The reagents used are of 'transistor' quality and all sample cleansing is carried out in polypropylene or teflon ware. The cleaned samples are handled with teflon-tipped tweezers. Ultrasonic agitation has been found useful in breaking up bubble formation during etching, in accelerating the attack of the reagents and in dispersion of the products throughout the solution. Several cycles of etch, rinse, and etch in fresh reagent are completed, and the final rinse is made under running deionized water. The samples are loaded immediately into the source chamber without drying, the surplus water evaporating away into the vacuum system. The cleaned specimens are rigorously kept away from organic solvents, since it was found that severe hydrocarbon contamination was obtained when acetone, alcohol or ether was used as a final wash liquid in order to accelerate drying.

As a final precaution against spurious surface effects a long pre-spark, equivalent to a integrated ion-beam current of 100 millimicrocoulombs, is made. This, besides removing the surface layers from the ends of the samples and allowing future exposures to be truly representative of the bulk material, also serves to coat the source parts and the source slit system with an evaporated film of the sample material. This appreciably assists in reducing 'memory' of previous matrices.

Before the photographic plate is exposed to the ion beam, the mass range to be covered must be selected and a choice of electrical parameters made to provide suitable source excitation conditions.

The mass range is determined by the strength of the magnetic field. This is variable in steps to cover mass ranges from 1-25 up to 7-250, as illustrated in Figure 2a. The expansion of the low mass end of the scale is valuable when multiply charged ions must be identified because the primary lines are obscured by background or totally interfered with.

The spark is controlled by an rf oscillator which can be varied with respect to pulse length and pulse repetition rate. It is necessary to adjust these controls to give a suitable ion beam intensity, so that the instantaneous current is neither so large as to overload the monitor amplifier, nor so small as to be comparable to the amplifier noise level. It is found, however, that the mass spectrum intensity varies in an apparently random manner with the settings of these controls. This is illustrated in Figure 2b, which shows the spectrum of a sample of indium containing added quantities of several impurity elements. The blocks of exposures are of four different pulse lengths at each of three different repetition rates. Although the integrated beam currents are equal in each exposure, the variation in line intensity is very marked. It is therefore imperative to retain the same pulse lengths and repetition rates throughout the whole series of

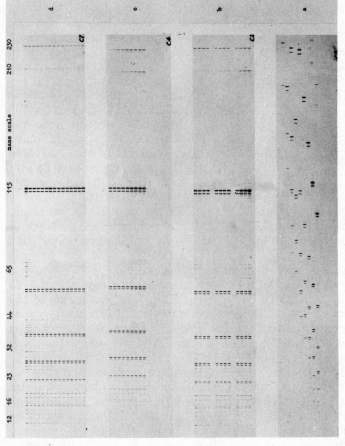

Figure 2. a – Variation of mass range by change in magnet current: lowest exposure, 7–250; 5th exposure, 4–120; 7th exposure, 3–60; 8th exposure, 1–32; top exposure, 1–24. b – Effect of change in spark length and frequency: pulse lengths of 25, 50, 100 and 200 μsec at 3000 c/s (lower block), 1000 c/s (center block) and 300 c/s (upper block). c – Effect of change in spark voltage: lowest exposure 60 kV, changing in 5 kV steps to 20 kV (upper exposure). d – Series of replicate exposures of equal value.

298

exposures on a plate, and not to increase these to reduce the time needed to make the longest exposures.

A further variable in the source excitation circuit is the spark voltage, and the value to which this is set has also a marked effect on the spectra produced. Figure 2c illustrates the effect of gradually increasing the spark voltage from about 20 kV to 60 kV. The exposures are all nominally equal, but the enhancement of the impurity lines is noticeable as the spark voltage increases. The greater tendency for molecular ion formation, such as In_2^+, with increasing spark energy is also indicated.

Figure 2d is a series of nominally equal exposures taken with constant source conditions and shows other features. The first (top) exposure indicates marked segregation of impurity elements at the surface of the sample, which has probably been caused by preferential dissolution of the matrix material during the etching procedure, or alternatively, of replating of dissolved impurities. The last ten or so exposures are more uniform in appearance and are probably more nearly representative of the bulk composition. A series of hydrocarbon lines is visible at masses 39-44, which decrease in intensity in each successive exposure as the contamination in the source chamber is gradually 'cracked' and removed from the system. The advantages of a long pre-spark before an actual sample determination are obvious.

It is found in practice that it is not easy to accommodate more than two samples during the course of a working day. The care that need be taken over sample preparation has been mentioned. The restrictions imposed on variation of the source parameters during analysis entail that the longest exposure required to reach detection limits of 1 in 10^8 to 1 in 10^9 takes upwards of one hour, and the total exposure period is of the order of two hours. Processing the plate is a relatively rapid procedure, but interpreting the mass spectrum and obtaining quantitative information is again lengthy. A complete analysis may take another three hours. Duplicate plates are taken wherever possible, and to guard against inhomogeneity in the sample material, specimens from different portions should be examined.

Interpretation of the Mass Spectra

Some typical plates are shown in Figure 3, which are of three aluminium ingots in various stages of purification. The upper is of a commercial super-purity grade taken from selected electrolytically refined stock. It contains noticeable quantities of iron, zinc, copper and silicon, and traces of rare earth and other impurities. The center plate is of a repeatedly electrolyzed sample showing reductions in the impurity level and the lower

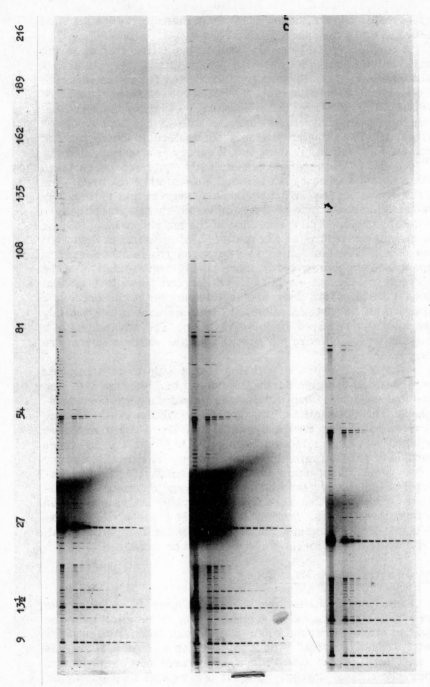

Figure 3. Aluminium Samples.

plate is of a zone-refined sample with a very low impurity level indeed.

The molecular ions Al_2^+, Al_3^+, Al_4^+, Al_5^+, etc., are prominent as are the charge transfer line at 20 1/4 and the charge transfer continua extending below masses 54 and 81. The halation around the main lines is caused by line broadening due to charge building up on the plate at high beam intensities and unable to leak away rapidly enough, and also by secondary emission from the emulsion under ion bombardment. These can both be reduced by working at low beam intensities, although the exposures take correspondingly longer to make.

A microphotometered record of part of the lower spectrum is given in Figure 4, and shows the components of the spectrum more clearly. Comparative analyses of these three samples are tabled in Figure 5; these were estimated by the visual method using the matrix line as an internal standard. Detection limits of impurities in aluminium and silicon are tabled in Figure 6, where data are listed for over seventy elements.

There are several possible sources of interferences which must be borne in mind when identifying mass lines.
(1) Multiply charged ions of major constituents
(2) Polyatomic ions of the major constituents, including ions of mixed isotopes
(3) Molecular ions, frequently oxides and carbides
(4) Charge transfer ions resulting from collisions in the analyser region
(5) Hydrocarbon lines originating from the pump oils
(6) Ions originating from residual gases in the source region, particularly oxygen, nitrogen and water vapour.
These lines are all featured in Figure 7 and where multiplets occur at a single mass number the lower limit of detection of the element so masked is automatically raised. For instance it is necessary to estimate sulphur from the S^{+++} line at 10-2/3 since the 32 line is masked by O_2^+; and it is frequently necessary to estimate aluminium by the Al^{++} line at 13-1/2 when the 27 line is masked by Fe^{++}. Small actual mass differences do exist between multiplets occurring at a particular mass number, but a high resolution is required to take advantage of these differences in all but a few cases. The resolution of the present instrument which is fitted with a .005" slit is approximately 1500, as illustrated in Figure 8, but to separate the important doublet at mass 32 (S^+, O_2^+) requires a resolving power of 1670, while to separate Al^+ from Fe^{++} at mass 27 requires a resolving power of almost 2300.

It is possible to reduce the extent to which polyatomic ions are formed by operating at low spark voltages, and the incidence of charge transfer ions is markedly dependent on the pressure in

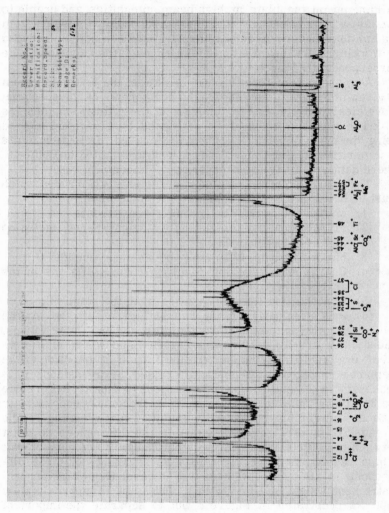

Figure 4. Microphotometer Trace of Mass Spectrum of Zone Refined Aluminium.

Aluminium Samples

Elements Definitely Detected	Concentration p.p.m. by Weight					
Ga	0.25		0.1			
Zn	10.0	(14.5)	0.4	(0.15)		
Cu	10.0	(5.0)	1.5	(1.8)	0.1	(0.001)
Fe	15.0	(23.0)	2.0	(3.6)		
Mn	0.5	(0.3)	0.3	(0.8)	0.5	
Sc	1.0	(1.2)	0.3	(0.3)	0.05	(0.08)
Cl	1.2		1.0			
S	5.0		1.5			
Mg	20.0		3.0			
Na	10.0		0.1		0.05	
B	1.2		0.1			
Si	5.0	(12.0)	2.0	(2.9)	0.3	(0.3)
Pb	0.3					
Nd	1.0					
Pr	0.15					
Ce	2.0					
La	0.5	(0.2)				
Ba	1.0					
Sb	1.0	(2.0)			< 0.01	(0.0005)

(Figures in parentheses were obtained by neutron activation analysis)

Figure 5

Detection Limits of Impurities in
ALUMINIUM

0.001 p.p.m.

I	Ba	Ce	Tb	Tm	Au	Bi	U
Cs	La	Pr	Ho	Lu	Tl	Th	

0.01 p.p.m.

Li	K	Co	Sr	Rh	In	Nd	Dy	Ta	Ir
Be	Ti	Cu	Y	Pd	Sn	Sm	Eu	W	Pt
B	Mn	As	Nb	Ag	Sb	Eu	Yb	Re	Hg
F	Fe	Rb	Ru	Cd	Te	Gd	Hf	Os	Pb

0.1 p.p.m.

Na	Si	S	Ca	V	Ni	Ga	Se	Zr
Mg	P	Cl	Sc	Cr	Zn	Ge	Br	Mo

Figure 6a

Detection Units of Impurities in
SILICON

0.001 p.p.m.

I	La	Ho	Bi	U
Cs	Tb	Tl	Th	

0.01 p.p.m.

Li	Mg	Ca	Cu	Se	Ru	Sb	Sm	Tm	Os
Be	Al	Sc	Zn	Br	Rh	Te	Eu	Lu	Ir
B	P	Ti	Ga	Zr	Pd	Ba	Gd	Hf	Pt
F	Cl	V	Ge	Nb	Ag	Pr	Dy	W	
Na	K	Cr	As	Mo	Sn	Nd	Eu	Re	

0.1 p.p.m.

S	Ni	Y	In	Yb
Fe	Co	Cd	Nd	Ta

1 p.p.m.

Mn	Sr

Figure 6b

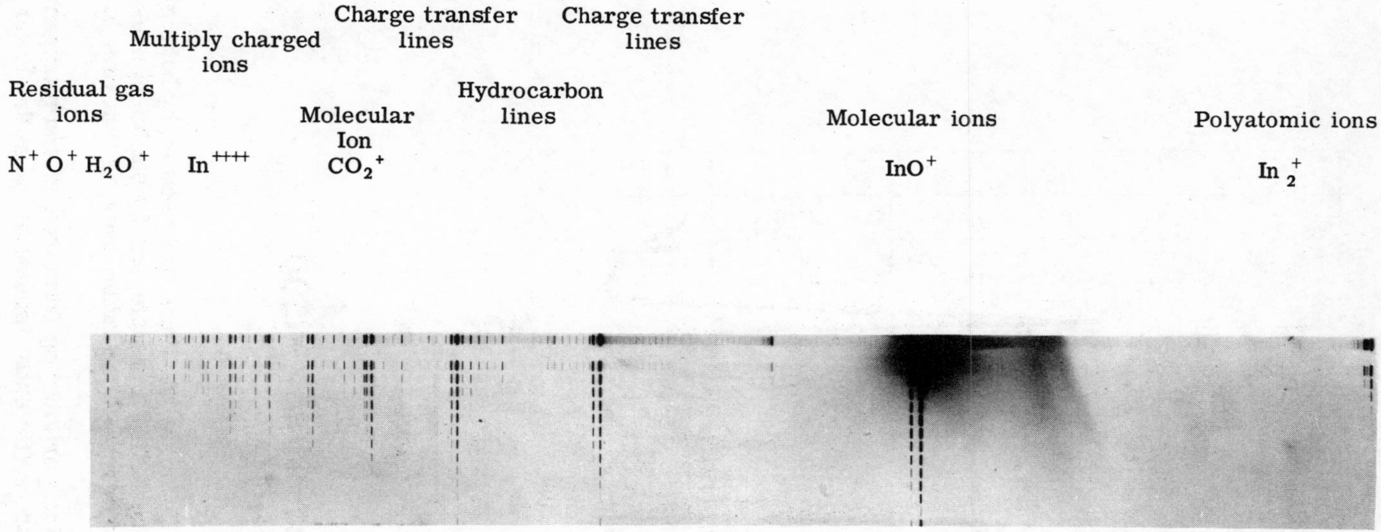

Polyatomic ions

In_2^+

Molecular ions

InO^+

Charge transfer lines

Charge transfer lines

Hydrocarbon lines

Multiply charged ions

Molecular Ion CO_2^+

Residual gas ions

N^+ O^+ H_2O^+ In^{++++}

Figure 7

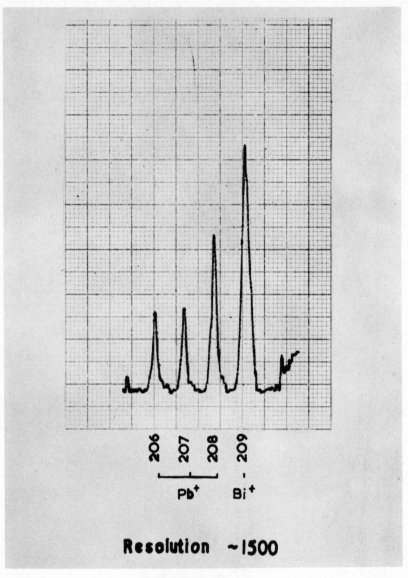

Figure 8

the analyser region. Hydrocarbon lines are reduced by baking the source region after loading a sample, and by sufficient pre-sparking, but this extends the time taken over an analysis to almost a day.

The background lines originating from oxygen and nitrogen in the source region are sufficiently intense to raise the lower

306

limit of detection to above 10 ppm. atomic, but the background level for carbon is possibly below 1 ppm. The lowest carbon level actually detected in indium is at present 2 ppm.

The accuracy with which determinations can be made using the visual method of estimating disappearance levels and an internal standard [1], is limited by a number of factors. (i) It is not easy to estimate the exact exposure at which a line just disappears; this is particularly true of the internal standard line, which is usually of the matrix material, and frequently still intense at the smallest measurable exposure. (ii) If it is necessary to use lines from multiply charged ions a factor is introduced which must be measured, and which is approximately 5 for each stage of ionization. (iii) The relative sensitivity of detection from element to element must be assumed unity if it is not already known from previous calibration with independently analysed standards. Evidence shows that this factor is in fact near unity for most elements, but the relative sensitivity of sulphur with respect to iron is more nearly 10. (iv) There is the assumption that the intensity of the ion beam is linear with concentration.

In spite of these approximations, the values obtained agree remarkably well with those obtained by other methods and are usually within a factor of three of the true value. This accuracy is often sufficient when concentrations of less than one part per million are under consideration.

Although the absolute accuracy is in question, relative measurements between similar samples have a high degree of significance. The repetitive precision of a number of determinations on a single sample of indium is illustrated in Figure 9; while a comparative survey of a number of indium specimens prepared by different techniques is given in Figure 10. A more complete analysis of a semiconductor grade indium is given in Figure 11; it is this sample that has a particularly low carbon content.

In order to calibrate the instrument and obtain a higher absolute accuracy it is necessary to collect data from a number of standardized samples, which are preferably made of hyperpure material with additions of impurity elements in a known range of concentration. However, before effective use of these standards can be made it is necessary to be able to control the precision with which the intensity of the blackening produced on the photographic plate can be related to the known concentration of the impurity element.

Microphotometry is the obvious choice of technique, but immediately the deficiencies of the Q2 emulsion are exposed. The emulsion is very thin, to minimize absorption of the incident ions in the gelatin layer, and therefore, very susceptible to

Elements Definitely Detected	Individual Determinations						Probable Value p.p.m. (weight)
Silicon	36	36	108	108	360	72	100
Phosphorus	1.1	1.6	2.8	1.0	1.0	0.5	1.3
Chlorine	5.4	13.0	5.4	5.4	2.5	2.5	6.0
Vanadium		1.9	0.6	0.6	0.3	0.2	0.7
Chromium		2.5	0.8	0.8	0.1	0.2	0.9
Manganese		0.3	0.2	0.2	0.06	0.1	0.2
Iron	2.2	2.8	0.7	2.2	0.5	1.0	1.5
Cobalt		0.1	0.2		0.07	0.04	0.1
Nickel		0.8	0.8	0.8	0.3	0.2	0.6
Copper	1.1	1.6	1.0	1.0	0.3	1.5	1.0
Zinc		0.7	0.5	0.5	0.1	0.2	0.4
Arsenic	0.9	0.3	2.7	1.0	0.1	0.3	1.0
Bismuth	2.5	2.5	7.5	7.5	4.0	4.0	4.5
Lead	0.7	1.5	1.5	1.5	0.5	1.5	1.2

Figure 9. Repeat Determinations on a Single Sample of Indium.

damage and it has a tendency to cover the plate unevenly. There is the tendency of the mass lines to broaden at high intensities and the occurrence of halation in the vicinity of the most intense lines leads to a variable background. Further, the working range of the emulsion is much shorter than that normally encountered on, say, plates used for optical emission spectrography. The evidence on the response of the emulsion to ions of different mass and energy is scant and this factor at least needs further investigation.

As a start in this direction an attempt has been made to devise a procedure of plate calibration that can eventually be

Indium Samples

Elements Definitely Detected	Concentration p.p.m. (atomic)					
	I	II	III	IV	V	VI
Fe	1.2	1.3	1	4.5	2	2
Cu	2	7	0.2	6.6	2	3
Zn	0.7	4	0.25	4.5	2	3
Ga	0.3	0.7	0.1	2	0.1	0.1
Cd	10	< 0.05	< 0.03	1	1	1
Sb	0.07	0.1		0.06	0.4	0.06
Sn	1	0.16	< 0.03	0.17	1	0.16
Hg	0.3			0.17	0.2	0.1
Pb	1.5	0.08		1	0.8	2
Bi	0.02			0.04	0.4	1
As	0.04	12	0.04	0.12	2	0.06
P	0.2	4	0.6	2	0.4	1
S	2	3	1	5	5	3
Cl	10	480	16	50	150	50
Tl	1	< 0.1			0.5	1

Figure 10

applied, with a series of standards of known concentrations, to determine factors such as the relative efficiency of detection for the individual elements, and to increase the precision and accuracy of subsequent determinations on unknown samples.

Churchill's two-line method of emulsion calibration [3] was used as a basis. A number of microphotometer readings of line intensities are taken of a pair of lines whose incident beam

Indium Sample
(Semiconductor Grade)

Concentration in p.p.m.

	Atomic	Weight
Bi	0.07	0.12
Sn	0.06	0.06
Br	0.03	0.02
As	0.01	0.007
Ga	0.003	0.002
Zn	0.3	0.2
Cu	1	0.6
Co	0.07	0.04
Fe	1	0.5
Mn	0.07	0.03
Cr	0.04	0.02
Ca	2	0.7
K	4	1.5
Cl	1	0.3
S	2	0.5
P	0.07	0.02
Si	3	0.7
Al	0.6	0.15
Mg	2	0.4
F	0.6	0.1
C	2	0.2

Figure 11

intensities bear a fixed relation R to one another. This latter ratio should remain constant and be completely independent of operating conditions, a requirement readily met by choosing a pair of isotopic lines - for instance ^{63}Cu and ^{65}Cu. A preliminary curve is plotted of the optical density of the weaker line against that of the stronger line as illustrated in Figure 12. These points are taken from a series of twelve plates from a single batch of emulsion on which the mass spectra were recorded of four aluminium-copper standards.

From this preliminary curve is constructed an absolute calibration curve as follows. A density, above which it will not be necessary to go during a normal analysis, is chosen and the density corresponding to a beam intensity R times less read off from the curve. This value is again applied to the curve and so on, and the resultant values replotted against R^n on a semi-logarithmic scale, as shown in Figure 13. This is an absolute gamma-curve from which relative optical densities can be directly translated into relative beam intensities.

Now the beam intensity producing a particular line in the instrument is proportional to the exposure X, the concentration of the element C, the isotopic abundance of the isotope in question a, and the efficiency of detection ϵ and inversely proportional to the square-root of the mass m, since the line width in the Mattauch arrangement is proportional to $\sqrt{m}$. Hence this curve can be used to compare known samples with unknown samples for the same element, and, if this curve is universal for all elements, between an internal standard element and a different element in one and the same sample, provided the respective ϵ values are known.

Evidence at the moment suggests that this may in fact be a universal curve for a number of elements since that constructed for tungsten (mass numbers 180-186) coincides with that for copper (mass numbers 63, 65). Further, the curves for multiply charged ions fall on that for the singly charged ion.

Using this curve the isotopic ratio of the two copper isotopes using the data from the mass spectra was calculated to be 2.30, 2.38, 2.16, 2.28, 2.25, 2.28, 2.21, 2.16, 2.15, 2.12, with a mean of 2.23 ± 0.08 in comparison with the accepted value of 2.24. Further the relative concentrations of the copper additions in the four aluminium alloys were determined and compared with those obtained by neutron activation analysis. The results, tabled in Figure 14, show remarkably good agreement.

CONCLUSION

The MS7 is a valuable addition to the range of physical instruments designed for trace analysis at very low levels.

311

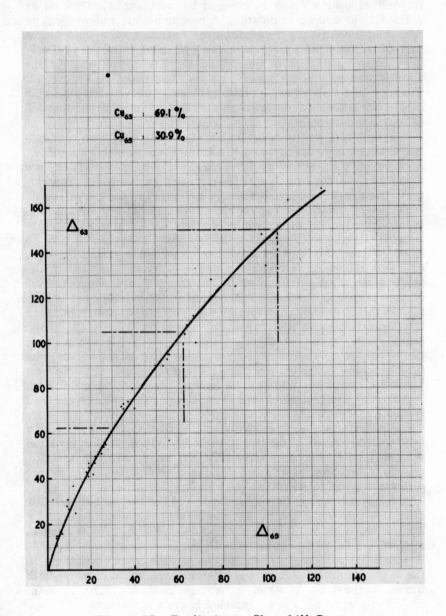

Figure 12. Preliminary Churchill Curve.

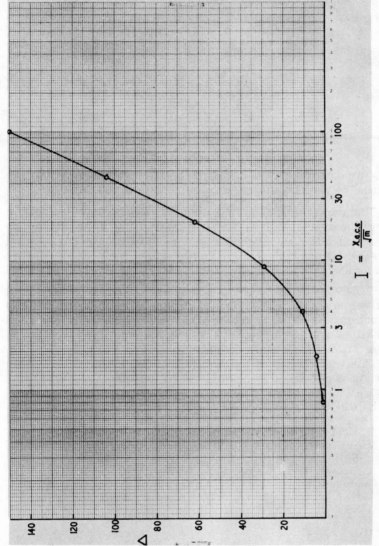

Figure 13. Q2 Emulsion Calibration Curve. Plot of Microphotometer Deflection Δ Against Incident Ion Beam Intensity I. (Optical Density of 1.0 = Deflection of 120.)

$$I = \frac{x_{acc}}{\sqrt{m}}$$

Aluminum Doped with Copper

	Relative Concentrations	
Sample No.	MS.7	Activation
I	1	1
II	1.35	1.30
III	2.61	2.50
IV	3.66	3.65

Figure 14

In its present state it is largely semi-quantitative, but it has the potential of yielding more accurate results in the future.

The low level of detection, the wide coverage of elements in a single analysis, and its simple presentation of the data make it very effective as a monitoring instrument for purification processes. Here comparative answers are frequently as significant as absolute values.

Since the time taken to produce a complete analysis is relatively long, it is not easy to foresee the use of the MS.7 in production control; it is rather a referee instrument. The need for skilled operators who understand its many complexities is also a disadvantage where routine work is concerned.

This work is part of the general research programme of the NPL and is published by permission of the Director.

REFERENCES

1. R. D. Craig, G. A. Errock and J. D. Waldron, Advances in Mass Spectrometry, p. 136, Pergammon Press, London (1959).
2. R. Brown, R. D. Craig, J. A. James and C. M. Wilson. This Conference.
3. J. R. Churchill, Ind. and Eng. Chem. (Anal. Edit.) 16, 653 (1944).

DISCUSSION

D. ANDRYCHUK (Texas Instruments): There is a technique in emission spectroscopy known as the Seidel function, which is used to straighten out the calibration curve. Have you checked to see if this applies to your type of work?

J. F. DUKE (National Physical Laboratory): We haven't used this but do know of it. However, I don't think it will extend our working range very much.

D. ANDRYCHUK (Texas Instruments): It might improve the precision of your method.

J. F. DUKE (National Physical Laboratory): That is a possibility.

ELECTRICAL AND MASS SPECTROGRAPHIC
ANALYSIS OF III-V COMPOUNDS

R. K. Willardson
Bell & Howell Research Center
Pasadena, California

ABSTRACT

A double-focusing mass spectrometer, utilizing a spark ionization source, was used to determine impurity concentrations in silicon, InSb, GaSb, AlSb, and GaAs. The major impurities identified in GaAs were carbon, oxygen, and silicon. Electron mobilities and carrier concentrations are found to be in acceptable agreement with those expected for the impurity concentrations shown to be present. Distribution coefficients for Zn, Cd, In, Ge, Sn, As, S, Se, and Te in GaSb were determined. The effects of ion clusters, multiple ionization, and residual gas background on the mass spectrographic analysis are discussed.

For many years mass spectrometers have been used for the analysis of gases and the identification of impurities in organic substances. Mass spectrometric studies have been used to determine the thermodynamic properties of both elemental and compound semiconductors [3, 4]. The application of a mass spectrometer to the detection of impurities in semiconductors was described by Hannay and Ahearn in 1954 [6]. This instrument used a spark source and was double-focusing. The sensitivity of this type of instrument was extended to 5 parts per billion (ppb) by Craig, Errock, and Waldron [2], who have more recently reported detection limits of less than 1 ppb in several elements. The instrument used in the analysis discussed in this article combines high sensitivity with high resolution (0.01 atomic mass units at mass 25) [10].

In the analytical field, mass spectrometry has much to offer. Mass spectrographic analysis gives a nearly uniform sensitivity of all elements, the rapidity of emission spectrography, and the high detection sensitivity of neutron activation analysis. In addition, it makes possible the detection of impurities existing as compounds and quantitative studies of surface impurities.

DESCRIPTION OF THE MASS SPECTROMETER

A schematic diagram of the basic instrument is shown in Figure 1. The combination of an electric and a magnetic sector acts as an achromatic lens and permits a sharp focus for ions of a range of energies, a feature that is indispensable in obtaining useful mass resolving power with the radiofrequency spark ion source. With this system it is possible in principle to place a photographic plate on the focal plane and record ions of all masses simultaneously; the present instrument covers a mass range of about 37:1, sufficient to record all the solid elements in a single exposure.

The Mattauch-Herzog tandem design is double-focusing to first order for ions of all masses [8]. However, control of the second order aberrations is important. One method is the addition of a certain amount of curvature [9] at the entrance boundary of the magnetic field and simultaneous adjustment of other appropriate parameters. This makes it possible to eliminate both of the second order velocity aberrations simultaneously for one point on the focal plane, thus permitting considerable improvement in resolution at that point and some improvement over the whole focal plane.

A Herzog shunt is used at the boundary of the magnetic field so that this boundary will be sharp and also so that its position and its effective shape will be accurately known. Stray fields in front of the Herzog shunt can produce a deflection which results in a displacement of a few thousandths of an inch of the focused ion beam. Ions which undergo a metastable transition or charge-exchange within that space are deflected differently from the stable ions, giving rise to the so-called "Aston bands" on the plates. To minimize these effects, magnetic shielding is provided where necessary to ensure that the stray magnetic field is very small throughout the region between the ion source and the boundary of the magnetic sector.

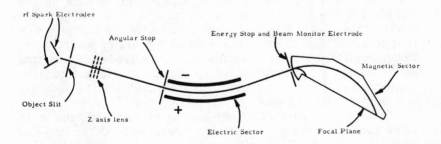

Figure 1. Basic Geometry of Mass Resolving System.

Another feature of the particular instrument used in this work is a three-element unipotential z-axis lens between the object slit and the electric sector for focusing in the direction parallel to the magnetic field. This lens increases the sensitivity of the instrument by about a factor of five.

The path length of the ion beam from the source to the photographic plate varies from about four to five feet, depending on the mass of ions. The large size is necessary to obtain separation of the masses of impurity isotopes from masses due to background in the analyses to be described. Three mercury diffusion pumps are used to evacuate the source, the electric sector, and the magnetic sector independently. Liquid nitrogen cold traps are used between the mechanical pump and the diffusion pump as well as between the diffusion pump and the sector being evacuated.

The theoretical limit of resolution of the instrument, with the .0025-inch wide object slit used in this work, and taking account of second order aberrations, is about 1:4000. Adjacent ion beams having masses differing by 1:2500 are clearly separated when the exposures are reasonably near the optimum; the mass of an isolated ion beam can be determined with an accuracy better than 0.01 atomic mass units.

OPERATION OF THE INSTRUMENT

The ions are produced by a radiofrequency spark between electrodes composed of the material to be analyzed. The frequency used is one megacycle. Typical operating conditions for the sparking and analysis of silicon, carbon, and several III-V compounds as well as more difficult materials such as selenium and beryllium are given in Table I. Although the ion accelerating voltage can be varied from 1000 to 20,000 volts, it is usually set at about 15,000 volts.

Optimum operating conditions depend on the nature of the sample. It is usually preferable to run with the pulse length and repetition rate adjusted to avoid appreciable heating of the sample and the evolution of volatile impurities at a disproportionate rate. Indium and gallium antimonide are exceptionally easy to spark, and in many cases several hours of sparking can be accomplished without repositioning the electrodes. Restarting of the spark or adjustment of sparking conditions during an exposure can cause variations in the relative numbers of singly and multiply charged ions.

Some of the ions are composed of clusters containing, in some cases, as many as eight or more atoms. Other ions are multiply charged. Each will be deposited on the photographic plate at a position corresponding to its charge to mass ratio.

318

Table I

Instrument Settings for Typical Analysis

Sample Electrodes	Ion Accelerating Voltage	R. F. Oscillator[a] Plate Voltage	Pulse Length Microsecond
InSb	16,000	3000	3.5
GaSb	16,000	4000	3.5
AlSb	16,000	3000	3.5
GaAs	16,000	5000	3.5
Si	16,000	4000	3.5
C	16,000	1400–4500	3.5
Se	16,000	1600	40[b]
Be	16,000	2000	3.5

[a]The R. F. sparking voltage is roughly 15 times the oscillator plate voltage.
[b]A 100 pulse/sec repetition rate was the maximum used.

Some multiply charged ions pass through the electric sector with a given charge, but pick up one or more electrons in the region between the electric and magnetic sector. These so-called charge-exchange ions are the result of a charge transfer process occurring between residual gas molecules and the positive ions in the beam. Since the ions lose a small amount of energy in the charge-exchange process, these lines are displaced one or two tenths of a mass unit towards the low mass end of the plate.* They not only produce extra lines on the plate but can also be smeared out and obscure lines of interest to the analysis.

DETERMINATION OF IMPURITY CONCENTRATION

A fraction of the ion beam is collected and integrated at the entrance to the magnetic sector by the beam monitor electrode.

*When a charge-exchange occurs with a loss of energy, the apparent mass of the ion is given by

$$m' = m \frac{q_1 (1 - 2\beta)}{q_2^2} ,$$

where m is the mass, q_1 the initial charge on the ion, q_2 the charge on the ion while it is in the magnetic field, and βv_0 the velocity change which occurs during the charge transfer between the positive ions and the residual gas molecules.

319

The charge collected is a direct measure of the number of ions in the part of the ion beam which enters the magnetic sector and exposes the photographic plate at the positions representative of the mass and the charge of the ions. The photographic plates used are $15 \times 2 \times 1/32$-inch glass coated with Ilford QII emulsion. In order to compare impurity concentrations varying by as much as a factor of a million, the exposure time and pulse repetition rate are used as adjustable parameters. Typical exposure values, times, and pulse repetition rates for InSb, GaSb, AlSb, and GaAs analyses are given in Table II. It is important to consider not only the density of a particular line on the photographic plate but also the total width of the lines.

Table II

Method of Obtaining a Range of Exposures

Exposure Coulombs	Typical Exposure Time Seconds	Repetition Rate Pulses/sec
6×10^{-7}	6000	2000
2×10^{-7}	2000	2000
6×10^{-8}	600	2000
2×10^{-8}	200	2000
6×10^{-9}	120	1000
2×10^{-9}	400	100
6×10^{-10}	120	100
2×10^{-10}	400	10
6×10^{-11}	120	10
2×10^{-11}	40	10
6×10^{-12}	12	10
2×10^{-12}	4	10
6×10^{-13}	1.2	10

Measurements of line density are made with a microphotometer in much the same way as with the photographic plates
obtained in emission spectrographic analysis. A calibration is
obtained by plotting the line density as a function of the logarithm
of exposure, i.e., the number of ions per unit area incident on a
particular section of the photographic plate. Figure 2 shows the
line density as a function of indium ions per unit area for exposures ranging from 2×10^{-12} to 2×10^{-7} coulombs. The exposure
times ranged from a few seconds to 35 minutes. The [113] In concentration ranged from 0.2 ppm to 2%. To obtain a quantitative
analysis, an exposure which gives a density between 0.1 and 1.0
is required for the element in question. Densities between 0.2
and 0.8 are preferred. Also it is desirable to derive the impurity
concentration from at least three density measurements on lines
of different exposures or of isotopes of the element.

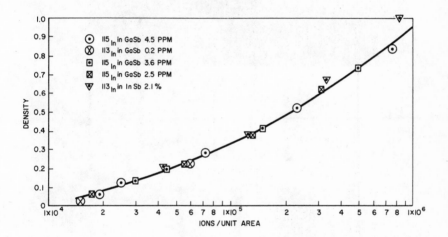

Figure 2. Line Density as a Function of Ions Per Unit Area on
the Photographic Plate (Data Shown for Indium and a Unit Area
of $0.0005 \times 0.075 = 38 \times 10^{-6}$ Square Inches).

Table II indicates that an analysis can consist of 13 or more
different exposures on a single photographic plate. In the analyses to be discussed in the next sections, a maximum exposure
of 2×10^{-7} coulombs was used. The time required to make the
necessary different exposures was about 1.5 hours. Two samples
were analyzed per day. The samples and photographic plate
were placed in the instrument in the evening or just before noon.
This allowed pump-down to 2 or 3×10^{-7} Torr overnight or
over the noon period. There did not appear to be a significant

321

difference in residual background between the 16-hour and 2-hour pump-down periods.

DISCUSSION OF SILICON MASS SPECTRUM

In addition to the lines formed on the photographic plate by the impurities and major constituents of the material being analyzed, lines are found which are caused by such background items as hydrocarbons and oxides, as well as the multiply charged ions, dimers and other polyatomic ions, and charge-exchange ions that have been mentioned. Examples of these are shown in Figure 3 which shows sections from a plate used in an analysis of high-purity silicon. Figure 3-A shows triply ionized

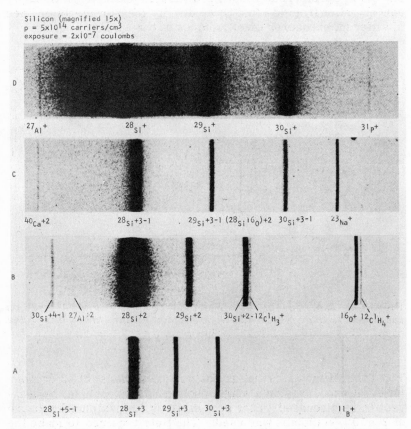

Figure 3. Enlargement of Sections from the Photographic Plate of a Silicon Mass Spectrographic Analysis. A. Mass 8 1/2 to 11 1/2; B. Mass 13.2 to 16.3; C. Mass 20 to 23 1/2; D. Mass 27 to 31.

isotopes ^{28}Si, ^{29}Si, and ^{30}Si having apparent masses 9-1/3, 9-2/3, and 10. The faint line to the extreme right is boron at mass 11. In the next row (3-B) the doubly ionized isotopes ^{28}Si, ^{29}Si, and ^{30}Si at masses 14, 14.5, and 15 are the most prominent. On the right side of the doubly ionized ^{30}Si at mass 15 is the hydrocarbon CH$_3$. Farther to the right the dark line is oxygen 16 with the weaker line being CH$_4$. On the third row from the bottom (3-C) are seen the charge-exchange lines at mass 21, 21.75, and 22.5 created by triply ionized ^{28}Si, ^{29}Si, and ^{30}Si picking up an electron in the region between the electric and magnetic sectors. The heavy smeared line at the upper left (3-D) is ^{28}Si. The two heavy lines to the right are the isotopes ^{29}Si and ^{30}Si. The weak line to the far left is aluminum, while the one on the right is phosphorus.

Figure 4 shows lines resulting from clusters of 2, 3, 4, 5, 6, and 7 atoms. On the bottom at the left is a charge-exchange and a dimer or cluster at mass 56. Two atoms of ^{28}Si are involved. The next line is a singly ionized dimer of ^{28}Si and ^{29}Si. This is followed by a charge-exchange doublet created by a doubly charged ^{29}Si picking up an electron, as the result of a charge transfer process occurring between residual gas molecules and the positive silicon ion. On the right is a dimer of ^{28}Si and ^{30}Si. Next is a dimer of ^{29}Si and ^{30}Si, which is followed by a charge-exchange doublet created by a doubly charged ^{30}Si picking up an electron. The last line is a dimer of ^{30}Si.

The next group of lines (4-B) shows first on the left a charge-exchange doublet of triply ionized ^{28}Si which picked up 2 electrons near the entrance to the magnetic sector. The remainder of the lines shown in the second group from the bottom indicate polyatomic clusters at masses 84, 85, 86, 87, 88. Each line represents a polyatomic ion consisting of ^{28}Si and 2 atoms of some combination of ^{28}Si, ^{29}Si, or ^{30}Si. Lines in the succeeding groups are singly ionized clusters of combinations of 4, 5, 6, and 7 atoms each of the silicon isotopes. Since ^{28}Si is 20 times as abundant as ^{29}Si and 30 times as abundant as ^{30}Si, all of the lines shown here are primarily due to ^{28}Si except the ones at mass 59 and 60. For larger exposures many additional lines resulting from the possible combinations of ^{29}Si and ^{30}Si would be obtained.

DISCUSSION OF GaAs MASS SPECTRUM

In Figure 5 silicon is seen as an impurity in GaAs. At mass 28 there are four lines consisting of ^{28}Si, ^{12}C ^{16}O, ^{14}N$_2$, and ^{12}C$_2$ ^{1}H$_4$ at masses 27.9769, 27.9949, 28.0061, and 28.0313

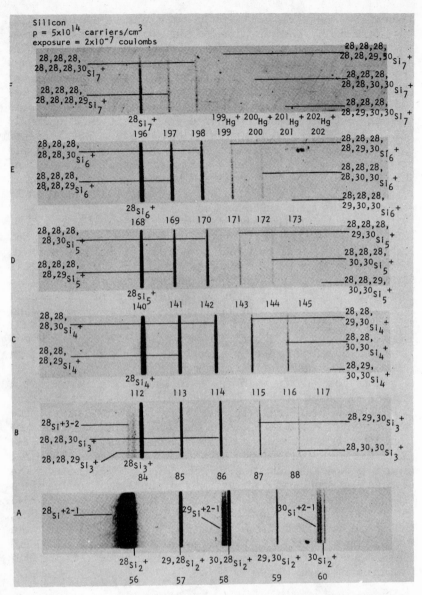

Figure 4. Enlargement of Sections from the Photographic Plate of a Silicon Mass Spectrographic Analysis. A. Mass 56 to 60; B. Mass 84 to 88; C. Mass 112 to 117; D. Mass 140 to 145; E. Mass 168 to 173; F. Mass 196 to 202.

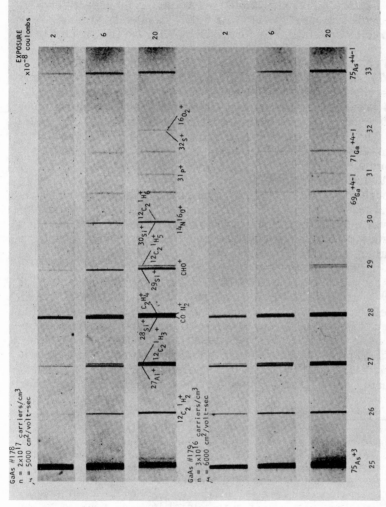

Figure 5. Enlargement of Sections Between Mass 25 and 34 from Photographic Plates Showing a Comparison of the Impurity Content in Two Gallium Arsenide Samples. Magnified 10x.

325

respectively.* Because of the large amount of silicon present, space charge broadening of the silicon line has obscured the $^{12}C\,^{16}O$ and $^{14}N_2$ lines and only the $^{12}C_2\,^1H_4$ line is visible. At mass 29 there is the triplet ^{29}Si, $^{12}C^1H^{16}O$ and $^{12}C_2\,^1H_5$, and at mass 30 is another triplet ^{30}Si, $^{14}N\,^{16}O$, and $^{12}C_2\,^1H_6$. In each case the line at the left is silicon. The lines near mass 29 have masses 28.9765, 29.0027, and 29.0391 respectively. A resolution of 1 part in 1100 or 0.026 mass units at mass 29 is required to separate $^{29}Si^+$ and $^{12}C\,^{16}O^1H^+$. On the photographic plate this corresponds to a separation of 0.002 inches.

The top three exposures in Figure 5 are for GaAs sample No. 178 which has a concentration of 2×10^{17} carriers/cm^3 and an electron mobility of 5000 cm^2/volt-sec. The bottom 3 exposures are for GaAs sample No. 179 which has a concentration of 3×10^{16} carriers/cm^3 and an electron mobility of 6000 cm^2/volt-sec. The bottom exposure in each case is 2×10^{-7} coulombs, the middle one 6×10^{-8} coulombs, and the top one 2×10^{-8} coulombs.

A fine line just visible on the photographic plate after an exposure of 2×10^{-7} coulombs corresponds to an impurity concentration of about 2 ppb. For sample 179 in Figure 5 the ^{30}Si line was a little more than just visible for the 2×10^{-8} coulomb exposure. This corresponds to about 40 ppb of $^{30}Si^+$ and gives a total of 1.2 ppm silicon, since $^{30}Si^+$ is only 3 percent of the total silicon present.

At mass 32 there is a doublet consisting of sulfur at 31.9721 and $^{16}O_2$ at 31.9898 which differ by 1 part in 1800. The line on the left corresponds to about 50 and 20 ppb sulfur in samples 178 and 179 respectively. The selenium and tellurium concentrations in these samples were less than 20 ppb.

In Figure 6 a doublet can be seen at mass 16 with CH$_4$ on the right and $^{16}O^+$ on the left. The concentration of oxygen is estimated to be about 1 ppm for the top sample and 2 ppm for

---

*All atomic masses reported here are given on the $^{12}C = 12$ mass scale. A table of all of the elements, their isotopic abundance, their mass to 6 significant figures reduced to the $^{12}C = 12$ mass scale, and the square root of their mass number as well as values for multiply ionized isotopes, dimers, probable hydrocarbons, and a few other compounds has been assembled, photographed on 16 mm microfilm, and donated to the subcommittee on Data and Nomenclature, ASTM Committee E-14 on Mass Spectrometry. A report SCR 245 "Table of Atomic Masses" which contains this information has been prepared by J. W. Guthrie, Sandia Corporation, Albuquerque, New Mexico. This report will be available from the Office of Technical Services, U. S. Department of Commerce, Washington 25, D. C., for sale to the general public.

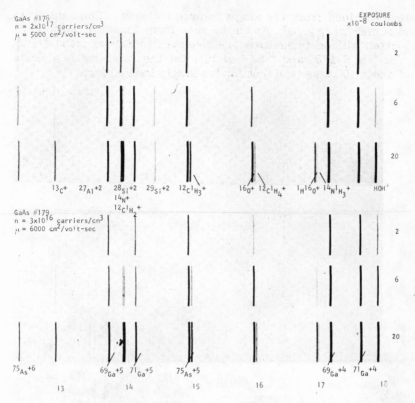

GaAs #178
n = 2x10^17 carriers/cm^3
μ = 5000 cm^2/volt-sec

EXPOSURE
x10^-8 coulombs

2

6

20

$^{13}C^+$ $^{27}Al^{+2}$ $^{28}Si^{+2}$ $^{29}Si^{+2}$ $^{12}C^1H_3^+$ $^{16}O^+$ $^{12}C^1H_4^+$ $^1H^{16}O^+$ $^{14}N^1H_3^+$ HOH$^+$
                      $^{14}N^+$
                      $^{12}C^1H_2^+$

GaAs #179
n = 3x10^16 carriers/cm^3
μ = 6000 cm^2/volt-sec

2

6

20

$^{75}As^{+6}$ $^{69}Ga^{+5}$ $^{71}Ga^{+5}$ $^{75}As^{+5}$ $^{69}Ga^{+4}$ $^{71}Ga^{+4}$
     13   14   15   16   17   18

Figure 6. Enlargement of Sections Between Mass 12 1/2 and 18 from Photographic Plates Showing a Comparison of the Impurity Content in Two Gallium Arsenide Samples.

the bottom sample. At mass 15 there is a doublet of CH_3 and quintuply ionized arsenic. The $^{75}As^{+5}$ completely masks doubly ionized $^{30}Si^{+2}$.* At mass 14.5 there is a doubly ionized $^{29}Si^{+2}$ line clearly visible on all 3 exposures of sample 178, but it is not visible for the sample 179 at the bottom of Figure 6. At mass 14 a triplet of $^{28}Si^{+2}$, $^{14}N^+$ and CH_2^+ can be seen. In this case $^{28}Si^{+2}$ is on the left and can be seen in all exposures except the lowest one for sample 179.

The doubly ionized silicon can be used as a qualitative check on the analysis, but since the ratio of multiply ionized ions may vary with sparking conditions this check is not as quantitative as

---

*Since it is the mass-to-charge ratio that is measured by a mass spectrometer, the apparent mass of an ion is its true mass divided by the degree of ionization.

that obtained from the singly ionized isotopes. The sensitivity is somewhat reduced. As can be seen from Figure 7, even triply ionized silicon impurities are observed ($^{28}\text{Si}^{+3}$ at mass 9-1/3, $^{29}\text{Si}^{+3}$ at 9-2/3, and $^{30}\text{Si}^{+3}$ at 10), but the intensity is a factor of about 100 less than that for the singly ionized form.

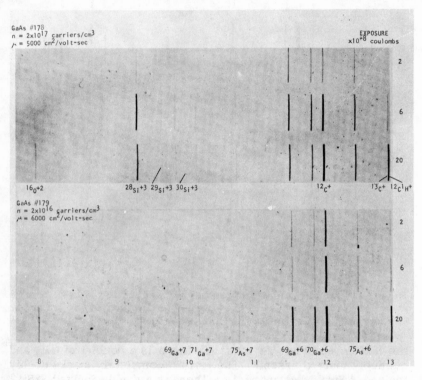

Figure 7. Enlargement of Sections Between Mass 8 and 13 from Photographic Plates Showing a Comparison of the Impurity Content in Two Gallium Arsenide Samples.

Since sodium has only 1 isotope (at mass 23) and this is completely masked by $^{69}\text{Ga}^{+3}$, multiply ionized sodium lines must be used to obtain even a semiquantitative analysis. The intensity of the multiply ionized ions decreases by about an order of magnitude per degree of ionization. Thus, the $^{69}\text{Ga}^{+9}$ line is not visible for a 2×10^{-7} exposure, while the density of the $^{23}\text{Na}^{+3}$ line at mass 7-2/3 will only be a factor of about 100 less than the $^{23}\text{Na}^{+}$ line. Hence, the triply ionized line at 7-2/3 atomic mass units is used for the detection of sodium, and the detection limit is about 200 ppb.

At mass 13 the doublet ^{13}C - $^{12}C^1H$, with a mass difference of 1:3300, may or may not be resolved depending on the settings of the instrument, relative intensities, total exposure, and other factors. However, the ^{13}C line density is derivable from the ^{12}C line density, and any excess density at mass 13 would then be attributable to $^{12}C^1H$.

DISTRIBUTION COEFFICIENT MEASUREMENTS

A few ppm of Ge, Sn, ZnS, CdSe, and InTe were added to a GaSb melt, and a single crystal of GaSb was pulled at 4 cm/hr. and a rotation rate of 6 rpm. The growth direction was <111>. Sections were cut from the ingot at positions representing the fraction which had just become solid when 5%, 30%, and 60% of the melt had been pulled. At the 60% position samples were taken from both the {111} facet and off the {111} facet. These samples were analyzed using the ion concentration to line density relationship given by the curve in Figure 2.

The results of these analyses are shown in Figure 8 and a summary is given in Table III. The column at the right is recent data given by R. N. Hall [5]. His results were obtained from Hall coefficient measurements on a number of GaSb crystals to which only the specified impurity had been added. In most cases reasonable agreement was found between the values obtained by Hall and those obtained by a single mass spectrographic analysis. The mass spectrographic results were consistent with the amount of impurity added and its expected distribution throughout the crystal. The 5% fraction gave concentration values for Te and Zn which were about 30% low compared to the extrapolation from the values at the 30% and 60% positions. This deviation could be caused by nonuniformity of the photographic plate or nonhomogeneity in the crystal. The indium concentration value at the 5% position was about 50% high. This may have been caused by "instrument memory" for the previous sample which was InSb. Indium did not appear to segregate, but arsenic, as expected, concentrated toward the first end to freeze. The arsenic, of course, was not preferentially added but came as a residual impurity in the antimony.

At the 60% position the concentration of selenium was 50% higher and the concentration of tellurium 100% higher on the {111} facet than off the {111} facet. This anisotropic segregation in GaSb is similar to that reported in InSb [1, 7], except that the ratio of concentration on the facet to that off the facet is not as large. A small concentration of copper, probably a residual impurity in the gallium, was detected on the facet sample, but not in any of the others. This indicated that copper also segregates anisotropically in GaSb as well as in InSb.

329

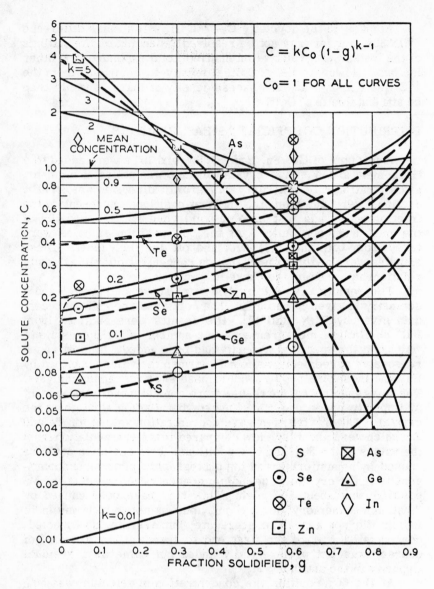

Figure 8. Segregation of Impurities in GaSb as
Indicated by Mass Spectrographic Analysis.

Table III

Distribution Coefficient Measurements
of Impurities in Single Crystal GaSb*

Solute Element	k_{eff} Determined in <111> Direction	k_{on} {111} Facet / k_{off} {111} Facet	Solute Concentration PPM	k_{eff} Other** Than <111> Direction
Zn	.16		7.2	.3
Cd	<.02		3.7	.02
In	~ 1	~ 1	2.9	
Si				1
Ge	.08		9.6	.2
Sn	<.02		5.9	.0002
As	2-4	0.5	6	
S	.06		7.2	
Se	.18	1.5	3.7	.4
Te	.4	2.0	2.9	.4

*Crystals pulled at 4 cm/hr with a rotation rate of 6 rpm.
**Data of R. N. Hall from individual preferential doping and Hall coefficient measurements, see reference 5.

The data on arsenic present a problem which should be investigated further. Its concentration on the {111} facet was only 50% of the value off the facet. The value on the facet at the 60% position is consistent with the off the facet values at the other positions and a distribution coefficient of about 4. However, if the 5% position value is ignored a distribution coefficient of 2 is obtained and a ratio 1/2 for the "on the facet" to "off the facet" concentrations. Since the study of anisotropic segregation is just beginning, and ratios less than 1 have not been suggested, the theoretical implications are significant.

The results of most studies of the distribution of impurities between the solid and liquid phases are based on the assumption that the preferentially added solute elements are completely dissolved in the liquid and homogeneously distributed. If the impurity is added in the form of a compound, as in the experiment discussed above, the amount of impurity actually in the liquid can be checked by comparison with the second impurity. In the case of indium and tellurium added as InTe, the magnitude of the amount of indium is unity so all of the InTe must have dissolved. The tellurium distribution coefficient is in agreement with the value obtained by Hall, and also with the value of 0.4

which we have found using individual element additions and Hall coefficient measurements. Since the selenium was added as CdSe, it is possible that the compound was not completely dissolved. This would mean that the value for the solute concentration is too high and the value for the segregation coefficient is too low for both Cd and Se. In the case of volatile impurities such as Cd and Zn the solute concentration can be reduced by evaporation of impurities from the GaSb in much the same manner as has been found to be so effective in InSb. Thus, volatilization of these impurities from GaSb can also result in a lower apparent distribution coefficient.

One analysis of an InSb sample doped with 30 ppb zinc indicated, in addition to the zinc, 600 ppb iron, 200 ppb chromium, 40 ppb nickel, 10 ppb manganese, and 60 ppb silicon. It soon became apparent that the ratio of these elements gave the composition of the stainless steel used for the sample holder. The $^{56}Fe^{+2}$, $^{58}Ni^{+2}$, and $^{60}Ni^{+2}$ from the stainless steel gave lines at mass 28, 29, and 30 which are only 0.009 atomic mass units larger than the corresponding ones for silicon and, hence, are difficult to resolve. This emphasizes the important factor of possible instrument-introduced errors. The new sample holders are made of tantalum, since tantalum has only one significant isotope ^{181}Ta and multiple ionization will not interfere with the even integer mass lines of other elements. If the samples are placed too close to the tantalum source aperture, stray sparks can also produce an appreciable number of tantalum ions. In analyses where tantalum is a significant impurity, and where a stray spark to the tantalum sample holder or source aperture would be important, these parts can be replaced with units made from other materials, e.g., rhodium.

The mass spectrometer has a memory for the major elements in a previous analysis unless it is carefully cleaned after each analysis. For example, GaAs sample 179 was run immediately after an AlSb sample and about 2 ppm aluminum is evident on the plate as a result of the aluminum residue in the source section. Gallium Arsenide 178 was run next, and it is seen that the memory effect is reduced, but the aluminum level indicated is still about ten times the amount actually in the GaAs. Disposable liners for the spark source housing can be used to minimize the contamination by materials from previous analysis.

Extreme care must be taken in cutting, etching, and handling samples when analyses of a few ppb are to be significant. The samples are cut to size (approximately $1/16 \times 1/16 \times 3/8$-inch) with a diamond saw. Silicon has been etched in NaOH and in an etch composed of 50 parts water, 20 parts 48% HF, 14 parts concentrated H_2SO_4, and 5 parts HNO_3 (by volume). The GaAs and GaSb were etched in 50 parts HNO_3 and 50 parts HCl. The AlSb was etched in HF and the InSb in a solution of 3 parts HF, 5 parts HNO_3, and 3 parts of glacial acetic acid. Impurities which are disproportionately abundant on the surface, either as a result of inadequate cleaning procedures or for other reasons, may be distinguished by the fact that their apparent abundance decreases on successive exposures as the electrode surfaces are eroded away by the spark.

An exposure of 2×10^{-7} coulombs requires about 1 milligram of InSb, AlSb, GaSb or GaAs. From Table II it can be seen that about 4 million spark pulses are required to produce this exposure. Each average spark pulse then uses about 2×10^{-10} grams of GaAs which has a volume of 5×10^{-11} cm^{-3}, and the penetration depth into the sample by the average spark is on the order of 4 microns. About 1 square millimeter of GaSb surface is sparked for the usual exposure of 2×10^{-7} coulombs, and a monatomic layer of an impurity would correspond to an impurity concentration of about 1 ppm in the total volume sparked. Sparking conditions can, of course, be varied to control the depth of penetration.

Another factor which complicates the analysis is the presence of compounds which survive the high energy spark. For example, in the GaAs mass spectrum AsO, GaO_2, Ga_2O, As_2O_2, and As_3O_3 are found in appreciable quantities, i.e., about 0.1 ppm. In many cases their quantity approaches that of a monatomic surface layer. Some of the bulk impurities may also be present in the form of compounds. It has not been definitely established that in some cases the CO_2 and hydrocarbon lines are not at least in part contributed by the sample. In analyses of beryllium it has been found that BeH^+ ions in quantities as high as several hundred parts per million can only be attributed to the beryllium sample.

DISCUSSION

In early work on InSb several ppm of zinc, cadmium, and tellurium were found to be the major impurities. Now only a few ppb of zinc and tellurium are detected in high-purity InSb. In the highest purity zone-refined InSb no impurities can be detected with the mass spectrometer, and their maximum concentration is believed to be less than 1 ppb.

Initially AlSb was p-type with a carrier concentration of $5-7 \times 10^{17}/cm^3$. It was thought that stoichiometry was the problem. However, heating the aluminum in a vacuum for 16 hours at $1000°C$ removed volatile impurities and a new limit of 2×10^{16} p-type impurities was encountered for AlSb. Mass spectrographic analysis has shown that the major impurity removed by the heat-treatment was magnesium. In GaSb a lower limit of 1.5×10^{17} p-type carriers/cm^3 has remained a stubborn and unexplained

333

obstacle. Many assume that stoichiometry is the answer. For both AlSb and GaSb no ordinary impurities with concentrations greater than 0.1 ppm are observed by mass spectrographic analysis. However, carbon and oxygen in quantities of about 1 to 5 ppm are observed. Some of these impurities definitely come from the residual background of the mass spectrometer, but some also appear to come from the AlSb and GaSb samples. Special analytical techniques will have to be developed before carbon can be ruled out as the 5 ppm residual impurity in GaSb.

In InAs and GaAs, silicon, carbon, and oxygen appear to be the main impurities which provide a 2-$4 \times 10^{16}/cm^3$ lower limit for the impurities in these compounds. Residual gas background again complicates the analysis for carbon and oxygen, and, in addition, the $^{12}C^{16}O$ line at mass 28 can in many cases be broad enough to hide the ^{28}Si. Multiple ionization of the ^{28}Si or the ^{29}Si and ^{30}Si isotopes reduce the sensitivity of the mass spectrometer for the detection of silicon, but a number of GaAs and InAs samples have been obtained for which silicon could not be the major impurity.

Silicon and carbon in InAs and GaAs are unusual impurities in view of their affinity for oxygen. Apparently oxygen is not present as an ordinary impurity but combines with silicon or carbon and reduces the carrier concentration. Thus, in part oxygen behaves like a p-type impurity, i.e., it can reduce the n-type carrier concentration. However, the Si-O scattering center seems to act as an electric dipole giving a $T^{1/2}$ dependence for the electron mobility. Some experimental observations suggest a C-H reaction which reduces the electron concentration in GaAs, but also reduces the electron mobility. Again, refined mass spectrographic techniques will be required to definitely correlate carbon, oxygen, and hydrogen contents with changes in sample preparation procedures and in electrical properties of GaAs.

It is of interest to mention that the mass spectrometer can be used to accurately determine experimentally the relationship between the carrier concentration and the Hall coefficient, i.e., $A = Rne$. For the precise analysis required, the photographic plate must be replaced by a more accurate ion detector such as an electrometer or electron multiplier. The total charge of one of the major constituents of the semiconductor, say arsenic, is also monitored. It should be possible to obtain the concentration of a few selected impurities to an accuracy of a few percent. Such measurements would be of great value in furthering our understanding of electronic transport phenomena in semiconductors.

SUMMARY

1. Impurities in compound semiconductors can be determined
    in concentrations which are, in many important cases, as
    low as 1 ppb.
2. Quantitative mass spectrographic studies of the segregation
    of a large number of impurities in a single pulled crystal
    have been made and found to be in reasonable agreement
    with the results obtained using individually doped crystals
    and Hall coefficient measurements.
3. High mass resolution is required to distinguish the impurities
    from normal background and other extraneous lines. Meas-
    urement of the position of the impurity line on the photo-
    graphic plate must be made to an accuracy of a few microns
    in order to identify it positively in the presence of other
    lines having nearly the same mass.
4. Extreme care must be taken to ensure that the impurity
    actually comes from the bulk of the material being analyzed
    and not surface, instrument, or other contamination.

ACKNOWLEDGMENTS

The author wishes to thank J. V. Leicht and D. M. Pollock
for their help in operating the mass spectrometer and aiding in
the analysis of the photographic plates, and expresses his
appreciation to W. P. Allred for the GaSb crystal with special
doping and to F. J. Reid of Battelle Memorial Institute for the
GaAs samples 178 and 179. Gratitude is expressed to C. F.
Robinson, W. M. Brubaker, G. D. Perkins, and C. E. Berry for
suggestions and valuable discussions.

This work was supported in whole or in part by the United
States Air Force under Contract AF 33(616)-5571, monitored by
the Materials Central, Wright Air Development Division, Wright-
Patterson Air Force Base, Ohio.

REFERENCES

1. W. P. Allred and R. T. Bate, J. Electrochem. Soc. 108, 258
    (1961).
2. R. D. Craig, G. A. Errock, and J. D. Waldron, "Advances in
    Mass Spectrometry," (J. D. Waldron, Ed.), Pergamon Press,
    London, 1959, pp. 136-156.
3. G. DeMaria, J. Drowart, and M. G. Inghram, J. Chem. Phys.
    31, 1076 (1959).
4. P. Goldfinger and M. Jeunehomme, "Advances in Mass Spec-
    trometry," (J. D. Waldron, Ed.), Pergamon Press, London,
    1959, pp. 534-546.
5. R. N. Hall, J. Appl. Phys. (To be published).
6. N. B. Hannay and A. J. Ahearn, Anal. Chem. 26, 1056 (1954).

7. K. F. Hulme and J. B. Mullin, Phil. Mag. 4, 1286 (1959).
8. J. Mattauch and R. Herzog, Z. Physik 89, 447, 786 (1934).
9. C. F. Robinson, U. S. Patent 2,851,608 (1958).
10. C. F. Robinson, G. D. Perkins, and N. W. Bell, "Proceedings of the International Instruments and Measurements Conference," Stockholm, Sweden, 1960 (to be published).

DISCUSSION

K. M. HERGENROTHER (Block Assoc.): Do you have any comment on what this half part per million in indium arsenide might be?

R. K. WILLARDSON (Bell and Howell Research Center): We think it is carbon in those cases where it is not silicon.

R. E. HONIG (RCA Laboratories): I have one comment and one question. I believe the concentration of carbon is practically impossible to detect because you have an irreducible carbon line in practically anything you spark, and it seems to be that this must be due to carbon monoxide as a background gas.

We have looked at quite a few plates and taken a few ourselves. There is an irreducible background at mass 12 corresponding to carbon and at mass 16, as you mentioned, corresponding to oxygen. Presumably they are surface impurities that dissociate and remain throughout the sparking of the sample.

Similarly, the hydrogenated lines that you mentioned with beryllium are not too surprising. I have seen hydrogenated and OH groups on various elements which exist when you sputter an element, as in the case of silicon, where you would observe not only silicon monoxide, SiO, but also SiOH, SiH, and so on.

You have mentioned minimum concentrations actually found of the order of a tenth of a part per million. Is that, at this moment, your limitation in detection sensitivity?

R. K. WILLARDSON (Bell and Howell Research Center): In the case of carbon and oxygen, the sensitivity varies from a tenth of a part per million up to two to three parts per million, and until we can eliminate the variability, the detection limit is something of the order of a part per million.

R. E. HONIG (RCA Laboratories): What about detection sensitivities for other elements beside carbon and hydrogen? What is the real lower limit in your instrument at this time?

R. K. WILLARDSON (Bell and Howell Research Center): As I mentioned before, to give a real lower limit on any particular element, you have to talk about the particular compound and other constituents. Using the microphotometer to obtain the density

336

for the line, it is about ten parts per billion. The weakest visible line is about a part per billion.

R. E. HONIG (RCA Laboratories): Have you observed parts per billion impurities in any sample?

R. K. WILLARDSON (Bell and Howell Research Center): We have observed zinc in indium antimonide in the three parts per billion range. However, this was determined by electrical measurements, but there may be some question as to exactly what impurity the line was due to.

R. E. HONIG (RCA Laboratories): Have you made internal standard measurements such as were discussed earlier by Dr. Duke, where you refer the concentration of impurity to the matrix material itself?

R. K. WILLARDSON (Bell and Howell Research Center): This was precisely what was done for indium and gallium antimonide.

D. M. JACKSON (General Electric Advanced Electronics Center): Can you give us the operating pressures in your instrument? And secondly, can you estimate how much trace impurity is introduced as a result of your electrode preparation, or alternately, from the glass bushings in your source?

R. K. WILLARDSON (Bell and Howell Research Center): Well, I can say that many months ago, when we first analyzed silicon, we had not received our diamond wheels and were using a boron carbide abrasive for preparing the sample. As a result our boron was extremely high.

This was before skills had been developed in etching the surface of the silicon, thereby removing surface boron. This illustrates a very important point. When you get into the parts per billion range, the sample handling techniques do not get easier just because you are using a mass spectrometer. You still have the contamination problem confronting you.

As to the point mentioned earlier with respect to the memory of the instrument; if you run a sample of any material and then, immediately after, run a sample of a different material, there will appear something on the order of one part per million of the first material, unless the source is very carefully cleaned between samples.

If the instrument is operated for months, as has been done, without cleaning it, then the analysis is practically meaningless for parts per billion analyses.

D. M. JACKSON (General Electric Advanced Electronics Center): What about the operating pressures?

337

R. K. WILLARDSON (Bell and Howell Research Center): The operating pressure is on the order of 2 to 3 times 10^{-7} mm. in the source.

L. R. WEISBERG (RCA Laboratories): Dr. Duke mentioned that to get detectable lines in the range of one to ten parts per billion requires a one to two hours exposure. How long an exposure is required to achieve the same in your instrument?

R. K. WILLARDSON (Bell and Howell Research Center): Dr. Duke mentioned that initially the MS-7 instrument was operated using a very high ion beam current. This causes a large spread of the ions on the plate, making the analysis very difficult. He mentioned that he had reduced his beam intensity so that it took about two hours for a 10^{-6} coulomb exposure. This is almost identical to what we require.

L. R. WEISBERG (RCA Laboratories): Can you achieve the same high ion beam intensity as the MS-7 in order to accomplish high sensitivity analyses?

R. K. WILLARDSON (Bell and Howell Research Center): Our instrument was basically designed as a high resolution instrument. One difference between the two instruments is that our slit width is 2-1/2 mils rather than the 10 mils of the MS-7 instrument. It is possible to widen the slit thereby obtaining a higher intensity beam.

L. R. WEISBERG (RCA Laboratories): Finally, one comment about your interpretation of the oxygen appearing with silicon or carbon in gallium arsenide. I tend to question this and also your interpretation that the lowering of mobility is due to ion pairing or the formation of dipoles. Dipole scattering is much less strong than simple ionized impurity scattering and could never be expected to explain the lowering of mobilities.

R. K. WILLARDSON (Bell and Howell Research Center): If oxygen is present in gallium arsenide as a neutral impurity, why does it reduce the carrier concentration when silicon and carbon are present?

L. R. WEISBERG (RCA Laboratories): I will be publishing a paper in the near future with possible explanations on this point. However, I have never stated that oxygen goes in as a neutral impurity, and in fact, have published an energy level in gallium arsenide that is believed due to oxygen.

R. E. JOHNSON (Texas Instruments): I would like to have the speaker clarify this particular point. If I interpret his remarks correctly, he says that the mass spectrograph shows that silicon and oxygen occur together in the gallium arsenide. Is that true?

338

R. K. WILLARDSON (Bell and Howell Research Center): No.

R. E. JOHNSON (Texas Instruments): Will you clarify your remarks about the phenomenon of dipole scattering due to the silicon oxygen, or clumping in the gallium arsenide?

R. K. WILLARDSON (Bell and Howell Research Center): I said that silicon and carbon are found as important impurities in the III-V compounds and that oxygen and possibly hydrogen appear to interact with them to change the effect of these impurities.

Further, I suggested that they come together in a complex, and that in mass spectrographic analysis one looks for complexes or compounds and is not restricted to purely elemental analysis.

R. E. JOHNSON (Texas Instruments): Have you some idea of the energy available in the volatilization process and the possibility of combinations of atoms existing as combinations throughout this process? Or is it possible that there would be complete separation into atomic species, or perhaps ionic, and then a recombination after the primary volatilization?

R. K. WILLARDSON (Bell and Howell Research Center): I think the best answer to this is that for each polyatomic ion there are up to as many as ten ions found on the plate.

R. E. JOHNSON (Texas Instruments): Of the same atomic species?

R. K. WILLARDSON (Bell and Howell Research Center): Right.

MASS SPECTROGRAPHIC EVIDENCE
FOR DEVIATIONS FROM
STOICHIOMETRY IN GaSb

Edward B. Owens and Alan J. Strauss
Lincoln Laboratory,* Massachusetts Institute of Technology
Lexington 73, Massachusetts

ABSTRACT

The purest GaSb now made is p-type. At room temperature this material contains free holes at concentrations between 1×10^{17} and 2×10^{17} cm^{-3}. In order to obtain additional evidence concerning whether the acceptors are impurity atoms or lattice defects associated with deviations from stoichiometry, GaSb has been analyzed with a spark source mass spectrograph which our calibration shows to be capable of detecting almost all impurity elements which are present at concentrations exceeding 1×10^{16} cm^{-3}. The only elements detected besides Ga and Sb were: (1) Si at a concentration of 5×10^{16} cm^{-3} or less and (2) C, O, H, and N, the levels of which were comparable to those obtained in blank runs, so that their concentration in the GaSb cannot be estimated. Of the latter elements, only carbon is likely to be a shallow acceptor in GaSb, and metallurgical evidence indicates that it should not be present at constant concentration in purified material. The analytical results therefore strongly increase the probability that the acceptors are lattice defects rather than impurity atoms.

The purest GaSb now made is p-type. At room temperature this material contains free holes at concentrations between 1×10^{17} and 2×10^{17} cm^{-3}. Free hole concentrations within this same rather narrow range have consistently been obtained in zone-refined ingots since 1953, when the electrical properties of GaSb were first described by Welker [9], and are now obtained without zone refining when the compound is prepared from commercial semiconductor grade gallium and antimony. The identity of the acceptors present in the purest material has never been established. The uniformity of samples prepared in different laboratories from different starting materials over such

---

*Operated with support from the U. S. Army, Navy, and Air Force.

an extended period suggests that the acceptors are predominantly lattice defects associated with deviations from stoichiometry, as Detweiler [1] first proposed, rather than impurity atoms. The hypothesis of stoichiometric deviations could be verified experimentally either by producing changes in acceptor concentration which could be attributed unambiguously to changes in stoichiometry or by using analytical techniques to demonstrate that the total concentration of acceptor impurities in the purest available material is less than 10^{17} cm^{-3}. (It should be noted that the acceptor concentration in the purest material is actually somewhat greater than the free hole concentrations measured at room temperature, since the acceptors have an ionization energy of about 0.025 ev [1,6] and consequently are not completely ionized at room temperature.)

An analytical investigation of the identity of the acceptors in high purity GaSb requires, ideally, an analytical method whose detection limit for every element is significantly below the observed acceptor concentration. A method which very nearly meets this requirement has become available with the development of the spark source mass spectrograph designed for analysis of solids. Therefore we have analyzed GaSb with a spectrograph which our calibration shows to be capable of detecting almost all impurity elements which are present at concentrations exceeding 1×10^{16} cm^{-3}. The results strongly increase the probability that the acceptors in the purest available GaSb are lattice defects rather than impurity atoms.

EXPERIMENTAL

The analysis was made with a mass spectrograph manufactured by Consolidated Electrodynamics Corp. Samples were cut from a single crystal of GaSb grown in a conventional resistance-heated crystal puller under an atmosphere of hydrogen. The raw material used in the puller was polycrystalline GaSb supplied by United Mineral and Chemical Corp. The free hole concentrations in various parts of the single crystal, as determined by Hall coefficient measurements at room temperature, ranged from 1.25×10^{17} to 1.55×10^{17} cm^{-3}, and the Hall mobilities were between 610 and 680 cm^2/v-sec.

The sample pieces were etched, washed thoroughly with distilled water, and dried before analysis. The pieces were sparked with a 75 kv, one Mc/s discharge in pulses 15 μsec long at the rate of 1000 pulses per sec. The accelerating potential was 15 kv. The detector was an Ilford Q-II photographic plate. A series of graduated exposures was made over the range between 10^{-7} and 10^{-12} coul on the plate. The plate was developed for four minutes in half-strength D-19 solution with mechanical agitation and automatically controlled temperature.

341

TREATMENT OF DATA

In order to interpret the analytical data obtained in the manner described, it is necessary to evaluate--for each possible impurity element--the minimum concentration which can be detected. We shall assume that the sputtering, ionization, and collection efficiencies are the same for all elements, so that the proportion of each element among the ions striking the photographic plate is the same as in the solid sample. For the present we shall also assume that the resolution of the mass spectrograph is sufficient to prevent interference between lines on the plate produced by ions of different isotopes, and that the proportions of the following ions are negligible: (1) residual gas ions not present in the solid sample, (2) dimers and higher polymers, (3) ions undergoing charge exchange.

If these assumptions are satisfied, the number of ions striking a particular position on the photographic plate during a specified exposure can be denoted by N_{ij}, the number of ions of isotope i of element X with charge j; N_{ij} is given by

$$N_{ij} = A_i \; B_j \; C_X N, \tag{1}$$

where A_i is the relative abundance of isotope i, B_j is the fraction of ions with charge j, C_X is the concentration of element X in the sample, and N is the total number of ions striking the plate during the exposure. The minimum concentration, C_{min}, of element X which can be detected is found by setting N_{ij} for the strongest line equal to N_{min}, the minimum number of ions required to form a detectable line on the plate:

$$C_{min} = \frac{N_{min}}{N} \cdot \frac{1}{A_1 \; B_1}, \tag{2}$$

where A_1 is the relative abundance of the most abundant isotope and B_1 is the maximum value of B_j for element X. Since the smallest value of A_1 for any element is 0.24, while the smallest value of B_1 which we have observed is 0.5, in the least favorable case $C_{min} = 8 \; (N_{min}/N)$.

In order to compare the analytical data with the results of Hall coefficient measurements, it is convenient to express C_{min} in atoms/cm^3. Consequently the quantity N in Equation (2) is replaced by the volume, V, of the solid sample which corresponds to the number of ions striking the photographic plate. Since the total charge on the impurity ions was negligible compared to the total charge on the ions of the major constituents, $V = Q/Zen$, where Q is the total charge striking the plate, Z is the average charge on the major ions, e is the electronic charge, and n is the number of atoms per cm^3 of the solid sample. In the present experiments, the maximum charge was 10^{-7} coul and the value of Z obtained by analysis of the GaSb data was approximately 2. Since n for GaSb = 3.5×10^{22} cm^{-3}, $V = 9 \times 10^{-12} cm^3$. Accordingly, for the least favorable case $C_{min} = (9 \times 10^{11})$ N_{min} cm^{-3}.

In order to obtain a reliable value for N_{min}, we have investigated in detail the relationship between the number of ions which strike the photographic plate at a given position and the intensity of the line produced by these ions. The calibration data were obtained by analysis of the spectra for GaSb and also for Pt. For each of the graduated exposures comprising the spectra, the lines associated with ions of the major constituents were identified. The number of ions (N_{ij}) producing each line was calculated on the basis of Equation (1) by setting the sample size for each exposure equal to Q/Ze, the total number of major ions striking the plate. The values of A_i used were obtained from the 1959 Nuclear Tables [7], while the proportions of the variously charged species were found by analysis of the spectra on the assumption that the darkening of the photographic plate produced by a fixed number of ions is independent of the charge on the ions.

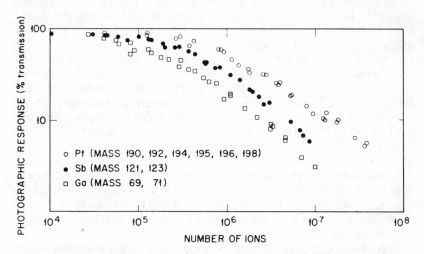

Figure 1. Calibration Curves for Ilford Q-II Emulsion.

Calibration curves for Ga, Sb, and Pt, obtained by plotting the measured values of N_{ij} on a log-log plot against the optical transmission of the corresponding lines measured with a micro-densitometer, are shown in Fig. 1. The small scatter of the points indicates that with the present instrumentation it should be possible to perform quantitative analyses accurate to within about 25%, provided that the number of impurity ions striking the plate exceeds about 10^5. Although at high values of N_{ij} the sensitivity of the photographic plate is seen to decrease markedly with increasing ion mass, convergence of the curves as the optical transmission approaches 100% shows that N_{min} is independent of mass. We estimate N_{min} to be approximately 10^4 ions; a number of lines corresponding to even smaller values of N have been observed. By using this value for N_{min}, we find that in the least favorable case the minimum concentration of an impurity element in GaSb which can be detected in the present experiments is approximately 1×10^{16} cm^{-3}, an order of magnitude below the acceptor concentration determined by Hall measurements, provided that there is no interference between lines produced by different isotopes and that the proportion of residual gas ions is negligible.

RESULTS AND DISCUSSION

The only elements detected, in addition to Ga and Sb, were Si, H, N, O, and C. In view of the detection limit of 1×10^{16} cm^{-3} just estimated, all undetected elements are effectively eliminated as possible sources of the predominant acceptors in the purest available GaSb; detailed consideration has shown that the presence of these elements would not be masked by interference due to the lines which are observed.

Since Si is known to be an acceptor in GaSb [2], a precise determination of its concentration would be particularly desirable. Unfortunately the line due to the most abundant isotope, Si^{28}, cannot be used for this purpose, since it conicides with a strong line due to residual CO ions. We have estimated the concentration on the basis of a line due to singly-charged Si^{29} (4.7% abundant) which was just visible on one out of three exposures of 10^{-7} coul. If the number of ions forming this line is taken as 10^4, the Si concentration would be only 5×10^{16} cm^{-3} even if only 50% of the Si ions were singly charged. This estimate suggests that Si atoms are not the predominant acceptors in GaSb, although they may make an appreciable contribution to the total acceptor concentration.

It is not possible to make any estimate of the concentrations of H, N, O, or C in the GaSb samples, since the intensities of the lines due to these elements and their compounds were comparable to those obtained in blank runs. On the basis of the analytical data, therefore, these elements cannot be eliminated as possible sources of the predominant acceptors in GaSb. Furthermore, they cannot be eliminated on the basis of definite evidence that they do not act as shallow acceptors in GaSb, since their electrical

344

properties in GaSb have not been investigated. However, the probability that any of these elements could be the source of the predominant acceptors does not seem very great. No evidence of electrical activity due to H has been reported for any III-V compound; the element is reported to be inactive in GaAs [8]. In addition, the acceptor concentration in GaSb is the same whether the material is prepared under an atmosphere of hydrogen or argon [4]. Nitrogen, as a Group V element, might substitute for Sb but would then be inactive; it too is reported to be inactive in GaAs [8]. If O, like other Group VI elements, substituted for Sb, it would be expected to be a donor; it is reported to act as a deep trap in GaAs [8].

In contrast to H, N, and O, C might be expected to be an acceptor in GaSb, since both Si and Ge are known to be acceptors in GaSb [2], and C itself is reported to be an acceptor in AlSb [5]. It is improbable that C atoms are the predominant acceptors in GaSb, however, since the acceptor concentration is the same whether the compound is synthesized in graphite crucibles or zone refined in quartz boats. Uniformity of C concentration in the presence or absence of elemental C seems unlikely, since it would seem to require that the effective distribution coefficient of C in GaSb be approximately unity at the limit of solubility.

On the basis of the above discussion, it can be concluded that the analytical results strongly increase the probability that the predominant acceptors in the purest available GaSb are lattice defects rather than impurity atoms, although elimination of Si and C as possible sources of the acceptors would require further analytical work or, in the case of C, an investigation of electrical activity, solubility, and distribution coefficient. Therefore the present results should encourage attempts to alter the acceptor concentration in GaSb by employing procedure designed to change the concentration of lattice defects. Such procedures would include the growth of GaSb crystals from Ga-rich melts at temperatures far below the maximum melting point and annealing-quenching experiments performed as a function of temperature.

If the predominant acceptors in pure GaSb are actually lattice defects, we suggest that these defects may be Ga vacancies. This speculation is motivated primarily by the agreement between the ionization energy (0.025 ev) of the acceptors in GaSb and the ionization energy (0.021 ev) of an acceptor level in GaAs which Whalen and Fuller [10] have attributed to Ga vacancies. In addition, Grimmeis [3] has proposed that an acceptor level of 0.19 ev in GaP is associated with Ga vacancies; the higher ionization energy might be expected in view of the fact that the energy gap of GaP (2.23 ev) is considerably larger than those of GaSb (0.69 ev) and GaAs (1.38 ev).

345

ACKNOWLEDGMENTS

The authors are grateful to P. L. Moody and R. L. MacLean for growth of the GaSb single crystal used for analysis and to R. N. Hall for communicating his results prior to publication.

REFERENCES

1. D. P. Detweiler, Phys. Rev. 97, 1575 (1955).
2. J. T. Edmond, Proc. Phys. Soc. 73, 622 (1959).
3. H. G. Grimmeiss, Philips Res. Repts. 15, 290 (1960).
4. R. N. Hall and J. H. Racette, J. Appl. Phys. 32, 856 (1961).
5. A. Hertzog, R. R. Haberecht, and A. E. Middleton, J. Electrochem. Soc. 105, 533 (1958).
6. H. N. Leifer and W. C. Dunlap, Phys. Rev. 95, 51 (1954).
7. K. Way (editor), "1959 Nuclear Tables," National Research Council, Washington, D. C., 1959.
8. L. R. Weisberg, F. D. Rosi, and P. G. Herkart, in "Properties of Elemental and Compound Semiconductors," edited by H. C. Gatos, Interscience Publishers, New York, N. Y., 1960, p. 49.
9. H. Welker, Z. Naturforschg. 8a, 248 (1953).
10. J. M. Whalen and C. S. Fuller, J. Appl. Phys. 31, 1507 (1960).

DISCUSSION

L. R. WEISBERG (RCA Laboratories): I think it is important to point out that there is very strong evidence that in all p-type compounds the number of acceptors and donors have been invariant even though the material is grown from a solution that is rich in either gallium or antimony. This is a strong negative suggestion against your evidence for the existence of stoichiometric deviation.

A. J. ROSENBERG (Chairman) (TYCO): Some work on this has been done in gallium antimodide, but more work has been done in other three-five compounds, and no change in the donor or acceptor concentration due to deviations from stoichiometry seems to have been found. In your own work in gallium arsenide, Dr. Weisberg, didn't you find an increasing acceptor concentration?

L. R. WEISBERG (RCA Laboratories): This was proven, I think, not to be due to deviations in stoichiometry.

E. B. OWENS (MIT, Lincoln Laboratory): I can comment on the mass spectrography part of this work, but may I ask my co-author to comment on the solid state physics aspect at this time?

A. J. STRAUSS (MIT, Lincoln Laboratory): I certainly agree that the type of evidence we are presenting in this paper is strictly negative evidence. My own estimation of the situation is this: We have, we think, succeeded in eliminating almost every element as a possible source of acceptors, assuming that the mass spectrography results are valid.

First of all, I think that we must examine each three-five compound individually. In the particular case of gallium antimonide, I do want to point out that there is a possibility that the width of the solidus region is so small that even growing the material from widely separated compositions in the melt might not show up a deviation from stoichiometry.

The second point I would like to bring out is, that the shape of the liquidus in gallium antimonide, as is the case in most of the three-fives, is extremely flat; because of this, one has to go to really large excesses of one or the other constituents in order to grow the solid compound from a melt at a temperature which is much below the maximum melting point. For this reason, I would expect that experiments with 5 to 10 percent gallium or antimony excess would show very great changes. However, I would certainly feel that evidence at 75 or 80 percent gallium would be pretty strong on the other side.

A. J. ROSENBERG (Chairman) (TYCO): Has this been done, Dr. Weisberg?

L. R. WEISBERG (RCA Laboratories): No careful study of this particular system has been made in contradiction.

A. J. STRAUSS (MIT, Lincoln Laboratory): I feel that we could take deviations from stoichiometry or, more generally, lattice defects, since they wouldn't have to be stoichiometric deviations, seriously enough to make a concerted effort to try to find out whether the acceptor concentration could be changed by means which would be expected to change the stoichiometry.

H. T. MINDEN (General Electric): In the particular sample you worked with, what was the hole concentration and what were the silicon and carbon concentrations? Is there a significant difference experimentally?

E. B. OWENS (MIT, Lincoln Laboratory): The free hole concentration ran between 1.25 to 1.55×10^{17} per cm^3. The silicon determination was run in three equal experiments. In only one of them did we detect silicon; the rest were well below the detection limit. We took the former as the worst case and calculated a value of 5×10^{16} cm^{-3}.

The carbon, as I have pointed out, cannot be estimated, because carbon lines are always present on the mass spectrogram. It varies from sample to sample, but not in any consistent fashion.

347

I think it is due to residual gases, or some other factor, and I cannot competently estimate the carbon content in this particular sample at this stage of development.

A. J. ROSENBERG (Chairman) (TYCO): Work at the Lincoln Laboratory has shown that an apparently irreducible donor concentration in mercury selenide, which is of the same general crystal structure as gallium antimonide, is due to a semimetallic behavior, that is, a crossing of the conduction bands in different portions of the K space. Could this also explain the behavior in gallium antimonide?

A. J. STRAUSS (MIT, Lincoln Laboratory): I doubt it. Our work on mercury selenide does not suggest that the limit is due to crossing of or overlapping of bands, but is really due to a stoichiometry in which the whole solidus region is on the mercury rich side of the 50 percent line. It is not certain that it is definitely connected with the overlap of bands. In this case, I don't think there is any question that the band structure is fairly typical for a three-five, although it has its complexities, and I doubt that there is too much connection between the two.

DETECTABILITIES OF THE ELEMENTS BY SEVERAL SPECTROGRAPHIC PROCEDURES

William C. Myers and W. M. Henry
Battelle Memorial Institute, Columbus, Ohio

INTRODUCTION

The emission-spectrographic laboratory is frequently required to analyze materials of construction, reagents, residues, and by-products associated with high-purity semiconductor research. These samples many times may contain a multiplicity of trace-element impurities and are often limited in size. The preferred method of analysis is usually one not requiring chemical treatment of the sample so the chance for contamination is low. The literature gives many methods of trace determinations not requiring chemical extractions, but little information is available on the direct inter-comparison of the detectabilities achieved by these methods. The purpose of the work reported here was to compare the limits of detectability obtained on a limited quantity of sample using one spectrograph and several methods of emission analysis. While a 1.5-meter-grating spectrograph was used for this work, the evaluation of these methods would be applicable to other spectrographs.

PROCEDURE

Standards Preparation. Two series of standards for the elements were prepared by successive graphite dilutions of master mixes of the elements' oxides. The concentrations of each element in these standards were diluted from 1.0 to 0.0001 per cent by factors of approximately 3.3. The standards were first ground and mixed by hand using a mortar and pestle, and then mechanically mixed and ground in plastic vials containing plastic balls. To keep line interference to a minimum, the first series was composed of the oxides of only 51 of the elements in a graphite matrix. The second set consisted of 17 rare-earth oxides in a graphite matrix.

349

Spectrograph and Excitation Source:

(1) A commercial 1.5-meter original grating spectrograph, having a reciprocal linear dispersion of 3.47 angstroms per millimeter at the film in the second order, was employed.
(2) A d.c. arc source was employed with a peak voltage adjustable to a maximum of 300 volts and a maximum arc current output of 15 amperes. Series resistance was used to control the current.
(3) An enclosed arc chamber similar to that used by Owen [7] was employed.

Experimental. A 5-milligram weight of each of the standards was tamped into a sample electrode. The following four methods of excitation were used on each of these standards: (1) d.c. arc in air, (2) d.c. arc in 70% argon—30% oxygen atmosphere, (3) cathode layer in air, and (4) cathode layer in 70% argon—30% oxygen atmosphere.

The spectrographic conditions for each of these methods is shown in Table 1.

The detection limits for each of the 68 elements were determined by visual observation of their spectral-line intensities on the photographic films.

RESULT AND DISCUSSION

The total-burn methods of excitation originally considered for trace analysis, in addition to the d.c.-arc method in air, were (1) the d.c.-arc excitation in a gas atmosphere [1,2,3,6,8, 10,11,12) and (2) the cathode-layer method of excitation [9].

The advantages of the use of the d.c.-arc excitation in a gas atmosphere are:
(1) Cyanogen bands can be reduced or eliminated by using a nitrogen-free gas, thus making additional sensitive lines available for use in analysis.
(2) The continuum background can be reduced by using special gas atmospheres.
(3) The arc temperature can be better controlled.
(4) Proper choice of gas atmospheres can increase the detectability of some of the elements.

The cathode-layer technique has the following advantages:
(1) Only a small quantity of sample is required, 5 milligrams or less.
(2) Increased detection limits are possible as a result of the migration of ions to the cathode, thus causing a greater concentration of the ions and neutralized metal atoms near the cathode.

350

Table 1

Spectrographic Parameters

	Cathode Layer		D.C. Arc	
	70% A— 30% O	Air	70% A— 30% O	Air
Sample Polarity	Negative*	Negative*	Positive	Positive
Slit Width, microns	20	20	20	20
Analytical Gap, mm	9	9	5	5
Amperes	15	15	10	10
Exposure Time, seconds	75	75	60	60
Weight of Standards, mg	5	5	5	5

Note: Lower sample electrode — High-purity preformed graphite cylindrical rod, 0.120 inch in diameter and 1.5 inches in length having a 0.096-inch-diameter cup with a depth of 0.25 inch centered on one end

Upper electrode — High-purity preformed graphite cylindrical rod, 0.242 inch in diameter and 1.5 inches in length having a 3/32-inch-wide undercut, 3/32 inch from one end and of a diameter of 0.125 inch on center

Film — Eastman Kodak Company, SA-1, 2200-3750 A, Second order
Eastman Kodak Company, 103-0, 3800-4500 A, Second order
Eastman Kodak Company, 4-F, 4400-7500 A, First order
Eastman Kodak Company, 1-N, 7600-9300 A, First order

*The top of the cathode sample electrode was continuously aligned to be 1/2 millimeter above the optical axis of the spectrograph during excitation.

Table 2

Detection Limits of Elements in Millimicrograms

Element	Symbol	Atomic No.	Cathode-Layer Excitation		D.C.-Arc Excitation	
			70% A—30% O$_2$	Air	70% A—30% O$_2$	Air
Aluminum	Al	13	1	0.5	100	500
Antimony	Sb	51	20	20	50	200
Arsenic	As	33	50	100	200	300
Barium	Ba	56	(20)	(20)	(50)	(150)
Beryllium	Be	4	<0.5	0.5	0.5	5
Bismuth	Bi	83	50	50	100	150
Boron	B	5	5	5	20	20
Cadmium	Cd	48	200	200	300	100
Calcium	Ca	20	0.5	0.5	2	30
Cerium	Ce	58	3,000	15,000	900	3,000
Cesium	Cs	55	(500)	(50)	(200)	(200)
Chromium	Cr	24	5	10	100	200
Cobalt	Co	27	10	5	100	20
Columbium (See Niobium)						
Copper	Cu	29	5	2	30	20
Dysprosium	Dy	66	300	2,000	90	900
Erbium	Er	68	80	300	90	300
Europium	Eu	63	200	600	40	600
Gadolinium	Gd	64	300	900	300	300
Gallium	Ga	31	5	5	50	300
Germanium	Ge	32	20	10	80	50
Gold	Au	79	100	50	30	100
Hafnium	Hf	72	50	100	500	300
Holmium	Ho	67	90	400	90	200
Indium	In	49	10	10	200	600
Iridium	Ir	77	50	80	300	200
Iron	Fe	26	5	2	80	80
Lanthanum	La	57	400	3,000	400	900
Lead	Pb	82	10	10	50	100
Lithium	Li	3	(0.5)	(0.1)	(10)	(40)
			300	20	2,000	2,000
Lutetium	Lu	71	30	90	50	50
Magnesium	Mg	12	1	1	3	10
Manganese	Mn	25	2	2	50	50
Mercury	Hg	80	100	200	50	15,000
Molybdenum	Mo	42	2	5	50	100

Table 2 (Continued)

Element	Symbol	Atomic No.	Cathode-Layer Excitation		D.C.-Arc Excitation	
			70% A—30% O_2	Air	70% A—30% O_2	Air
Neodymium	Nd	60	2,000	6,000	600	2,000
Nickel	Ni	28	10	20	50	50
Niobium	Nb	41	50	50	500	100
Osmium	Os	76	10	20	500	200
Palladium	Pd	46	5	10	70	100
Phosphorus	P	15	500	1,000	2,000	5,000
Platinum	Pt	78	5	20	50	60
Potassium	K	19	(5)	(8)	(20)	(300)
			2,000	300	20,000	30,000
Praseodymium	Pr	59	900	4,000	700	3,000
Rhenium	Re	75	500	2,000	500	2,000
Rhodium	Rh	45	30	40	50	300
Rubidium	Rb	37	(100)	(20)	(100)	(100)
Ruthenium	Ru	44	10	30	200	400
Samarium	Sm	62	2,000	2,000	300	2,000
Scandium	Sc	21	10	20	200	300
Silicon	Si	14	5	10	30	100
Silver	Ag	47	1	0.5	5	10
Sodium	Na	11	(<1)	(<1)	(5)	(30)
			80	80	2,000	3,000
Strontium	Sr	38	5	5	20	500
Tantalum	Ta	73	400	400	1,000	1,000
Tellurium	Te	52	50	600	500	2,000
Terbium	Tb	65	300	2,000	300	900
Thallium	Tl	81	100	20	1,000	800
Thorium	Th	90	2,000	2,000	900	2,000
Thulium	Tm	69	30	90	20	30
Tin	Sn	50	5	5	100	200
Titanium	Ti	22	5	30	30	30
Tungsten	W	74	500	1,000	1,000	1,000
Uranium	U	92	400	900	400	900
Vanadium	V	23	5	10	50	200
Ytterbium	Yb	70	3	3	20	30
Yttrium	Y	39	8	60	20	20
Zinc	Zn	30	100	100	200	500
Zirconium	Zr	40	20	100	50	300

Note: Figures enclosed in parentheses are for wavelengths above 4500 A. Underlined figures indicate the best detection limit for the element.

353

The advantages of the two methods were later combined by using the cathode-layer technique in a gas atmosphere.

The 70% argon—30% oxygen gas mixture was chosen as an atmosphere for simultaneously detecting both the refractory and highly volatile elements. Other ratios of these gases have not been investigated.

Table 2 gives the detection limits for each of these methods of excitation for 68 elements.

The cathode-layer technique in the argon-oxygen atmosphere provides the best simultaneous detection limits for 47 of the elements. The next best method is the cathode-layer technique in air; this yields the best simultaneous detection limits for 28 of the elements.

The least desirable excitation is that provided by the d.c arc in air, which fails to utilize the full sensitivity of the carbon arc.

The excitation conditions used in these analyses were those considered to be the best for a general analysis for all of the elements. Improved detection limits can be obtained in many cases for a particular element by using conditions selected specifically for that element [4,5]. Examples of these conditions include buffers, special gas atmospheres, selective volatilization of the elements predetermined by moving-plate studies [6,8], special electrodes, carriers, and superposition of several exposures on a high-contrast film.

The detection limits of course will vary with the matrix, but the use of a graphite matrix gives one a good estimate of the detection limits attainable for any one method.

REFERENCES

1. S. J. Adelstein and B. L. Vallee, Spectrochim. Acta 6, 134-8 (1954).
2. E. M. Hammaker, G. W. Pope, Y. G. Ishida and W. F. Wagner, Appl. Spectroscopy 12, 161-163 (1958).
3. D. O. Landon and A. Arrak, "Stabilization of DC Arc Using a Stallwood Jet," Paper presented at Pittsburgh Conference on Analytical Chemistry and Applied Spectroscopy (1960).
4. A. J. Mitteldorf, The Spex Speaker 1, No. 1 (1956).
5. A. J. Mitteldorf, The Spex Speaker 1, No. 2 (1956).
6. G. H. Morrison, R. L. Rupp and G. L. Klecak, Anal. Chem. 32, 933-935 (1960).
7. L. E. Owen, J. Opt. Soc. Amer. 41, 139 (1951).
8. R. L. Rupp, G. L. Klecak and G. H. Morrison, Anal. Chem. 32, 931-933 (1960).
9. L. W. Strock and V. M. Goldschmidt, "Spectrum Analysis with the Carbon Arc Cathode Layer," Adam Hilger, Ltd., London, England (1936).
10. R. E. Thiers, Appl. Spectroscopy 7, 157-163 (1953).

11. B. L. Vallee and S. J. Adelstein, J. Opt. Soc. Amer. 42, 295-299 (1952).
12. B. L. Vallee and R. W. Peattie, Anal. Chem. 24, 434-444 (1952).

ABBREVIATIONS

d.c. .... direct current
mm .... millimeters
mg .... milligrams
A .... angstroms
Spectrochim. Acta .... Spectrochimica Acta
Anal. Chem. .... Analytical Chemistry
J. Opt. Soc. Amer. .... Journal of the Optical
                                 Society of America
Appl. Spectroscopy.............. Applied Spectroscopy

DISCUSSION

J. F. DUKE (National Physical Laboratory, England): Do you think the limits shown (Table 2) are equally applicable to the solution technique on graphite and your techniques, that is, the actual mixed oxides in graphite?

W. C. MYERS (Battelle Memorial Institute): Yes, I believe so. I might further add that our instrument is an astigmatic instrument, and perhaps better detection limits could be obtained with a stigmatic instrument which is preferable.

A SPECTROCHEMICAL METHOD FOR THE DETERMINATION OF TRACE IMPURITIES IN INDIUM

J. F. Duke
National Physical Laboratory
Metallurgy Division
Teddington, Middlesex, England

ABSTRACT

The development of a spectrochemical method for the determination of trace elements in high purity indium is described. The impurities are chemically separated from the matrix and converted into an aqueous solution of their chlorides. The solutions are concentrated and transferred to a flat, undercut, graphite electrode which is dried, and excited by a 15 amp D.C. arc in an oxygen-argon atmosphere. The spectra are recorded with a 3.4 metre Ebert mounting grating spectrograph.

Copper is used as an internal standard and calibration is by comparison with a solution standard. The sensitivity of detection of nearly thirty elements is below 1 microgram and in several cases below 0.01 microgram. Satisfactory recovery from the chemical procedures has been demonstrated using synthetic solutions.

INTRODUCTION

The problem posed was to devise procedures for the analysis of trace elements in high purity indium metal at levels down to 0.1 parts per million. Since the demands of semiconductor research on the analytical laboratory are frequently varying, it was also desirable that the procedures should be equally applicable to the analysis of some other matrix at a later date, either directly or with the minimum modification. It was of further advantage if the determination could be made on modest amounts of sample.

Time being at a premium, it was decided to seek a method, not necessarily of the highest possible accuracy or sensitivity, which would accommodate the largest possible number of elements, rather than concentrate on individual impurities one by one.

The success of emission spectrographic methods in allied fields has recently been demonstrated by a number of workers [1], although the rival claims have often been difficult to establish in true perspective. Nevertheless optical spectroscopy held promises of the requisite sensitivity, adequate accuracy and, an important point, the facility of simultaneous determination of a number of elements. A high resolution grating instrument was available for this investigation.

PRELIMINARY WORK

The simplest method is undoubtedly direct excitation of the sample. A small globule of relatively impure indium was held in a graphite cup electrode and excited by spark discharges from both a Hilger condensed spark source and from a source modelled on the lines of the BNFMRA unit [2]. Various combinations of circuit parameters were chosen and a series of exposures of differing length were made to discover the conditions of optimum background density. Excitation by a direct current arc was also attempted. The range of discharge currents had to be limited to below 6 amps since higher amperage values caused excessive distillation and sputtering of the sample, rapidly fouling the excitation chamber. It became obvious that in no case could the required sensitivity be obtained and that a preliminary separation of the impurities from the bulk of the indium would probably be essential.

Previous experience in this laboratory led us to believe that the necessary sensitivity might be attained with an impregnated graphite technique. This would require that the impurities be removed from the indium matrix by a chemical procedure and concentrated into a small volume, since a simple solution technique would still offer little advantage over direct excitation. The problem of reagent blanks would be raised, but this would be compensated to a certain extent by the ease of calibration with the aid of synthetic solutions and an internal standard.

It was expected that the limit of detection using the available spark sources would still not be entirely adequate and indeed this was found to be the case. Both Morrison and Pink [3], and Owens [4] have demonstrated the application of a Jaco Varisource (which can produce a soft spark with multiple discharge per half-cycle) in establishing low levels of detection. However, this equipment was not available and it was decided to investigate D.C. arc techniques instead.

DEVELOPMENT OF SPECTROGRAPHIC METHOD

A Jarrel-Ash 3.4 metre Ebert spectrograph was used in this investigation. This has a plane grating ruled at 15,000 lines per inch and has a linear dispersion of 5 Angstroms per millimetre in the first order. It has a marked gain in line-to-background ratio over the Hilger Littrow quartz prism spectrograph and superior dispersion above 3600 A.

Initial difficulties were encountered on account of the narrow aperture of the instrument, which is only 1-1/2 mm wide x 8 mm high, 45 cm from the slit. Arcs show a tendency to shift laterally and fall outside this region. Total stabilization of the arc stream is virtually impossible and so the effect was minimized by partially defocussing the cylindrical lens in the optical system.

Electrodes were fabricated from high purity graphite (Johnson Matthey grade 2B; National Carbon Co. grade AGKSP) in the form of 1/4 inch diameter rod. A number of electrode shapes were tried in an endeavour to satisfy the following criteria:

    (i)   complete absorption of the test solution without crust formation

   (ii)   a stable arc stream

  (iii)   complete passage of the sample into the arc in less than 30 seconds

  (iv)   a temperature sufficiently high to give good sensitivity without too early distillation of the more volatile elements

   (v)   maximum mean sensitivity for the greatest number of elements.

The shape finally decided on is shown in Figure 1. The counter electrodes were 90° cones.

A water-cooled arc chamber was constructed to permit the use of different surrounding atmospheres (Figure 2). It is basically a pyrex glass cylinder fitted with brass end-plates and carrying optically flat silica windows. It is mounted on a normal Gramont arc stand.

Arcing in air at current strengths between 5 and 20 amperes produced considerable cyanogen banding. Pure argon atmospheres produced flaming and instability of the arc stream and gave much reduced sensitivities. Pure oxygen atmospheres led to a burn rate which was too rapid; this, in turn, resulted in reduced sensitivity for the more volatile elements. Mixtures of argon and oxygen appeared suitable between the limits 30% to 70% argon. Background effects were considerably reduced and arc stability was satisfactory. Flow rates greater than 0.5 litres per minute were found necessary to avoid fouling of the chamber windows.

Figure 1. Graphite Electrodes Before and After Arcing (X⁴)

To evaluate the change of parameters in the above tests, standard solutions were prepared containing some twenty representative elements at concentrations between 0.1 and 10 micrograms per millilitre. These solutions were made in sulphuric, perchloric and hydrochloric acid media to check the effect of different anions. The solutions also contained copper to the extent of 10 milligrams per millilitre to act as the internal standard. Tests were run in pairs, 0.05 millilitres of solution being transferred to each of two electrodes.

It was found that greater sensitivity could be obtained with chloride solutions than with either sulphates or perchlorates. It was further found that greater reproducibility could be obtained if the concentration of the copper internal standard was doubled.

At this stage it was possible to standardize a spectrographic procedure, which has been followed without modification for the remainder of the investigation, based on the use of chloride solutions.

Preparation of Standards

A series of solutions containing more than forty individual metallic elements at a concentration of 1 milligram per millilitre

Figure 2. Arc Chamber.

was prepared from the highest purity materials available
dissolved in 'transistor'· grade hydrochloric acid supplied by
B.D.H. Ltd. These stock solutions were diluted as required to
produce five composite standards containing 0.1, 0.33, 1.0, 3.3
and 10 μg per millilitre respectively of each element. To avoid
precipitating easily hydrolysable elements, the hydrochloric acid
concentration was never allowed to drop below 1N. One millilitre of each solution was taken and 2 milligrams of copper in

the form of cupric chloride solution added. Each solution was carefully evaporated to dryness in a microbeaker and the residue redissolved in 0.1 millilitre of 6N hydrochloric acid. This was divided equally between two electrodes in order to record duplicate spectra as described below.

Preparation of Electrodes

The electrodes were hand turned from rod immediately before use and stored in a steel block maintained at 120°C on an electric hotplate. The electrodes were not pre-arced since this did not appreciably affect the electrode blank, and further, the original porosity of the graphite was sufficient to absorb completely the test solution, provided this was strongly acid.

0.05 millilitres of the test solution was placed on each of two electrodes with the aid of a calibrated micro pipette and allowed to soak into the hot graphite. The drop should evaporate away smoothly without leaving a crust. After drying the electrodes were stored hot until used.

Spectrographic Method

A 15 ampere D.C. arc was finally chosen, with an exposure time of 30 seconds. The lower electrode, containing the sample was made the cathode and the analytical gap adjusted to an initial value of 4 millimetres. No attempt was made to maintain this spacing during the burn although major lateral displacements of the arc were corrected manually by bodily displacing the arc chamber. The 1:1 argon-oxygen atmosphere was passed through the arc chamber at a rate of 1 litre per minute. The spectrographic conditions are summarised in Table 1.

Calibration

The spectra produced from the synthetic solution standards were inspected visually and an estimate made of the lower limits of determination for the various elements they contained. These are shown in Table 2. At the same time approximate working graphs were constructed, comparing the intensity of the lines listed in Table 3 with that of lines from the copper internal standard. Plate calibration was with a normal 2:1 step sector and 2.5 ampere iron arc.

A series of replicate spectra were taken, using a fresh electrode and standard solution each time, to check the reliability of the evaporation technique. The intensities of the various impurity lines were found to reproduce well, even those of elements with reputably volatile chlorides such as iron, tin, antimony and

Table 1

Spectrographic Conditions

Instrument	Jarrel-Ash 3.4 m Ebert
Grating	15,000 Lines/inch
Waveband	2150–4650 A
Dispersion	5 A/mm : 1st order
Slit width	10 μ
Electrodes	1/4 in. diam. graphite
	lower (-ve) : undercut with flat top
	upper (+ve) : 90° cone
Analytical gap	4 mm (not maintained)
Arc	15 amp D.C. continuous
Atmosphere	argon + oxygen (1:1) at 1 1/min.
Exposure	30 seconds
Plates	2 x Kodak B10
Development	3 min. in 1D2 at 20°C
Calibration	2:1 step sector with 2.5 amp iron arc

Table 2

Limits of Detection (μg)

Li	1.0	Ti	0.05	Rh	0.1
Na	0.02	Zr	0.1	Pd	0.05
K	0.02	Hf	+	Pt	0.3
Rb	+			Au	5.0
Cs	+	V	0.01		
		Nb	3.0	Zn	0.2
Be	0.002	Ta	+	Cd	0.2
Mg	0.01			Hg	5.0
Ca	0.002	Cr	0.03		
Sr	0.1	Mo	0.1	Ge	+
Ba	2.0	W	3.0	Sn	0.3
				Pb	+
Al	0.01	Mn	0.02		
Ga	+	Fe	0.1	As	0.2
Sc	+	Co	0.25	Sb	2.0
Y	0.05	Ni	0.1	Bi	0.2
Eu	0.1				
Yb	0.02			Se	+
				Te	3.0

+ — over 10

Table 3

Lines Used for Estimation of Concentration

Al	3944.0	Na	3302.3
Al	3961.5	Na	3303.0
As	2780.2	Nb	3094.2
Ba	4554.0	Ni	3414.8
Be	3130.4	Pb	3683.5
Be	3131.1	Pd	3421.2
Bi	3067.7	Pt	2830.3
Ca	3968.5	Rh	3434.9
Cd	3261.1	Sb	2598.1
Co	3405.1	Sn	3262.3
Cr	4245.3	Ti	3349.0
Eu	3907.1	V	3184.0
Fe	2483.5	W	4008.8
Hg	2536.5	Y	3600.7
K	4044.7	Yb	3694.2
Mg	2795.5	Zn	3302.6
Mn	2794.8	Zn	3302.9
Mo	3132.6	Zr	3392.0
Mo	3170.3		

arsenic. This gave confidence in later assigning recovery figures to the chemical separation procedures. Some variation was found in the intensities of aluminium, magnesium and silicon lines, but this was adjudged caused by variation of the blank values rather than by inconsistencies in electrode preparation.

Interferences

It was expected that small quantities of indium would still be found in the processed samples even after rigorous chemical separation. The effect of small quantities of indium on the electrode was explored using the composite solution standards. Amounts up to 100 micrograms showed no effect; but as the quantity was increased above this value the overall intensity of the spectrum was seen to decrease. There was no apparent difference, however, in the ratio of the intensity of the impurity line to that of the copper internal standard line for most elements. Direct interference with the determination of cadmium, tin and particularly lead, however, was detectable and it was decided that a maximum of 500 micrograms of indium was all that could be tolerated.

Small amounts of nitric acid were found to have no deleterious effect, on the other hand traces of sulphuric and perchloric

363

acids severely depressed sensitivities. There was no interference by small quantities of hydrobromic acid.

DEVELOPMENT OF CHEMICAL
SEPARATION PROCEDURES

While the spectrographic method was being established,
parallel investigations were made into chemical separation
procedures. The aim was to remove the impurities from 1 gram
of indium (or in exceptional cases 10 grams), convert them to
chlorides and concentrate them into a volume of 0.1 millilitres
without loss or addition and without a carry through of more than
500 micrograms of indium.

The most important criteria to be satisfied were that the
procedures should be efficient, few in number, each as comprehensive as possible, simple from the point of view of manipulation and exceedingly economic in the use of reagents. These
latter points were to minimise the risk of adventitious contamination and to maintain the blank figure at the lowest possible
level.

Of the possible experimental techniques it was decided to
concentrate on solvent extraction and precipitation processes
since these are relatively rapid operations compared with electrolysis, ion-exchange or distillation processes for example.

Solvent Extraction Procedure

The extraction of halides from aqueous solutions into im-
miscible organic solvents such as ethers, and the influence
thereon of acid concentration, has been demonstrated by many
authors [5]. Specific and efficient extractions can readily be
obtained in a number of cases. Recently, Pohl [6] has investigated the extraction of metallic bromides into diisopropyl ether
from hydrobromic acid solutions, with special reference to the
separation of indium from impurity elements. He concluded that
indium, along with thallium and gold, could be almost totally extracted from 4 - 5N hydrobromic acid. Under these conditions
iron, arsenic, gallium, antimony, tin and tellurium are partially
extracted, but practically all other metallic elements with stable
bromides remain in the aqueous phase. With this information
as a guide, a procedure for isolating over thirty elements from
indium was devised.

The extraction of indium tribromide by diisopropyl ether
was checked for various acid concentrations, using equal volumes of each phase. Over 98% extraction was obtained from 4N
hydrobromic acid, and the efficiency of extraction increased

364

slightly at higher acid strengths. Twenty millilitres of diisopropyl ether would readily accommodate three grams of indium tribromide, i.e., one gram of indium.

Distillation of hydrobromic acid at atmospheric pressure yields a constant boiling mixture containing approximately 48% of HBr (8.8 normal). For simplicity's sake it was decided to extract from 24% (4.4 N) solutions. 'Analar' hydrobromic acid was redistilled in a silica fractionating still at 5 millilitres per minute, only the central 200 millilitres being retained from 500 millilitre batches. Polythene bottles were used for storage.

Diisopropyl ether (Hopkin and Williams G.P.R.) was shaken with a strong solution of sodium sulphite to remove peroxides and redistilled over calcium chloride in a silica fractionating still. The fraction boiling between 67.5°C and 68.5°C was collected and stored in polythene away from the light.

Deionised, distilled water was used throughout the investigation.

One gram of indium was etched to remove surface impurities and dissolved in 8 millilitres of 48% hydrobromic acid. The solution was made up to 10 millilitres with 24% hydrobromic acid and shaken for one minute in a separating funnel with 20 millilitres of diisopropyl ether, which had previously been equilibrated with 10 millilitres of 24% hydrobromic acid. The aqueous layer was drawn off and the aethereal layer backwashed with 1 millilitre of 24% hydrobromic acid, the washing being added to the aqueous extract. The combined aqueous phase was then shaken with a further 20 millilitres of equilibrated diisopropyl ether, which was separated and backwashed as before.

Two milligrams of copper carrier in the form of a cupric chloride solution was added to the final aqueous extract and the resultant solution gently evaporated to dryness. The residue was redissolved in 0.1 millilitre of 6N hydrochloric acid ('transistor' grade) and spotted on to two electrodes as described in the spectrographic procedure. An outline of the whole operation is given in Table 4.

Operations were done as far as possible in silica vessels. Originally platinum crucibles were used for the solution and evaporation stages, but considerable pick-up of platinum was noticed and their use was discontinued.

Studies with radioactive isotopes of indium showed that from 1 gram of indium present originally, 15 milligrams persisted in the aqueous layer after the first extraction, and less than 200 micrograms after the second. This was considered satisfactory from the spectrographic point of view.

Preliminary recovery figures from 10 μg synthetic samples as determined spectrographically are shown in Table 5. These confirm Pohl's figures, although there are some additions that

Table 4

Extraction Procedure

Dissolve 1 gm Indium in 8 ml of 48% (8.8N) HBr
Make up to 10 ml with 24%
Extract with 20 ml diisopropyl ether
Backwash ether layer with 1 ml 24% HBr and combine
    aqueous layers
Extract with another 20 ml diisopropyl ether
Backwash as before
Add 2 mg copper carrier and evaporate to dryness

     Less than 200 μg of indium remain in the
     aqueous layer after this double extraction

Table 5

Recovery from Extraction Procedure

Greater than 95%

    Li Na K Rb Cs Be Mg Ca Sr Ba Al Sc Y Eu Yb
    Ti Zr V Cr Mn Co Ni Rh Pd Pt Cd Pb Bi

Between 25% and 95%

    Zn Fe Mo Nb W

it will be desirable to confirm by an independent method such as radioisotope tracers or polarography. To the elements listed the remainder of the rare earths can probably be added. Of the elements with poor recovery figures only zinc is at present not covered by an alternative procedure.

Precipitation Procedures

Cupferron, the ammonium salt of nitrosophenylhydroxylamine, will precipitate a number of elements from cold acid solutions. Indium is not precipitated provided the acid concentration is approximately 0.5 normal and that tartaric acid is present. The cupferride precipitate can be collected, converted to oxides by gentle ignition and finally converted to chlorides in a form suitable for the standard spectrographic procedure. This was made the basis of a method for separating a further twelve impurities from indium using copper as a 'carrier' element.

One gram of indium was dissolved in 6 millilitres of 6N hydrochloric acid ('transistor' grade) and the solution gently evaporated to dryness. The residue was redissolved in 10 millilitres of 0.5N hydrochloric acid and 2 milligrams of copper added as cupric chloride. The copper has a twofold action: it acts as a precipitate collector as well as an internal standard for the spectrographic procedure. 0.2 grams of tartaric acid were added and the solution cooled to room temperature.

Four millilitres of a 6% solution of 'Analar' cupferron were added and the mixture allowed to stand for one hour. The resultant precipitate was filtered off through a washed 7 cm Whatman No. 40 paper. The paper was transferred to a silica dish and carefully dried. It was then ignited in a muffle furnace to convert the cupferride precipitate to oxides and to remove all carbonaceous matter.

The residue was dissolved in 1 millilitre of 6N hydrochloric acid with the addition of 0.2 millilitre of concentrated nitric acid (also 'transistor' grade). The solution was evaporated almost to dryness and 0.1 millilitre of 6N hydrochloric acid added in preparation for the spectrographic determination.

The outline scheme of this separation is given in Table 6 and the recoveries obtained from synthetic samples are shown in Table 7.

Table 6

Precipitation Procedure 1

Dissolve 1 gm Indium in 6 ml of 6N HCl
Evaporate and redissolve in 10 ml of 0.5N HCl
Add 2 mg copper carrier and 0.2 gm tartaric acid
Cool and add 4 ml of 6% cupferron solution
Filter precipitate through a 7 cm No. 40 Whatman
     Filter paper
Transfer filter to a silica dish
Dry on hot-plate and ignite to oxides
Dissolve oxides in 1 ml 6N HCl plus 0.2 ml 16N HNO_3
Evaporate solution almost to dryness

Indium sulphide is not precipitated in 0.5 normal hydrochloric acid solution, whereas several metallic sulphides are. It was decided to attempt to utilize this as the basis of another separation scheme, again relying on a copper carrier and using the standardised spectrographic finish. Ten elements could be covered.

One gram of indium was dissolved in 6 millilitres of 6N hydrochloric acid and the solution evaporated to dryness. The residue was dissolved in 10 millilitres of 0.5N hydrochloric acid;

Table 7

Recovery from Precipitation Procedures

Cupferride	Sulphide

Greater than 95%

Cupferride	Sulphide
Sn Ti Zr Hf	Mo Pd Sb Bi
V Nb Ta Mo	Au Hg Cd
W Fe Bi	

Between 25% and 95%

Cupferride	Sulphide
Pd	Rh Pt As

2 milligrams of copper carrier were added and the solution warmed to about 60°C. Hydrogen sulphide gas from a generator was passed slowly through the solution for 10 minutes, the solution being allowed to cool meanwhile. This sulphide precipitate was removed with the aid of a King filter stick and washed thoroughly with 0.5N hydrochloric acid saturated with hydrogen sulphide.

The precipitate and its pulp pad were transferred to a silica dish and dissolved with gentle heating in 1 millilitre of 6N hydrochloric acid with the addition of 0.2 millilitres of concentrated nitric acid. The solution was filtered and carefully evaporated to dryness, the residue being taken up in 0.1 millilitres of 6N hydrochloric acid in readiness for the spectrographic determination.

The outline procedure is given in Table 8. Recoveries obtained using synthetic samples are listed in Table 7, where it is seen that the method is satisfactory for seven elements, with the possible addition of three more.

Table 8

Precipitation Procedure 2

Dissolve 1 gm Indium in 6 ml of 6N HCl
Evaporate and redissolve in 10 ml of 0.5N HCl
Add 2 mg copper carrier and warm solution
Pass H_2S for 10 minutes
Remove sulphides on filter stick and wash
    with 0.5N HCl containing H_2S
Transfer precipitate and dissolve in 1 ml 6N HCl
    plus 0.2 ml 16N HNO_3 with gentle heat
Filter and evaporate solution to dryness

In an attempt to short circuit the procedure the direct spectrographic analysis of the sulphide precipitate was tried. The precipitate was washed well in a centrifuge tube and dispersed under diethyl ether. A small quantity of graphite powder was introduced and the whole thoroughly mixed and finally centrifuged. The resulting pellet was transferred to a graphite cup electrode and excited under a variety of conditions. In no case, however, could the required sensitivity be attained and so this approach was abandoned.

BLANK VALUES

The bugbear of all chemical separation procedures is the unwelcome introduction of additional impurities from reagents and apparatus in the course of the operations. If this is large in relation to the true values in the sample the results obtained can be completely invalidated. Careful purification of all reagents is necessary and they must be used in minimal quantities. The most hygienic conditions possible must be rigidly adhered to and the amount of manipulation kept as low as practicable. It is frequently preferable to attain only 90% efficiency in an operation rather than to risk doubling the blank value by repeating it.

A blank run was made in parallel with all determinations made during this investigation. Typical results for the three procedures followed are shown in Table 9. These blanks are composite figures, arising partly from the reagents — iron and aluminium in particular; partly from atmospheric contamination — most probably calcium and magnesium; and partly from the graphite electrodes — vanadium. These five elements are the only ones where blanks seriously affect the ultimate sensitivity.

A fairly satisfactory state of affairs is indicated although there is still room for improvement.

Discussion

At this stage of the investigation it is possible to detect twenty metallic elements in a one gram sample of indium at a concentration of 0.1 parts per million:

Na K Be Mg Ca Sr Al Y Eu Yb Ti Zr V Cr Mo Mn Fe Ni Rh Pd

A further eight elements can be detected at the part per million level:

Li Co Pt Zn Cd Sn As Bi

369

Table 9

Blank Values (μg)

Bromide Separation		Cupferride Separation		Sulphide Separation	
Fe	0.5	Fe	3.0	As	0.3
Al	0.3	Sn	1.0		
Mg	0.3	Mo	1.0		
Ca	0.1				
V	0.1				
Cr	0.03				
Mn	0.02				

Following elements below the detection limit:	Ti	
	Zr	
	Hf	Rh
Li Na K	V	Pd
Be Sr Ba	Nb	Pt
Y Yb Eu	Ta	Au
Ti Zr Mo	W	Cd
Co Ni Rh	Pd	Hg
Pd Pt W	Sb	Sb
Zn Cd Bi	Bi	Bi
		Tl

If a ten gram sample is taken another seven elements can be detected at the part per million level:

Ba Nb W Au Hg Sb Te

The analysis of a typical sample is given in Table 10.

The precision at present attainable is estimated at approximately ±50%, when interpolating visually between the fixed values on the standard plates, which, although not as high as is generally reckoned possible with a refined spectrographic technique, is nevertheless acceptable for trace analysis at this level.

Future work will be divided into four phases with the following aims:

1. Improvement of the spectrographic limits of detection of those elements covered by the present separation schemes but which have particularly poor spectrographic sensitivity.
2. Development of procedures to cover the elements omitted from the present schemes, particularly Cu Ag Ga Tl Se and Te.

370

Table 10

Indium Sample

Elements definitely detected	Concentration in p.p.m. (weight)
As	0.5
Sn	0.5
Na	0.05
Mg	1
Ca	0.3
Al	1
Cr	0.05
V	0.1
Mn	0.1
Fe	3
Ni	1
Cd	15

3. Improvement of the blank figures where these interfere with the ultimate sensitivity — Fe Al Mg Ca.

4. Increasing the precision of the determinations.

It is expected that this spectrochemical method will lend itself readily to the detection of impurities in other materials of interest in semiconductor research. With appropriate modifications to the chemical separation procedures analysis of almost all 2B, 3B, 4B, 5B and 6B sub-group elements could be accomplished.

The work described above was carried out on behalf of the Admiralty (C.V.D. working party on the trace analysis of semiconductors), and is part of the general research programme of the National Physical Laboratory and published by permission of the Director.

REFERENCES

1. W. M. Saltman and N. H. Nachtrieb, Analytical Chemistry 23 1503 (1951). J. A. Norris, ASTM Special Technical Publication 221 23 (1957). R. E. Heffelfinger, et al., Analytical Chemistry 30 112 (1958). C. G. Baird, Applied Spectroscopy 13 29 (1959). J. H. Oldfield and E. P. Bridge, AML report B/153(M) (1960).
2. A. Walshe, Bulletin of the BNFMRA 201 60 (1946).
3. J. M. Morris and F. X. Pink, ASTM Special Technical Publication 221 39 (1957).
4. E. B. Owens, Applied Spectroscopy 13 105 (1959).

5. G. H. Morrison and H. Frieser, Solvent Extraction in Analytical Chemistry, Wiley, New York (1957).
6. F. A. Pohl, Zeitschrift für Analytische Chemie 161 108 (1958).

DISCUSSION

R. A. KRAMER (Alcoa Research Laboratories): I thought it would be of interest to know that Mr. Currier of our Analytical Staff has applied practically the same type of analysis to determine impurities in gallium; for some elements down to the parts per billion level.

ELECTRON GUN-TYPE EXCITATION SOURCE FOR SPECTROGRAPHIC DETERMINATION OF O₂, N₂, H₂, P, S AND HALOGENS IN GALLIUM ARSENIDE

Dmetro Andrychuk and Charlie E. Jones Jr.
(Contribution from the Central Research Laboratories,
Texas Instruments Incorporated
Dallas, Texas.)

INTRODUCTION

The object of this research was to develop a spectrographic method for the determination of non metallic impurities in GaAs. Spectroscopic sources have been developed for the determination of non metals in solids, but none of them have been applied to semiconductor materials. V. A. Fassel [1] and his co-workers have developed methods for the determination of oxygen in steels and titanium, and extended the technique to nitrogen and hydrogen. J. R. McNally, G. R. Harrison, and E. Rowe [2], using the hollow cathode technique, obtained sensitivities in the tens of parts per million for oxygen, sulfur, fluorine and chlorine in graphite.

The hollow cathode technique showed good sensitivity for a large variety of elements; hence, it was first applied to the GaAs material.

HOLLOW CATHODE

In a conventional D.C. arc, GaAs does not melt, but volatilizes by decomposition. The arsenic volatilizes from the outside of the crystal towards the inside, with the gallium remaining in the electrode as the crystals of GaAs gradually decompose. After the arsenic, the gallium begins to volatilize, the volatilization proceeding until the gallium is consumed.

In the hollow cathode technique, using graphite electrodes, the volatilization is similar to that just described, except that it proceeds until about 25% of the arsenic is removed from the sample, when the nature of the discharge changes in character and the volatilization stops. With the sample in the cathode it was not possible to find the experimental conditions that would cause the volatilization to go to completion. For instance, changes

373

in the sample electrode shape to reduce conduction heat losses, the helium pressure or the current magnitude were unsuccessful. It was felt necessary to volatilize the GaAs completely for a correct analysis.

Next the polarity of the voltage to the hollow cathode electrodes was reversed. With the sample in the anode, complete volatilization was possible. The difficulty now was finding the gas pressure and voltage that would enable easy striking of the discharge and eliminate contamination from the cathode since the cathode hot spot wanders unpredictably, striking the cathode supports or any other undesired spot. It was to circumvent these last two difficulties that the electron gun type cathode was tried. It was planned eventually to operate in a vacuum but first an atmosphere of helium was tried.

ELECTRON-GUN TYPE SOURCE

The final arrangement of the components can best be understood with the aid of Figure 1. The anode consists of two parts, the sample anode made from a deeply undercut N.C. 4018 graphite electrode, and an auxiliary anode in the form of a ring made from a tantalum sheet. Both are connected to the positive of a 200 volt D.C. supply through a current divider network. Quartz chimneys enclose these anodes; the inner one serves to confine the discharge to the sample bearing portion of the electrode, the outer one concentrates the discharge column.

The cathode is made of 0.002 x 0.062 x 6.0 inch tantalum, corrugated and shaped into a ring. It is heated by an isolation transformer of 500 watt capacity. One end of the cathode is connected to the negative of the power supply.

The chamber is constructed from pyrex and metal cylinders with provision for water cooling. It is connected to a vacuum system and a helium supply. Two helium supplies are used; one is from a cylinder to return the chamber to atmospheric pressure for sample loading, the other is a glass chamber containing two tantalum and calcium electrodes between which a discharge may be struck to reduce the residual oxygen and hydrogen content of the helium.

For recording spectra, observation is made along the discharge column, the image of the top of the sample electrode is formed upon the slit of the spectrograph by means of the lens and 45° mirror. The diameter of the filament cathode is so chosen that no light from it falls upon the photographic emulsion. By using a 20 micron slit in a 1.5 meter Bausch & Lomb spectrograph and limiting the exposure times to one minute or less, the black body radiation from the glowing electrode when loaded with a sample is sufficiently reduced to enable the observation of the

374

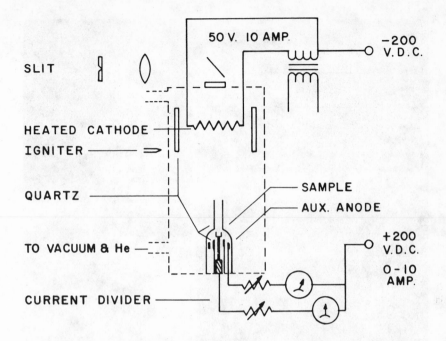

Figure 1. Schematic Diagram of the Electron Gun Type Source.

oxygen spectral lines at 7772 A. For wavelengths below 4500 A continuum presents no problem.

The appearance of the source is shown in Figure 2.

To prepare the system for operation, it is first evacuated for a few hours, then returned to atmospheric pressure with cylinder helium when the sample electrode may be loaded and introduced into the system. The system is again evacuated and purged a few times with purified helium. Next a discharge is struck between the cathode and the auxiliary anode for 30 seconds using 3 amperes. This aids in the outgassing of the chamber. The system is evacuated again and filled with purified helium to 150 microns of mercury pressure. It is now ready for the exposure.

The discharge is initiated by first turning on the filament and the D.C. power supply, then starting a Tesla coil outside the chamber a few inches from the glass wall in the vicinity of the cathode. The current in the discharge is regulated by controlling the cathode filament temperature. Care must be taken that the internal impedance of the power supply is sufficiently large to prevent the discharge current from increasing rapidly out of control, as the impedance of the arc discharge is not ohmic in character.

Figure 2. Physical Appearance of Electron Gun Type Source.

Unlike the hollow cathode, no provision was made for circulating the gas through a purification system and its effect was not investigated.

CHARACTERISTICS OF THE SOURCE

The temperature of the sample anode reaches an estimated value of 2500 to 3000 degrees Centigrade. Its magnitude is directly proportional to the discharge current and inversely to the gas pressure and the surface area of the anode. Convection currents occur in the gas within the chimney over the anode. For pressures above 100 microns of mercury the convection carries the volatilized sample into the chimney and hence into the discharge. Below 50 microns the convection flow appears to be reversed.

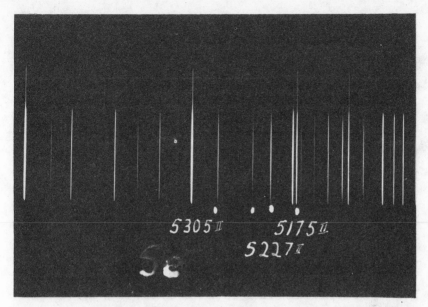

Figure 3a. Selenium Spectrum, 0.02% in GaAs. Current 5 amps,
75 Seconds Exposure, 150 Microns He Pressure.

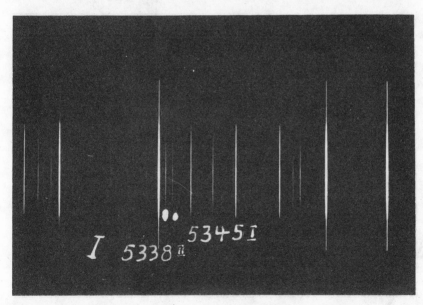

Figure 3b. Iodine spectrum, 0.7% as KI in GaAs.
Other Conditions Same as 3a.

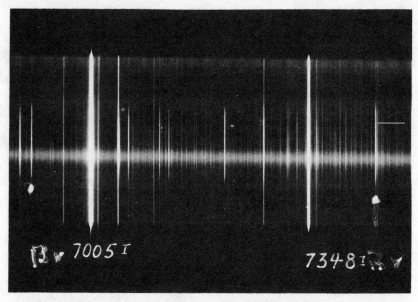

Figure 3c. Bromine Spectrum, 0.7% as NH$_4$Br in GaAs.
Other Conditions Same as 3a.

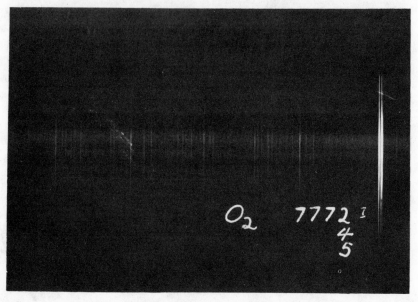

Figure 3d. Oxygen Spectrum, residual gas.

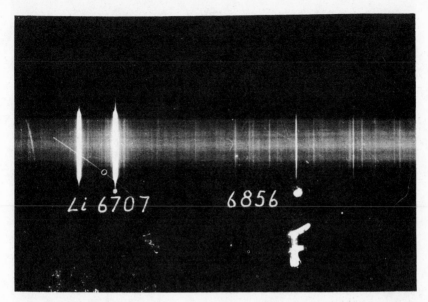

Figure 3e. Spectrum of fluorine that was adsorbed on silicon.

Some of the spectra recorded are shown in Figure 3 (a) to (e). The sensitivities for the various elements in GaAs were estimated using standards synthesized by the addition of appropriate salts to the GaAs. Spectra were obtained and from the intensity of the lines a sensitivity was estimated. The results are summarized in Table I.

The ability of the source to excite the spectra of the gases and halogens is attributed to the high excitation potential of the energy levels in the helium atom which transfers its energy to the sample atoms by collisions of the second kind.

The sensitivity attained (0.05%) is inadequate for most semiconductor analyses, while the outgassing of the source components seriously interferes with the determination of oxygen and hydrogen. On the other hand, the ability of the source to volatilize even materials having high boiling points coupled with the provision for controlling the excitation of the vapour independently of the sample volatilization warrants further study and development of this source.

DETERMINATION OF FLOURINE ADSORBED ON SILICON

The source was applied to the determination of flourine adsorbed by silicon surfaces from etching solutions. Two sets of standards were prepared, one using crushed silicon and lithium fluoride, the other crushed silicon and ammonium bifluoride.

Table I

Sensitivity in GaAs

Element Spec Line	Salt Used	% Element Detected	Estimated Sensitivity
Cl 7414 A 7255 6094	NH_4Cl	0.1	0.05%
N 7468 7442	NH_4Cl	0.04	0.04
F 7426 7399 6856	GaF_3	0.14	0.05
Br 7426 7349 7005	NH_4Br	0.7	0.1
I 7469 7402	KI	0.7	0.1
S 6312 6305 6787	PbS	0.2	0.1
Se 4730 4739 6056 6303	Se	0.02	0.02
H 6562 4861		Outgassing interference	
O 7772 7774 7775		Outgassing interference	
P 5253 5296	P_3O_5	Spectra excited	

The two sets of standards gave identical working curves within experimental error. The precision and accuracy were checked and are presented in Table II.

Table II

Results on Fluorine Determination

Sample	Spectrographic	Chemical
1	0.028%	0.010%
Coef. Var.	30%	

ACKNOWLEDGMENT

The authors wish to express their appreciation for the encouragement and moral support received from Dr. T. S. Burkhalter and P. F. Kane during this research.

This paper was presented at the Pittsburgh Conference on Analytical Chemistry and Applied Spectroscopy in Marcy 1961.

REFERENCES

1. V. A. Fassel and R. W. Tabeling, Spect. Acta, 8, 201, 1956.
2. J. R. McNally, G. R. Harrison, and E. Rowe, Jour. Opt. Soc. Amer., 37, 93, 1947.

ANALYSIS OF IMPURITIES IN SEMICONDUCTORS BY MEANS OF SPECTROSCOPY

M. Balkanski
Laboratoire de Physique de l'Ecole Normale Supérieure
Paris, France

I. INTRODUCTION

The analysis of matter is qualitative when the nature of the studied substance is determined and quantitative when the concentration of each atom present per unit volume is found. We shall examine a series of possibilities of qualitative and quantitative analysis by means of spectroscopy and magnetic resonance taking as an example impurities contained in Silicon.

The examined impurities are of two groups: neutral impurities which do not give free carriers; and electrically active impurities, which accept or give up free charge carriers. We shall first consider the neutral impurities because their study is more of a specific problem in Infra-Red spectroscopy.

The position of the absorption peaks due to a neutral impurity in Silicon is specified by the Silicon-Impurity binding. In the case of electrically active impurities, transitions from the ground to any excited state are not specific for the chemical nature of the impurity. The impurity nature is specified by its ionization energy. This point will be discussed later.

II. INFRA-RED SPECTROSCOPY

1. Neutral impurities

The study of electrically neutral impurities and especially atomically dispersed oxygen in Si and Ge has received considerable attention during recent years [14]. Other neutral impurities like Carbon [1] and Nitrogen [16] in Si have also been studied recently. In all cases it is possible to observe absorption bands in the I.R. region of the spectrum which are characteristic for the impurity.

The presence of dissolved atomic oxygen [13] in Si gives rise to three absorption bands at 8.3, 9.0 and 19.5μ. The most prominent peak is at 9μ and is specific for oxygen in Si. In the case of carbon dissolved in Si a characteristic absorption band is found [1] at 12.2μ; for Nitrogen the absorption band seems to be at $10.6\,\mu$.

The absorption band attributed to oxygen occurs at the same wave length as an absorption band produced by a fundamental molecular vibrational mode in silicon dioxide and silicates in general [15].

The absorption band observed in Si containing C is at the same wave length as the fundamental vibrational band in SiC. In the case of Nitrogen in Si the strong absorption observed at $10.6\,\mu$ is also observed in Si_3N_4.

The interpretation of these absorption bands is thus based on the fact that when the neutral impurity is atomically dispersed in the lattice the observed I.R. absorption bands correspond to Si-O; Si-C or Si-N molecular vibrations.

It is then possible to establish a direct correlation between the value of the absorption coefficient of the peak characterizing the impurity and the number of oscillators and, consequently, the number of impurity atoms.

In the case of Oxygen in Si it has been established that the absorption maximum of the band at 9μ is proportional to the Oxygen concentration determined by vacuum fusion gas analysis. Another technique, based on the effect of Oxygen upon the precipitation of Li, gives good agreement with the optically determined Oxygen concentration [22]. High precision X-ray and density studies [3], as well as analysis of the optical fine structure of the Oxygen absorptions in Si, supported the suggestion that Oxygen occupies interstitial lattice sites while being bound to two neighboring Si Atoms [15].

In the case of C in Si if one admits that SiC is ionic with a density of $4.84 \cdot 10^{22}$ pairs of ions per cubic centimeter, it is possible to calculate the concentration of C atoms in Si to obtain an absorption coefficient of 10 cm^{-1} .

The number of normal modes is 3Nt where N is the number of unit cells and t is the number of atoms per unit cell. In SiC there are 2 atoms per unit cell and $4.84 \cdot 10^{22}$ unit cells per cm^3. For each unit cell there are 6 normal modes, 3 acoustical and 3 optical. Only the 2 transverse optical modes contribute to the light absorption. The number of optically active modes is then:

$$M = \frac{2 \cdot 3Nt}{6Nt} = 9.68 \cdot 10^{22} \text{ cm}^{-3}$$

The absorption coefficient at the Reststrahl band in SiC is of the order of $1.7 \cdot 10^5$ cm^{-1} . The absorption for one oscillator should be equal to:

$$1.76 \cdot 10^{-18} \quad cm^{-1}$$

One can admit four stretching optically active vibrations which are observed at 12.2μ. An absorption coefficient of $10 cm^{-1}$ will then correspond to $1.4 \cdot 10^{18}$ carbon atoms per cm^3. Fig. 1 shows the absorption spectra of a series of samples intentionally doped with C. The concentrations of C deduced from the absorption spectra for each sample are given.

2. Interaction between neutral impurities

The maximum solubility of oxygen in Si at the melting point has been found to be approximately 2×10^{18} atoms per cm^3. When samples containing atomically dispersed oxygen are annealed at several hundred degrees centigrade, donor states up to 10^{17} per cm^3 can be formed. The concentration of these states can now be found by electrical measurements. Kaiser [14] suggested that SiO_4 complexes formed during the annealing are responsible for the donor activity. It is possible to follow spectroscopically the loss of dissolved oxygen; this loss should be a factor of four greater than the number of donors appearing.

Oxygen-Carbon interaction in Silicon is under investigation presently in our Laboratory. When Oxygen is added in Si containing C as a neutral impurity two interesting effects are observed.

First: The solubility of oxygen increases with the carbon concentration. Concentrations of Oxygen up to 7.10^{19} have been observed when the initial carbon concentration is 4.10^{18}.

Second: The 12.2μ absorption band attributed to C-Si vibrations in displaced toward larger wavelengths.

3. Electrically active impurities

The absorption spectra of almost all donor and acceptor centers are now well established. The main features of these spectra are interpreted in terms of the effective mass approximation. The impurity, considered as a localized electrical charge which acts on a weakly bound electron by the coulomb field, gives an hydrogen-like assembly whose spectrum is determined by the electron effective mass. In these conditions all donors should have the same absorption spectrum. According to this simplified picture it will be impossible to distinguish the impurity nature only from the absorption spectrum.

At large distances the energy state of a weakly bound electron will be discribed by the Schrödinger equation:

$$- \frac{h^2}{2 m^*} \nabla^2 - \frac{e^2}{\kappa r} \; F \; (r) = E \; F \; (r)$$

where m* is the appropriate effective mass [4].

384

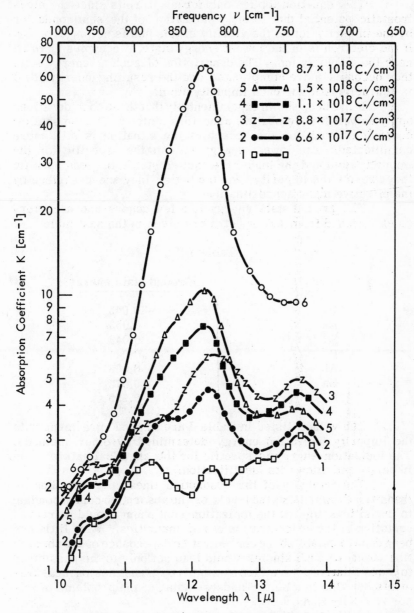

Figure 1. Absorption Spectra of C Doped Si.C Concentration for Each Sample is Calculated from the Absorption Coefficient at 12.2μ.

This equation applies only for large orbits since the electrostatic potential due to the polarization of the semiconductor by the impurity ion in the vicinity of this ion is no longer $e/\kappa r$. If the electron is in the lowest energy state, it occupies an orbit near the impurity ion. The description of such an energy state thus becomes more complicated and the resulting energy level is characteristic for each impurity atom.

It has been shown experimentally that these considerations apply as well for the shallow acceptors states as for the shallow donors, although for the acceptors the situation is still more complicated. The lowest energy state is then specific for the impurity atom and the higher the excited states, the less specific they are for the impurity, and the better they are described by the effective mass approximation.

The ground state energy of a few donors and acceptors as established from I.R. spectra are given in the next table:

Table I

Impurity	Ground state energy
P	- 0.045
As	- 0.053
Sb	- 0.043
B	0.044
Al	0.068
Ga	0.072
In	0.155

The values listed in Table I are in good agreement with the impurity ionization energy determined by other methods. The ionization energy is specific for the chemical nature of an impurity and allows its identification.

The intensity of the absorption lines corresponding to transitions toward excited levels or the absorption corresponding to transitions toward the ionization continuum should be representative of the concentration of the impurities. Very little has been done to establish the concentration dependance of the absorption spectra. Such studies would lead not only to the possibility to a quantitative determination simply by transmission measurements but also to a better understanding of the problems of impurity interactions.

R. Newman [21] has established the absorption spectra of B, Al, and Ga in silicon. He mentions that at 21°K the details of the spectra (relative position, line shapes, intensities) differ for the different acceptors. Below an acceptor concentration of about 10^{16} cm^{-3} the shapes of the spectra are concentration independant.

Above 10^{16} cm^{-3} the spectral lines begin to broaden and by ~ 10^{18} cm^{-3} the line structure disappears almost completely.

All spectra present a series of sharp bands due to transitions from the ground state of the impurity to one of its discret states. These absorption peaks are followed by an absorption continuum which indicates transitions from the ground to an ionized state lying in either the valance or conduction band. If one traces the curves representing the variation of the absorption coefficient of any of the peaks or of the continuum at a given frequency as a function of the impurity concentration one obtains a straight line in a logarithmic plot.

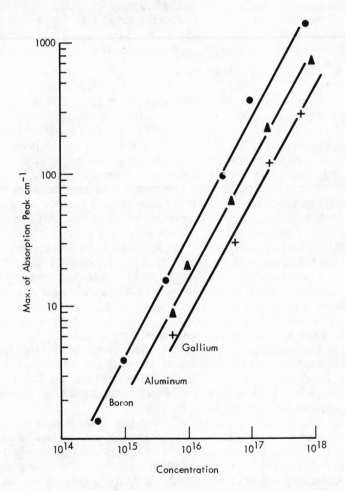

Figure 2. Absorption coefficient corresponding to the transition 1s - 2p as a function of the impurity concentration.

387

The impurity concentrations are deduced from resistivity measurements according to Carlson [5]. There is a direct relation between the number of occupied states and the absorption coefficient. Calibration curves such as those given in Fig. 2, permit the interpolation of the results for samples where the impurity concentration is unknown. Thus from the value of the absorption coefficient at a given frequency it is immediately possible to deduce the donor or acceptor concentration.

III. MAGNETIC RESONANCE

Another very specific method for identifying impurities in semiconductors such as Ge and Si is magnetic resonance which also gives indications as to their concentrations. The best performance of the method should be in the very low concentration range where the impurity atom interacts only with the host lattice.

1. Electron spin resonance

It has already been mentioned that the shallow impurity states lie close in energy to the bottom of the conduction band and to the top of the valence band. The electron bound to a donor state behaves as if it were in a Bloch state near the band edge, which is modulated by the weak coulombic interaction of the donor ion. The donor state wave functions are constructed from Bloch states at the band edge multiplied by a modulating function which itself obeys an effective mass equation [17]. There is a degeneracy in the ground state associated with the fact that the Bloch wave can be chosen from any of the several valleys. Group theoretical analyses [18] show that the sixfold degenerate state of Silicon, for example, will be split into a single, doublet and triplet.

Low temperature electron-spin resonance experiments measure the hyperfine interactions between the localized donor electron and nuclear moments with which it interacts. The hyperfine interaction is proportional to the square of the electronic wave function at the position of the nuclei.

The resonance spectra are characteristics for the nature of the impurity. The interaction between the electronic spin S and the nuclear spin I of the donor atom split the two energy levels $(S = \pm 1/2)$ into $2I + 1$ sublevels giving a hyperfine structure of $2I + 1$ lines.

The P nuclear spin is 1/2 and the resonance pattern [9] of P donors in Si consists of a well resolved doublet. For As, $I = 3/2$, giving a quartet; Sb nuclei have spins $I = 5/2$ and $I = 7/2$ and experimentaly the superposition of a strong sextet and a weaker octet is observed. It is thus evident that at low concentrations the donor nature will be easily identified by the electron spin resonance spectrum.

Recently resonance spectra have been established for many impurity systems in Si, such as Li, Bi, Au, Cu and the transition metals V, Cr, Mn [20], Fe [19], Ni, Pd and Pt. Two species of sulfur [6] also have been detected. Many of these impurities form complexes when they are associated with lattice imperfections or with neutral impurities like Oxygen, which makes the interpretation of their resonance absorption spectra more complicated but leads to more information as to the real situation of the impurity in the semiconductor lattice. Woodbury and Ludwig [25] have studied in some detail the spin resonance of five transition metals in Si and found that each element exists in an isolated form in Si and undergoes no distortion from the site of maximum symmetry.

For $(V^{51})^{++}$, $I = 7/2$, eight narrow hyperfine lines are observed and, in addition, each hyperfine line is split into three fine structure lines since $S = 3/2$. For $(Cr^{53})^{+}$, $I = 3/2$, there are $2\,S(S = 5/2)$ well resolved fine structure lines each of which is split into four by the hyperfine interaction (in all five groups by four identical lines). For Mn^{55} there are three possible states Mn^{-}, Mn^{++}, and Mn_4° , each one giving a characteristic spectrum: six hyperfine lines each split into two by a second order hyperfine term for Mn^{-}, five fine structure lines each split into six by hyperfine interaction for Mn^{++} . Fe° gives one line showing pronounced structure.

An increase of the impurity concentration above 10^{16} cm^{-3} brings the impurity atoms sufficiently close together so that their electron spins are coupled strongly by the exchange interaction [24]. The electrons then act as a unit which responds to the average magnetic field produced by the hyperfine coupling to the nuclei involved. The pattern consists then of lines spaced at half the interval of single impurities but extending over the same total range. The two electrons form a system described by quantum numbers $S = 1/2 \pm 1/2 = 1$ or 0 and $M = S, S - 1 \ldots \ldots -S$ interacting with the two nuclear spins described by m_1 and m_2. The hyperfine lines are now spaced by the energy: $a/2\,M(m_1 + m_2)$. The spacing is $a/2$ rather than a and the number of lines $4\,I + 1$ instead of $2\,I + 1$. The intensity of the satellite lines will not be uniform. The relative intensity of lines starting from one end of the pattern will be $1 - 2 - 3 \ldots 3 - 2 - 1$.

As the concentration increases more than two impurities may interact and give still more complicated patterns. The interaction becomes larger with increase of concentration and the satellite lines build in intensity and become broader. In the case of extremely high concentrations, the exchange coupling is so strong that we have a metal with completely non localized electrons.

All these particularities, directly related to the concentration, allow the establishment of calibration curves in such a way that one could afterwards, for a given sample, tell not only the nature of the impurity present but also its concentration from a single measurement.

2. Effects of nuclear spin resonance

a. Electron spin-lattice relaxation times.

The effect of concentration is not only on the electron spin resonance pattern, but also acts on the electron spin-lattice relaxation time, T_1, under the effect of the nuclear spins of Si^{29}.

Interaction of the electron spin S and the nuclear spin $i = 1/2$ of Si^{29} atoms gives an hyperfine spliting of the levels we just considered. This interaction leads to an unhomogeneous broadening of the spectral lines. This interaction makes energy exchanges possible between the nuclear spins of Si^{29} and the lattice. This is the major contribution to the spin-lattice relaxation time, T_1, of the nuclear spins. The concentration dependance of the spin lattice relaxation times suggests another method for direct determination of the impurity concentration by a measurement of nuclear magnetic resonance which is an easy experiment.

Because of the long relaxation times it is necessary to use adiabatic fast-passage detection. The nuclear spins being polarized in a magnetic field $H_0 > H_1$, the resulting magnetic moment M_0 of the sample, directed along H_0, is reversed during an adiabatic passage over the resonance. After this it tends with a time constant, T, toward its new equilibrium value M corresponding to the final magnetic field H_1.

G. Galleron [10] has built equipment for nuclear magnetic resonance at low temperature consisting of a nuclear resonant cavity with crossed coils, a 5 Mc quartz oscillator, a compensation bridge and a large band amplifier. The fast-passage method has been used at $4.2°K$ to measure a relaxation time of $T_1 = 10$ min. by detecting the nuclear resonance line of Si^{29} as shown in Fig. 3.

A comparison of the relaxation times [23] for samples with different free carrier concentration show that T_1 is inversely proportional to the carrier concentration for the high conductivity samples, but approaches an asymptotic value in the purer samples. Here we have a method for deducing the impurity concentration be measuring the relaxation times not only in n-type materials but in p-type samples as well. Fig. 4 gives results obtained by Shulman and Wyluda [23].

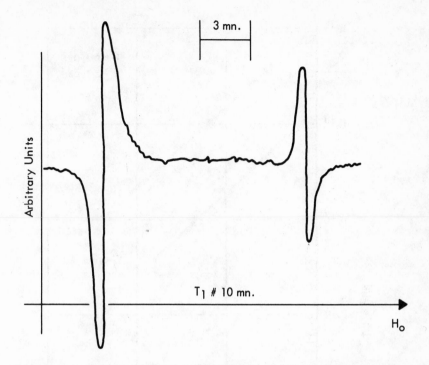

Figure 3. Nuclear Resonance of Si^{29} Containing $10^{17} P/cm^3$ at 4.3°K. The Second Line Corresponds to Fast Passage Over the Resonance in the Opposite Direction 3 min After the First: $T_1 = 10$ min.

More recently Honig and Stupp [12] have done an extensive study on the concentration dependance of the electron spin-lattice relaxation in phosphorus doped silicon. This kind of study is promising for a better understanding of impurity concentration effects in semiconductors.

b. Electron-nuclear double resonance (ENDOR)

Feher [7] has developed a technique involving electron-nuclear double resonance (ENDOR) which increases the resolution obtainable in ordinary paramagnetic resonance experiments by several orders of magnitude. This technique allows a detailed study of donor electronic structure [7] and of the concentration effects on the electron spin relaxation [8].

3. Combined optical and magnetic resonance methods

Combined optical and magnetic resonance techniques open a new field for interesting investigations on the impurities in

391

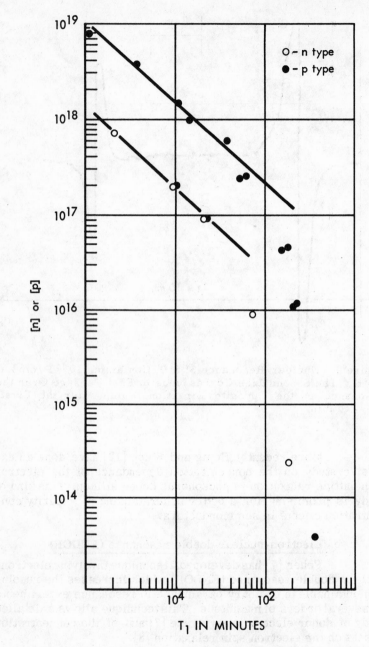

Figure 4. Spin-Lattice Relaxation Times Versus
Free Carrier Concentration.

semiconductors. Some preliminary measurements confirm this opinion. From electron spin resonance and photoconductivity experiments [11] performed on samples of phosphorus—doped silicon with boron compensation—it has been possible to determine the ratio of P^+ ion trapping cross section to neutral B trapping cross section for conduction electrons as well as the rate of transfer from P to B at various impurity concentrations. These techniques allow accurate determinations of the ratio of donor concentration to compensating acceptor concentration and permit the control of the number of ionized impurities in a given sample at low temperatures.

In n-type Si containing N_D donors and N_A acceptors, the electron spin resonance signal is due to the number of neutral donor states N_D^o. When such a sample is irradiated with light, creating free electron-hole pairs which are trapped by the ionized impurities the N_D concentration is built up, and the rate of electron transfer from N_D^o to N_A^o is much lower than the rate of electron-hole pairs generation. The resonance signal in this case is $(1 - N_A/N_D)^{-1}$ times the original signal and the compensation N_A/N_D is directly determined. Spin resonance on donor impurities in compensated p-type silicon has also been observed [2]. Normally there is no paramagnetism in p-type silicon associated with the presence of donors as compensating impurities. These donors are positively charged having lost their electrons to the acceptor atoms.

Irradiation with light which induces electron hole pair creation leads to the appearance of resonance absorption typical of the donor present as compensation. The amplitudes of the lines increase with the absorbed photon flux eventually reaching saturation. These resonance lines are due to electrons captured by the donors which become neutral and paramagnetic.

The nature of the donor could be specified if one now induces ionization transitions at specific frequencies transferring the captured electron to the conduction band. One can observe simultaneously the characteristic optical absorption and the decrease of the resonance signal. I.R. spectroscopy coupled in this way with magnetic resonance should give more detailed information on the electron structure of impurities and their concentration interaction.

Optically produced electrons trapped on donor centers give resonance lines whose maximum amplitudes added to amplitudes of signals from samples with known donor concentrations allow a determination of the compensation donor concentration in a p-type sample. Concentrations calculated from the Hall coefficient at low temperatures confirm very well the concentrations obtained by optically induced paramagnetic resonance. This method may be used in the determination of compensation

393

in p-type silicon as well as the type of impurity and its concentration. Such a method supplies much more information and a more accurate determination of concentration than electrical measurements such as the Hall effect for example.

One should point out also that other methods like photo-conductivity for example induced by optical transitions from impurity centers are available although these methods are not yet fully explored.

An ideal situation would be that at least in an initial period determinations of the nature and concentration of impurities could be done by all these methods on identical samples and the results controlled by electrical, chemical and mass spectroscopy methods. Once calibration curves are established, giving the signal intensity as a function of the concentration in well specified conditions, it will then be easy to make a fast determination by a single measurement in the given conditions. A large effort in this direction is certainly suitable.

REFERENCES

1. M. Balkanski, W. Nazarewicz et E. Da Silva, C.R. 251, 1277 (1960).
2. G. Bemski and B. Szymanski, J. Phys. Chem. Solids 17, 173, (1960).
3. W. L. Bond and W. Kaiser, J. Phys. Chem. Solids 16, 44, (1960).
4. E. Burstein, E. E. Bell, J. W. Davisson and M. Lax, J. Phys. Chem. 57 849 (1953).
5. R. O. Carlson, Phys. Rev. 100, 1075 (1955).
6. R. O. Carlson, R. N. Hall and E. M. Pell, J. Phys. Chem. Solids, 8, 81 (1959).
7. G. Feher, Phys. Rev. 114, 1219 (1959).
8. G. Feher, and E. A. Gere, Phys. Rev. 114, 1245 (1959).
9. R. C. Fletcher, W. A. Yager, G. L. Pearson, A. N. Holden, T. W. Read and F. R. Merritt, Phys. Rev. 94, 1392 (1954).
10. G. Galleron, Technical Report C.E.N. Saclay.
11. A. Honig and R. Levitt, Phys. Rev. Letters 5; 93 (1960).
12. A. Honig and E. Stupp Phys. Rev. 117, 69 (1960).
13. H. J. Hrostowski et R. H. Kaiser, Phys. Rev. 107, 966 (1957).
14. W. Kaiser paper presented at the Prague Conf. for a summary see W. Kaiser, H. L. Frisch and H. Reiss, Phys. Rev. 112, 1546 (1958).
15. W. Kaiser, P. H. Keck and C. F. Lange, Phys. Rev. 101, 1264 (1956).
16. W. Kaiser et C. D. Thurmond, J. Appl. Phys. 30, 427 (1959).
17. W. Kohn, vol. 5 of Solid State Physics, New-York, Academic Press Inc. (1957).
18. W. Kohn and J. M. Luttinger, Phys. Rev. 97, 1721 (1955), ibid 98, 915 (1955).
19. G. W. Ludwig, R. O. Carlson and H. H. Woodbury, Bull. Am. Phys. Soc. 4, 22 (1959) id. 4, 144 (1959).

20. G. W. Ludwig, H. H. Woodbury and R. O. Carlson, J. Phys. Chem. Solids 8, 490 (1959), H. H. Woodbury, R. O. Carlson and G. W. Ludwig, Bull. Am. Phys. Soc. 4, 22 (1959).
21. R. Newman, Phys. Rev. 103 (1956).
22. E. N. Pell. Proceedings of the Brussels Conference on Solid State Physics (1958).
23. R. C. Shulman and B. J. Wyluda, Phys. Rev. 103, 1127 (1956).
24. C. P. Slichter, Phys. Rev. 99, 479 (1955).
25. H. H. Woodbury and G. W. Ludwig, Phys. Rev. 117, 102 (1960).

DISCUSSION

D. ANDRYCHUK (Texas Instruments): We have observed molecular vibration bands in silicon as well as the ionization of impurities. However, for gallium arsenide at room temperature, and at liquid hydrogen or helium temperatures, we have never observed any absorption due to impurities present. Will you comment on gallium arsenide or indium antimonide?

M. BALKANSKI (University of Paris): In the case of III-V compounds, it seems that the most convenient method is that of measuring the reflectivity due to free carriers. As to the identification of the impurities, no work has been done by us on these compounds, but it seems that the free carrier concentration is high enough to cover the bands due to impurities. One would need very low impurity concentration material in order to start this study.

D. ANDRYCHUK (Texas Instruments): It seems that the most promising route is photoconductivity.

M. BALKANSKI (University of Paris): Photoconductivity will be certainly a very promising route, but I didn't have time to cover this aspect.

P. H. KECK (General Telephone and Electronics Laboratories): You have shown that the solubility of oxygen in silicon is enhanced by carbon. How did you prepare the silicon crystals containing oxygen and carbon? Was there a carbon monoxide or dioxide atmosphere present during crystal pulling?

M. BALKANSKI (University of Paris): The samples were prepared by cracking trichlorosilane, containing some hydrocarbons. A spectrum was then taken confirming the presence of carbon. The crystal was then heated for twelve to sixteen hours in a pure oxygen atmosphere, whereby oxygen is introduced. The oxidized surface is then removed and the spectrum again recorded. Certain single crystals which were pulled were found to contain oxygen initially; these were also used for our studies.

P. H. KECK (General Telephone and Electronics Laboratories): What absorption have you used for boron and the other impurities you have shown? (Figure 2).

M. BALKANSKI (University of Paris):   These are transmission measurements in the region of 35 to 45 microns.   The
spectra start at 27 microns.   Any transition is characteristic of
the concentration and gives exactly the same straight line as a
function of the concentration.   Only the shape and position of the
pattern is characteristic of the nature of the impurity.

C. S. FULLER (Bell Telephone Laboratories):   I would like
to comment that using electron spin resonance to detect and determine donor states in silicon, as Dr. Balkanski has mentioned,
is certainly feasible.   This was shown by Fletcher and his co-
workers some years ago.

However, as I pointed out in my talk, this method does not
apply to acceptor states in silicon, unless the acceptor is strained,
because of the degeneracy of the valence band.

M. BALKANSKI (University of Paris):   The band due to the
acceptor state is very large and, therefore, it is not used in
electron spin resonance.

But then, the effect on the $T_1 - 1$ in the acceptor state, according to Schulman's work, will give a means of defining the concentration.   This then is a nuclear resonance.

THE HALL EFFECT AS AN ANALYTICAL TOOL IN ULTRAPURE SILICON AND GERMANIUM

Claude A. Klein and W. Deter Straub
Research Division
Raytheon Company
Waltham, Massachusetts

ABSTRACT

The analysis of extrinsic Hall effect data provides the most sensitive means of estimating the impurity content of ultrapure semiconductors. Difficulties in getting reliable results arise mainly from the need to know the Hall coefficient factor with sufficient accuracy. This paper describes work performed on high-resistivity p-type silicon and germanium in order to better appreciate the Hall coefficient factor behavior, and, by the same token, to improve the evaluation of impurity concentrations.

NOMENCLATURE

E_f : Fermi energy (ev)

E_i : energy of state i (ev)

E_o : ground state energy (ev)

H : magnetic field (gauss)

K_A : equilibrium constant (cm^{-3})

N_A : acceptor concentration (cm^{-3})

N_D : donor concentration (cm^{-3})

N_v : density of states (cm^{-3})

397

R : Hall coefficient ($cm^3/coul$)

R_o : 300°K Hall coefficient ($cm^3/coul$)

T : temperature (°K)

β : impurity scattering parameter

γ : magnetic field parameter

μ : drift mobility (cm^2/v-sec)

μ_H : Hall mobility (cm^2/v-sec)

μ_I : impurity mobility (cm^2/v-sec)

μ_L : lattice mobility (cm^2/v-sec)

σ : conductivity (mho/cm)

e : electronic charge (1.60×10^{-19} coul)

f_A : hole trapping probability

g_i : degeneracy of state i

g_o : ground state degeneracy

h : Plank's constant (4.14×10^{-15} ev sec)

k : Boltzmann's constant (8.62×10^{-5} ev/°K)

m_o : electronic mass (9.11×10^{-28} g)

m* : density of states mass (g)

n : free electron density (cm^{-3})

p : free hole density (cm^{-3})

r : Hall coefficient factor

r_o : 300°K Hall coefficient factor

398

I. INTRODUCTION

Nature and concentration of the electrically active impurities are critical factors in most investigations of semiconducting materials. Even in ultrapure specimens of germanium and silicon, specimens with free carrier densities of 10^{13} cm^{-3} or less, transport processes can be affected by impurities, whose concentrations must therefore be accurately known. Many attempts have been made to develop readily applicable suitable techniques; galvanomagnetic measurements appear to provide the most reliable indications [12].

It is well known, for instance, that the room-temperature value of the Hall coefficient in germanium or silicon can be related to the net concentration of active centers. Measurements as a function of temperature, on the other hand, may yield indications on the total number of such centers. An exploitation of the Hall effect for this purpose requires however a certain amount of care, mainly because of the Hall coefficient factor behavior. This factor connects the Hall coefficient to the carrier density and ipso facto to the impurities. Unfortunately, it depends upon the magnetic field intensity, the energy-band structure, and the carrier scattering mechanism in a fairly complex way [1, 2]. In this paper we shall attempt to take the Hall coefficient factor issue into consideration and develop a scheme that should allow to perform an accurate impurity concentration analysis on relatively pure specimens.

In Section II we discuss briefly the procedure used to collect the experimental data shown in Figures 2-8. Section III outlines the theoretical treatment on which rests the detailed p-type silicon analysis of Section IV. Section V refers to p-type germanium and presents some Hall coefficient factor results that were found useful in the framework of an investigation of gold-doped specimens [7].

II. EXPERIMENTAL CONSIDERATIONS

Shape and size of our samples are similar to those described by Debye and Conwell [3]. Though they were not cut along any specific crystallographic direction but perpendicularly to the crystal axis, the [111] direction was found in general to be parallel to the applied magnetic field. The magnetic field strength was maintained close to 2500 gauss throughout the temperature range, whereas the electric field (constant current technique!) never exceeded 1 v/cm, so as to avoid carrier heating effects. A six-point recorder was used to program the measuring cycle, which included temperature, dc Hall signal, and conductivity voltage, before as well as after reversal of the magnetic field.

Great care was taken to reduce the experimental scatter and to assure a high degree of reproducibility. Measurements performed on the same specimen after repeated surface treatments and contact preparations lead to the conclusion that, on the average, the error does not exceed 3% at most temperatures.

III. THEORETICAL CONSIDERATIONS

In a conventional semiconductor with N_A acceptor and N_D donor impurities per unit volume, electrical neutrality implies that

$$n + N_A^- = p + N_D^+ , \tag{1}$$

if n and p are the free electron and hole densities. Let us consider, for example, a p-type specimen $(N_A > N_D)$ with a Fermi level that remains relatively close to the valence band. The electron density can then be neglected $(n \ll p)$, and all the donors are presumably ionized $(N_D^+ = N_D)$. If f_A represents the probability to find an acceptor center in a neutral state of charge, that means with a bound hole, we have therefore

$$p = (N_A - N_D) - N_A f_A . \tag{2}$$

The group III acceptors give rise to a set of discrete energy levels in the immediate vicinity of the valence band, but they can trap only one hole per center [9]. The trapping probability is then given by

$$f_A = \frac{\sum\limits_i g_i \exp\left[(E_i - E_f)/kT\right]}{1 + \sum\limits_i g_i \exp\left[(E_i - E_f)/kT\right]}, \tag{3}$$

where the summation has to be performed over all the levels [5]. Figure 1 displays the energy level system associated with boron impurities in silicon. The diagram is based on the ground state energy (E_o) determination reported in Section IV, on Hrostowski and Kaiser's transmission experiments in so far as the positioning of the excited levels $(E_i, i = 1, 2, \ldots, 8)$ is concerned [6], and on Schechter's evaluation of the degeneracies g_i [9]. Introducing the effective density of states in the valence band, N_v, and assuming that a Maxwell-Boltzmann approximation is acceptable (low carrier densities!), we can write

$$p = N_v \exp\left(- E_f/kT\right) \tag{4}$$

400

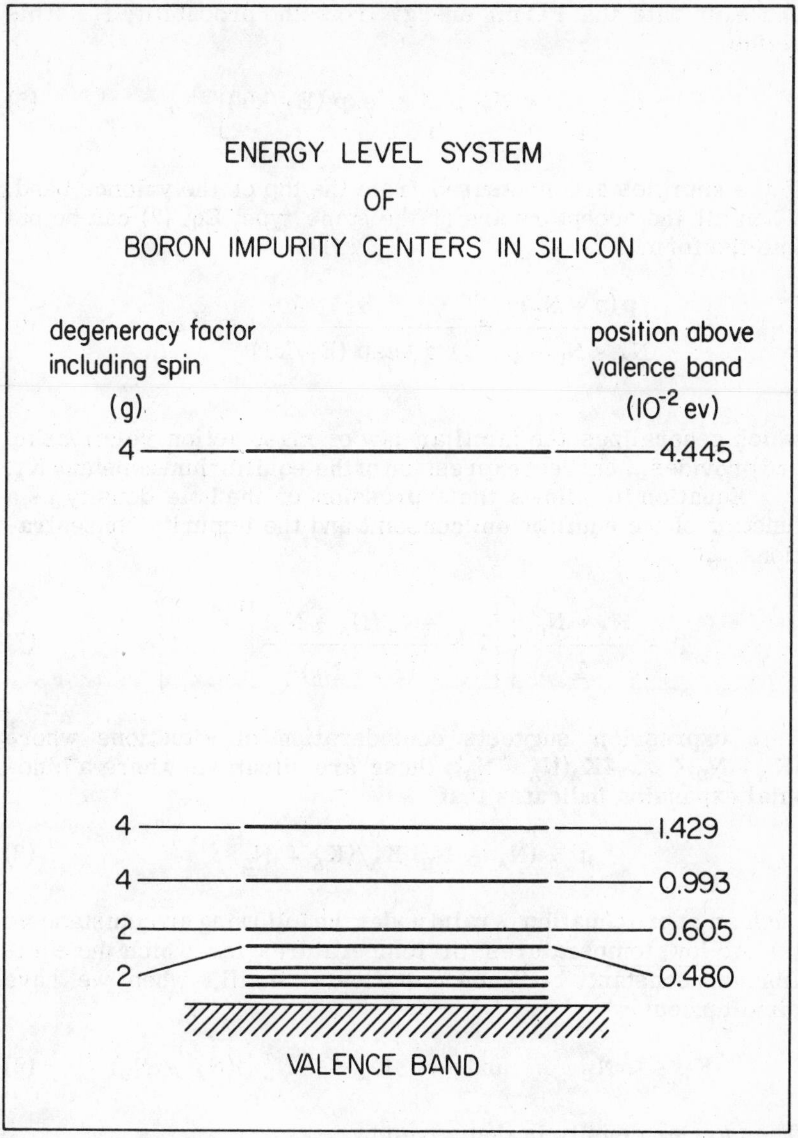

Figure 1. Energy Spectrum and Degeneracies of
Boron Acceptor States in Silicon.

and eliminate the Fermi energy from the probability f_A. This yields

$$f_A = \left[1 + N_v/p \sum_i g_i \exp{(E_i/kT)} \right]^{-1} , \tag{5}$$

if the energies are measured from the top of the valence band. When all the acceptors are of the same type, Eq. (2) can be put into the form

$$\frac{p(p + N_D)}{N_A - N_D - p} = \frac{N_v}{\sum_i g_i \exp{(E_i/kT)}} = K_A , \tag{6}$$

which generalizes the familiar law of mass action relationship and provides a correct expression of the equilibrium constant K_A.

Equation (6) allows the expression of the hole density as a function of the equilibrium constant and the impurity concentrations:

$$p = \frac{K_A + N_D}{2} \left\{ \left[1 + \frac{4K_A (N_A - N_D)}{(K_A + N_D)^2} \right]^{1/2} - 1 \right\}. \tag{7}$$

This expression suggests consideration of situations where $(K_A + N_D)^2 \gg 4K_A(N_A - N_D)$; these are situations where a binomial expansion indicates that

$$p \approx (N_A - N_D) K_A/(K_A + N_D) . \tag{8}$$

Such an approximation is valid under the following circumstances: (a) At low temperatures, or temperatures for which the equilibrium constant becomes relatively small, when we have simultaneously*

$$K_A \ll N_D \quad \text{and} \quad K_A \ll N_D^2/4(N_A - N_D) . \tag{9}$$

The carrier density is then given by

$$\boxed{p = (N_A - N_D) K_A/N_D} . \tag{10}$$

---

*Note that the second inequality is automatically satisfied as a consequence of the first one, when the degree of compensation, N_D/N_A, does not exceed 80%.

(b) At high temperatures, or temperatures for which the equilibrium constant becomes very large, when we have simultaneously*

$$K_A \gg 4(N_A - N_D) \qquad \text{and} \qquad K_A \gg N_D . \qquad (11)$$

The carrier density may then be approximated according to

$$\boxed{p = (N_A - N_D) (1 - N_D/K_A)} , \qquad (12)$$

which describes the temperature dependence in the exhaustion region—where p remains practically equal to the net impurity concentration $(N_A - N_D)$—and its immediate vicinity.

In Section IV we shall demonstrate how the formulae (10) and (12), in conjunction with resistivity and Hall effect data, may lead to reasonably accurate indications on the impurity content of p-type silicon samples. Prerequisite is the availability of the equilibrium constant K_A and of the true carrier concentration in the situations delimited by the inequalities (9) and (11). According to Eq. (6), K_A involves the effective density of states in the valence band,

$$N_v = 2 \left(2 \pi m* kT/h^2\right)^{3/2}$$
$$= 2.51 \times 10^{19} (m*/m_o)^{3/2} (T/300)^{3/2} , \qquad (13)$$

and the expression

$$\sum_i g_i \exp (E_i/kT)$$
$$= g_o \exp (E_o/kT) \sum_i (g_i/g_o) \exp [(E_i - E_o)/kT] , \qquad (14)$$

which is entirely determined by the energy states of the acceptor impurity. If their characteristics are known, it becomes a straightforward matter to evaluate K_A. The carrier density, on the contrary, requires delicate handling. In a nondegenerate

---

*Note that the second inequality is automatically satisfied as a consequence of the first one, when the degree of compensation, N_D/N_A, does not exceed 80%.

semiconductor the relationship between carrier density and Hall coefficient,

$$p = r \,/\, Re \,, \qquad\qquad (15)$$

includes namely the so-called Hall coefficient factor r. As shown by Beer and Willardson [2], this factor is best described in terms of the dimensionless parameters

$$\gamma = (9 \,\pi/16) \left(\mu_L H/10^8 \right)^2 \quad \text{and} \quad \beta = 6 \, \mu_L/\mu_I \,, \qquad (16)$$

the mobilities μ_L and μ_I referring to lattice and impurity scattering, respectively. In a constant temperature situation, γ conveys the effect of the magnetic field, and β expresses the influence of ionized impurities. The Hall coefficient factor depends upon γ and β in a complicated fashion, but simplifications occur in two cases:

(a)   for $\gamma \ll 1$, $r = \mu_H/\mu$ (17)

(b)   for $\gamma \gg 1$, $r = 1$.   (18)

In an experiment as a function of temperature the Hall coefficient factor behavior becomes an intricate affair because β and γ both vary. In the lattice scattering range γ remains usually very small, at least with standard magnetic fields, and r is given by the Hall- to -drift mobility ratio. Since μ_L exhibits a strong temperature dependence in most semiconductors, γ may become much larger than one at low temperatures; this may entail the appearance of galvanomagnetic fine structure effects in the transition region [8].

IV. APPLICATION TO p-TYPE SILICON

Utilizing the formalism outlined in the previous section, we shall now attempt to analyze data collected on p-type silicon samples cut from two different crystals labelled M-11 (floating-zone silicon) and K-121 (crucible-grown silicon). The Hall coefficients, more precisely the two 1/Re vs 1000/T curves, are confronted in Figure 2; obviously, M-11 must be much purer than K-121. This is confirmed in Figure 3, which shows that in the temperature range where impurity scattering effects become noticeable, the Hall mobility of the floating-zone specimen ($\approx 10^5$ cm^2/v-sec) exceeds that of crucible-grown material by a whole order of magnitude.

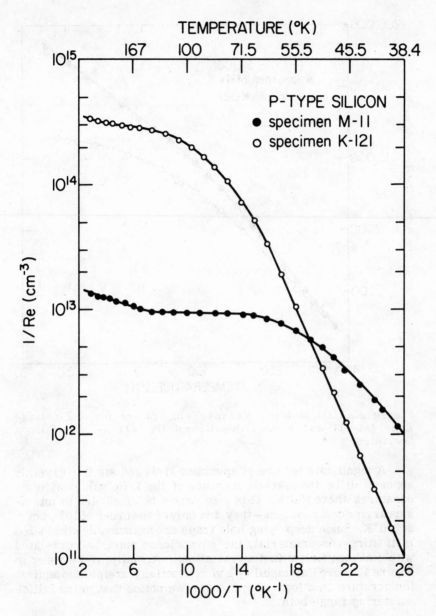

Figure 2. Reciprocal Product of Hall Coefficient and Electronic Charge, as a Function of Temperature, for a Floating-Zone (M-11) and a Crucible-Grown (K-121) p-Type Silicon Specimen.

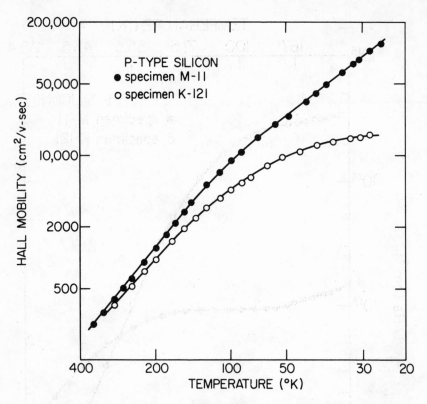

Figure 3. Hall Mobility Versus Temperature for a Floating-Zone (M-11) and a Crucible-Grown (K-121) p-Type Silicon Specimen.

A significant feature of specimen M-11 and similar crystals appears to be the marked increase of the 1/Re values at temperatures above $150°K$. This rise cannot be attributed to intrinsic carrier contributions—they are only of the order of 10^{11} cm^{-3} at $300°K$. Since deep-lying hole traps are presumably eliminated in floating-zone material, the phenomenon must be correlated with Hall coefficient factor variations. Actually, if we refer to Figure 4, where Hall mobility and conductivity are plotted against temperature on a logarithmic scale, we notice that in the lattice scattering range both

$$\mu_H = R\sigma \qquad \text{and} \qquad \sigma = ep\mu \qquad (19)$$

obey $T^{-\alpha}$ laws, namely $T^{-3.0}$ and $T^{-2.7}$, respectively. This implies that μ_H/μ, and therefore r, varies approximately as

406

$T^{-0.3}$ down to 150°K or even below.* In fact, a second look at Figure 2 suggests that the Hall coefficient factor should rapidly flatten out, since this would result in an essentially constant carrier concentration down to the liquid nitrogen temperatures, as predicted by Eq. (12) for highly-purified material (low donor concentration!) such as M-11. Specimen K-121 also exhibits a temperature-dependent $1/R$ behavior in a region where exhaustion is expected. The $T^{-0.195}$ dependence indicated by the least squares fit in Figure 5 is consistent with the reduced Hall and drift mobility slopes observed on this specimen (see Figure 3), although these slope variations may surprise, since they occur under circumstances where impurity scattering effects are supposed to be negligible. Both specimens, however, have a Hall mobility of approximately 370 cm²/v-sec at 300°K. Assuming that a drift mobility of 480 cm²/v-sec, as measured by Ludwig and Watters for holes in high-resistivity silicon [11], is a good figure for our specimens, it follows that $r(300°K) \approx 0.77$. We are now in a position to evaluate the free carrier densities in the exhaustion region, and, ipso facto, to estimate the net impurity concentrations $(N_A - N_D)$. They are listed in Table I.

At low temperatures, the excited levels of group III acceptors in silicon do not really contribute to the hole trapping process. This makes it attractive to consider Eq. (10) for two specific purposes: (a) identification of the acceptor impurity via the ground state energy E_o; (b) evaluation of the compensating donor concentration when $(N_A - N_D)$ is available. For the sake of convenience (dimensionless parameters!), we shall rewrite Eq. (10) as follows:

$$\frac{R_o}{R}\left(\frac{T}{300}\right)^{-3/2} = \frac{\exp(-E_o/kT)}{\mathcal{N}(r/r_o)}, \qquad (20)$$

where R_o and r_o refer to the 300°K values, whereas $\mathcal{N}$ stands for $N_{Do}(m^*/m_o)^{-3/2}/(2.51 \times 10^{19})$.

Figure 6 exhibits the left-hand side term of Eq. (20), as measured for specimen K-121, versus the reciprocal temperature below 60°K. It is apparent that an exponential law governs the behavior of $(R_o/R)(T/300)^{-3/2}$. If we assume that the r and m^* variations are essentially negligible in comparison to the $1/R$ decrease at temperatures below 50°K, a least squares fit might provide the ground state energy of the acceptor centers.

---

*We are implicitly assuming that in this temperature range the impurities remain completely ionized ($p = p_o = N_A - N_D$), hence that the temperature dependence of the conductivity is entirely due to drift mobility variations.

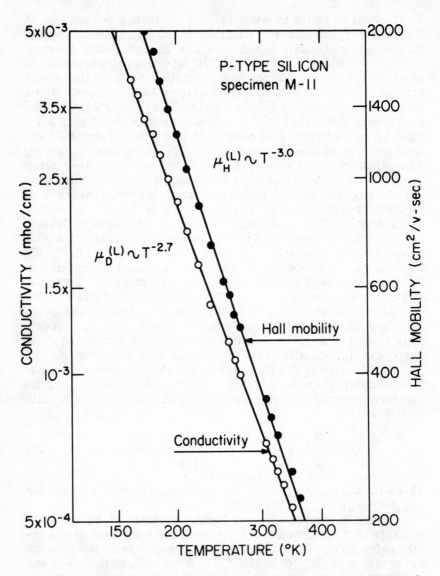

Figure 4. Temperature Dependence of the Hall Mobility and Conductivity (or Drift Mobility) in the Lattice Scattering Range of a Floating-Zone p-Type Silicon Specimen.

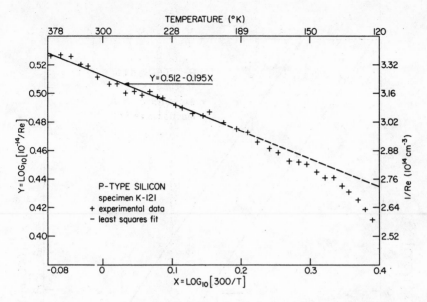

Figure 5. Temperature Dependence of the Reciprocal Product of Hall Coefficient and Electronic Charge for a Crucible-Grown p-Type Silicon Specimen in the Exhaustion Region.

The fit shown in Figure 6 corresponds to $E_o = 0.04445$ ev and identifies the centers as boron atoms. On the basis of recent infrared spectral measurements, Zwerdling et al. estimate the ionization energy of holes as (0.0441 ± 0.0003) ev in a transition from the boron ground state to the $p_{3/2}$ band maximum in silicon [13]. The fair agreement between optical and thermal activation energies is noteworthy and illustrates the degree of reliability of our Hall effect equipment.

The low-temperature slope of specimen M-11 also identifies boron as the dominant impurity, but develops only below 30°K (see Figure 2). This signifies that in the range of validity of Eq. (20) the high-field approximation—that means $r = 1$—might be justified even at our field strength of 2500 gauss. It is then a straightforward matter to evaluate the parameter π and to deduce the donor concentration; with $g_o = 4$ and $(m^*/m_o)^{3/2} = 0.48,$* we get $N_D \approx 3.7 \times 10^{11}$ cm^{-3}. Owing to the considerable uncertainty attached to the density of states mass, this figure may only be accurate within about 30%. It can nevertheless be

---

*This value of the density of states mass for holes in silicon was obtained according to the method of Lax and Mavroides [10] from the latest cyclotron resonance data [4]; actually $(m^*/m_o)^{3/2}$ = 0.48 ± 0.15.

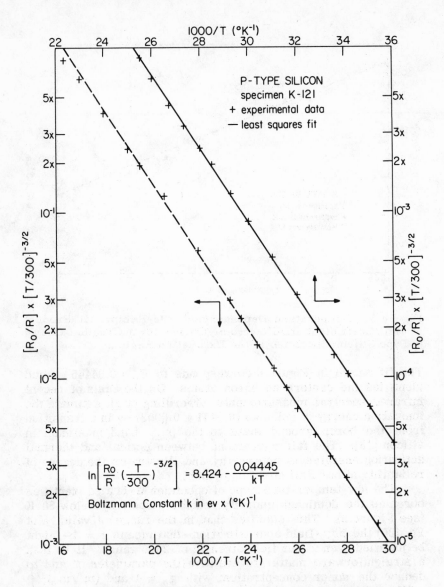

Figure 6. Boron Ground State Activation Slope as Indicated by Low-Temperature Hall Effect Measurements on a Crucible-Grown p-Type Silicon Specimen; R_o is the $300°$K Hall Coefficient.

Table I

Impurity Concentrations in Two p-Type Silicon Specimens Representative of Floating-Zone and Quartz-Crucible Grown Material.

Specimen	M-11 (Floating-Zone)	K-121 (Quartz-Crucible)
Room-Temperature Resistivity (ohm-cm)	1330	53
Net Impurity Concentration (cm^{-3})	$(1.00 \pm 0.05) \times 10^{13}$	$(2.50 \pm 0.10) \times 10^{14}$
Donor Concentration (cm^{-3})	$\sim 3.7 \times 10^{11}$	$\sim 3.8 \times 10^{14}$
Total Concentration (cm^{-3})	1.1×10^{13}	$\sim 1.0 \times 10^{15}$
Compensation N_D/N_A (%)	4	60

stated that the degree of compensation does not exceed 5% in commercially available floating-zone material of the M-11 grade. This is not so with pulled silicon, as we shall see in the next paragraph.

The activation energy slope of specimen K-121 covers a temperature range where the variations of β and γ confuse the Hall coefficient factor issue and make it questionable to assume $r = 1$ [1]. It is impossible therefore, to extract the true π value from the least squares fit of Figure 6. This difficulty, which is always encountered in highly-compensated material, prevents a determination of the donor concentration on the basis of Equation (10) alone. Since we have recognized the acceptor centers as boron atoms, and since Figure 1 provides us with a reasonable picture of the energy spectrum, we may then attempt to proceed via Equation (12). Let us rewrite this equation in the notations of Equation (20),

411

$$\ln\left(\frac{R}{R_o}\right) - \ln\left(\frac{r}{r_o}\right) = \frac{N_D}{K_A} = \frac{\displaystyle\hbar \sum_i (g_i/g_o) \exp(E_i/kT)}{(T/300)^{3/2}}, \quad (21)$$

and plot the right-hand side term as in Figure 7.* On the same diagram let us locate the $\ln(p_o/p)$ values deduced from the measurements in the hypothesis of a $T^{-0.195}$ dependence of the Hall coefficient factor. (We assume that the deviation from the straight line in Figure 5 is entirely due to carrier removal effects.) In spite of the fact that our "subtraction" procedure exaggerates the experimental scatter, the confrontation reveals that $\hbar \approx 1.25 \times 10^{-4}$. The donor concentration should thus be of the order of 3.8×10^{14} cm^{-3}, which means that the compensation might hit 60% (see Table I). It remains, of course, to check if the approximation (12) is valid in the considered temperature range—in other words, if the inequalities (11) are satisfied. Since K_A exceeds 10^{16} cm^{-3} at 125°K, we may indeed apply Eq. (21). Hence, we must attribute the odd trend of the upper $\ln(p_o/p)$ points to the onset of anomalies in the temperature dependence of the Hall coefficient factor.

V. APPLICATION TO p-TYPE GERMANIUM

The arguments developed in Sections III and IV emphasize that an investigation of the Hall coefficient factor must precede any serious evaluation of impurity concentrations in nondegenerate semiconductors. In this context we present Figure 8, which describes the Hall coefficient factor behavior of p-type germanium specimens with carrier densities of up to 10^{15} cm^{-3}, at magnetic field strengths of about 2500 gauss. The three curves illustrate typical results deduced from Hall coefficient measurements performed on a variety of highly-purified gallium-doped samples.**

Specimen ZBD-23 reflects the behavior of ultrapure material (less than 10^{14} electrically active impurities per cubic centimeter). We notice that a "high-field plateau" situation is apparently reached at temperatures below 77°K. If this is indeed

---

*The degeneracies of the four "upper" excited states are not available [9]. These states are presumably twofold or fourfold degenerate, and N_D/K_A has been spread out in consequence. Note that in the temperature range of Figure 7 excited states contribute to the hole trapping process in the amount of up to 40%.

**Accurate determinations of the compensating donor content would require measurements at liquid helium temperatures; they have not been made.

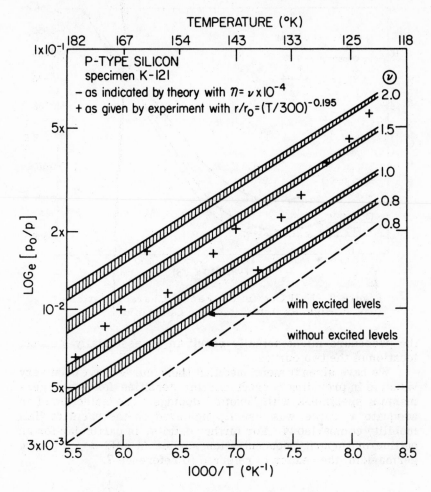

Figure 7. Carrier Removal Process at High Temperatures in a Crucible-Grown p-Type Silicon Specimen; p_o is the 300°K Hole Concentration.

the case, the ZBD-23 curve may be positioned according to the scale on the left of Figure 8, since r is known to be strictly equal to one in the high-field region. Specimens with hole densities exceeding 10^{14} cm^{-3} exhibit rather prominent fine structure characteristics, which prevent an unambiguous determination of the absolute Hall coefficient factor values. The GRT-15 and GT-44 points have therefore been plotted on a reduced scale normalized at 300°K. Since we have reasons to believe that the room-temperature value of μ_H/μ does not depend too strongly upon the impurity content, at least in the 10^{14}-10^{15} cm^{-3} range,

413

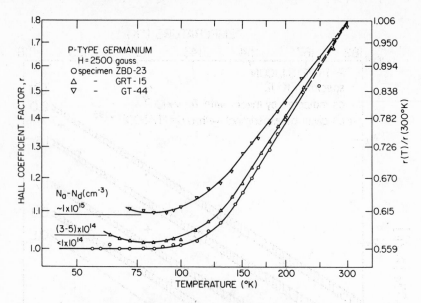

Figure 8. Hall Coefficient Factor Characteristics of
High-Resistivity p-type Germanium.

the procedure might actually result in an essentially correct
location of the two curves.

We have already mentioned that these curves have been very
valuable in providing correct carrier densities for p-type germanium specimens with "exotic" dopings. The selection of an
adequate r curve was usually achieved on the basis of Hall
mobility comparisons. For further details, in particular for an
outline of impurity concentration studies in gold-doped p-type
germanium, the reader is referred to reference 7.

VI. CONCLUSION

An accurate impurity content evaluation on the basis of Hall
effect studies involves elements such as Hall coefficient factor,
excited energy levels, and quantum-mechanical degeneracies,
whose significance has only recently been appreciated. We
believe that the approach delineated in Section III enables us to
take these factors properly into account, and may therefore lead
to correct estimates of the net and total concentration of electrically active impurities in homogeneous semiconductors. The
scheme has been illustrated in an application to p-type silicon
specimens representative of commercially available materials,
and calls for the following comments:

1. The validity of the low-temperature and high-temperature approximations (10) and (12) is critically dependent upon the amount of compensating impurities; self-consistency must be established a posteriori.

2. The accuracy of the net impurity content evaluation is conditioned by the availability of adequate drift mobility data in the lattice scattering range.

3. The evaluation of the compensating impurity concentration involves always the density of states mass, which entails some uncertainty.

4. The evaluation of the compensating impurity concentration in poor material may involve the excited states and their degeneracies in a fashion visualized, for instance, in Figure 7.

5. The use of high magnetic fields would eliminate much of the Hall coefficient factor difficulties and appears, therefore, strongly advisable.

6. The availability of correct impurity content and energy level figures may provide valuable indications on the Hall coefficient factor behavior in the "fine-structure region," simply as a result of confronting Eq. (7) with carefully taken 1/Re data; work of this nature is in progress at the authors' laboratory.

REFERENCES

1. A. C. Beer, J. Phys. Chem. Solids 8, 507 (1959).
2. A. C. Beer and R. K. Willardson, Phys. Rev. 110, 1286 (1958).
3. P. P. Debye and E. M. Conwell, Phys. Rev. 93, 693 (1954).
4. R. N. Dexter, H. J. Zeiger, and B. Lax, Phys. Rev. 104, 637 (1956).
5. H. Y. Fan, "Solid State Physics," Academic Press Inc., New York, 1955, Vol. 1, pp. 283-365.
6. H. J. Hrostowski and R. H. Kaiser, J. Phys. Chem. Solids 4, 148 (1958).
7. C. A. Klein and P. P. Debye, "Proceedings of the International Conference on Semiconductor Physics, Prague 1960," Publishing House of the Czechoslovak Academy of Sciences, Prague, 1961, pp. 278-281.
8. C. A. Klein and W. D. Straub, Bull. Am. Phys. Soc. 4, 28 (1959).
9. W. Kohn, "Solid State Physics," Academic Press Inc., New York, 1957, Vol. 5, pp. 257-320.
10. B. Lax and J. G. Mavroides, Phys. Rev. 100, 1650 (1955).
11. G. W. Ludwig and R. L. Watters, Phys. Rev. 101, 1699 (1956).
12. E. H. Putley, "The Hall Effect and Related Phenomena," Butterworth & Co., London, 1960.
13. S. Zwerdling, K. J. Button, B. Lax, and L. M. Roth, Phys. Rev. Letters 4, 173 (1960).

SPACE-CHARGE CURRENT MEASUREMENT AS A TECHNIQUE FOR THE ANALYSIS OF TRACE IMPURITIES IN ULTRAPURE MATERIAL

Roland W. Smith
RCA Laboratories
Princeton, N. J.

The term insulator is generally applied to materials of very low electrical conductivity. One of the principal purposes of this paper is to indicate that very pure wide-bandgap crystals, i.e., insulators, can pass relatively large currents and that the analysis of this current provides a very simple and extremely sensitive technique to determine extremely low impurity densities in ultrapure materials.

To understand the space-charge current technique for trace analysis we begin with a physical description of an insulator and indicate some of the factors that determine the degree of conductivity that can be obtained. An ideal insulator is a crystal in which the valence band full of electrons is appreciably separated from the conduction band. At room temperature and in the absence of other means of excitation, the density of electrons in the conduction band is negligible. If electrons are

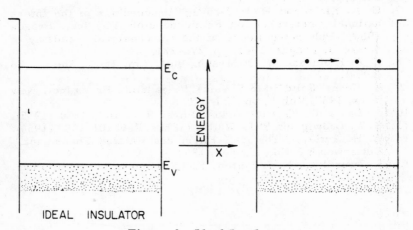

Figure 1. Ideal Insulator.

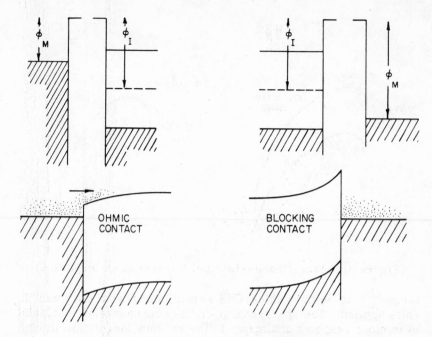

Figure 2. Metal-Insulator Contacts.

introduced into the conduction band by any means, then these carriers are entirely free to move in the crystal and to drift as a current in an applied electric field. There are many ways of introducing electrons into the conduction band. The simple and direct means we will be interested in here is by injection from an ohmic contact. With appropriately matched work functions, the metal acts as a reservoir of electrons which can maintain, even at room temperature, relatively large current densities in the crystal. A contact with this basic characteristic is called an ohmic contact. This is to be contrasted with a blocking contact in which a high barrier limits the supply of electrons from the metal into the insulator to negligible proportions.

Consider next the plane parallel arrangement of an insulator and two ohmic contacts. An applied voltage fills the crystal with electrons injected from the cathode. The total charge is given by $Q = CV$. The current of these electrons through the crystal is space-charge limited. The current density is given by

$$J = 10^{-13} \; \mu k \; \frac{V^2}{L^3}$$

where μ = mobility, K = dielectric constant, V = applied voltage, and L = electrode separation. As an example the current density

417

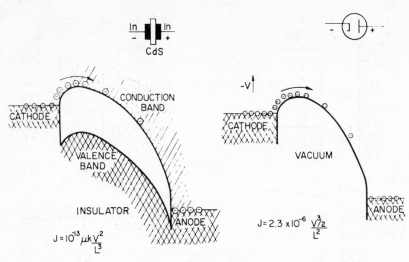

Figure 3. Space-Charge-Limited Current in an Insulator.

through a 10 micron thick CdS crystal is ~1 amp/cm^2 with 3 volts applied. The space-charge limited current in an insulator is in most respects analogous to the vacuum thermionic diode.

The expression $J \propto (V^2/L^3)$ assumes that all the injected electrons remain in the conduction band, and applies only for an ideal or trap-free insulator. Real crystals, of course, are far from ideal, and even ultrapure samples contain many

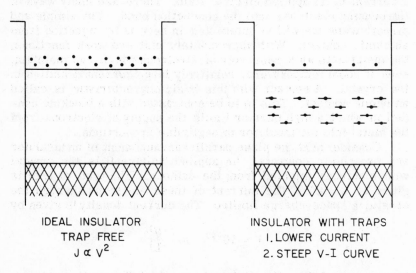

Figure 4. Effect of Traps on Space-Charge Current in an Insulator.

418

imperfections, such as traps or states within the forbidden zone into which electrons fall and become immobilized. Traps drastically modify the current-voltage characteristic of an insulator. The two main effects of traps are to reduce the magnitude of the current observed and to cause the current to vary steeply with voltage. Thus for a fixed voltage and for the same size sample, the same total number of electrons are injected into the crystal, while the actual number of electrons in the conduction band, free to move, is determined by the density and distribution of states into which the electrons fall. The essence of the space-charge current trace analysis technique is to deduce the density and distribution of states from the form of the measured current-voltage curve. Until recently the current that could be measured through insulators was too low to be readily used for analysis. More pure materials and better contacts have changed the situation. A virtue of the space-charge current technique is that the measurements become easier the better the material.

As a demonstration of the space-charge current technique we will take data from a particular CdS crystal. Fig. 5 shows a log V, log I plot of the equilibrium dark current through the crystal. There are two distinct branches to this curve we wish to emphasize. In the lower part of the curve I is proportional to V^2. This is followed by a transition region to the point, V_{TF}, where I varies very steeply with voltage. The trap-free V^2 characteristic expected for this crystal is shown in the upper left for comparison. This particular dark curve has an especially simple interpretation as may be seen with the aid of Fig. 6. The initial conditions with the crystal in the dark and with low applied voltage place the Fermi level deep in the forbidden band. As the voltage is increased more electrons are injected into the crystal. Most of these electrons fall into the traps; however, a small but significant fraction remain in the conduction band. As a result of this redistribution the steady-state Fermi level moves up in the forbidden zone and in a sense scans the trapping states. It can be shown that when the Fermi level scans a trap-free region below a single trap level that the current varies of V^2, and that the depth of the trap, E_T, can be obtained from the displacement, θ, of the observed curve from the trap-free curve. With further increase in voltage the traps at, E_T, become filled and the current increases very steeply as the Fermi level passes through. Since most of the injected charge is in the traps the trap density can be obtained from the traps-filled voltage and the capacitance of the crystal. The Fermi level has passed through the trap at V_{TF}, but at $V_{TF}/2$ it is centered at the trap. The current at $V_{TF}/2$ then gives an independent measurement of the trap depth, E_T.

419

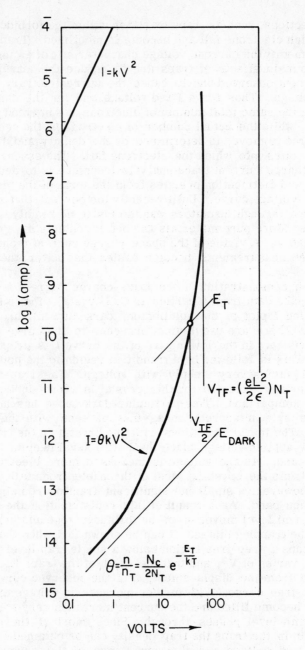

Figure 5. Thermal Equilibrium Space-Charge-
Limited Dark Current in a CdS Crystal.

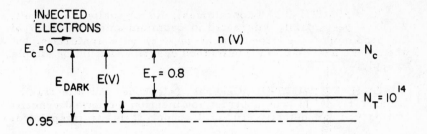

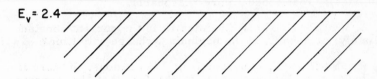

Figure 6. Discrete Trap Determined from Data in Figure 5.

In summary the measurements indicate a discrete trap at 0.8 ev below the conduction band of a density of 10^{14} per cc.

REFERENCES

1. N. F. Mott and R. W. Gurney, "Electronic Processes in Ionic Crystals." Oxford University Press, New York (1940).
2. M. A. Lampert, Phys. Rev. 103, 1648 (1956).
3. M. A. Lampert, A. Rose and R. W. Smith, J. Phys. Chem. Solids 8, 464 (1959).
4. A. Rose, Phys. Rev. 97, 1538 (1955).
5. R. W. Smith and A. Rose, Phys. Rev. 97, 1531 (1955).
6. R. W. Smith, RCA Review, 20, 69 (1959).

DISCUSSION

L. R. WEISBERG (RCA Laboratories): At low temperature, silicon would be considered an insulator also. Could this method be applied to silicon?

R. W. SMITH (RCA Laboratories): There is no reason why it couldn't. Dr. Larabee of our laboratory is working in this region, so he may have the answer very soon.

C. ROSENBLUM (Chairman) (Merck): You have mentioned cadmium sulfide. Have you applied this to materials other than the cadmium sulfide?

R. W. SMITH (RCA Laboratories): No. Actually, we haven't. We have been mainly interested in cadmium sulphide. Part of the problem is the procurement of very pure materials, but when these are available, the method described should be simple to apply.

G. H. SCHWUTTKE (General Telephone and Electronics Laboratories): In your abstract you mention the lowest concentration you can detect is 10^{-6}. I wonder if this is misprinted.

R. W. SMITH (RCA Laboratories): It must be. The lowest impurity density that we have determined were of the order of 10^{14} atoms per cubic centimeter.

G. H. SCHWUTTKE (General Telephone and Electronics Laboratories): That sounds more reasonable.

G. A. WOLFF (Harshaw Chemical): Is the current constant immediately, or does it, in the beginning, change with time?

R. W. SMITH (RCA Laboratories): Yes it does. If there is one difficulty with the method, it is the fact that the current takes a very long time to reach equilibrium at room temperature. For instance, a day or so may be required for equilibrium to be established when moving to a new point. This is due to the fact that, as the voltage is increased, more charge is injected. The injected carriers must then settle down in traps and this may require a long time. In cadmium sulphide, to look at traps 8/10 of a volt below the conduction band, this amount of time is required.

G. A. WOLFF (Harshaw Chemical): In aluminum nitride, there is a similar behavior. Each point required a long time and equilibrium is really never attained.

"DETERMINATION OF SMALL STOICHIOMETRIC DEVIATIONS IN OXIDE MONOCRYSTALS"

Herbert B. Sachse
Keystone Carbon Company, St. Marys, Pennsylvania

ABSTRACT

The determination of small stoichiometric deviations of 1 milliatom/mole in oxide monocrystals is possible with rather good accuracy, independent of the type of deviation (surplus or deficiency).

A. INTRODUCTION

The important role of stoichiometric deviations in semiconductors is well known and dates back to the classical investigations of the electronic conductivity of CuI with small I surplus [1]. Later LeBlanc and Sachse [6] reported similar effects with the oxide semiconductors NiO, CoO, MnO and Cu_2O. As example, between the compositions NiO and $NiO_{1.05}$ the conductivity increases by a factor 10^6.

Also O-deficiencies can have a strong influence on the electrical conductivity. In this case the classical examples are TiO_2 and ZnO. Between TiO_2 and $TiO_{1.995}$ the resistivity at room temperature decreases by a factor 10^{10}. Simultaneously the activation energy drops from 1.65 ev to .27 ev [9]. Monocrystals of TiO_2 (Rutile) make this transition at 600°C in pure hydrogen within 5 minutes. By stoichiometric deficiency undetectable with normal chemical analysis the dielectric loss can increase by a factor 10 - 100, while simultaneously the apparent dielectric constant increases from approximately 100 to more than 15,000 [10,12]. Further work with O-deficient TiO_2 monocrystals was done by Breckenridge and Hosler [2] and Cronemeyer [4].

When O-deficient synthetic crystals of pure ZnO with an initial resistivity of 0.3 - 0.7 ohm centimeter and an activation energy of ~ .01 ev are annealed for 30 hours at 900°C in oxygen, a final resistivity of $2.5 \cdot 10^5$ ohm centimeter and a gap of .04 ev is reached [5]. This last figure is still far below the theoretical energy gap for intrinsic semiconduction in ZnO.

In a number of other oxides the influence of the O-pressure on the electrical properties has been investigated without knowledge of their stoichiometric deviation.

These few facts show the urgent need to define semiconducting compounds very well by their stoichiometric deviation before electrical investigations are started. Numerous other examples could be given. This holds true still more for monocrystals where grain boundary effects, which might overshadow nonstoichiometry, are absent. During recent years increasing emphasis has been laid on basic investigations of electrical and thermal properties of oxide monocrystals [8,11]. A strict comparison of their results makes it not only desirable but imperative to know the degree of stoichiometry.

B. OXIDES WITH OXYGEN SURPLUS

The stoichiometric surplus of oxide can be determined by the iodometric method which dates back to Bunsen. The oxide is dissolved in hydrochloric acid in the presence of potassium iodide, and its active oxygen, the surplus of oxygen over that in the valence state of the metal in the dissolved chloride, oxidizes an equivalent amount of iodide ions to iodine.

For oxide powders with a reasonable dissolution rate, this method can be used as described by Bunsen [3]. The spontaneous oxidation of iodide ions by atmospheric oxygen must be prohibited. This is no serious problem if dissolution times on the order of hours are involved. However, with dissolution times of days and weeks, the diffusion of the atmospheric oxygen into the reagents represents a source of error, which becomes increasingly intolerable with a decreasing stoichiometric surplus of oxygen. This is the case when densely sintered bodies or even single crystals have to be investigated that need up to 3 weeks for complete dissolution. A modified Bunsen method was necessary to deal with these cases.

A reasonable approach to this problem was made by Sachse [6], who sealed the oxide to be investigated with the reagents into a test tube and added a small amount of sodium carbonate to the acidic solution immediately prior to sealing to replace the air in the small remaining gas volume by carbon dioxide. Deviations down to 1 atomic % oxygen can be determined this way.

Further improvements were necessary to increase the sensitivity and reliability of the method for much smaller concentrations of surplus oxygen. The complete elimination of all parasitic oxygen was necessary. This involved the removal of the oxygen dissolved in the reagent solution and adsorbed on the surface of the single crystal chips or powder and on the glass walls. Evacuation seemed advisable. Under practical conditions, a

424

vacuum of 50 to 80 mm. of mercury was sufficient, as the reagent solutions developed partial pressures of hydrochloric acid and water, resulting in a heavy boiling of the liquid [7].

PROCEDURE

Chips of the crystal to be investigated were crushed to a relatively coarse powder and placed in a thin-walled glass tube approximately 2 mm. in inside diameter and 25 mm. in length with one open end. Subsequently, this glass tube was inserted into a borosilicate glass reaction tube 10 to 12 mm. in inside diameter and 15 cm. in length. After adding reagent solutions of 7 ml. of hydrochloric acid (d = 1.2) and 3 ml. of potassium iodide (n = 0.1), the neck of the tube was rinsed with a minimum amount of distilled water and subsequently connected to a high vacuum system with a manometer.

After reaching a vacuum on the order of 50 mm. of mercury, the reagent solution was pumped for a period of 10 minutes. Fifteen minutes of gentle boiling at this vacuum were sufficient to remove most of the parasitic oxygen. It was necessary that the pressure not be reduced below the specified values to avoid substantial losses of hydrochloric acid which might have resulted in a reduced dissolution rate. Small amounts of hydrochloric acid and water, which escaped, were condensed in a trap cooled with liquid oxygen. During this evacuation process, the tube with the specimen was completely degassed and slowly filled with reagent solution. In addition to the efforts to remove the oxygen from the reagents, blank tests were run with the reagent solution only, but with the corresponding metal chloride added to reproduce the conditions in the analysis of the specimen.

After sealing, the reaction tubes were stored in an oven at 65°C. in the dark and opened after complete dissolution had taken place. The dissolution rate could be increased by removing the crystal powder from the specimen tube by placing the entire reaction tube upside down at an angle of 45°.

After complete dissolution, the reaction tubes were broken open and rapidly rinsed out with oxygen-free water. A surplus of 0.01N thiosulfate was added and back-titrated with 0.002N bichromate using starch, grade Baker c.p. 1-4006 for iodometry, as indicator.

RESULTS

The analyses were calculated so that the oxygen surplus found by titration was subtracted from the weight of the specimen. This yielded the value for the hypothetical amount of stoichiometric metal oxide and indicated the amount of metal in the specimen (Table 1). In a separate investigation it was found that

425

Table I

Results of Metal Oxide Analyses

	Oxide	Specimen Weight Gram	Metal Milliatoms	Surplus Oxygen Microatoms	Formula	Probable Error In Gram-Atom Oxygen
A	MnO	0.1172	1.64	32	MnO $_{1.0195}$	±0.0002
B	MnO	0.088	1.24	0.93	MnO $_{1.00075}$	±0.0002
C	CoO	0.0891	1.18	4.54	CoO $_{1.0039}$	±0.0003
D	CoO (a)	0.2772	3.9	23.8	CoO $_{1.0061}$	±0.0003
D	CoO (a)	0.2760	3.89	21.3	CoO $_{1.0055}$	±0.0003
D	CoO (a)	0.1334	1.88	10.4	CoO $_{1.0055}$	±0.0003
E	NiO	0.129	1.73	1.81	NiO $_{1.00104}$	±0.0003
E	NiO	0.1504	2.01	1.94	NiO $_{1.00097}$	±0.0003
F	NiO (a)	0.1361	1.83	2.26	NiO $_{1.00124}$	±0.0005
G	NiO	0.1310	1.75	0.56	NiO $_{1.00032}$	±0.00012

(a) Specimens received from Nippon Telegraph and Telephone Public Corp., Japan; the others from General Electric Research Laboratory.

426

the standardization of the solutions, which were used for the titration, had a probable error of $\pm2\%$, if a microburet was used to reduce reading errors at the buret, and a white background promoted the recognition of the end point. The probable error in a series of blanks stored the same time under the same conditions as the oxide specimens was $\pm7\%$. The influence of this error on the result decreases with the amount of surplus oxygen to be determined. For the first specimen of MnO in the table the oxygen ratio of blank and specimen is only 0.1. Therefore, the probable error of the blank represents in this case only $\pm1\%$ of the surplus oxygen; in most other cases the percentage of the probable error is higher.

The MnO monocrystal was evidently inhomogeneous, as confirmed also by electrical measurements and appearance. CoO and NiO monocrystals appeared very homogeneous and their oxygen surplus apparently did not depend very much upon their origin.

Electrical measurements by vacancy diffusion with NiO-specimen G yielded a composition $NiO_{1.0003}$ in good agreement with the chemical determination of this very small O-surplus.*

C. OXIDES WITH O-DEFICIENCY

It would be unrealistic to base the calculation of small stoichiometric oxygen deficiencies on the analytical determination of the bulk ratio of metal and oxygen. The possible deviation would be submerged in the usual tolerance level, as in the case of O-surplus. Analytical methods, which only respond to the deficiency, are normally based on oxidimetric analysis with permanganate or ceric sulfate as oxidizing agents.

Small O-deficiencies in polycrystalline CuO, TiO_2 and earth aklalititanates can easily be determined by dissolving these materials in H_2SO_4 in presence of a sufficient Fe^{3+} - surplus. The following reactions take place:

$$Cu^+ + Fe^{3+} = Cu^{2+} + Fe^{2+}$$
$$Ti^{3+} + Fe^{3+} = Ti^{4+} + Fe^{2+}$$

The produced Fe^{2+} is titrated with $KMnO_4$.

This method can naturally be extended to other oxides which tend to O-deficiency, such as ZnO, V_2O_5, etc. One condition has to be met, that the ions with the highest valence are stable in aqueous solution.

In the case of TiO_2 monocrystals this method failed entirely due to the fact that the dissolution rate was practically nil.

---

*Private communication from G. A. Slack, General Electric Research Lab., Semiconductor Division.

Neither heating nor stirring or the application of other acids than H_2SO_4 accelerated the reaction. In cases where an electronegative element is involved, such as Ti, the usual approach is a caustic or carbonate melt which forms the titanate (zincate, vanadate, respectively). Since the melting process requires temperatures at which the oxygen-deficiency would disappear spontaneously by oxidation in air, a vacuum melting procedure was developed, which gave excellent results.

D. APPARATUS AND PROCEDURE

A few chips of the TiO_2 monocrystals were melted with 6 grams of 55 mole percent Na_2CO_3 + 45% K_2CO_3 in a platinum crucible, A, of 20 ml volume. This crucible was placed on a porous brick pad within a Vycor tube B, which was surrounded by a water cooled 5 turn induction coil C to be energized with 400 kc/s. After evacuation of the Vycor tube to less than 10^{-3} mm Hg. stopcock D was closed. It was found that application of premolten carbonate lumps reduced the outgassing time considerably. For the following 4 hours, often overnight, permanence of vacuum was observed at the manometer E, and if no leakage was found, the hf-field was slowly built up under renewed short pumping until the entire batch of carbonate was molten and reached a temperature of approximately 950°C. The progress of the dissolution of the crystal chips could be observed visually through the clear melt and it required normally not more than 3 hours. According to the reaction: TiO_2 + Na_2CO_3 = Na_2TiO_3 + CO_2, the dissolution is accompanied by a fine bubbling which ceases after the reaction is completed.

For small deficiencies it is advisable to reduce the reaction temperature to 920°C and to keep the CO_2 pressure below 0.6 mm. Thus the O-dissociation pressure of CO_2 is well matched to the O-equilibrium pressure of TiO_2.

After cooling and removing crucible A from the Vycor tube, the solid cone of frozen melt containing the formed titanate could be easily taken out and was broken into a few large lumps, which were transferred into a Pyrex tube F. A surplus of diluted H_2SO_4 + $Fe_2(SO_4)_3$ was added to dissolve the salt cone and then the Pyrex tube was immediately closed with a stopcock fitted to the tube by a ground joint (size 29/42). The dissolution process due to the relatively large lumps was sufficiently slow (2 hours) that the evolved CO_2 could be pumped off in a controlled manner without losing any liquid. Although the applied liquids had been freed from oxygen by bubbling with nitrogen, the additional CO_2-evolution helped to rinse out any traces of oxygen completely, as shown by blank tests with known amounts of metallic Fe. After complete dissolution of the salt cone, the formed Fe^{2+}-ion was titrated with 0.02 n—$KMnO_4$.

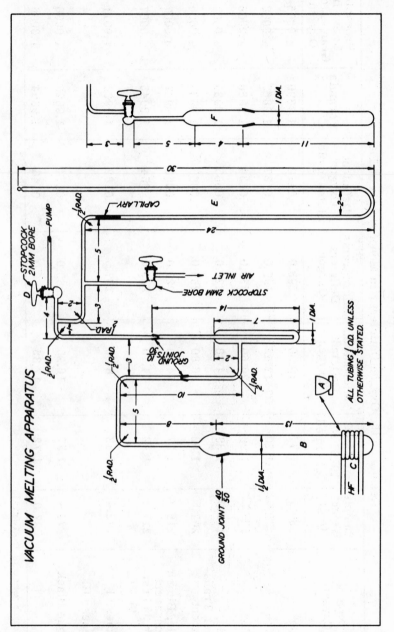

Figure 1. "Vacuum Melting Apparatus".

429

Table II

Results on the Oxygen Deficiency in Monocrystals of TiO_2

Type of Crystal	Sample Weight (mg)	ml KMnO $.0207$ N Consumed	Microatoms Deficient Oxygen	Micrograms Deficient Oxygen	Deficient Oxygen Atoms/mole	Formula	Probable Error In Gram-Atom Oxygen
Linde*	130.5	1.77	18.30	293.0	.0110	1.9890	±.0005
Linde*	72.7	1.20	12.43	199.0	.0137	1.9863	±.0008
Linde*	123.3	1.99	20.60	330.0	.0134	1.9866	±.0005
Linde, Bluish Trans-parent	176.0	1.38	14.30	229.0	.0065	1.9935	±.0007
	207.5	1.62	16.80	269.0	.0065	1.9935	±.0006
Linde, Bluish Transparent after 36 hrs. 700°C in air	216.0	1.37	14.20	227.0	.0053	1.9947	±.0007
	217.2	1.42	14.70	235.0	.0054	1.9946	±.0007
Japanese I	42.4	0.83	8.60	137.5	.0162	1.9838	±.0011
Japanese II: Opaque Black	74.8	1.57	16.25	260.0	.0174	1.9826	±.0006
	97.0	1.72	17.85	286.0	.0146	1.9854	±.0006

*Inhomogeneous material

Table II
(Continued)

Results on the Oxygen Deficiency in Monocrystals of TiO_2

Type of Crystal	Sample Weight (mg)	ml KMnO .0207 N Consumed	Microatoms Deficient Oxygen	Micrograms Deficient Oxygen	Deficient Oxygen Atoms/mole	Formula	Probable Error In Gram-Atom Oxygen
Japanese II: (Cont.)							
Bluish Trans- parent	149.0	1.57	16.25	260.0	.0088	1.9912	±.0006
Static Vacuum	107.7	1.25	12.90	207.0	.0095	1.9905	±.0008
Static Vacuum	224.7	1.91	19.80	317.0	.0070	1.9930	±.0005
Continuous Pumping	157.8	1.20	12.40	198.5	.0079	1.9921	±.0008
Japanese III:							
Static Vacuum	209.1	1.88	19.50	312.0	.0075	1.9925	±.0003
Continuous Pumping	201.7	1.79	18.50	296.0	.0073	1.9927	±.0003
Large Chips (3 hours)**	112.1	1.03	10.70	171.0	.0076	1.9924	±.0006

**Partial dissolution to check homogeneity

F. RELIABILITY AND ULTIMATE SENSITIVITY

The accuracy of the described method depends, as already shown for oxides with O-surplus, on the strict exclusion of parasitic oxygen. Serious errors can hardly be expected during the melting process in high vacuum, however the dissolution of the melt cone in aqueous solutions still might introduce traces of dissolved oxygen.

Since it was difficult to introduce well-defined O-deficiencies into TiO_2-monocrystals, blank tests were made only for the wet phase of the dissolution process. Small portions of pure iron wire (.002" diameter) equivalent in reduction value to the observed O-deficiency were dissolved under the same conditions as the titanate containing melt cones and the Fe^{+2} produced was titrated. The observed deviation was within ±0.8 microatoms iron resulting in the same probable error in O-deficiency. With crystal samples of more than 100 mg, the deficiency value is accurate within ±5%, for larger sample weights even better.

The possibility of a spontaneous O-loss of the crystals, especially of those with low deficiency during the heating in vacuum, caused some concern. According to thermodynamic calculations, the dissociation pressure of TiO_2 at the temperature of the carbonate melt would be smaller than 10^{-4} mm. The fact that the same O-deficiency was found whether the melting point was performed with or without continuous pumping indicated that apparently no oxygen was lost during the dissociation. A possible interference for very small deficiencies (<0.0002 atoms/mole) is under investigation.

It should be kept in mind that the accuracy is finely limited by the blank. If larger crystal specimens are available for analysis, the sensitivity limit could easily be boosted by another order of magnitude.

G. ACKNOWLEDGMENT

The author wishes to thank Keystone Carbon Company for granting permission to publish this information and Mr. Gordon L. Nichols for his valuable assistance.

REFERENCES

1. K. Baedeker, Ann. Phys. 22, 749 (1907); and Ann. Phys. 29, 566 (1909).
2. R. G. Breckenridge, and W. R. Hosler, Phys. Rev. 91, 793 (1953).
3. R. W. Bunsen, F. P. Treadwell, and W. T. Hall, "Analytical Chemistry, Quantitative Analysis," 9th ed., Vol. II, p. 598, Wiley, New York, 1958.

4. D. C. Cronemeyer, Phys. Rev. 87, 876 (1952).
5. O. Fritsch, Ann. Phys. 22, 375 (1935).
6. M. LeBlanc and H. Sachse, Abhandl. Sächs. Akad. Wiss. Leipzig, Math.-naturw. Kl. 1, 82, 133 (1930).
7. H. B. Sachse, Analytical Chemistry 32, 529, April 1960.
8. G. A. Slack and R. Newman, Phys. Rev. Letters 1, 59 (1958).
9. E. J. Verwey, Phil. Tech. Rd. 9, 47, (1947).
10. E. J. Verwey, Phil. Tech. Rd. 10, 232 (1949).
11. E. Yamaka, and K. Sawamoto, Phys. Rev. 112, No. 6, 1861 (1959).
12. A. Zerfoss, R. G. Stokes and C. H. Moore Jr., J. Chem. Phys. 16, 1166 (1948).

DISCUSSION

J. P. CALI (Air Force Cambridge Research Laboratories): Have you tride the potassium-sodium carbonate fusion using pressures of inert atmospheres, rather than a vacuum, in order to suppress oxygen evolution?

H. B. SACHSE (Keystone Carbon): We have done this in nitrogen, at reduced pressure. However we feel that as soon as nitrogen is introduced at normal pressures, then there is the problem of removing the last traces of oxygen.

It might be of interest for those of who have worked in the field of oxide semiconductors to know that Mr. Slack of the General Electric Semiconductor Division sent us a few crystals to analyze. At the same time, the determination of the oxygen surplus in nickel oxide was measured by electrical means using a vacancy diffusion technique. By our method we found 0.32 milliatoms per mole in nickel oxide. The physical method gave a value of 0.30.

M. R. LORENZ (General Electric Research Laboratories): You mentioned a band gap for TiO_2 of 1.65 to 2.07 ev. Are you referring to pure stoichiometric TiO_2? Is this the optical band gap value?

H. B. SACHSE (Keystone Carbon): I referred to stoichiometric TiO_2, and these values refer to the thermal band gap.

TRACE ANALYSIS IN SEMICONDUCTOR
CRYSTALS BY X-RAY DIFFRACTION MICROSCOPY

G. H. Schwuttke
General Telephone and Electronics Laboratories, Inc.
Bayside Laboratories
Bayside 60, New York

ABSTRACT

X-ray diffraction microscopy has been used successfully to reveal dislocation structures in single crystals. In this paper its application in the detection of minute impurities in the semiconductor lattice will be described. The visibility of dislocations is determined chiefly by the angle between the Burger's vector and the Bragg reflecting plane. When the Burger's vector lies in the Bragg reflecting plane, the dislocations are either invisible or have very low visibility. Impurities are known to migrate to dislocations and precipitate along dislocation lines. It will be shown that these precipitates then enhance the visibility of dislocations in the diffraction image and that, consequently, such a contrast change can be used to detect minute impurities. The detection of microsegregation, cluster formation and random precipitation is also possible and will be discussed.

INTRODUCTION

Quite recently the domain of X-ray studies in the field of crystal perfection was greatly extended by the discovery that it is possible to observe individual dislocations by the diffraction of X-rays. Almost simultaneously several investigators published results demonstrating that this new technique, called X-ray diffraction microscopy, is very effective in mapping dislocations in single crystals [1-5]. We have investigated the potentialities of this technique for the detection of impurities in semiconductor crystals and have found that segregation, cluster formation and precipitation exerts a strong influence on the diffraction image [6-8]. In this paper additional information on the application of X-ray diffraction microscopy for the detection of minute traces of impurities in silicon is presented.

434

EXPERIMENTAL

X-ray diffraction microscopy can be performed in two different ways, both leading essentially to the same results. The first is based on the phenomenon of anomalous transmission of X-rays in crystals and the second utilizes the effect of primary extinction of X-rays. The results discussed in this paper were obtained by a method based on the primary extinction effect. Techniques using primary extinction rely upon the fact that strain present in the neighborhood of imperfections reduces the primary extinction otherwise present in a nearly perfect crystal. As a direct consequence of primary extinction it is found that the integrated intensity reflected by a perfect crystal is proportional to the structure factor, while the integrated intensity reflected by an imperfect crystal is proportional to the square of the structure factor. Therefore, an imperfect area in an otherwise perfect crystal will reflect more intensity than its surroundings and can be made visible.

If we consider the diffraction by a slab of a crystal, we have to distinguish between the two cases sketched in Figure 1, (a) the Bragg or reflection case and (b) the Laue or transmission case. In both cases imperfections present in the slab will affect the diffracted beam as explained. A topographic picture of the disturbance present can be obtained if a high-resolution photographic plate is placed as near as possible to the crystal. In the reflection case the film is located in front of the crystal, whereas in the transmission case the film is placed behind the crystal. Disturbances in the lattice can be studied in detail by optical magnification of the photographic image.

The technique selected to conduct our experiments is the transmission method introduced by Lang [4]. In this method a narrow X-ray beam is made to pass through a crystal oriented with suitable crystal planes at the Bragg angle. If crystal and recording film are placed on the same support and are translated in a direction parallel to the film, the beam can be made to scan a considerable area of the crystal. A stationary screen prevents the direct beam from striking the film. The experimental set-up is sketched in Figure 2. Here S_1 is a slit system defining a beam 25 mm in height, C_r is the crystal, S_2 is the stationary slit, and F is the photographic plate.

SAMPLE PREPARATION

The micrographs presented in this paper were taken on Ilford nuclear plates with Mo radiation at 50 kv and 20 ma. Exposure time for 25 mm scanning width, with G-5 emulsion, 100 μ thick, was one hour. The recorded crystal area is thus

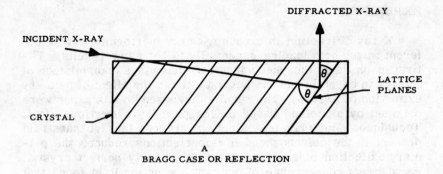

A

BRAGG CASE OR REFLECTION

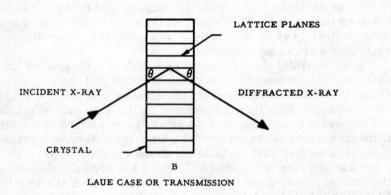

B

LAUE CASE OR TRANSMISSION

Figure 1. Bragg and Laue Case for Reflection of X-Rays.

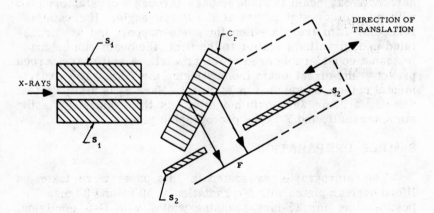

Figure 2. Experimental Set-Up.

25 mm^2. The silicon wafers were cut from the bulk material approximately 1.2 mm thick, as sketched in Figure 3. The large

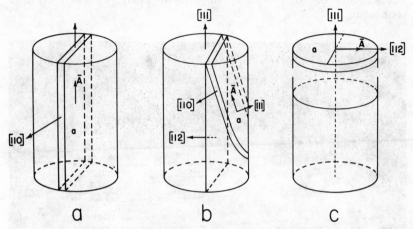

Figure 3. Orientation of Crystal Wafers Relative to Bulk Crystal.

lateral face, a in Figure 3, is a low index face such as (111), (110), (112), or (100); the face was oriented optically to better than 1/2 degree of arc [9]. After cutting and lapping, the wafers were etched for approximately 5 minutes in a solution of 5 parts HNO$_3$, 3 parts HF and 5 parts acetic acid to remove the surface layer. After etching, the crystal thickness was ~1 mm. The photographic plate was placed perpendicular to the diffracted beam.

Infrared pictures were taken for comparison with the X-ray micrographs. These were obtained with a closed-circuit TV system equipped with an infrared sensitive videcon connected to a microscope [10].

OBSERVATIONS AND DISCUSSION

Segregation

Segregation effects are conveniently studied in silicon crystals pulled from a quartz crucible. Since such crystals are known to contain oxygen, microsegregation can be observed [11]. Figure 4 is an X-ray diffraction micrograph of a silicon crystal. The wafer was cut from a crystal grown in the (100) direction as shown in Figure 3a. The picture was obtained by reflecting the X-rays from planes perpendicular to the growth axis. The striations observed run perpendicular to the growth axis and are due to segregation of oxygen [7, 12]. The sensitivity of this method is comparable to that of the 9 μ absorption method [13]. Variations of oxygen concentration, computed from the absorption coefficient, of 10^{16} atoms cm^{-3} have been recorded by this technique.

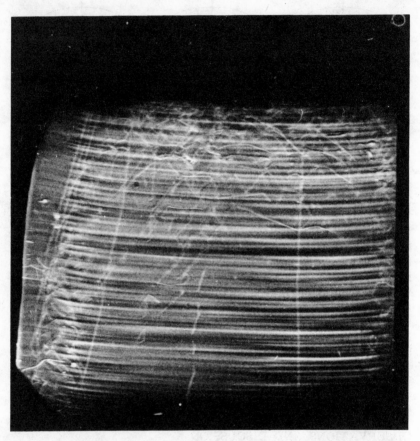

Figure 4. Oxygen Segregation in Silicon. Reflection Perpendicular to Growth Axis. Crystal Cut According to Figure 3a.

Figure 5 shows an X-ray image of the same crystal wafer as seen in Figure 4; in this case, however, the image was obtained by reflecting the X-rays from planes parallel to the growth direction. It is interesting to observe that for this reflection the oxygen striations are not visible.

If silicon containing oxygen is heat treated at 1000°C for several hours, the oxygen is known to precipitate as SiO_2 and form clusters [11]. Figure 6 is an X-ray picture of a silicon wafer heat treated at 1000°C for several hours. The striations

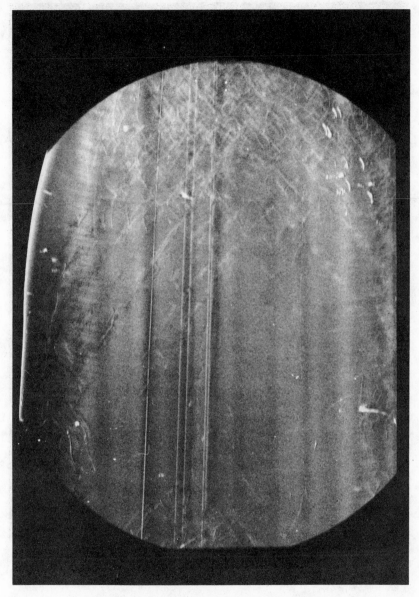

Figure 5. Oxygen Segregation in Silicon.
Reflection Parallel to Growth Axis.

now appear much sharper and in addition are visible in reflections both parallel and perpendicular to the growth axis. This effect has an important consequence in that it is possible to differentiate between impurities in solution, e.g., oxygen in silicon

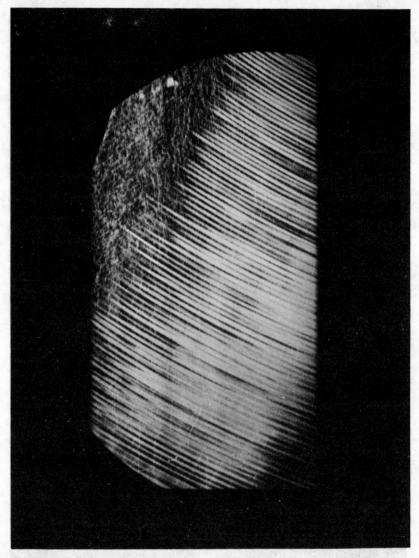

Figure 6. SiO$_2$-Clusters in Silicon After Heat-Treatment
of Wafer at 1000°C. (220)-Type Reflection.

before the heat treatment, and precipitated impurities, e.g., SiO$_2$ in silicon after heat treatment. By means of this effect, for instance, we were able to conclude that As in a highly doped germanium crystal, showing strong microsegregation, did not form a second phase [14].

PRECIPITATION

Precipitation effects were investigated in silicon containing copper precipitates. In such crystals X-ray results can be verified directly by infrared microscopy. Figure 7 represents an

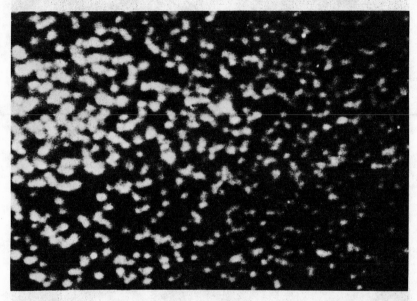

Figure 7. Precipitation of Copper in Silicon of Zero Dislocation Density. (220)-Type Reflection. Crystal Cut According to Figure 3c.

X-ray image of a silicon wafer of zero dislocation density after copper was diffused into it at 900°C for 15 minutes and subsequently quenched to room temperature within a few seconds to achieve precipitation. The solubility of copper in silicon at 900°C has been given by Struthers [15] as 10^{17} atoms cm^{-3}. Since no care was taken to obtain saturation, the concentration of copper in this sample is probably smaller than 10^{17} atoms cm^{-3}. Figure 8 is an infrared picture of the same crystal shown for comparison. In both the X-ray picture and the infrared picture, random precipitation is clearly visible.

Another example of precipitation is seen in Figure 9. The silicon wafer shown in this diffraction image contains approximately 10^{18} copper atoms/cm^3. The diffusion temperature was 1200°C. Interesting details are revealed: heavy precipitation in certain areas is observed; large clusters have formed in some spots, and precipitation along dislocation lines is found. Figure 10 is an infrared picture of the same wafer for comparison.

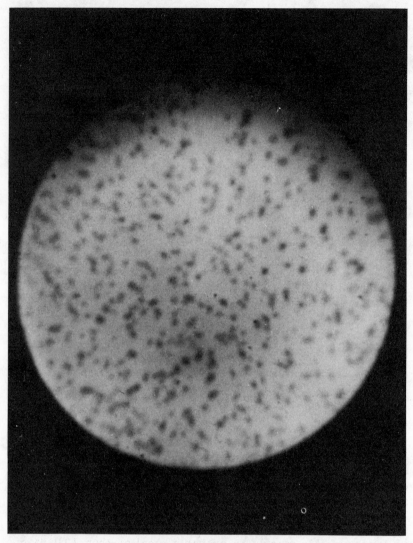

Figure 8. Infrared Photomicrograph of Silicon
Wafer Shown in Figure 7.

DISLOCATIONS

Figure 11 is a diffraction micrograph taken using (220) type
planes; it shows dislocations lying in a (111) slip plane. Figure 3a explains how the wafer was cut from the bulk crystal.
The slice is a 1.2 mm thick cut from a crystal grown in the (111)
direction parallel to one of the three octahedral planes that make

442

Figure 9. Copper Precipitation in Silicon. (111)-Type
Reflection. Crystal Cut According to Figure 3a.

an angle of 19-1/2 degrees with the (111) growth direction. In
cooling the crystal during growth, slip occurred in the octahedral
planes introducing the dislocations seen in the micrograph.

Dislocations propagated by growth from the seed into the
crystal (the seed was near the smaller end) are seen in Figure 12.
The wafer is a 1.2 mm thick cut parallel to a (112) plane containing the (111) growth axis as shown in Figure 3b. The dislocations introduced through the seed grow out with the growing
crystal. Some edge-type dislocation, generated by plastic deformation are also seen in the micrograph. The picture is a
result of using (220) type planes for the reflection of X-rays.

The visibility of individual dislocation lines in the diffraction micrograph is determined by dislocation density and orientation of the dislocation line relative to the reflecting net plane.
Dislocation lines are recorded photographically as lines of enhanced intensity. As mentioned previously, this is a consequence
of the difference in the integrated intensity reflected by a "perfect" and an "imperfect" crystal area. Therefore the dislocation density must be low enough for these lines to be individually
distinguishable, and low enough so that the regions between dislocations are sufficiently perfect to approximate the conditions
of diffraction by a perfect crystal.

443

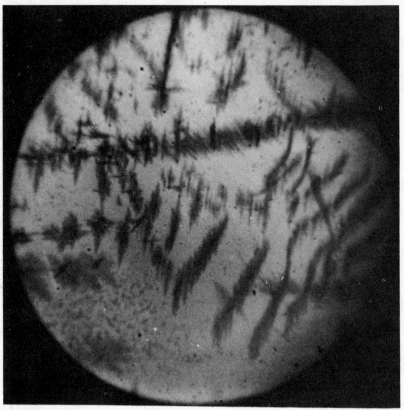

Figure 10. Infrared Picture of Crystal Shown in Figure 9.

Dislocations produce a maximum of enhanced intensity in the X-ray image when the latter arises from Bragg reflection against a plane perpendicular to the Burger's vector [4]. If the Burger's vector is parallel to the reflecting net-plane, the line is invisible or only very slightly visible in the image. This is seen very clearly in Figure 13 which represents two different (220) reflections of a silicon wafer cut in accordance with Figure 3b. The change in dislocation contrast is especially distinct for the dislocation loops in the lower halves of the pictures.

Our investigations lead to the conclusion that the usual rule describing the visibility of dislocations breaks down if impurities have precipitated along dislocation lines. Consequently, an excellent means is provided to find minute traces of impurities since impurities are known to migrate to dislocation lines and to precipitate along them. This is demonstrated in Figure 14. This figure shows a section of silicon wafer containing a dislocation group which is clearly visible in 14a but not visible in 14b because a different reflection was used. The dislocation group

444

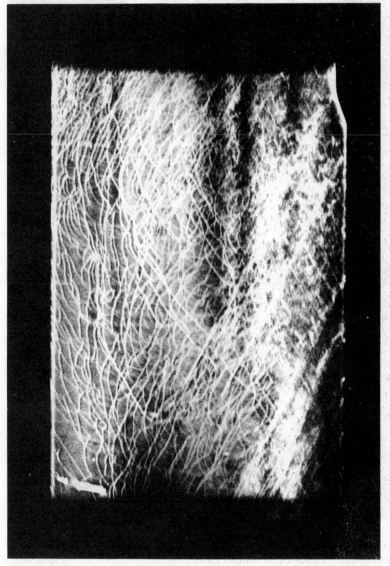

Figure 11. Dislocations in Octahedral Plane. (220)-Type Reflection. Crystal Cut According to Figure 3b.

Figure 12. Dislocations Propagated by Growth and Dislocations
Introduced by Plastic Deformation. Crystal Cut According to
Figure 3a. (220)-Type Reflection.

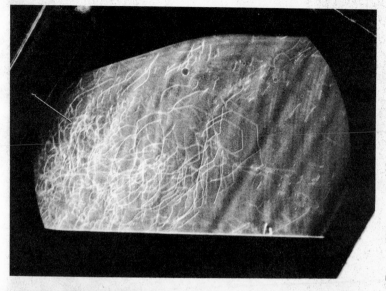

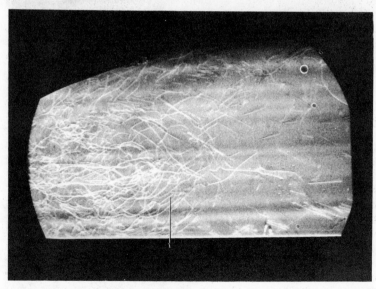

Figure 13. Visibility of Dislocations Depending on Different Reflections. Diffraction Vector given by Arrow. Crystal Cut According to Figure 3b.

447

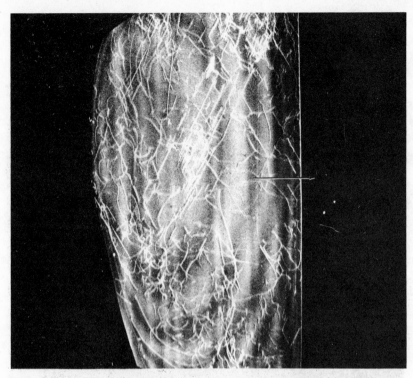

Figure 14. Change in Contrast of Dislocations in Diffraction Image Induced by Precipitates. a - Before Copper Diffusion, Dislocation Group Visible. Crystal Cut According to Figure 3b. Diffraction Vector given by Arrow. (220)-Type Reflection.

seen in 14a was generated by plastic deformation; therefore one can assume that these dislocations are relatively free of impurities. The micrograph shown in Figure 14c is that of the X-ray image of the same wafer after copper diffusion at 900°C for ten minutes and subsequent quenching to room temperature within seconds to achieve precipitation. The X-ray image of 14c is identical with that of 14b except that it was taken before copper diffusion. The dislocation group and several other dislocations not seen in 14b have become clearly visible in 14c due to copper precipitation along the dislocation lines.

The effect just described can be used for trace analysis because minute traces of impurities along dislocations can be found with extreme sensitivity. Figure 15 shows an infrared picture of a dislocation line containing copper precipitates. From size and spacing of the copper needles the maximum number of copper atoms along a 1-cm dislocation line can be estimated to be not larger than 10^{15} atoms, assuming the

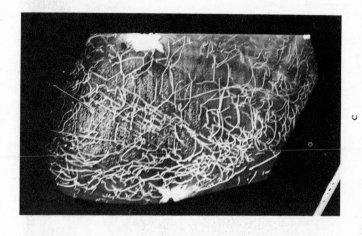

c

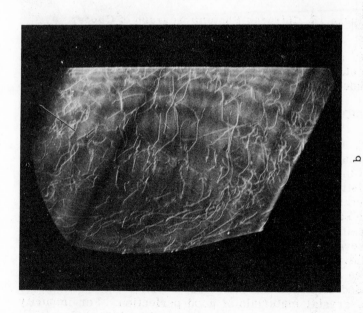

b

Figure 14. Change in Contrast of Dislocations in Diffraction Image Induced by Precipitates. b--Before Copper Diffusion, Dislocation Group Not Visible; c--The Same Picture as (b) but After Copper Diffusion. Dislocation Group Visible.

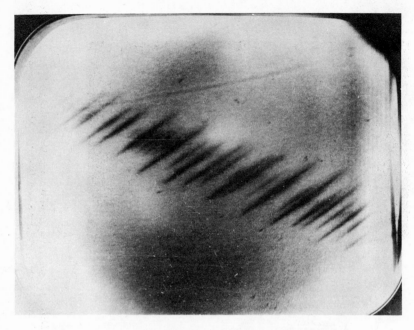

Figure 15. Infrared Photomicrograph of Copper
Precipitation Along Dislocation Line.

precipitate to be pure copper. We have found that this concentration is sufficient to nullify the usual rule describing the conditions under which dislocations in an X-ray image are visible.

CONCLUSIONS

X-ray diffraction microscopy by extinction contrast has been demonstrated to be quite effective in the detection of minute traces of impurities in the semiconductor lattice. The technique has the distinct advantage that it is non-destructive, and therefore structure defects can be correlated with electrical properties of the same sample. The method is a very general one. It is not possible to identify the kinds of impurities, but it is possible to reveal their presence and their distribution throughout the crystal. Precipitation, segregation and cluster formation can also be detected. The high sensitivity of the method enables it to be used for trace analysis. The technique is applicable to all single crystal materials of good perfection. For impurity studies the dislocation density should not exceed 10^4 dislocation/cm^2. This is not a severe restriction for semiconductor crystals since in this field the art of crystal growing is well advanced.

The technique is relatively simple to handle and requires only moderate additions to standard X-ray equipment.

It should be a powerful tool for the investigation of preferential segregation of impurities [16], the study of diffusion of impurities along dislocation lines and their subsequent precipitation [17], and the study of formation of metal precipitates in junctions [18]. The method has been used successfully for impurity studies in Ge, Si, and GaAs.

ACKNOWLEDGMENT

The author gladly thanks Dr. P. H. Keck for advice and encouragement, Mr. E. Jungbluth and Mr. R. Modena for the help in performing the measurements and Mr. P. K. Marshall for growing most of the silicon crystals.

The research reported in this paper was sponsored by the Electronics Research Directorate of the Air Force Cambridge Research Laboratories, Air Force Research Division, Air Research and Development Command, under Contract Number AF 19(604) 7313.

REFERENCES

1. G. Borrmann, W. Hartwig and H. Irmler, Z. f. Naturforschung 13a, 423 (1958).
2. H. Barth and R. Hosemann, Z. f. Naturforschung 13a, 792 (1958).
3. J. B. Newkirk, Phys. Rev. 110, 1465 (1958).
4. A. R. Lang, J. Appl. Phys. 29, 597 (1958), J. Appl. Phys. 30, 1748 (1959).
5. U. Bonse, Z. f. Physik 153, 978 (1958).
6. G. H. Schwuttke, Semiconductor Symp. ECS, Spring Mtg. 1960, Chicago, Ill., Fall Mtg. 1960, Houston, Texas.
7. G. H. Schwuttke, J. Electrochem. Soc., 108, 163 (1961).
8. G. H. Schwuttke, AIME Symp. on Direct Observation of Imperfections, March 1961, St. Louis, Mo.
9. G. H. Schwuttke, J. Electrochem. Soc., 106, 315 (1959).
10. G. H. Schwuttke, Sylvania Technologist, XIII, 122, (1960).
11. W. Kaiser, P. H. Keck, C. F. Lange, Phys. Rev. 101, 1264 (1956).
12. G. H. Schwuttke, P. H. Keck, O. Weinreich, J. Electrochem. Soc., 105, 706 (1958).
13. W. Kaiser, P. H. Keck, J. Appl. Phys. 28, 882 (1957).
14. G. H. Schwuttke, Semiconductor Symp. ECS, Spring Mtg. 1961, Indianapolis, Indiana.
15. J. D. Struthers, J. Appl. Phys. 27, 1560 (1956).
16. J. A. M. Dickhoff, Solid State Electronics, 1, 202 (1960).
17. R. Bullough, R. C. Newman, J. Wakefield and J. B. Willis, J. Appl. Phys. 31, 707 (1960).
18. A. Geotzberger and W. Shockley, J. Appl. Phys. 31, 1821 (1960).

DISCUSSION

B. SELIKSON (Raytheon): Will you explain why the photographs in the first series, (Figures 4-6), all show the lines as quite regular and parallel to each other, whereas in the following photographs, (Figures 11-15), they are shown crossing each other?

G. H. SCHWUTTKE (General Telephone and Electronics Laboratories): This effect is due primarily to the directions in which the crystals were cut.

C. H. LI (General Instrument): Can you identify the impurities by noting the rates of precipitation at different temperatures? Each impurity presumably would precipitate with different activation energies.

G. H. SCHWUTTKE (General Telephone and Electronics Laboratories): In this case, you would have to follow the precipitation behavior as a function of temperature. This is a possibility, but has not been done at our laboratory.

C. H. LI (General Instrument): There are some data in the literature showing different activation energies. It is not particularly related to silicon, but the phenomenon is more or less the same.

E. A. LEARY (Martin Company): You referred to the method as non-destructive, and you are using a transmission technique. How thick is that slab?

G. H. SCHWUTTKE (General Telephone and Electronics Laboratories): Well, this depends on several factors. First of all, the kind of material is important; second, the kind of radiation used. Since maximum contrast is required, so that the imperfections show up as clearly as possible, one chooses the crystal's thickness so that the product of the absorption coefficient times crystal thickness approximates one for this particular technique.

E. A. LEARY (Martin Company): You were using molybdenum radiation?

G. H. SCHWUTTKE (General Telephone and Electronics Laboratories): Yes. But if one chooses, say tungsten radiation, penetrations of 10 millimeters of silicon are possible and the contrast is still good.

M. J. VOGEL (IBM): In single crystals of electroluminescent zinc sulphide phosphors, the banding was also noted by Goldberg. Have you examined this type of single crystal for the precipitation of copper? Crystals which are electroluminescent contain copper and chlorine and the location of the copper is a problem.

452

G. H. SCHWUTTKE (General Telephone and Electronics Laboratories): Not as yet, but we are working on this and if precipitation exists, then we should be able to find it.

L. R. WEISBERG (RCA Laboratories): Do you have any correlations between your observations and changes in the electrical properties of these crystals?

G. H. SCHWUTTKE (General Telephone and Electronics Laboratories): We have done some investigations aimed at finding preferential segregation and have results where the visual image shows the difference of impurity concentration. This can be correlated with electrical properties.

METHODS FOR THE DETERMINATION
OF SELENIUM IN ARSENIC, GALLIUM,
AND GALLIUM ARSENIDE

E. L. Bush and E. H. Cornish
Standard Telecommunication Laboratories, Ltd.
Harlow, Essex, England

ABSTRACT

Two methods for the determination of selenium are described. The first, a colorimetric method involving the use of asymmetric diphenylhydrazine, has a sensitivity of 0.1 μg of selenium in one drop. The reagent blank is low so that a gallium arsenide sample weight of 10g or more could probably be used.

The second method is polarographic, and involves the use of arsenic acid as a base electrolyte when analysing elementary arsenic or gallium arsenide. In this electrolyte the maximum sensitivity is 0.005 μg. With gallium, a hydrochloric acid electrolyte is used and the sensitivity is then 0.02 μg. Although heavy metals and oxidising agents may cause interferences in the method, these can be eliminated by the procedures described.

INTRODUCTION

Selenium, as indeed are all the Gp VI elements, is an important n-type dopant in the Gp 3/5 compound semiconductors. Although it is not so commonly distributed as are, for example, oxygen and sulphur, its analysis is by comparison fairly simple because the selenium content of reagents is generally low, leading to desirably low blank values. Various methods have been recorded for the determination of selenium. Amongst the most sensitive which may be mentioned is that in which selenious acid is reduced by iodide in acid solution to elementary selenium [7]. Using this method, 1 μg can be detected.

Another colorimetric method involves the oxidation of pyrrole to the dyestuff pyrrole blue by selenious acid. When carried out in concentrated phosphoric acid solution, the sensitivity is maximised by the addition of ferric ions, and is then 0.5 μg of selenium [1]. Selenide ions in solution are able catalytically to increase the reduction rate of methylene blue by sulphide ions. In this test 0.08 μg of selenium has been detected [6].

454

Yet another colorimetric test, of even greater sensitivity, (0.05 μg) is that in which selenious acid is used to oxidise asymmetric diphenylhydrazine to produce the violet coloured quinoneanildiphenylhydrazone [5]. This method was further developed in the present study.

Another, less sensitive, test for selenious acid involves the precipitation of free selenium from a selenite solution by solid thiourea [4] which has an identification limit of 2 μg. In this method tellurium interferes although 5 μg of selenium may be detected in the presence of 25 μg of the former element.

Another method produces a red-blue fluorescent precipitate when a solution of 10% thiourea is added [3]. Heavy metals do not interfere, and the identification limit is 5 μg of selenium.

1, 8 naphthylene diamine reacts in acetic acid solution with selenites to yield a brown product, the detection limit of which is 1 μg as selenium dioxide [8].

These methods are all largely independent of the presence of tellurium and may, indeed, be used for the analysis of tellurium for selenium. All are semi-quantitative since the final colour measurement is by eye and is not instrumental.

It was felt that none of these methods was sufficiently sensitive or suitable for application to gallium arsenide analysis, although the method of Cheng [2] using the reagent 3 3' diaminobenzidine has been applied to the analysis of metals, including arsenic, and can be used to measure down to 0.03 ppm of selenium in a 20 g sample, using a spectrophotometric finish.

The method of Cheng was used to analyse some samples of selenium which had been separated from an arsenic matrix using a tellurium carrier. It was found however that the lower limit of detection was only 1 μg. It was not felt desirable to increase sensitivity by increasing the sample size substantially above 1 g in view of the small amounts of material which are produced in many experiments on semiconducting compounds.

EXPERIMENTAL

1. The Asymmetric Diphenylhydrazine Method

This method was selected as being potentially the most sensitive. Although the reaction with selenium is not specific, it is possible to detect 0.05 μg of selenium by using precautions to avoid interferences. Iodates, permanganates, bromates, peroxides, tungstates, molybdates, ferric and cupric salts interfere [9]. If these are present, they may be removed by evaporation of the sample solution with concentrated hydrochloric acid followed by treatment with a solution containing oxalic acid and ethylene diamine tetracetic acid. This procedure destroys

the oxidising acids and complexes the metal ions. As this hydrazine reagent gives no reaction with oxides of tellurium, it seemed
desirable to use this latter element as a carrier for the initial
separation of the small amount of selenium which is likely to be
present in the samples being analysed. In this way the final test
liquid volume could be kept small, and the main bulk of gallium
and arsenic would be removed. In fact, the method finally adopted
to separate the selenium from the matrix element was that due
to Veale [9]. The method as applied to arsenic or gallium arsenide was to dissolve in a minimum quantity of warm aqua regia,
about 10 ml being suitable for a 1 - 2 g sample; to this was added
a solution of 1 mg of tellurium as tellurite. The mixture was
evaporated to a syrup, avoiding overheating which would tend to
convert the arsenic present to a less-readily soluble pyroarsenic
acid. The residue, after solution in 2N hydrochloric acid, was
reduced with hydrazine hydrochloride by heating first momentarily to the boiling point and then maintaining at 60°C for one
hour. This ensured complete reduction to elementary selenium
and tellurium. After cooling and centrifuging, the supernatant
liquid containing gallium and arsenic was discarded, and the
precipitate washed to remove any contamination by these elements. The residue was then dissolved in one drop of concentrated nitric acid to oxidize selenium to selenious acid and the
solution was evaporated just to dryness.

Recovery of selenium by this technique was checked using
radioactive selenium 75 as a tracer. The method employed was
to dissolve 1 g of gallium arsenide in 1:1 hydrochloric acid/nitric
acid mixture. To this was added about 1 μg of radioactive
selenium of known activity. A solution containing 1 mg of tellurium was also added. After carrying out the separation procedure, the activities of both the precipitate and of the supernatant liquid were checked. The recovery of selenium varied
between 94% and 105% in six determinations. The activity found
in the supernatant liquid was in every case negligible.

This method differed from that of Veale in that the use of
sulphuric acid was avoided. Veale employed this reagent to remove excess nitric acid, and to bring about complete precipitation of relatively large amounts of tellurium. In the present
case only small amounts of tellurium were to be precipitated
and to effect this an excess of the hydrazine reductant was employed. Furthermore, the use of such a large amount of sulphuric acid would have given a very high blank value for selenium.
In the reduction procedure described both arsenic and gallium
remain in solution, since the reduction conditions are not such
as would precipitate them.

The test drop of solution, which may have been treated with
hydrochloric, oxalic and ethylene diamine tetracetic acids as

necessary to remove interfering ions, was then transferred to a porcelain plate which had been treated with a silicone fluid to eliminate wetting and drop spreading. To this solution were added two drops of asymmetric diphenylhydrazine in glacial acetic acid. In parallel with the test solution were run solutions of known selenium concentration. After 5 - 10 minutes of colour development, the colour of the test sample was then compared visually with that of the range of standards. The reagent blank was normally less than 0.1 μg.

Using this technique it proved possible to detect 0.1 μg selenium present in one drop. Thus, using a 2g sample of gallium arsenide, the detection limit is 0.05 ppm. As the reagent blank is reasonably low, it is considered that a sample of 10 g or more of gallium arsenide could perhaps be processed without significant loss of sensitivity.

Although a reflectometer could be used to measure the drop colours instrumentally, it was felt that such a procedure would be unsatisfactory in view of the stringent timing required and the temperature control which would be necessary to ensure reproducible colour formation. For this reason, an alternative method for analysis of selenium was turned to.

2. Polarographic Methods

The application of the cathode-ray polarograph to the determination of selenium seemed particularly attractive as arsenic acid itself is a suitable electrolyte for selenium. In this way it proved possible, in the case of arsenic samples, to avoid a separation of the type carried out during the colorimetric test. In the method finally adopted, the arsenic sample of 1 g was dissolved in aqua regia and repeatedly evaporated with nitric acid to ensure complete oxidation of the tri-valent arsenic. The residue was diluted with 4 ml of water and the cathodic selenium wave measured at the peak potential of -0.85 v. Tri-valent arsenic at -0.95 v, and particularly lead at -0.75 v, did not give troublesome interference since both these contaminants can be shown up anodically as waves and their amounts compensated for. The maximum sensitivity of this method was 0.005 μg of selenium. With more than a 1 g sample of arsenic, spurious waves were obtained at about -1.0 volts, the leading edge of which interfered with the selenium wave. It was not always possible to reproduce these spurious waves and indeed a 1.5g sample of arsenic has been processed without their appearing, but it was felt best to standardise on a sample weight of 1 g to avoid the possibility of interferences from this source.

In the case of gallium alone, the most suitable base electrolyte is hydrochloric acid, the concentration of which must be not less than 0.5 N in order to avoid the precipitation of a basic

457

gallium nitrate during the initial solution in aqua regia. The excess nitric acid is removed by two evaporations with added hydrochloric acid. The final electrolyte acid concentration is not critical, but can lie suitably in the range 0.5 - 1 N. In this electrolyte the height of the selenium wave is not so great as in arsenic acid, so that the detection limit is raised to 0.02 μg, the peak potential of the selenium wave being at -0.42 volts. The limit of sample size which can be used is 0.5 g. This is because spurious waves sometimes appear as in the case of arsenic; this raises the detection limit to 0.04 ppm.

Aqua regia is also used as an initial solvent for gallium arsenide samples. The excess nitric acid is removed by evaporation with hydrochloric acid. It is of course essential to remove the nitric acid to avoid precipitation of a basic gallium nitrate. With 6.7N (constant boiling) hydrochloric acid, after making up the sample volume to 5 ml, the gallium is extracted with di-isopropyl ether which has previously been equilibrated with 6N hydrochloric acid. In this extraction process, more than 99% of the gallium is removed into the organic layer. The liquid is centrifuged to remove droplets of gallium-containing solvent from the aqueous phase, and the bottom layer is separated and oxidised with two drops of nitric acid, then evaporated. As this phase now contains all the arsenic and none of the gallium, it can be treated as a simple arsenic sample, provided the nitric acid oxidation is carefully carried out to remove excess organic solvent which can, if present, give rise to spurious interfering waves. The oxidation could also be carried out by perchloric acid, but there may be difficulties in purifying this reagent, so that nitric acid is to be preferred. As gallium arsenide contains approximately 50% of arsenic, a 2g sample may be used, giving a final solution which is equivalent to a 1g sample of arsenic. The sensitivity for selenium in this method is again 0.005 μg, i.e., 0.0025 ppm for a 2g sample.

INTERFERENCES

In the polarographic methods described, traces of tellurium do not interfere, but the tellurium carrier technique used in the colorimetric tests cannot be used as the ratio of tellurium to selenium would then be excessive.

In the arsenic acid electrolyte, tri-valent arsenic at -0.95 volts and particularly lead at -0.75 volts can be shown up anodically, and hence their interference with the selenium wave be compensated for. However, in the hydrochloric acid electrolyte these interfering waves have relatively more effect because the selenium wave is smaller. Other likely impurity elements in gallium, arsenic or gallium arsenide do not interfere, as their waves are well separated from that of selenium.

RESULTS

Table 1 shows some results which have been obtained, using both methods of analysis and several different samples of gallium, arsenic and gallium arsenide. Agreement between the two methods is reasonable.

Table I

Selenium Content of Samples

Sample	Colorimetric method (ppm)	Polarographic method (ppm)
Gallium 1	< 0.05	< 0.04
2	-	< 0.04
Arsenic 1	0.1	-
2	< 0.05	0.005
3	-	0.005
4	2.5	2.7
5	6	-
Arsenic trioxide	3.3	3.0
Gallium arsenide 1	0.6	0.5
2	-	0.5
3	-	0.005
4	-	0.005

CONCLUSIONS

Two methods are described, which are applicable to the determination of selenium in arsenic, gallium and gallium arsenide. The colorimetric method has a sensitivity of 0.05 ppm for a 2 g sample, although it is probable that this could be increased by using a larger sample weight. The method has the advantage of simplicity, and few resources are needed to carry it out. The disadvantage is that it is not really suitable for an instrumental finish, and relies purely on a visual comparison of a sample colour with a set of standards. A colour comparison chart could not be made to represent these standards as the colour produced depends to some extent on the concentration and age of the reagent, and the time and temperature for colour development.

In the polarographic analysis of samples which on dissolution yield unsuitable electrolytes or interfering waves, the tellurium carrier method described could probably be used for an

459

initial separation of selenium from the matrix. Final separation from excess tellurium could then be achieved by oxidation and paper chromatography of the anions. Using a butanol-methanol mixture, a tellurite remains at the starting point of the chromatogram while the selenite travels sufficiently for a clean separation to be made.

The polarographic method described has the advantage of greater sensitivity in the cases of arsenic and of gallium arsenide, although some samples of gallium arsenide have been shown to contain the lowest concentration of selenium which can be detected. It is felt therefore that any further development in the production of semiconductor-purity gallium arsenide will need a parallel development of sensitivity of the method.

ACKNOWLEDGMENT

Thanks are due to **Mr. G. King**, Director of Research of Standard Telecommunication Laboratories, for permission to publish this paper.

REFERENCES

1. R. Berg and M. Teitelbaum, Mikrochemie (Emich Festschrist) 23 (1930)
2. K. L. Cheng, Anal. Chem., 28, 1738 (1956)
3. M. H. Evans, Chem Abstracts, 32, 8299 (1938)
4. P. Falciola, Chem Abstracts, 21, 3580 (1927)
5. F. Feigl and V. Demant, Mikrochim. Acta, 1, 322 (1937)
6. F. Feigl and Ph. W. West, Anal. Chem, 19, 351 (1947)
7. N. S. Poluektoff, Mikrochemie, 15, 32 (1934)
8. F. Feigl, "Spot Tests" Elsevier Publishing Company London (1954) p. 321
9. C. R. Veale, The Analyst, 85, 133 (1960)

DISCUSSION

M. C. GARDELS (MIT, Lincoln Laboratory): In your paper you mention oxidizing the arsenic to the plus 5 state. Did this not oxidize the selenium any higher than a plus 4 state, or is selenium being reduced at the electrode?

E. H. CORNISH (Standard Telecommunication Laboratories, England): No, we are reducing at the electrode and under these conditions there is no problem with oxidation.

D. H. WILKINS (General Electric): What volume sample are you running on the polarograph?

E. H. CORNISH (Standard Telecommunication Laboratories, England): In the work I have described it was 4 milliliters, but we are now working on a microcell which requires only 0.2 milliliter, which will materially help, of course, in reducing the blank.

A NEW METHOD FOR THE DETERMINATION OF MICROQUANTITIES OF CARBON IN SEMICONDUCTORS: APPLICATION TO SILICON AND GERMANIUM

L. Ducret and C. Cornet
Centre National d'Etudes des Telecommunications
Issy les Moulineaux, Seine, France

INTRODUCTION

The sensitivity of the classical method for the analysis of carbon, which consists in the determination of the amount of carbon dioxide formed after oxidation of material under analysis, is insufficient for the determination of carbon traces in high purity semiconductor materials. By substituting sulfur for oxygen, a method with much higher sensitivity has been developed. The principle of the method is as follows: if, by reaction with sulfur vapor at a suitable temperature and pressure, the material undergoing analysis is converted to sulfides, it is probable that carbon traces are quantitatively and parallelly converted to carbon disulfide since these elements combine rather easily. The quantitative determination of this substance, which can be collected by dissolution in an organic solvent, has been the object of many studies and its determination in trace quantities in diverse solvents has become a classic one. The limit of sensitivity of the method is of the order of one p.p.m.

The general operational scheme for the determination is the following: the material to be analyzed, in pulverized form or otherwise, is placed, along with a small excess of pure sulfur, under vacuum in a quartz or glass tube. This tube is heated to a temperature suitable for the formation of the sulfides of the principle constituents, as well as carbon disulfide. After cooling, one extremity of the tube is broken within an organic solvent such as benzene which rises into the tube and dissolves the traces of carbon disulfide present. The quantitative determination of this compound is then carried out by the Higgins-Pollard method, which consists in reacting the carbon disulfide with diethylamine to form diethyl-dithiocarbamic acid according to the following reaction:

$$CS_2 + HN\begin{matrix} C_2H_5 \\ \\ C_2H_5 \end{matrix} \longrightarrow S=C\begin{matrix} SH \\ \\ C_2H_5 \\ N \\ C_2H_5 \end{matrix}$$

With certain metallic cations, such as the cupric ion, this acid forms colored salts soluble in benzene and suitable for colorimetric analysis.

APPLICATION TO SILICON

The method of operation described is taken partly from the work of Gabriel and Alvarez-Tostado [1]. These authors have shown that silicon and sulfur combine directly, but with some difficulty. The reaction,

$$Si + 2S \longrightarrow SiS_2 + 59.9 \text{ kcal.}$$

takes place at elevated temperatures and requires a glass wool catalyst. We have found that the reaction takes place in the presence of quartz wool at $1000°C$. At this temperature the vapor pressure of sulfur (diatomic at $1000°$) is several atmospheres. Under these conditions the formation of carbon disulfide is greatly enhanced. It is well known that these elements combine easily over a rather large temperature range, thus rough limits of 600 to $1300°C$ can be fixed. The temperature and speed of reaction depend essentially upon the physical state of the carbon and the vapor pressure of the sulfur. This has been shown by Markovskii [2], Stull [3], Trotter [4], and the kinetic studies of Guerin and Adam-Gironne [5,6].

I. EXPERIMENTAL

In the following, it should be noted that the major precautions taken are those to avoid contamination by carbon from atmospheric dust and from the normal handling of the tubes.

a. Sample Preparation

Before grinding the silicon, the agate mortar and pestle, the screen and the spatulas are washed in a chlorinated solvent such as dichloroethane, then in pure alcohol and rinsed in double-distilled water (quartz distilling apparatus). These are then dried in a dessicator. The silicon is then ground within a glove box without ventilation and sifted (screen 19, AFNOR).

The sulfur is prepared by adding an excess of reagent grade hydrochloric acid to a solution of sodium thiosulfate. The resulting sulfur is filtered in a glass crucible through a No. 4 fritted disc, rinsed with double-distilled water and dried in a desiccator.

b. Preparation of Quartz Tubes

The quartz tubes which are often made by compression through a graphite template, are initially heated for one hour at 800°C in a stream of oxygen. The quartz wool employed is subjected to the same treatment.

The initial dimensions of a typical reaction tube are as follows: 15 cm in length, 0.7 cm interior diameter and 0.9 cm exterior diameter. At one extremity of such a tube a "swan's neck" with an open point is formed. A female standard taper joint is formed at the other extremity. After these operations the tube is reheated at 800°C in a stream of oxygen. After cooling and immediately upon leaving the furnace, the tube is sealed at the standard taper end with a quartz wool plug and the point of the swan's neck is sealed.

c. Tube Filling

The quartz wool plug is pushed to the bottom of each tube and the pulverized silicon and the sulfur are placed in contact with it. The amount of silicon placed in the tubes is based upon the experimental fact that "pure" silicon contains approximately 500 p.p.m. of carbon. For each analysis 3 samples of 5, 10, and 15 mg of silicon each and a constant excess of sulfur are placed in the tubes. These are then sealed under vacuum (10^{-2} mm Hg) at a length of about 10 cm. The filled tubes are then heated between 1000 and 1100°C for one hour. The formation of small white platelets of silicon sulfide is evidence that a reaction has taken place.

d. Carbon Disulfide Analysis

When cool, the swan's neck is broken in a polyethylene beaker containing 4 ml of reagent grade benzene. The liquid then rises into the tube nearly completely filling it. Care is taken to orient the tube so that the total wall area comes into contact with the benzene. The other end of the tube is then broken and the benzene placed in a separatory funnel. The tube and the beaker are then rinsed with 2 ml of benzene which is also placed in the separatory funnel.

Five ml of a solution of sodium hydroxide (approx. 1 N) are placed in the above and thoroughly stirred in order to eliminate any traces of hydrogen sulfide formed by the hydrolysis of the silicon sulfide in the small amounts of water contained in the solvent and the atmosphere. The benzene is then mixed with 5 ml of double-distilled water. Note here that verification has shown that these operations do not eliminate any trace of carbon disulfide.

Five drops of diethylamine are added to the benzene solution. This is agitated for one minute with 5 ml of a 1 % aqueous solution of copper sulfate. The mixture is then decanted for 15 min. in the absence of light and the separated organic layer is diluted to exactly 10 ml. If the optical density of the above is too large, one ml is diluted, say, five times.

The colorimetric analysis is done with a Jean-Constant apparatus at 435 mμ in a one cm cell. A control is made under the same conditions using pure benzene. The calibration is made in the following way: a titrated solution of carbon disulfide in benzene (about 1 gm. per liter) is prepared and weighed into a volumetric flask. Using various dilutions a calibration curve is drawn.

II. RESULTS

a. A test performed by placing sulfur only in the reaction tube gave zero for carbon disulfide analysis.

b. The following table lists the results for two typical analyses.

	Sample weight (mg)	Optical density (after dilution)	Carbon content (in p.p.m.)
	5	0.063	1355
Silicon A	10	0.120	1290
	15	0.185	1330

(no dilution)

	5	0.210	903
Silicon B	10	0.395	850
	15	0.605	866

The carbon content of diverse silicon semiconductor samples analyzed varies between 500 and 2000 p.p.m.

c. The verification of the method was carried out in the following way: the analysis if a silicon sample revealed the presence of 1700 ± 50 p.p.m. of carbon. This sample was then

464

used to pull a 20 gm crystal doped by adding silicon carbide such that the carbon content would increase by 1000 p.p.m. The crystal was then treated as indicated above and the new analysis showed 2700 ± 70 p.p.m. of carbon.

APPLICATION TO GERMANIUM

The above experimental method applies in the case of germanium. However, since germanium contains much less carbon than silicon, the sample taken for analysis must be larger (100 mg for example). In addition, the total volume of benzene used may be limited to 5 ml.

The carbon content of diverse samples analyzed is between 5 and 10 p.p.m.

REFERENCES

1. H. Gabriel and C. Alvarez-Tostado, J.A.C.S. 74, 262 (1952)
2. L. Markovskii, Khim. Prom. 10, 15 (1946)
3. Stull, Ind. Eng. Chem. 41, 1968 (1949)
4. I. F. Trotter, ibid. 42, 570 (1950)
5. H. Guerin and J. Adam-Gironne, C. R. 238, 583 (1954)
6. J. Adam-Gironne, Bul. Soc. Chimique, 732 and 1234 (1954)

DISCUSSION

C. ROSENBLUM (Chairman) (Merck): The very high concentration of carbon in silicon recalls some work done several years ago at our laboratory on germanium. Powdered germanium was heated in oxygen, and the gases which were formed were condensed and identified as carbon dioxide. In germanium a very high concentration of carbon was found, of the order of 500 parts per million, as I recall. In view of this observation, do you think this procedure might be adapted to the determination of carbon in silicon?

N. BALKANSKI (University of Paris): My personal feeling is that this method might be a bit optimistic for the determination of carbon in silicon.

J. F. DUKE (National Physical Laboratory, England): Some work has been done in Britain on the examination of carbon in silicon by oxidization using a lead oxide flux. By this method a carbon content on the order of 5 to 20 ppm has been determined.

D. H. WILKINS (General Electric): I would like to verify the work Dr. Duke refers to; the same procedure has been used in this country; by utilization of a conductimetric determination, carbon concentrations down to this order of magnitude have been achieved.

III

PHYSICAL PREPARATION, PURIFICATION, AND MEASUREMENTS OF SEMICONDUCTOR MATERIALS

HORIZONTAL ZONE PURIFICATION OF SILICON IN NON-REACTIVE CRUCIBLES

Duncan M. Lamb
Sylvania Electric Products Inc.
Chemical and Metallurgical Division
Towanda, Pennsylvania

and

John L. Porter
Sylvania Electric Products Inc.
Semiconductor Division
Woburn, Massachusetts

ABSTRACT

Although the techniques employed commercially in the horizontal zone melting of germanium have been generally satisfactory, numerous difficulties have been experienced in applying similar techniques to the zone melting of silicon. These difficulties have stemmed primarily from the fact that at the temperature of molten silicon, contamination of the silicon by the material of the vessel has resulted. In addition to the chemical problem of contamination, mechanical problems resulting from wetting of the vessel walls by molten silicon and adherence of solidified silicon to the walls have been encountered. Heretofore, the problem has been approached by attempting to find a suitable material for the zoning vessel.

This paper describes a method for the horizontal zone purification of silicon in a receptacle which is maintained non-reactive with respect to molten silicon by a method which is independent of the vessel material. More particularly, the walls of the vessel containing the silicon are cooled so that the surfaces in contact with the silicon are at a temperature below the melting point of the silicon and of the container. As a result, the molten silicon does not attack or wet the walls of the container and there is no adhesion upon solidification of the silicon. Zone purification in "cold-wall" containers has produced large ingots of high-purity uncompensated silicon.

469

INTRODUCTION

Although the techniques employed in the horizontal zone melting of germanium have been generally satisfactory, numerous difficulties have been experienced in applying similar techniques to the zone melting of silicon [1]. These difficulties have stemmed primarily from the fact that at the temperature of molten silicon, contamination of the silicon by the material of the vessel [2] has resulted. Heretofore, the problem has been approached by attempting to find a suitable material for the zoning vessel. Although other techniques such as the "floating-zone" [3,4] method do not require a crucible, there are certain limitations and difficulties, e.g., zone length stability, cross-sectional area, one molten zone per pass, etc.

This paper describes a method for the horizontal zone purification of silicon in a receptacle which is maintained non-reactive with respect to molten silicon. Zone purification of silicon in "cold-wall" containers has produced large ingots of uncompensated silicon.

EXPERIMENTAL

Of the various materials investigated, such as quartz, refractory carbides, nitrides, none were suitable as a crucible material because of their reactivity with molten silicon. Since no material was found that is capable of retaining molten silicon without attack, a workable method resolved itself into a technique for making the receptacle non-reactive with respect to molten silicon. It was discovered that if the vessel (quartz, copper, steel, tantalum) containing the silicon are maintained at a temperature substantially below that of molten silicon then no reaction takes place. In order to accomplish this, the walls of the vessel are maintained in direct contact with a liquid coolant. The molten silicon does not, under these conditions, attack or wet the walls of the container and there is no adhesion between the silicon and the container upon solidification of the silicon. Thus, the primary problems involved in handling and processing molten silicon are surmounted.

The first such water-cooled vessel was constructed of a quartz test tube immersed in a container of water. A charge of silicon was melted in the tube by means of an RF coil which was also immersed in the water. When the melt was allowed to freeze, the silicon did not wet or adhere to the cold quartz nor was there any evidence of reaction of the silicon with the quartz vessel.

Attempts to perform zone-melting by immersing a 50-mm diameter quartz tube and a travelling RF coil in a water bath

met with mixed success. Figure 1 shows this system. Formation of steam on the outer surface of the quartz tube opposite the
molten zone decreased the heat transfer and frequently allowed
the quartz to become hot enough so that the molten silicon would
adhere upon freezing, thus cracking the quartz. Some improvement was noted when the water bath was vigorously agitated opposite the molten zone.

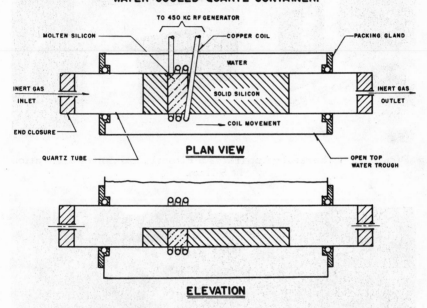

Figure 1. Zone Refining of Silicon in a Water-Cooled Quartz
Container.

Experiments along these lines led to the design of a water-
cooled silicon zone-refining system consisting of two concentric
tubes, the outer one Pyrex and the inner one quartz, with water
flowing in the annular space between them. An RF coil surrounded the outer tube. Molten zone movement was accomplished
by moving the tube. Figures 2 and 3 show the laboratory equipment for this system. Figure 4 shows a zone-refined silicon
ingot which was made in the laboratory apparatus.

Figures 5 and 6 show prototype production equipment designed to zone-refine silicon in water-cooled quartz tubes. The
use of the "double-pipe" heat exchanger principle permitted high
water velocity past the molten zone, thus eliminating the formation of steam. Inert ambients such as argon, helium, or hydrogen
were used successfully. On several occasions vacuum was used.

471

Figure 2. Laboratory Apparatus for Horizontal Zone Purification of Silicon.

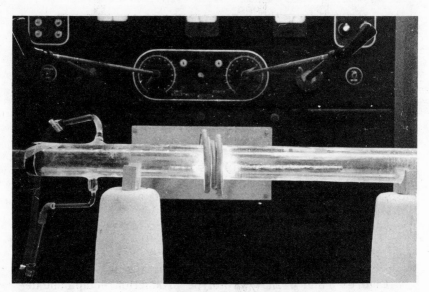

Figure 3. Close-Up of Molten Zone in Laboratory Horizontal Zone Purification Apparatus.

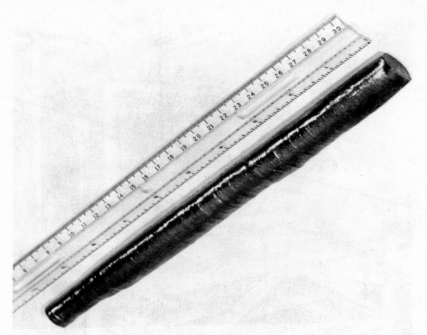

Figure 4. Silicon Ingot Made in Laboratory Apparatus.

Figure 5. Prototype Production Horizontal Zone Purification
Machine for Silicon (First Model, Cold Wall Quartz).

473

Figure 6. Prototype Production Horizontal Zone Purification Machine for Silicon (Second Model, Cold Wall Quartz).

Figure 7. Water Cooled Metal Boat for Horizontal Zone Purification of Silicon.

The same idea was extended to metal containers. The first such water-cooled metal boat was constructed of a plurality of small diameter copper tubes in the form of a small trough; each tube was individually cooled from its own water source. A charge of silicon was melted on the cooled tubes by RF induction. There was no evidence of reaction or adhesion between the silicon and cold metal. Molten silicon by virtue of its very high surface tension, remains within the container, even though no positive seal is provided between the adjacent tubes defining the container. Figure 7 will show this in more detail.

The container is constructed so that metal manifolds close the end of the trough. These manifolds include a hollow chamber into which each of the tubes opens.

474

Figure 8. Prototype Apparatus for Zone Purification of Silicon in Water Cooled Metal Boats.

Figure 9. Close-Up of Silicon Molten Zone in Water Cooled Metal Boat.

Figure 8 shows the apparatus used for zone-purification. A cylindrical tube of clear quartz encircles the container. End closures form seals around the inlet and outlet tubes and seal the openings at the ends of the quartz tube. The container is thus supported within the tube while an inert ambient such as hydrogen or argon is used as a protective atmosphere. An induction heating coil encircles the container and quartz tube. Movement of the container through the coil is obtained by a suitable driving means.

In zone-purifying an ingot of silicon, a quartz-enclosed graphite block is used to initiate the RF pickup. As the silicon is heated to a higher temperature by radiation from the graphite block, its resistivity is reduced sufficiently to permit direct coupling. If the silicon is of low resistivity initially (say in the 0.5-ohm cm range), then the graphite block need not be used since the silicon will couple directly. Figure 9 shows a close-up of the molten zone. It is believed that a very thin layer of solid silicon (or oxide) is present at the interface between the molten silicon and the cold container.

Figures 10 and 11 show top and bottom views of a zone-purified bar which was prepared in a water-cooled copper boat. Figure 12 shows results after zone purification of silicon having an initial resistivity of 25 ohm cm, p-type.

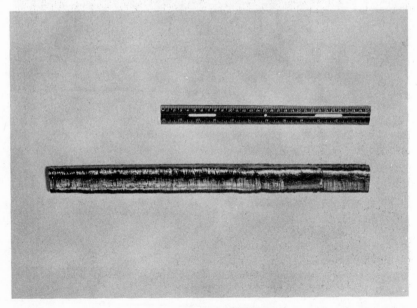

Figure 10. Top View of Zone Purified Silicon Bar Prepared in Water Cooled Metal Boat.

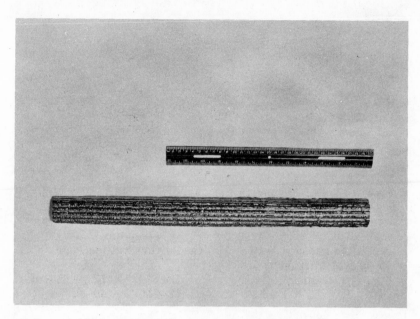

Figure 11. Bottom View of Zone Purified Silicon Bar Prepared
in Water Cooled Metal Boat.

	Resistivity		
Zones*	Front	Center	Tail
29	1600	175	12

*Velocity - 8"/hour

Figure 12. Resistivity of Silicon Purified in Water
Cooled Metal Boat.

The cut-off point for the tail was approximately two zone
lengths from the end. The conductivity remained p-type but the
very tips showed a gradual increase in n-type contamination.

Figure 13 shows a quantity of zone-refined silicon ingots.
These ingots were made in a 50-mm ID water-cooled quartz
tube.

Resistivity profiles of the level portion of two silicon ingots
which were zone-refined in water-cooled quartz are shown in
Figure 14. All of the original silicon used in these experiments
was in the 15-30 ohm cm, n-type range. Total bar length was
between 40 and 60 cm.

Figure 13. Silicon Ingots Zone Purified in 50-mm Diameter Water Cooled Quartz Tubes.

cm Along Level Portion of Ingot	ohm cm On Polycrystalline Ingot	
	Lot # 43-42	Lot # 40-33
2	580	1190
4	555	1010
6	555	1060
8	555	1030
10	505	1070
12	580	1120
14	705	980
16	655	870
18	605	1060
20	505	1190
22	555	
24	580	
Cond. Type	P	P

Figure 14. Resistivity Profile of Silicon Zone Purified in Water Cooled Quartz.

In order to eliminate the possibility of melting unrefined silicon on subsequent passes, zone-refining was carried out from the center of the ingot towards each end. In the horizontal zone-refining of large-diameter bars unmelted silicon forms the dam at each end to prevent the silicon from "running out" which would make the bar longer and thinner. A study on one such bar was made by the floating-zone technique. This particular bar had been given nine zoning passes from the center to the ends. The

478

level center section, between the p-n junctions, was cut from the ingot and a one-centimeter-square bar was cut from it to be used in floating-zone evaluation. Data from this experiment are displayed in Figure 15.

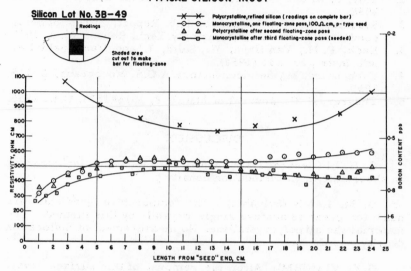

Figure 15. Floating-Zone Study of Silicon Ingot Zone-Purified in Water Cooled Quartz Tubes.

Resistivities on the zoned bars were comparable to those of single crystals grown from the same material. Resistivity correlation is very similar to that which one obtains with "poly" and single-crystal germanium in the higher resistivity ranges.

The processing involved can vary quite widely depending upon the initial impurity level and impurity identity. The water-cooled metal boat has been used mainly in processing low-grade types. However, life-time data, resistivity profiles, and device characteristics indicate a superior product after zone-purification—when compared to the original material. After zone-refining, the only significant impurity that is left is boron since all other impurities have favorable segregation coefficients and have been swept out by zone purification.

CONCLUSION

It has been demonstrated that through the technique of forming a "cold surface" a crucible can be maintained non-reactive for containing molten silicon. Through the use of such a receptacle

479

large-area silicon bars have been zone refined, resulting in silicon of a much improved quality.

REFERENCES

1. Taft, E. A. and Horn, F. H., Journal of the E.C.S. 105, p. 81, 1958.
2. Shockley, W., Semiconductor Lab. Report, "Prep. of Semiconductor Materials," Quarterly Tech. Report No. 1, 1957.
3. Keck, P. H., Van Horn, W., Solid, J. and MacDonald Rev. Sci. Instr., 25, 331 (1954).
4. Tanenbaum, M., Semiconductors A.C.S. Monograph, p. 118, 1959.
5. Theurer, H. C., Journal of Metals 8, 1316-1319, Oct., 1956.

DISCUSSION

C. H. LI (General Instrument): Does water cooling introduce an abnormally high dislocation density?

D. M. LAMB (Sylvania): The temperature gradients are much too great to achieve single crystals by this method. The material was all polycrystalline. No measurement of dislocation density was made.

G. G. VIA (IBM): After the removal of this surface layer, did you see how the surface of the quartz looked after several refining processes?

D. M. LAMB (Sylvania Elec. Prod. Inc.): The inner surface of the quartz tube was covered with a brown material.

G. G. VIA (IBM): After the removal of this brown material, did you find any modification in the surface of the quartz?

D. M. LAMB (Sylvania Inc.): Not if the process was working properly. If wetting of the quartz did not occur and temperature balance was right, then the quartz was quite smooth.

W. TILLER (Chairman) (Westinghouse Research Laboratories): Has this process applied to any materials other than silicon?

D. M. LAMB (Sylvania): No, it has not been applied to other materials.

FREE CONVECTION IN ZONE MELTING

W. R. Wilcox* and C. R. Wilke
Lawrence Radiation Laboratory and
Department of Chemical Engineering
University of California
Berkeley, California

ABSTRACT

When zone refining is conducted under free-convection conditions several interesting phenomena occur. First of all, the degree of purification is influenced by the heat-transfer conditions, i.e., by the size of the container, by the orientation of the zone, by the heat input to the zone and by the thermal expansion properties of the melt. Secondly, the degree of purification is much greater when the fluid of lower density (between the bulk zone and the freezing interface) is on the bottom rather than on the top. As might be expected, insertion of an axial rod of high thermal conductivity into the zone increases the free convection, and hence also increases the separation. Free-convection conditions also cause shifting of the zone with respect to the heater--generally upwards.

In order to understand these phenomena quantitatively, zone melting studies were made using two organic systems, naphthalene-β-naphthol and naphthalene-benzoic acid. These systems represent the two simplest types of binary solid-liquid phase behavior, namely isomorphous and simple-eutectic forming. Solid mixtures from these systems were enclosed in 5 to 20 mm glass tubes and pulled through a stationary heater which generated the liquid zone. By using the experimental data, correlations were developed which enable estimation of the separation and of the zone position for various free-convection conditions in zone melting.

INTRODUCTION

Free convection is fluid motion caused by density variations resulting from temperature and/or concentration variations within the fluid [4]. In zone melting, and in related fractional

---

*Present address: Pacific Semiconductors, Inc., Lawndale, Calif.

solidification processes, we have nonhomogeneity of both temperature and concentration in the melt. The concentration variation results from segregation at the freezing interface, and the temperature variation results from heat transfer to and from the melt and to the freezing and melting solid.

The degree of separation attained in zone refining depends, among other things, on the degree of mixing in the zone. Intuitively, free convection can be expected to influence this mixing. Indeed, with resistance heating, and for all but zones of very small diameter, free convection is the sole mechanism for mixing in the zone. However, free convection still plays a role in mass transfer in the zone even when appreciable forced convection occurs [1, 3]. Hence free convection probably also affects the mass transfer rates when inductive heating is utilized. The stirring caused by induction may, in addition, be largely confined to the surface of the melt because of a high frequency "skin effect." This paper will deal exclusively with zone melting in tubes with the zone heated primarily by conduction from a resistance heater. The mass transfer, therefore, will be due only to free convection and to molecular diffusion. Nevertheless some of the results are expected to apply qualitatively to other situations.

In this work zone melting was studied experimentally by using two organic systems, naphthalene-β-naphthol and naphthalene-benzoic acid. These systems represent the two simplest types of binary solid-liquid phase behavior, namely isomorphous and simple-eutectic forming. The complete phase diagrams and other pertinent physical properties have been determined and are given elsewhere [6]. Mixtures of 10% by weight of β-naphthol and of benzoic acid were melted, poured into glass tubes of nominal diameters 5 to 20 mm, and quickly frozen for the zone-refining experiments. Molten zones were generated by means of heating tape wrapped around a concentric glass tube. The zone-melting tubes were pulled through this heater, thereby effectively moving a single zone in the opposite direction. The tubes were cooled by concentric cooling chambers through which mixtures of water and ethylene glycol at various temperatures were pumped. The experimental arrangement is shown schematically in Figure 1, and is described in greater detail elsewhere [6].

In this sort of arrangement, bulk mixing of the zone results primarily from the free-convection currents generated at the tube walls by transfer of heat from the heater, through the tube walls, to the zone. A diagram of these currents is given in Figure 2, which is based on observation of the flow patterns of a suspension of fine aluminum lactate powder in a molten naphthalene zone. The upward flow at the wall is a natural consequence

482

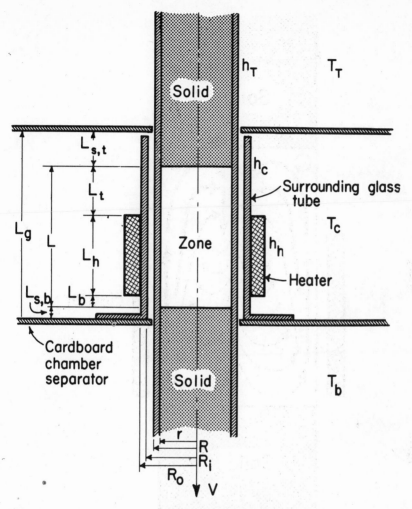

Figure 1.   Diagram Showing Various Thermal Parameters in
Zone-Melting Apparatus.

of the decrease in density of the melt as its temperature
increases.   Therefore the fluid traveling up is hotter than that
traveling down, and so more solid is melted above the heater
than below it.   Thus the zone extends farther above the heater
than below it, at least at low zone travel rates. If the fluid density
varied oppositely with temperature, as in the case of water
between 0 and 4°C, then the zone position with respect to the
heater would be exactly reversed, as would the thermal free-
convection currents.

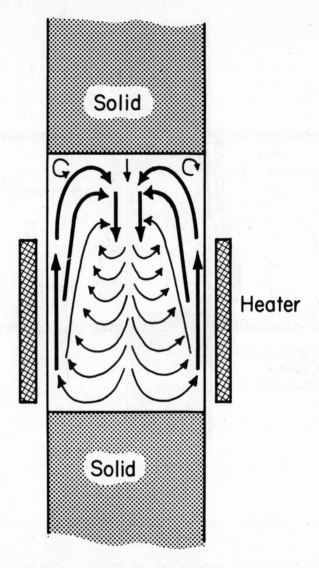

Figure 2. Diagram of the Observed Laminar
Free-Convection Currents in a Zone of Naphthalene in a 10-mm Pyrex Tube. Currents
were Made Visible with a Suspension of Fine
Aluminum Lactate Powder.

HEAT TRANSFER

A multiple linear regression analysis was made of heat-transfer data for 41 verticle zone refining runs in an attempt to define the parameters affecting zone position in the experimental conditions. The heat-transfer calculations are outlined in detail elsewhere [6]. The various parameters were varied over the following ranges:

r   (inside radius of tube) : 1.75 to 8.75 mm.
T_m (melting point) : 77 to 84°C.
V   (zone travel rate) : 0 to 2.70 cm/hr.
T_b (mean coolant temperature) : -11.0 to 65.3°C.
L_h (length of heater) : 1.37 to 2.32 cm.
L   (length of zone) : 1.30 to 4.48 cm.

The best correlation of the data was found to be:

$$\frac{L_{ch}}{L} = -0.014 + 0.54 \left[\frac{r}{L} \frac{Q_{tot}}{(q_t + q_b)} \right]^{1/4} \tag{1}$$

where

L_{ch} is the distance from the upper solid-liquid inter-face to the center of the portion of the heater actually adjacent to the zone, and not to solid material.

Q_{tot} is the rate of heat transfer from the heater to the zone.

$(q_t + q_b)$ is the rate of axial heat conduction out the two ends of the zone.

The average error of the above correlation was 7.9%, as is illustrated in Figure 3. Obviously this is not a general correlation. The zone travel rate does not appear in the expression, yet at high enough zone travel rates the zone will obviously be dragged along with the tube. This means that for the zone travel rates studied here the rate of heat transfer by convection currents in the zone was much larger than the rate of latent-heat liberation at the freezing interface and of the rate of latent-heat absorption at the melting interface. Physical properties (such as viscosity, density, and coefficient of thermal expansion) were not included in the correlation since they were not varied over an appreciable range in these experiments. The correlation is interesting nevertheless, because (L_{ch}/L) is the fraction of the zone above the center of the heater while $(r\,Q_{tot}/4\,L\,(q_t + q_b))$ is the ratio of heater input per unit area of glass tube around the zone to the heat per unit area removed through the solid at both ends of the zone.

485

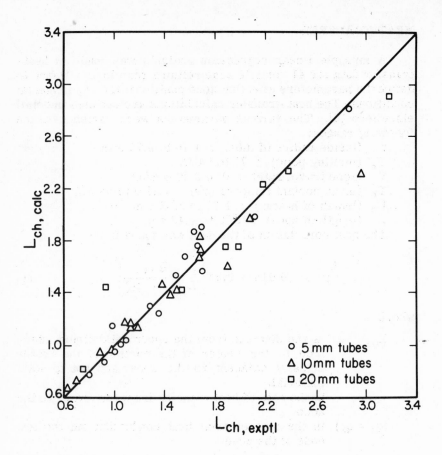

Figure 3. Comparison of Calculated (Eq. 1) with Experimental
Zone Locations for Vertical Zone Melting.

Obviously, the correlation breaks down when the zone lies entirely within the heater, for in this case $(L_{ch}/L) = 0.5$ exactly, by definition.

For horizontal runs the same effect which caused the zone to be mostly above the heater tends to make the zone spread at the top. No systematic study was made of this phenomenon, although it was observed that the spreading was worse for larger tubes and for higher coolant temperatures, as might be anticipated.

MASS TRANSFER

When free-convection currents such as those just described are in operation, the bulk of the zone is actually well stirred.

Near the solid-liquid interfaces, however, these free-convection currents die out, leaving a boundary-layer of nearly stagnant fluid adjacent to the interfaces. In such a situation the degree of purification depends largely on the resistance to mass transfer at the freezing interface. Since the boundary-layer there is nearly stagnant the separation depends, in turn, on its thickness. This mass-transfer resistance may be idealized by the equivalent-film model. A completely stagnant and uniform fluid film is assumed to reside at the freezing interface. The thickness of this film is such that its mass transfer resistance is the same as that of the true boundary layer and convection patterns. Beyond the stagnant film, in the bulk zone, complete mixing is assumed. In other words, impurity is rejected by the solid at the freezing interface, moves through the stagnant film by molecular diffusion into the bulk of the zone, and is instantly mixed with it. During this transfer process the impurity is diffusing upstream against the flow of liquid moving to the freezing interface (considering the freezing interface itself to be stationary). With these considerations the solid-phase concentration-profile resulting from a single zone pass of a material with a constant distribution coefficient may be given by [6]

$$\frac{w_s}{w_0} = 1 - (1 - k) \exp \left(-k \frac{z}{L} \frac{\rho_s}{\rho_l} \right) \tag{2}$$

In this equation,

w_s = the concentration of impurity in weight fraction at point z.

w_0 = the original impurity concentration.

z = the distance to a point where material first froze out of the zone.

L = zone length.

ρ_s = solid density.

ρ_l = liquid density.

k = the effective distribution coefficient, i.e., w_s / w_l at any specific time, and is given by Eq. (3).

w_l = the bulk, or average, zone concentration at the instant w_s comes out at z.

In Eq. (2) k is given by

$$k = \frac{k_0}{k_0 + (1 - k_0) \exp \left(-\frac{\delta V}{D} \frac{\rho_s}{\rho_l} \right)} \tag{3}$$

487

where

 k_0 = the ratio of solid to liquid concentration at the freezing interface, w_s/w_i, which may, for all practical purposes, be taken as the equilibrium distribution coefficient as read from the phase diagram.

 w_i = concentration of impurity in the liquid zone at the freezing interface.

 δ = equivalent-film thickness.

 V = velocity of zone travel through the charge.

 D = diffusion coefficient of impurity in the liquid zone.

For a simple-eutectic forming system a similar analysis yields only the steady-state bulk zone concentration, i.e., it yields the zone concentration after the zone has passed through an infinitely long charge. It is given by

$$\frac{w_l}{w_0} = 1 + \left(\frac{e}{w_0} - 1\right) \exp\left(-\frac{\delta V}{D} \frac{\rho_s}{\rho_l}\right) \tag{4}$$

where e is the impurity concentration of a eutectic mixture.

In the present experiments the zone was passed down a charge so long that the steady state had, to a close approximation, been attained. After a single zone pass the re-frozen material, including the zone at run-end, was cut into sections which were analyzed for their compositions. Use of 10% by weight mixtures of β-naphthol and of benzoic acid made analyses by ordinary methods practical. A spectrophotometer was used for the β-naphthol analyses and an acid-base titration for the benzoic acid [6]. The resulting data were processed by calculating what is defined as the "total separation," S_t. This is the weight of impurity (per unit cross-sectional area of charge) that is stripped from, or perhaps added to, the original charge by the passage of a single zone. S_t may be expressed by the following equation, which also serves to define P, the "purification factor."

$$P = \frac{S_t}{\rho_l\, w_0} = \int_0^\infty \left|\frac{w_s}{w_0} - 1\right| \left(\frac{\rho_s}{\rho_l}\right) dz$$

$$= \int_0^L \left|\frac{w_l}{w_0} - 1\right| dx \tag{5}$$

where x is the distance into the zone from the freezing interface. These integrals were evaluated experimentally by a summation of the analytical results of the run. Conversion of these results to equivalent-film thicknesses was accomplished by substitution of Equations (2), (3), and (4) into (5) and performing the integrations to yield

$$\delta = \left(\frac{D}{V}\right)\left(\frac{\rho_l}{\rho_s}\right) \ln \frac{P}{L\left|1 - 1/k_0\right|} \qquad (6)$$

for a material with a constant distribution coefficient, and

$$\delta = \left(\frac{D}{V}\right)\left(\frac{\rho_l}{\rho_s}\right) \ln \frac{P}{L\left|\dfrac{e}{w_0} - 1\right|} \qquad (7)$$

for a simple-eutectic forming system.

A preliminary correlation of the data, for runs in which the tube was pulled down, revealed two rather surprising results:

1. A decrease in coolant temperature caused an increase in the equivalent-film thickness for naphthalene-β-naphthol and a decrease in it for benzoic acid-naphthalene. Based on our previous free-convection considerations we should expect only a decrease with lower ambient cooling temperatures, since more cooling means more gross free-convection currents are generated in the zone.
2. Increasing the zone travel rate decreased the equivalent-film thickness. Previous considerations predict no such effect.
3. The equivalent-film thickness was an order of magnitude thicker for the β-naphthol-naphthalene runs than for the benzoic acid-naphthalene runs.

To rationalize these facts we must re-examine the sources of free convection in the zone. As mentioned before, the majority of the free-convection currents are generated by the transfer of heat from the heater to the zone. However, additional free-convection currents are generated by heat transfer from the zone to the freezing interface. In addition, however, another driving force for free convection was introduced at the freezing interface by the segregation which occurred there. Since the mass transfer resistance right at the freezing interface is the most significant one to the separation, this driving force might be expected to impose itself strongly on the observed separation, even if it does not greatly affect the bulk stirring of the zone.

The segregation at the freezing interface changed the concentration and hence the density at the freezing interface as compared to that of the bulk zone. The effect of these

489

concentration-induced density changes may either hinder or augment the density changes with temperature, according to whether the density is increased or decreased by the concentration change due to segregation. For the present mixtures and experimental arrangement the concentration-density effect hindered convection for the β-naphthol mixtures and increased the ·convection for the benzoic-acid mixtures. Assumption of control of the mass transfer resistance at the freezing interface by the free convection currents generated there is the only method known to the authors that will explain the experimental results given above. Accordingly those results may be explained, by using this assumption, as follows:

1. Since lowering the coolant temperature decreased the intensity of the free-convection currents generated at the freezing interface for β-naphthol mixtures, the density change due to the concentration change must have been greater than the density change due to heat transfer. Thus increasing the heat input to the zone actually opposed the concentration-generated density-difference and increased the equivalent-film thickness. For benzoic-acid mixtures, however, the concentration and temperature effects were additive, so increasing either one decreased the equivalent-film thickness.

2. Increasing the zone-travel rate increased the concentration difference between the bulk zone and the liquid at the freezing interface,* thus strengthening the free-convection currents.

3. For the β-naphthol mixtures the density of the fluid was actually heavier at the freezing interface (which was on the bottom of the zone in these runs) than in the bulk zone [6, 8]. This naturally was a great deterrent for free convection. The opposite was true, of course, for the benzoic-acid mixtures.

In order to obtain a final correlation with some fundamental significance and general validity, a theoretical analysis was made of simultaneous heat and mass transfer in free convection [7]. This, of course, is exactly the situation encountered in zone melting. The analysis was made for vertical flat plates, but, based on previous heat transfer experience, may be expected to hold in form for other situations, only the constant changing. Accordingly the equivalent-film thickness could be represented by an expression of the type

---

*See Equations (10) and (11).

$$\frac{\delta}{r} = \frac{a}{|F|} \tag{8}$$

where a is a constant which depends on the particular geometry under consideration, and must, in general, be evaluated empirically.

$$F = Pr^{-1/4} Sc^{1/2} [Gr + (Pr/Sc)^{1/2} Gr']^{1/4}$$
for Sc > Pr and
$$= Sc^{1/4} [Gr' + (Sc/Pr)^{1/2} Gr]^{1/4} \text{ for Pr > Sc.}$$

Gr = Grashof number for heat transfer,
$(g r^3 \beta) (T_0 - T_\infty)/\nu^2$.

Gr' = Grashof number for mass transfer,
$(g r^3 \alpha) (w_i - w_l)/\nu^2$.

Sc = Schmidt number, ν/D.

Pr = Prandtl number, ν/A.

A = thermal diffusivity, $k_t/c_p \rho_l$.

g = acceleration due to gravity (taken as positive for flow up, and negative for flow down).

T_0, T_∞ = temperatures at interface and in bulk zone, respectively.

α = concentration densification coefficient,
$(1/\rho_l) (\partial \rho_l /\partial w)_T$.

β = temperature densification coefficient,
$(1/\rho_l) (\partial \rho_l/\partial T)_w$.

To extend this correlation to the present situation additional empirical factors, $(r/L)^b$ and $(LV/D)^c$, were introduced to account for the geometry and for the mass transfer resistance in the part of the zone lying outside the boundary layer at the freezing interface, respectively. This gives a final equation of the form:

$$\frac{\delta}{r} = \frac{a}{|F| (r/L)^b (LV/D)^c} \tag{9}$$

For the present experiments $(w_i - w_l)$ in Gr' is given by

$$(w_i - w_l) = \left(\frac{1}{k_0} - 1\right) w_0 \left[1 - \exp\left(-\frac{\delta V}{D} \frac{\rho_s}{\rho_l}\right)\right] \tag{10}$$

for material with a constant distribution coefficient, and by

$$(w_i - w_l) = \left(\frac{e}{w_0} - 1\right) w_0 \left[1 - \exp\left(-\frac{\delta V}{D} \frac{\rho_s}{\rho_l}\right)\right] \tag{11}$$

491

for a eutectic-forming system. The term $(T_0 - T_\infty)$ in Gr could not be calculated exactly, since T is neither known nor capable of indirect calculation from the present data. Consequently $(T_0 - T_\infty)$ was taken to be a constant fraction of the difference in temperature between the ambient cooling temperature and the melting point, T_0. This is reasonable because when one increases the other also increases, since more heat must be transferred and rates of heat transfer are always roughly proportional to temperature drops. Fortunately the magnitude of Gr is such that the exact value of it is not very critical. In any event this fraction was evaluated by trial and error to give the best fit of the data to Equation (9) by using a multiple linear-regression routine on an IBM 650 digital computer. It turned out to be 0.001, which is reasonable. The value for b was found to be 0.439 and for c, 0.258. The value of "a" depended on the particular geometry of the experiment and is given in Table I for various situations.

Table I

Values of the Constant "a" in Eq. (9) for Various Conditions		
Condition	$(Gr' + (Sc/Pr)^{1/2} Gr)$	
	> 0	< 0
Vertical, pulling down	6.64	66.4
Vertical, pulling up	6.64	9.95
Horizontal	9.61	impossible
Vertical, pulling down, glass tube inside	6.24	--
Horizontal, glass tube inside	3.98	impossible
Vertical, pulling down, thermocouple inside	5.98	30.2
Vertical, pulling up, stainless steel tube inside	---	3.32

Experimentally the various terms in Equation (9) were varied over the following ranges:

δ - 0.0104 to 3.87 cm.

$|Gr'/r^3|$ - 9.36 x 10^3 to 2.06 x 10^5 cm^{-3}.

$|(Sc/Pr)^{1/2} (Gr/r^3)|$ - 905 to 2,400 cm^{-3}.

(r/L) - 0.0412 to 1.09.

(LV/D) - 1.10 to 130.

Experimental and calculated equivalent-film thicknesses based on the above calculations are compared in Figures 4 and 5. Although the correlation is obviously far from perfect, it would appear to substantiate qualitatively the theoretical considerations outlined above. The values of "a" shown in Table I are

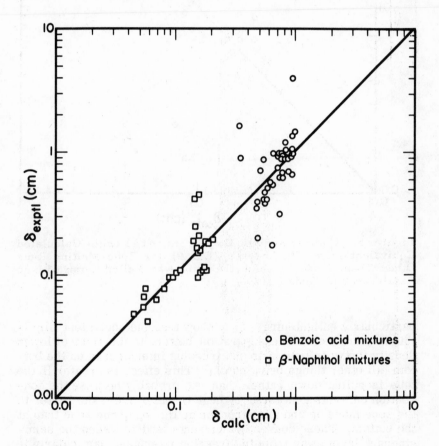

Figure 4. Comparison of Experimental with Calculated Equivalent-Film Thicknesses (Eq. 9) for Zone Melting Runs in which the Tube was Pulled Down with no Axial Tubes or Rods in it.

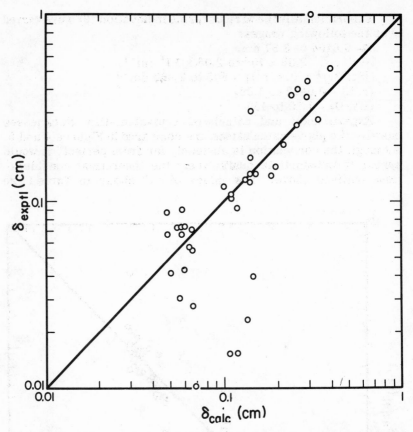

Figure 5. Comparison of Experimental with Calculated Equivalent-Film Thicknesses (Eq. 9) for Zone Melting Runs Other Than Those in which the Tube was Pulled Down with no Axial Tubes or Rods in it.

particularly enlightening. They show that the equivalent film is thinner, and hence the separation better, if the fluid of lower density (between bulk zone and freezing interface) is on the bottom (all other things being equal). This effect is greater if the tube is pulled down rather than up; probably because the convection currents generated by heat transfer from the heater to the zone move up and are stronger at the top of the zone than at the bottom. These convection currents tend to sweep the semi-stagnant layer away from the freezing interface, particularly if it is on the top of the zone where the currents are strongest. Hence, for situations in which the fluid of lower density is on top, a term containing the heat transfer parameters for heating of the zone should be included in the equivalent-film thickness

494

correlation. Unfortunately the present data are not sufficiently precise and detailed to permit a more refined analysis.

An especially interesting observation based on Table I is that insertion of a rod or tube of high thermal conductivity (such as the glass tube, thermocouple leads, and stainless-steel tube in the present experiments) into the zone lowers the equivalent-film thickness. Such a rod or tube conducts heat from the zone faster than the liquid and so draws heat from the liquid. This generates additional free-convection currents which in turn lower the equivalent-film thickness.

CONCLUSIONS

Qualitatively the conclusions on heat transfer can be summarized as follows:

1. For normal fluids which expand upon heating, the zone will extend farther above the heater than below it, unless the zone travel rate is sufficient to drag the zone with the tube.
2. With increased tube diameter the curvature of the solid-liquid interfaces increases and the size of the zone tends to increase.

The mass transfer results may be summarized by the following:

1. The orientation for optimum separation depends on the density behavior of the fluid with concentration and temperature changes occurring in the zone. In general the separation is best when the fluid of lower density (between the bulk zone and the freezing interface) is on the bottom.
2. Insertion of a rod or tube of thermal conductivity much greater than that of the zone increases the separation.
3. Separation increases as the radius of the tube increases.
4. The equivalent-film thickness decreases, but of course the separation decreases too, as the velocity of the zone increases.

Of particular significance to this conference is the observation that the correlation for mass transfer, Equation (9), is subject to simplification for many instances of ultra-high purification. When the object of zone refining is to produce material of ultra-high purity usually the starting charge is already quite pure. For such a situation $(w_i - w_l)$ is very small and so $Gr > Gr'$ (provided that $\beta \ll \alpha$ is not true and that k_o does not differ greatly from unity). Hence the term containing Gr' may be dropped from the expression for F to yield

$$F = Sc^{1/2} \ Pr^{-1/4} \ Gr^{1/4}. \qquad (12)$$

If, on the other hand, the substance being purified has a high thermal conductivity (as for liquid metals), then Pr $\ll$ Sc and so Gr $\gg$ (Pr/Sc)$^{1/2}$ Gr'. This condition, of course, also yields Equation (12). A combination of both high thermal conductivity and high purity makes the simplification to Equation (12) even more exact. The significance of the above is that for ultra-high purification, or for metallic materials, the optimum separation in zone refining is generally obtained if the tube is moved up, i.e., the zone moves down, which means the freezing interface is on the top of the zone. Needless to say, other factors, such as the collection of a bubble at the upper interface during zone motion, can invalidate this.

Finally it should be noted that zone refining is useful not only for the ultra-purification of semiconductors themselves, but also for the preparation of other high purity materials for the semiconductor industry, such as high-purity dopants and solvents. An apparatus similar to the one utilized for these experiments would be a practical laboratory tool for such purifications.

ACKNOWLEDGMENTS

The development of the analytical methods and the performance of the multitude of routine analyses were accomplished by the Analytical Group of the Nuclear Chemistry Division, Lawrence Radiation Laboratory.

The machine work on the experimental equipment was expertly handled by the Accelerator Technicians.

W. R. Wilcox is grateful for the financial support provided by fellowships from the General Electric Foundation, the National Science Foundation, and the Dow Chemical Company.

This work was performed under the auspices of the United States Atomic Energy Commission.

NOMENCLATURE

A — thermal diffusivity, $k_t/c_p\rho_l$ (cm^2/sec).

a, b, c — empirical constants.

d — differential operator.

D — diffusion coefficient, molecular diffusivity (cm^2/sec).

e — weight fraction of impurity at eutectic point.

g — acceleration due to gravity (taken as positive for flow up, and negative for flow down).

k_0 — distribution coefficient, w_s/w_l, at equilibrium.

k — effective distribution coefficient, w_s/w_l.

k_t — heat transfer coefficient (cal/sec °C cm).

L — length of zone (cm).

L_h — length of heating-tape heater (cm).

L_{ch} — distance from the center portion of the heater adjacent to the zone to the upper solid-liquid interface (cm).

$\ln(x)$ — natural logarithm of x, i.e., logarithm of x to the base e.

P — purification factor, $S_t/\rho_l w_0$ (cm).

q_b — rate of axial heat conduction into the lower solid-liquid interface from the zone (cal/sec).

q_t — rate of axial heat conduction into the upper solid-liquid interface from the zone (cal/sec).

Q_{tot} — rate of heat transfer from the heater to the zone (cal/sec).

r — inside radius of the zone melting tube (cm).

S_t — total separation, i.e., the mass of impurity removed from (or added to) the charge per unit cross-sectional area due to a single zone pass down a very long charge (g/cm^2).

T_0 — temperature at the freezing interface, assumed to be the melting point (°C).

T_∞ — temperature in the bulk zone (°C).

V — zone travel rate (cm/sec).

w_i — concentration of impurity in the liquid at the freezing interface (wt. frac.).

w_l — concentration of impurity in the bulk zone (weight fraction).

w_0 — initial uniform concentration of impurity (weight fraction).

w_s — concentration of impurity at a distance z from the first material frozen out of the zone, and in equilibrium with w_i (weight fraction).

x — distance into the zone from the freezing interface (cm).

z — distance along the tube from the point where solid first came out of the zone (cm).

α — concentration densification coefficient, $(1/\rho_l)\,(\partial \rho_l/\partial w)_T \times (1/\text{wt. frac.})$.

β — temperature densification coefficient, $(1/\rho_l)\,(\partial \rho_l/\partial T)_w \times (°C^{-1})$.

∂ — partial differential operator.

δ — equivalent-film thickness. That hypothetical thickness of stagnant fluid at the freezing interface which has a mass transfer resistance equivalent to that physically observed (cm).

ν — kinematic viscosity (stokes, cm^2/sec).

ρ_l — density of the liquid zone (g/cm^3).

ρ_s — density of the solid (g/cm^3).

$\exp(x)$ — e^x

Gr   — Grashof number for heat transfer, $(g\,r^3\beta)\,(T_0 - T_\infty)/\nu^2$ (dimensionless).

Gr'   — Grashof number for mass transfer, $(g\,r^3\alpha)\,(w_i - w_l)/\nu^2$ (dimensionless).

Pr   — Prandtl number, ν/A (dimensionless).

Sc   — Schmidt number, ν/D (dimensionless).

REFERENCES

1. A. Acrivos, AIChE Journal 4, 285 (1958).
2. J. A. Burton, R. C. Prim, and W. P. Slichter, J. Chem. Phys. 21, 1987 (1953).
3. F. H. Garner and J. M. Hoffman, AIChE Journal 6, 579 (1960).
4. W. H. McAdams, "Heat Transmission," Ch. 7, McGraw-Hill Book Co., Inc., New York, N. Y. (1954).

5.   W. G. Pfann, "Zone Melting," John Wiley and Sons, Inc., New York, N. Y. (1958).
6.   W. R. Wilcox, "Fractional Crystallization from Melts," UCRL-9213, Lawrence Radiation Laboratory, Berkeley, 1960, and Ph. D. Dissertation, University of California, Berkeley, 1960.
7.   W. R. Wilcox, "Simultaneous Heat and Mass Transfer in Free Convection," UCRL-8807, Lawrence Radiation Laboratory, Berkeley, August 1959, and Chem. Eng. Science 13, 113 (1961).

DISCUSSION

P. M. GRUZENSKI (NBS): What is your estimate of the thickness of this equivalent film?

W. R. WILCOX (Pacific Semiconductors Inc.): In these particular cases, it was about a tenth of a centimeter but it can vary widely.

B. A. GRUBER (Monsanto): Is this really a free convection case since your molten zone is restrained by a tube along the sides? Wouldn't this also affect your observed segregation coefficients?

W. R. WILCOX (Pacific Semiconductors): First of all, let me say that the dependence on the radius of the tube was very small.

Secondly, the smallest tube was not small enough to eliminate free convection. This was verified by deriving a theoretical equation for pure diffusional mass transfer in zone melting [6]. The experimental segregation coefficient was much higher than would be predicted from these results. It must be concluded, therefore, that some form of stirring was taking place.

W. C. BENZING (Merck): I would like to continue this line of questioning. The length parameters should also have an effect in free conductive mixing. Therefore, the length of the zone should be an important parameter.

W. R. WILCOX (Pacific Semiconductors): That is true. In the equation derived there was an empirical length factor for the zone introduced but it did not have an appreciable effect.

J. R. O'CONNOR (MIT Lincoln Lab.): On the slide where you showed stream lines, you showed a small vortex at the upper portion of the fluid. Doesn't this have more effect than a density mass transport? For example, in these regions one would have zero fluid momentum.

W. R. WILCOX (Pacific Semiconductors): That is true. There is some interchange, of course, with other fluid streams passing by. It is very difficult to take these effects into account.

W. TILLER (Chairman) (Westinghouse): Can you give a measure of how much delta changes due to the temperature effect as ·contrasted with the density effect? Is one more important than the other?

W. R. WILCOX (Pacific Semiconductors): This depends on the particular situation. In my particular case the mixtures were quite concentrated – 10 per cent by weight – and so the concentration effect was an order of magnitude larger than the temperature effects. For ultrapurification the reverse situation would no doubt be true.

W. TILLER (Chairman) (Westinghouse Research): Can you very simply state how Delta depends upon some temperature differential and/or upon some velocity differential? Presumably, from your theoretical treatment, you could get a Delta variation as a function of the external conditions.

W. R. WILCOX (Pacific Semiconductors): Roughly, Delta depends upon the temperature difference between the coolant and the melting point to the minus 1/4th power. In other words, as the temperature difference goes up, the equivalent film thickness goes down.

P. H. KECK (General Telephone and Electronics): We have made many passes on silicon (up and down) and we could not notice any difference in segregation depending on the direction of these zone passes. Perhaps the effect, which you have noted here, is not very big. However, heating the zone with rf fields introduces large convection currents in the liquid zone.

W. R. WILCOX (Pacific Semiconductors): That is true. The induction induced convection currents would possibly dominate in this case.

W. TILLER (Chairman) (Westinghouse): It would seem to me that, if the zone is symmetrical with respect to the heat source or the driving fluid, that it shouldn't matter whether the zone goes up or down for very dilute solutions. Do you have a top effect because your freezing interface is further outside the heat source than the melting interface?

W. R. WILCOX (Pacific Semiconductors): No. The lower interface has a higher density than the bulk zone and so free convection is inhibited there. At the upper interface, you have also a higher density than in the bulk zone, which tends to make the fluid drop and free convection is enhanced.

W. TILLER (Chairman) (Westinghouse): When one has a symmetrical situation the primary flow velocity up the outer side and circulating around the top has to have continuing paths through the bottom zone.

W. R. WILCOX (Pacific Semiconductors): Except that I believe the free convection current will die out by the time they get down to the bottom.

SOME EXPERIMENTS RELATING TO
THE ZONE REFINING OF TIN

A. F. Armington and G. H. Moates
Air Force Cambridge Research Laboratories,
L. G. Hanscom Field,
Bedford, Massachusetts

Zone refining has been a uniquely effective method of purification in the last few years. Its effectiveness has been demonstrated in several fields of materials preparation, particularly in the electronics industry. Although the theory of zone refining is fairly well understood [6] the theoretical efficiency is not attained, owing to parameters which are not accounted for by theory. The purpose of this paper, is to investigate and give examples of some of these parameters.

Some zone refining of tin has been reported in the literature [1, 8, 9] and it was felt that this would be a good material to investigate because of its negligible vapor pressure at the melting point [4]. The existence of other work in the field also gave the advantage of comparison.

Apparatus and Procedure - Two types of zoning apparatus were used in this study. One was an automatic single heater zoner in which temperature, rate of passage, ambient gas and container shapes could be varied. In addition, it had two heat inputs controlled by a microswitch so that additional heat could be supplied at the start of each pass in order to melt the charge. The major portion of these studies were carried out with this zoner.

The second zoner was also an automatic apparatus with five heaters placed four inches apart. This apparatus was not as versatile in that the rate of passage and shape of the container were not variable. In addition, the sample was enclosed in a sealed container. Thus this zoner had several limitations: (1) zone-passage rate of two inches per hour; recycling of zoner every two hours. (2) Closed container (at atmospheric pressure) for sample. (3) Quartz-tube container, 1/2-inch diameter and 20 inches length; no variation of ambient gas.

In these experiments the zone length varied from 1-1/2 to 2-1/2 inches and with exception of samples subjected to a large number of passes, all were zone leveled in each direction three times before start of zoning. In some cases the ends were cut off after zone leveling, however, this did not appear to produce any significant change in results. The samples were generally about 1/2-inch diameter, the sample charge 12 inches long for single-pass experiments, and 20 inches long for multipass experiments; the rate of passage, 2 inches per hour. After the zoning was completed, the sample was cut into one-inch pieces and sent for analysis. Most samples were etched in dilute HNO_3 and cleaned with lens tissue before analysis.

The samples were analyzed spectroscopically in the following manner. Approximately 0.20 gm. was placed in a shallow cup, undercut electrode. The cavity wall was turned down to approximately 0.010 inch. This sample was burned to completion in a 10 amp d-c arc and a moving plate spectrum recorded on Kodak 103-0 spectrum analysis plates. A second sample of tin converted to the oxide was mixed in a one to one ratio with ultrapure graphite. A 10 mg sample of this oxide and graphite mixture was burned to completion in a 10 amp d-c arc. These spectra were recorded in the conventional manner on spectrum analysis number one plates. Duplicate samples of the oxide were run, and where possible, duplicate analysis on the metal samples were also run. The limits of detectability of impurities in tin are shown in Table 1.

TABLE I

MINIMUM DETECTABLE AMOUNTS*

Ag	0.001	Fe	0.04	Pb	0.01
Al	0.040	Ge	0.03	Sb	0.01
As	0.1	In	0.035	Si	0.025
Bi	0.01	Mg	0.002	Ti	0.025
Cr	0.05	Mn	0.002	V	0.2
Cd	0.01	Ni	0.02	Zr	0.02
Ca	0.01	P	0.2		
Cu	0.005				

*In parts per million.

Two grades of tin were used in this work. For some experiments Mallinckrodt Analytical Reagent grade mossy tin was used; for the remainder, Vulcan EHP tin. The latter had been zoned in Pyrex for twenty passes by the manufacturer. Typical analysis for both tin samples are shown in Table 2.

TABLE 2
IMPURITIES IN TIN−AS RECEIVED*

ELEMENT	MALLINCKRODT	VULCAN
Ag	0.5	<1
Al	0.8	18
As	<50	<50
Cr	<1.0	<1.0
Cd	<10	<10
Cr	<1	<1
Cu	30	7
Fe	35	20
Mg	<1	5
Mn	<1	<1
Ni	1	<5
Pb	∿500	<1
Si	1	<40
Ti	ND	<1
Zn	ND	<20
Zr	ND	<1
B	B<1	Hg >100 (In one
Bi	300	analysis)
Co	<1	
Sb	∿100	Other elements ND

*In parts per million
ND=Not detected

RESULTS AND DISCUSSION

It is the purpose of this paper to evaluate some of the experimental factors of zone refining and it is not intended to be a comprehensive survey. Some factors such as mass transfer and the effect of zoning angles will not be treated at all.

Leaching study - The leaching of four container materials was investigated by melting high purity tin in boats of the material to be tested for a two hour period followed by slow cooling of the tin. During the experiment, the tin was protected by an argon flow. The container materials tested were Pyrex, quartz, commercial graphite (99.5% purity) and United-high purity graphite which was reported to have less than 10 ppm impurities. Leaching was assumed to occur if the average concentration of the impurities leached from one container was more than twice the average concentration from the other containers. Leaching was also assumed to occur if an impurity (not present in the initial tin) was found after the experiment. The results obtained indicate that the high purity graphite is the most satisfactory material and Pyrex the least satisfactory. Table 3 shows some

504

TABLE 3

AVERAGE SPECTROSCOPIC ANALYSIS OF TIN IN CONTACT WITH DIFFERENT CONTAINERS*

ELEMENT	GRAPHITE			QUARTZ			PYREX	
	1	2	3	1	2	3	1	2
Ag	0.5	0.5	0.7	0.5	0.6	0.4	0.3	>0.1
Al	0.5	1.3	1.3	>0.5	>0.5	>0.5	>0.5	>0.5
Cd	6	14	1.4	ND	ND	ND	9	18
Co	>1	>1	>1	5	5	1	4	4
Cu	40	36	30	36	70	55	170	85
In	41	30	15	40	45	39	43	45
Ge	12	15	18	16	9	11	10	10
Ni	1	0.7	0.9	12	15	8	14	12
Si	1	4	4.5	1	>1	1	1	>1

*All values in parts per million.
ND = Not detected.

TABLE 4

LEACHING IN TIN

MATERIAL	ELEMENTS LEACHED
PYREX	Cd, Co, Cu, Ni, Fe
QUARTZ	(Co), Ni, Bi, Cu, In
COMMERCIAL GRAPHITE	Al, Cd, Si, (Co), Ni
HIGH PURITY GRAPHITE	(Co), (Ni)

of the analytical results of this study. Some of the quartz and
high purity graphite results, determined from much longer exposure times, are not included in this table. Table 4 gives a
summary of all the leaching studies. The parentheses indicate
only minor leaching.

Segregation Coefficients - The approximate segregation
coefficients were evaluated primarily to see if leaching had any
effect on the shape of the segregation curves. However, no definite effect could be found. All experiments were performed at
a zoning rate of 2-inches per hour. Thus, the segregation coefficients determined were not theoretical but effective segregation
coefficients. They were determined from extrapolation of the
segregation curves to zero passage through the ingot. The shape
of the curves was not sufficiently reproducible to warrant comparison with standard curves, in order to evaluate the segregation coefficient in this manner, or to make calculations to estimate the segregation. These values are shown in Table 5 where
they are compared with the estimates of other workers. In
general, there seems to be good agreement between the various
authors on this Table with one exception, i.e., Bi which in this
study shows a considerably larger segregation coefficient than

TABLE 5

EFFECTIVE SEGREGATION OF IMPURITIES IN TIN

ELEMENT	THIS STUDY	I	8	9
In	1.7-2.3			
Sb	<0.3	<I	<I	
Fe	2.5-3.3	>I		>I
Cu	1.1-2	>I	>I	>I
Bi	4.5 (in graphite, 3 runs) 1.5 (one run in SiO$_2$)		~I	
Pb	2-3	>I	>I	>I[1]
Ni	<0.6	>I	>I	
Zn			>I	
As		>I		
CONTAINER RATE	GRAPHITE SiO$_2$ (2 in/hr)	UNKNOWN (probably graphite)	PYREX (4 in/hr)	PYREX
PASSES	I	50	20	I

506

in the case of the Russian workers. The latter workers did not actually determine segregation coefficients but stated that the bismuth could not be efficiently separated. They further stated that after prolonged zoning the bismuth content was reduced along the first twenty percent of the ingot. Their results are based on fifty passes. One other exception to total agreement between authors in Ni. In this study, the effective segregation coefficient for Ni in tin was found to be less than one for two experiments in which a representative curve could be found. Two other experiments were performed which gave undefinable curves. This will be discussed again later in this paper.

The majority of the experiments in the present study were performed using graphite containers. However several experiments were performed using quartz in order to determine if the thermal conductivity of the boats affected the resultant segregation curves. With the exception of one Bi result, no measurable change in the shape of the segregation curves could be detected. Therefore, the authors concluded that thermal conductivity is not an important factor in this case. However, in a case unlike tin where the sample itself has a low thermal conductivity, the conductivity of the container material might affect a change in the curve. This assumption is based on the concept that a highly conductive container will result in non-uniform cooling of the zone front as it moves along the ingot.

Equilibrium segregation coefficients can be roughly estimated from phase diagrams where these are available. Since most tin systems have been subjected to equilibrium studies and have been reported in the literature, it might be of interest to compare the equilibrium segregation coefficient with the effective segregation coefficient derived from the present work and that of previous authors. The phase diagrams used were reported in Hansen [3]. The results for the equilibrium segregation coefficients are shown in Table 6 where they are compared with experimental data. It is found that out of ten cases, only three experimental (K_{eff}) agree with the theoretical (K_o) result. The value of K_o was determined from the slope of the liquidus and solidus on the one hundred percent tin side of the phase diagrams. Thus, they probably are not absolutely reliable since the number of determinations near this point is not known. However, it appears that the segregation coefficient found from phase diagrams may not be reliable in practice.

Multipass Experiments - In addition to the single pass zoning discussed previously, several multipass experiments were performed to determine how the results of such experiments would compare with those predicted by calculations. The tin in this case was subjected to more than 500 zone passes using the equipment already described. This number of passes was selected

TABLE 6

COMPARISON OF EQUILIBRIUM SEGREGATION COEFFICIENTS WITH EXPERIMENTAL VALUES

ELEMENT	K_o	K_{eff}	No. of AUTHORS REPORTING
Fe	>1	>1	3
In	<1	probably >1	1
Sb	>1	<1	3
Cu	<1	>1	4
Bi	<1	$\sim$ or >1	2
Pb	<1	>1	4
Ni	>1	2*	2-1
Co	<1	>1	1
Zn	<1	>1	1
As	>1	>1	1

*Some disagreement.

TABLE 7

IMPURITY CONCENTRATION IN ZONED TIN

ELEMENT	STARTING TIN	ZONED TIN	AS OXIDE CONCENTRATION
Ag	<1	ND	0.2
Al	8	0.5	>50
As	<50	ND	ND
Cr	18	ND	ND
Cd	3	1	15
Fe	16	2	45
Mg	4	<0.1	15
Mn	<1	ND	<0.1
Ni	<5	ND	40
Pb	<1	ND	5
Si	18	1	
Ti	<1	ND	
Zn	20	ND	
Zr	<1	ND	
Sb	3	12	22

ND = Not detected.

508

since it was felt that the ultimate distribution possible under the conditions used in this work could be attained in this manner. The results shown are for the central part of the ingot where the concentration is minimized both for segregation coefficients greater than and less than one. The original concentration of these impurities is also shown. With the exception of iron, no quantitative conclusions can be drawn between those results and those predicted by segregation coefficients, since the concentration of most impurities is below the limit of detectability. Iron shows an 8-fold decrease as a result of zoning. Copper shows only a 3-fold decrease, although analysis at the low concentration may not be too reliable. If theoretical purification were to be achieved, it would be expected that both of these impurities would be below the level of spectroscopic detection. The increase in antimony was unexpected as preliminary leaching studies did not detect antimony from quartz. However, there seems to be no other explanation for the presence of such a large amount of antimony.

Approximate effective distribution coefficients (<1 or >1) were taken from the slope of the segregation curves, in order to compare them with other results. Some of the impurities in this case were impurities which could not be evaluated in the previous work. With the exception of nickel, the segregation coefficients compare favorably. It is suspected that the value of 0.6 found in the earlier portion of this study is in error. The segregation coefficients in the multipass zoning experiments are in somewhat better agreement with the theoretical coefficients deduced from the phase diagrams, although the agreement is still far from perfect.

Oxide Formation - In the multipass zoning experiments, a noticeable oxide layer was found building up on the surface which appeared to be impervious. This layer was too thin to separate in order to get a direct analysis. However, in one experiment, large discrepancies were found between the two methods of analysis used for this work. The oxide analysis of this run is shown in Table 7 along with the metal. The distribution of impurities in the oxide analysis was more uniform along the length of the ingot. This appears to support the belief that these impurities are oxides which are included in the oxide layer on the surface.

Two related experiments were performed. First, a tin sample was etched after zone levelling, and zoned in vacuum to see if the oxide layer was an important factor in the zoning results. No detectable difference was noted in either the shape of the curves or the estimated segregation coefficients.

In the other experiment a sample of tin was melted, partially oxidized and held molten for several hours to determine if the oxide could act as a precipitating medium for the impurities in the tin.

509

TABLE 8
EFFECTIVE SEGREGATION COEFFICIENTS FROM MULTIPLE ZONING STUDIES

ELEMENT	K	K_o^*
Co	>1	<1
Cu	>1	<1
Fe	>1	<1
Ge	>1	>1
Hg	>1	>1
Ni	>1	>1
Pb	>1	<1

*From phase diagrams.

TABLE 9
COMPARISON OF OXIDE LAYER IMPURITIES TO MATRIX IMPURITIES

ELEMENT	Ag	Al	B	Cr	Mg	Mn	Cd	Ni	Pb
IN TIN	0.1	0.4	0.4	0.05	1.0	0.01	0.7	97	6.0
IN OXIDE LAYER	2.0	3.9	5.3	9.5	5.0	0.5	ND	26.5	13

ND=Not detected.
Elements contained in about equal concentration
As, Co, Cu, Fe, Sb, Si, Ti, Zr, Mo.

In this experiment the tin was coated with oxide, particularly around the bottom of the ingot. It can be seen in Fig. 9 that several elements are present in a higher concentration in the oxide layer than in the bulk of the tin. Some of these elements are Ag, Al, B, Cr, Mg and Mn, Pb. Since these elements are all shown to be at least twice as concentrated in the oxide as in the

510

melt, it appears that some purification could be achieved by this method, the oxide being easily separated from the metal.

These results indicate that the zone refining is not totally effective in the purification of tin--the principal impurity remaining being antimony. In order to increase the purity of the material, a sample from the middle portion of a multipass zone-refined ingot was vacuum melted overnight in a graphite crucible. The analysis of the material before vacuum melting is shown in Table 7. The impurities after vacuum treatment were in parts per million: $Cu < 1$, Fe 2, $Si < 1$, $Ge < 1$, and $Mg < 1$ or a total impurity concentration between 2-6 ppm. This represents the best purity attained in this laboratory, although other authors [2, 5] using different techniques, have reported a higher purity.

SUMMARY

Zone refining by itself is not sufficient to produce tin in the ultra-high purity range unless subjected to additional treatment. High purity graphite is the best container material for the zone refining of tin. Theoretical segregation coefficients for impurities in tin are not in good agreement with the effective segregation coefficients. There is a possibility that impurities tend to be more concentrated in the oxide rather than the tin.

ACKNOWLEDGMENTS

All spectrographic analyses were made by Metal Hydrides, Incorporated under contract AF19(604)-3469. The authors should also like to acknowledge Mr. Joseph R. Weiner for his assistance in the work.

REFERENCES

1. A. Y. Baimakov, et al, Tsvethye Metal, 29, No. 8, 51 (1956).
2. W. Brenner, New York University, Private Communication.
3. M. Hansen, "Constitution of Binary Alloys," McGraw Hill Co., N. Y. (1958).
4. "International Critical Tables," Vol. III, P. 207, McGraw Hill, N. Y. (1933).
5. V. Kudrik, Accurate Specialties Co., Private Communication.
6. W. G. Pfann, "Zone Melting," John Wiley and Sons, Inc., N. Y. (1958).
7. W. G. Pfann and K. M. Olsen, Phys. Rev., 89, 322 (1954).
8. R. H. Taylor, formerly of Vulcan Detinning Co., Sewaren, N. J. Private Communication.
9. M. Tanenbaum, A. J. Goss, and W. G. Pfann, Trans. AIME, 200, 762 (1954).

DISCUSSION

J. F. MILLER (Battelle): Did you look for transfer impurity gradients in the metal itself? We have found higher impurity concentrations in the metal which was near the boat than in the center portion. I wonder whether this is really an oxide effect or whether it is an effect due to other factors.

A. F. ARMINGTON (AFCRL): We have not looked at this.

L. R. WEISBERG (RCA): In studies of segregation in gallium, we found that there was a marked effect of the crystallinity on the segregation because gallium is an anisotropic material and apparently impurities were being trapped at grain boundaries. Now, since tin is tetragonal and also anisotropic, the same effect may be occurring here.

W. TILLER (Chairman) (Westinghouse): How pure was the argon that you used? It is very important in this case.

A. F. ARMINGTON (AFCRL): The argon used was passed through Molecular sieves. It was not the extra high purity which can be used.

W. TILLER (Chairman) (Westinghouse): When you use this kind of argon you often find that segregation coefficients do not agree with phase diagrams because of the impurity content of the argon.

A. F. ARMINGTON (AFCRL): We made 500 passes where no argon was present and K still went in the wrong direction. These were sealed containers.

W. TILLER (Chairman) (Westinghouse): Was there an oxide layer on this material?

A. F. ARMINGTON (AFCRL): Yes, there was some oxide.

W. TILLER (Chairman) (Westinghouse): The reason that I ask these questions is that we have studied Ni and Pb in tin and find that $K \leq 1$ for both whereas I notice that you report $K \geq 1$ for Pb. We have also observed grain boundary segregation of nickel in tin. There appears to be a fair amount of oxygen left in tin after zone refining. One further question on the K value of nickel in tin. I had noticed that there is a eutectic at 231°C (one degree below the melting temperature of tin) and because of this the K value of nickel should be less than unity. Would you comment on this?

A. F. ARMINGTON (AFCRL): We got less than unity in some cases. In general, the literature reports K 1. Then when we subject this sample to a large number of passes, our values agreed with the literature.

512

FLOATING-ZONE REFINING OF GALLIUM ARSENIDE

F. A. Cunnell, W. R. Harding and R. Wickham
Services Electronics Research Laboratory,
Baldock, Hertfordshire, England

INTRODUCTION

The suitability of various crucible materials which have been used in the preparation and processing of gallium arsenide has been discussed in previous publications [2,6]. Quartz is generally regarded as being the most suitable material for the purpose, although the problem of contamination of gallium arsenide by silicon, and possibly oxygen, from the quartz is well known. It is this problem which has led to the application of floating-zone refining to the compound gallium arsenide. The technique was developed originally by Keck and Golay for processing silicon [7]. Since then it has been applied to the zone melting of refractory metals and more recently to GaAs, [8,4] and GaP [5].

A very simple equipment was used by the authors in their early efforts to refine gallium arsenide by floating zoning [3]. Some of the problems encountered in the early work were discussed in a publication which described an improved equipment designed to minimize the difficulties of the operation [4]. The present account describes an alteration in the design and operation of the latter equipment which should lead to an improvement in the purity of the gallium arsenide produced. Since much of the design is unaltered a complete description of the present equipment will not be given here and readers are referred to the original publication for details. An appreciation of the essential features of design can be obtained by reference to Figs. 1 and 2.

EQUIPMENT DESIGN

One of the noteworthy features of the equipment is a quartz work tube which, though demountable, is capable of limiting the rate of the loss of arsenic to the exterior to a small value when one atmosphere arsenic pressure is maintained internally. This is achieved by the use of a piston-type 'seal'. The open end of the quartz tube is closed by a quartz rod, fifteen millimetres in diameter, which is a sliding fit in the tube over a length of about

513

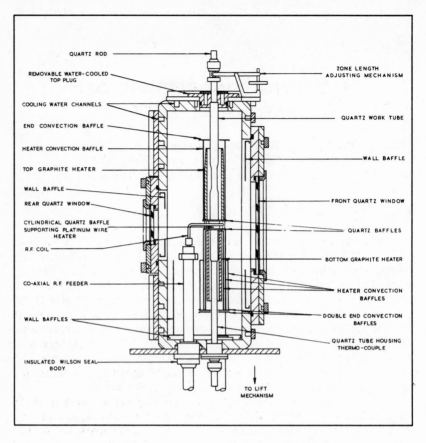

Figure 1. General Arrangement of the Equipment.

six centimetres. Both the internal surface of the tube and the surface of the rod over the length of the 'seal' are ground and lapped individually to a fine finish so that free movement of the rod in the tube is possible with a clearance on the diameter of only five to ten microns. In the initial conception of the apparatus it was decided to impede the loss of arsenic through the 'seal' by maintaining a pressure of nitrogen outside the work tube in excess of the arsenic pressure inside the tube. It was necessary, therefore, to provide a heater system in which the power dissipation along the work tube was non-uniform in order to combat the effect of convection losses in the gas. As improved techniques for fabricating the quartz seal were developed it became evident that arsenic loss rates as low as several milligrammes per hour of operation were attainable provided a nitrogen ambient was maintained. However, since the nitrogen was a possible source of contamination, the operation of the equipment under

514

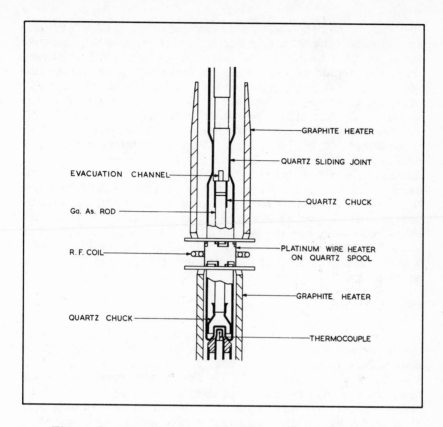

Figure 2. Arrangement of the Work Tube and Heaters.

vacuum conditions was to be preferred provided, that as a result
of the change, the rate of loss of arsenic was not increased
excessively. Experiments in vacuo showed that although the rate
of loss of arsenic was substantially increased it was still possible to have ten to twenty hours of operation without increasing
the capacity of the arsenic reservoir above one gramme. Consequently, the equipment was converted for operation in a good
vacuum and the graphite heater system modified to restore a
suitable temperature profile along the work tube. The alloy box
which surrounds the heaters and the work tube was modified to
enable a high speed oil diffusion pump complete with cold trap
and flap-valve assembly to be attached. A pressure of 10^{-5} mm
of Hg can be obtained.

EQUIPMENT OPERATION

Operation is very similar to that already described [4] except
for the outgassing of the work tube and contents prior to closing

515

the 'seal'. The preparation and mounting of the gallium arsenide is unaltered. The work tube containing the ingot to be processed is supported in the furnace system with the quartz rod withdrawn from the region of the 'seal'. In this position the work tube space is in easy communication with the box. A monotonic temperature distribution along the work tube is created with the arsenic reservoir at approximately 250°C and the seal at 650°C. By this means arsenic trioxide present in the arsenic reservoir is sublimed out of the system. After about thirty minutes at a pressure of 10^5 mm of Hg and under the above thermal conditions the 'seal' is closed by lowering the quartz rod. The temperature of the arsenic reservoir is raised to 605°C, at which temperature arsenic exerts a vapour pressure of 0.9 atmospheres, and the power delivered to the upper furnace is adjusted to maintain a higher temperature than 605°C at all other points along the work tube. Once steady thermal conditions are attained a molten zone is formed at the junction of the seed and the gallium arsenide rod and zoning is commenced.

DISCUSSION

Prior to the conversion of the equipment to high vacuum operation, outgassing of the work tube and contents could not be done satisfactorily with the work tube mounted in the box. This was due to the non-uniformity in the temperature distribution along a heater system which was designed to operate in a nitrogen atmosphere and yet was required to operate in vacuo during outgassing. A preliminary outgassing was performed on the work tube and contents in a separate vacuum and heater system before they were mounted. A final low temperature bake in the box was given at a pressure of 2.5×10^{-3} mm of Hg, the best pressure attainable with the previous vacuum equipment. During the course of the zoning some nitrogen leaked into the work tube. The nitrogen was described as oxygen-free and had been treated to remove moisture, but the possibility of some gaseous impurities being transported with the nitrogen cannot be ignored.

It was found that under these conditions a scum always appeared on the ingot when a molten region was first formed. In order to prevent the scum promoting polycrystallinity in the zoned rod, an initial annular zone was formed at the extreme upper end of the ingot. This had the effect of gettering the work tube space and thereafter a butt join could be made between seed crystal and ingot without the formation of further scum.

In view of the probable role of oxygen as an impurity in gallium arsenide [1] it is obviously important to improve the outgassing of the work tube. It is also equally important from the point of view of general gaseous contamination to eliminate the influx of nitrogen during the zoning. Both of these sources of impurity are probably best reduced by the conversion of the equipment to high vacuum operation. It is significant that since making the conversion there is no longer any evidence of scum on the surface of the ingot.

While the change to vacuum operation has brought the disadvantage of an increased rate of loss of arsenic it is possible that this feature may also be an advantage in allowing volatile impurities, present in the gallium arsenide initially, to escape more freely from the work tube space. In this respect it may well prove worthwhile to use a 'seal' which allows the largest tolerable arsenic loss rate. A simplified calculation shows that the rate of viscous flow of gas along an annular channel is proportional to Δd^3 where Δd is the difference in the internal diameter of the tube and the external diameter of the quartz rod. Consequently only a small change in Δd is required to produce a pronounced change in the arsenic loss.

Thermal equilibrium conditions in the equipment are established much more quickly in vacuum operation than in a nitrogen ambient. This, together with the facility for completing the outgassing treatment with the work tube in its position in the box, reduces the time which is required before zoning can commence. In addition the elimination of convection losses in the heater system has led to more efficient use of the power input.

RESULTS

Gallium arsenide ingots prepared from the purest available gallium and arsenic by the horizontal Bridgman technique [2] are typically n-type with an electron concentration in the range 10^{16} to 10^{17} cm^{-3} and an electron mobility between 5,500 and 6,000 cm^2. volt^{-1} sec^{-1}. After several zone passes in the floating-zone equipment such ingots are normally converted to material with a very high resistivity over most of the zoned length. The variation in resistivity along a zoned rod after five passes is shown in fig. 3. An explanation for the occurrance of high resistivity material has been given by Allen [1]. He postulates a compensation mechanism involving donor impurities, probably silicon, and some other centres which provide deep-lying energy levels for electrons. Allen has suggested that the latter centres are due to oxygen in the lattice since high resistivity gallium arsenide can also be formed by preparing the compound in the presence of limited amounts of oxygen. Conversion from low to high resistivity material by zone refining is probably due to a reduction in the donor concentration to a level below that which the oxygen content of the material is capable of compensating. Mass-spectrographic analysis of a relatively impure floating-zoned

517

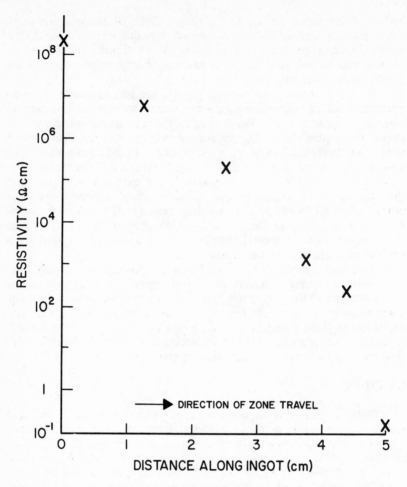

Figure 3. Distribution of Resistivity Along Floating-Zoned
GaAs Ingot.

rod has shown that silicon, which is believed to be the predominating donor impurity in our material segregates in the direction of zone travel. The accumulation of silicon could therefore account for the low resistivity found at the extreme end of the rod which is referred to in fig. 3.

Hall constant measurements have been made on high resistivity samples but, in the absence of a satisfactory model for the scattering processes occurring in high resistance material, it is not possible to deduce mobility values.

High resistance, floating-zoned rods have been analyzed using a mass-spectrograph. The only elements detected in the material

518

were silicon (approximately 0.2 parts per million, atomic) at the extreme end of the zone traverse and phosphorus (approximately 0.03 parts per million, atomic).

In the course of the work it has been found essential to eliminate all metal parts from the work tube assembly. Some early experiments were performed using pure molybdenum and pure tantalum chucks but in every case the gallium arsenide was heavily contaminated. Simple quartz chucks have, therefore, been designed which sacrifice some precision in the mounting of the gallium arsenide rods but which nevertheless prove quite satisfactory.

ACKNOWLEDGEMENTS

The authors are indebted to Mr. F. E. Birbeck for assistance in the design of the apparatus, to Dr. P. Bennett for mass-spectrographic analysis of samples, to Mr. C. H. Gooch for the electrical measurements, and to the Admiralty for permission to publish the work.

REFERENCES

1. J. Allen, Nature, 187, p.403, (1960).
2. F. A. Cunnell, 'Preparation of III-V Compound Semiconductors', Reinhold Publishing Company, (1961). (In press.)
3. F. A. Cunnell, J. T. Edmond, and W. Harding, "Solid-State Electronics," 1, 2, p. 97, (1960).
4. F. A. Cunnell, and R. Wickham, J. Sci. Inst., 37, 410 (1960).
5. C. J. Frosch, M. Gershenzon, and D. F. Gibbs, Symposium Battelle Memorial Institute, (1959).
6. C. Hilsum, and A. C. Rose-Innes, "Semiconducting III-V Compounds," Pergamon Press, London, (1961). (In press.)
7. P. H. Keck, and M. J. E. Golay, Phys. Rev., 89, 1297 (1953).
8. J. M. Whelan, and J. H. Wheatley, J. Phys. Chem. Solids, 6, 169 (1958).

DISCUSSION

H. T. MINDEN (General Electric): You mentioned the spitting, which many of us have observed. In addition, there is an evaporation of gallium arsenide from an rf heated zone to form an actual evaporated film rather than any molten liquid transfer. Do you observe this?

F. A. CUNNELL (Services Electronics Research Lab., England): We do, in fact, observe this. The extent to which this happens seems to be rather variable.

519

S. J. SILBERMAN (General Electric): Have you considered possible chuck rotation to insure uniformity?

F. A. CUNNELL (Services Electronics Research Lab., England): Well, we have considered it, but not for very long with this equipment. We have recently started to build a gallium arsenide puller, which is based on much the same sort of system, that is, a rotating, sliding quartz joint on a bigger scale. With this, we intend to rotate.

W. C. ERDMAN (Bell Telephone): What have you found? Are your limits on zone length? How short may the zone be made?

F. A. CUNNELL (Services Electronics Research Lab., England): With a 6 millimeter rod the zone length would be around 6 millimeters a square section. Clearly, there is a problem here in that one has to be sure that the zone is completely molten.

W. C. ERDMAN (Bell Telephone): Does this require rather critical control?

F. A. CUNNELL (Services Electronics Research Lab., England): Yes. I must confess that when we first started this work I had hoped that this would not be a problem. However, the furnace needs constant observation.

DISLOCATIONS OF SILICON SINGLE CRYSTALS GROWN BY THE FLOATING ZONE METHOD

K. Akiyama
Matsushita Electric Ind. Co., Ltd.
Kadoma, Osaka, Japan
J. Yamaguchi
Osaka University
Higashinoda, Osaka, Japan

INTRODUCTION

Dislocations of silicon single crystals grown by the floating zone method were examined by the copper decoration method and also by the X-ray Borrmann's method [1]. It is usually said that single crystals grown by the floating zone method are inferior to those grown by the pulling method with regard to dislocation. Crystals we examined were prepared in our Laboratory, Du Pont Co. Inc., and Siemens Co. Ltd.

Dislocation patterns of those three kinds of crystals are almost similar to each other and their densities are of (1 to 4) X 10^4 per cm^2. The interface between solid and melt during the crystal growth was observed by p-n junction method, and the relations between the generation of crystal imperfection and the shape of interface will be reported. Some origins of dislocations in floating zone crystals are studied. A suggestion to enhance their perfections will also be presented.

EXPERIMENTAL PROCEDURES

Experimental procedures adopted here of observing dislocations by the copper decoration method are just the same as those developed by Dash [2, 3]. The infrared image tube used is RCA 6032A, whose spectral sensitivity is limited at 1.3μ in the longer wave region. The objective of the microscope is of 10 and 40 times magnification.

Most of the crystals are grown with the (111) direction parallel to the growth axis and are sectioned along the (110) plane or the (210) plane including the growth axis and also along the (111) plane perpendicular to the growth axis. Slices of the crystals are lapped and decorated with copper.

521

In order to observe the interface of solid and melt during the growth, a small piece of p-type impurity is placed in a small hole in a n-type ingot. As the doped impurity diffuses immediately in a molten zone, the p-n junction after doping gave a picture of the interface. After passing the zone the crystal is cut and the p-n junction is delineated by copper plating [4].

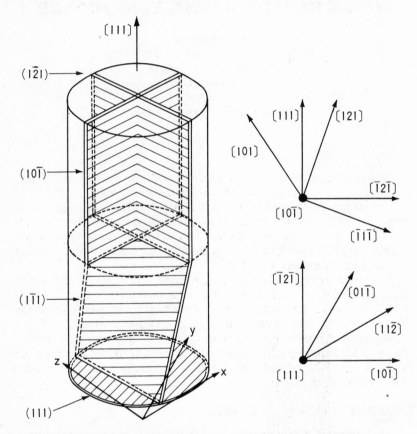

Figure 1. Schematic Diagram of Observation Planes and Direction of Crystallographic Orientations.

RESULTS

Almost all dislocations lie on (111) planes perpendicular to the growth axis and also on (111) planes inclined to the growth axis.

Figure 2 shows a dislocation pattern on a (110) plane. The growth axis is directed upward on the plane. Dislocation lines run along the $\langle 110 \rangle$ direction, their glide plane being the (111)

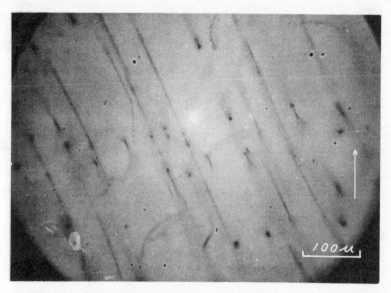

Figure 2. Dislocation Pattern in Floating Zone Crystal,
(110) Plane, X 40.

plane. The black dots represent points where the lines bend toward the direction perpendicular to the plane. Such a bent line
makes a curve and reappears at another consecutive dot. Some
of the lines are curved due to thermal stress. Figure 3 shows a
dislocation pattern on a (111) plane. Some lines run upward in
the <110> direction and other along another < 110> direction on
the plane. Both intersect at 120 degrees to each other. Three
fold points are seen in the figure, the interval between them being
about 100μ. These patterns are often observed on a (111) plane.
Figure 4 shows a pattern on a (110) plane. The growth direction
is upward. The right side of the figure is the circumference of
the crystal. Most of the lines run along the <110> direction and
also along the <211> direction perpendicular to the growth axis.
Figure 5 shows a pattern on a (111) plane. The dislocation patterns on this plane have many more curves than those on a (110)
plane.

It was already reported that an imperfection in a crystal has
a close relation with a curvature of interface between solid and
melt in pulling crystals [4]. It could be expected that the curvature of the interface in the floating zone method would be less flat
than that in the pulling method. Observation of interfaces by the
p-n junction method was carried out. Figure 6 shows two examples of a curved interface. The shape of the interface of

523

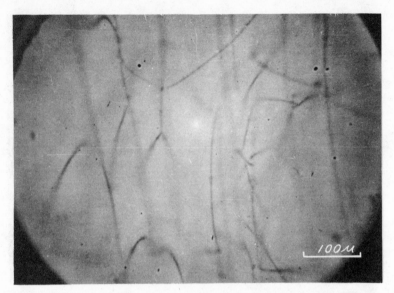

Figure 3. Dislocation Pattern in Floating Zone Crystal, (111) Plane, X 40.

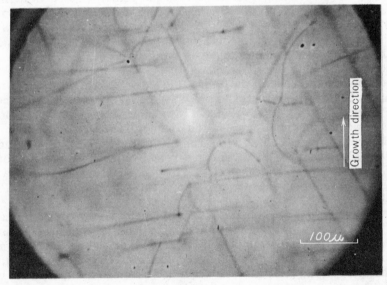

Figure 4. Dislocation Pattern in Floating Zone Crystal, (110) Plane, X 40.

524

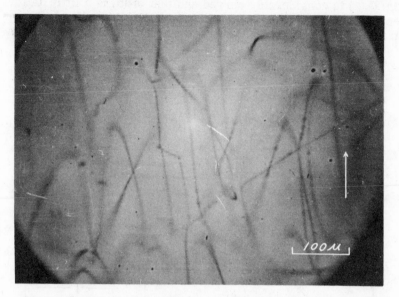

Figure 5. Dislocation Pattern in Floating Zone Crystal, (111) Plane, X 40.

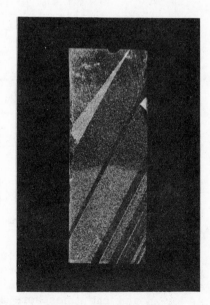

Figure 6. Interface Between Solid and Melt During Crystal Growth.

Fig. 6 (a) is considerably curved and that of (b) is a little flatter because of improvement of the heating coil. An acute temperature gradient in the radial direction can be found from the radius of curvature.

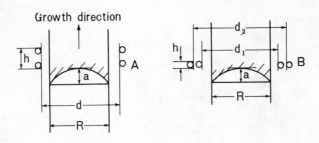

Coil	d (d_1, d_2)	h	R	a	Etch pits $\times 10^{-4}/cm^2$	
					Minimun	Surface
A	26	7.7	12	4.0	———	———
A	21	9.0	12	3.0	3.0	9.0
A	21	9.0	13	3.2	———	———
* A	21	9.0	12	2.8	4.0	12.0
B	21, 31	4.0	12	2.1	2.0	6.5
B	21, 29	5.0	12	2.4	3.2	10.0
B	21, 29	3.0	13	1.4	1.5	4.5

(Length in mm)

Atmosphere H_2 gas,   Rotation $\begin{cases} 10 \text{ r.p.m.} \\ * 0 \text{ r.p.m.} \end{cases}$

Figure 7. Curvature of Interface vs. Growth Condition.

Figure 7 shows the relation of the radius of curvature vs. growth condition. The form of the heating coil has the closest effect on the curvature and coil type B is preferable to type A. As for an ambient atmosphere hydrogen is preferable to argon. The rotation of the seed has no detectable effect on the interface shape.

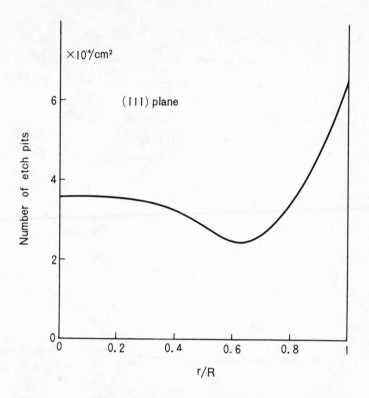

Figure 8. Radial Distribution of Etch Pit Densities on (111) Plane.

Radial distribution of etch pit densities on a (111) plane is shown in Fig. 8. The etch pit density at the circumference of the crystal is twice as great as at the center and there is a region of minimum density between them just as in pulled crystals [5, 6]. This is consistent with the assumption that there is a tangential compression at the center and a tangential tension at the surface due to the change of temperature distribution.

The extreme multiplication of dislocations in the seed was noticed to take place when high frequency heating was applied. A pulled crystal having an etch pit density of less than $100/cm^2$ was used as a seed. The etch pit density increases to more than 10^5 per cm^2 after only one heating cycle of about 1400°C. Radial distribution of the etch pit density after being heated up to around melting point is shown in Fig. 9. Seeds used in this experiment were pulled crystals having etch pit densities of less than $100/cm^2$. Line No. (4) in the figure represents the distribution of the densities in the crystal after being subjected to three heating cycles. The curve shows that there is only a slight increase beyond curves

527

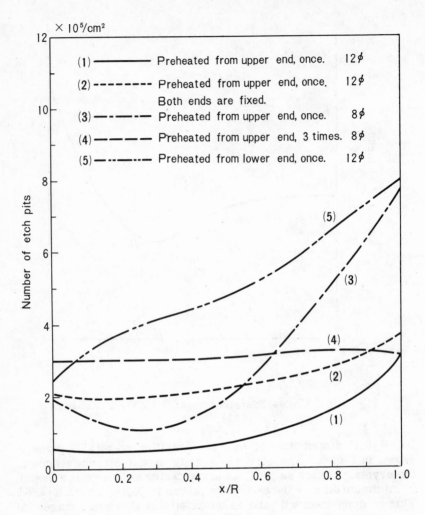

Figure 9. Distribution of Etch Pit Densities in Seed
Crystals after High Frequency Heating.

of crystals subjected to one heating cycle. An increase of etch
pit density could not be observed when the seed was heated in a
resistance furnace up to the same temperature. There may be
other factors which contribute to the occurrence of remarkable
increase of etch pits other than the large temperature gradient.
Some examples of dislocation patterns at the heated portion are
shown in Figs. 10, 11 and 12. In some of the figures dislocations
similar to Dash's observation [1] in plastically deformed crystals
are seen.

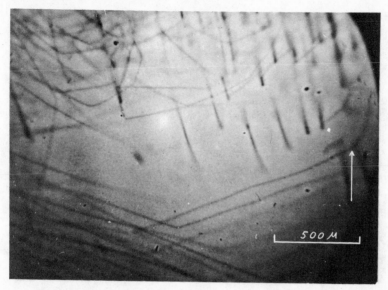

Figure 10. Dislocation Pattern in a Seed Crystal after High Frequency Heating. (Around 1000°C).

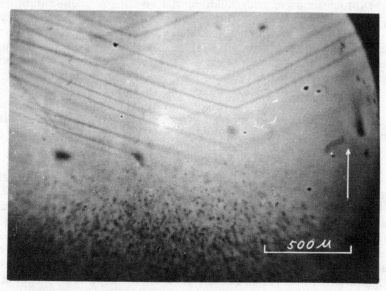

Figure 11. Dislocation Pattern in a Seed Crystal after High Frequency Heating. (Around 900°C).

529

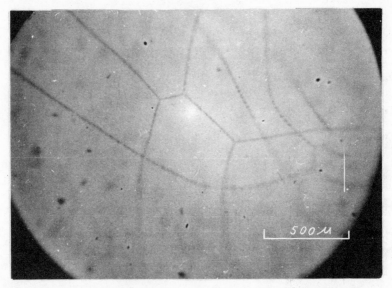

Figure 12. Dislocation Pattern in a Seed Crystal
after High Frequency Heating. (Around 850°C).

Dislocations generated during the seeding process might be
expected to grow towards the surface of the ingot, because they
lie on (111) planes which are inclined toward the growth axis.
But actually an etch pit density of about 3×10^5 per cm^2 at the
start of growth does not decrease over the whole length of the rod
regardless of growth condition. When a seed of small diameter
is used and if the diameter of the rod is enlarged at some portion to the desired size, it is possible to prevent propagation of
dislocations generated in the seeding process. The etch pit
density of the upper part decreases to a density of around $10^3/$
cm^2.

Radial distribution of etch pit densities on a (110) plane at
the region where the diameter is increasing is shown in Fig. 13.
The figure shows that the decrease of etch pits is very large near
the surface of the ingot where the highest etch pit density exists.
The interface between solid and melt at the portion where the
diameter of the rod is changing is shown in Fig. 14. The observed
dislocation pattern in this portion shows less curved lines. This
suggests that the thermal stress is rather relaxed in this region.
The lattice perfection may be improved if these conditions are
fulfilled throughout the whole length of the rod.

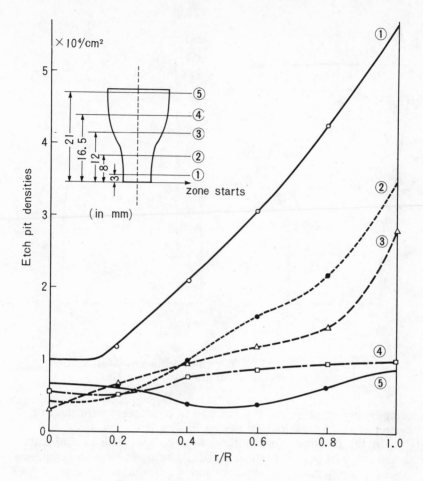

Figure 13. Radial Distribution of Etch Pit Densities in the Portion where Diameter of Rod is Changing.

CONCLUSION

Observations of dislocation patterns which seem to be peculiar to floating zone crystals have been presented. The profile of the interface between solid and melt during the crystal growth has informed us that there is a considerable temperature gradient in the radial direction. The authors are now trying to solve the problem of the temperature distribution in the rod during crystal growth by the Liebmann method with the aid of an IBM 650 [7]. The solution obtained shows that there is an acute temperature gradient at the surface of the rod near the interface. Radial

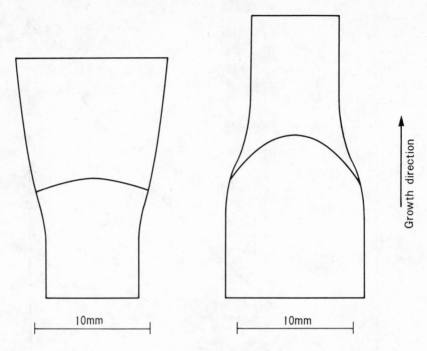

Figure 14. Interface Between Solid and Melt in the
Portion where the Diameter of Rod is Changing.

temperature distribution in the rod is consistent with the distribution of etch pit densities shown in Fig. 8.

In the floating zone method a large increase of dislocation
densities will occur even in heating the seed by high frequency
power. Propagation of dislocation thus generated can be reduced by increasing the diameter of the rod. The idea of maintaining such a condition during growth may be used to improve
the crystal perfection.

ACKNOWLEDGEMENTS

The authors are grateful to Prof. Z. Nishiyama and Dr. E.
Matsuura for their helpful discussion and also wish to thank our
colleagues Dr. Y. Hamakawa and Messers S. Kubo, E. Ichinohe
and E. Adachi for their assistance in experiments and observations.

REFERENCES

1. Von G. Borrmann, W. Hartwig, and H. Irmler, Z. für Naturforshung, 13a, 423 (1958).
2. W. C. Dash, J. Appl. Phys., 27, 1193 (1956).
3. W. C. Dash, "Dislocations and Mechanical Properties of Crystals," J. Wiley and Sons, New York, p57 (1957).
4. A. J. Goss and R. E. Adlington, Marconi Rev., 22, 18 (1959).
5. P. Pennig, Philips Res. Rep., 13, 79 (1958).
6. J. Hornstra and P. Pennig, Philips Res. Rep., 14, 237 (1959).
7. K. Akiyama, J. Yamaguchi and K. Morishita, Reported on the Annual Meeting of I.E.E. of Japan, April 9, 1961.

DISCUSSION

R. J. LOMBARDO (DuPont): I would like to comment that Dr. Akiyama's work parallels some work we have done with the delineation of a floating zone interface. These results agree closely with the information we have obtained.

The shape of the interface can be easily changed from convex, to flat, to concave at the freezing surface. We have also found that it is possible to control the etch pit density at the surface of the crystal such that this very wide disparity between the center of the crystal and the outside edges is eliminated.

W. TILLER (Chairman) (Westinghouse): When the dimension of the sample decreased, your slide showed that the solid-liquid interface became more convex to the liquid. Under these conditions, I would have expected that the interface would tend to flatten and then become concave. Was this just a schematic drawing or do you have experimental data to show that this is what happens when one changes the sample dimensions?

K. AKIYAMA (Matsushita Electric Industrial Co., Japan): That is the result of an experiment using the p-n junction method.

W. TILLER (Chairman) (Westinghouse): I noticed small dots in the region where you did not have dislocations. Do you think these were, in fact, dislocation loops due to vacancy supersaturation in those regions?

K. AKIYAMA (Matsushita Electric Industrial Co., Japan): This is just assumption, but I think these are voids caused by precipitated vacancies.

EXPERIMENTS WITH FLOATING-ZONE SILICON

A. J. Goss
Marconi's Wireless Telegraph Co., Ltd.
Chelmsford, Essex, England

ABSTRACT

A vacuum apparatus with an internal R.F. coil is briefly described and some experimental problems are discussed. Floating zone crystals of 2 cm diameter were grown in this apparatus, with high resistivity and lifetime. The dislocation density, in the seed and in the crystal was high, however, with greater than 10^4 etch pits cm^{-2}. Variation of the growth conditions and of the interface shape gave no reduction in dislocation density. Seeds had to be reduced to less than 1 mm diameter and crystals pulled from a molten silicon pool to produce crystals with dislocation density ~ 10 cm^{-2}. Diffused diodes prepared from high dislocation density floating zone silicon were less satisfactory than diodes from pulled silicon except in those experiments in which phosphorus was present.

INTRODUCTION

Silicon crystals are an essential part of semiconductor technology. Single crystals prepared by the normal pulling technique suffer from the disadvantages associated with the solution of oxygen and other impurities from the quartz crucible. The floating-zone (f.z.) technique, which has been described in detail [1, 2], avoids such contamination and produces homogeneous crystals of high purity and lifetime with very uniform cross-section. However, the dislocation density, by etch pit counts, is of the order of 10^4 cm^{-2} or greater in most samples of f.z. silicon prepared in this and in other laboratories. This is in marked contrast to pulled silicon crystals in which, by the use of a small seed (Dash [3]), crystals of low dislocation density, i.e., 10 cm^{-2}, may be grown regularly. A similar disparity has been observed in GaAs between crystals grown in the horizontal method (Richards [4]) and f.z. GaAs crystals (Cunnell and Wickham [5]). While high dislocation f.z. material is suitable for certain devices, e.g., rectifiers, it is generally agreed that a more reasonable density would be advantageous, as may be judged from the results with diffused silicon diodes given below.

534

Hence, the present work is particularly concerned with the problem of dislocations in f.z. silicon.

APPARATUS

Two basic types of f.z. apparatus are used for silicon.
(1) The silicon is enclosed in a quartz or similar tube with the R.F. coil external to the tube, as described by Buehler [1].
(2) The silicon and the internal R.F. coil are in a larger enclosure, usually a vacuum chamber, as described by Parmee [6].
After experiments with both arrangements the apparatus with an internal R.F. coil was found to have the advantages of close electrical coupling between the R.F. coil and the work, good conditions for vacuum pumping, good visibility and ready access for modification of the growth conditions. The same apparatus also suffers from disadvantages due to contamination from the R.F. coil, difficulties in the use of gas atmospheres and vacuum seals. In this laboratory several f.z. units with an internal R.F. coil have been successfully used for crystal growth experiments and a brief description of this type of apparatus is given below.

The work chamber was a stainless steel drum (9" or 12" I.D.) water cooled, with ports for R.F. power entry, viewing, doping, etc., as shown in Figure 1. A conventional oil diffusion pump system (Edwards High Vacuum, Ltd.) pumped the system to give an indicated vacuum of 10^{-5} mm of mercury, or better. Liquid nitrogen traps were fitted but not always used. Power was provided by R.F. generators (English Electric Co., Ltd.) via a current transformer to a fixed R.F. coil. The coil was usually two turns of silver tube (0.100" O.D. x 0.010" wall) with coil diameter to suit the work. For ingots of nominal 20 mm diameter a coil of 25 mm internal diameter was generally preferred.

The silicon was held in two chucks made of various materials, e.g., stainless steel, molybdenum, carbon or quartz. In the apparatus shown in Figure 1 the whole drive mechanism was external to the vacuum chamber and independent movement of the two chucks in all senses was possible. In another apparatus both chucks were mounted inside the vacuum chamber on a stainless steel carriage and moved up or down in unison by means of a screw driven through a Wilson seal. Separate movements of the chucks, except for rotation, were then not available.

APPARATUS PROBLEMS

A number of problems have arisen during crystal growth experiments, in particular, problems associated with R.F. heating. The choice of a suitable R.F. frequency has been discussed

535

Figure 1. Vacuum Floating Zone Apparatus.

elsewhere [1, 6, 7] and the range 1 to 5 Mc/s appears to be advantageous. In this laboratory experiments with 400 Kc/s frequency, have, in fact, shown marked disadvantages of this low frequency. The zone was slow to heat and, before molten, reached a length such that it would easily fall out. A frequency of 2 Mc/s or 4 Mc/s has therefore been used for all f.z. crystal growing.

Fluctuations in R.F. power were troublesome in particular at low frequency (50 c/s or 300 c/s) and caused oscillations in the molten zone. Power control by voltage regulation has been found preferable to power control by the use of grid-controlled rectifiers, the latter tending to give low frequency power fluctuations. The vacuum seal to carry the R.F. power into the work chamber has also presented difficulties, and a simple design, readily demountable, is shown in Figure 2. Two discs of P.T.F.E. support the silver tubes and the R.F. coil. These discs are clamped onto an O-ring on the work chamber and, at the same time, compress O-rings on the silver tubes to form a complete vacuum seal.

Finally, a problem which is intrinsic to all vacuum f.z. experiments, is the deposition of silicon on water cooled surfaces. With the internal R.F. coil it was found that a deposit of loose silicon and silicon whiskers soon grew on the coil (Figure 3a)

536

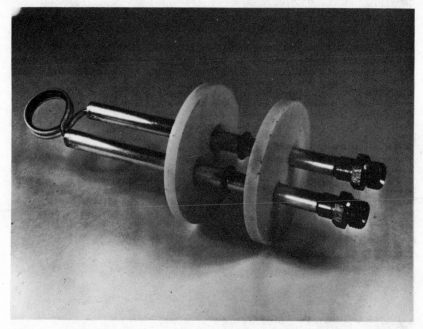

Figure 2. R.F. Coil Assembly (2.5 cm. I.D.).

and then became detached from the coil and nucleated twins on
the growing crystal. A quartz sleeve on the coil prevented the
loose silicon deposit but the most satisfactory solution was to
sand-blast the R.F. coil. An adherent silicon film formed on the
rough coil (Figure 3b) which had a higher surface temperature
than a smooth coil, and many hours of operation were possible
before cleaning was necessary. No contamination of silicon has
been observed which could be ascribed to coil materials.

CRYSTAL GROWTH

(a) Large seeds, 1.5 - 2 cm diameter

Conventional techniques for the preparation of f.z. crystals
have been described elsewhere [1, 2]. Similar techniques were
used in this laboratory to grow crystals of silicon, from several
suppliers, using seeds and ingots of nominal 2 cm diameter.
Resistivities in the range 500 to 1400 ohm cm p-type were
obtained after five zone passes in vacuum, all crystals being
grown with [111] longitudinal axes. The minority carrier lifetime in these crystals, measured by a chopped light method, had
a wide range of values from 50 μsec to 1500 μsec. Lifetime
values, which showed no correlation with resistivities, were

Figure 3. Silicon Deposit on the R.F. Coil,
(A) Smooth Coil, (B) Roughened Coil.

increased in some samples but not in others by further zone refining. All crystals showed an etch pit density greater than 10^4 cm^{-2} and further experiments were therefore carried out to study the problem of this high dislocation density.

The shape of the solid-liquid interface between the seed and the ingot (i.e., at seed-on) and the dislocation densities in the seed are important, since these dislocations are propagated along the ingot. Crystals were grown with seeds of known dislocation density, maximum 10^2 cm^{-2}, prepared from pulled silicon crystals 1.5 to 2 cm diameter, held in the lower chuck in the f.z. apparatus. With an n-type seed and p-type ingot the seed-on could be shown by chemical staining or with powdered barium titanate under reverse bias (Figure 4). Dislocation etching (Dash [3], p. 461) could also be used but it was slow and varied with resistivity value and type. Figure 4a shows a typical seed-on interface, similar to those described by Braun [8], and far from the ideal flat interface.* The seed (at the bottom) is seen to extend up into the molten zone, indicating a cold central core which is well known to experimenters by its persistence after the zone appears to be completely molten. The corresponding dislocation density is observed to be greater than 10^4 cm^{-2} with prominent slip patterns in the seed and the ingot. This normal interface shape is due to the R.F. heating, which is localized in the periphery of the silicon, and to thermal conduction along the ingot. Optical measurements in these experiments indicated a longitudinal surface temperature gradient, approximately linear, of 200 to 250°C cm^{-1} for both stationary and moving ingots. A considerable radial temperature gradient may be estimated, e.g., 50°C cm^{-1} from Figure 4a.

Although crystals were grown with the zone moving up at rates of 2 to 10 cm h^{-1}, no significant reduction in the dislocation density was observed in any ingot. A zone pass in the reverse, i.e., downward direction was very difficult due to zone instability.

It was considered desirable to reduce the seed-on curvature and hence the strain in the crystal while plastic. Changed thermal conditions were therefore used in the following series of experiments.

(1) The silicon seed was normally held in a metal chuck, e.g., stainless steel or molybdenum. As an alternative a thermal insulator was substituted and the seed stood on a flat quartz plate on the end of a quartz tube held in the metal chuck. A reduction in the seed-on curvature was then observed, depending on other factors such as the seed length.

---

*A recent paper by J.H. Braun and R.A. Pellin (J. Electrochem. Soc. 108, 969, (1961)) discusses silicon f.z. interface shapes.

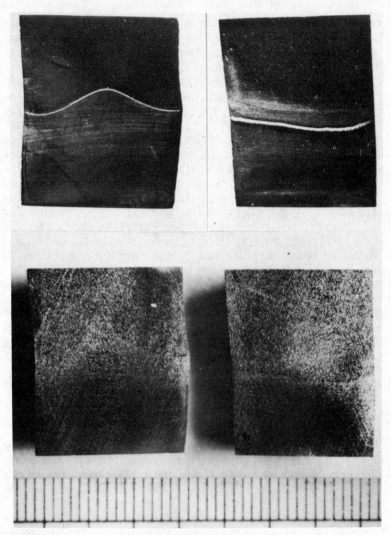

Figure 4. Seed-on Interfaces and Dislocations,
(A) 3 cm Seed Length, (B) 1-1/2 cm Seed Length.

(2) The flow of heat along the insulated seed depended on its length. Figure 4a shows the interface obtained with a seed 3 cm in length and Figure 4b with a seed 1-1/2 cm in length. The longitudinal temperature gradient was 100-150°C cm^{-1} in the latter case, i.e., about one half of the normal gradient. A reverse seed-on curvature was obtained without improvement in the dislocation density.

(3) Thermal conditions were also modified by a heat reflector or heat source around the seed. A quartz cylinder with a

nickel film of approximately 300 Å thickness (not heated by R.F.) and also a small furnace, resistively heated to 1000°C, were used. In both cases a flatter interface was obtained than without the heater but no reduction in the dislocation density after seed-on was observed. (Figure 6 shows an example with smaller seeds.)

(4) The seed-on curvature was also reduced by rotation of the seed and of the ingot. No change in dislocation densities or electrical properties of the rotated crystals could be detected.

(b) R.F. heating effects

Crystal growth with seeds greater than 1.5 cm diameter had shown that all such seeds contained a high dislocation density below seed-on. R.F. heating was therefore used to raise to a high temperature without melting, selected silicon crystals with dislocation densities less than 10^2 cm^{-2}.

A normal crystal growth was simulated with a seed 4 cm in length, held in molybdenum fingers, heated to 1200°C and moved out of the R.F. field at 12 cm h^{-1}. The crystal showed a slip pattern characteristic of f.z. seeds. In the series of experiments that followed the thermal insulation was increased and the seed-length and the rate of cooling reduced. A crystal 1 cm in length standing on quartz could be moved out of the R.F. field at 1 cm h^{-1} and severe slip avoided. However, any sample heated to 1300°C was found to show marked slip patterns. Examples of the dislocation densities before and after heating are shown in Figure 5. Other arrangements of carbon heaters and reflectors were also used but without success.

In contrast, when silicon was heated in a resistance furnace to 1200°C, under near isothermal conditions, dislocations were not introduced. Penning [9] has discussed the effect of thermal strain introduced by rapid cooling and it is obvious that normal silicon samples, heated by an R.F. field suffer in the same way.

(c) Small seeds, 1.0 - 0.05 cm diameter

To reduce the thermal strain due to R.F. heating, seeds of smaller diameters were used in the lower chuck of the f.z. apparatus. Examples of the crystals grown are shown in Figure 6. A low dislocation density seed, 1.0 cm diameter, was used to grow a crystal of 1.9 cm diameter and the resulting dislocation pattern and interface shape may be seen in Figure 6a. Dislocations were generated in a 2 cm length of the solid seed. In a second similar experiment thermal strain was reduced by surrounding the seed with a furnace at 1000°C, but as seen in Figure 6b, although the interface shape was improved 4 mm of

541

Figure 5. Dislocations Due to R.F. Heating.

the seed were of high dislocation density. Similar results were obtained with seeds of 5 mm diameter.

Seeds less than 5 mm diameter would not couple directly into the R.F. field and a carbon cylindrical heater, 1 cm outside diameter, was fitted therefore to heat these seeds. At the same time the seeds were screened from the field and from thermal strain. In this way seeds of 2 mm diameter were used for crystal growing, although the difficulties of joining the molten tip of the upper ingot on to the top of the seed were considerable and only one experiment in four was at all successful. Under these conditions, even with the seed-on interface inside the carbon cylinder, slip patterns were found in the seed and the dislocation densities in the grown crystals were high.

Experiments with very small seeds, less than 1 mm diameter, were made by crystal pulling from a melt on the top of the lower ingot, as has been described by Dash [3, 10]. Seed crystals were prepared by cutting 1 mm × 1 mm sections from low dislocation density pulled crystals and tapering one end in HF:HNO$_3$ mixture. These seeds were held in a quartz capillary or in a graphite rod with a tapered hole, attached to the upper chuck. The ingot, in the lower chuck, was slightly tapered and gave a stable hemispherical melt 1.5 to 2 cm diameter with R.F. heating at 2 Mc/s frequency. The small seed, about 1/4 mm diameter, heated up on touching the melt surface and a satisfactory

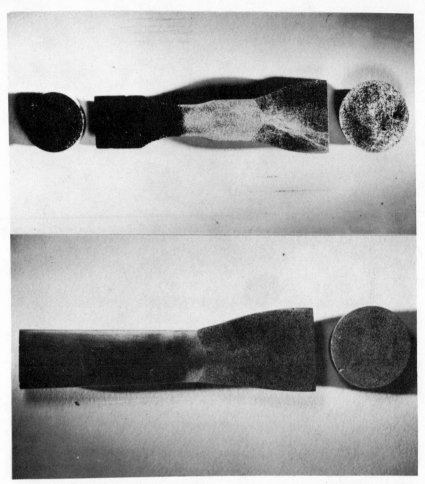

Figure 6. Seed-on Interface and Dislocations, (A) 1 cm Diameter
Seed, (B) 1 cm Diameter Seed and Heater.

seed-on was obtained. Dash's technique was then used, the seed
being pulled at 60 cm h^{-1} for several cm giving crystal 2 to 3 mm
diameter with dislocation density < 10 cm^{-2}, as shown in Figure 7. Small notches which were visible in the melt interface in
[211] directions, corresponding to growth flats on the crystal,
were used to confirm that single crystal was continuing to grow.
A combination of power control and of rates of movement of
silicon into and out of the molten pool were used to grow the
crystal out to larger diameters, approximately 1 cm being the
maximum at the time of writing. Smooth changes in growth
conditions were necessary to avoid the introduction of dislocations.

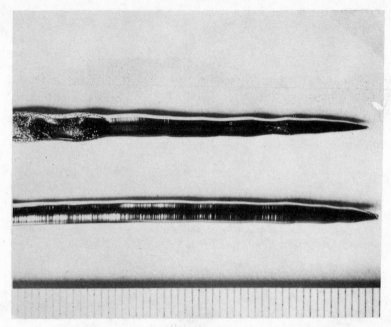

Figure 7. Low Dislocation Density f.z. Silicon.

DIODES PREPARED FROM f.z. SILICON

To compare high dislocation density f.z. silicon with pulled crystal silicon for device application, a number of simple diodes were prepared. Samples of silicon of the two materials of comparable resistivity received identical processing, as far as possible, and measurements of reverse characteristics were made with pressure contacts.

Alloy diodes were formed on polished n-type silicon slices by heating pure aluminium wire (0.010" diameter) in contact in an argon atmosphere. An $HF:HNO_3$ etch was used subsequently to minimize leakage. For silicon of 0.06 ohm cm resistivity a sharp breakdown at 10-12V with leakage less than 1 μamp at 140°C was observed for both materials. For silicon of 6 ohm cm the breakdown was 150-200V. These simple tests detected no difference between f.z. and pulled silicon crystals.

Diffused diodes were formed on diamond polished slices, using several diffusants, with junction depths of 5-10 μ, except for deep diffused slices with simultaneous boron and phosphorus treatment. Mesa diodes of 0.025 inch diameter, and smaller, were made by wax masking and etching. The results, given in Table 1 give the percentages of satisfactory diodes, i.e., those diodes with μamp leakage and sharp breakdown.

544

Table 1

Diffused Diode Results

Diffusant	Silicon	Mesa Size Inch	Satisfactory Diodes
Gallium	F.Z; 0.06 ohm cm, N	.025	0 - 30%
	Pulled; 1 ohm cm, N	.025	< 50%
Gallium	F.Z; 0.06 ohm cm, N	.010	10 - 30%
	Pulled; 1 ohm cm, N	.010	> 50%
Boron	F.Z; 0.06 ohm cm, N	.001 .003	10%
	Pulled; 0.06 ohm cm, N	.001 .003	~ 100%
Phosphorus	F.Z; 0.4 ohm cm, P	.010	~ 100%
	Pulled; 0.2 - 1.0 ohm cm, P	.010	~ 100%
Gallium + P treatment 1000°C	F.Z; .06 ohm cm, N	.010	~ 95%
	Pulled; 1 ohm cm, N	.010	~ 100%
Simultaneous B, P*	F.Z; 6 ohm cm, N	.070	~ 100%
	Pulled; 6 ohm cm, N	.070	~ 100%

*Results from L. J. Bayford, English Electric Valve Co., Chelmsford, England.

It is observed (Table 1) that where a degradation occurred, f.z. silicon was less satisfactory than pulled silicon. In particular those diodes made from silicon into which gallium or boron alone was diffused gave poor results, whereas phosphorus diffusion or phosphorus treatment gave good results. The same slices of silicon were also examined by infra-red transmission. Impurities which diffused into f.z. silicon during gallium diffusion at 1220°C resulted in decoration of dislocations, as shown in Figure 8a. A section of the same silicon slice is shown in Figure 8b after phosphorus treatment at 1000°C and the decoration of dislocations is no longer visible. It would appear, therefore, that the high dislocation density was associated with fast diffusion of

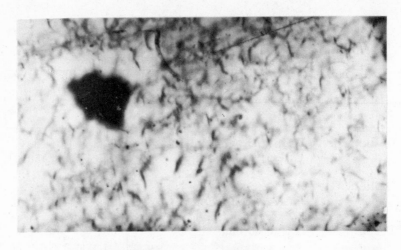

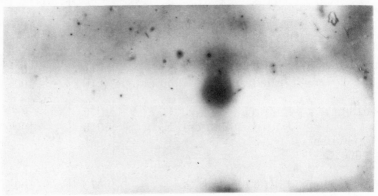

Figure 8. Infra-red Observation: (Magn. x 160 Before Reduction). (A) Impurity on Dislocations in f.z. Silicon, (B) Impurity Gettered by Phosphorus on f.z. Silicon.

impurity, e.g., copper, which was sited on dislocations and gave poor device characteristics. Phosphorus removes the impurity and improves the diodes in a manner similar to that reported by Goetzberger and Shockley [11].

F.Z. SILICON DOPING

Doping of f.z. silicon has been described by Kolb and Tanenbaum [12] for p-type resistivities. Crystals of 1 cm diameter, doped with aluminium to 0.3 and 5 ohm cm resistivity, showed a maximum of 5% variation of resistivity. N-type doping with phosphine in a gas f.z. apparatus has been used by Goorissen and van Run [13]. In the vacuum f.z. apparatus used in the present experiments p-type doping presented no problem but n-type doping was difficult because of evaporation losses from the zone. Phosphine has been used with a doping tube within a cm of the molten zone but the efficiency of doping was low, as may be seen from results given in Table 2.

Although the cross-sectional uniformity of resistivity was reasonable, i.e., ± 10% variation within 3 mm of the periphery of a 22 mm diameter slice, the proportion of phosphine used was very low, 0.02% and therefore unsatisfactory when compared with doping in a gas system [13].

Table 2

Phosphine Doping

Phosphine Dope atoms/min	Doped Resistivity ohm cm	$N_{D/min}$ in Silicon	% Phosphine as Donor
54×10^{19}	0.05	10×10^{16}	.02
9.4×10^{19}	0.09	6.6×10^{16}	.07
9.4×10^{19}	0.16	3×10^{16}	.03
2.7×10^{19}	0.6	0.6×10^{16}	.02
0.3×10^{19}	δR	0.06×10^{16}	.02

ACKNOWLEDGMENTS

The author is indebted to Dr. E. Eastwood, Chief of Research, Marconi's Wireless Telegraph Co., for permission to publish. The contributions of many members of the laboratory in experimental work and discussions are gratefully acknowledged.

REFERENCES

1. E. Buehler, Rev. Sci. Inst. 28, 453 (1957).
2. W. Bardsley, Research 12, 183 (1959).
3. W. C. Dash, J. Appl. Phys. 30, 459 (1959).
4. J. L. Richards, J. Appl. Phys. 31, 600 (1960).
5. F. A. Cunnell and R. Wickham, J. Sci. Inst. 37, 410 (1960).
6. J. L. Parmee, The Engineer, 209, 979 (1960).
7. J. E. Keister, W.A.D.C. Tech. Report, 57-618, July 1958.
8. J. H. Braun, Electrochem. Soc. Meeting, Texas, Oct. 1960.
9. P. Penning, "Halbleiter und Phosphore," F. Vieweg Braunschweig, 1958, p. 482.

10. W. C. Dash, J. Appl. Phys. 31, 736 (1960).
11. A. Goetzberger and W. Shockley, J. Appl. Phys. 31, 1821 (1960).
12. E. D. Kolb and M. Tanenbaum, J. Electrochem. Soc. 106, 597 (1959).
13. J. Goorissen and A. van Run, Proc. I.E.E. Pt. B. Supp. No. 17, p. 858, 1959.

DISCUSSION

C. H. LI (General Instrument): I would like to comment on the dislocation density. When we diffuse slices at $1200°C$, you increase a dislocation density by a factor of 10 or 100. I am citing this in order to raise a suspicion. That is, the role of the interface or the shape of the interface may not be as important as we think.

Specifically, in Mr. Akiyama's slide, he has a dislocation distribution versus radius. The shape of this curve coincides with the residual stresses left in a rod quenched in water, so that it is just a simple matter of residual stress. I would say, in order to produce low dislocation floating zone silicon, we should do these things: (1) Increase the diameter of the silicon; (2) Increase the diameter of the coil so that you get less coupling; (3) Lower the frequency of the rf power so as to heat the center more than the surface; (4) Use vacuum in preference to nitrogen so as to reduce surface cooling; (5) Use after heaters and things like that. This process would give less residual stress and would equalize the temperature so as to produce a low dislocation density. In addition, I would also like to point out the difference between the floating zone process and ordinary crystal growing. For crystal growing, the silicon ingot is heated by a large area melt, whereas, in the floating zone process, the crystal is cooled by a water-cooled rf coil. This difference is very appreciable.

J. R. O'CONNOR (M.I.T. Lincoln Lab.): With regard to the last speaker, I would like to mention that Dash and others have actually taken a crystal which had zero dislocations out of the melt, allowed it to freeze, put it back into the melt and then grew a crystal which was still dislocation free. The large thermal stresses caused by this process produced no dislocations.

W. TILLER (Chairman) (Westinghouse): Yes. He has also used seeds which have a great number of dislocations and, by reducing their dimensions during crystal growth, he has removed the dislocations in a small section. Then, grown dislocation-free crystals result even though large thermal stresses are present. Since no dislocations are in the crystal, there are no sources for slip.

A. J. GOSS (Marconi Research Lab., England): Having taken the precaution of talking to Dash before I came here, we agree strongly that there is quite a difference between growing crystals

548

in the floating zone machine and growing crystals in a crystal puller. In a crystal puller, one is dealing with a uniform enclosure and one can do all sorts of things. For example, one can take a seed out, then replace it, and go on pulling a dislocation free crystal. You cannot do this in a floating zone arrangement. You have to be a most patient soul to get a centimeter diameter dislocation free crystal. Any sudden variation that you may make in the growth conditions introduces dislocations.

As you say, one can increase the resistance to thermal shock by having it dislocation free, but you still cannot take liberties with the system. One has to be very cautious.

W. R. WILCOX (Pacific Semiconductors): What was your source of phosphorous diffusant? After diffusion was there a surface deposit?

A. J. GOSS (Marconi Research Laboratories, England): P_2O_5 was used and a phosphorous glass was formed.

W. R. WILCOX (Pacific Semiconductors): I would like to say in reference to the previous comments on the introduction of dislocations during diffusion that Cy Prussan of our laboratories has recently observed that dislocations are introduced in dislocation-free silicon during diffusion because of a lattice contraction due to the impurities. In general, these dislocations do not reach the junction. Finally, the total number of dislocations introduced is roughly proportional to the surface concentration.

W. P. ALLRED (Bell and Howell): Did you ever perform the experiment where you started out simulating the Czochralski method, as you do with the very small seed, and then gradually convert this to a full scale floating zone where the top portion is equal to the bottom?

A. J. GOSS (Marconi Research Laboratories, England): We are working on this method. We are relatively inexperienced in this -- a hundred or so pulls. We can get out to about one or two centimeter diameter. It would be unwise, I think, to say whether you would ever finally get out to the full zone dimension.

CRYSTAL GROWTH OF III-V COMPOUNDS

Worth P. Allred
Bell & Howell Research Center
Pasadena, California

ABSTRACT

Crystal growth of GaAs, InAs, AlSb, GaSb, and InSb by the Czochralski technique is discussed. The GaAs and InAs crystals are grown in an arsenic atmosphere within a sealed system using a magnetic puller. The AlSb is grown in a helium atmosphere whereas hydrogen is used while InSb and GaSb crystals are being pulled. The source of impurities, such as contamination from the crucible, atmosphere, and starting materials of the III-V compounds, is discussed. Mass spectrographic analysis of AlSb shows copper, carbon, and oxygen to be the major impurities, while in GaAs silicon, oxygen, and carbon are the impurities usually introduced during synthesis. It has been found that impurities can be introduced into InSb from an atmosphere of hydrogen during the crystal growing operation. The use of palladium-purified hydrogen eliminates this contamination problem. Handling of the material prior to crystal growth is also discussed.

The need for large single crystals of the III-V compounds has caused the development of a large variety of crystal growing systems. Particular problems characteristic to the compound being grown dictate the type of puller to be used.

When designing any crystal grower, there are three fundamental factors that should be considered which influence the crystal to grow polycrystalline. These conditions are growth rate, shape of liquid-solid interface, and nucleation particles.

The factors which control growth rate can be subdivided into temperature control, vibration of the melt or seed, and pulling rate. Temperature variations, although momentary, cause the interface to vary in growth rate. The crystal will be found to twin if the rate of solidification exceeds the rate at which the crystal can grow. The intermetallics are particularly prone to twin because of too high a growth rate. This is due to the difficulty of maintaining an absolute stoichiometric melt. Vibration of the melt and seed cause the meniscus to be pulled up momentarily. If the meniscus moves up relative to the melt, it is cooled, causing accelerated growth. The rate of seed withdrawal plus the momentary rates of growth caused by temperature fluctuation and vibrations must never exceed the ability of the crystal to reproduce its natural lattice structure.

The liquid-solid interface should be either flat or slightly convex. If the interface grows concave the crystal will twin easily.

Oxide particles on the melt stick to the edge of the crystal. As the seed is withdrawn, material grows from the oxide producing new crystal growth. Oxides are particularly detrimental if the crystal grows with a concave interface.

INDIUM ANTIMONIDE AND GALLIUM ANTIMONIDE SINGLE CRYSTALS

Of the III-V compound crystals, indium and gallium antimonide are the most easily grown. Indium antimonide with a melting temperature of 525°C and GaSb with a melting point of 702°C require a relatively simple system in which to grow the crystals. The most difficult problem encountered is that of oxide scum which is often observed on the melt. This oxide frequently causes twinning of the crystal. It is, therefore, essential that the crystal pulling system be vacuum tight, with a minimum of outgassing of internal parts. For this reason it is desirable that the system contain only quartz in the region of high temperature. A gas atmosphere free from oxygen or water is also necessary. Water can be removed from helium and hydrogen by passing the gas slowly through liquid nitrogen traps.

Proper preparation of the starting material will further reduce the amount of oxide scum. If the compound is to be used as the starting material, it should be etched with an etch which does not leave an oxide residue on the surface of the material. It should be emphasized that the etch can be a source of contamination. Precautions should be taken if ultrapure crystals are expected. For InSb, a CP4A etch of 5 parts nitric, 3 parts hydrofluoric, and 3 parts acetic acid can be used. After etching, the InSb should be washed thoroughly with ultrapure water. For cleaning GaSb prior to pulling, a one-to-one mixture of concentrated hydrochloric and nitric acid is satisfactory. After etching, the GaSb should also be washed in ultrapure water. It is important, when washing the material, that a liberal flow of water be used to wash away the acid. It has been observed that diluting the acid with water leaves an oxide coating on the material which produces a surface slag upon melting.

551

If the elements are to be used for the starting materials, they can be etched to remove surface oxide. Oxides can be removed from indium by etching the indium with concentrated HCl. This etch leaves a precipitate of indium chloride which can be effectively removed by heating the indium in a vacuum to approximately 600°C.

Antimony can be cleaned with the CP4A etch described for etching InSb. A fresh etch solution should be used with each charge of antimony as an exhausted etch will produce oxides on the antimony surface. After the etch a liberal washing is again essential.

Oxides can be cleaned from gallium by etching in diluted hydrochloric acid. The solution can be warmed to speed the process, if desired. After the gallium has been etched and washed with distilled water, it is advisable to solidify the gallium before it is transferred to the pulling system.

Despite the most meticulous cleaning and handling steps, it is often observed that a light scum of oxide exists. Since even the slightest oxide can cause the crystal to twin, it is important that this remaining oxide be removed. By using the double crucible method, the remaining oxide can be eliminated.

Figure 1 is a drawing of an InSb, GaSb crystal puller [1]. After the elements have been reacted and the residual oxygen in the system gettered, an inner crucible with a small hole in the base is inserted into the melt. The lip of the hole of the inner crucible protrudes beneath the surface of the melt allowing oxide-free InSb from beneath the surface to enter the inner crucible, the oxide scum thereby being trapped between the two crucibles. Extremely oxidized surfaces can be removed by this technique. The rod which lowers the inner crucible is then withdrawn and the pull started. Figure 2 is a photograph of InSb single crystals grown in this type of puller.

For ultrapure InSb crystal growth, it is imperative that an ultrapure atmosphere be provided. Ordinary tank helium or hydrogen is not always suitable for this work. It has been shown that after starting an InSb crystal in vacuum, the introduction of tank hydrogen, which had been passed through a liquid nitrogen trap, introduced 1×10^{16} p-type impurities per cm^3. Hydrogen which had been purified by diffusion through palladium at 350°C produced no measurable increase in carrier concentration (i.e., less than 1×10^{14} carriers/cm^3).

ALUMINUM ANTIMONIDE CRYSTAL GROWTH

Although single crystals of AlSb have been grown by several investigators during the past few years, [2, 3, 7, 11] the compound remains one of the more difficult of the III-V crystals to grow.

552

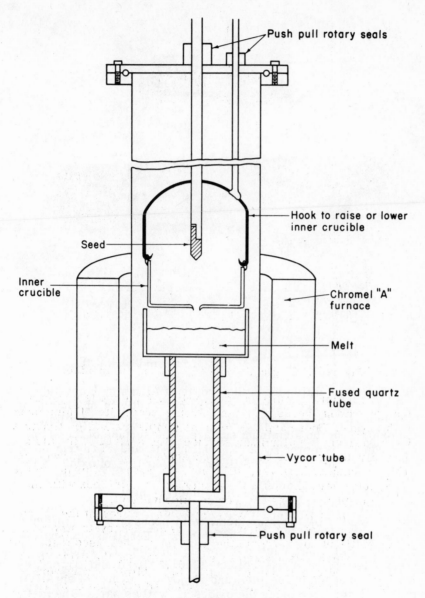

Figure 1. Indium Antimonide, Gallium Antimonide
Crystal Puller.

553

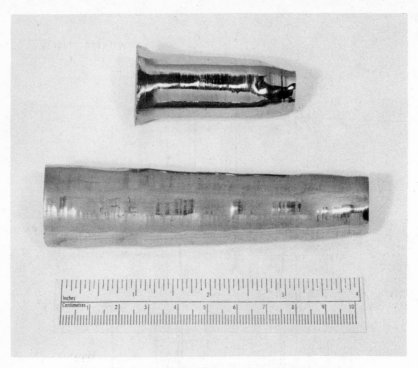

Figure 2. Single Crystals of Indium Antimonide.

The major difficulty in the growth of AlSb single crystals is that of oxides, because of the extreme reactivity of aluminum with oxygen. There appears to be no simple method to eliminate the oxide from the aluminum surface. The surface of the aluminum can be removed by a 95% phosphoric and 5% nitric etch. This technique, however, still leaves a coating of oxide on the aluminum melt. Lapping the aluminum in a dry box with inert gas atmosphere offers little or no improvement.

Since it is difficult, if not impossible, to prevent the formation of oxides on the aluminum, it is necessary to improvise other methods to overcome the problem. Schell used a shallow crucible which was caused to swirl, throwing the oxide to the outer edge where it was collected [10]. Allred and coworkers froze the surface of the melt and removed it by use of an Al_2O_3 probe [3], thus removing the oxides as well as part of the melt. Later it was found that the oxide could be removed from the aluminum by a simple heat-treatment technique [2]. Figure 3 is a drawing of an AlSb crystal growing system. The aluminum is heated to 1000°C in a vacuum for several hours. Upon melting, the aluminum is observed to be covered with a tenacious coating of oxide. After several hours, however, this oxide has disappeared [2].

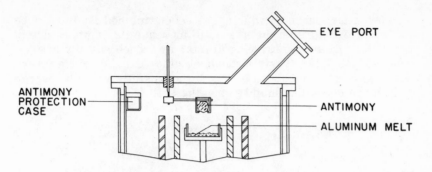

ANTIMONY PROTECTION CASE

EYE PORT

ANTIMONY

ALUMINUM MELT

Figure 3. Aluminum Antimonide Crystal Grower.

Although there is little doubt that some of the oxide is removed by sublimation, it is doubtful that this is the major mechanism by which the oxide leaves. It has been observed that the
oxide scum splits near the center of the aluminum melt with the
oxide-free gap widening with time. If an evaporation process
was involved, it would be expected that the oxide would be removed fastest at the edge of the crucible where the melt is
hottest, and not at the center. It has also been noted that if the
oxide is freed from the crucible walls, it never leaves, but remains floating on the surface of the melt. From the above ab-
servations the conclusion drawn is that as the melt vibrates, the
oxide is forced against the walls of the crucible where it adheres
to the side wall. As the aluminum moves back, the oxide is
pulled toward the edge of the crucible. The vibrations thereby
cause a pumping action on the oxide which pulls the oxide to the
edge of the crucible.

After the oxide is removed from the surface of the aluminum
melt, the crystal growing system is filled with an inert gas that
has been passed through liquid nitrogen traps to remove water
vapor. Helium has been used with success as the atmosphere
gas. The antimony is then moved over the hot aluminum and
allowed to melt, dripping into the crucible. An oxide-free melt
can be produced by this technique.

Seeding of the melt is always a critical point in any crystal
growth from the melt. The seeding of AlSb melts is complicated
because of the oxide on the surface of the AlSb seed. As yet there
has not been a technique developed which will yield an oxide-free
surface on the AlSb seed. The oxide can cause nucleation of new
crystals. There are two ways in which to minimize the effect of
this oxide.

If a large seed is used the seed can be pushed beneath the
surface of the melt about 1/4 of an inch. The seed is withdrawn
after the surface of the seed has been melted away, thus removing
the oxide. The oxide remains upon the melt surface, however,

555

as a potential source of twinning. A second method used to reduce the effect of oxides on the seed is to increase the temperature of the melt, forcing the growing crystal to reduce sharply in size. The newly seeded crystals caused by the oxide are thus forced out. Both techniques can be used successfully with the degree of success depending mainly upon the skill of the operator.

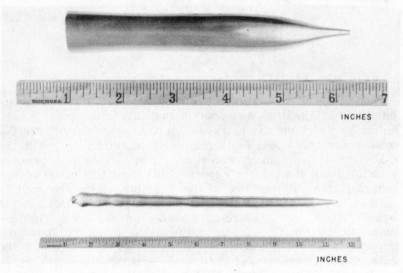

Figure 4. Single Crystals of Aluminum Antimonide.

Figure 4 is a photograph of single crystals of AlSb grown by this technique. Antimony is rather volatile at the melting point of AlSb, and a considerable amount is lost during the reacting and pulling period. A slight excess of antimony (approximately 1 percent) can be added to compensate for this loss. If the aluminum is heat-treated in the system, enough aluminum is usually lost to balance the loss of antimony during the pulling operation. The striations at the bottom of the long thin AlSb crystal (Fig. 4) are caused by a nonstoichiometric melt.

INDIUM ARSENIDE AND GALLIUM ARSENIDE SINGLE CRYSTAL GROWTH

The crystal pullers used for the growth of single crystals of both InAs and GaAs are, of necessity, more complicated than those used for compounds with less volatile elements. An arsenic pressure of approximately 0.3 atmospheres for InAs and approximately 0.9 atmospheres for GaAs must be maintained over the melt during the entire growing period. This necessitates heating the crystal growing chamber to a minimum of about 570°C for InAs and 608°C for GaAs. Due to the reactivity of arsenic at this temperature, the construction materials inside the system are limited to materials such as quartz, graphite, or the more stable oxides and nitrides.

Since push-pull rotary vacuum seals are not practical at these temperatures, it has been necessary to develop new techniques for the growth of this material.

Of the various crystal pullers that have been developed for growing InAs and GaAs, the two most widely used are the

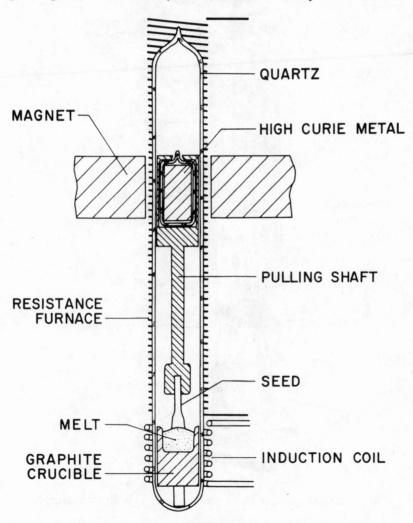

Figure 5. Magnetic Type Crystal Puller [7].

557

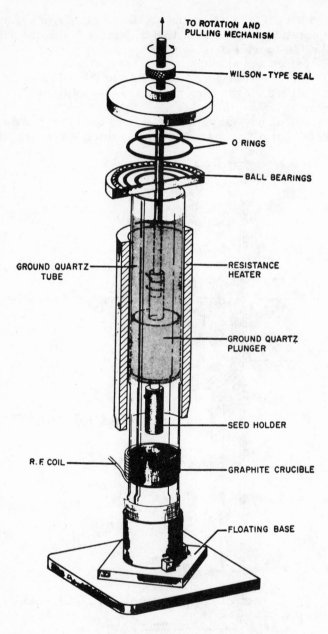

TO ROTATION AND
PULLING MECHANISM

WILSON-TYPE SEAL

O RINGS

BALL BEARINGS

GROUND QUARTZ
TUBE

RESISTANCE
HEATER

GROUND QUARTZ
PLUNGER

SEED HOLDER

R.F. COIL

GRAPHITE CRUCIBLE

FLOATING BASE

Single-crystal furnace for materials with volatile constituent.

Figure 6. Syringe Type Crystal Puller [6].

558

syringe [8] and magnetic [5] pullers. The syringe (Fig. 6) depends upon a precision-fit piston that limits the amount of arsenic which escapes from the pulling chamber. An inert gas is usually used to decrease the mean-free-path of arsenic, thus reducing the arsenic loss. An excess of arsenic is provided to replace the arsenic lost during operation.

The magnetic puller developed by Gremmelmaier [5] (Fig. 5) uses a completely sealed system and, therefore, does not lose arsenic during the pulling operation. The seed motion is supplied by magnetic coupling through the quartz tube.

There are advantages and disadvantages to both types of systems. The precision quartz for the syringe puller is expensive and easily broken by jamming of the precision parts. The loss of arsenic can also be a problem if the growing time is prolonged.

Since the vapor pressure of arsenic changes exponentially with temperature, small changes in arsenic temperature will cause large changes in the stoichiometry of the melt. The control of the arsenic pressure is, therefore, extremely critical when excess arsenic is used in the puller. A definite advantage of the syringe puller is that the piston to which the seed is attached can be driven by direct drive. Smooth pulling and rotation is, therefore, easily achieved. The system can also be readily opened for reloading.

The magnetic puller has the disadvantage of requiring the quartz capsule to be cut open and resealed for each crystal. Smooth rotation of the seed is also difficult to obtain. Principal advantages in using the magnetic puller are that high precision quartz is not necessary and the loss of arsenic is eliminated.

Eliminating the loss of arsenic enables the stoichiometric composition of the melt to be controlled very simply. By using only enough arsenic to produce stoichiometry and allowing a small excess to produce the required pressure in the pulling chamber, the temperature control problem for the arsenic pressure can be eliminated. The only condition to be met is that the ambient temperature be above that which would normally produce an arsenic pressure equal to the dissociation pressure of the compound. Thus, large changes in temperature produce only small changes in the stoichiometry of the melt. Another advantage, when the elements are used as the starting material, is that the ambient temperature can be rather high, producing a high pressure of arsenic which decreases the reaction time. The arsenic pressure remains high until all the arsenic (except that used as atmosphere) is reacted and stoichiometry realized.

One of the major problems in the growing of single crystals of InAs and GaAs is that the quartz tube just above the melt often becomes coated with material and visibility is lost. This coating is comprised of the oxides as well as evaporated indium or

559

gallium. If the oxides have not been properly removed from the melt, this condition is more pronounced. Removal of the oxides of InAs and GaAs can be achieved by a one-to-one mixture of hydrochloric and nitric acid. Cleaning of the elements--gallium and indium--has been discussed in a previous section. Oxides are removed from the arsenic by hydrogen reduction or by sublimation of the oxide at elevated temperatures. The coating of the quartz window area can be completely eliminated if the area is continually heated to a temperature near that of the molten compound. A partial pressure of inert gas such as helium will reduce the evaporation of the compound.

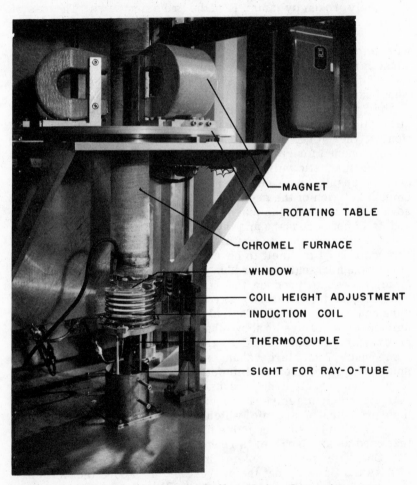

Figure 7. Magnetic Puller Under Operation.

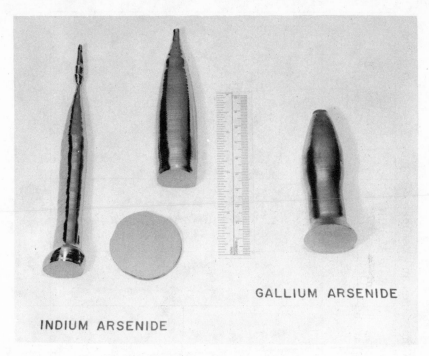

GALLIUM ARSENIDE

INDIUM ARSENIDE

Figure 8. Single Crystals of InAs and GaAs.

Figure 7 is a photograph of a magnetic puller under operation. A few of the crystals that have been grown in this system are shown in Fig. 8. Crystals in excess of 1.5 inches in diameter have been grown with the major limitation of size being the diameter and volume of the crucible.

IMPURITIES IN SINGLE CRYSTALS

Although crystal growth by the Czochralski technique can yield large single crystals of very low dislocation density, the ultimate of purity is usually produced in a horizontal system where purification by zone refining can be used. Crystals produced by the horizontal method are usually high in dislocations due to wetting of the boat. Table I gives the published electron mobility, hole mobility, and estimated impurity level of boat grown and pulled single crystals. The impurity content is estimated by comparing the measured carrier mobility with empirical mobility as a function of impurity concentration curves. The pulled crystals are those which the author has grown using commercially available high-purity elements and the techniques described in this paper. An exception is InSb for which the zone-refined compound was used. They do not represent the highest

561

Table I. Carrier Mobilities in High-Purity III-V Compounds and Estimated Impurity Concentrations

	Electron Mobility cm²/v-sec 77°K		Estimated Total Impurity Concentration n/cm³	Hole Mobility cm²/v-sec 77°K		Estimated Total Impurity Concentration n/cm³
	Boat Grown	Pulled		Boat Grown	Pulled	
InSb	620,000 [4]	500,000*	4×10^{14} 2×10^{14}		10,200	8×10^{14}
GaSb		6,000 [11]	1×10^{18}		2,200	2×10^{17}
AlSb		360	2×10^{17}	3,000	3,700	2×10^{16} 4×10^{16}
InAs	67,000 [6]	70,000	2×10^{16} 4×10^{16}			
GaAs	17,000 [13]	9,000	$2-4 \times 10^{16}$ 1×10^{17}			
InP	23,400 [12]	5,000	6×10^{16} 1×10^{17}			

*Pulled from zone-refined indium antimonide.

purity which has been obtained in pulled crystals. The impurity values for the boat grown crystals are published values and also do not necessarily represent the highest purity materials yet produced.

In almost every case the impurities are higher in the pulled crystals than those produced by the horizontal method. With the exception of GaAs and possibly InAs, this increase in impurity concentration is not due to the method of crystal growth. The boat grown crystals represent crystals grown from elements which had undergone extensive purification. In many cases the material was also zone refined after reaction.

The pulled crystals were grown from the purest elements available without any attempt at further purification. In GaAs, where the melt is known to be contaminated by the quartz crucible, there is a definite increase of impurity concentration in the pulled crystals. Doping from the quartz crucible is a major problem. The very nature of the Czochralski technique requires the temperature at the periphery of the crucible to exceed that near the center of the melt. The contamination rate from the quartz crucible is, therefore, accelerated. It is possible, however, to use other crucibles for the growth of GaAs, thus eliminating the contamination due to silicon from the crucible.

Mass spectrographic analyses of GaAs crystals grown in quartz boats show the material to contain considerable silicon and carbon. The presence of large quantities of oxygen is also observed. It is probable that the silicon is introduced from the quartz crucible. The carbon might be introduced from graphite parts in the pulling system. Residual oxygen in the system would react with the graphite, forming carbon dioxide which could ultimately react with the melt. Carbon, copper, and oxygen, identified by the mass spectrometer, are found to be impurities in AlSb. The high level of carbon probably comes from the graphite heater used in the system.

INDIUM PHOSPHIDE AND GALLIUM PHOSPHIDE CRYSTAL GROWTH

Single crystals of InP and GaP grown by the Czochralski method are still a challenge for the future. The problems of growing single crystals of InP and GaP are similar to those of growing GaAs and InAs. The high dissociation pressures at the melting points are the major differences.

Indium phosphide, which has a melting point of $1060°C$, must be grown under an atmosphere of approximately 15-20 atmospheres, while GaP, which melts at about $1500°C$, requires between 30 and 50 atmospheres to maintain stoichiometry. Since quartz will not stand these temperatures and pressures, it is necessary to enclose the puller in an autoclave which can be pressurized to a pressure near that of the phosphorus pressure used to produce stoichiometry.

It is probable that single crystals can be pulled from non-stoichiometric melts. Slow growth rates, extremely good temperature control, and a minimum of vibrations of the seed and melt become very important when growing from solutions. The farther the melt is from stoichiometry the slower the growth rate must be. Vibrations of the melt, sudden changes in the melt temperature, and rapid pulling rates, produce twinning of the crystal due to fast (although momentary) growth rates. If the rate of growth exceeds the rate of diffusion of excess indium or gallium away from the growing interface, the crystal will incorporate elemental indium and gallium and thus be forced to twin.

Because of the high melting point of GaP, the choice of crucible is limited to materials such as graphite, Al_2O_3, BN, or AlN. Quartz can be used satisfactorily for InP crystal growth.

CONCLUSIONS

Large single crystals of most of the III-V compounds can now be grown in a routine fashion. Although the crystal growing system of GaAs and InAs is more involved than that of Si or Ga, the actual pulling of the material is no more difficult. In general, the pulled crystals are less pure than single crystals grown by horizontal zone refining. If zone-refined material were used, however, comparable purity would be expected. Gallium arsenide and possibly InAs appear to be doped with silicon from the quartz crucibles in which they are grown. Crucibles made from other materials will probably be used in the future. Pulling of large single crystals of InP and GaP is practical. When the need for these materials is sufficient, the crystals will be grown.

In studies of the growth of single crystals of InSb [9] and GaSb, it has been observed that the effective segregation coefficient of Te and Se varies from less than one "on the [111] facet" to greater than one "off the facet" region. Now that reproducible single crystals of GaAs and InAs can be pulled, the effect of facet growth on segregation coefficients will be studied. Segregation coefficients in InP and GaP will also be investigated when these crystals can be pulled reproducibly.

REFERENCES

1. W. P. Allred, R. T. Bate, J. Electrochem. Soc. 108, 258 (1961).
2. W. P. Allred, W. L. Mefferd, and R. K. Willardson, J. Electrochem. Soc. 107, 117 (1960)

3. W. P. Allred, B. Paris, and M. Genser, J. Electrochem. Soc. 105, 93 (1958).
4. R. T. Bate, R. K. Willardson, and A. C. Beer, J. Phys. Chem. Solids 9, 119 (1959).
5. R. Gremmelmaier, Z. f. Naturf. 11a, 511 (1956).
6. T. C. Harmon, H. L. Goering, and A. C. Beer, Phys. Rev. 104, 1562 (1956).
7. A. Herczog, R. R. Haberecht, and A. E. Middleton, J. Electrochem. Soc. 105, 533 (1958).
8. P. L. Moody and C. Kolm, Rev. Sci. Instr. 29, 1144 (1958).
9. J. B. Mullin, Electrochem. Soc. Abstracts 9, 176 (1960).
10. H. A. Schell, Z. Metallk. 49, 140 (1958).
11. A. J. Strauss, Phys. Rev. 121, 1087 (1961).
12. K. Weiser and M. Glicksman, J. Electrochem. Soc. 105, 728 (1958).
13. R. K. Willardson and J. J. Duga, Proc. of the Phys. Soc. 75, 280 (1960).

DISCUSSION

A. J. ROSENBERG (Tyco): You comment that in the case where the advancing surface of the crystal is convex, that you were able to obtain single crystal growth, whereas, when it is concave, it is more difficult to obtain good growth. Now, in all the III-V compounds, there is evidence for anisotropic segregation, particularly on the (III) plane. This is commonly associated with faster growth on the (III) surface. Now these two ideas are contradictory. That is, a convex interface gives you single crystal growth with anistropic segregration, whereas the reverse presumably causes twins, but gives you a more uniform impurity distribution. How do you reach a compromise here?

W. P. ALLRED (Bell and Howell): When we grow with an interface of this shape on the (III), we create a large area in this crystal that is actually a (III) plane. Now, say we draw an isotherm in the melt. Our crystal doesn't like to grow on a (III) face and so it lags the isotherm. It is hard to nucleate on this plane. When a crystal starts to grow on a (III) face, it grows very, very slowly. The only growth that takes place is due to supercooling. In other directions there are favorable planes, fast growth planes, where growth occurs very rapidly. In these regions of very fast growth, trapping of impurities takes place. Now, if the absorption of impurities on the surface takes place like Mullen has reported then one expects the segregation coefficient to become greater than one in this region.

W. TILLER (Chairman) (Westinghouse): Is it impossible to grow with a flat interface?

W. P. ALLRED (Bell and Howell): If you could grow with a very flat interface, you would get homogeneous material. Looking at the (110), the facets are not in the middle. They are out on the edge of the ingot. Now, this will minimize the amount of material that has this high impurity level in it.

A. J. STRAUSS (M.I.T. Lincoln Laboratory): With respect to this last point we have done some growing on other orientations--either the (110) or (100). For these orientations there are no problems. Whatever facet there may be is so far out to one side that you don't see it.

W. P. ALLRED (Bell and Howell): The thing is that it depends on the shape of your interface. If your interface is very, very flat on the (110), you won't see anything. If it is very curved, then you will see a large facet.

A. J. STRAUSS (M.I.T. Lincoln Laboratory): In tellurium doped indium antimonide, we have been able to grow crystals where the tellurium concentration has been constant to better than 5 per cent. At least, it is constant within the limits of our measurement.

M. R. LORENZ (General Electric): For the aluminum antiomonide grown crystals, you mentioned a crucible. Could you tell me the material you used?

W. P. ALLRED (Bell and Howell): Aluminum oxide.

M. R. LORENZ (General Electric): You mentioned the oxide film. It has been reported by the Alcoa people that aluminum oxide forms a suboxide which is volatile and this may be the one which disappears.

Now, the next question is, have you observed the interaction of the aluminum oxide with the aluminum antimonide in the melt? Actually, we have observed a very strong diffusion of either aluminum oxide into the aluminum antimonide or aluminum antimonide in the aluminum oxide. You cannot see the original interface of the crucible.

W. P. ALLRED (Bell and Howell): Let me say this. I know that we get samples of oxides, aluminum oxide. When we pull a crystal and then try to melt it back, we get material off the surface of the aluminum antimonide crystal that I can only attribute to aluminum oxide. However, the reason for this leaving the surface is not because it all evaporates.

M. D. BANUS (M.I.T. Lincoln Laboratory): You mentioned using autoradiography techniques. Would you outline the systems you have studied with this?

W. P. ALLRED (Bell and Howell): Well, I have only studied indium antimonide. However, we are going to start studying gallium arsenide, indium arsenide and the phosphides just as soon as I can grow them reproducibly. However, in gallium antimonide we do find this effect with a mass spectrometer. We know where the facets are and we get large differences. However, a detailed radiographic study has not been made.

M. D. BANUS (M.I.T. Lincoln Laboratory): What isotope do you use with your indium antimonide?

W. P. ALLRED (Bell and Howell): I used radioactive tellurium.

M. D. BANUS (M.I.T. Lincoln Laboratory): We have been working with sulphur 35 and indium antimonide. We observed these facet effects. Have you noticed any effects of the rotation rate on the concentration of your dopant on and off the facet?

W. P. ALLRED (Bell and Howell): I haven't done any detailed study on this. I have some pretty concrete views that a lot of the earlier work that was done were observations of facet growth, even in silicon and germanium.

H. T. MINDEN (General Electric): Do you have any way in a given material of varying the shape of the interface in the Czochralski technique?

W. P. ALLRED (Bell and Howell): Yes. You can vary the type of heater that you are using. You can vary the loss of heat from the ingot, and you can change them quite drastically. You can change them from convex to concave very easily.

W. ZIMMERMAN (N.R.L.): You mentioned the necessity for very careful temperature control. I would like to say that we agree with you wholeheartedly on this. What techniques do you use to maintain a steady temperature during growth?

W. P. ALLRED (Bell and Howell): For indium antimonide I use a resistance furnace that is very well insulated and has a fair amount of heat lag. There is no air gap between it and the tube so that convection is eliminated.

SOURCES OF CONTAMINATION IN GaAs CRYSTAL GROWTH

L. Ekstrom and L. R. Weisberg
RCA Laboratories, Princeton, N. J.

ABSTRACT

Current evidence indicates that the purity of GaAs is now limited by contamination during crystal growth, rather than by the purity of the starting materials. A careful study has been carried out to identify sources of such contamination in the preparation of GaAs. Vacuum baking of gallium at $650°C$ for several hours in a quartz boat to remove oxides was found to increase the copper content, but not the silicon or other spectrographically detectable impurities. Back diffusion of impurities from a contaminated high vacuum pump was observed to affect properties of GaAs even when pressures of 10^{-6} torr were maintained. Sealing under vacuum of large (20 mm) diameter quartz ampoules introduces significant quantities of silicon and copper onto the inner ampoule walls, which subsequently contaminate arsenic vapor when heated to above $1000°C$. During growth, it was found that there is no appreciable diffusion of atmospheric gases through quartz at $1200°C$. However, nearly 10^{18} molecules of gas are released due to outgassing of the walls. The most serious contamination, especially with silicon, occurs from the reaction between the GaAs melt and the quartz boat, and the reaction increases rapidly with increasing melt temperature.

I. INTRODUCTION

The application of GaAs for transistors and transistor-like devices requires a material of extremely high purity in single crystal form. Past efforts to increase the purity of GaAs have centered on the purification of the component elements, gallium and arsenic, because of the existence of impurities that could not readily be removed from GaAs by zone refining. The impurity content of commercially available gallium and arsenic has now been reduced to the point where it is comparable to or below the amount of impurities introduced into GaAs by contamination during its preparation. The following evidence supports this conclusion.

568

First, emission and mass spectrographic analysis have detected impurities, such as silicon and copper, in GaAs in concentrations greater than that present in the starting materials. Second, series of GaAs crystals produced from the same lots of gallium and arsenic have had widely varying electrical properties. However, variations in the lots of gallium and arsenic have produced only minor changes in the electrical properties of the resulting GaAs. Third, special purification treatments carried out for gallium and arsenic have improved the properties of other compounds such as InAs, but have had little or no effect on the properties of GaAs.

For these reasons, this investigation was carried out to determine the sources of such contamination and thus provide proper guidance in devising improved methods of preparation. The investigation is specifically concerned with the horizontal Bridgman technique of crystal growth; however, the results are applicable to other methods of crystal growth. The details of the preparation of a GaAs growth ampoule for this growth technique are described in the following section. In subsequent sections each step in this procedure is carefully examined for possible sources of contamination. Throughout this paper, it is implicit that careful precautions were taken to remove the obvious contamination sources such as dust and similar foreign matter, to use gloves where required, etc.

II. PREPARATION OF GaAs

The arsenic was received in chunks each weighing approximately a gram, sealed in a Pyrex ampoule in 50 or 100 g lots. After being opened, the Pyrex ampoule was stored under vacuum in a larger Pyrex ampoule, sealed by a vacuum stopcock. The gallium is received in a polyethylene bag as a large lump. To remove pieces, the gallium was cooled to liquid nitrogen temperature, placed in "Glassine" paper bags, and cracked by squeezing in a vise. It was subsequently stored in these bags within a closed glass jar inside an airtight cabinet.

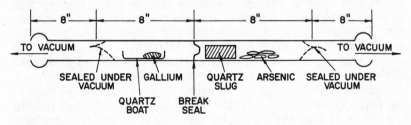

Figure 1.   GaAs Growth Ampoule.

The ampoule, shown in Fig. 1, consists of a quartz tube of 20 mm bore with a ball joint at each end and a breakseal dividing it into two chambers. All quartz ware, including the tube, growth boat, and slug for rupturing the breakseal, was cleaned by first washing it in a detergent such as "Alconox," then treating it with aqua regia, then etching with a 1:1 mixture of HF and HNO_3, and finally cleaning in a mixture of triple distilled HNO_3 and HCl. Each step was followed by extensive rinsing in triple distilled water; and after the final rinse, the water was removed using transistor-grade acetone which was drained, and the quartz allowed to dry in air. The quartz slug and the arsenic were loaded in air into one chamber of the tube, and the tube was then connected through a liquid nitrogen trap to a diffusion pump and evacuated. The arsenic was heated in a vacuum of below 10^{-6} torr for 1 hour at 300°C to remove surface oxides, and then that section of the ampoule was sealed under vacuum after first collapsing the tube with a broad flame produced by a brass hydrogen-oxygen torch.

Next, the growth boat containing solid gallium was placed in the other chamber of the tube, which was then evacuated before the gallium was melted. A vacuum heat treatment of 3 hours at 650°C was given to remove oxides of gallium as Ga_2O, after which the gallium was refrozen and the ampoule sealed off using the same technique as for the arsenic section. The final ampoule is shown in Fig. 1.

After the breakseal was ruptured by causing the quartz slug to strike it, the GaAs was synthesized and grown into a crystal in a typical two zone horizontal Bridgman furnace [1]. In synthesizing the GaAs, the entire system was brought up to the arsenic reservoir temperature of about 600°C, and then the temperature of the reaction zone containing the molten gallium was gradually raised to about 1260°C. The crystal was then grown by moving the entire furnace over the stationary quartz tube at a rate of about 1 cm hr^{-1} for a total period of 16 hours.

III. EFFECTS OF CLEANING AND HANDLING PROCEDURES

It was first determined whether the ordinary rinsing with distilled water is sufficient to remove the acids used for cleaning. This was found by measuring the resistivity of the water after each rinse. A 1:1 mixture of $HCl-HNO_3$ was placed in a quartz ampoule for one hour. This mixture was then discarded and replaced with deionized water, which remained in the ampoule for various times (usually 10 sec). After a number of rinses, the rinse water was also boiled in the ampoule. Typical results are shown in Table I. It can be seen that even ten rinsings with cold deionized water is not sufficient to remove all traces of

Table I. Effect of Rinsing Treatment on Removal of
Acids from Ampoules

Rinse No.	Conditions	Water Resistivity (megohm- cm)
0	Original water	2
4		.035
5		.2
6	All rinses through No. 10	.3
7	in ampoule for 10 sec.	1.0
8		1.5
9		1.8
10		2
11	Boiled for 1/2 hour	.8
12	10 sec	2
13	Boiled for 1-1/2 hours	1.8
14	10 sec	2
15	10 sec	2

impurities subsequent to acid cleaning. Instead, it is at least necessary to boil the water for a half hour in the vial.

Experiments were also carried out to determine if the cleaning procedure itself was adequate. Many variations were tested, such as treating different ampoules with HF only, HF followed by aqua regia, or aqua regia alone, using non-distilled acids, eliminating the acetone rinse, etc. It was noted that a scouring agent such as "Ajax" should be avoided since it is not dissolved by aqua regia. Variations were also attempted in the handling of the elements such as weighing out and transferring gallium as a liquid rather than a solid [2], the use of filter paper instead of "Glassine" paper, and plastic instead of stainless steel forceps. Despite all of these variations, no difference could be seen in the properties of the resulting GaAs. The conclusion can be drawn that the cleaning procedure used for quartz and the handling techniques for the elements are not significant variables compared to contamination sources described in the sections to follow.

IV. EFFECTS OF VACUUM BAKING AND SEALING

During the vacuum annealing of the gallium and arsenic to remove oxides, and the subsequent sealing of the evacuated ampoules, there are several ways in which contamination might occur. The three which have been investigated are back diffusion of impurities from the vacuum pump, reaction between gallium and the quartz boat during bakeout, and evolution of material from the quartz while it is being sealed.

A. Contamination from Vacuum Pumps

Both oil and mercury diffusion pumps have been used in the preparation of GaAs ampoules, and no significant difference was noted in the purity of the resulting GaAs. On certain occasions, the vacuum pumps have been cleaned or new vacuum pumps have been used. In general, this has caused no improvement in the properties of the GaAs, except on one occasion[2]. In this case, a series of crystals were produced with electron mobilities on the average below 4000 cm^2 v^{-1} sec^{-1}. Many variations were attempted, but the mobilities did not improve until the mercury diffusion pump was dismantled and cleaned. The resulting change in the mobility is shown in Fig. 2. The points with the attached bars indicate crystals of GaAs produced from the same lots of gallium and arsenic. Not all crystals grown are included in the graph, because some were doped or else grown under special conditions. The importance of a clean vacuum system is manifest from these results. However, this result is somewhat surprising since the system was producing vacuums of the order of 10^{-6} torr both before and after the cleaning. At this pressure, the number of residual gas molecules in the ampoule is about 10^{13} while the change in properties corresponds to 10^{17} atoms or more. It would appear that material was continuously diffusing back from the pump through the trap and condensing on the walls.

In further tests of the effects of vacuum systems, the vacuum grease in the ball and socket joints used to attach the cold trap and growth ampoule to the vacuum system was replaced by black vacuum wax. This wax does not have a tendency to flow out of the joint into the system, and reportedly has a vapor pressure of only 10^{-8} torr at room temperature. However, this substitution did not improve the purity of GaAs prepared with this vacuum system.

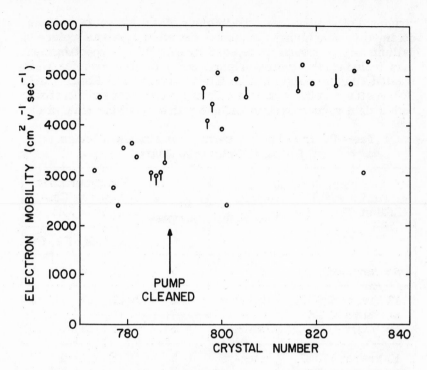

Figure 2. Electron Mobility of GaAs Crystals Before and
After Cleaning of the Mercury Diffusion Pump.

B. The Vacuum Baking of Gallium

The next possibility is that gallium might react with the quartz boat during the vacuum anneal and become contaminated, especially with silicon. Gallium is known to react with quartz readily at higher temperatures [3], so there was reason to suspect that this reaction might also be occurring at 650°C to a significant extent. To test this possibility, gallium samples were subjected to the same annealing conditions used in preparing an ampoule, except that the annealing time was increased to 12 hours from the usual 3 hours to exaggerate any effects. Changes in the impurity content of the gallium were determined by emission spectrographic analysis before and after the anneal. In each case, several samples were analyzed, and the reported impurity concentration is the geometric mean of the results. This averaging process was necessary, since the spectrographic analysis was semiquantitative and accurate to within only a factor of three. To differentiate between bulk contamination of the gallium and impurities which collect on or segregate to the surface of the gallium, two types of samples were taken for analysis. The first

573

consisted of pieces from the interior of a 5 g ingot of gallium, obtained by fracturing the ingot. The other type was a piece of gallium small enough to be used directly in the spectrograph, thus including the entire original surface. The samples were treated simultaneously in a suitably compartmented boat. Table II shows the results of such a heat treatment on the gallium using both a tight vacuum system and one with a small air leak. It can

Table II. Impurities Introduced During the Vacuum
Baking of Gallium in Quartz

Gallium Treatment	Type of sample	No. of samples	Spectrographic Impurity Content in ppm.			
			Si	Mg	Fe	Cu
As received	-	5	<.1	.3	2	<1
12 hrs. at 650°C, pressure of 3 x 10⁻⁶ torr	interior	2	<.1	.2	1	2
	exterior	3	<.1	.3	2	3
12 hrs. at 650°C, pressure of 5 x 10⁻⁵ torr (air leak)	interior	2	1	<.1	2	<1
	exterior	3	5	.5	3	1

be seen that no detectable silicon contamination occurs due to the baking process at 650°C provided there is no oxygen present. However, one of the oxides of gallium apparently attacks quartz at this temperature. It can also be seen that there is no evidence for iron and magnesium contamination, but that the copper content is increased. The copper could be leached from the quartz boat, since quartz is known to contain copper that easily diffuses out [4].

C. Sealing of the Ampoule

During the sealing of the ampoule the quartz is heated above its softening point. The quartz vaporizes with some decomposition at these temperatures, and redeposits in part on cooler portions of the quartz as manifested by the appearance of a rough white film. The decomposition products include oxygen[5] which could enter the ampoule, as could the gases from the oxy-hydrogen flame. Thus, the sealing procedure might first introduce gaseous impurities into the ampoule; second, directly contaminate gallium or arsenic within the ampoule; and third, contaminate the inner ampoule walls and thereby contaminate the arsenic vapor during growth.

The first possibility was investigated by attaching a thermocouple gauge to a quartz ampoule, which was subjected to the same cleaning and vacuum baking process used for growth ampoules. After sealing of the ampoule, the pressure in the ampoule was below the 10^{-3} torr detection limit of the gauge, indicating that a total of less than about 5×10^{15} gas molecules are trapped in the ampoule due to the sealing process. This represents a comparatively negligible amount of contamination in a GaAs crystal, which is usually about 4 cm^3 in volume.

The possibility of direct deposition of decomposition products onto the gallium was investigated by preparing an ampoule containing a compartmented boat with both large and small gallium samples similar to the experiment described in Sec. IVB. After the usual vacuum baking and freezing, the quartz ampoule was sealed at a point beyond the boat and vacuum pump. Thus, if there were a flow of material towards the vacuum pump, it would enhance the effects of deposition. Subsequent to the sealing, the samples were spectrographically analyzed. The results are shown in Table III, which also includes results for a similar experiment with arsenic. The analysis of the interior samples of gallium indicates that no accidental introduction of impurities occurred during the vacuum baking within the limits of error. It can be concluded, therefore, that direct deposition of impurities onto the elements is not a significant source of contamination.

Table III. Impurities Introduced During the Sealing of an Ampoule

Material and Treatment	No. and type of sample	Spectrographic Impurity Content in ppm			
		Si	Mg	Fe	Cu
Gallium (as received)	5	<.1	.5	3	<1
Gallium (after vacuum bake and sealing)	2 interior	<.1	1	nd	1
	3 exterior	<.1	1	1	1
Arsenic (as received)	3	.1	<.1	nd	nd
Arsenic (after vacuum bake and sealing)	3	<.1	nd	nd	nd

The third experiment on the sealing of quartz tubing dealt with the possibility of the deposition of impurities on the ampoule walls from the sealing operation with subsequent contamination of the arsenic vapor during crystal growth. The procedure was again designed to duplicate the conditions prevailing in the growth of GaAs. A 20 mm bore quartz ampoule, cleaned in the usual manner, was degassed in vacuum for 2 or 3 hours at 700°C, cooled, and about 0.3 gm of arsenic was then introduced without breaking the vacuum. This amount of arsenic was calculated to be just sufficient for complete vaporization. After vacuum baking to remove arsenic oxides, the ampoule was sealed under vacuum and placed in a two zone furnace for periods of about 16 hours with the sealed end held at 1220°C and the opposite end at 600°C. After this treatment, care was taken to cool the ampoule slowly and at the cooler end first. In this manner the arsenic condensed in the form of lumps, rather than as large area thin sheets. The condensed arsenic was recovered by breaking the ampoule. Changes in the impurity content of the arsenic were determined by spectrographic analyses before and after this exposure to quartz. In all cases, the arsenic starting material was found to contain only two impurities: copper at or below the detection limit of 1 ppm, and silicon at or below 0.2 ppm. For each run, four samples of arsenic were analyzed. The reported impurity concentration represents the geometric mean of the four results.

The typical contamination of arsenic that is observed due to the sealing is shown in the first two rows of Table IV for two separate runs. A large increase in both the silicon and copper content of the arsenic can be seen. To try to enhance this effect, several runs were made in which multiple seals were performed on the ampoule, each seal being made closer to the arsenic. The results of one such run using 6 seals is shown in the third row. The absence of a proportional increase in the contamination is probably caused by much of the vaporized material depositing very close to the seal, so that most of the contamination comes from only the last seal.

Table IV. Effect of Sealing Quartz on Contamination of
Arsenic after Heating at 1220°C for 16 Hours

No. of Seals	Quartz Bore (mm)	Spectrographic Analysis (ppm)	
		Si	Cu
1	20	3	4
1	20	4	9
6	20	10	7
1	6	.05	<1
1	6	.2	1

576

In the above experiments, the possibility existed that the arsenic simply attacked the quartz walls, and the contamination was not related to the sealing process. To test this possibility, ampoules were constructed with the 20 mm bore quartz ampoule terminating with 6 mm bore tubing. Much less heating is required to seal 6 mm bore quartz tubing than 20 mm bore tubing so less quartz is vaporized. As shown in Table IV in the last two rows, this reduces the arsenic contamination to below the limits of detection.

Next, the effect of temperature on the above reaction was investigated. To exaggerate any effects so that they could be easily observable, four to five seals were made on the 20 mm bore tube for each run. The sealed end of the ampoule was held in different runs at 700°C, 1000°C, and 1220°C while the opposite end was held at 600°C. To improve reliability, separate runs were made two or three times at each temperature. The results in Table V represent geometric averages of 8 or 12 analyses. The usual contamination discussed previously is shown in the first row. It can be seen that reducing the temperature to only 1000°C is not sufficient to remove the contamination completely; and to do so, a temperature as low as 700°C must be employed.

Table V. Contamination of Arsenic at Various
Temperatures due to Sealing of 20 mm Bore Quartz Tubing

No. of runs	No. of seals	Temp. (°C)	Spectrographic Analysis (ppm)	
			Si	Cu
3	5	1220	4	3
3	4	1000	1	1
2	4	700	.1	1

V. CONTAMINATION DURING CRYSTAL GROWTH

A. Gaseous Impurities from Quartz

In general, it is known that fused quartz can release considerable quantities of gases when heated, and is quite permeable to both helium [6] and hydrogen [7] at elevated temperatures. The latter fact suggests that atmospheric gases might also diffuse through the quartz ampoule at the melting temperature of GaAs. Therefore, the effect of both diffusion through and desorption from quartz has been investigated at temperatures used during GaAs crystal growth.

577

The literature on the diffusion of gases other than H_2 and He through fused quartz is conflicting, and does not include studies above 1000°C. T'sai and Hogness [7] report no observable diffusion of air through quartz at 1000°C. Nevertheless, based on Barrer's [8] data, Dushman[9] calculates a permeability rate for N_2 at 1100°C high enough to allow over 10^{19} N_2 molecules to enter an ampoule during a routine crystal growth. However, Barrer's work failed to take account of the outgassing of quartz. In order to distinguish between diffusion and degassing as the source of this gas, experiments were conducted with an apparatus similar to that of T'sai and Hogness [7].

The present apparatus consisted of two fused quartz tubes, one inside the other, and so connected that the outer one could be either evacuated or open to the atmosphere. The inner tube was connected to a thermocouple gauge, and to a diffusion pump by means of a stopcock. After the inner tube was evacuated with the diffusion pump, the stopcock was closed and the rate at which the pressure increased in the inner tube was measured. Every 12 hours the stopcock was again opened, and the process repeated. In this way the rate at which gas collected in the inner tube was obtained when it is alternately surrounded by air and by vacuum for these 12 hour periods. A temperature of 1200°C was used throughout, because it is the maximum temperature to which an evacuated fused quartz tube can be heated in air for several hours without collapsing.

The typical results of one of these experiments are shown in Fig. 3. The units of the ordinate are chosen to correspond to the maximum area of fused quartz that is heated above the melting point of GaAs in a routine crystal growth. It can be seen that the rate at which gas is collected is independent of whether there is air or vacuum around the tube. Thus, the amount diffusing through the walls is below the detection limit of the experiment, which is estimated to be 2×10^{15} molecules hr^{-1}. Furthermore, the fused quartz used in these tests was about 1/2 as thick as that used in a standard growth ampoule. It is also noteworthy from Fig. 3 that the rate of evolution decreases exponentially with time, which is not to be expected for the general case of the permeation of gases through a wall from a relatively large source such as the atmosphere. Nevertheless, this type of behavior was always observed. Thus, the diffusion of gases through the quartz walls during crystal growth is not considered an important source of contamination of GaAs.

To determine the number of molecules entering the ampoule during the usual 16 hour growth period due to the desorption, apparatus similar to that previously described was used but with no outer tube. The results are shown in Table VI. In the first line is shown the number of gas molecules desorbed from the

578

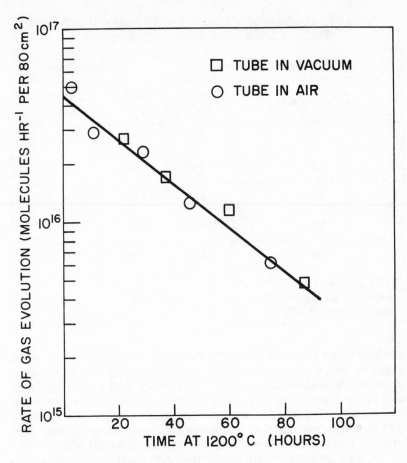

Figure 3. Time Dependence of the Rate of Gas Evolution From Fused Quartz at 1200°C.

section of the ampoule containing the gallium. The second line gives the molecules desorbed from the arsenic end of the ampoule. Therefore, a total of nearly 10^{18} molecules of gases enter the growth ampoule, which could dope a 20 g GaAs crystal to a level of roughly 3×10^{17} cm^{-3}.

The effect of predegassing at 1100°C and 1200°C is shown by the data in the third and fourth lines in Table VI. It can be seen that predegassing is not very effective since the rate of degassing is quite slow, which is also indicated by the data in Fig. 3. As would be expected, predegassing at the higher temperature is always more effective. The fraction of the total degassing that is due to adsorbed gases as compared to absorbed gases is indicated in the final two lines of Table VI. Prebaking the ampoule

Prebaking Treatment		Outgassing	
Time (hrs.)	Temp. (°C)	Temp. (°C)	Total Gas Molecules
3	650	1200	7×10^{17}
1	350	650	2×10^{17}
40	1100	1200	3×10^{17}
40	1200	1200	2×10^{17}
80	1200	1200	8×10^{16}
100 hrs. at 1200°C, exposed to air at 25°C, then 3 hrs. at 650°C		1200	2×10^{17}

at 1200°C for 80 or 100 hours reduces the evolution of absorbed gases to below 10^{17} molecules. Subsequently, a short exposure to the air will introduce 2×10^{17} adsorbed molecules, which is a sizable fraction of the total number of molecules desorbed from quartz that has not been prebaked. Therefore, quartz ware that has been prebaked and subsequently exposed to air will still introduce significant contamination during GaAs growth.

A preliminary mass spectrometric analysis of the gases evolved from quartz in vacuo has been obtained by R. E. Honig [10]. His results were reported as percentage of the total gas evolved at 600°C and at 1150°C. The analysis at 1150°C was obtained after the quartz had been prebaked at 1200°C for about one hour. The amount of helium evolved was not investigated. The results are given in Table VII. In accord with these results is the separate observation that most of the gas evolved at 600°C can be condensed at liquid nitrogen temperature, while very little of the gas evolved at 1200°C is thus condensible. Even if one assumes that hydrogen is not harmful to GaAs, there is still a total of 3×10^{17} molecules of water vapor and 7×10^{16} molecules of carbon monoxide introduced into the growth ampoule due to the desorption from both its sections. Finally, it has been found that the presence of arsenic in the reaction tube will increase by an order of magnitude the number of molecules of the major species of gaseous molecules found in the growth ampoule [11].

Component	Percentage at 600°C	Percentage at 1150°C
H_2O	68.7	17.5
CO	8.2	7.5
CO_2	5.5	3.0
H_2	5.0	71
HF	4.5	-
NO	2.2	-
N_2	2.0	0.8
O_2	1.6	0.2
HCl	1.4	-
BF_3	0.8	-
SiF_4	0.1	-

B. Contamination from the Boat

It has been previously found[1] that silicon is the main donor in GaAs, and tests have shown that the major source of silicon contamination is due to a reaction of molten GaAs with the quartz boat. The type of contamination that occurs is shown in Table VIII. The crystal was grown with a maximum temperature in the range 1265 to 1275°C. It is seen that both copper and silicon are introduced; however, the copper segregates to the tail end of the crystal due to its small distribution coefficient. There is also some evidence for a little magnesium contamination.

The contamination shown in Table VIII is not due to the sealing process, since it depends strongly on relatively small

Table VIII. Impurities Introduced into GaAs during
Crystal Growth

Sample	Spectrographically Det. Imp. (ppm)			
	Si	Mg	Fe	Cu
Gallium (as received)	<.1	.5	3	1
Arsenic (as received)	<.1	.1	-	1
GaAs Front	3	1	-	1
Middle	1	.3	-	<1
Tail	10	1	-	10

Table IX. Properties of n-type GaAs Crystals Grown at Various Temperatures

Maximum Growth Temp. (°C)	300°K		78°K	
	$n(cm^{-3})$	$\mu(cm^2V^{-1}sec^{-1})$	$n(cm^{-3})$	$\mu(cm^2V^{-1}sec^{-1})$
1265 to 1275	3.4×10^{17}	2210	2.8×10^{17}	2290
	2.5×10^{17}	3300	2.4×10^{17}	2880
	1.4×10^{17}	3500	1.1×10^{17}	3960
	1.6×10^{17}	3650	1.5×10^{17}	3950
	3.7×10^{17}	3790	2.5×10^{17}	3680
1255 to 1265	1.4×10^{17}	4100	1.3×10^{17}	4250
	2.6×10^{17}	3700	2.4×10^{17}	3700
	6.5×10^{16}	4000	5.0×10^{16}	5470
1250 to 1255	9.3×10^{16}	4550	7.5×10^{16}	5300
	4.1×10^{16}	4850	3.4×10^{16}	7250
	2.8×10^{16}	4320	2.1×10^{16}	7460*
	5.4×10^{16}	5300	4.3×10^{16}	7850*
	5.9×10^{16}	4550	4.8×10^{16}	5200

*Grown at higher speeds

582

variations of the growth temperature. The effect of the maximum temperature to which the melt is heated is shown in Table IX. It can be seen that higher growth temperatures simultaneously increase the electron (or silicon) concentration, and decrease the electron mobility. The scatter in the data in Table IX is due in part to the use of non-uniform preparative techniques for all of the crystals. It should be remembered that in these tests 16 hour growth periods were used, so that the melt remained at or near the elevated temperatures for periods of several hours. An extremely rapid change in the stability of quartz at these temperatures is also manifest by the amount of devitrification of the quartz ampoule. After a 16 hour run at 1270°C, the devitrification is so bad that the quartz becomes opaque; while at 1250°C devitrification causes only slight clouding. It can be concluded that reaction of the GaAs melt with the quartz boat constitutes the major source of contamination.

VI. CONCLUSIONS

A study has been carried out of the contamination introduced during the preparation and growth of GaAs by the horizontal Bridgman technique in a quartz ampoule and quartz boat. The major source of contamination, especially with silicon, is due to reaction of the GaAs melt with the boat. Contamination with silicon and copper has also been observed during sealing of the quartz ampoules; with copper during vacuum baking of gallium; and with water vapor and carbon monoxide during growth due to outgassing of quartz. Contamination has also been observed to occur due to back diffusion of impurities from a vacuum system.

Atmospheric gases were not observed to diffuse through quartz at the growth temperature; and the cleaning procedures used for the quartz had no significant effect on the properties of GaAs. No direct reaction of gallium with the boat was observed during vacuum baking at 650°C.

VII. ACKNOWLEDGMENTS

The authors are grateful to Mr. E. A. Miller and Mr. E. J. Stofko for important technical assistance. They are indebted to Mr. H. H. Whitaker for the spectrographic analyses, and to Dr. F. D. Rosi for continued interest and encouragement throughout this work. This research has been sponsored by the Electronics Research Directorate of the Air Force Cambridge Research Laboratories under Contract No. AF19(604)-6152.

583

REFERENCES

1. L. R. Weisberg, F. D. Rosi, and P. G. Herkart, "Properties of Elemental and Compound Semiconductors," Metallurgical Society Conference, Vol. 5, Interscience Publishers, Inc., New York (1960), p. 25.
2. P. G. Herkart, Private Communication.
3. L. M. Foster and R. A. Kramer, J. Electrochem. Soc. 107, 189C (1960).
4. J. T. Edmond and C. Hilsum, J. Appl. Phys. 61, 1300 (1960).
5. H. L. Schick, Chem. Rev. 60, 331 (1960).
6. D. E. Swets, R. W. Lee, and R. C. Frank, J. Chem. Phys. 34, 17 (1961).
7. L. S. T'sai and T. Hogness, J. Phys. Chem. 36, 2595 (1932).
8. R. M. Barrer, J. Chem. Soc. 1934, 378 (1934).
9. S. Dushman, "Scientific Foundations of Vacuum Technique," J. Wiley and Sons, New York (1949), p. 534.
10. R. E. Honig, Private Communication.
11. S. Skalski and R. Foehring, Private Communication.

DISCUSSION

G. L. VANWINKLE (Melpar): Did you make any analysis to determine what the impurities were that come from your vacuum diffusion pump?

L. EKSTROM (RCA): No, we didn't.

G. L. VANWINKLE (Melpar): I am curious why you used the mercury diffusion pump instead of the oil. We usually use the oil diffusion pump to eliminate the problem of back diffusion in mercury.

L. EKSTROM (RCA): We have used both oil and mercury diffusion pumps and have noticed no difference in the properties of the gallium arsenide.

R. A. KRAMER (Alcoa): We have done extensive work at Alcoa on the reaction of gallium with quartz. Can you distinguish between the reactivity of gallium arsenide and gallium? We feel it is the reaction of gallium with quartz rather than gallium arsenide that introduces contamination.

L. EKSTROM (RCA): Certainly the gallium arsenide melt reacts much more slowly with quartz at 1250°C than does gallium. The exact species in the gallium arsenide melt that causes the reaction may be gallium, but this question cannot be answered at the present time.

R. A. KRAMER (Alcoa): That is true, but still gallium is heated up to temperature before the arsenic is introduced and so it must be the gallium that is reacting with the quartz.

L. R. WEISBERG (RCA): The last table indicates that the main contamination is due to the reaction of the gallium arsenide melt with the boat, and not the gallium during the heating period.

PREPARATION OF CRYSTALS OF THE
ALLOY SYSTEM Bi-Sb-Se-Te

David A. Puotinen
Energy Conversion Group
Department of Electrical Engineering
Massachusetts Institute of Technology
Cambridge, Massachusetts

ABSTRACT

This paper describes the preparation of crystals of the quaternary alloy system $Bi_{24} Se_6 Sb_{(60+x)} Te_{(150-x)}$ where x varies from -8 to +12. This system has recently been investigated by Merck and others because of its reported high figure of merit. The samples were prepared by a modified and carefully controlled Bridgman process. By this technique, large crystals have been obtained over the entire alloy system. Separate direct measurement of a, k, and ρ on the first material to crystallize indicate that a figure of merit approaching 3×10^{-3} $(K°)^{-1}$ may be obtained in this system.

ACKNOWLEDGMENT

Financial support for this research was provided by the United States Air Force through the Air Force Cambridge Research Laboratories under Contract AF19(604)-4153 with the Energy Conversion Group, Department of Electrical Engineering, Massachusetts Institute of Technology. Although this paper is based upon work sponsored by the U. S. Air Force, it has not been approved or disapproved by that agency.

I.   INTRODUCTION

The alloy system $Bi_{24} Sb_{60+x} Se_6 Te_{150-x}$ has been the subject of a number of investigations because of the possible applications of these alloys in thermoelectric devices. An investigation by Merck and Company [6] reported values of thermal conductivity as low as .010 w/cm°C and indicated that a figure of merit approaching 4×10^{-3} $(K°)^{-1}$ may be obtained. The formal composition of this system may be regarded as a melange of sesquitellurides with excess tellurium:

585

$$(Bi_2Se_3)_2 \cdot (Bi_2Te_3)_{10} \cdot (Sb_2Te_3)_{\frac{60+x}{2}} \cdot (Te)_{(30-\frac{5}{2}x)} \cdot$$

Thus as x is varied from -8 to +12, the amount of "excess" tellurium approaches zero. X-ray analysis of Bridgman ingots has shown that in the region of x = 0 the alloys formed are iso-morphous with bismuth telluride [6]. In this paper are presented the results of a study of the temperature variation of the Seebeck coefficient and the electrical resistivity of the crystals grown from melts of different x values. All data presented are from one-centimeter long slugs of the first material to crystallize in a Bridgman ingot. It should be noted in particular, that the chemical composition of each specimen will not, in general, be representable by a simple x value, but is instead the composi-tion which is in equilibrium with a melt of that x value.

II. EXPERIMENTAL

A. Specimen Preparation

The crystal specimens were prepared by sealing aliquot portions of semiconductor grade materials in vacuo in Vycor ampoules, RF induction mixing, and Bridgman processing. The bismuth, selenium, and tellium used were ASARCO's semicon-ductor grade and the antimony was Ohio Semiconductor's grade Sb-1. With the exception of the tellurium, and some of the selenium, the materials were used as supplied. It was found to be necessary to purify further the tellurium by molecular dis-tillation [8] to avoid the introduction of oxide impurities. These oxides not only act as acceptor atoms [4,5] but also react with the tube walls to form an oxide cement. In addition all ampoules were carbonized by pyrolytic decomposition of absolute ethanol to insure that the crystals would not adhere to the Vycor wall. Residual tars were removed by boiling in ethyl alcohol. Speci-mens were RF induction mixed for at least three hours to insure homogeniety, and were processed in a Bridgman furnace with a drop rate of .2 inch/hour. The Bridgman furnace is equipped with water cooling baffles so that a temperature gradient of 200C°/inch is maintained at the freezing point of the sample [1].

B. Measurements

(1) Room Temperature Measurements

Room temperature measurements of the electrical proper-ties of the first material to crystallize were made on a wet lapped surface of the ingot. The Seebeck coefficient, α, was

586

measured with a hot probe and is reported relative to copper. Resistivity measurements were made by either two- or four-point probes. With the exception of the composition $x = -4$, thermoelectric and resistivity profiles of different ingots of the same gross composition have been essentially identical.

(2) Measurements with Temperature

The temperature dependence of the Seebeck effect and the resistivity were measured in the apparatus shown in Figure 1. The thermal conductivity was measured in a vacuum cryostat which has been described in detail by H. Lyden [3]. Values of thermal conductivity were calculated from measurements of the heat flow through a one-centimeter slug of material.

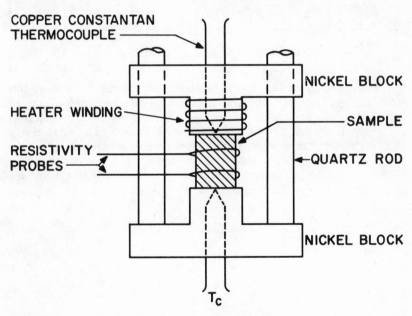

Figure 1. Apparatus for the Measurement of the Seebeck Coefficient and Resistivity.

III. RESULTS AND DISCUSSION

All of the parameters reported in this paper were measured on one-centimeter slugs of the first material to crystallize in a Bridgman ingot. A chemical analysis based on the method of Reed [7] was performed on two samples of the first material to crystallize. The results of this analysis shown in Table I emphasize that the gross composition of the melt may not represent the true sample composition.

587

Table 1

Chemical Composition of the First Material to Crystallize

Constituent	X = 0		X = +6	
	Found	Theoretical	Found	Theoretical
Se	1.3 ± 0.3	2.5	1.4 ± 0.3	2.5
Te	58.4 ± 0.4	62.5	58.1 ± 0.4	60.0
Sb	29.4 ± 1.2	25.0	30.2 ± 0.4	27.5
Bi	10.9 ± 0.3	10.0	10.3 ± 0.3	10.0
Total Atomic %	100.0 ± 2.2	100.0	100.0 ± 1.4	100.0

The results of the room temperature measurement of the electrical resistivity and the Seebeck coefficient are shown in Figures 2a and 2b where the resistivity and Seebeck coefficient are plotted against gross sample composition. The resistivity is a maximum at x = -8, decreases monotonically until x = 0, and then remains fairly constant for the rest of the range. The Seebeck coefficient is a maximum at x = -8 and falls monotonically through the entire range. The room temperature thermal

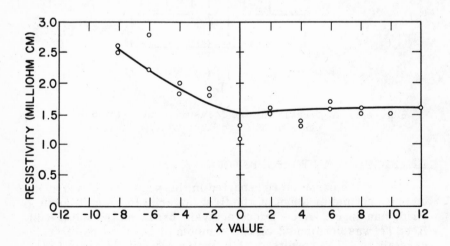

Figure 2a. Electrical Resistivity (at room temperature) as a Function of Gross Sample Composition.

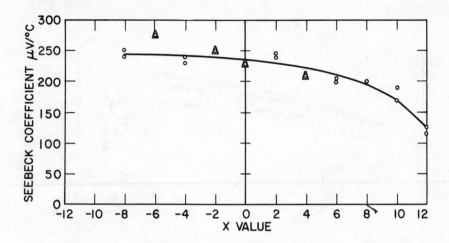

Figure 2b. Seebeck Coefficient (at room temperature)
as a Function of Gross Sample Composition

conductivity of five specimens is plotted against gross sample
composition in Figure 3. The thermal conductivity varies slowly
with x and has a broad minimum at x = 0 where it reaches the
value of 12.0×10^{-3} w/cmC°.

In Figure 4 are shown the temperature variations of the
Seebeck coefficient for five specimens in this series of alloys.

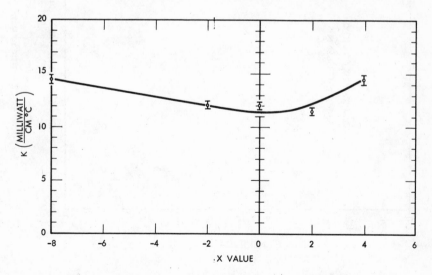

Figure 3. Thermal Conductivity (at room temperature)
as a Function of Gross Sample Composition.

589

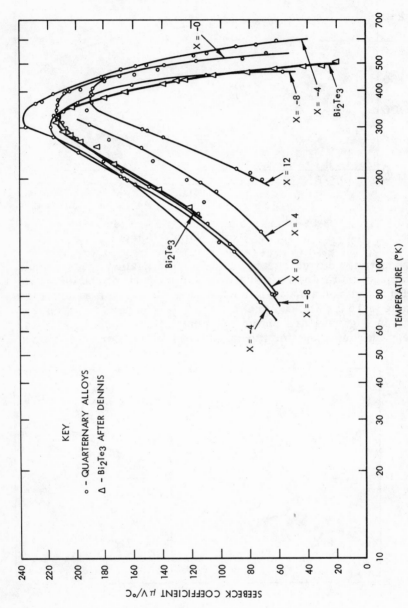

Figure 4. Temperature Variation of the Seebeck Coefficient.

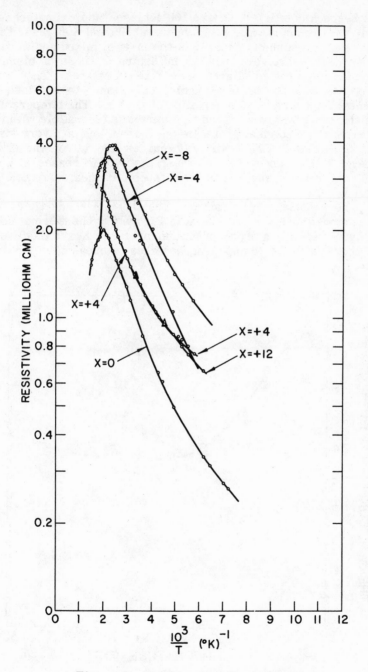

Figure 5. Temperature Variation of the
Electrical Resistivity.

The Seebeck coefficient (above 100°K) rises approximately linearly with temperature, peaks between 300 and 400°K and then decreases presumably because of the onset of mixed conduction. These curves are very similar in feature to those of bismuth telluride but peak at slightly higher temperatures. They may be compared with the temperature variation of α obtained by Dennis[2] for the parallel orientation of Bi_2Te_3. The temperature variation of resistivity shown in Figure 5 is compatible with the idea that the electrical properties of these alloys are very similar to Bi_2Te_3. The resistivity curves are all of the same general shape: above 120°K° the resistivity increases at $T^{1.1}$ to $T^{1.5}$ until the specimens start becoming near intrinsic at about 500K°.

The temperature variation of the thermal conductivity for the composition x = +4 is shown in Figure 6. The thermal conductivity reaches a broad minimum near 200°K and then rises as the electronic component becomes increasingly prominent.

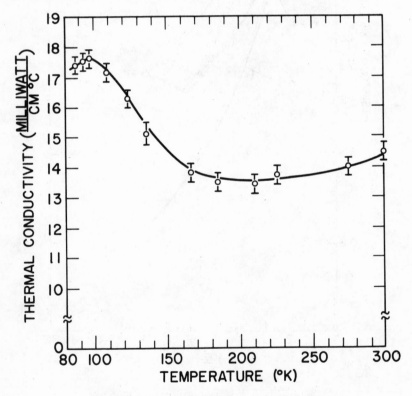

Figure 6. Temperature Variation of the Thermal Conductivity.

592

The electrical properties of these alloys are very similar to those of bismuth telluride. The thermal conductivity, however, may be as low as .012 w/cm°C which is a substantial improvement over Bi_2Te_3. As a direct result of this lower value of thermal conductivity, a figure of merit ($\alpha^2/\rho k$) of 3×10^{-3} $(K°)^{-1}$ may be readily obtained from these alloys. The possibility of improving the electrical properties by controlled doping remains to be investigated.

ACKNOWLEDGMENT

The author is indebted to Mr. J. Bills for performing the chemical analysis. Especial thanks are due to Mr. Henry Lyden for measurements of the thermal conductivity.

REFERENCES

1. AFCRC TN 60-125, Theoretical and Experimental Research in Thermoelectricity. Scientific Report No. 1.
2. J. H. Dennis, Anisotropy of Thermoelectric Power in Bismuth Telluride. Technical Report 377. Research Laboratory for Electronics, M.I.T., 1961.
3. First Joint Progress Report of the Laboratories for Molecular Science and Molecular Engineering, Theoretical and Experimental Research in Thermoelectricity, p. 80-85, 1961.
4. R. A. Horne, Journal of Applied Physics, 30 No. 1, p. 393.
5. W. D. Lawson, Journal of Applied Physics, 22 No. 12.
6. Pollack et. al., Structural Investigation in Thermoelectric Materials, Merck, Sharpe, and Dohme Progress Report No. 1, 1960.
7. J. F. Reed, Analytical Chemistry, 32, p. 662, 1960.
8. B. D. Wedlock and F. M. Norton, The Purification of Tellurium by Distillation. Conference on the Ultrapurification of Semiconductor Materials, 1961.

DISCUSSION

F. K. HEUMANN (General Electric): I think your lattice conductivity agrees quite well with what other people have found for this system. What did you say the Z value was for undoped material?

D. A. PUOTINEN (M.I.T. Energy Conversion Laboratory): We can get a Z of 3 with this material.

F. K. HEUMANN (General Electric): Did you investigate the homogeneity of these ingots?

D. A. PUOTINEN (MIT): We have not investigated them by X-ray techniques. However, we are investigating them by X-ray fluorescence. This method seems to indicate that they are reasonably homogeneous.

W. TILLER (Chairman) (Westinghouse): What was the freezing rate of these crystals?

D. A. PUOTINEN (MIT): The growth rate was about two tenths of an inch per hour.

W. TILLER (Chairman) (Westinghouse): Do you think that also applied in the first centimeter, there was no supercooling?

D. A. PUOTINEN (MIT): There should not have been. The factor of supercooling is one thing which we have not investigated. The crystals were grown in a Bridgeman furnace which has a temperature gradient of 300°C per inch.

A. J. ROSENBURG (Tyco): Since you have not made X-ray measurements of this material, do you have any basis to assume that it is single phase? This particular system has been investigated by a number of people and I believe there is general agreement that it is two phase system.

D. A. PUOTINEN (MIT): The material that we are reporting on is the first material to crystallize. Now, it is very possible that toward the end of the Bridgeman ingot we are reaching a two phase region so I would really have no comment beyond that.

CONDENSATION OF EVAPORATED ZINC AND CADMIUM ON SILICON SURFACES

W. H. G. Helwig
Standard Elektrik Lorenz AG
Nürnberg, West Germany

Generally, no condensation occurs if zinc or cadmium is evaporated in high vacuum on non-metallic substrates at room temperature. Vapor atoms impinging on the surface have a certain "average life" of mobility during which they can re-evaporate if they have no possibility of condensation.

The average life of metals such as zinc, cadmium and also mercury is so long that re-evaporation is likely to occur [6]. Condensation of these metals will happen only under one of the following conditions:

(a) Decreasing the substrate temperature below the critical temperature under which progressive condensation will take place. Under this condition the "average life" is reduced so far that re-evaporation is practically non-existent [6,9]. The critical temperature of zinc and cadmium is exceptionally low (-81 up to -297°F) [7].

(b) Increasing the vapor density beyond the "critical density" and so increasing the possibility of forming atom pairs from impinging vapor atoms during the "average life." These atom pairs cannot re-evaporate and form the nuclei for the condensation of subsequent atoms [1,2,6].

(c) Coating of surfaces which act as nuclei themselves as, e.g., several kinds of clean metal surfaces [4].

(d) Surfaces which do not meet condition (c) can be pre-sensitized with certain deposits acting as nuclei. The thickness of these deposits very often can be much less than that of a mono-atomic layer [3,5,8] (this method is, e. g., used for the production of metallized paper capacitors).

However, condensation of zinc or cadmium under the condition (c) can be prevented by certain deposits which can be detected in this manner [4,5]. Hence, in using the condensation effect one has a very sensitive method to make visible and to localize surface regions with different probabilities of condensation. Since this method detects very thin coatings it seemed reasonable also to use it for semiconductor surfaces as, e.g., silicon.

The arrangement used for the first experiments is explained in Figure 1. The distance between sample and crucible was 1.57". Pre-weighed quantities of zinc and cadmium were used and evaporated completely. A removable mask was provided to protect the sample against first evaporating impurities.

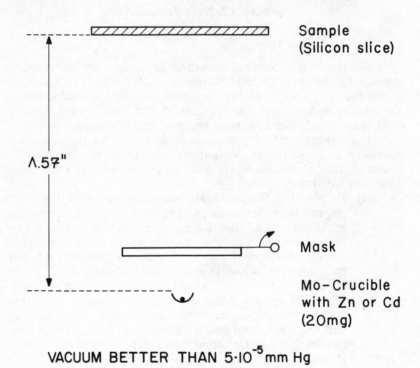

Figure 1. Arrangement for Depositing of Zn or Cd on Silicon Surfaces.

In order to test the condensation on silicon without any coatings, very clean surfaces were produced by fracturing single crystals in high vacuum. Afterwards these surfaces were exposed to the cadmium vapor. Figure 2 shows cadmium crystallites condensed preferably at the plane regions of the fractured surface and at the conchoidal edges. Etching off the cadmium by means of diluted HNO_3 proves that the light scattering is due to the cadmium condensed crystallites and not due to the

596

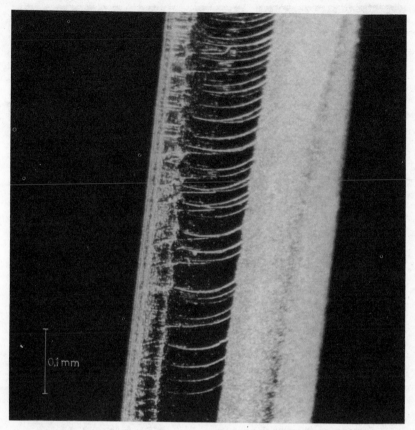

Figure 2. Fresh Fractured Silicon Surface, Evaporated
with Cd (dark field illumination).

roughness of the fractured surface. Figure 3 illustrates that
the so cleaned surface does not any longer cause a scattering in
dark field illumination.

Quite another behavior was found after coating of surfaces
etched with CP8, afterwards washed with deionized water and
then dried. In this case there are irregularly distributed areas
(Figure 4) in which condensation had taken place. There is no
correlation between the crystal structure or defects in silicon
and the described distribution of the condensed areas. This can
be shown by using surfaces with etchpits produced by Dash-
etching. The same irregular distribution of these condensation
areas was found, where, however, etchpits were coated, too
(Figure 5). Etchpits in the uncoated areas remained also un-
covered.

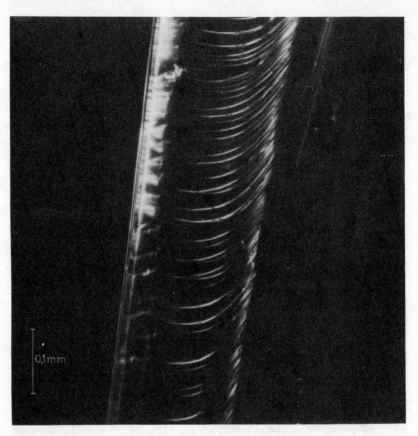

Figure 3. Fresh Fractured Silicon Surface, Cd-Layer
Removed (dark field illumination).

A close correlation exists between the structure of condensation and the treatment after etching. The already shown ir-
regularities were present when the silicon slices after etching
and washing were just touched with filter paper in order to
remove the remaining water. Removing the water by wiping
caused a wiping structure on the condensed metal layers (Figure 6). The final treatment of the silicon surfaces after etching
obviously influences the formation of very thin coatings preventing the kind of condensation taking place on really clean surfaces.

It should be mentioned in this connection that a microscopic
examination of the tested samples also revealed effects (ref. to
Figure 7) which, obviously, are not in any way related to the
effects above described.

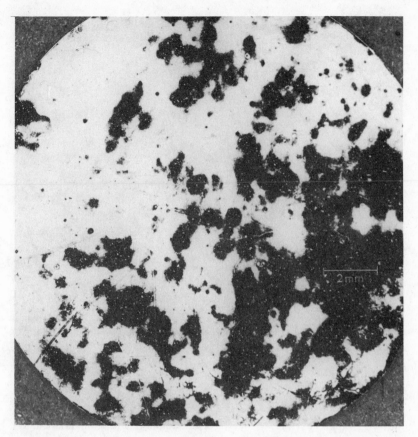

Figure 4. Silicon Slice, Etched with CP8, with Condensed
Zn Layer (dark field illumination).

Dust particles accidentally reaching the silicon surface before the high vacuum coating are surrounded with halos free of any
condensation. Obviously the gas emitted from these dust particles in the high vacuum has deflected the impinging metal atoms.

Final interpretation of the results and complete analysis of
coatings preventing the condensation is not yet possible, but it
can be assumed that oxide layers which still remain on the surface after the usual etching are the cause [5]. This is corrobo-
rated by the fact that a very uniform condensation can be
reached by treating the etched surfaces in diluted HF which removes still remaining oxide layers. Such a surface still keeps
its properties even after being exposed to distilled or deionized
water, whereas oxidizing reagents like H_2O_2 again prevent the
ability of condensation. Figure 8 demonstrates a silicon surface

599

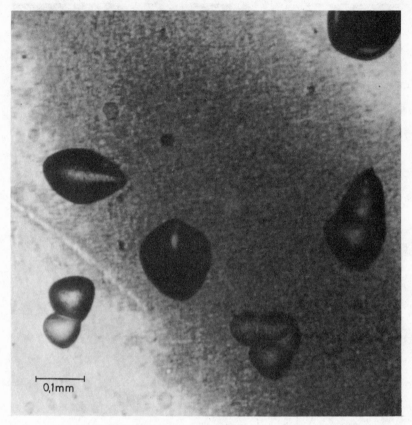

0,1mm

Figure 5.   Etchpits on Silicon Surface in Evaporated and
Nonevaporated Areas.

treated with HF and afterwards with water of different purity
and H_2O_2 respectively. One can easily see that H_2O_2 prevents
condensation completely.

CONCLUSION

A method was described which allows to localize different
surface regions on silicon which can be developed by evaporated
zinc or cadmium layers. Though the causes of the said effects
are not yet completely known, it seems to be possible to use the
method, because of its high sensitivity, for investigating the influence of etch-treatments on the cleanness of semiconductor
surfaces. Those investigations could prove its importance, e.g.,
for studying the wetting properties of the semiconductor material
using alloying techniques.

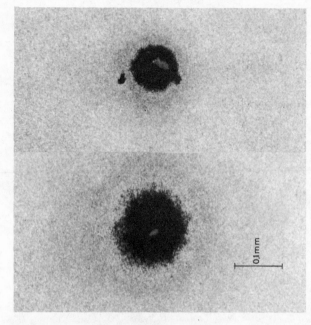

Figure 7. Prevention of Condensation Around Gas-Emitting Particles on the Silicon Surface (dark field illumination).

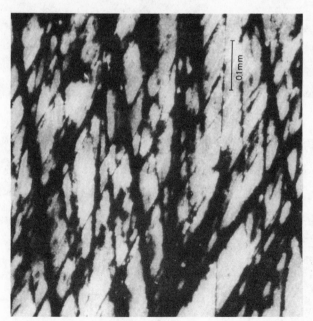

Figure 6. Etched Silicon Surface with Wiping Structures, Developed by Cd-Evaporation (dark field illumination).

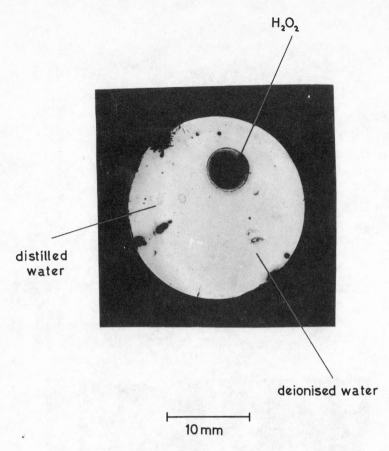

Figure 8.   Etched and HF-Treated Silicon Slice With
Dried Drops of Various Liquids.

REFERENCES

1. J. Cockcroft, Proc. Roy. Soc. (London) A 119, 293 (1924).
2. R. W. Ditchburn, Proc. Roy. Soc. (London) A 141, 169 (1933).
3. R. Fraser, "Molecular Beams," Cambridge University Press
    (1931).
4. L. Holland and K. Hacking, Electronic Engineering, July,
    296 (1954).
5. H. König, H. J. Löffler and F. Lappe, Glastechn. Ber. 28,
    131 (1955).
6. I. Langmuir, Proc. Nat. Acad. Sci. (US) 3, 141 (1917).
7. H. Mayer, Vakuum-Techn. 4, 1 (1955).
8. E. Traub, Zs. f. angew. Physik 1, 545 (1949).
9. R. W. Wood, Phil. Mag. 30, 300 (1915).
10. R. W. Wood, Phil. Mag. 32, 364 (1916).

DISCUSSION

O. J. MARSH (HUGHES SEMICONDUCTORS): What was the temperature of the material when you evaporated cadmium?

G. HELWIG (Standard Elektrik Lorenz AG): The silicon was at room temperature.

K. REINITZ (Delco Radio): After the etching treatment, how long was the sample exposed to air before the evaporation was started?

G. HELWIG (Standard Elektrik Lorenz AG): Only a very short time. As soon as possible, the samples were placed in the vacuum chamber.

K. REINITZ (Delco Radio): Did you put the sample in your vacuum chamber dry or wet?

G. HELWIG (Standard Elektrik Lorenz AG): Immediately after etching, the samples are practically dry and are immediately put in the chamber.

C. H. LI (General Instrument): Are you sure these are dust particles? We have examined silicon wafers after treatment with different solvents or etches and can produce marks like these hallo marks. They are not necessarily dust particles. They are just throwing marks of a very complicated process such as surface evaporation.

G. HELWIG (Standard Elektrik Lorenz AG): These are really dust particles because under the microscope I can see that there are lines on the surface.

A. J. ROSENBERG (Chairman) (Tyco): The nature of dried surfaces of silicon or germanium after CP4 or similar etches is very obscure.

PURIFICATION METHODS IN THE STUDY OF SEMICONDUCTOR SURFACES*

J. A. Dillon, Jr.
Department of Physics, Brown University
Providence, Rhode Island

ABSTRACT

Since the surface properties of semiconducting materials are quite sensitive to small amounts of contamination, the study of such properties requires special techniques for both preparing and analyzing the surfaces. High-temperature heating, evaporation, vacuum cleaving, vacuum crushing, and ion bombardment followed by annealing are all discussed. Particular attention is given the latter method since in some applications it has certain advantages over other techniques. The method is applicable to both polycrystal and single-crystal samples and to the various crystal planes of the latter. It is particularly useful in cases where stable films are not readily removable by high-temperature heating or in which diffusion of film components might alter the surface electrical properties. It is essential however that the experimental conditions be controlled so that the surface is not etched by the bombardment or contaminated by sputtered material. Preliminary studies using a method such as low-energy electron diffraction are also required to determine both the feasibility and the operating conditions necessary in the application of the technique to a particular material.

INTRODUCTION

Regardless of the state of bulk purification, the preparation of an atomically clean solid surface is a problem of great complexity. Contamination can arise from a number of sources. It can be in the form of a chemical film residual from etching or it might be due to gaseous adsorption from the ambient. It can also be due to the diffusion of impurities from the bulk to the surface or the unintentional result of a particular surface treatment. Since very small fractions of an impurity monolayer alter

---

*This work is supported by the U.S. Air Force Cambridge Research Laboratories, Bedford, Mass.

both the surface and bulk chemical and electrical properties of a semiconductor, a number of special techniques have been developed to prepare surfaces which are atomically clean. It is obvious that such methods must be applied under ultra-high vacuum conditions. At a pressure of 10^{-6} mm Hg sufficient atoms or molecules strike a surface per second to form an adsorbed monolayer if one assumes a sticking coefficient of unity. The work must therefore be carried out at pressures several orders of magnitude lower than this so that sufficient time will elapse between the cleaning process and the adsorption to allow for meaningful measurements. With modern vacuum techniques it is possible to achieve pressures of the order of 10^{-9} mm Hg even in large systems, and the use of getters or ion-pumping components permits the reduction of the partial pressures of the active gases in the ambient to negligible values. In this paper we shall assume the utilization of such techniques, and shall outline and compare several of the methods which have been employed in the cleaning of semiconductor surfaces.

HIGH-TEMPERATURE HEATING

One of the oldest and most widely used methods of removing impurities from solid surfaces is high-temperature heating in vacuum. In its application to the surface studies of semiconductors, a number of unexpected and interesting results have been found. Low-energy electron-diffraction studies indicated that for the case of germanium single crystals a stable film remaining after chemical etching could not be completely removed even though the samples were heated just below the melting point [1]. When the film was removed by another technique (argon ion bombardment), a study of the adsorption properties of the clean surface demonstrated that the tenacious, residual film had properties quite different from those of adsorbed oxygen which could be removed by heating at only 500°C [2,3]. The important point illustrated by these results is that all surface films do not react in the same way to vacuum heating, and that some sensitive method must always be used in new circumstances to evaluate the effectiveness of the cleaning process. Electron diffraction [1,3], secondary emission [4], surface conductivity [5], and the kinetics of oxygen adsorption [6] are among the methods which have been used to judge the degree of cleanliness obtained.

In many cases it is desirable to use more than one evaluation technique, since one method might be more sensitive to certain types of contamination than others. Silicon is a case in point. It has been demonstrated by a number of methods that silicon surfaces heated at temperatures of 1000°C or higher are essentially free of contamination [7]. However, there is also ample evidence to indicate that some of the impurities present on the surface before heat treatment diffuse into the bulk when the temperature is raised [8,9,10]. This is particularly true of boron contamination which is present in Pyrex systems and which is discussed at some length in a later section. Although the heating produces a clean surface, the electrical properties of the material are quite different from those which would have been observed in the absence of the diffused layer. It has also been shown that adsorbed oxygen diffuses, at least in part, into the bulk when silicon is heated [11]. Although low-energy electron-diffraction would indicate that such a surface was clean, photoelectric emission data would definitely indicate the presence of a diffused layer.

The realization that diffusion into the interior can play an important role in the removal of surface layers must be kept in mind in the use of the heating process lest in the act of producing a clean surface in a two-dimensional sense, one actually contaminates the bulk.

Diffusion at high temperature can also work in the opposite direction so as to deposit non-volatile contaminants from the bulk onto the surface. For both nickel [12] and silicon [3], carbon which appears as a natural impurity in the lattice has been observed on the heated surfaces. Conditions in such experiments have been varied sufficiently to ascertain that the carbon actually came from the interior and not from the ambient. When this interstitial carbon arrives at the active silicon surface it can form a layer of silicon carbide. If a particular silicon sample contains considerable carbon, this diffusion process can be very troublesome when heat treatment is used as the cleaning process.

As is the case with any cleaning method, care must be taken to avoid unintentional contamination of the sample. If electron bombardment is used for heating, the filaments must be shielded to prevent evaporation onto the samples. The sample mounting arrangement must also be designed to minimize the possibility of sample contamination.

A further difficulty which can be encountered in high-temperature heating is the appearance of thermal etching. Certain crystalline planes are more stable than others, and when evaporation takes place these planes can be developed at the expense of others. In this way thermal etch patterns can be created on heated surfaces. This is an undesirable situation whenever one is attempting to measure a parameter which is asymmetrical with respect to crystalline orientation. The conditions under which such etching takes place are functions of the particular material, the temperature, and the ambient pressure. Silicon crystals can be heated at 900°C in high vacuum for many hours without evidence of thermal etching, whereas an increase in temperature of about two hundred degrees results in pronounced etching [11,13]. If the ambient pressure is increased to about 10^{-6} mm Hg, the etching can be observed at lower temperatures.

A problem of particular complexity in the cleaning of semiconductor surfaces is due to the fact that in some cases the heat treatment itself determines certain of the bulk and surface parameters. For example, it is well known that silicon, which contains oxygen, can be varied in resistivity by either quenching or annealing the sample [14]. It was found that the work function for oxygen-doped silicon could also be changed by either radiation quenching or slowly cooling the samples from a temperature of 1000°C. The adsorption properties of silicon were also different depending on the heat treatment [3]. Law has reported changes in bulk conductivity and trap density due to precipitation effects of certain impurities when silicon is heated at temperatures in excess of about 900°C [9]. It is quite apparent that the condition of a heated semiconductor can be far from simple.

In summary, high-temperature heating can be used to advantage as a surface cleaning method provided that the following precautions are taken.

1. A sensitive technique is used to determine the degree of cleanliness.

2. Steps are taken to identify and eliminate diffused layers resulting from the heating.

3. The experimental arrangement has been designed to avoid contamination during the heating process.

4. Conditions of temperature and pressure are controlled to minimize thermal etching.

5. Effects of heat treatment on electrical properties of the semiconductor are understood.

ION BOMBARDMENT AND ANNEALING

When it was recognized that the chemical films due to the etching process were not removed from germanium by heating alone, the process of ion bombardment or sputtering was used to remove the films [1,2,3]. In this process the energy of ions incident upon a solid is at least partially transformed into lattice vibrations in the solid. These vibrations can achieve such amplitudes that surface atoms are ejected. The actual mechanism of the sputtering process has not been completely determined, but it is apparently dependent on the incident ion energy. At lower energies, of the order of a few hundred electron volts, the lattice vibration model with its resultant preferential ejection appears to be well established, while at much higher energies a form of radiation-damage theory seems to be needed. At any rate, surface layers can be removed from a solid by the process.

Electron-diffraction studies indicated that an ion-bombarded surface was broken up and that annealing in high vacuum was necessary to produce a clean, single-crystal surface. The annealing process also removed the gas atoms which had been occluded in the surface during the bombardment. Because this technique has been widely used in the study of metal and semiconductor surfaces, we shall summarize certain of the important points which must be considered in its application.

The success of the method depends in part on a thorough outgassing of the bulk of the solid. If this has not been achieved, gas from the interior can diffuse to the surface during annealing. For this reason a number of cycles of high-temperature heating, ion-bombardment, and annealing must be used before the optimum conditions are attained. For each material the proper operating conditions must be determined by observing the effects of the cleaning with a sensitive method such as low-energy electron diffraction.

The annealing conditions are different for different materials and must be determined before the method can be applied with success to a particular material [15]. It is conceivable that there are some substances to which the method could not be applied. A binary compound in which the sputtering rates for the components were quite different might well develop a non-stoichiometric surface on ion bombardment. It is also possible that the annealing conditions for some materials would be such that one could not anneal out the damage caused by the bombardment. In diamond, for instance, the electron-diffraction patterns obtained after etching and vacuum heating were obliterated by argon-ion bombardment. Subsequent annealing at temperatures as high as 1100°C did not restore the patterns [16]. There is a possibility that the temperature required for annealing in this case is higher than the temperature at which a graphite layer forms on vacuum heating. Thus the usual application of the bombardment method does not appear too fruitful for this material.

Just as heating can result in thermal etching, so also can ion bombardment result in the development of surface etching. For this reason the cumulative bombardment must be kept at the smallest possible value. Cumulative bombardments of several hours at ion energies of about 500 ev and current densities of about 100 μ amps/cm^2 can be used without causing any serious etching of the surfaces of germanium or silicon [17].

The experimental conditions must be such that there is no possibility of sputtering impurities onto the semiconductor sample. The argon gas used in the bombardment must be highly purified to avoid introducing active gases into the sample. Passing the gas through an active getter just before its admission to the apparatus has been found to be effective. The pressure of the gas during the bombardment should be maintained at a value below one micron. At higher pressures, the mean free path in the gas is so short that some of the material removed by the sputtering can be returned to the surface. This effect is so pronounced at pressures of about 10^{-1} mm Hg that prolonged bombardment results in the appearance of visible films on the sample surface.

The ion-bombardment cleaning process has been shown to be particularly effective in removing impurities which diffuse either to or from the surface. As has been mentioned in a previous section, carbon can diffuse to the surface of some materials and remain there as a contaminant. By using ion bombardment it is possible to remove such carbon, and by cycling processes of heating and bombardment one can deplete the amount of the impurity in the bulk so that the rate of diffusion at the annealing temperature becomes quite small. In this way a clean, carbon-free surface can be obtained.

The bombardment technique is also of great advantage in the elimination of the p-type films which have been detected on both germanium and silicon samples heated in Pyrex systems [8,9,10]. The contamination responsible for the formation of these layers is an oxide of boron which is transferred from the Pyrex walls to the sample by water vapor in the initial stages of evacuation. Some of this oxide remains on the crystal and is reduced when the sample is heated. The free boron thus released can diffuse into the crystal to form a p-type layer which extends several microns into the lattice. Once such a diffused layer is formed it can be removed by prolonged or high-current density bombardment. It has been shown that a total argon-ion bombardment of 10^{19} ions/cm^2 is required to remove such a film. The danger of using such large cumulative bombardments lies in the fact that excessive bombardment is known to produce surface etching. The alternative method of avoiding these films is to ion bombard the surface before the high-temperature heating. In this way the contamination can be removed, and it has been found possible to heat such a surface for many hours without the appearance of the film. The bombardment required for the removal of the impurity before heating is only 5×10^{17} ions/cm^2, a substantial reduction from the amount required once the diffused layer has been created. Since there is always the danger that some component of residual films might diffuse into the lattice on heating, it seems that the use of ion bombardment before heating should become a standard technique in surface studies.

VACUUM CLEAVING

With single crystals of certain materials it is possible to cleave the samples in such a way as to expose fresh surfaces in vacuum [18]. This method is not as widely applicable as the two methods previously discussed in that only certain preferred cleavage planes are involved, and the difficulty of cleavage varies considerably from one material to another. However, a number of semiconductors have been studied in this manner, and the results deserve consideration. Haneman [19], using the low-energy electron-diffraction method, has studied surfaces of bismuth telluride crystals which had been cleaved in vacuum and also cleaned by the ion-bombardment and annealing process. The surface structures and the gaseous adsorption properties of the surfaces prepared by these two methods were identical. Studies which have been made of the electrical properties of cleaved silicon surfaces, however, have indicated differences between the properties of the cleaved surfaces and those prepared by ion bombardment and annealing [20]. The reasons for these differences have not yet been explained. Possibly related to these discrepancies are the questions of whether all cleaved surfaces are necessarily free of strain and defect when formed, and whether such imperfections might influence the surface properties. If annealing should be required to relieve strains, the problem then arises of the possible diffusion of impurities from the bulk to the surface if the sample has not previously been thoroughly outgassed. Without more information than is available at present, it is therefore somewhat dangerous to assume in all cases that a cleaved surface is necessarily an ideal one.

VACUUM CRUSHING

Much interesting information concerning the kinetics of gaseous adsorption on germanium and silicon has been obtained in experiments utilizing crushing techniques [21]. In such experiments a high-purity sample is crushed in high vacuum or in the presence of the gas under study so that a very large surface-to-volume ratio is obtained. In these cases it is apparent that the majority of the surface exposed must be clean, and if care is taken to insure free passage of the gas through the powdered material and if sintering effects are accounted for, this method can be quite effective in the study of adsorption kinetics. Results obtained by ion-bombardment cleaning and by crushing are essentially the same for the study of the adsorption and desorption of oxygen at germanium surfaces [22].

Limitations of the method include the facts that it does not allow the study of the properties of different crystal planes and that the effects on surface properties of the numerous edges and defects created by the crushing are not well known.

EVAPORATED FILMS

Another method which has found some application in semi-conductor studies is that of evaporating fresh films of the semi-conductor under study and examining the properties of the surfaces so formed [23]. Although results obtained by this method and some of the other cleaning processes are in general agreement, one occasionally finds discrepancies. For example, the kinetics of oxidation of germanium as observed in the crushing experiments of Green are different in some details from those observed for evaporated films by Law [24].

There is a good deal of evidence to suggest that an evaporated film of some materials can contain defects which influence some of the surface properties. Problems of this type have been considered for the case of metal films [25], and there is no reason to doubt that they are also important in consideration of the results of semiconductor film research.

SUMMARY

In this brief discussion of surface cleaning, we have obviously not been able to include all the existing techniques. Certain ones, such as high-field evaporation or reduction in hydrogen, which might find occasional application have been omitted. From the melancholy recital of possible difficulties which has been given in this paper, it should be clear that no particular method can be assumed to be perfect in every case. Each has its advantages and its limitations. The encouraging thing is that we do know a lot more about cleaning techniques than we did when the interest in clean semiconductor surfaces began approximately ten years ago. We have probably learned at least as much about such processes as ion bombardment as we have about the semiconductor surfaces to which they have been applied. There is still very much to learn—but in what worthwhile field does this situation not exist?

REFERENCES

1. H. E. Farnsworth, R. E. Schlier, T. H. George, and R. M. Burger, J. Appl. Phys. 29, 1150 (1958).
2. J. A. Dillon, Jr. and H. E. Farnsworth, J. Appl. Phys. 28, 174 (1957).
3. R. E. Schlier and H. E. Farnsworth, J. Chem. Phys. 30, 917 (1959).
4. H. D. Hagstrum, J. Phys. Chem. Solids 14, 33 (1960).
5. P. Handler, Semiconductor Surface Physics (University of Pennsylvania Press, Philadelphia, 1957), p. 23.

6. M. Green and I. A. Liberman, Proceedings of the International Conference on Semiconductor Physics, Prague 1960 (Publishing House of the Czechoslovak Academy of Sciences, Prague, 1961) p. 536.

7. F. G. Allen, J. Eisinger, H. D. Hagstrum, and J. T. Law, J. Appl. Phys. 30, 1563 (1959).

8. F. G. Allen, T. M. Buck, and J. T. Law, J. Appl. Phys. 31, 979 (1960).

9. J. T. Law, J. Phys. Chem. Solids 14, 9 (1960).

10. J. A. Dillon, Jr. and R. M. Oman, Proceedings of the International Conference on Semiconductor Physics, Prague, 1960. (Publishing House of the Czechoslovak Academy of Sciences, Prague, 1961) p. 533.

11. J. A. Dillon, Jr. and H. E. Farnsworth, J. Appl. Phys. 29, 1195 (1958).

12. H. E. Farnsworth and J. Tuul, J. Phys. Chem. Solids 9, 48 (1958); R. E. Schlier and H. E. Farnsworth, Advances in Catalysis IX, 434 (Academic Press, New York 1957).

13. H. E. Farnsworth, R. E. Schlier, and J. A. Dillon, Jr., J. Phys. Chem. Solids 8, 116 (1959).

14. W. Kaiser and P. H. Keck, J. Appl. Phys. 28, 882 (1957); C. S. Fuller and R. A. Logan, Jr., J. Appl. Phys. 28, 1427 (1957).

15. D. Haneman, J. Phys. Chem. Solids 14, 162 (1960).

16. H. E. Farnsworth and J. Marsh, Bull. Am. Phys. Soc. II, 5, 349 (1960).

17. J. A. Dillon, Jr. and R. M. Oman, J. Appl. Phys. 31, 26 (1960).

18. D. Haneman, J. Phys. Chem. Solids 11, 205 (1959).

19. D. Haneman, Phys. Rev. 119, 563 (1960).

20. D. R. Palmer, S. R. Morrison, and C. E. Dauenbaugh, Phys. Rev. Letters 6, 170 (1961).

21. M. Green, J. A. Kafalas, and P. H. Robinson, Semiconductor Surface Physics, University of Pennsylvania Press, Philadelphia (1957), p. 349.

22. A. J. Rosenberg, P. H. Robinson, and H. C. Gatos, J. Appl. Phys. 29, 771 (1958).

23. C. A. Neugebauer, J. B. Newkirk, and D. A. Vermilyea, (editors), Structure and Properties of Thin Films, John Wiley & Sons, Inc., New York (1959).

24. M. Green, J. Phys. Chem. Solids 14. 77 (1960).

25. H. E. Farnsworth, Proc. Phys. Soc. 71, 703 (1958).

DISCUSSION

C. H. LI (General Instrument): I would like to get some quantitative estimates as to the requirements of cleaning the surfaces of semiconductor devices.

J. A. DILLON (Brown Univ.): The clean surface experiments described in this paper have been devoted to obtaining fundamental information about the nature of the surfaces involved.

I do not think that it is possible to make any general statements as to practical applications in device fabrication. This would depend on the particular device being considered. There are practical implications of course. As an example one might consider some of the recent work which has been done with binary compounds. Certain of these materials can be oriented in such a way that opposite faces of the same crystal slab exhibit an asymmetry in atomic species. Quite frequently the surface properties of these faces are different. This may account in part for some of the difficulty which has been encountered in making devices from these compounds.

GRAIN BOUNDARIES AS IMPERFECTIONS OF PLANAR EXTENT, THEIR MODEL AND ELECTRONIC PROPERTIES

H. F. Matare
TE KA DE
Nuremberg, Germany

INTRODUCTION

The nonchemical imperfections in semiconductor crystals, which include vacancies, interstitials, and dislocations, are a major class of crystal imperfections. They can be either statistically distributed or ordered as in grain boundaries of low and medium angles of misfit. Vacancies and interstitials are considered as phonon- or radiation-generated equilibrium imperfections whose random distribution causes changes of important material constants such as the diffusion constant, dielectric constant, resistivity, mobility, etc. Dislocations, on the other hand, are more complex primary imperfections and have a rather localized and pronounced influence on the mechanical and electrical properties of crystals. The latter are to be considered here. In the nomenclature of F. Seitz we shall deal with "imperfections having linear extent" and add to these "imperfections having planar extent" (grain boundaries) in the body of the crystal.

I. DEVELOPMENT OF THE GRAIN BOUNDARY MODEL FROM THE EDGE DISLOCATION

A physically meaningful classification of the different types of dislocations should be based on energy rather than on geometric properties. The types of lattice disturbances known for some time are identified mostly from their mechanical appearance rather than from their energy relations to the matrix.

Since here our concern is with those dislocations that have a marked influence on the electrical properties of the crystal, we shall deal only with the edge dislocation and the superposition of edge dislocation pipes in grain boundaries.

Edge Dislocations

The most important type of lattice disturbance is the edge dislocation because the extra half plane necessary to produce an edge dislocation causes a distinct zone of mechanical misfit with a dilation and a compression region. In Figure 1 the simple cubic structure of an edge dislocation is schematically drawn to show the free bonds at the end of the extra half plane; the resulting compression region is at the left and the dilation region at the right, where the adjacent atomic planes converge to restore the ordered lattice. In this hypothetical cubic case, and also in the actual diamond lattice, the "pipes" formed by these dilation regions are typical of an edge dislocation and may be made visible as etch pits on the surface of imperfect crystals.

For an isolated edge dislocation we may consider two regions:

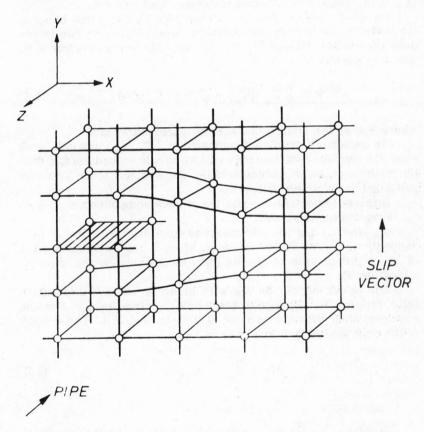

Figure 1. Hypothetical Cubic Model of an Edge Dislocation.

(a) A narrow field disturbance in the immediate vicinity of the dislocation (radius of the order of magnitude of a lattice constant).

(b) A wider region of elastic strain.

The continuum theory may be used to compute the elastic strain energy because the lattice configuration in the immediate vicinity of a dislocation is without importance for the energy situation at larger distances from a dislocation center. This treatment is much older than the theory of dislocations and is known from elasticity theory [1]. The far-reaching elastic field of a dislocation is determined by the Burger's vector and the slip plane only. The Burger's vector is defined as a closure failure arising in a cycle in perfect crystal material surrounding the dislocation. We want to deduce an expression for the strain energy of a dislocation. If we assume a linear relationship between stress and strain-tensor (Hooke's law) this energy is 1/2 the product of stress and strain. (Appendix 1.)

Since the strain energy corresponds to the work done on the body by the forces that cause the dislocation, we can introduce the surface forces T_x, T_y, T_z and the displacements u, v, w at any surface S:

$$E = \frac{1}{2} \int_S (T_x u + T_y v + T_z w) \, ds \qquad (1.1)$$

where E = strain energy of material enclosed within S.

An external force T (components T_x, T_y, T_z) per unit area over the surface S of the body causes single valued elastic displacements (u, v, w). Reciprocally the surface force T can be produced by the dislocations.

In plane deformation only the stress components σ_{xx}, σ_{yy}, σ_{xy} have to be considered.

σ_{xx} and σ_{yy} are the normal stresses along the x- and y-axis respectively. The shear stress σ_{xy} ($=\sigma_{yx}$) acts in the direction of the y (or x) axis on planes perpendicularly to the x (or y) axis (Fig. 1).

The shear stress on the slip plane of an edge dislocation (slip vector $\perp$ to slip plane) therefore is given by σ_{xy} and the corresponding displacement is Burger's vector b. The energy of the edge dislocation site is then:

$$E_\perp = \frac{b}{2} \int_S \sigma_{xy} \, ds \qquad (1.2)$$

Equation (1.2) is an important expression for the density of strain energy and can be modified so that one can calculate the energy per dislocation in terms of surface forces in the following way. Assume a cylindrical cut surrounding a dislocation pipe with radius r_1 large compared to the pipe-radius r_0 ($\simeq 10^{-7}$ cm), such that there is a negligible stress field at this distance, e.g., $r_1 = 1$ cm. (The stress decreases with $1/r$.) Then we may write for the energy of the edge dislocation:

$$E_{\perp} = \frac{b}{2} \int_{r_0}^{r_1} \sigma_r \ dr \tag{1.3}$$

The radial stress function can be expressed in terms of the shear modulus, lattice constant and Poisson's ratio, using the classical Volterra derivation for the stress function [2,3]:

$$\sigma_r = \frac{\mu b}{2\pi \ r} (1 - \nu), \tag{1.4}$$

in which

μ = shear modulus ($\simeq 10^{12}$ dynes/cm^2 for germanium) [7],
ν = Poisson's ratio ($\simeq 0.4$ for germanium).

This leads to the form

$$E_{\perp} = \frac{\mu b^2}{4\pi \ (1 - \nu)} \ \log \left(\frac{r_1}{r_0}\right) \ [\text{dynes}] \tag{1.5}$$

We shall use this formula later in determining the influence of the stress field energy on the electrical properties of crystals.

Dislocation Planes

The transition from an edge dislocation to a dislocation plane is made by assuming a stabilizing boundary energy perpendicular to the individual dislocation pipes. In the case of a misfit between large crystallographic regions, or when adjacent pipes have to arrange in a minimum energy situation lineage will form. This type of dislocation has the smallest energy interdependence and does not fall into the boundary category. The corresponding angles of misfit lie in the range of a few minutes of arc. It is difficult to grow lineage boundaries artificially by arranging seed crystals at low angles. The energy perpendicular to the edge pipes is too small to establish a coherent growth of the boundary in the host matrix under normal temperature conditions: $\pm 0.1°C$ at $1000°C$. This energy

617

increases with increasing tilt angle up to a value of 25 degrees for most crystals of the diamond type [4].

The shear stress on the slip plane of a dislocation may then be expressed by the sum of the individual stress components σ_{xy} (x, y) in the x-y plane:

$$S = \sum_n \sigma_{xy} (x, nD) \qquad (1.6)$$

where

D = dislocation spacing,
n = number of individual dislocations.

Following (1.1), the energy of the dislocation pipe is b/2 times the shear stress integrated over the slip plane:

$$E_{\perp} (D) = \frac{b}{2} \int_o^{\lambda} \sum_n \sigma_{xy} (x, nD) \, dx \qquad (1.7)$$

in which b is Burger's vector. When $\lambda \to \infty$ the crystal is infinitely large.

The strain energy is composed of three parts, assuming the surface of the body to be free from external forces. These are
(a) the self energy of the first dislocation as given by formula (1.5)
(b) the self energy of the second dislocation, and
(c) the mutual interaction energy.

We use σ_{xy} from the classical local shear-stress expressions [3] (see (1.4)).

$$\sigma_{xy} = \mu b/2\pi (1 - \nu) \frac{x (x^2 - y^2)}{\left(x^2 + y^2 \right)^2} \qquad (1.8)$$

We may then write the energy per dislocation (1.7):

$$E_{\perp} = \frac{\mu b^2}{4\pi (1 - \nu)} \int_{r_o}^{\infty} \sum_{n = -\infty}^{+\infty} \frac{x\left(x^2 - y_n^2\right)}{\left(x^2 + y_n^2\right)^2} \, dx \qquad (1.9)$$

The sum can be evaluated by Fourier series transformation [3], and the whole expression will then lead to the well-known expression for the unit-area energy of the boundary (1.10):

$$E_{\perp} = \frac{\mu b}{4\pi (1 - \nu)} \theta (A - \log \theta) \, [\text{ergs/cm}^2] \qquad (1.10)$$

618

where

$A = 1 + \log (b/2\pi \, r_o) = $ constant, and
$\theta = b/D = $ lattice constant/dislocation spacing = tilt angle.

This expression was first derived in a rigorous way by Read and Shockley [8]. Comparisons with experimental data have shown that (1.10) is valid up to higher angles of misfit $(\theta > 25°)$, even beyond the range of the validity of the assumptions [4].

The salient features of the theoretical curve are a rapid rise of E with θ at small values of θ, and a relatively broad, flat maximum (at 25° for most crystals). In general, the experimental values are scattered around the theoretical curve, but in certain cases energy cusps are clearly measured for certain distinct angles of misfit. For example, see the curves of Greenough and King [4], Figure 2, where the ratio of grain-boundary energy to surface energy is plotted for Ag.

Figure 3 gives a schematic view of a symmetrical grain boundary and the energy components.

The explanation of these deviations from a monotonic E versus θ curve can be found by considering the possible twin-like orientations in the lattice in which the majority of the dangling bonds are replaced by "repaired" bonds. J. A. Kohn [6] has considered the possible cases of first- and second-order twinning. It is important to note here that Mott's picture of a glassy grain-boundary structure (unordered material) has become less likely as progress is made in understanding the grain boundary structure. It is believed now that low- and medium-angle grain boundaries (angle of tilt $1° < \theta < 25°$) represent ordered structures and can as such be represented by a dislocation model. More support for this will be evident from electrical data given in Section 2. Amelinckx [5] has described in a general way boundaries that can be built from two sets of dislocation lines. The densities of dislocations are derived on the basis of Frank's formula for a general grain boundary:

$$\sum_i b_i = \vec{\omega} \cdot \vec{r}, \qquad (1.11)$$

where

$\sum_i b_i$ = sum of the Burger's vectors of the dislocation lines cut by r.

$\vec{r}$ = arbitrary vector lying in the contact plane

$\vec{\omega}$ = rotation vector.

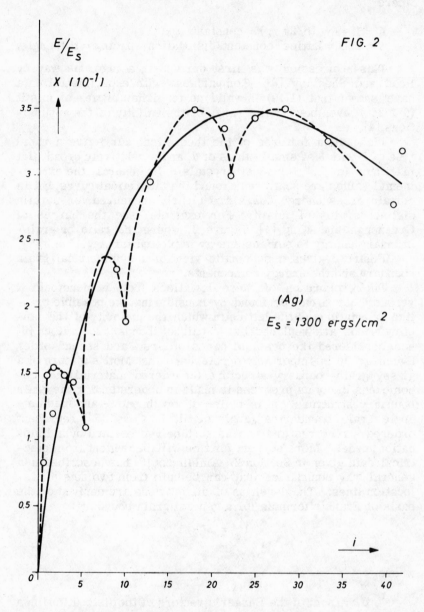

Figure 2. Ratio of Grain Boundary Energy E to Surface Energy E_s in Silver. (E_s = 1300 ergs/cm^2.) Measurements by E. P. Greenough and R. King: J. Inst. Metals, 79, p. 415-427 (1951).

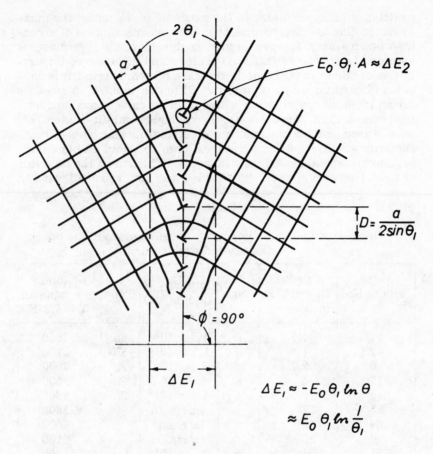

Figure 3. Model of Grain Boundary Plane Perpendicular to Dislocation Pipes. Symmetric Case $\emptyset = 90°$, Tilt-Angle θ_1. Dislocation Energy $E_0 . \theta_1 . A$ (A = Constant, E_0 = Specific Energy Amount). Elastic Energy = $E_0 \theta_1 \ln 1/\theta_1$.

The resulting dislocation models for boundaries and intersecting sets of dislocations were found in sodium chloride crystals [5]. Even in the cases of junctions of several tilt boundaries the corresponding dislocations were discovered in actual crystals. It may be concluded that the low-angle boundaries and, to a certain degree, the medium-angle boundaries are ordered structures obeying the laws of the mathematical dislocation models.

Recently the Read-Shockley model for grain boundaries was confirmed for Germanium in the range of tilt angles of $1° \ldots 15°$ [9]. For higher angles of misfit the grain boundary energy begins to be independent of θ. It must be assumed that the model may be applied also in the range up to 25° since the maximum is flat and micro-cracking [10] and dissolution of structure occurs only at even higher angles of misfit. It must be assumed furthermore that also preferential diffusion of impurities is of minor importance in the case of symmetric tilt boundaries of medium angle of misfit. Diffusion studies on crystals grown from bicrystal seeds with sufficient care to avoid screw-type dislocation (seed rotation) and higher misfit-angles [12] have shown that even sensitive electrical measurements (conductivity at different temperatures down to liquid Helium temperature) cannot reveal any impurity influence on the behavior of these boundary planes. (See Table 1 and Reference 13 and 14.)

Table 1

Dependence of Grain Boundary Sheet Resistivity ρ on Doping of Crystal

Sample No.	ρ (bulk) T = 300°K (ohm-cm)	Type	Impurity N (atoms/cc)	Type	ρ^* (ohms per square) T = 4.2°K
7	1.3	n	1.4×10^{15}	Sb	7800
42	1.6	n	1.1×10^{15}	Sb	5100
6	2.7	n	7×10^{14}	Sb	7500
17	4	n	4.5×10^{14}	Sb	3600
3	5	n	4×10^{14}	Sb	3600
35	27		intrinsic		3600
64	30		intrinsic		5600
29	36		intrinsic		4100
31	4	p	2×10^{14}	Ga	11200
9	1.75	p	3×10^{14}	Ga	8200
11	1.1	p	8×10^{14}	Ga	10200
12	1.1	p	8×10^{14}	Ga	11200
27			10^{16}	Cu	2900
15			10^{16}	Cu	3700
Tweet [14]				Au	8000

It can be understood however that the small angle boundary or lineage boundary is most sensitive to impurities and much influenced by diffusion processes since it has a small stabilizing energy, a wide reaching Cottrell atmosphere and no pronounced overlap between dilatation and compression regions.

The grain boundary diffusion problem is complicated by the definition of the diffusion with respect to the bicrystal orientation. In the case of small tilt angles the values of the diffusion coefficients $D_{\parallel}$ and $D_{\perp}$, parallel and perpendicular to the

622

dislocation lines, are very different. They are more and more equal for increasing tilt angle θ. In this case both coefficients should also approach the value of D, the bulk diffusion coefficient in the monocrystal material. In principle the misorientation of the bicrystal (angle of rotation, r and of twist, t; see ref. 12) should have a pronounced effect on the grain boundary diffusion and the ratio $D_{||}/D_{\perp}$. These conditions have not yet been studied carefully and are not available in the literature. By a general theoretical reasoning the following relations with respect to the diffusion coefficients should prevail if an ideal tilt bi-crystal with misorientation r = 0 and twist t = 0 and with grain boundary plane orientation $\phi = 90°$ (orientation of the grain boundary plane with respect to the tilt axis) has been produced:

$$\theta : \; <1° \rightarrow |D_{||}| \gg |D_{\perp}|, \; (D_{||} \approx 10^6 \, D_{\perp}), \; |D_{\perp}| \approx D$$

$$\theta : \; 1° \rightarrow 20° \rightarrow |D_{||}| \geqq |D_{\perp}| \rightarrow |D|$$

$$\theta : \; 20° \rightarrow 90° \rightarrow |D_{\perp}| = |D_{||}| \gg |D|$$

One may consider the properties of a bicrystal interface from the standpoint of surface physics as an internal surface layer. The analogy between a clean surface and a grain boundary plane has been worked out recently more clearly by Handler and Portnoy [15] of Urbana, Illinois. They showed that surfaces cleaned under high-vacuum (p $< 10^{-8}$ Torr) by electron bombardment perform degenerate conductivity behavior and strong p-type properties in the case of germanium as do the bi-crystal interfaces. The overlapping wave-functions begin to take over the conductivity mechanism after all oxygen bonds have been eliminated.

II. ELECTRONIC PROPERTIES OF BICRYSTAL INTERFACES

The Space Charge Region

The specific charge distribution introduced into a crystal by a line imperfection suggests a cylindric space charge around the dislocation pipe. The dislocation has the tendency to accept electrons to form double dangling bonds. If not all the bonds are occupied the filling factor f is different from 1 and given by

$$f = D/a \tag{2.1}$$

where

D = spacing between dangling bond levels ($\approx \operatorname{cosec} \alpha$),
a = spacing between filled levels (compare 17).

We assume now that a dislocation acceptor level E_2 is introduced into a N-type crystal such that E_2 lies below the Fermi level. In germanium E_2 is approximately .2 eV below the conduction band and is found to be an acceptor level in all cases. In silicon with a larger band gap a dislocation donor level might lie in the gap and thus create a N-type boundary.

It is possible that the electrons in dangling bonds form donors but it seems more probable that in silicon conduction electrons move into the dangling bond levels forming doubly charged centers which then represent donor levels with an energy level above the Fermi-level.

In germanium this level might fall into the conduction band. N-type behavior of grain boundaries in silicon has been found.

We assume that, in general, the spacing between added electrons in free orbitals is at least as small as the spacing between impurity centers [22], even in the case of high impurity ranges.

The structure of a medium angle grain boundary as developed so far is based upon the mathematical model of a contact plane with equidistant bonds (Figure 3). From this representation a number of predictions may be deduced concerning the energy and the electrical effects of the overlapping wave functions of the free bonds in this plane.

Shockley's picture of a continuous band of energy levels, half full, because the spin of each electron can have either of two values, applies to medium angle boundaries, as experiments with dislocation planes have shown.

If one looks for the high conductivity of dislocation pipes, measurements of the conductivity changes due to randomly introduced dislocations are not conclusive. Observations (Gallagher and Pearson, Read and Morin) showed that dislocations may make a specimen less, rather than more, conducting. This is understandable and depends on the position of the space-charge cylinders introducing blocking layer action and thus the longitudinal high conductivity of a pipe does not appear, but the barrier layer may increase the apparent resistivity of the sample.

It is not easy to arrange dislocation pipes in a geometrical fashion for $\theta < 1°$ since their stabilizing energy is very small. For $1° > \theta < 25°$ the growth is stable.

Let us assume now that Fermi statistics are still valid for the filling factor f for a spacing: a between filled free orbitals small compared with the normal impurity spacing in the semiconductor:

$$ f = \frac{1}{1 + \exp\left[(E_2 - E_F)/kT\right]} \qquad (2.2) $$

624

The radius R of the space charge cylinder is obtained from:

$$\frac{1}{a} = \pi R^2 (N_d - N_a) = \frac{1}{D\{1 + \exp[(E_2 - E_F)/kT]\}} \quad (2.3)$$

or

$$R \left[\frac{1}{\pi D(N_d - N_a)\{1 + \exp[(E_2 - E_F)/kT]\}}\right]^{1/2} \quad (2.4)$$

Typical values for N-type Ge ($N_d - N_a = 10^{15}$ cm^{-3}) with f = 1/10 lie between 10^{-4} and 10^{-3} cm.

The radius of the space charge cylinder of the pipes is therefore large compared to: a, the mean spacing between filled levels. It is even large compared to the mean spacing L between excess donors in the bulk, which in the above case is:

$$L = (N_d - N_a)^{-1/3} \simeq 10^{-5} \text{ cm} \quad (2.5)$$

It is therefore obvious that lateral overlap of the pipes in medium-angle grain boundaries is so complete that the grain-boundary plane acts like a homogeneous layer.

Occupation of Dislocation Acceptor Centers

For the explanation of the high blocking voltages of grain-boundary planes we need some information on the occupation of dangling bond levels.

The statistics applicable to the occupation of the dislocation centers or to the filling factor f depend on the geometry of the dislocations. We made use of the Fermi-distribution function under the assumption that the spacing D between dangling bonds is smaller than the spacing between filled levels. We define, in accordance with Read, the energy of interaction of two electrons in adjacent sites as

$$E_0 = e^2/kD \quad (2.6)$$

e = unity electric charge,
k = dielectric constant.

The interaction energy between electrons in nearest filled sites is therefore:

$$f E_0 = e^2/ka \quad (2.7)$$

625

We can now define several regions for the spacing a between added electrons and the subsequent interaction energies.

1. $f E_0 \ll kT$
2. $f E_0 < kT$
3. $f E_0 \simeq kT$
4. $f E_0 > kT$

Cases 1 and 2 are typical for small spacing between filled sites and/or high temperatures. Cases 3 and 4 are the low temperature cases and/or the case of a high filling factor.

At low temperature and high dislocation densities, the original charge density q_o in boundary states is given by the relation between $f E_0$ and kT. A voltage applied to the grain boundary barrier will strongly increase the number q of actual charges present at both barrier sides. The ratio q/q_o is proportional to f and may be larger than unity if carriers are available. They may be made available by a cross voltage applied to such a structure or by light injection or other means. We shall see later that this fact plays a major role in the explanation of the behavior of grain boundary planes where voltage can be applied. (Appendix 2.)

More would have to be added to this concerning dislocation scattering the influence on mobility and recombination of randomly distributed dislocations. (See: 16.)

Electrical Properties of Medium Angle Grain Boundary Planes

The most probable model for the medium angle grain boundaries as derived from the foregoing considerations may be described by Figure 4. The overlapping of the dilation and compression regions is so complete that a general increase of the forbidden gap results. $(E + \Delta E/2)$, where $\Delta E \approx$ the maximum width of the gap at the compression points. The arrangement of the dislocation pipes in a minimum energy situation by this overlap is a reason for the stable growth of such boundaries. The electrical consequence for the grain boundary plane may be a high injection efficiency when it is used as a p-type layer in pn-structures [21-23]. Other electrical properties of grain boundary planes have been measured by Taylor and coworkers using accidentally grown bi-crystal structures [19]. These measurements have been refined by using artificially grown by-crystals [12] in which the growth conditions and deviations from the ideal tilt-boundary have been clearly observed [20-23].

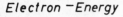

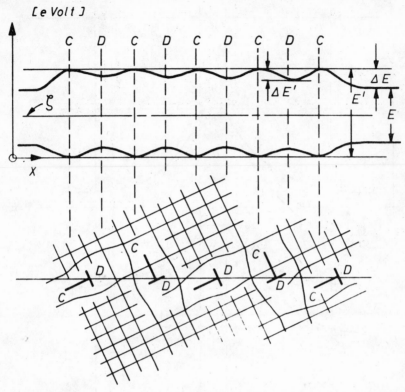

Figure 4. Model of Medium Angle Grain Boundary Plane and Corresponding Electronic Band Structure.

With high resistivity bulk-material (germanium doped with antimony) blocking voltages of such boundary layers can reach high values. The question of the origin of high blocking voltages and strong p-type behavior of the interface (impurity contribution by diffusion or segregation excluded) may be answered by an electronic model summarized in Figure 5. The number of acceptor levels in the interface may be as high as 10^{12} cm^{-2} which explains that even in p-type doped material the grain boundary plane has p^{+}-character. It is important to note that the additional energy levels in the forbidden gap have the character of recharging centers which means that acceptance of a free electron may lead to a surplus of negative charge and transform the Cis-acceptor into the Trans-donor [18]. In addition to the dense packing of acceptors in the small medium layer

627

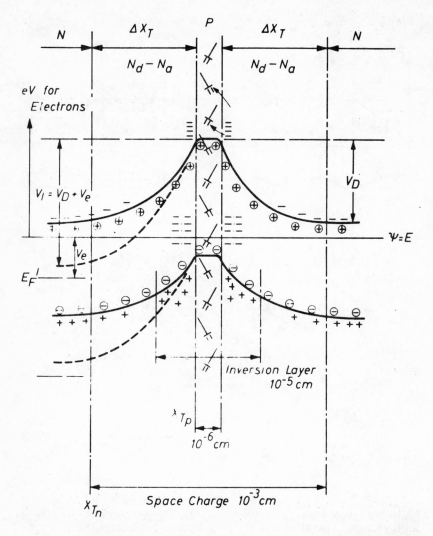

Figure 5. Model of Electronic Band Structure Perpendicular to Bi-Crystal Interface: $\oplus$ = Fixed Ionized Donors, $\ominus$ = Fixed Ionized Acceptors, - = Free Electrons, + = Free Holes.

free holes assemble in the valence band to form the inversion layer region of 10^{-5} cm width. The space charge region may extend further out into the crystal from either side of the interface. Considering the grain boundary field produced by the dangling bonds we may start with Poisson's equation for an equal distribution of ionized donors at both sides:

628

$$\frac{d^2 V}{dx^2} = \frac{-4\pi \rho}{k} \qquad (2.8)$$

ρ = space charge density,
k = dielectric constant,
x = distance from point x = 0.

For the potential V the solution of Equation (2.8) may be written in the most simple case

$$V = \frac{-2\pi \ x^2 \ \rho}{k} \qquad (2.9)$$

For the field strength one has

$$E = \frac{dV}{dx} = - \int_0^\ell \frac{4\pi \ \rho}{k} \qquad (2.10)$$

or

$$E^2 = 16\pi^2 \ \rho^2 \ \ell^2/k^2 \qquad (2.11)$$

E in (2.11) is the maximum field-strength at the barrier layer and ℓ = the depth of the space charge zone. (Δx_T in Figure 7.) This gives for the potential

$$V = \frac{k \cdot E^2}{8\pi \ eN} \qquad (2.12)$$

N = impurity density
e = unity charge.

For the case of different impurity densities at both sides of the bi-crystal interface the measurable voltage difference is given by Eq. (2.13)

$$V_e = V_1 - V_2 = \frac{k}{8\pi \ e} \left(\frac{E_1^2}{n_1} - \frac{E_2^2}{n_2} \right) \qquad (2.13)$$

As Taylor and coworkers have shown the field is 0 for a critical applied voltage of the order of magnitude given by Eq. (2.14)

$$V = \frac{2\pi}{k \ eN} \cdot q_o^2 \qquad (2.14)$$

629

This critical voltage should at maximum amount to less than 1 Volt. Since the barrier voltage is much higher (in pulsed operation even up to a few 100 Volts) (see Figure 6) one must assume that the factor q_o in formula (2.14) which is representative for the equilibrium number of charges in the grain boundary layer can increase with voltage applied. (See Appendix 2.)

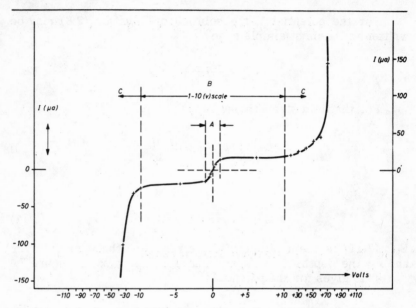

Figure 6. Typical J(V)-Characteristic of Bi-Crystal with Ohmic Contacts at Both Ends.

Another important property of the grain boundary plane is the degenerate behavior of this conducting plane if Indium-alloyed contacts have been applied which show rectifying property with respect to the bulk material. As Figure 7 shows the activation energy for the temperature dependence of the resistivity of the grain boundary plane is very small even in the range of liquid-Helium temperatures. The high temperature value is almost maintained. The important difference in the conducting behavior between a grain boundary plane and a normal mono-crystal structure can be evaluated with the aid of Figure 7 since it shows the usual strong increase in resistivity of a normal mono-crystal compared to the resistivity of the grain boundary layer at the same scale.

More would have to be added with respect to the unusual photoelectric properties of these layers (see References 21-23) and with respect to the field-effect at these interfaces and its temperature independence (see Reference 24).

630

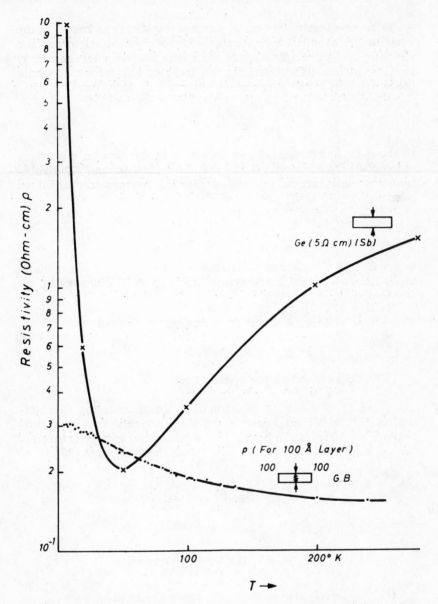

Figure 7. Comparison of Resistivity Versus Temperature (°K) for Mono-Crystal (5 Ω cm, Antimony-Doped) and Bi-Crystal Sheet with Indium-Alloyed Contacts. Bi-Crystal Resistivity Computed for a 100 Å Layer.

631

Appendix 1

The continuum theory of crystal elasticity is based on the equilibrium conditions of a deformed body subjected to surface and volume forces. The latter ones may also be represented by surface forces (tensions). In the case of anisotropic crystals these are defined by symmetric tensors σ_{ik} such that

$$\sum_k \sigma_{ik} \; df_k$$

is the i-th component of the force to be applied to a surface element df of an internal cut to maintain equilibrium. The relations between stress σ_{ik} and strain ε_{mn} tensors are assumed linear (Hooke's law)

$$\sigma_{ik} = \sum_{mn} C_{ik,mn} \; \varepsilon_{mn}$$

where $C_{ik,mn}$ = tensor of fourth degree (elastic constant tensor). Since tensors σ_{ik}, ε_{mn} are symmetric, the elastic energy is

$$E = 1/2 \sum_{ik} \sigma_{ik} \; \varepsilon_{ik} = 1/2 \sum_{ik,mn} \varepsilon_{ik} C_{ik,mn} \; \varepsilon_{mn}$$

Appendix 2

The corresponding statistics are:

Case 1: The strong dilution of filled sites or the rarification of the added electrons along the dislocation yields a non-degenerate Maxwellian behavior. A minimum energy treatment can be applied. The filling function has then the form [17]

$$f = \int \frac{k \; \ell n \; [(N_d - N_a)/N_a]}{E'_s \; (f) + 3 \; E_0} \; dT$$

where

$$E'_s \; (f) = \frac{\delta \; E_s \; (f)}{\delta f}$$

E_s (f) = electrostatic energy per added electron.

Case 2: Here f is already large enough so that the W ways of arranging N electrons over the sides have approximately the same energy and Fermi statistics apply:

$$f = \frac{1}{1 + \exp\left[(E_A - E_F)/kT\right]}$$

where

E_A = dislocation acceptor level,

E_F = Fermi level,

$\Delta E = E_F - E_A \simeq 0.3$ eV for acceptor states below the Fermi level.

For n_A acceptors per unit volume in the energy state E_A a number $n_A \times f$ is occupied or neutral. This number is:

$$n_A^* = n_A \frac{1}{\exp\left[(E_A - E_F)/kT\right] + 1}$$

The concentration of the negatively charged acceptors is then

$$n_A \cdot f = n_A^- = n_A - n_A^*$$

$$= n_A \left[\frac{1}{\exp(E_F - E_A)/kT + 1} \right]$$

$$f = \frac{1}{e^{\Delta E/kT} + 1}$$

Since ΔE is small we have here the situation of a distribution of quantum states coincident with the Fermi level, or $f = 1/2$ is the maximum filling factor.

Cases 3 and 4: Either T is small or D has decreased such that the wave functions of adjacent dangling bonds overlap. (Extreme case D = b = lattice constant). In this case each electron moves in the average field of all other electrons. The Bohr radius

$$a = k h^2/m^* e^2 = 85 \text{ Å}$$

k (dielectric constant) = 16,

m^* (effective mass) = 0,1m

h = Plancks constant/2π

for normal Ge samples may be even larger due to changes in k (higher in the compression region) and m.

One can show [19,20,22,24] that the number of charges q in the grain boundary is a function of the voltage applied to the barrier, V_e. This relation is:

$$q = q_o/2 \left[1 + (1 + eV \; e/\phi)^{1/2} \right]$$

ϕ = work function,

e = unity charge,

V_e = applied external voltage,

q_o = initial number of charges,

q = actual number of charges.

For larger voltages V_e the ratio q/q_o may reach values of 1 and more.

REFERENCES

1. A. Seeger: "Theorie der Gitterfehlstellen," Encycl. of Physics, ed. S. Fluegge, Springer-Verlag, p. 383-665 (1955).
2. A. Seeger: (see Reference 1) p. 481.
3. A. H. Cottrell: "Dislocations and Plastic Flow in Crystals" The Clarendon Press, Oxford, pp. 34 ff. (1953).
4. W. T. Read, Jr.: "Dislocations in Crystals," McGraw-Hill Book Co., New York, p. 160 (1953).
5. S. Amelinckx and W. Dekeyser: "The Structure and Properties of Grain Boundaries," Solid State Physics, ed. F. Seitz and D. Turnbull, Vol. 8, 1959, Academic Press, p. 325-499.
6. J. A. Kohn: The American Mineralogist, 43, p. 263-284 (1958).
7. W. Shockley: "Electrons and Holes in Semiconductors," D. Van Nostrand Co., New York, 1950, p. 334.
8. W. T. Read, Jr. and W. Shockley: "Dislocation Models of Grain Boundaries," "Imperfections in Nearly Perfect Crystals," ed. W. Shockley, J. H. Hollomon, R. Maurer and F. Seitz, John Wiley and Sons, New York, 1952, p. 352-376. W. T. Read: "Dislocations in Crystals," McGraw-Hill Book Co., 1953.
9. R. S. Wagner and B. Chalmers: J. Appl. Phys. 31, 581-587 (1960).
10. J. H. van der Merwe: Proc. Phys. Soc. 63, 616-637 (1950).
11. H. F. Mataré: Z. Phys. 145, 206-234 (1956).
12. H. F. Mataré and H. A. R. Wegener: Z. Phys. 148, 631-645 (1957). E. Billig and P. J. Holmes: "Defects in Diamond-Type Semiconductor Crystals." Advances in Electronic and Electron Phys. 10, p. 71-105, Academic Press (1958).
13. H. F. Mataré, B. Reed and O. A. Weinreich: Z. Naturforschung, 14a, 281-284 (1959). B. Reed, O. A. Weinreich, and H. F. Mataré: Phys. Rev. 113, Nr. 2, 454-456 (1959).
14. A. G. Tweet: Phys. Rev. 99, 1182-1189 (1955).

15. P. Handler and W. M. Portnoy: Phys. Rev. 116, 516-526, (1959).
16. W. Bardsley: "The Electrical Effects of Dislocations in Semiconductors," Progress in Semiconductors 4, Heywood and Co., London, 1960, p. 157-203.
17. W. T. Read, Jr.: Philosoph. Magazine, 45, 775-796, (1954); 45, 1119-1128, (1954); 46, 111-131, (1955).
18. W. Schottky: "Halbleiterprobleme," Vieweg and Sohn, Braunschweig, p. 85 ff (1956).
19. W. E. Taylor, N. H. Odell and N. Y. Fan: Phys. Rev. 88, 867-875, (1952).
20. H. F. Mataré: Z. Naturforschung, 10a, 640-652, (1955).
21. H. F. Mataré: J. Appl. Phys. 30, 4, 581-589, (1959).
22. H. F. Mataré: "Anisotropy of Carrier Transport in Semiconductor Bi-Crystals," Solid State Physics in Electronics and Telecommunications, Vol. 1, Part 1, 1960, p. 73-96, Academic Press, London and New York.
23. H. F. Mataré: The Proc. of the Inst. of Electrical Engineers, 106, Part B, Supplement No. 15, 293-302, (1959).
24. O. A. Weinreich, H. F. Mataré and B. Reed: Proc. Phys. Soc., 73, 969-972, (1959).

APPLICATION OF SIEMENS METHOD TO MEASURE THE RESISTIVITY AND THE LIFETIME OF SMALL SLICES OF SILICON

Jun-ichi Nishizawa, Yuzo Yamoguchi
Naotoshi Shoji and Yoshio Tominaga
Research Institute of Electrical Communication
Tohoku University

1. INTRODUCTION

It is important to measure the resistivity and the lifetime of semiconductor materials when refining or crystallizing them and fabricating devices. Recently an apparatus for measuring lifetime and resistivity was reported by Siemens [1,2] which allowed the measurements to be made without directly contacting an electrode. This method has been adapted for use with small slices of semiconductor materials, similar to that found in the production line. In the experimental work to follow, silicon was used to show the value of the method.

The apparatus for measuring the resistivity is based on the "Q-meter principle." An L-C-R series circuit was coupled with a high frequency (100 Mc/s) source and was tuned to the source by adjusting a variable condenser. Then the maximum value of the voltage-drop along the inductance L was measured. The resistivity is determined by comparing it with a previously calibrated curve of the maximum voltage versus the resistivity.

The apparatus for measuring the lifetime was based on the photo-conductive-decay method. When the light pulse of a xenon lamp is applied to the surface of a small slice of silicon through a mica or a polyethylene sheet, it modulates the conductivity in the bulk material and the impulse detected by an F-M detector is reproduced on a cathode-ray tube. The lifetime of a small slice of semiconductor material is easily measured by this method.

2. MEASURING APPARATUS

(1) Resistivity

a) Principle and Circuit

The series resonant circuit based on the "Q-meter principle" consisted of inductance L, condenser C and the electrode. A small slice of silicon, encapsulated in a mica or a polyethylene sheet, was placed on the electrode and contacted capacitively.

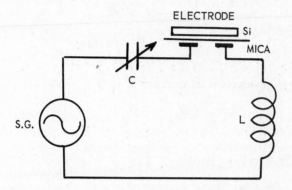

Figure 1. Simple diagram of the apparatus for measuring the resistivity: silicon crystal was wrapped in polyethylene sheet or put on the mica sheet.

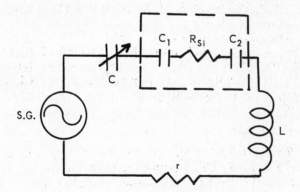

Figure 2. Equivalent circuit of electrode which is the part shown in dotted lines.

This circuit is shown in Figure 1 and its equivalent circuit in Figure 2. Here, R_{si} is the known resistivity, C_1 and C_2 are the capacitance between a specimen and the electrodes and r the total sum of the resistivity in the circuit. When this circuit is tuned with the source by adjusting the condenser C, the current I flows through the circuit.

$$I = \frac{V}{r + R_{si}} \tag{1}$$

where V is the applied high frequency voltage. Angular frequency is

$$\omega_0 = 1/\sqrt{LC_0}, \tag{2}$$

where

$$C_0 = (1/C + 1/C_1 + 1/C_2)^{-1}$$

The voltage V_L across inductance L is described by:

$$V_L = \omega_0 L \, I$$

$$= \frac{R_0}{R_{si} + r} V \tag{3}$$

$$= Q \, V,$$

where

$$R_0 = \omega_0 L = Q(R_{si} + r). \tag{4}$$

If the voltage applied from the cathode follower circuit is held at a given value, the relation of the resistivity R_{si} versus voltage V_L is shown in Figure 3. (The point of inflexion is $R_{si} = r$ on the semi-log scale.)

The high frequency 100 Mc/s, which is generated in the modified "Colpitts Oscillator" using tube 6BC4, is applied to the grid of tube 6J6 and is added to the R-L-C series resonant circuit through the cathode-follower circuit of tube 6J6 to minimize the variation of the voltage due to the variation of circuit elements, R, C.

b) Electrode

The structure of the electrode buried in a plastic plate is shown in Figure 5. The results indicated in Figure 3 are obtained by using the electrode as shown in Figure 5.

When the electrode is not covered perfectly with the specimen, the value of the resistivity is apt to be in error. Therefore, the electrode must be carefully covered. This effect is shown in Figure 6.

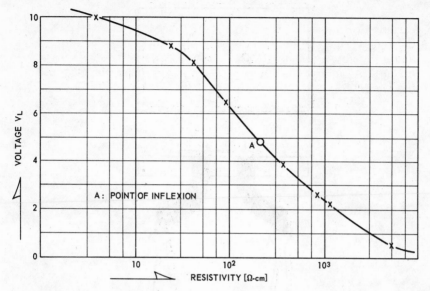

Figure 3. The relations of the resistivity vs. the maximum voltage along the inductance L. The crossed points, X, are the measured values and A is the point of inflexion which can be moved to the range of high resistivity if the sum of total resistivity in the circuit is made large.

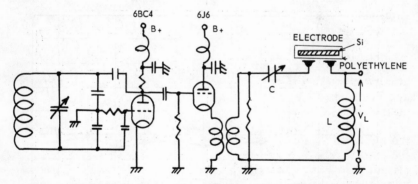

Figure 4. The apparatus for the measurement of the resistivity. R-L-C series resonant circuit was tuned by adjusting the variable condenser, C, while measuring the maximum voltage V_L on the P.V.V.

c) Results of measurement

At first the resistivity of a small slice was measured by the other method, and the relations of V_L to R_{si} from which the resistivity is obtained is given as shown in Figure 3. The measurement of high resistance slices, it can be obtained as

639

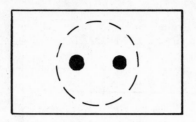

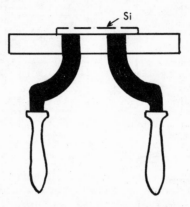

Figure 5. The electrode for measuring the resistivity of small slices.

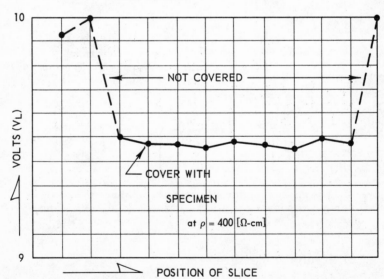

Figure 6. The effect of not covering the specimen; shift of 0.5 volts from the true voltage causes an error of a few hundred ohm-cm on the semilog scale in this graph.

640

follows: the point of inflexion A in Figure 3 moves to the range of high resistivity when r (the total sum of the circuit resistivity) is made large, even though the output voltage V_μ across inductance L decreases (as indicated in section (a)). No difference between the measured valued of resistivity of slices with the surface lapped, etched and cut are recognized. The skin depth in a semiconductor can be calculated at 100 Mc/s by

$$\delta = \sqrt{\frac{\rho}{\pi f \mu,}} \ [m] \ (M.K.S.) \tag{5}$$

where μ is permeability, f the frequency at (100 Mc/s), ρ, the resistivity, (100 ohm-cm). δ is a few centimeters. The skin effect did not appreciably effect the measurement even for values less than 1 mm.

The ripple of B source to the apparatus and the supply voltage to the P.V.V. must be kept stable within a few percent.

(2) Measurement of lifetime

a) Principle and circuit

The measurement of lifetime is based on the photoconductive decay method. The difference between the D. C. current method and this method is that the cutting or soldering of the specimen is not required and the measurement can be done without contaminating the specimen by contacting it with electrode capacitively.

The principle of the detector circuit is as follows: the electrode on which small slices are put, is in parallel with the tank circuit of the oscillator. When the light pulse is applied to small slices, the output power is modulated by the variation of the semiconductor conductivity, and the frequency modulation at the same time.

The modulated signal is detected by using the "Travis circuit." The high frequency, 100 Mc/s, was used to closely couple the specimen with the electrode. The block diagram of this apparatus is shown in Figure 7. The light pulse was given to the slice by a xenon discharge tube to which a D. C. high voltage is applied through the R-C blocking circuit.

This pulse interval is 10 μsec, and the period 2 ~ 20 c/s. The detector circuit of the lifetime apparatus is shown in Figure 8. The center frequency is 116 Mc/s and the frequency band width 12 Mc/s.

b) Electrode

The electrodes, indicated in Figure 9, are 3 mm in width, 4 mm in length and 2 mm apart and, thus, are suitable for

641

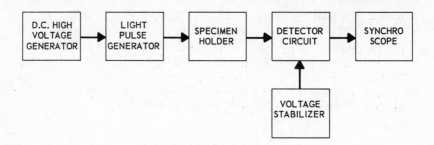

Figure 7. Block diagram for the measurement of the lifetime.

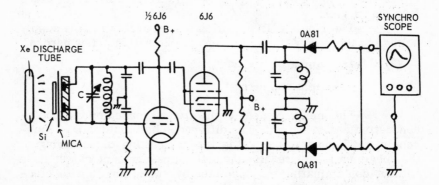

Figure 8. The detector circuit containing the modified
"Colpitts oscillator" and "the Travis circuit."

the measurement of the resistivity of a silicon slice. Also, for
the sake of decreasing an error caused by silicon surface recombination, only the light pulse through the silicon filter was
applied to the crystal.

c) Results of measurement

Decay pulses were reproduced on a synchroscope.
The lifetime was obtained by a reading on the horizontal scale
as height is decayed to 1/e. When small slices are being measured, the oscillator may deviate slightly from the tuned point,
resulting in decreased sensitivity and power output. This may
be corrected by varying condensor C (Figure 8). For lower
resistivity silicon the "Q" of the tuned circuit will drop due to
dissipation in the sample; and as the tank damping is increased,
the output power decreases. Similarly, the tank independence
will be increased with decreasing dissipation.

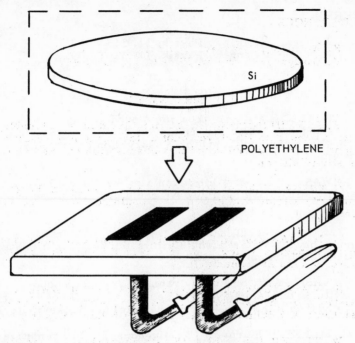

POLYETHYLENE

Figure 9. Electrode for the measurement of lifetime.

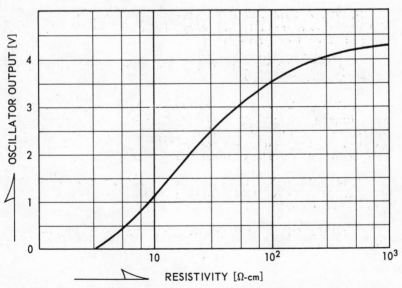

Figure 10. Output voltage of "Colpitts oscillator" due to the variation of the resistivity when the light pulse is applied to the specimen.

REFERENCES

1. K. Wolfgang, Z. angew. Physik. 11, 346 (1959).
2. K. Wolfgang, Z. angew. Physik. 11, 351 (1959).

DISCUSSION

F. J. REID (Battelle): You mentioned lack of trouble with surfaces and data which you quoted for fairly low resistivity of silicon. Have you duplicated this observation on extremely high resistivity silicon?

S. IWASA (Univ. of Pennsylvania): We did not have a high resistivity silicon available, so we could perform these experiments.

H. M. MANASAVIT (Autonetics): Your data indicates that one must have a wafer about 80 mils thick before resistivity measurements are meaningful.

S. IWASA (Univ. of Pennsylvania): Yes, it depends on the resistivity of the sample you are dealing with. If you have high resistivity then it indicates that you have to have thicker material.

W. TILLER (Chairman) (Westinghouse): How sensitive do you expect this procedure to be?

S. IWASA (Univ. of Pennsylvania): When you have low resistivity this method is not very sensitive, namely, the whole thing is about 10^{-1} ohm-cm.

F. J. REID (Battelle): Did you say this process measured the surface resistivity?

S. IWASA (Univ. of Pennsylvania): We wondered whether we were measuring surface resistivity or bulk resistivity, and in order to obtain this information we changed the surface, using a difference finish such as a copper surface or a etched surface. The results do not show much change either way.

J. M. HIRSHON (Philco): If you were to use a paralled circuit, would you have better measurements than when you were measuring in series?

S. IWASA (Univ. of Pennsylvania): There is no good reason why we chose the series circuit process. We should investigate this.

THERMODYNAMIC PROPERTIES OF CUBIC BP
AND OF RHOMBOHEDRAL B₆P

B. D. Stone, F. V. Williams,
R. A. Ruehrwein, and G. B. Skinner
Chemical Research Department, Research
and Engineering Division,
Monsanto Chemical Company,
Dayton 7, Ohio

INTRODUCTION

The preparation of cubic boron phosphide by a number of methods was described in a previous paper [1]. One of these methods, the reaction

$$BCl_{3(g)} + \frac{3}{2} H_{2(g)} + \frac{1}{4} P_{4(g)} \rightleftharpoons BP_{(c)} + 3HCl_{(g)} \qquad (1)$$

was studied in detail. This communication gives some thermodynamic properties derived from temperature dependence studies of this equilibrium reaction. Thermodynamic quantities for the dissociation reaction [1]

$$BP_{(c)} \rightleftharpoons \frac{1}{6} B_6 P_{(c)} + \frac{5}{12} P_{2(g)} \qquad (2)$$

are also given.

EXPERIMENTAL

Reaction (1) - Formation of BP - A mixture of BCl_3 and H_2 gases was passed over a boat containing red phosphorus in a 22 mm fused silica tube, heated to a temperature to give the desired phosphorus vapor pressure. The silica tube extended into a second furnace which was heated to the desired reaction temperature. This hot reaction zone was packed with rings made from 8 mm Vycor tubing to provide a large surface for deposition of the BP. The exit gas stream was burned in the atmosphere. Temperatures were controlled to ±2°C by electronic controllers

645

operated by thermocouples attached to the outside of the silica tube at the center of each furnace. The flow rates of BCl_3 and H_2 were measured by calibrated floating-ball flowmeters and the phosphorus vapor flow was measured by the weight loss from the boat per unit time. At the end of the run, the BP product was removed from the Vycor rings and the silica reaction tube by etching with HF. It was then dried and weighed.

For reaction (1), the equilibrium constant is

$$K_1 = \frac{(P_{HCl})^3}{(P_{BCl_3})\ (P_{H_2})^{\frac{3}{2}}\ (P_{P_4})^{\frac{1}{4}}} \tag{3}$$

where P is the partial pressure of each gas. Since three moles of HCl are formed per mole of BP deposited, the equilibrium flow rate of HCl in moles per minute is equal to three times the number of moles of BP deposited per minute. The equilibrium flow rates of BCl_3, H_2 and P_4 were calculated by correcting the initial flow for the HCl formed according to equation (1). Since the total pressure was one atmosphere, the partial pressure of each gas is equal to its mole fraction in the gas stream; i.e., its equilibrium flow rate in moles per minute divided by the sum of the flow rates. The partial pressure of P_4 in the gas stream was corrected for the effects of dissociation

$$P_4 \rightleftharpoons 2P_2$$

by an appropriate calculation based on the published equilibrium constant for the dissociation reaction[2]. The partial pressures thus obtained were used in equation (3) to calculate the equilibrium constant.

Reaction (2) - Dissociation of BP - A weighed sample of BP was placed in a graphite boat inside a graphite reactor designed to maintain a constant temperature over the length of the boat. The entire assembly was placed in a fused silica tube and the reactor heated by an induction heater while a measured stream of argon was passed through the tube. After a measured time interval at the desired temperature, the induction heater was shut off and the weight loss of the sample determined. The weight loss was converted to volume of P_2 vapor per unit volume of argon, which equals the partial pressure of P_2 in atmospheres as the total pressure was one atmosphere. It was assumed that the products were only P_2 and B_6P, as given in equation (2), so the equilibrium constant is

$$K_2 = (P_{P_2})^{\frac{5}{12}} \tag{4}$$

RESULTS AND DISCUSSION

The results of a number of experiments on the reaction of BCl_3 with H_2 and P_4 are given in Table I.

Table I

Experimental Results on Formation of Cubic BP by the Reaction $BCl_3 + \frac{3}{2} H_2 + \frac{1}{4} P_4 \rightleftharpoons BP + 3HCl$

T(°K)	Moles H * / Moles BCl$_3$	G.-Atoms P* / Moles BCl$_3$	% Conversion** to BP	K$_{eq.}$
1193	2.86	1.74	37	0.58
1193	4.17	3.27	55	1.19
1293	3.54	1.67	49	1.34
1293	3.69	2.61	58	1.79
1293	5.59	1.91	61	1.44
1293	3.10	3.01	49	1.35
1293	6.98	4.51	67	1.07
1543	5.84	2.94	66	2.36

*In initial reaction mixture
**Based on BCl_3

There is considerable scatter of the points obtained at lower temperatures, perhaps due to equilibrium not being reached in the sojourn time in the reaction zone, even though the bulk of the product BP was found in the front half of the reaction zone. Although only one run was made at 1543°K, there could be no question of equilibrium being established in this case as all the BP was condensed in a narrow band about 5 cm wide at the front edge of the zone. Therefore, in obtaining an Arrhenius type equation for the temperature dependence of the equilibrium constant, a least-squares calculation was made, with the condition that the highest temperature point is given exactly by the equation. The result is

$$\log K_1 = 1.740 - \frac{2,110}{T} \tag{5}$$

where T is the absolute temperature. Thus, $\Delta H° = 9,660$ cal, $\Delta S° = 7.96$ cal/deg, and $\Delta F°$ is -1,490 cal at 1400°K.

Since thermal functions of BCl_3 [3], H_2 [4], P_4 [5] and HCl [4] are known, it could be calculated that the entropy of BP at 1400°K is 24.56 cal/deg/mole. If the specific heat of BP follows a Debye[6] curve, and C_p is taken equal to C_v, then the Debye characteristic

647

temperature, θ, is 680°K. This is not an unreasonable value, but it does seem a little low compared to θ values for other hard materials, as listed in Table II. Most of these characteristic temperatures have been calculated from the data summarized by Kelley [7].

Table II

Debye Temperatures for Hard Solids

Material	θ, °K	Material	θ, °K
W	260	SiO (quartz)	890
Mo	380	Al_2O_3	930
CaO	560	SiC	1130
Si	620	BeO	1180
MgO	740	B	1320
TiN	740	B_4C	1370
TiC	860	C(diamond)	1860

Experimental results for the dissociation of BP are given in Table III.

Table III

Experimental Data for the Reaction
$$BP \rightleftharpoons \frac{1}{6} B_6P + \frac{5}{12} P_2$$

T(°K)	Argon Flow Rate (ml/min)	Wt. Loss (g/1 of argon)	Partial Pressure P_2(mm)	$K_{eq.}$
1473	22	0.0189	5.7	0.130
	23	0.0120	3.6	0.107
	23	0.0127	3.8	0.110
	22	0.0136	4.1	0.114
	11.5	0.0201	6.0	0.133
	4.6	0.0212	6.4	0.137
1523	8	0.0441	13.1	0.184
	13.5	0.0341	9.5	0.161
	4.6	0.0575	15.8	0.206
	5.9	0.0257	7.7	0.147
	10.2	0.0420	12.6	0.181
	8.8	0.0412	12.4	0.180
	3.7	0.0450	13.5	0.187
1573	9.4	0.0839	25.1	0.241

Again, a least-squares curve passing through the highest-temperature point was calculated. The equation is

$$\log K_2 = 3.764 - \frac{6,890}{T} \tag{6}$$

from which $\Delta H° = 31,530$ cal, $\Delta S° = 17.22$ cal/deg and $\Delta F°$ at $1500°K$ is $5,690$ cal. Using Stevenson and Yost's value for the entropy of P_2, and the Debye θ of $680°K$ for BP, it is found that θ for B_6P is $650°K$.

This value of θ for B_6P does seem quite low, since one would expect B_6P to resemble B_4C in structure. Because of the high atomic weight of phosphorus, θ for B_6P should be a little less than that of B_4C; perhaps $1200°$ to $1300°K$ would be reasonable. Therefore, a new calculation was made in which it was assumed from the outset that θ for B_6P was $1250°K$. With this assumption, no value of θ for BP could satisfy both equations (5) and (6), of course, and both these equations had to be changed slightly in slope. The method of doing this was (a) to continue to require that the line pass through the highest-temperature point in each case, and (b) to increase the standard deviation of the experimental points from the line by the same factor in each case. The new equations are

$$\log K_1 = 1.377 - \frac{1,550}{T} \tag{7}$$

$\Delta H° = 7,090$ cal, $\Delta S° = 6.30$ cal/deg, $\Delta F°$ at $1400°K = 1,730$ cal

$$\log K_2 = 3.134 - \frac{5,900}{T} \tag{8}$$

$\Delta H° = 27,000$ cal, $\Delta S° = 14.34$ cal/deg, $\Delta F°$ at $1500°K = 5,480$ cal

The corresponding θ for BP is $780°K$, which seems a little more satisfactory than the previous value. In calculating these new equations, the standard deviation of the points was increased by only 25%, and the largest difference between the new and old curves was about one standard deviation.

Taking literature values [3,4,5] for the heat contents, and using a θ of $780°K$ for BP, ΔH for Reaction (1) is $7,700$ cal at $298°K$. The same references give heats of formation of BCl_3 and HCl, while Rossini et al. [8] list the heat of formation of $P_{4(g)}$. Therefore, one finds that for the reaction

$$B_{(c)} + P_{(white)} \rightarrow BP_{(c)} \quad \Delta H(298°K) = -19,900 \text{ cal}$$

The experimental error in this value is about 3,000 cal, largely because of uncertainty in the slope of the log K versus $1/T$ curve.

In a similar way, ΔH for Reaction (2) at 298°K is +28,900 cal, from which using literature values and the above heat of formation of BP, one finds

$$6B_{(c)} + P_{(white)} \rightarrow B_6P_{(c)} \quad \Delta H(298) = -31,000 \text{ cal}$$

Here, the experimental error could be as high as 25,000 cal, because there is an uncertainty of a few thousand calories in the heat of formation of $\frac{1}{6} B_6P$. However, the values 19,900 and 31,000 cal seem to be in a reasonable relationship to one another, since one would expect that the first atom of phosphorus reacting would give out more heat than the subsequent ones.

Hoch and Hinge [9] have studied the thermal dissociation of BP using the Knudsen effusion method. For reaction (2), they found $\Delta H(298) = +31.2$ kcal, which compares quite well with our value of +28.9 kcal.

REFERENCES

1. F. V. Williams and R. A. Ruehrwein, J. Am. Chem. Soc., 82, 1330 (1955).
2. T. D. Farr, "Phosphorus, Properties of the Element and Some of Its Compounds," Tennessee Valley Authority Chemical Engineering Report No. 8, Wilson Dam, Alabama (1950) p. 16.
3. W. H. Evans, D. D. Wagman, and E. J. Prosen, unpublished results, reported to the U. S. Atomic Energy Commission in National Bureau of Standards Report No. 4943 (1956).
4. National Bureau of Standards, "Selected Values of Chemical Thermodynamic Properties," Series III.
5. D. P. Stevenson and D. M. Yost, J. Chem. Phys. 9, 403-8 (1941).
6. P. Debye, Ann. Phys. 39, 789 (1912).
7. K. K. Kelley, Bureau of Mines Bulletin 477 (1948).
8. F. D. Rossini, D. D. Wagman, W. H. Evans, S. Levine, and I. Jaffe, "Selected Values of Chemical Thermodynamic Properties," National Bureau of Standards Circular 500 (1952).
9. M. Hoch and K. S. Hinge, Abstracts of Papers, 138th Meeting of the American Chemical Society, New York, N.Y., September 11-16, 1960, p. 85.

DISCUSSION

W. R. WILCOX (Pacific Semiconductors): What did you use for your vapor pressure data for the res phosphorous?

B. D. STONE (Monsanto Chemical): We used the TVA pamphlet and the quantities quoted therein. However, in determining our flow rates, it turned out that you couldn't calculate what to expect. It had to be done empirically for a given temperature and a given hydrogen flow rate. However, for the thermodynamic calculations, the values given in TVA's pamphlet were used for determining the thermodynamic values.

THERMODYNAMIC PROPERTIES OF ANTIMONY TELLURIDE AND BISMUTH TELLURIDE

B. W. Howlett and M. B. Bever
Department of Metallurgy
Massachusetts Institute of Technology

ABSTRACT

The heats of formation of the V-VI compounds, $Sb_2 Te_3$ and $Bi_2 Te_3$ have been measured in a metal solution calorimeter. The melting points of both compounds and the heat of fusion of $Bi_2 Te_3$ have been measured in a constant-temperature-gradient calorimeter. These data shed light on the stability of these compounds.

As part of an investigation of the thermodynamic properties of various intermetallic compounds, the heats of formation, heats of fusion, heat capacities and melting points of antimony telluride and bismuth telluride are being investigated. Such data are needed for thermodynamic calculations and are also of interest in interpreting the nature of these compounds.

Materials. A coarse-grained ingot of stoichiometric bismuth telluride was obtained from the Air Force Cambridge Research Laboratories. Stoichiometric antimony telluride was obtained from the Lincoln Laboratory, Massachusetts Institute of Technology, as an ingot consisting mainly of a single crystal. The elemental antimony, bismuth and tellurium required for the measurement of the heats of formation of the compounds were obtained from the American Smelting and Refining Company; they were reported to be 99.999+% pure.

Calorimetric Methods. The heats of formation were measured by metal solution calorimetry with bismuth as a solvent. In this technique the difference between the heat effect on solution in liquid bismuth of the compound and a mechanical mixture of its components, adjusted for changes in composition of the solvent bath, is the heat of formation of the compound at the temperature from which the samples are added to the bath. Details of the equipment and technique have been described [6,8].

The heats of fusion, heat capacities and melting points were measured in a constant-temperature-gradient calorimeter. The principle of this calorimeter was proposed by Smith [7]. In this technique, the time required for heating the specimen through a known temperature interval under a known temperature gradient is compared with the time required for a standard specimen to be heated through the same temperature interval under the same temperature gradient. A description of this calorimeter will be published [4]. This technique yields heat capacities and the heat effects of phase changes. It also lends itself to an accurate determination of the temperatures of phase changes because undercooling and superheating effects are largely eliminated; however, the limitations of temperature measurement still apply.

Results. The measured heats of formation of the compounds and the heat of fusion of bismuth telluride are listed in Table 1. The Table also lists the observed melting points of both compounds.

Table 1

	Sb_2Te_3	Bi_2Te_3
Heat of Formation, ΔH°_{273}, cal/g-atom	$-2,700 \pm 15$	$-3,700 \pm 50$
Heat of Fusion, ΔH_f, cal/g-atom	--	4,140
Melting Point, $^{\circ}C$	618.5 ± 0.5	584.5 ± 0.5

The literature contains a value of the heat of formation of bismuth telluride [2]. This value is $-1,600 \pm 600$ cal/g-atom or approximately half the value found in the present investigation. The earlier value was obtained by extrapolation by an unspecified method and is not likely to be of high accuracy.

A heat of fusion of $5,800 \pm 200$ cal/g-atom has been reported [1] for bismuth telluride. This value was obtained by a method of quantitative thermal analysis due to Oelsen [5,6]; the specimen had to be encapsulated, which may have interfered with the accuracy of the method.

The melting temperature of bismuth telluride of $584.5 \pm 0.5^{\circ}C$ compares with a value of $585^{\circ}C$ given by Hansen [3]. The melting temperature of antimony telluride of $618.5 \pm 0.5^{\circ}C$, found in this investigation, lies within the range given by Hansen, which extends from 606 to $630^{\circ}C$.

It is probable that Wagner's analysis [9] can be used to derive the free energies of formation of antimony telluride and bismuth telluride from their heats of formation and heats of fusion. However, special allowances will have to be made for the solubility ranges of the compounds and the uncertainties in the phase diagram of antimony telluride will further complicate the application of this analysis. The heats of formation give an approximate indication of the stability of these compounds. They are small and the stability of the compounds is correspondingly small. It may be noted that although antimony telluride has a higher melting point, it has a smaller heat of formation than bismuth telluride.

Acknowledgements. Support of this work, which is part of a larger investigation, by the Air Force Cambridge Research Laboratories under Contract No. AF19(604)-5588 is acknowledged. Thanks are due to Mr. J. R. O'Connor for supplying the bismuth telluride and to Dr. A. J. Rosenberg for the antimony telluride. The authors thank Mr. B. Howell for technical assistance.

REFERENCES

1. G. F. Bolling, J. Chem. Phys. 33, 305 (1960).
2. G. Gattow and A. Schneider, Angew. Chemie 67, 306 (1955).
3. M. Hansen, "Constitution of Binary Alloys," McGraw-Hill, Inc., New York, 1958.
4. B. W. Howlett, to be published.
5. W. Oelsen, K. H. Rieskamp and O. Oelsen, Arch. Eisenhüttenw. 26, 253 (1955).
6. W. F. Schottky and M. B. Bever, Acta Met. 6, 320 (1958).
7. C. S. Smith, Trans. AIME, 137, 236 (1940).
8. L. B. Ticknor and M. B. Bever, Trans. AIME, 194, 941 (1952).
9. C. Wagner, Acta Met. 6, 309 (1958).

DISCUSSION

W. ZIMMERMAN (Naval Research Lab.): Two related questions: You stated that you have a bath that was kept at a temperature of plus or minus 0.002°C - I am curious to know how you maintain this accuracy and what means you used to measure it?

B. W. HOWLETT (MIT): This is a bath containing about 1000 pounds of molten salt. The salt is a lithium, potassium, sodium nitrate mixture. It is stirred extremely rapidly and has a very high thermal mass. The bath is contained in an iron pot with a heater on the outside. The heater power is from a stabilized A.C. source. A platinum resistance thermometer in a Wheatstone bridge is used to control the temperature. The out-of-balance current is fed to a mirror galvanometer, which reflects a light beam into a photocell. The output of this cell is amplified and fed to a saturable reactor which is in series with

654

a control winding immersed in the salt. Using these techniques we can get this stability of control for periods of half an hour or so. The long-term stability is not guite as good. The temperature of the salt bath is measured by two iron-constantan thermocouples in series contained in a Vycor sheath immersed in the salts. This inables us to measure changes in temperature of the salt of the order of 0.002 degrees centigrade. The absolute temperature of the salt is only known to about ± 1 degree centigrade, but this is not important with a difference method.

A. J. ROSENBERG (Chairman) (Tyco):   It would seem that the free energy would depend, quite sensibly, upon the stoichiometry of the system.   Would there be a substantail change in measuring the free energies as a function of the crystal composition at either end of the solidus at a given liquidus temperature?   That is, on either the bismuth or tellurium rich side?

B. W. HOWLETT (MIT):   There may be appreciable differences.   This is something which is well worth studying.